33

W9-CEZ-541

80⁰⁰
88E

Nigeria

WORLD BIBLIOGRAPHICAL SERIES

General Editors:

Robert G. Neville (Executive Editor)

John J. Horton   Ian Wallace

Hans H. Wellisch   Ralph Lee Woodward, Jr.

John J. Horton is Deputy Librarian of the University of Bradford and currently Chairman of its Academic Board of Studies in Social Sciences. He has maintained a longstanding interest in the discipline of area studies and its associated bibliographical problems, with special reference to European Studies. In particular he has published in the field of Icelandic and of Yugoslav studies, including the two relevant volumes in the World Bibliographical Series.

Ian Wallace is Professor of Modern Languages at Loughborough University of Technology. A graduate of Oxford in French and German, he also studied in Tübingen, Heidelberg and Lausanne before taking teaching posts at universities in the USA, Scotland and England. He specializes in East German affairs, especially literature and culture, on which he has published numerous articles and books. In 1979 he founded the journal *GDR Monitor*, which he continues to edit.

Hans H. Wellisch is Professor emeritus at the College of Library and Information Services, University of Maryland. He was President of the American Society of Indexers and was a member of the International Federation for Documentation. He is the author of numerous articles and several books on indexing and abstracting, and has published *The Conversion of Scripts* and *Indexing and Abstracting: an International Bibliography*. He also contributes frequently to *Journal of the American Society for Information Science*, *The Indexer* and other professional journals.

Ralph Lee Woodward, Jr. is Chairman of the Department of History at Tulane University, New Orleans, where he has been Professor of History since 1970. He is the author of *Central America, a Nation Divided*, 2nd ed. (1985), as well as several monographs and more than sixty scholarly articles on modern Latin America. He has also compiled volumes in the World Bibliographical Series on *Belize* (1980), *Nicaragua* (1983), and *El Salvador* (1988). Dr. Woodward edited the Central American section of the *Research Guide to Central America and the Caribbean* (1985) and is currently editor of the Central American history section of the *Handbook of Latin American Studies*.

VOLUME 100

Nigeria

Robert A. Myers

Compiler

CLIO PRESS

OXFORD, ENGLAND · SANTA BARBARA, CALIFORNIA
DENVER, COLORADO

British Library Cataloguing in Publication Data

Myers, Robert A.
Nigeria. – (World bibliographical series; 100).
1. Nigeria. Bibliographies
I. Title   II. Series
016.9669

ISBN 1–85109–083–5

Clio Press Ltd.,
55 St. Thomas' Street,
Oxford OX1 1JG, England.

ABC–CLIO
130 Cremona Drive,
Santa Barbara, CA 93117, USA.

Designed by Bernard Crossland,
Typeset by Columns Design and Production Services, Reading, England.
Printed and bound in Great Britain by
Billing and Sons Ltd., Worcester.

THE WORLD BIBLIOGRAPHICAL SERIES

This series, which is principally designed for the English-speaker, will eventually cover every country in the world, each in a separate volume comprising annotated entries on works dealing with its history, geography, economy and politics; and with its people, their culture, customs, religion and social organization. Attention will also be paid to current living conditions – housing, education, newspapers, clothing, etc. – that are all too often ignored in standard bibliographies; and to those particular aspects relevant to individual countries. Each volume seeks to achieve, by use of careful selectivity and critical assessment of the literature, an expression of the country and an appreciation of its nature and national aspirations, to guide the reader towards an understanding of its importance. The keynote of the series is to provide, in a uniform format, an interpretation of each country that will express its culture, its place in the world, and the qualities and background that make it unique. The views expressed in individual volumes are not necessarily those of the publishers.

VOLUMES IN THE SERIES

Contents

Contents

Contents

Contents

Preface

This bibliography emphasizes, as nearly as possible, the uniqueness of Nigeria, while at the same time retaining a sense of the nation's West African setting. History, ethnic groups, politics, economics, literature and the arts receive special attention but more than three dozen other subjects are covered also. Included within the 1,150 annotations are details of numerous other works of value. Access to all of these is facilitated by the detailed index of authors, titles and subjects. Not only is this an attempt to provide material on important topics from Abuja to Zaria, but it also contains references to exoteric subjects ranging from embroidered hats and truck art to proverbs and names. Above all, the goal of this volume has been to present both the general reader and the specialist with a useful compilation of significant resources to enhance the study and understanding of Africa's most populous and complex nation. Since many entries concern West Africa, *Nigeria* should serve also as a valuable resource for the larger region.

This volume is the end product of a difficult process of selecting entries from an enormous body of material. Books and doctoral theses have received primary consideration over journal articles. In some instances, government reports or publications with corporate authors have been chosen when they seemed to best represent a subject. Criteria for selection have been varied but include importance as a standard work, high quality and coverage of a specific topic. In some cases, availability has dictated inclusion; there are undoubtedly worthy Nigerian publications which have not been accessible in the data bases and libraries I have searched. Usually, more recent materials were selected over older studies; however, works of unique and enduring value are included, sometimes at the expense of more specialized recent works. In a very few areas, such as science and technology, there was a scarcity of publications suitable for inclusion. Emphasis is on works in English, but a few of the most significant volumes in French and German are included.

The large number of publications on Nigeria is striking. Residents of the former British colony have published at a prolific rate since before independence in 1960. Tens of thousands of Nigerians have studied abroad, especially in Britain and the United States, with many writing dissertations and theses for advanced degrees. Students at Nigerian universities have written vast numbers of theses over the last forty years. Nigeria's own publishing industry, producing numerous volumes in Nigerian languages as well as in English, is certainly one of the most, and possibly the most, vigorous in Africa. Because of its importance in African history and politics, its large population, its many writers, and the richness of its cultures, languages and artistic creations, Nigeria has been a magnet for students of the continent. The result of all these facts is that everything written about Nigeria and by Nigerians would fill a substantial library.

It would have been possible to have compiled a selective bibliography twice as large as this one without loss of quality. A few examples may reinforce the point. *Dissertation Abstracts International* records 1,281 doctoral dissertations written on Nigeria between 1861 and early 1989; many others have been written on particular ethnic groups, languages and other topics. Major collections may contain thousands of entries under 'Nigeria'; the New York Public Library, for example, has catalogued more than 2,400 items since just 1972. Writers Chinua Achebe, Cyprian Ekwensi, Wole Soyinka and Amos Tutuola sustain a flourishing publishing enterprize; their fiction and essays together with critical studies of their works number, conservatively, in the hundreds. One scholar believes that more may have been written on the arts of south-western Nigeria than on the rest of Africa put together. Standard bibliographies on the Yoruba and Hausa include 3,488 and 1,281 entries respectively, excluding the publications of the last decade. Members of the University of Ibadan Faculty of Medicine published 3,788 articles between 1948 and 1980. Among the numerous prolific writers about Nigeria, one scholar stands out. A. H. M. Kirk-Greene has authored several hundred individual publications on the country, many of them essential historical, linguistic, and political studies. The list could be much longer. I have attempted to make a just and balanced selection that is representative of the wealth of publications.

Popular and professional periodicals and newspapers published in Nigeria are numerous, although many have had a short life and issues of others appear irregularly. Only the most well-known or important of these could be included, (high quality Africa-oriented journals published outside Nigeria have been omitted).

One of the emphases of this compilation, which makes it particularly valuable, is bibliographies. Since it has been possible to include only a fraction of the available works on most topics, I have provided as broad a bibliographic base as possible. Most books, articles, theses and reports on Nigeria can be located through a bibliographic citation in this volume. Bibliographies are included in the relevant topical chapters, while those of a more general nature form their own chapter.

Nigeria includes all relevant works from the Ibadan History Series, the Cambridge University Press African Studies Series, and the International African Institute's Ethnographic Survey of Africa, as well as most of the books by Nigerian authors in the Heinemann African Writers Series. Each year numerous valuable works are published in Nigeria. I have attempted to include as many as possible of the best of these, especially those published by Nigeria's oldest university press, Ibadan University Press.

Printed materials from Africa can be difficult to obtain. Two excellent sources of Nigerian (and other African) books, pamphlets and government publications are Hogarth Representation, 1 Birchington Court, Birchington Road, London N8 8HS, England, and African Imprint Library Serivces 410 West Falmouth Highway, Box 350, West Falmouth, MA 02574 USA. The recently formed African Books Collective, a consortium of African publishers of whose founding members nearly half are Nigerian, provides an important outlet for current books of all types. Its provisional address is c/o Hans Zell Associates, 11 Richmond Road, P.O. Box 56, Oxford OX1 3EL, England.

Entries are arranged alphabetically by the name of the author within each section or subsection. If there is neither author nor corporate author, entries are listed by the first non-article word in the title. Multiple entries by the same author are arranged chronologically.

Users should note that every attempt has been made to record titles, authors' names, Nigerian words and phrases as they are in each original source. In some cases authors and publishers have included diacritics and in others they have not. These have not been standardized throughout this volume. Within the index alternative spellings are indicated in parentheses. The first entry in the index and the names used on the map represent the most commonly found versions. In addition, it many be useful to know that 'northern' (and 'southern', 'eastern' and 'western') Nigeria refer to general geographic regions, while 'Northern' (and 'Southern', 'Eastern' and 'Western') Nigeria refer to the regions politically constituted during various periods of the country's history. I have followed the usage as it is in each work cited. The First Republic refers to Nigeria during 1960–66; Second Republic refers to the second attempt at democratic government, 1979–83. The University of Ife changed its name to

Preface

Obafemi Awolowo University in 1987. University Press Limited in Ibadan (Three Crowns Building, Jericho, P.M.B. 5095) should not be confused with Ibadan University Press (c/o University of Ibadan, Ibadan, Oyo State).

A work of this breadth inevitably incurs many debts. The compilation and selection of entries was greatly facilitated by an Alfred University Faculty Summer Research Grant to study at the libraries of Harvard University, the National Museum of African Art Library, and the Library of Congress. Additional research was done at Cornell University in Ithaca, New York. I must thank the staff of Alfred University's Herrick Memorial Library, particularly reference librarian Frank McBride and periodicals librarian Pam Lakin. This compilation would not have been possible without the skills and persistence of Linda Hardy and Trevor Jones who obtained literally hundreds of the volumes through interlibrary loan. Indeed, this bibliography is notable in that the vast majority of its entries can be obtained in the United States cost-free through the interlibrary loan system, and undoubtedly, at the libraries of major universities throughout the world, notably that of the African Studies Centre in England which has an outstanding collection.

This undertaking has benefited from the assistance of many individuals who sent reprints and lists of their publications, offered suggestions or otherwise made its completion possible. I thank J. F. Ade. Ajayi, G. I. Akenzua, Martha Anderson, Holly Bedell, Joseph Butler, Mark W. DeLancey, Larry Diamond, Elizabeth Eames, Janet Frederick, Beverly Ann Gray, Curtis Huff, A. H. M. Kirk-Greene, Murray Last, Bernth Lindfors, Joyce Lowe, Otwin Marenin, Bill Miles, Cheryl Monroe, Joseph Nevadomsky, Ayo Ogundipe, Bisi Ogunleye, Ikponmwosa Osemwegie, Simon Ottenberg, D. D. O. Oyebola, Sam E. Oyovbaire, Tola Olu Pearce, Linda Rhoad, Ron and Diane Schaefer, Sayre P. Schatz, Nancy J. Schmidt, Timothy Shaw, Richard Sklar, M. G. Smith and especially Vic and Virginia Yurkewich. I am particularly grateful for suggestions made by Janet Stanley of the National Museum of African Art, Smithsonian Institution, Washington, DC. Of course, none of these people is responsible for any errors or omissions or the final selection of entries.

I wish to thank also *WBS* Executive Editor Robert G. Neville for his support and Rachel Houghton and (for *Dominica*) Susan Haberis for their invaluable editorial skills.

I thank my wife, Cathie Chester, for her inspiring generosity.

Robert A. Myers
1989

xiv

Introduction

The Federal Republic of Nigeria is located in West Africa, surrounded by the Francophone countries of Benin, Niger and Cameroon, with Lake Chad in its north-eastern corner and a southern coastline on the Atlantic's Bights of Benin and Biafra. Geological forces in the form of enormous petroleum reserves, and historical factors resulting in a large, dynamic population have combined to make Nigeria one of Africa's most important states. With only three per cent of the continent's land area but perhaps twenty per cent of its population, Nigeria has been described as the 'Brazil of Africa', the 'Texas of Africa' and the 'giant of Africa'.

Nigeria is the fourteenth largest African nation. In area its 923,768 square kilometres (356,669 square miles) occupy a region nearly four times the size of the United Kingdom or slightly larger than the American states of California, Oregon, Washington and Maine combined. The distance from Badagri (or Badagry) in Nigeria's south-west corner to Lake Chad is about 1,370 kilometres (851 miles), nearly the distance from London to Barcelona or from New York to Chicago. Through the country for 1,175 kilometres (730 miles) flows the River Niger, nearly one-third of the rivers' length. The Niger is joined by the River Benue, 797 kilometres (495 miles), at Lokoja and diffuses into the many smaller rivers and creeks of the large Niger Delta. Other tributaries of the Niger include the Sokoto, Kaduna and Anambra Rivers; there are nineteen other rivers of more than 120 kilometres.

Much of Nigeria's terrain is not dramatic, despite being varied. A spectrum of vegetation zones range from thick coastal mangroves and rain forests in the south, covering twenty per cent of the country, to successively dryer savannah regions in the extreme north ending with the marginal Sahel. Nigeria's basically uniform land mass is relieved by scattered plateaux and heights including: Chappal Waddi (2,419 metres, 7,936 feet) in the Gotel Highlands on the Cameroon border; Vogel Peak (2,042 metres, 6,700 feet); Shere Hill (1,872 metres, 5,841 feet) on the Jos Plateau; the Oban Hills (1,004 metres, 3295 feet); and Idanre Hill (981 metres, 3217 feet), the highest point in south-western Nigeria. At the new federal capital of Abuja, an inselberg of bare ancient granite known as Zuma Hill rises as an impressive landmark.

Both natural events and human activities are posing significant threats to the Nigerian environment. Northern Nigeria is increasingly faced with the problem of the slow expansion of the Sahara desert, and wood continues to be the primary source of cooking fuel. In the south, shifting cultivation and logging take a high toll on the forests. In July 1988, the Niger Delta port of Koko in Bendel State featured in international headlines when 10,000 barrels of Italian toxic waste were discovered.

Animal life in Nigeria is diverse, but nowhere, not even in the popular Yankari Game Reserve, do large mammals exist in the numbers found in East Africa. There is growing pressure on the country's wildlife as a growing human population, faced with worsening economic conditions, expands its farmlands and turns to 'bush meat' as a source of food. The Nigerian Conservation Foundation, set up in 1982, has intensified efforts to protect a number of endangered species, among them lowland gorillas and chimpanzees. At the Hadejia Nguru Wetlands Project, a 890,000-acre tract of land at the intersection of Kano, Bauchi and Borno States, conservationists are attempting to save one of the most important resting and wintering sites for migrating birds in West Africa. Here one may once have found forty-five per cent of the bird species recorded in Nigeria, including the Crowned Crane, Nigeria's national bird.

Nigeria is endowed with valuable mineral resources. Sub-bituminous coal has been mined at Enugu since 1915. Commercial tin mining has gone on in the Jos Plateau since 1906, with tin, for half a century, among the country's most important exports. Nigeria is the world's largest producer of columbite, a source of the rare elements niobium and tantalum. Iron ore deposits exist in Kwara State, although the low concentration of iron has been one of the factors impeding the development of the country's steel industry. Gemstones, including sapphire, topaz, turmaline, aquamarine and amethyst, are mined both legally and illegally in Plateau and Kaduna States.

Above all, Nigeria's recent history has been dominated by the sulphur-free petroleum deposits in and near the Niger Delta. Although oil exploration began in 1908, the first strike was not announced until 1953. Commercial production by British Petroleum and Royal Dutch Shell began in December 1957. From 6,000 barrels daily in 1958, production in 1966 reached 418,000 barrels daily or 152,000,000 barrels for the year, selling at US$2.17 a barrel. Nigeria joined the Organization of the Petroleum Exporting Countries (OPEC) in 1971 and by 1974 annual production had risen to more than 823,000,000 barrels at an average price of $14.69 each. Nigerian oil production peaked in 1979 at 2.5 million barrels a day. By July 1980, Nigeria's 'Bonny Light' crude oil brought $37 a barrel on the world market, a price which reached $40 briefly in early 1981, before sliding to $33.75 in 1983 and to $10–12 a barrel in mid-1986, with prices throughout 1988 fluctuating from $15–18 per barrel.

The United States has been the major market for Nigerian oil, taking about one-half of all exports, with the Netherlands, France and the GFR also buying large quantities. In 1986, the most recent year for which statistics are available, Nigeria was the fourth largest source of imported oil for the United States; it had been the second largest supplier from 1975 to 1981. Nigeria was the fifth largest producer in OPEC in 1986 and was estimated to have reserves of sixteen billion barrels, 2.23 per cent of the world's reserves. In 1986, 1,127 oil wells produced about 1.3 million barrels a day, more than any other African nation; this rate would use up known reserves in about forty years. Nigeria's current OPEC quota is 1.355 million barrels of oil a day. Nigeria's highly regarded oil minister Alhaji Rilwanu Lukman has been OPEC president since 1986. The Nigerian National Petroleum Corporation (NNPC) controls production by Shell, in which it has an eighty per cent interest, and by Mobil, Agip-Phillips, Elf-Aquitaine, Texaco, Ashland and Pan Ocean oil companies, in all of which it has sixty per cent interests. The petroleum is refined at Port Harcourt, Warri and Kaduna. Nigeria is estimated to have forty-six billion cubic feet of natural gas, 1.34 per cent of the world's total proven reserves. At present, however, the gas is simply burned off creating huge flares throughout the petroleum-rich region.

Nigeria is estimably the eighth most populous nation in the world but all statements about the current population and, therefore, all population-based statistics must remain estimates. The censuses of 1911, 1921 and 1931 were entirely unsystematic. In 1952–53 the first modern census counted 30.42 million Nigerians, but can make no great claims for accuracy. The May 1962 census of 45.6 million people was so politicized that its results were cancelled. The 1963 census held from 5–8 November counted 55,670,055 Nigerians. Despite its controversial procedures and numbers, it proved politically acceptable because it gave the three regions of the country approximate parity. Results from the 1973 census were cancelled because its provisional total of 79.76 million showed a dramatic population increase in the northern regions and an improbable decrease in the Western State. The next census is being planned for 1991.

Introduction

The Nigerian government uses an estimated 2.5 per cent rate of annual increase from 1963 to calculate official population statistics. International organizations use an estimate of 2.9 per cent annual growth rate or higher based on small carefully controlled sample surveys. *The World Bank Atlas 1988*, for example, uses a 3.3 per cent annual growth rate resulting in a 1987 population of 106,736,000. The Population Reference Bureau estimates Nigeria's 1988 population at 111.9 million based on a 2.9 per cent growth rate. At this rate, the population will double in twenty-four years. Whatever the actual count, there is no question that Nigeria's population is at least twice that of any other African nation, that it exceeds the combined populations of all other West African states, and that its growth rate outpaces the growth of available resources and social services.

Other population statistics are informative. Nigeria's crude birth rate (births per 1,000 population) is forty-six, its crude death rate (deaths per 1,000 population) is seventeen, and its infant mortality rate (annual number of deaths of infants under one year old per 1,000 births) is 122. All three rates are higher than those in the developing world in general, but not higher than those for many other African countries. At least forty-five per cent of the population is under age fifteen, but only two per cent is over age sixty-five, a demographic pattern similar to most other African countries (*1988 World Population Data Sheet* Washington, DC: Population Reference Bureau, 1988, data based on United Nations statistics).

With an estimated 22.8 per cent of the population living in cities, Nigeria is the seventh most urbanized country in black Africa. The Yoruba people of south-western Nigeria have a long tradition of living in towns and cities, many of which are among Nigeria's largest. Metropolitan Lagos was estimated to have more than five million residents in 1986; Ibadan, sometimes called the 'largest indigenous city in black Africa' has substantially more than one million. Kano and Kaduna are the largest cities of northern Nigeria, while Ogbomosho, Oshogbo, Ilorin, Abeokuta, Port Harcourt, Zaria, Ilesha, Onitsha, Iwo, and Ado-Ekiti, were all officially estimated to have more than 200,000 people in July 1975. Urban growth rates are estimated at between eight and ten per cent per year, reflecting high rates of rural-urban migration. Population density is estimated at more than 100 people per square kilometre. Distribution is uneven, however, with Oyo, Kano, Sokoto, Imo, Kadune, Anambra and Cross River States sharing large populations and Niger State having one of the lowest concentrations (*Africa South of the Sahara 1989*, London: Europa, 1988, p. 790, 799; *The world in figures*, Boston, Massachusetts: G. K. Hall, 1988, p. 89–90).

Nigeria has been host to large numbers of workers from

neighbouring countries. In January 1983 two million aliens were expelled, more than one million of whom were from Ghana. Although the country's borders remained officially closed throughout 1983–85, many of the workers returned, with the result that another 700,000 people, of whom about 300,000 were Ghanaians, were forced out in May 1985. It is likely that many illegal aliens remain in the country or have returned once again. However, many Nigerians have studied abroad or emigrated. In 1980, more than 20,000 Nigerian students studied in the United States, a number exceeded only by the Iranian student population.

Nigeria is one of the most ethnically diverse countries in Africa and, relative to its size, the world. Scholars suggest that 395 mutually unintelligible languages are spoken and the country's leading geographer has written that there are 434 ethnic groups in Nigeria. Exactly how many groups and languages there are depends upon the terms used to define them. Many of the groups identified have only a few thousand members, with the result that Nigeria's population is dominated by the Hausa-Fulani, the Yoruba, and the Igbo, concentrated in the north, the south-west and the east, respectively. According to the 1963 census, these three groups comprised 57.8 per cent of the total population. In the 1980s, it is thought that ten groups (Hausa-Fulani, Yoruba, Igbo, Kanuri, Tiv, Edo, Nupe, Ibibio and Ijaw) account for nearly eighty per cent of the population.

Religion is an important and sensitive dimension of Nigerian society. In 1963, 47.2 per cent of the population was Muslim, 34.5 per cent Christian, and 18.3 per cent practised traditional beliefs. Northern Nigeria is overwhelmingly Islamic. All three belief systems exist throughout the southern parts of the country, with Islam practised more in the west and Christianity in the east. A December 1980 clash in Kano between the militant followers of Alhaji Muhammad Marwa, known as Maitatsine, and government troops resulted in several thousand deaths, including that of Maitatsine. The populist movement, fuelled by the economic distresses of the oil boom, was officially banned, but this did not prevent its spread to other urban areas. Clashes between members of the group and authorities caused a combined estimate of two thousand deaths in Maiduguri in October 1982, Yola in February-March 1984 and Gombe in April 1985. In March 1987 conflict between Muslim and Christian youths began in Kafanchan, Kaduna State, and spread across several other northern states. The Nigerian government has continuously emphasized its secular nature. However, when it was announced in February 1986 that Nigeria had joined the Organization of the Islamic Conference, non-Muslims expressed their concern.

It is not known when the area today known as Nigeria was first

Introduction

settled by humans; the archaeological investigation of Nigeria's past is still in its infancy. The establishment of the oldest identified cultural phase, Nok, is based on more than 150 remarkable terracottas, the earliest sculptures from sub-Saharan Africa, and evidence of primitive iron-working. Nok artefacts have been found in a 240 square mile area in central Nigeria and are dated from at least 500 BC to AD 200 and may be as early as 900 BC. Other dramatic archaeological and serendipitous discoveries include the magnificent 'bronze' objects from a ninth century AD tomb of a priest-king near Igbo-Ukwu, first discovered in 1938. The naturalistic bronze and terracotta heads discovered at Ile-Ife in 1910 and 1938, dated from about 1200 AD, are unique in the history of African art and are surpassed in their artistry by no sculptures anywhere in the world. Objects from Tada and Owo are also justifiably well known, but most famous of all are the brass castings and carvings from the Benin Kingdom, some dating from the fourteenth century AD. Members of the British Punitive Expedition of 1897 were astonished by the quality and number of these and took several thousand objects home with them to pay for their venture. Today, Benin art is found scattered throughout the world's great museums and commands premium prices when it appears, rarely, for sale.

Many of the ethnic groups occupying present-day Nigeria have been part of complex kingdoms for centuries. Only the most important and best known can be mentioned. The (Kanuri) Kanem-Borno Empire dominated the Lake Chad area from the thirteenth century well into the nineteenth century. The seven Hausa states of Kano, Katsina, Zazzau (Zaria), Daura, Gobir, Rano and Biram controlled the northern central area and had adopted Islam as the state religion by the end of the fifteenth century. Hausa influence spread to other states to the west and south of this area, including Zamfara, Kebbi, Yawuri, Nupe, Gwari, Kwararafa and Yoruba areas. In the early-nineteenth century, Usman dan Fodio, a Fulani scholar, led a *jihad*, an Islamic holy war, against the kings of Hausaland. By his death in 1817, he had established Islamic rule from the new Fulani capital of Sokoto throughout what is now northern Nigeria and had begun to penetrate south of the River Niger in the western areas.

In the south-west a group of Yoruba-speaking kingdoms (Awori, Egbado, Lagos, Ijebu, Ife, Ijesa, Igbomina, Ekiti, Owo and Ondo among them) came to be dominated by Oyo between the fifteenth and eighteenth centuries. To their east the Benin Kingdom controlled a large area from the 1400s to its conquest by the British in 1897. East of the Niger lies a region densely populated by Igbo small village democracies. Although not united into larger kingdoms, these communities are linked often through kinship, trade and religion. Along the Niger and Benue is the Middle Belt, a broad area of enormous ethnic complexity which includes the kingdoms of the Busa, Nupe, and Igala, as well as the Idoma and Tiv, which, like the Igbo, are classified as 'stateless societies'. In the eastern Niger Delta were the city states of Bonny, Elim Kalabari, Brass-Nembe and Okrika which rose to prominence during the Atlantic slave trade. Trade in the western Delta was dominated by the Itsekiri Kingdom of Warri. In the south-eastern corner the Efik state of Old Calabar united separate communities at the mouth of the Cross River.

Contact between Nigerian peoples and Europeans dates at least to 1480 when two Portuguese ships explored along the Bight of Benin and bought slaves. The trade in slaves, who were supplied in the hundreds of thousands by coastal groups, many of whom were made wealthy and powerful in the process, characterized relations with Europeans until the early-nineteenth century. More than three centuries of coastal slave trade with Europeans established an extensive network for accumulating victims through raids and wars in far-reaching areas, and intensified the slave societies already in existence in the region. Without question, the magnitude and duration of the Atlantic trade transformed local societies both along the coast and in the hinterlands. As well as slaves, although to a much lesser extent, ivory, precious woods, and Benin pepper were traded for guns and gunpowder, cloth, liquor, tobacco, metal items, and copper and iron bars.

Large numbers of captives from what is now Nigeria survived the Middle Passage and carried with them their culture, religion and languages to New World slave-holding societies. These influences survive throughout the Caribbean and in South America and today remain strongest in parts of Cuba and Brazil. Portuguese slavers introduced a 'Brazilian' architectural style to nineteenth-century buildings in Lagos.

High mortality from yellow fever and malaria confined Europeans to coastal areas until the early-nineteenth century when a handful of intrepid explorers, led by a lust for adventure and geographic curiosity rather than by greed or God, penetrated the interior. Mungo Park on his second expedition in 1805–06 traced the Niger from Timbuktu to Bussa (now covered by Kainji Reservoir) where he was killed. Walter Oudney, Dixon Denham and Hugh Clapperton in 1823–25 crossed the Sahara and explored from Lake Chad to Kano and Sokoto. Hugh Clapperton and Richard Lander journeyed overland from Badagry to Bussa, Sokoto and Kano in 1825–27. In 1830 Richard Lander and John Lander confirmed finally that the series of rivers and channels of the delta area formed the mouth of the Niger. Soon afterwards, the British government began to sponsor expeditions, beginning with MacGregor Laird's in 1832.

In 1807 the British abolished the slave trade, but despite their efforts both the Portuguese and the independent slavers of several nationalities continued their highly profitable trade for another eighty years. During this time market interests shifted from slaves to palm-oil. The increasingly lucrative palm-oil trade attracted British merchants to search for cheaper means to control the trade and ways in which they might deal directly with inland palm-oil producers and circumvent the coastal middlemen. Christian missionaries brought their religion and European education as they indirectly contributed to the development of more extensive trade relations between local peoples and the British. A Methodist mission opened at Badagry in 1842; the Church Missionary Society began work in Abeokuta in 1846 and at Onitsha in 1857. The Church of Scotland Mission at Old Calabar in 1846 was the first Presbyterian mission in West Africa. After Dr. William Balfour Baikie's expedition journeyed up the Niger to Lokoja in 1854 without fatalities, the protection quinine offered against malaria became widely known. From then on, the West African door was opened to European activities.

Formal British relations with the area which became Nigeria began in 1849 with the appointment of John Beecroft as Consul for the Bights of Benin and Biafra. His headquarters were on the island of Fernando Po, a healthier location than the mainland. The British attacked Lagos and deposed its king in November 1851 as part of their efforts to suppress the slave trade. Benjamin Campbell was appointed consul for Lagos and the Bight of Benin in 1853; he established residency on the island. By 1861 it became necessary to suppress local rulers again; this time Lagos was made a British Colony. By the 1893 the British had secured peace treaties with all of the Yoruba groups in the broader area. Along the River Niger, George Dashwood Goldie Taubman (later knighted as Sir George Taubman Goldie) consolidated British companies into the United African Company by November 1879. He managed to secure a monopoly under a Royal Charter for what was renamed the Royal Niger Company after the Berlin Conference of 1884–85. As a result of Goldie's domination of trade throughout the Niger basin, Britain lay claim to much of today's Nigeria. British treaties with states in the delta were grouped under the Oil Rivers Protectorate in 1887, which became the Niger Coast Protectorate in 1893. After 1897 the British controlled all of what became south-western Nigeria. The name 'Nigeria' was coined in January 1897 by Flora Shaw in an article in the London *Times* to describe the Royal Niger Company's territories. The Royal Charter granted to Goldie was withdrawn in 1900 and his company's territories south of Idah on the Niger were merged with the Niger Coast Protectorate to form the Protectorate of Southern Nigeria. Territories north of Idah became the Protectorate of Northern Nigeria, headed by Sir Frederick Lugard. Lugard, motivated to no small degree by a need to check French expansion from the north, extended British control throughout Northern Nigeria with the conquest of Kano and the Sokoto Caliphate in 1903. With some exceptions, nearly all of present-day Nigeria was brought under British rule by 1905.

So modern Nigeria took shape. The Lagos Colony and Protectorate and the Protectorate of Southern Nigeria were unified in 1906 to form the Colony and Protectorate of Southern Nigeria with Lagos as its capital. On 1 January 1914 Lugard supervized the amalgamation of the Colony and Protectorate of Southern Nigeria with the much poorer Protectorate of Northern Nigeria into the Colony and Protectorate of Nigeria; he presided over the new colony as Governor General. In both large regions he had established a system of Native Administration emphasizing indirect rule through existing political systems. The approach worked brilliantly in the north but poorly in the south-west, and hardly at all in the 'stateless societies' of the south-east. Thus, the Nigerian state was created in 1914, although its present boundaries were not fixed until 1961 when the northern part of the Cameroons administered by the British became Nigerian. Although Chief Obafemi Awolowo asserted in 1947 that 'Nigeria is not a nation. It is a mere geographical expression', the country was explored, exploited, developed and forged into a modernizing sovereign state over the short span of eighty years, a remarkable feat given its size and complexity.

The British placed great emphasis on road building, often with forced labour, and on railway construction, both of which were essential in developing the domestic and export economies. At the same time, they impelled the production of cash crops, especially palm-oil, cocoa, and rubber in the south, and groundnuts and cotton in the north. Control over tin and coal mining remained exclusively in the hands of companies run by expatriates and these industries contributed little to revenues for the Colony, which was operated by taxes collected from its residents directly and indirectly, through, for example, export duties on cash crops.

The roots of Nigerian nationalism lie in assertions for greater participation in government early in this century. By 1922 changes initiated by Governor Hugh Clifford established the Nigerian Legislative Council for Lagos and Southern Nigeria: ten of its forty-six members were Nigerians. As a result of public agitation after World War II, the Richards Constitution of 1947 was adopted; this

Introduction

created a national legislative council and three regional legislative councils. The conservatism of this constitution was attacked by the nationalist organizations which had recently been formed. The National Council of Nigeria and the Cameroons (NCNC), founded in 1944 and led by Dr. Nnamdi Azikiwe, joined the Action Group (AG) led by Obafemi Awolowo and the Northern People's Congress (NPC) led by the Sardauna of Sokoto, Ahmadu Bello and Abubkar Tafawa Belewa in combined agitation for change. The 1951 Macpherson Constitution granted elections through electoral colleges, rather than directly, and created ministerial positions. In the 1954 Constitution Nigeria became a federation of three states, each of which had its own premier and governor. Lagos became a federal territory. By 1956 the Eastern and Western Regions were granted self-government, followed by the Northern Region in 1959. Increasingly, these moves toward independence strengthened the autonomy of the regions and contributed to their mutual rivalry. Federal elections in 1959 were contested along regional lines. Not surprisingly, the most populous Northern Region and the NPC dominated.

Nigeria became independent from Britain on 1 October 1960 with Alhaji Sir Abubakar Tafawa Balewa as Prime Minister and Minister of Foreign Affairs. The country was organized following the British Westminster parliamentary model, which allowed fervent regionalism to dominate issues. On 1 October 1963, the country became the Federal Republic of Nigeria and remained within the British Commonwealth. A complex series of political events, constitutional difficulties, ethnic allegiances, and social unrest followed by violent, corrupt elections in 1964 and 1965, paved the way for the first of the six unplanned changes of government which have occurred in independent Nigeria. Since 1960 Nigeria has been run by a civilian government for slightly less than ten years.

The First Republic ended on 15 January 1966 when junior army officers assassinated Chief S. L. Akintola, the Premier of the Western Region, Sir Ahmadu Bello, the Premier of the Northern Region, Tafawa Balewa, the Prime Minister, Chief Festus Okotie-Eboh, the Federal Minister of Finance, and most of the senior army officers, who were primarily northerners. Major-General J. T. U. Aguiyi-Ironsi (an Igbo) emerged as leader of the army and head of state. His reliance on other Igbo officers and dissolution of the country's regional organization aroused fears of southern domination in the north. In May of 1966, bloody riots in northern cities broke out, directed against the southerners, especially Igbos who were the most numerous migrants in the north. Northern army officers assassinated Ironsi and many other Igbos in the army on 29 July 1966 and order was achieved by Lt.-Colonel Yakubu Gowon, the Army

Chief of Staff and a Christian northerner from the Middle Belt.
The change of government proved futile as an attempt to restore
national unity. Thousands more Igbos were killed in an even bloodier
series of massacres by northern army members in September and
October 1966. The popular military governor of the Eastern Region,
Lt.-Colonel Chukwuemeka Odumegwu Ojukwu called home all
Igbos and proceeded to govern the state as if it were independent of
the federation. Compromise efforts at a meeting between the
Nigerian government and Ojukwu in Aburi, Ghana, in January 1967
failed. By 30 May 1967, the Igbo consultative assembly declared the
Eastern Region the independent 'Republic of Biafra'. When the
Biafran army invaded the Mid-Western Region on 6 July, the nation
was plunged into a civil war which lasted for thirty months and cost
an estimated 100,000 military casualties and almost two million
civilian deaths, nearly all in the secessionist state.

The bitter war of attrition attracted the involvement of foreign
powers, with several African states (including Ivory Coast, Gabon,
Tanzania and Zambia) recognizing Biafran independence. A successful
propaganda campaign by Biafra attracted popular financial support in
the United States and Western Europe, and French military and
technical assistance, while the United Kingdom and the USSR
supported the federal government. Gradually federal forces strangled
the rebel state and Ojukwu escaped to exile in the Ivory Coast
leaving Lt.-Colonel Philip Effiong to surrender on 12 January 1970.
By the war's end the federal government had armed forces of about
250,000 men, Africa's largest. (This was reduced to 180,000 by 1979
and in July 1987 stood at 94,500, including a navy with 5,000 men and
an air force with 9,500.)

To General Gowon's credit, peaceful reconciliation between the
secessionists and the nation was pursued vigorously and, aided
immeasurably by the swelling oil wealth, reconstruction of the war-
torn areas quickly began. Unfortunately, while successfully attending
to healing war wounds, Gowon lost political and economic control of
the country. Nigeria was transformed by oil revenues on a scale that
no black African nation has experienced before or since. Poor
planning and management, deficient infrastructure, acute port
congestion, growing corruption in both national offices and within the
governments of the twelve states, and events surrounding the failure
of the 1973 census contributed to Gowon's downfall. The final blow
came when he announced in 1974 that military rule would continue
indefinitely rather than ending in 1976 as planned. On 29 July 1976,
when Gowon was in Kampala, Uganda, at an Organization of
African Unity (OAU) summit conference, he was overthrown in a
bloodless coup by General Murtala Mohammed.

Introduction

The new régime was immensely popular. Mohammed provided decisive leadership, replaced some 10,000 officials throughout the country and promised to return the country to civilian rule by October 1979. However, army unrest resulted in an attempted coup on 13 February 1976, in which Mohammed was assassinated by Lt.-Colonel Bukar Dimka. Lt.-General Olusegun Obasanjo, the Chief of Staff of the armed forces, quickly assumed control of the goverment and continued Mohammed's policies. Nineteen states were created from the twelve already in existence. A national programme of free Universal Primary Education was begun and seven new universities were created. A major goal of the government was to draft a workable constitution for the Second Republic. Already, however, tremors in the economy were felt from oil revenue fluctuations which forced Obasanjo to make unpopular budgetary cuts.

The constitution which marked the second effort at democratic government rejected the Westminster system in favour of an American-style presidential system. A strong president, with the vice president on the same ticket, needed at least twenty-five per cent of the vote in two-thirds of the nineteen states and a majority of the national vote, to win. The bicameral legislature would elect the president in the absence of sufficient national votes. The president's cabinet consisted of at least one minister from each state. One of the most contentious issues for the new constitution was the relation of the Islamic Sharia court system to the new federal judiciary, an issue which has also plagued preparations for the Third Republic. The Second Republic's constitution emphasized Nigeria's 'federal character' in an effort to speed national integration.

Offices for the new Republic were contested vigorously. The Federal Electoral Commission (FEDECO) recognized five national political parties: the Unity Party of Nigeria (UPN), a Yoruba-based party headed by Chief Obafemi Awolowo; the National Party of Nigeria (NPN), a largely northern-based party whose presidential and vice presidential candidates were, respectively, Alhaji Shehu Shagari of Sokoto and Dr. Alex Ekwueme, an architect from Anambra State; the People's Redemption Party (PRP), also northern-based and led by Alhaji Aminu Kano; the Nigerian People's Party (NPP), whose candidate was Dr. Nnamdi Azikiwi; and the Greater Nigeria People's Party (GNPP), which split from the NPP and was led by its presidential candidate, wealthy Borno State businessman Alhaji Waziri Ibrahim. In the voting, which took place during July and August 1979, the NPN won between thirty-six and thirty-eight per cent of the seats in the house, the senate and the state assemblies, and seven of the nineteen state governorships. Shagari (NPN) received 5.7 million votes, Awolowo (UPN) 4.9 million, Azikiwi

(NPP) 2.8 million, Kano (PRP) 1.7 million and Ibrahim (GNPP) 1.6 million. Shagari won at least twenty-five per cent of the vote in twelve states, but not thirteen. FEDECO, supported by the supreme court, ruled that he needed only 16.67 per cent in the thirteenth state, and so he won the election and was sworn in on 1 October 1979.

The Second Republic was faced with insurmountably difficult tasks. Political tensions among the parties remained high. The transition from the Westminster to the new US-government model was more complicated than expected. Fair distribution of oil revenues among the federal government, the states and the local governments proved more difficult; the division of the 'spoils of office' absorbed vast sums. The government's five-year development plan (1981–85) was based on the expectation that the oil wealth would remain high. This resulted in overly ambitious budgets and development projects. Nigeria became dependent upon imports of all sorts to satisfy newly acquired tastes for consumer goods and for foods such as wheat which had never been a part of the Nigerian diet. As oil revenues collapsed in 1981, the goverment was caught with an unmanageable level of debt and was forced to trim budgets and to introduce austerity measures.

It was against this backdrop that the country prepared for elections in August–September 1983. The NPN spent enormous sums to assure success, contributing to a growing cynicism about political ethics in the country. Shagari was re-elected with twelve million votes, forty-seven per cent of those cast; Awolowo was second with about eight million votes. The NPN won thirteen of nineteen state governorships and a substantial majority in the legislatures. The cost of this purchased success was the complete loss of public confidence in democratic government.

President Shagari's second term of office lasted only three months. The Second Republic was overthrown on 31 December 1983 by the military, led by Major General Muhammadu Buhari, acting as head of a Supreme Military Council (SMC) of nineteen members. Corruption in government, blatant waste of oil revenues, an economy and society completely out of control and the distortions of the 1983 elections all contributed to the change of government. Rigidity coupled with the unpopular level of austerity which was imposed to repair the excesses of the Second Republic resulted in Buhari's overthrow on 27 August 1985, by Major General Ibrahim Babangida, heading an Armed Forces Ruling Council (AFRC), with twenty-eight members. An attempted coup led by Major-General Vatsa on 20 December 1985 was unsuccessful; thirteen of the conspirators, including Vatsa, were executed in February 1986.

Introduction

The AFRC has followed a systematic course for the return of government to civilian control on 1 October 1992, two years later than originally planned. Political parties and former politicians, as well as members of the AFRC, are banned from political participation and candidates for office must first be screened by the National Electoral Commission. Non-party based local government elections were held in December 1987 and again in March 1988 and a 450-member constituent assembly was elected in April 1988, with another 113 members nominated by the AFRC. The constitution for the Third Republic establishing a two-party system and a civilian president with a six-year term of office was completed in March 1989.

Administratively, Nigeria continues to undergo organizational changes. In 1947, the country was divided into the Northern, Eastern and Western Regions. Nigeria became a federation of three regions with its capital at Lagos in 1954. The Mid-Western Region was created out of the Western Region in 1963. On 27 May 1967, the regions were divided into twelve states (Lagos, Western, Mid-Western, Rivers, East-Central, South-Eastern, Kwara, Benue-Plateau, North-Western, North-Central, Kano, and North-Eastern). In principle, the creation of these states occurred to enhance the 'federal character' of the country, to give greater voice to minority ethnic groups and to disperse political process and power. Seven new states were created in April 1976 bringing the total to nineteen: Lagos, Ogun, Ondo, Oyo, Bendel, Rivers, Imo, Anambra, Cross River, Kwara, Benue, Plateau, Niger, Sokoto, Kano, Kaduna, Bauchi, Borno and Gongola. The country was divided into 312 local government areas (LGAs). A Federal Capital Territory was added in 1979 as plans got underway to transfer the nation's capital to a more central location in Abuja. In the early 1980s the possibility of creating as many as forty states was debated; in 1987 the total number of states was increased to twenty-one when Katsina and Awka Ibom were created in order to simplify any governmental decisions requiring support from two-thirds of the states. Despite discussion over further subdivisions, the military government placed a moratorium on the creation of new states.

Throughout most of this century, agriculture has been the basis of Nigeria's economy, accounting for eighty-five per cent of exports in the late 1950s. At one time Nigeria was the world's largest exporter of groundnuts and palm products (palm-oil and palm kernels) and the second largest exporter of cocoa. Cocoa remains the only substantial non-petroleum export. Rubber and timber were once significant but their production and their value as exports, like that of palm kernels, has declined to an insignificant level. Groundnuts are now consumed on the local markets and cooking oil must be imported to meet domestic demand.

xxviii

Cash crops and food crops for local consumption have been overwhelmingly in the hands of traditional small-scale farmers. Subsistence crops of rice, maize, sorghum, millet and particularly taro (coco yam), yams and cassava, have become more important than ever before with the ban on food imports. Both the Buhari and Babangida governments have made agricultural development and self-sufficiency of food production essential goals of their economic recovery plans. To accomplish this a variety of measures have been instituted, including: incentives in the forms of easier loans to farmers; tax relief for agricultural ventures using local materials; projects to supply seeds and fertilizers to farmers; and a decree to facilitate the purchase of land for commercial farming.

Self-sufficiency in food production will require the reversal of a twenty-year trend. From the early 1970s, earnings from oil dominated the Nigerian economy so completely that the agricultural sector was neglected, despite lipservice to agricultural development projects. Nigeria became a large-scale importer of food, especially of wheat and rice from the United States, rather than the exporter it had been traditionally. From 1960 to 1986, agriculture's share of export earnings dropped from seventy-five per cent to three per cent, while the share of oil grew to ninety-seven per cent of total export earnings and seventy per cent of all government revenues.

As soon as oil money began to pour in during the 1970s, government budgets expanded to spend it and creditors extended large loans on the assumption that the country's new-found wealth made it a good risk. When the world's oil markets became saturated and the price of oil dropped, Nigerian dreams and budgets were caught at lofty levels and had to be scaled down quickly. As a result, the oil boom became a bust; because expectations were raised so high and so suddenly and then dashed, some have even described petroleum as a curse.

Despite prolonged negotiations and heated public debate throughout the mid-1980s, Nigeria has resisted taking loans from the International Monetary Fund (IMF). Yet the government has met nearly all conditions initially established by the IMF for a loan including devaluation of the naira and, more recently, reduction of subsidies for electricity and gasoline; Nigeria seems poised to accept a loan should one prove both financially beneficial and politically tolerable. The spartan 1989 budget, based on estimated oil revenues of $14 a barrel, continues the Nigerian structural adjustment programme. Meanwhile, Nigeria's foreign debt, Africa's second largest after Egypt, put at $26 billion by the government and at $30 billion by creditors, must still be serviced. To do this in 1988, the government spent a painfully high forty-five per cent of its revenue but nevertheless achieved a favourable balance of trade. Throughout the years of austerity in the 1980s, the Nigerian military governments have consistently discharged financial responsibilities both to creditors and to the international organizations to which Nigeria belongs. The price for this slow path to economic stability has been high. Plans for free schooling and health care have been either cut back drastically or abandoned. Roads and bridges remain in dangerous states of disrepair. The crime rate has soared. By November 1988, the consumer price index, according to the Central Bank of Nigeria, had increased nearly ninefold since 1975. In 1988, the World Bank reclassified Nigeria from a 'middle income' country to a 'low income' country. The naira which was valued at 1.37 per US$, or £0.90, in July 1983, was worth only 0.24 per US$, or £0.13, in June 1988 and 0.14 per US$, or £0.08, in March 1989. Nigerian annual per capita income dropped from $770 in 1983 to $370 in 1987, a level comparable with Haiti's per capita income in 1987, $360. Because of the declining oil income, the GNP contracted from $72,190 million in 1986 to $39,533 million in 1987. From 1980 to 1987, the GNP declined at an average of five per cent per year, while during 1986–87, it dropped 7.7 per cent. On the positive side, according to *The World Bank Atlas 1988* (Washington, DC: World Bank, 1988, p. 8), school enrolment (the number of children in primary and secondary school, expressed as a percentage of the number of school-age children) increased from thirty-seven per cent in 1970 to sixty-four per cent in 1985, the largest gain made in any of the sixteen largest developing countries. Life expectancy at birth increased from forty-three to fifty-one per cent between 1970 and 1987. Unfortunately, the total fertility rate (the number of children a woman will bear during her lifetime) for Nigerian women was 6.9 in 1987, the same it had been in 1970. Nigeria was the only country among the sixteen largest developing countries where the fertility rate did not decline during this period.

In a survey of 130 nations called the 'International human suffering index' (Washington, DC: Population Crisis Committee, 1987), living conditions in Nigeria were considered to be better than those in only eighteen other countries. Among the ten measures contributing to this low ranking were: claims that less than one-half of the adult population is literate, and that less than one-third of the population has access to clean drinking water; the high infant mortality rate; a high rate of rural-urban migration; high rates of unemployment and under-employment; and a poor use of available energy resources.

Lagos is notable among Nigerian cities, not because it is the nation's capital and largest city, but for its reputation as a difficult place in which to live. An official press release of the early 1980s explaining the government's move to the new centrally located and planned capital, Abuja, reports that 'perennial traffic jams, intolerable congestion, chaotic sanitary situation, inadequate social amenities, and alarming crime rate have become Lagos's trademark'. Infamous for traffic jams called 'go-slows' which can turn a drive across town into a sweltering half-day long excursion, and unreliable electricity and telephone services, Lagos was also rated the world's most expensive city in 1982 and 1983. It is now one of the cheaper capital cities, however, since the devaluation of the naira. The unruly city was featured in November 1983 on the American CBS News television programme '60 Minutes' as 'probably the world's worst' capital. In an effort to improve Lagos's image, for the past two years the military government has required residents to spend three hours on the last Saturday each month cleaning the city as part of the National Environmental Sanitation Exercise.

No description of modern Nigeria can omit mention of its general highway and traffic problems. The nation has an extensive road network (107,990 kilometres or 67,102 miles in 1980) which was used, in 1981, by 262,000 passenger cars and 91,000 commercial vehicles. Yet while malaria, diseases prevented by immunization and diarrhoea from unsanitary water still cause high loss of life among the very young, the greatest danger to adults is travel on the nation's highways. Failure to repair and maintain roads and bridges, absence of vehicle safety standards and road marks, lack of driver training and eyesight testing, overcrowded commercial vehicles, and an enthusiasm for high-speed driving are among the factors combining to give Nigeria the worst traffic accident record in the world. Only recently did the newly created Federal Road Safety Corps begin to address the severe problem by setting the first highway speed limits.

Modern Nigeria is a land of enduring continuities and striking contrasts, a land in which centuries old patterns co-exist with modern technology. Visitors to contemporary Nigeria enter a country characterized by an extremely vigorous entrepreneurial spirit not found in neighbouring states: Nigeria has been described as a nation of traders. Buying and selling, marked by continuous negotiations, permeate most aspects of daily life. Nigerians are known for the energy, enthusiasm and ambitious self-confidence with which they conduct themselves.

Despite Nigeria's shortcomings since independence, Nigerians have important reasons to be proud. They have successfully endured a bitter civil war with remarkably little lasting animosity. Although the military forcefully seized control of the government from civilians, on balance it has governed with benevolence and acted in the interests of the larger society. Nigeria continues to seek a republican form of government as the best way to match the needs of individuals and groups with the requirements of nationhood. The country has contributed leaders, scholars and creative individuals to the world; a body of Nigerian literature and works of both traditional and modern art exist for which any nation would deserve praise. The first Nobel Prize awarded to an African was given to Nigerian writer Wole Soyinka on 16 October 1986, and Chinua Achebe is the African novelist most widely read.

Although problems lie ahead, Nigerians have reasons for optimism. In a short period of time they have created a dynamic society from an extremely diverse collection of peoples. Despite cleavages of ethnicity, religion, politics, and class, Nigerians remain irrepressibly committed to democratic political and capitalist economic systems. Nigeria continues to be a leader on the African continent. As a result of the diaspora over the last three decades, Nigerians are now found in large numbers and in positions of influence far beyond the country's borders. In little more than a generation of independence, the nation has gained invaluable experience for the future. The many obstacles Nigerians have to overcome will be met with resourcefulness, determination and drive, and they stand every chance of accomplishing any reasonable goals. Confronted by their present difficulties, Nigerians can take heart in a popular slogan which combines characteristic cynicism and optimism: 'no condition is permanent'.

The Country and Its People

1 **Ethics in Nigerian culture.**
Elechi Amadi. Ibadan, Nigeria; London: Heinemann Educational,
1982. 120p. map. bibliog.
A fascinating, informative examination of indigenous Nigerian philosophy and moral
behaviour. The prominent author of several fictional works and a non-fictional civil
war diary *Sunset in Biafra* (London: Heinemann, 1973. Reprinted, 1982. 184p.
(African Writers Series, 140)) uses his personal experience and the historical and
anthropological work of others to examine religion, secret societies, murder, theft and
adultery, *awuf* ('bribery, corruption or any gain obtained through trickery, dishonesty
or sharp practice', p. 82), slavery, goodness and other practices and values. Amadi
condems sexual discrimination and urges that ethics be taught in Nigerian schools. In
his *Socio-ethical issues in Nigeria* (q.v.), Nwachukwuike S. S. Iwe discusses a similarly
wide range of social issues and makes recommendations.

2 **The development of modern Nigeria.**
Okoi Arikpo. Harmondsworth, England: Penguin, 1967. 176p. map.
bibliog. (Penguin African Library, AP 21).
This book offers a perceptive and wide-ranging survey of the new nation, attempting
'to explain how Nigeria came to be what it is today. Emphasis has . . . been laid on the
social forces – political, economic and cultural – which have determined the nature and
direction of constitutional change. The central theme of the book is that Nigeria is
neither a geographical expression nor a historical accident . . . [but rather] a single
economic unit' (p. 13). The author describes Nigerian cultural and colonial history,
constitutional evolution, nationalism, tribalism, factionalism and the collapse of the
First Republic. The 'Bibliographical note' (p. 167–69) directs readers to important
sources.

1

3 Modern Nigeria.

Guy Arnold. London: Longman, 1977. 192p. 3 maps. bibliog.

Arnold assesses Nigeria's development and potential in 1975 and early 1976. Chapters provide informative summaries of post-independence history, politics, the petroleum industry, the Third National Development Plan, development problems, agriculture, education and manpower, corruption, neocolonialism and the press. Appendices contain General Murtala Mohammed's speech on assuming power, 30 July 1975, census comparisons, state changes, oil production data from 1972 to the first quarter of 1975, banks, growth rates of demand and production in 1975, and General O. Obasanjo's broadcast to the nation, 14 Febuary 1976. An important volume on contemporary Nigeria is *Social Change in Nigeria* (New York; Harlow, England: Longman, 1986. 261p.) edited by Simi Afonja and Tola Olu Pearce. Its ten chapters authored by the editors and Ladun Anise, Oladimeji Alo, Leo Dare, Carolyne Dennis, Sheilah Clarke Ekong, and Funmi Oluruntimehin (all except Anise are members of the faculty of the University of Obafemi Awolowo University) cover theoretical perspectives, family patterns, politics, bureaucracy, social inequality, religion, the medical system, social structure, and the law.

4 Le Nigeria contemporain. (Contemporary Nigeria.)

Edited by Daniel C. Bach, foreword by Etienne L. Dalemont. Paris: Éditions du C.N.R.S. (Centre National de le Recherche Scientifique), 1986. 336p. 18 maps. bibliog.

This excellent volume contains a wealth of diverse information. The first part has six survey chapters, on demography and cultural geography by Georges Courade, on history and historiography by Elisée Soumonni, on urbanization by John O. Igué, on politics by the editor and Mouftaou Laleye, on political economy by Johny Egg and Jean Philippe, and on art and society by Virginia Coulon and Alain Ricard. Part two (p. 195–212) is a detailed listing by Francoise Meynard of collections of Nigerian periodicals in Belgium, France and Switzerland with the years of each periodical held and the address of each depository. Part three (p. 215–324) by the editor and Marie-Elisabeth Bouscarle is another high standard bibliography of 1,538 French-language articles, books and theses on Nigeria, organized into fifteen topical categories and indexed by author.

5 Nigeria: magic of a land.

Ola Balogun. Paris: Éditions J. A., 1978. 191p. map. (Grand Livres Series).

This spectacular 'coffee-table book' by Nigerian author and film-maker Balogun with full-page colour photographs by Bruno Barbey, gives a realistic portrayal of the exuberant and vibrant qualities of Nigerian life. It was published in French as *Nigéria: du réel à l'imaginaire* (Paris: Éditions J. A., 1978.191p.).

6 Nigeria: twenty years of independence.

Edited by Bridget Bloom, with contributions by Tony Hawkins, Martin Dickson, Ian Rodgers, Mark Webster, Michael Holman. Ibadan, Nigeria: Spectrum Books, 1980. 148p. maps. bibliog. (A Financial Times Survey).

A comprehensive survey for the non-specialist by six *Financial Times* journalists who visited Nigeria during August and September 1980. Topics covered include agriculture, communications, the economy, finance, energy, industry, politics, unions, manpower, law and education. The chapter 'Doing business' (p. 27–40) with its 'visiting an executive,' 'newspapers are never dull' and list of addresses of the ministries and key officials is particularly useful. One of the best current accounts is the *Financial Times'* 'Survey: Nigeria' (8 March 1988). African news editor Michael Holman, and contributors Tony Hawkins, Nicholas Woodsworth, Peter Montagnon and Victor Mallet provide first-rate information on politics, the economy and social conditions in a sixteen-page special report.

7 Nigeria.

Sir Alan Cuthbert Burns, Reuben Kenrick Udo. In: *Encyclopaedia Britannica*, 1986, 15th ed., Macropaedia, vol. 29, p. 901–14, 933. 3 maps. bibliog.

An especially informative survey of the country, its physical and human geography, economy, administration and social conditions, cultural life and history. Briefer accounts of 'Nigeria' and 'Nigerian theater' are in the Micropaedia of the same edition vol. 8, p. 702–04. Current political and economic information appears in the annual *Britannica book of the year*.

8 Katsina: profile of a Nigerian city.

Gretchen Dihoff. New York: Praeger, 1970. 166p. map.

The author, an American who lived in Katsina with her family for two years, describes the ancient walled city from a non-academic viewpoint. She covers ethnic groups, history, Islam, the Emir of Katsina, sports and social life, the Hausa life cycle, education, agriculture, health, and local crafts and industries. Many subjects are illustrated with photographs.

9 Nigeria.

Ernest Dunbar. New York: Franklin Watts, 1974. 85p. map. bibliog. (A First Book).

This well-illustrated volume introduces the history, ethnology, resources and government of Nigeria to children of primary school age. The author is a former *Look Magazine* senior editor who has written on numerous African topics. The bibliography lists several other children's books on Nigeria. Nicholas Freville's *Let's visit Nigeria* (London: Burke, 1985. 95p. 3rd rev. ed.) describes natural resources, foods, geography, history, culture and peoples of Nigeria and includes 'A visit to a small village'.

10 How to be a Nigerian.

Peter Enahoro. Ibadan, Nigeria: Caxton, 1971. 79p.

A famous, witty, satirical examination of Nigerian 'national character' by a prominent Nigerian journalist and publisher. The volume consists of short anecdotal essays on tribalism, 'The chairman', etiquette, noise, greetings, grumbling, oratory, 'dash' (bribery or 'service charge'), mourning, telephone operators, bureaucrats, taxi drivers, newspapers, sex, patience, the English language, Lagosians, foreigners and humour. Enahoro (1935– .) was editor of the *Daily Times*, where many of these sketches first appeared in 1966, under the pseudonym 'Peter Pan' (q.v.). Another informative view of Nigerian behaviour is given in anthropologist Elizabeth A. Eames' article 'Navigating Nigerian bureaucracies, or 'Why can't you beg?' she demanded' in *Work in*

The Country and Its People

modern society: a sociological reader, edited by Lauri Perman (Dubuque, Iowa: Kendall/Hunt, 1986, p. 166–72).

11   **Nigeria struggles with boom times.**
   Noel Grove.   *National Geographic*, vol. 155, no. 3 (March 1979), p.
   413–44. map.

A survey of the state of the country, combining factual information and anecdotes with the upbeat *National Geographic* style. Writes Grove, 'A livelier, more responsive people I have never met. I was hustled, jostled, even threatened by Nigerian citizenry, but so was I gently cared for by strangers when I lay ill. I was turned away from meetings with public officials sensitive about publicity, but I was never turned away from a home' (p. 413). Excellent colour photographs by Bruno Barbey enliven the article. Other *National Geographic* articles on Nigeria include 'Progress and pageantry in changing Nigeria' by W. Robert Moore, vol. 110, no. 3 (Sept. 1956), p. 325–65, which documents Queen Elizabeth II's visit, and Hden Trybulowski Gilles' 'Nigeria: from the Bight of Benin to Africa's desert sands', vol. 85, no. 4 (May 1944), p. 537–68.

12   **The most African country: a survey of Nigeria.**
   Nicholas Harman.   *The Economist*, vol. 282, no. 7221 (23 Jan. 1982),
   p. 1–46 survey. 2 maps.

Presents a critical view of 'the giant of Africa'. In his survey of politics, the economy, agriculture, demography and a wide range of problems, the reporter was frustrated by a lack of hard data. 'This is the first survey published by *The Economist* in which every single number is probably wrong. There is no accurate information about Nigeria. Nobody knows, within a margin of error of about one-third, how many people the country contains, where they live or how much they produce' (p. 4). Letters objecting to the article's harshness appeared in issues of 20 Feb. (p. 4) and 27 Feb. (p. 8). Harmon also authored a sequel, 'After the ball: a survey of Nigeria' in *The Economist*, vol. 299, no. 7444 (3 May 1986), p. 1–42 survey, which examines this 'nation with a hangover' (p. 4). He reports on the inflated naira, population, agriculture, politics and the economy.

13   **Nigeria: giant of Africa.**
   Peter Holmes, preface by M. O. Akanbi.   London: Oregon, 1985.
   208p. 7 maps. bibliog.

A spectacular portrayal of the country and its people, on the nation's twenty-fifth anniversary of independence. Following a general essay (p. 13–23), the volume has sections of photographs on the land, the rivers, the people, four major geographic regions, nature, agriculture and development. Notes on the photographs, a brief bibliography (p. 207) and an index complete a fine volume. The production of the book was sponsored by the National Oil and Chemical Marketing Company of Nigeria.

14   **First things first: meeting the basic needs of the people of Nigeria. Report
   to the Government of Nigeria by a JASPA basic needs mission.**
   International Labour Office, Dudley Seers.   Addis Ababa, Ethiopia:
   International Labour Office, Jobs and Skills Programme for Africa,
   1981. 256p.

A critical evaluation of the basic needs of the Nigerian people, providing eight technical papers with observations and statistics on health, agriculture, food and nutrition, water, housing, health services, education, work, income and government. Past and present priorities are reviewed, and numerous suggestions made for a more socially oriented strategy for achieving higher levels in each of these areas. The ILO study, the first of its type in Africa, was conducted by the mission of ten people who completed their four months' fieldwork in December 1979. Dudley Seers of the University of Sussex Institute of Development Studies was Chief of Mission.

15 **Nigeria at the crossroads: a nation in transition.**
J[o] O[gbonnaya] Irukwu. London: Witherby, 1983. 324p. bibliog.

This volume surveys modern Nigerian society, including marriage and the family, religion, culture and 'the Nigerian way of life – life and death as seen by the typical Nigerian', political events from 1914 to 1979 and the economy. The author is cautiously optimistic about the country's future but asserts that success will require unselfishness and the placing of nation above tribe. He has been President of the Nigerian Insurance Association and has also published *Insurance law and practice in Nigeria* (Ibadan, Nigeria: Caxton, 1978, 3rd ed. 394p.) and *Reinsurance in the third world* (London: Witherby 1982. 266p.)

16 **Nigeria: reorganization and development since the mid-twentieth century.**
Charles Jarmon. Leiden, Netherlands; New York: E. J. Brill, 1988.
169p. bibliog. (Monographs and Theoretical Studies in Sociology and Anthropology in Honour of Nels Anderson, publication 23).

In this broad, integrative study of post-independence Nigeria, the author develops a theme of the rôle played by political institutions in national development. Chapters address the indigenization movement, the impact of civilian and military governments, the modern economy and wage ineqality, religion and political dimensions of education, and the rôle of cities in national development. In the appendix, the author, a sociologist at Howard University, Washington, DC, reports on his visit to an Igbo village (Obaku) in 1974.

17 **The Africans.**
David Lamb. London: Bodley Head; New York: Random House, 1983. 363p. map. bibliog.

The Africans is a lively, often critical, portrait of the continent as seen by the author during his extensive travels and interviews over four years while bureau chief for the *Los Angeles Times* in Nairobi, Kenya. 'Nigeria: the future is now' (p. 299–312) is a relatively brief account of 'the most exciting country in all of the Third World,' 'the Brazil of Africa' (p. 299). Nigeria 'moves to the rhythm of money, big money that springs from its plentiful oil wells' (p. 299). While full of information, this chapter lacks
the depth, accuracy and insights of his chapters on East Africa. The volume concludes with a statistical profile of Africa and a short bibliography (p. 349–51).

18 **Dreams and deeds: achievement motivation in Nigeria.**
Robert A. Levine, with the assistance of Eugene Strangeman, Leonard Unterberger. Chicago: University of Chicago, 1966. 123p. bibliog.

A fascinating study of underlying psychological factors in Nigeria's three largest ethnic groups and their potential functions in economic development. Guided by David C. McClelland's studies of need-achievement levels in diverse populations, the author

5

analyses data gathered from 342 male secondary school students (65 Hausa, 33 Northern Yoruba, 106 Southern Yoruba, 138 Ibo), students' dream reports and essays and from a variety of independent sources. He identifies a cluster of behavioural dispositions (achievement motivation, concern with self-improvement, non-authoritarian ideology, favourable attitude toward technological innovation, rapid advancement in Western education and Western-type occupational hierarchy) in which the Ibo rank high, the Hausa low and the Yoruba higher than average.

19 **Nigeria, the land, its art and its people: an anthology.**
Edited by Frederick Lumley. London: Studio Vista, 1974. 124p. map. bibliog.

The thirty-two historical and literary selections included in this volume 'aim to capture the spirit and ethos of a nation, Nigeria, its people and its places' (p. 12). The anthology contains excerpts from larger works by Mungo Park, Richard Lander, Mary Kingsley, Sir Richard Burton, Hugh Clapperton, Chinua Achebe, Amos Tutuola, Wole Soyinka, Cyprian Ekwensi and Flora Nwapa, among others. The volume is richly illustrated with reproductions of older prints and contemporary and historical photographs, seven in colour by Werner Forman, and contains brief 'Notes on authors and further reading' (p. 120–22).

20 **Take a trip to Nigeria.**
Keith Lye. London: Franklin Watts, 1983. 32p. map. (Take A Trip To Series).

For young children, this book gives a colourful overview of the country and the many lifestyles of its peoples. Basic 'facts about Nigeria' and an index are included. Other recent children's books include Carol Barker's *Village in Nigeria* (London: Adam & Charles Black, 1984. 25p.) which shows, in colour photographs and text, life in Aye-Ekan, a Yoruba village of Kwara State, and her *A family in Nigeria* (Minneapolis, Minnesota: Lerner, 1985. 31p. (Families the World Over Series)) in which she describes the daily activities of a twelve-year-old boy in a village.

21 **Nigeria: a country study.**
Edited by Harold D. Nelson. Washington, DC: The American University, Foreign Area Studies, 1982. 358p. 4th ed. 18 maps. bibliog. (Area Handbook Series; Department of the Army, DA Pam 550–157).

The most recent edition of this extremely informative handbook, based on scholarly works, official reports of governmental and international organizations, journals and newspapers, contains five chapters following a chronology of events, country profile and introduction. These are: 'Historical setting' by Robert Rinehart (p. 1–71); 'The society and its environment' by Irving Kaplan (p. 73–136); 'The economy' by Donald P. Whitaker (p. 137–86); 'Government and politics' by Jean R. Tartter (p. 187–234); and 'National security' by Frederick Ehrenreich (p. 235–85). The appendices have a wide range of information and the extensive bibliography (p. 309–43) is excellent. Earlier editions of this handbook appeared in 1961, 1964 and 1971. A fifth edition is planned in the early 1990s. Of great interest is the forthcoming volume in the series 'Westview Profiles. Nations of Contemporary Africa' *Nigeria*, edited by Timothy M. Shaw, Julius O. Ihonvbere (Boulder, Colorado: Westview, 1990).

22 **Nigeria.**
Sir [Cecil] Rex Niven. London: Benn; New York: Praeger, 1967. 268p.
map. bibliog. (Nations of the Modern World).
'This book is an attempt to describe the complicated country in as many aspects as possible' (p. 9). The author, who served in the Administrative Service of Nigeria from 1921 to 1959 and was President and Speaker of the Northern House of Assembly from 1947 to 1959, provides an account of Nigeria's economy, transport system, education, arts, health, administration and politics up to 1966. His numerous other works include *A short history of Nigeria* (Ikeja, Nigeria: Longmans of Nigeria, 1937, 9th ed., 1965. 294p.), *How Nigeria is governed* (London: Longmans, 1961. 4th ed. 180p.) and a *Short history of the Yoruba peoples* (London: Longmans, Green, 1958. 135p.).

23 **Nigerian life and culture: a book of readings.**
Edited by O. Y. Oyeneye, M. O. Shoremi. Ago-Iwoye, Nigeria: Ogun State University, 1985. 373p. bibliog.
This collection of fourteen essays covers diverse aspects of Nigerian culture, and includes: the editors' 'The concept of culture and Nigerian society'; A. R. Akintimehin's 'Precolonial political institutions and government in Nigeria'; B. Okuwa's 'Traditional kingdoms in Nigeria: indirect rule and its impact on traditional government in Nigeria'; M. A. Kwamena-Poh's 'Evolution of modern Nigeria (c. 1850–1979)'; S. O. Osagie's 'The concept of material culture and comtemporary issues in Nigeria'; O. Y. Oyeneye's 'Marriage and family'; O. O. Odugbemi's 'Nigerian culture and space utilization with special reference to Yorubaland'; M. O. Oyelade and A. T. Shonubi's 'Management practices in Nigerian traditional agriculture'; M. O. Shoremi's 'Indigenous associations in Nigeria'; A. T. Oduyale's 'Education in a Yoruba traditional set-up'; E. A. Odumuyinwa's 'Traditional religion in Nigeria with particular reference to the Yoruba'; O. Ogunba's 'Agemo: the orisa of the Ijebu people of south-eastern Yorubaland'; J. A. I. Bewaji's 'African beliefs'; and the editors' 'Toward a cultural revival'. The editors compiled this volume for their course by the same title at Ogun State University, Ago-Iwoye, Nigeria.

24 **Nigeria in pictures.**
John Frederick Schultz, Lerner Publications Geography Department.
Minneapolis, Minnesota: Lerner Publications, 1988. rev. ed. 64p. maps.
(Visual Geography Series).
This is one of the best children's introductions to Nigeria, full of colour and black-and-white photographs, relevant maps and graphs. The text is divided into chapters on the land, history and government, the people and the economy.

25 **Nigeria.**
Walter Schwarz. New York: Praeger, 1968. 328p. 3 maps. bibliog.
(Praeger Library of African Affairs).
This study is one of the most readable, informative accounts of the country and its peoples. The author weaves together history, colourful descriptions, literature and sociology, but appropriately emphasizes economics and politics. The result is a thorough overview of the new nation. For example, the chapter 'Behind the elite' discusses rural society, the unemployed, the working class, the middle class, the tycoons, the professionals, the chiefs, the politicians, the expatriates, Nigerian society, justice, education, the civil service, the press, religion, art and leisure. The

The Country and Its People

bibliography (p. 307–11) is useful. The author succeeds in writing a balanced, sympathetic description of the nation while it was embroiled in civil war.

26 **Friends, Nigerians, countrymen.**
Mabel Segun. Ibadan, Nigeria: Oxford University, 1977. 74p.

The well-known humourist, writer and 'international table-tennis star' has compiled seventeen of her amusing looks at Nigerian life which were broadcast over Nigerian radio between 1961 and 1974. Selections include 'Looking for a job', 'Who has seen a witch', 'Polygamy – ancient and modern', 'Family planning in Nigeria' and 'On being a good cook'. Each story is illustrated by Dele Morgan. Segun is President of the Children's Literature Association of Nigeria. Among her other publications are *Olu and the broken statue* (Ibadan, Nigeria: New Horn. 1985. 68p.) and *Conflict and other poems* (Ibadan, Nigeria: New Horn. 1986. 49p.).

27 **The Guardian Nigerian handbook, 1982–3.**
Edited by Michael Simmons, Ad'Obe Obe. Glasgow; London: Collins, 1982. 183p. 14 maps. bibliog.

A concise, useful and interesting guide to many facets of the country. Numerous writers describe Nigeria in some forty-six brief essays grouped under a general introduction, including: 'Foreign relations', 'The economy', 'National character', 'Education', and 'Business briefing'. Other titles include: 'State of the nation', 'Party profiles', 'Nigeria and the wider world', 'OPEC', 'Trade unions', 'Women', 'The states, towns and cities' (with twelve town plans), 'Abuja', 'Travelling in Nigeria', 'Rock music', 'The education programme', 'Officialdom', 'Advertising' and 'Tips and hints'. Statistics, photographs and useful addresses appear throughout. A list of important dates concludes the volume. The second edition of *The Guardian Nigerian handbook, 1983–84* was published to coincide with the 1983 elections.

28 **Nigeria: the land and its peoples.**
Richard Synge. London: Macdonald Educational, 1975. 63p. maps. bibliog. (Countries Series).

A colourful, richly-illustrated volume in a series aimed at younger students. The slender book is packed with information on topics including geography, family life, fashion, sports, education, religion, customs, foods, music, arts and crafts, history and governemnt. Special reference pages concentrate on human and physical geography, history, the arts and the economy and include a gazetteer. The earlier *Getting to know Nigeria* by Sam Olden (New York: Coward-McCann, 1960. 64p.) is profusely illustrated by Hans Petie and takes the reader on a descriptive tour of the country. It contains a brief historical outline and a pronunciation guide to the numerous Nigerian terms introduced in the text.

29 **Africa: the people and politics of an emerging continent.**
Sanford J. Ungar. New York: Simon & Schuster, 1986. 543p. map. bibliog. rev. ed. (A Touchstone Book).

An excellent introduction to the continent with an emphasis on economic and political aspects and on relations between the United States and black Africa. Lengthy chapters are devoted to Liberia, Nigeria, Kenya and South Africa. 'Nigeria: black power' (p. 121–61) is a sober, balanced, informative look at the country's development contemporary achievements and problems, which states that, 'For the country in

8

Africa that has, in important respects, come the farthest, there is still far to go' (p. 161). The appendix contains a statistical profile of forty-four countries; the bibliographic essay (p. 487–92) contains a practical list of references.

30 **Nigeria: the political and economic background.**
Royal Institute of International Affairs [C. H. Walton, R. M. Prothero, Ivor Stanbrook]. London; Ibadan, Nigeria; New York: Oxford University, 1960. 141p. 8 maps. bibliog.
This short book, published to coincide with independence, offers an authoritative survey of Nigeria's people, history, constitutional development, government and economic resources. The economic survey describes agriculture and forestry, mineral resources, industrialization, transport and communications, external trade, finance and planning for development. Economic data as well as area and population statistics are included.

31 **Background notes: Nigeria.**
United States Department of State, Bureau of Public Affairs, Office of Public Communication, edited by Juanita Adams. Washington, DC: Government Printing Office, Sept.1984. 7p. map. bibliog. (Department of State Publication, 7953. Background Notes Series).
A succinct, highly informative publication which gives a basic overview of the country. Standardized categories include a statistical profile, people, history, government, travel notes, political conditions, economy, defence, foreign relations, US–Nigerian relations, principal US officials and a brief reading list.

32 **Nigeria.**
Wilson Quarterly, vol. 4, no. 1 (winter 1980), p. 56–95. bibliog.
In this special issue, three articles describe the Nigerian economy, politics and society, and writers: Sayre P. Schatz's 'Moving up' (p. 57–69); Pauline H. Baker's 'Lurching toward unity' (p. 70–80); and Charles R. Larson's 'New writers, new readers' (p. 81–92). A series of selections from Nigerian literature and books for background reading are also included (p. 93–95). In 1980, of 215 books published in the Heinemann African Writers Series, fifty-two were by Nigerian authors; South African writers were second with twenty-three books. Pranay Gupte's 'Nigeria: oil-rich and nervous' in *The Atlantic*, vol. 247, no. 1 (Jan. 1981), p. 4, 6–8, 10–11, is a cogent analysis of Nigerian politics and economy skillfully woven throughout his interview with President Shehu Shagari. 'Nigeria is undoubtedly the giant of this huge continent. . . Nigeria sees itself as the peacemaker of this continent, but not necessarily as the banker' (p. 10).

Periodicals

33 **Annual Report on Nigeria.**
Great Britain, Colonial Office. London: HM Stationery Office,
1946–58. map. bibliog.

The British Colonial Office reports provide informative standardized surveys of the
colony's administration, population, government, and economy. This report supersedes
the Colonial Office's *Annual report on the social and economic progress of the people of
Nigeria*, published from 1914 to 1938.

34 **The Nigeria Handbook.**
Lagos: Government Printer; London: Crown Agents; Lagos: Patike
Communication. 1920– . irregular.

Each of these volumes is a rich resource of information on the country. *The Nigeria
Handbook* for 1953 (London: Crown Agents for the Colonies on behalf of the
Government of Nigeria, 12th ed., 339p.) is considered to be particularly useful in
describing Nigeria at that time. It is well illustrated, has appendices with economic
statistics, government lists and a practical bibliography (p. 272–88). Among its ten
maps are five large separate sheets devoted to geology, forestry, the provinces, the
divisions and physical features. The thirteenth edition did not appear until 1970. *The
Nigeria Handbook* for 1985 (Lagos: Patike Communication, 176p.) is a Silver Jubilee
issue containing information on the government, economy, tourism, a who's who, the
press, music, business and several special essays by Chief J. O. Irukwu, Ekpo Eyo,
Sylvester Utomi, Dennis Odife and others. The *Nigeria yearbook* (Lagos: Daily Times)
has been published in most years since 1952 and provides a useful directory to
businesses and government.

**Land and people in Nigeria: the human geography of Nigeria and its
environmental background.**
See item no. 36.

Nigeria.
See item no. 41.

Nigeria in maps.
See item no. 55.

Nigeria: a travel guide. Supplementary notes on Benin (formerly Dahomey).
See item no. 64.

Survive Lagos.
See item no. 68.

History of Nigeria.
See item no. 153.

A short history of Nigeria.
See item no. 154.

Groundwork of Nigerian history.
See item no. 162.

A history of Nigeria.
See item no. 163.

Nigerian history and culture.
See item no. 169.

The Nigerian civil war.
See item no. 315.

Nigerian slangs: a dictionary of slangs and unconventional English used in Nigeria.
See item no. 446.

Women in Nigeria today.
See item no. 519.

The trouble with Nigeria.
See item no. 528.

Nigeria: background to nationalism.
See item no. 577.

Nigeria between dictatorship and democracy.
See item no. 596.

West Africa: Nigeria and Ghana.
See item no. 609.

The Federal Republic of Nigeria.
See item no. 634.

The political economy of Nigeria.
See item no. 640.

Political economy of Nigeria.
See item no. 687.

Nigerian capitalism.
See item no. 708.

Nigeria: economy and society.
See item no. 717.

Nigeria Magazine.
See item no.1107.

Geography and Geology

Geography and climate

35 **Geographical literature on Nigeria, 1901–1970: an annotated bibliography.**
Compiled by Wilson O. Aiyepeku. Boston: G. K. Hall, 1974. 214p. map.

An excellent listing of 1,441 briefly-annotated items arranged by topic covering, for example, cartography and methodology to medical geography, land use and management and many other topics. Appendices include ranked lists of 'core authors', of periodicals analysed, and a list of bibliographies consulted. The work is indexed by author, place and subject. A good related book is Sanford H. Bederman's compilation *Africa: a bibliography of geography and related disciplines; a selected listing of recent literature published in the English language* (Atlanta, Georgia: School of Business Administration, Georgia State University, 1974. 3rd ed.) which contains 776 references to Nigeria among its 3,629 entries.

36 **Land and people in Nigeria: the human geography of Nigeria and its environmental background.**
Keith M. Buchanan, J. C. Pugh, foreword by L. Dudley Stamp.
London: University of London, 1955. 252p. 172 maps. bibliog.

Although dated, this impressive study is still one of the finest basic geographies of the country. Topics include the environmental setting, the human pattern, the agricultural economy, forest reserves, mining and industry, transport and public and social services. A substantial section on 'Disease as an element in the Nigerian environment' (p. 41–57) was contributed by Professor A. Brown. The volume contains 172 maps and diagrams and sixteen plates of photographs.

37   **Eastern Nigeria: a geographical review.**
      Barry Floyd.   London: Macmillan, 1969. 359p. maps. bibliog.

This is a comprehensive geographical appraisal of Eastern Nigeria up to mid-1967,
based on the author's teaching and research during 1962–66 at the University of
Nigeria, Nsukka, where he was Acting Head of the Department of Geography. The
volume provides an impressive survey of the peoples, the physical setting and
economic activities of the region in its eighteen chapters, numerous maps, tables, and
fifty-three photographs. The appendix contains 'The succession of geologic strata in
Eastern Nigeria, with an outline of their lithology and related topography' (p. 315–17)
and the bibliography (p. 318–43) is extensive.

38   **A geography of Western Nigeria.**
      James Grant.   Cambridge: Cambridge University, 1960. 95p. maps.

A highly-informative, descriptive account of the geography of the Western Region of
Nigeria using the device of an imaginary journey through the area. The book, well-
illustrated with maps, photographs and figures, was written for 'the junior classes of
secondary schools, . . . [and] may also be found useful in primary schools and teacher
training colleges' (Preface, p. iv). Its author was formerly Vice-Principal, Government
Teacher Training College, Ibadan, Nigeria.

39   **A geography of the eastern provinces of Nigeria.**
      J. H. Jennings, S. O. Oduah.   Cambridge: Cambridge University,
      1966. 208p. maps.

Though somewhat dated, this geography contains a wealth of information on south-
eastern Nigeria, including the Niger Delta. Climate, farming, village life, resources,
cities, industrialization and government are mong the many topics discussed through
the vehicle of a journey in the region. One hundred-and-thirty figures include
numerous maps, diagrams and photographs. The book was intended for secondary
school students and has study questions at the end of each chapter.

40   **The land and peoples of West Africa.**
      Akin L[adipo] Mabogunje.   In: *History of West Africa.* Edited by
      J. F. A. Ajayi, Michael Crowder. New York: Columbia Univeristy,
      1976. 2nd ed. Vol. 1, p. 1–32. 5 maps. bibliog.

An authoritative overview of geography and its impact on human culture in the region:
'. . . there is no doubt that much in the history of West Africa becomes understandable
when set against the background of the character of the land on which the events took
place' (p. 1). Nigeria is prominent in the description, for example, 'of the 434 ethnic
groups within Nigeria, . . . nearly 300 are found within [the Guinea savannah] zone.
Most of them number less than 50,000 people and only two groups over 100,000' (p.
5). Mabogunje is Professor of Geography and former Dean of the Faculty of Social
Sciences at the Univeristy of Ibadan, Ibadan, Nigeria. He is one of Nigeria's most
distinguished geographers.

41 **Nigeria.**
W. T. W. Morgan, preface by Akin L. Mabogunje, foreword by J. M.
Houston. London, New York: Longman, 1983. 179p. maps. bibliog.
(The World's Landscapes).

The author, Lecturer in Geography at the University of Durham and in 1976–78,
Visiting Professor of Geography at the University of Jos, Jos, Nigeria, describes
succinctly Nigerian geology, climate, ecosystems, human geography, 'townscapes' and
urbanization in this well-illustrated volume.

42 **A geography of Nigerian development.**
Edited by J. S. Oguntoyinbo, O. O. Areola, M. Filani. Ibadan,
Nigeria: Heinemann Educational (Nigeria), 1983.
2nd ed. 456p. maps. bibliog.

This second edition is an expanded version of the papers from the Regional
Conference of the International Geographical Union, Nigeria, originally published in
1978. Twenty-seven papers are grouped under the headings: 'Physical basis of Nigeria's
development', the 'Human factor in Nigeria's development', 'Agricultural development',
'Industrial development', 'Transport and trade', and 'Regional planning'. Authors
include Akin L. Mabogunje, R. K. Udo, G. J. A. Ojo, and E. O. Adeniyi, among
others. Topics include climate, water resources, mineral and energy reserves, soil and
vegetation resources, pests and disease, population, livestock, recreation and tourism.

43 **The climates of West Africa.**
[Simon] Oyediran Ojo. London; Ibadan, Nigeria: Heinemann
Educational, 1977. 219p. maps. bibliog.

An impressive, copiously illustrated description of the region's climates. Numerous
maps of the continent, the region and of Nigeria and data-filled tables present an
enormous amount of information, often technical, on solar radiation and sunshine,
temperature, evaporation, atmospheric moisture, rainfall, winds, regional climatic
patterns, microclimatology, bioclimatology and paleoclimatology. The bibliography
(p. 210–14) provides a lengthy list of relevant materials. The author (1939– .) wrote his
1969 University of California, Los Angeles, doctoral dissertation on *Energy balance,
climatology and livestock potential in Nigeria* and has published extensively. He was
Senior Lecturer in Geography, University of Lagos, Nigeria at the time of publication.

44 **Nigeria: a descriptive geography.**
W. A. Perkins, Jasper H. Stembridge. Ibadan, Nigeria: Oxford
University, 1966. 3rd ed. 184p. maps.

First published in 1957, this useful book is described in the foreword as 'primarily
intended for the use of pupils in the middle and upper forms of Secondary Schools who
are preparing for the School Certificate and similar examinations', and for students in
the teacher training colleges. The chapters cover topics such as geology, climate, fauna
and vegetation, products, travel, and trade as well as each of the states. The third
edition contains a new chapter on Mid-Western Nigeria, which was created 9 August
1963. The numerous figures, maps and photographs are informative.

45 **Geographical regions of Nigeria.**
    Reuben K[enrick] Udo. Berkeley; Los Angeles, California: University
    of California, 1970. 212p. maps. bibliog.

In twenty chapters arranged in three parts, 'The coastlines of Guinea', 'The middle belt' and 'The Nigerian Sudan and the eastern borderlands', the author presents a comprehensive study of Nigerian geography. An enormous amount of information is contained in the lucid text, the eighty-four maps and diagrams and the fifty-two photographs. A brief postscript 'The Nigerian political scene' (p. 208–10) relates the study to the bloody civil war being waged when it was written. This book remains the most thorough geography of the nation for the general reader. At the time of publication, Dr. Udo was a Senior Lecturer in Geography at the University of Ibadan, Ibadan, Nigeria. His *A comprehensive geography of West Africa* (New York: Africana, 1978. 304p.) provides an excellent geographic study of the region and includes a chapter on Nigeria (p. 225–49).

46 **Official standard names gazetteer: Nigeria.**
    United States Board on Geographic Names. Washington, DC:
    Geographic Names Division, US Army Topographic Command, May
    1971. 641p. map.

This gazetteer contains about 42,000 official standard names approved by the United States Board on Geographic Names. Each name is given geographic coordinates and an administrative division location. 'The basic name coverage corresponds generally to that of maps at the scale of 1:250,000' (Foreword, p. i).

47 **Towards a Nigerian urban policy.**
    Joseph Uyanga. Ibadan, Nigeria: Ibadan University, 1982. 211p.
    7 maps. bibliog.

The author examines in detail urban resources, urban land policies, transportation, urban traffic and the problems and prospects of Nigerian urbanization. Important statistical tables show 182 urban centres ranked according to population by the 1963 census, growth for selected cities and urban and rural populations in 1963 and 1972.

Periodical

48 **The Nigerian Geographical Journal.**
    Ibadan, Nigeria: University of Ibadan, Department of Geography, April
    1957– . annual.

The Nigerian Geographical Association's journal contains a wide range of articles on Nigerian geography including topics such as land use, demography, planning, transport, disease, soil studies and many others. Of recent interest is H. I. Ajaegbu's 'Orientation for Nigerian geography in the 1980s: the need for medical geographical studies' vol. 24, nos. 1,2 (June and Dec. 1981), p. 3–13.

Annals of Borno.
See item no. 1103.

Savanna. A Journal of the Environmental and Social Sciences.
See item no. 1110.

Nigeria.
See item no. 1139.

Geology and natural resources

49 **Proceedings of the conference on African geology held at the University of Ibadan from 7–14 December 1970 in commemoration of the tenth anniversary of the founding of the Geology Department.**
Edited by T. F. J. Dessauvagie, A. J. Whiteman. Ibadan, Nigeria: University of Ibadan, Department of Geology, 1972. 668p. maps. bibliog.

Among the fifty-one papers included are geological studies, some in French, of Niger, Botswana, Angola, Cameroon, Côte d'Ivoire, Sierra Leone, Libya, Liberia, Republic of South Africa, Algeria and Tanzania, but the overwhelming majority concern aspects of Nigerian geology. Papers are grouped into eight categories: 'Basement complex and pre-Cambrian rocks'; 'Alkaline rocks and ring complexes'; 'Cretaceous rocks of Nigeria and adjacent areas'; 'Tertiary rocks of Nigeria'; 'Quarternary rocks and geomorphology of Angola, Chad, Côte d'Ivoire, Nigeria and Sahara'; 'Regional geology'; 'Structural geology'; 'Others, and excursions in Nigeria'. Maps and diagrams abound; several plates are included.

50 **Fossil vertebrates of Nigeria.**
L. B[everly] Halstead, Jennifer Middleton. *Nigerian Field*, vol. 41, no. 2 (June 1976), p. 55–63; vol. 41, no. 3 (Sept. 1976), p. 129–33; vol. 41, no. 4 (Dec. 1976), p. 166–74. bibliog.

The authors describe the history of previous research on Nigerian fossil vertebrates and illustrate descriptions of Eocene creatures (an albatross, a leathery turtle, a sea-snake, and a whale), Palaeocene crocodiles and Cretaceous crocodiles, a Mosasaur lizard and a giant tortoise. See also Beverly Halstead's 'Hunting pre-historic reptiles in Nigeria' *Nigerian Field*, vol. 38, no. 1 (March 1973), p. 4–14, for an account of the expedition to the Sokoto area.

51 **Geology of Nigeria.**
Edited by C. A. Kogbe. Lagos, Nigeria: Elizabethan Publishing, 1976. 436p. maps. bibliog.

This volume, based on the papers presented at the January 1974 Conference on Nigerian Geology sponsored by the Centre for Advanced Studies at the Univeristy of Ife, is replete with information. Its twenty-eight chapters and three abstracts provide a comprehensive survey of the outstanding aspects of the geology of Nigeria. The papers are divided into six sections: pre-Cambrian and Upper Palaeozoic basement; volcanic rocks and the younger granite province; sedimentary basins; quarternary sediments; hydrogeology and economic geology and abstracts. Most papers contain data, illustrative material, diagrams and/or maps. The editor was secretary of the conference and was in the Department of Geology, University of Ife (now Obafemi Awolowo University), Ile-Ife, Nigeria.

52 **Water resources and economic development in Nigeria.**
Akin L. Mabogunje. In: *Ecology and economic development in tropical Africa.* Edited by David Brokensha. Berkeley, California: University of California, Institute of International Studies, 1965. p. 147–59. bibliog. (Research Series, no. 9).
This paper describes 'how the water resources of Nigeria are being developed to respond to the crisis posed by the increasing tempo of economic development in the country' (p. 147). The author describes Nigeria's groundwater and surface water resources, the water supplies of urban centres, industrial use of water and trends in the development of water resources, and states that 'There is no accurate estimate of the magnitude of the water resource potential in Nigeria' (p. 148).

53 **Energy in Nigeria.**
Richard Synge. London: Middle East Economic Digest, 1986. 145p. 4 maps. (A MEED Perspective).
An extremely valuable survey and analysis of Nigeria's energy resources, with emphasis on the oil industry, natural gas and electric power. Discussions include the history of the oil industry, Nigeria's rôle in OPEC, problems with electric power, export prospects, the effects of the 'post-1982 crisis,' and Nigeria's energy future. Appendices (p. 105–45) present additional information from the Fourth National Development Plan and Programmes of the Nigerian National Petroleum Corporation as well as oil production data. The author was assistant editor of the *African Research Bulletin* and *Africa Contemporary Record*, 1968–75 and has worked for Africa Economic Digest (AED) since 1980. An impressive comprehensive account of Nigerian geology described systematically from the viewpoint of the petroleum explorationist is Arthur Whiteman's *Nigeria: its petroleum geology, resources and potential* (London: Graham & Trotman, 1982. 2 vols.). It is rich in maps, statistics and history, with more than 340 figures and extensive selected references (vol. 2, p. 376–81).

Annals of Borno.
See item no. 1103.

Savanna. A Journal of the Environmental and Social Sciences.
See item no. 1110.

Nigeria.
See item no. 1139.

Maps and atlases

54 **Historical atlas of Africa.**
General editors, J. F. Ade Ajayi, Michael Crowder, geographical editor Paul Richards, linguistic editor, Elizabeth Dunstan, cartographic designer, Alick Newman. London, New York: Cambridge University, 1985. [167]p. bibliog.

A magnificent volume containing sixty black-and-white and seventy-two large colour maps displaying a vast amount of information on the continent's geography, history politics and economics. 'Event' maps, 'process' maps, and 'quantitative' maps cover topics from 'Relief and rainfall' and 'Tsetse fly, trypanosomiasis and livestock' to 'Africa in world trade c. 1600' and 'Decolonisation and independence'. The atlas is the product of fifty-seven contributors, many of them Nigerian or with experience in Nigeria, and was funded by numerous corporate sponsors, a large proportion Nigerian. *An atlas of African history* by J. D. Fage (New York: Africana, 1978. 2nd ed., 79p. 71 maps) and *African history in maps* by Michael Kwamena-Poh, John Tosh, Richard Waller, Michael Tidy (Harlow, England: Longman, 1982, 76p. 36 maps) are both excellent sources of cartographic information on West African and Nigerian historical background.

55 **Nigeria in maps.**
Edited by K. M. Barbour, J. S. Oguntoyinbo, J. O. C. Onyemelukwe, J. C. Nwafor. New York: Africana, 1982. 148p. maps. bibliog.

A remarkable compendium of information displayed in fifty-eight data-filled maps and discussed in sixty chapters by twenty-one contributors, most of whom are geographers at the University of Ibadan, Ibadan, Nigeria. The contents are arranged in nine parts: 'General'; 'Physical geography'; 'Pre-history and historical and political evolution'; 'Social conditions'; 'Agriculture and fisheries'; 'Rural and urban life'; 'Manufacturing and power'; 'Commerce'; and 'Communication, transport and planning'. The final chapters describe 'Regional inequalities' and 'Problems, prospects and challenges of the Nigerian scene'. Two appendices, 'Summary of the main mineral resources of Nigeria' and 'Archaeological sites and dates', followed by a glossary of terms and a detailed bibliography (p. 143–48) complete the volume. 'Languages' (p. 46–48) lists and locates 395 languages and dialect clusters.

56 **Nigeria.**
Central Intelligence Agency. Washington, DC:CIA, 1985. scale 1:3,000,000.

A clearly designed colourful map of the country with smaller maps showing population, linguistic groups, economic activity, gas and oil fields, vegetation and Nigeria's location in Africa and relative size to the United States. It is available from the National Technical Information Serivce, 5285 Port Royal Road, Springfield, VA 22161, order no. PB 85-928033.

57 **The national atlas of the Federal Republic of Nigeria.**
Federal Surveys, introduction by Olumuyiwa Adebekun, foreword by
Chief R. Oluwole Coker. [Lagos: Federal Surveys], 1978. 136p.
An invaluable compilation of cartographic information on Nigeria, produced by a team
of at least thirty-two named specialists (including K. M. Barbour, S. A. Agboola,
G. E. K. Ofomata, P. O. Sada, and A. L. Mabogunje). Large colour maps in the folio
volume are grouped in topics covering physical aspects, flora and fauna, climatology,
human geography and rural economy, trade and industries, and twelve town maps
(scale 1:50,000). Useful descriptions accompany each map. The maps were drawn and
printed by Federal Surveys, Lagos, between 1968 and 1977. Town maps are from
1973-76.

58 **Republic of Nigeria. Catalogue of maps (June 1971).**
Lands and Surveys Division. Lagos: Survey Division, Ministry of
Works and Housing, 1971. 110p. maps.
'This catalogue lists all map series published by the Lands and Surveys Division of the
Federal Ministry of Works and Housing, and those series published by the Survey
Departments of the Northern, Mid-Western, Eastern and the Western States and those
published by the Department of Geological Surveys etc.' (Introduction, p. 1).
Ordering information and prices are included. The address is Director of Lands and
Surveys, Federal Ministry of Works and Housing, Lands and Surveys Division, P.M.B.
12596, Lagos, Nigeria. An earlier catalogue was published in (Lagos: Survey Division,
June 1969. 104p.).

59 **Macmillan road map of Nigeria.**
Macmillan. Ibadan, Nigeria; Lagos: Macmillan Nigeria Publishers,
1982. Scale 1:1,500,000.
An attractive map showing vegetation regions, main roads and state boundaries.
Distances between major cities are shown, as are latitude and longitude of larger towns
and cities. This map is available from Macmillan Nigeria Publishers, Editorial and
Sales Office, Scheme 2, Oluyole Industrial Estate, Lagos-Ibadan Expressway, P. O.
Box 1463, Ibadan, Nigeria. The Bartholomew World Travel Map, *Nigeria* (Edinburgh,
Scotland: John Bartholomew, 1982. Scale 1:1,500,000) is excellent. The three best, and
readily available, maps of the region are Bartholomew's World Travel Map, *Africa
North-West* (Edinburgh, Scotland: John Bartholomew, 1983. Scale 1:5,000,000);
Michelin's *Afrique Nort et Ouest/Africa North and West* (Paris: Michelin, 1983. Scale
1:1,400,000 (no. 153)); and Shell's *Africa North and West* (Frankfurt, GFR: VWK,
1983. Scale 1:4,000,000).

60 **Lagos street atlas.**
Macmillan. London; Basingstoke, England: Macmillan, 1985. 147p.
Represents an excellent colour atlas of Lagos for residents and visitors alike. Maps
are scale 1:10,000, and there is an explanation of vehicular access rules for Lagos,
together with lists and addresses of high commissions, embassies, federal ministries,
state liaison offices and hotels, plus an index of street names. The actual cover title is
Winnay Lagos street map. Enemsi's new map of greater Lagos (Yaba, Nigeria: Nigerian
Mapping, 1981. scale 5 cm.:1km.) is a large, colour map of the city which includes a
street index.

Geography and Geology. Maps and atlases

61 **The Federal Republic of Nigeria at a glance.**
Okpaku Communications. Lagos, New York: Third Press International/Okpaku Communications for the Federal Ministry of Information, [n.d.] scale 1:2,000,000.

A large map, emphasizing the states, expressways, and game and forest reserves, with a smaller inset showing the location of Nigeria in Africa. The reverse contains descriptions of the land, the people, government, Lagos, climate, tourist information with lists of hotels and their telephone numbers in each state and several colour photographs. It is available from Third Press International, Division of Okpaku Communications Corporation, P.O. Box 7680, Lagos, Nigeria, or 1995 Broadway, New York, New York 10023. The Nigerian Mapping Company's *Road map of Nigeria* (Yaba, Nigeria: Nigerian Mapping, 1980. 3rd. ed., scale 1:2,000,000) is an excellent map showing vegetation, terrain and roads with an index to towns and cities on one side and practical maps of nineteen state capitals on the other. It is available from the Nigerian Mapping Company Ltd., 22 Moor Road, Yaba, Lagos State, Nigeria.

62 **Oxford atlas for Nigeria.**
Cartographic Department of Clarendon Press with the advice of F. C. A. McBain. London; Ibadan, Nigeria: Oxford University, 1968. rev. ed., 1978. [78]p.

Only pages ii–vii and 1–21 concern Nigeria and West Africa (the remainder consists of a world atlas), but there is considerable useful information in this atlas. Maps are of varying scales. The 'Gazetteer of Africa' (7p.) locates a large selection of cities and geographic features. *Nigeria in maps: eastern states* edited by G. E. K. Ofomata (Benin City, Nigeria: Ethiope, 1975. 146p. bibliog.) is intended as the first in a series aiming to eventually cover the entire country. The editor and eighteen contributors, including A. E. Afigbo, M. O. Ijere and P. O. Sada, provide maps for Anambra, Imo, Rivers and Cross Rivers States and discussions on fifty-one topics covering *inter alia* geology, climate, vegetation, demography, land use, major cities, education, food crops, minerals and mining, ports and tourism. The bibliography (p. 144–46) contains 128 references.

An agricultural atlas of Nigeria.
See item no. 738.

Land resources of central Nigeria: agricultural development possibilities.
See item no. 744.

Nigeria.
See item no. 1139.

20

Travel guides

63 Visiting Midwestern Nigeria.
Compiled by Ignatius A. Atigbi.   Lagos: Nigerian Tourist
Association, [n.d.] 58p. 3 maps.

This informative, illustrated guide for visitors and travellers through Mid-Western
State (now Bendel State) of southern Nigeria describes tourist sites, the 'history,
people and language', 'historic Benin', other towns throughout the state and hotel
amenities. It contains fold-out maps of Benin City and the state and a double-page
map of Warri, plus a mileage chart for the cities and towns of the state.

**64 Nigeria: a travel guide. Supplementary notes on Benin (formerly
Dahomey).**
Elizabeth Harris.   Flushing, New York: Aburi Press, 1977. 191p.
10 maps. bibliog. (Let's go to Africa Series).

One of the few practical, detailed guide books devoted to Nigeria, this volume includes
general information such as 'What to eat in Nigeria and where' and 'What to buy and
where' as well as information on health care, hotel accommodation and nightlife,
village customs, picture-taking, residence in Nigeria and a glossary of Nigerian terms.
Featured cities are Lagos, Ibadan, Kano, Enugu, Benin City, Kaduna, Jos and Port
Harcourt, for each of which a small map is included. There is a useful list of Nigerian
festivals which includes the time and location of each and a recommended reading list
(p. 174–78). The supplementary notes on Benin are brief (p. 179–91). Aburi Press is at
Box 130, Flushing, New York 11368. J. O. Ayoade's 'Outdoor recreation and tourism
in Nigeria', *Nigerian Field*, vol. 42, pt. 4 (Dec. 1977), p. 22–29, also describes Nigeria's
diverse tourist resources and includes maps showing the forest and game reserves,
cultural resources, and the transportation network.

65 Bright continent: a shoestring guide to sub-Saharan Africa.
Susan Blumenthal.   Garden City, New York: Anchor/Doubleday, 1974.
545p. maps.

Although the financial information is now outdated, the author brings insight to her
comments on twenty-four countries, to make this one of the most informative guides
available. The Nigerian chapter (p. 167–95) includes descriptions of Lagos, Kano, Jos,
Kaduna, Ibadan, Benin City, Enugu and other cities. 'Getting around Nigeria' and
'Leaving Nigeria' are discussed briefly. The author's solitary travels in Africa for two
years form the basis of her book. Another important guide is Philip M. Allen and
Aaron Segal's *The traveler's Africa: a guide to the entire continent* (New York:
Hopkinson & Blake, 1973). Allen's chapter on Nigeria (p. 593–620) provides a
forthright assessment of 'Getting in and out', 'Getting around within Nigeria', 'Where
to stay', 'What to see and do', 'Local attitudes' and other topics.

66 West African travels: a guide to people and places.
Sylvia Ardyn Boone.   New York: Random House, 1974. 430p. maps.
bibliog.

Fourteen countries are described for the tourist. The chapter on Nigeria (p. 309–49)
focuses on Lagos and on Ibadan, 'the largest indigenous African city'. Particularly

21

useful are the first and last chapters, 'Perspectives' and 'ABCs of coping', giving practical insights on how to make the most of the trip.

67 A guide to Kaduna, the capital of Northern Nigeria.
Compiled by Kenneth James Bryant. Zaria, Nigeria: Gaskiya, [1959]. 38p. 2 maps.

This illustrated guide, though dated, offers useful descriptions of important buildings and covers the history of the city; it also contains a fold-out map. Bryant compiled two similar guides, *Kano, gateway to Northern Nigeria* (Zaria, Nigeria: Gaskiya, 1959. 38p.) which contains a fold-out map, and *Kwara State tourist guide* (Ilorin, Nigeria: Government Printer, 1980. 32p.) which surveys this western state. A. H. M. Kirk-Greene's *This is Northern Nigeria: background to an invitation* (Kaduna, Nigeria: Government Printer, 1956. 96p.) remains a valuable guide to the region.

68 Survive Lagos.
Elizabeth Cox, Erice Anderssen. Ibadan, Nigeria: Spectrum, 1984. 143p. 2 maps.

Presents an immensely useful and informative guide. The authors cover everything from the history of Lagos, shopping, housing, hotels, and transport to customs and etiquette, language, cuisine, recipes, doing business in Lagos and much more. The 'Leisure' section (p. 79–143) describes clubs and organizations, restaurants and nightlife, beaches, 'trips up country', gardening and bird watching in Lagos and visits to neighbouring countries. Numerous colour photographs appear throughout. It is available from Spectrum Books, Sunshine House, Second Commercial Road, Oluyole Estate, P.M.B. 5612, Ibadan, Nigeria, or Safari Books (Export) Ltd., P.O. Box 316, Portman House, 32 Hue Street, St. Helier, Jersey, Channel Islands.

69 Guide to West Africa: the Niger and Gambia River route.
Kim Naylor. London: Michael Haag, 1986. 224p. 7 maps.

A practical guide for travellers to northern Nigeria, Niger, Mali, Senegal and Gambia, generously illustrated with photographs by the author and with city maps. For Nigeria, the focus is on Kano (p. 37–43). The appendix describes the West African travels of Mungo Park, Gordon Laing, René Caillie and Heinrich Barth. *Backpacker's Africa: a guide to West and Central Africa for walkers and overland travellers* by David Else (Chalfont St. Peter, England: Bradt; Edison, New Jersey: Hunter, 1988. 248p.) also includes a section on Nigeria (p. 187–94) which describes Lagos, Kano, the Jos Plateau, Yankari Game Reserve and Kainji Lake National Park. The Touring Club Suisse's *Transafrique: descriptions de routes* [Trans-Africa: descriptions of the routes] (Geneva: Touring Club Suisse, 1983. 6th ed. 425p.) contains routes through Nigeria and sketchy city maps of Enugu, Ibadan, Kaduna, Kano and Lagos.

70 West Africa: a travel survival kit.
Alex Newton. Berkeley, California; Victoria, South Yarra, Australia: Lonely Planet, 1988. 460p. maps.

An excellent, up-to-date guide book and introduction to sixteen West African countries with useful preliminary material (p. 7–92) on the region. The Nigerian section (p. 342–75) contains a historical summary, descriptions of the people, geography and practical information on the major Nigerian cities, Obudu Cattle Ranch and Yankari Game Reserve. There are simple maps for Nigeria, Lagos, Benin City,

Kaduna, Kano and Sokoto. Geoff Crowther's *Africa on a shoestring* (Berkeley, California; Victoria, Australia: Lonely Planet, 1986. 3rd ed. 752p.) contains a chapter on Nigeria (p. 436–55) with useful basic information on visas, accommodation, transportation and city plans for Lagos, Kano, Kaduna, Ibadan and Enugu.

71 **Traveller's guide to West Africa.**
Edited by Alan Rake. London: IC Publications; Edison, New Jersey: Hunter, 1988. 7th ed. 274p. maps.

In addition to a 'country-by-country' guide to twenty West African nations, this volume contains brief sections on climate; 'Do's and don'ts'; 'A guide to package tours' by Roger Murray; 'Peoples of the Niger' by Peter B. Clarke; 'An African's guide to the traveller' by Nii K. Bentsi-Enchill; 'Gastronomic adventures in West Africa', and an 'Introduction to West African literature' by Alistair Niven. The Nigerian chapter (p. 208–35) offers an overview of the country, discusses major sights in each state and lists hotels by state in addition to offering standard information on entry regulations, how to get there, embassies in Lagos, transport and food. It states, '. . . Nigeria does not actively encourage tourism although there are many new hotels and communications have been improving rapidly' (p. 208). The fifth edition was published in 1983 and the sixth edition in 1986.

Information Lagos: a comprehensive reference/directory for businesspeople in Nigeria.
See item no. 1113.

Explorers', Travellers' and Missionaries' Accounts

Nineteenth century

72 **A narrative of the expedition sent by Her Majesty's government to the River Niger, in 1841. Under the command of H. D. Trotter.**
William Allen, T. R. H. Thomson. London: Richard Bentley, 1848.
Reprinted, New York, London: Johnson Reprint, 1967. 2 vols. 2 maps.
(Landmarks in Anthropology Series).
An account of the expedition up the River Niger sponsored by the Society for the Extinction of the Slave Trade and for the Civilization of Africa. Three ships, the *Albert*, the *Sudan*, and the *Wilberforce* set out with 145 Europeans and 158 Africans and West Indians to promote trade, open up the interior and to establish a model agricultural farm. The expedition was a complete failure, especially because the Europeans failed to use their quinine to prevent malaria. Following the journal, appendices contain financial, medical, geological and natural history reports as well as 'Vocabularies of the Edeeyah, Dulla, or Cameroons, Mimbia, and fishmen languages' and 'On the Kru, Edeeyah, and Bimbia languages' by R. G. Latham, M.D. See also C. C. Ifemesia's 'The "civilizing" mission of 1841: aspects of an episode in Anglo-Nigerian relations' in the *Journal of the Historical Society of Nigeria*, vol. 2, no. 3, (Dec. 1962), p. 291–310.

73 **Narrative of an exploring voyage up the Rivers Kwo'ra and Bi'nue (commonly known as the Niger and Tsadda) in 1854.**
William Balfour Baikie. London: John Murray, 1856. Reprinted, London: Frank Cass, 1966. 456p. map.
An account of the expedition up the Niger and Benue Rivers led by physician W. B. Baikie (1825–64). The sixty-six voyagers (twelve Europeans and fifty-three 'persons of colour') left England 24 May 1854 aboard the 100-foot schooner *Pleiad*, built by former River Niger explorer Macgregor Laird and John Laird, and returned 3 February 1855. Baikie provides details of his encounters and observations of numerous

24

Explorers', Travellers'and Missionaries' Accounts. Nineteenth century ethnic groups, difficulties of the expedition and prospects for trade along the rivers. The appendix contains a 'Treaty between King Pepple of Bonny and the chiefs of Andony', commentary on 'The languages of the countries bordering on the Kwo'ra and Bi'nue' and lists of alternative names for features, towns and tribes in the region. A large fold-out map of 'The Rivers Kwo'ra and Bi'nue with the adjoining countries' prepared by John Arrowsmith in 1856 and a detailed view of the *Pleiad* are included.

74 **The Sultanate of Bornu, translated from the German of Dr. A. Schultze with additions and appendices.**
P. A. Benton, A. Schultze.   London: Oxford University, 1913.
Reprinted, London: Frank Cass, 1968. 401p. 2 maps. bibliog. (Cass Library of African Studies, General Studies, no. 50).

Dr. Schultze describes the history, climate, flora, fauna, population and 'commerical conditions and prospects' of Bornu (the Kanuri area of north-eastern Nigeria) around the turn of the century. To this P. A. Benton has added twenty-one appendices including lists of butterflies and kings of Bornu, meteorological observations for 1905–11, ethnological notes, unpublished correspondence regarding W. Oudney, D. Denham and H. Clapperton's mission to Bornu and other historical notes. Another major account of Kanem-Bornu is that by Gustav Nachtigal (1834–85) originally published as *Sahara und Sudan* (Berlin: Weidmannsche Buchhandlung, vol. 1, 1879, vol. 2, 1881; Leipzig: F. A. Brockhaus, vol. 3, 1889) and translated, introduced and provided with excellent notes by Allan G. B. Fisher and Humphrey J. Fisher as *Sahara and Sudan* (London: C. Hurst; Atlantic Highlands, New Jersey, 1987. 3 vols.). Volume three, *The Chad Basin and Bagirmi* (London: C. Hurst; Atlantic Highlands, New Jersey: Humanities Press, 1987. 519p.) contains his description of travels in Kanem-Bornu in 1871–72 and includes three separate map sheets.

75 **In the Niger country by Harold Bindloss together with James Pinnock's Benin: the surrounding country, inhabitants, customs and trade**
Harold Bindloss, James Pinnock.   Edinburgh, London: William Blackwood, 1898; Liverpool: Journal of Commerce, 1897. Reprinted, London: Frank Cass, 1968. 397p. 3 maps. (Cass Library of African Studies, Travels and Narratives, no. 48).

Bindloss primarily describes his travels to Liberia, the Gold Coast, Lagos, Akassa, the Forcados River, Warri, New Benin, Sapelli and Bonny and some of the local customs he observed. Pinnock's account is more of 'the surrounding country' than of Benin. The text (p. 341–97) is his lecture delivered to the Geographical Societies of Liverpool and Newcastle-on-Tyne and is heavily illustrated with photographs and sketches from *The Graphic* and *Black and White*.

76 **Missions to the Niger.**
Edited by E. W. Bovill.   Cambridge: Cambridge University for the Hakluyt Society, 1964, 1966. 4 vols. maps. bibliog. (Hakluyt Society, Series II, vols. CXXIII, CXXVIII, CXXIX, CXXX).

Vol. 1 contains 'The journal of Friedrich Hornemann's travels from Cairo to Murzuk in the years 1797–98' and 'The letters of Major Alexander Gordon Laing, 1824–26'. Vols. 2–4 are more important for the study of the European exploration of northern Nigeria as they concern the Bornu Mission, 1822–25, a reprint of the 'Narrative of travels and discoveries in northern and central Africa in the years 1822, 1823, 1824' (and extending into 1825) by Major Dixon Denham (1786–1828), Hugh Clapperton

(1788–1827) and the late Doctor Walter Oudney (1790–1824), originally published by John Murray in 1826. The narrative is fully annotated by the editor who also contributed an excellent lengthy introduction in vol. 2 (p. 3–127). Vol. 4 contains a bibliography (p. 781–84) and an index. Each volume has maps and plates.

77 **Abeokuta and the Cameroons mountains: an exploration.**
    Richard F[rancis] Burton. London: Tinsley Brothers, 1863. 2 vols.

In October 1861, the author left Fernando Po for Lagos from where he ascended the Ogun River to Abeokuta, the chief city of the Egba Yoruba. All of vol. 1 (333p.) concerns the trip, the author's literate observations on the country and the Egba, their customs and warfare and finally the possibilities of growing cotton there (he is doubtful that it will work). Vol. 2 (306p.) describes the return to Lagos in December and includes the treaty made with the Alake and chiefs of the Egba in November 1861. Most of the volume concerns the ascent of the Cameroon mountains, with botanical, zoological and meteorological lists appended. Burton's *Wanderings in West Africa from Liverpool to Fernando Po* (London: Tinsley Brothers, 1863. Reprinted, New York, London: Johnson Reprint, 1970. 2 vols. map) recounts his trip from England to Fernando Po to assume the consulship. Vol. 2 reports his views of Cape Coast Castle, Accra, Lagos, the Niger Delta, Bonny and Calabar. Numerous footnotes and Burton's enormous breadth of experience make this a lively and often humourous personal narrative.

78 **Journal of a second expedition into the interior of Africa from the Bight of Benin to Soccatoo to which is added the journal of Richard Lander from Kano to the sea-coast, partly by a more eastern route.**
    Hugh Clapperton, Richard Lander, introduced by 'J. B.'   London: John Murray, 1829. Reprinted, London: Frank Cass, 1966. 355p. map.

The first of these journals (p. 1–254) relates Hugh Clapperton's overland expedition from Badagry beginning 7 December 1825, to Sokoto where he died of dysentery 13 April 1827. The second (p. 257–327) is that of his servant Richard Lander who relates how he was captured from 20 November 1826 to 30 April 1828 and taken to Kano before he eventually made his way back to Badagry. An English-Yoruba vocabulary and meteorological tables are included (p. 328–55). The volume begins with a 'Short sketch of the life of Captain Clapperton by Lieutenant-Colonel Clapperton' and an introduction. A large fold-out map shows the routes of Clapperton and Lander.

79 **Travels and explorations in Yorubaland, 1854–1858.**
    William H[enry] Clarke, edited and introduced by J. A. Atanda.
    Ibadan, Nigeria: Ibadan University, 1972. 297p. 3 maps. bibliog.

The editor's informative introduction (p. xi–xxxvii) provides the context for Baptist missionary Clarke's detailed account of mid-nineteenth century Yoruba territory. Clarke's narrative is notable not only for its 'descriptive analysis of the history, the environment, and the political and cultural organization of the Yoruba society' (p. xvii), but also because he wrote without prejudice. Clarke (13 April 1829–71) describes the flora and fauna, geology, government, social life, agriculture, commerce, language, art and religion of the Yoruba people.

80 **Journal of an expedition up the Niger and Tshadda Rivers undertaken by Macgregor Laird in connection with the British government in 1854.**
Samuel Crowther, introduced by J. F. A. Ajayi. London: Seeley, Jackson & Halliday, 1855. Reprinted, London: Frank Cass, 1970. 2nd ed. 234p. map. (Missionary Researches and Travels, no. 15).

Historian J. F. Ade Ajayi in the 'Introduction to the second edition' (p. vii–xvii) describes the historical setting of the expedition aboard the steam-vessel *Pleaid* up the Niger and Benue Rivers. In addition he argues that Samuel Crowther's account is his 'most important book apart from his publications on the Yoruba language' (p. ix) and 'remains the most useful account of this crucial aspect of a major revolutionary period of Nigerian history' (p. xvi). Crowther records the expedition's progress from Abeokuta on 12 June up the rivers and back to Fernando Po on 7 November 1854. The voyage was notable for its discoveries and for the survival of the Europeans. In the appendices, Crowther describes 'The countries on the banks of the Niger and Binue' (*sic*) (p. 199–207) and in a 'Comparison of languages' (p. 208–29), he provides wordlists in English, Yoruba, Igana and Doma.

81 **Search for a place: black separatism and Africa, 1860.**
M. R. Delany, Robert Campbell, introduced by Howard H. Bell. Ann Arbor, Michigan: University of Michigan, 1969. 250p. map.

A reprint of the reports of two black Americans who travelled through the Yoruba-speaking areas of West Africa in 1859 and 1860 searching for places to establish settlements for black American emigrants. Delany's *Official report of the Niger Valley exploring party* (p. 23–148) provides details of the separatist movement itself as well as his observations on Liberia and Yorubaland. Campbell's *A pilgrimage to my motherland. An account of a journey among the Egbas and Yorubas of Central Africa, in 1859–60* (p. 149–250) (1st ed., New York: Thomas Hamilton; Philadelphia: The Author, 1861. 145p.) offers a fuller account of the expedition in diary form. The original contains a map of 'The Aku country with the course of the Niger' and an engraving of Campbell in Yoruba dress. Campbell was one of the 'Commissioners of the Niger Valley Exploring Party'. The introduction (p. 1–22) sheds light on the backgrounds of these men and on the movement they represented.

82 **Equiano's travels, his autobiography: the interesting narrative of the life of Olaudah Equiano, or Gustavus Vassa the African.**
Olaudah Equiano, abridged, edited and introduced by Paul Edwards. London: Heinemann, 1967. 198p. bibliog. 3 maps. (African Writers Series, 10).

The famous story of Olaudah Equiano, an Igbo captured and sold as a slave when he was ten years old, and who eventually bought his freedom and lived in England. Edwards provides an excellent introduction and notes to this account in Dawsons of Pall Mall's reprint of the 1789 original, *The life of Olaudah Equiano*, in the Colonial History Series (London, 1969, 2 vols.). His introduction to the African Writers Series edition is highly informative, but briefer. The 1837 edition has been reprinted (New York: Negro Universities, 1969. 294p.).

83 **The Niger journal of Richard and John Lander.** Edited, abridged and introduced by Robin Hallett. New York: Praeger, 1965. 317p. 2 maps. bibliog. (Travellers and Explorers Series).

By abridging the Landers' 175,000 word account of their 1830–31 explorations to about 100,000 words, providing an informative introduction, an epilogue, appendices of their instructions and equipment, a bibliography (p. 302–4), a place-name index, gazetteer and general index, the editor performed a valuable service. He considers this 'surely one of the most entertaining narratives of travel ever written' (p. 35). Richard Lander (1804–34) died in Fernando Po after being wounded on his second trip. John (1806–39) died in London. Of interest also is William Bascom's examination of 'Lander's routes through Yoruba country' in *The Nigerian Field*, vol. 25, no. 1 (Jan. 1960), p. 12–22. The original appeared as *Journal of an expedition to explore the course and termination of the Niger: with a narrative of a voyage down that river to its termination* (London: John Murray, 1832, 3 vols. Rev. ed., New York: Harper & Brothers, 1842. 2 vols.) and contained a fold-out map, 'The course of the Quorra, the Joliba or Niger of Park from the journals of Mess. Richard and John Lander with their route from Badagry to the northward in 1830'.

84 **The voyage of the *Dayspring*, being the journal of the late Sir John Hawley Glover, R.N., G.C.M.G., together with some account of the expedition up the Niger River.** A. C. G. Hastings, introduced by Lady Elizabeth Glover. London: John Lane, 1926. 230p. map.

This volume is Lieutenant John Glover's story (p. 28–201) in letter form of his venture from Liverpool (7 May 1857) up the 'River Niger to Boussa (27 Jan. 1858) as surveyor on the W. B. Baikie expedition. Hastings introduces, elaborates upon throughout and concludes the account with proud flourishes of Empire. The *Dayspring* was seventy-six feet long, yawl-rigged, weighed seventy-seven gross tonnes, was powered by a thirty horse-power engine and carried eighteen European men. The ship foundered on rocks in the Niger and parts of its engine are preserved at Jebba. The expedition never reached Sokoto, its destination, nor was Glover able to reach there on his overland efforts in 1859. Glover later spent fourteen years in Africa and served as Governor of Lagos for two terms.

85 **Seventeen years in the Yoruba country. Memorials of Anna Hinderer, wife of the Rev. David Hinderer, C.M.S. missionary in western Africa, gathered from her journals and letters.** Anna Hinderer, introduced by Richard B. Hone. London: Seeley, Jackson & Halliday, 1873. 3rd ed. 343p. map.

An account of mission work in Ibadan from 1851 (briefly) and early 1853 through to 1862 and the later 1860s. The volume contains seven illustrations. Miss [Charlotte Maria] Tucker's *Abbeokuta; or, sunrise within the tropics. An outline of the origin and progress of the Yoruba mission* (New York: Robert Carter, 1853. 278p. 2 maps) provides a slightly earlier history of missionary work among the Yoruba, especially the Egba' of Abeokuta during the 1840s and 1850s, with particular comment on the evangelical efforts of Rev. J. C. Müller, Rev. D. Hinderer, John Baptist Dasalh and the early mission schools. A fifth edition of this book was published in London by James Nisbit in 1856, which contains a fold-out 'Map of Yoruba and the adjacent countries' and a 'Rough sketch of ground plan of Abbeokuta (from memory)'.

86 **Denham in Bornu: an account of the exploration of Bornu between 1823 and 1825 by Major Dixon Denham, Dr. Oudney and Commander Hugh Clapperton and of their dealings with Sheik Muhammad El Amin El Kanemi.**
H[ugh] A[nthony] S[tephens] Johnson, D. J. M. Muffett. Pittsburgh, Pennsylvania: Duquesne University, 1973. 266p. map. bibliog.
(Duquesne Studies. African Series, 4).
Extensive extracts from the explorers' journals are interspersed with the authors' explanatory accounts of the expedition. The result is a highly readable and informative narrative.

87 **Travels in West Africa, Congo Français, Corsico and Cameroons.**
Mary H[enrietta] Kingsley. London: Macmillan, 1897. Reprinted, Boston, Massachusetts: Beacon, 1988. 5th ed. 741p. 2 maps.
(Virago/Beacon Travelers Series).
This well-known account primarily covers the author's second voyage from 23 December 1894 to 30 November 1895. Literate, personal and full of insight, this volume relates her observations from Sierra Leone to Angola, including brief descriptions of Lagos, Brass and Bonny of the Niger Delta and Calabar, where she spent most of her time between January and May. The Beacon edition contains Elizabeth Claridge's 1982 introduction. The third edition (London, 1965) has an informative introduction by John Flint, as does the third edition of *West African studies* (London: Frank Cass; New York: Barnes & Noble, 1964. 507p. map). Here Kingsley (1862–1900) offers 'reflection at a deeper level than the earlier *Travels in West Africa*' (Introduction, p. xliii). This volume contains numerous references to the peoples of southern Nigeria. This edition of the 1899 original by Macmillan has a fold-out map of West Africa, twenty-seven illustrations and Flint's excellent introduction (p. xxxiii–lxvii).

88 **Barth's travels in Nigeria: extracts from the journal of Heinrich Barth's travels in Nigeria, 1850–1855.**
Selected, edited and introduced by A[nthony] H[amilton] M[illard] Kirk-Greene. London; Ibadan, Nigeria: Oxford University, 1962. 300p. 6 maps. bibliog. (West African History Series).
An 'essential Barth', prefaced by a biography (p. 1–72), the first in English. Kirk-Greene attempts to give Barth (1821–65), one of Africa's most neglected eminent explorers, the attention he deserves. The majority of the volume contains excerpts from Barth's journal 'written in a style that is neither exemplary nor particularly absorbing' (p. 44). Selections concern: Katsina, 1851; Kano, 1851; the Hausa-Bornu borderland, 1851; Bornu, 1851; Adamawa, 1851; a base in Bornu, 1851–52; from Bornu to Katsina, 1852–53; Sokoto, 1853; from Sokoto to Bornu, 1854–55; and his return journey, 1855. 'Barth was proud, priggish and prickly, but he was a brave man, a fine scholar, and an outstanding traveller' (p. 44). Several maps, seven figures and twelve plates are from the original *Travels and discoveries in North and Central Africa, being a journal of an expedition undertaken under the auspices of H. B. M.'s government in the years 1849–1855* (London: Longmans, Green, 1857; New York: Harper, 1857–59; Reprinted, London: Frank Cass, 1965. 3 vols.).

Explorers', Travellers' and Missionaries' Accounts. Nineteenth century

89 **West African travels and adventures: two autobiographical narratives from Northern Nigeria.**
Translated and annotated by A. H. M. Kirk-Greene, Paul Newman.
New Haven, Connecticut; London: Yale University, 1971. 255p. 2 maps. bibliog.

Part one is 'The life and travels of Dorugu', translated and annotated by Newman (p. 27–129), the story of a Hausa boy who travelled with Heinrich Barth across the Western Sudan between 1850 and 1855. Part two is 'The story of Maimaina of Jega, Chief of Askira', translated and annotated by Kirk-Greene, 'an account of the British occupation of northern Nigeria at the turn of the century told fifty years later by a Nigerian chief who participated in these events' (p. 2). In addition two short works in Hausa are republished, with a selection from *Magána Hausa* by J. F. Schön (1885) and *Labarin Mai maina na Jega, Sarkin Askia* (the above work in Hausa), recorded reminiscences made in 1956 by Kirk-Greene and published in 1958.

90 **Narrative of an expedition into the interior of Africa by the River Niger, in the steam vessels *Quorra* and *Alburkah* in 1832, 1833 and 1834.**
Macgregor Laird, R. A. K. Oldfield. London: Richard Bentley, 1837. Reprinted, London: Frank Cass, 1971. 2 vols. map. (Cass Library of African Studies, Travels and Narratives, no. 68).

Macgregor Laird describes the expedition, which failed as a commercial venture because only nine of forty-eight Europeans survived, but which succeeded in navigating up the Niger from the delta to its confluence with the Benue. The expedition left Liverpool on 19 July 1832 and returned on 1 January 1834, following stops at Calabar and Fernando Po. The junior surgeon of the expedition, R. A. K. Oldfield provides a more extensive account (vol. 1, p. 307–451, and most of vol. 2) and includes his medical observations. Following a general chapter on trade with Africa, the appendix contains meteorological tables and vocabulary in English, Hausa and Eboe (Igbo).

91 **Africa discovery: an anthology of exploration.**
Margery Perham, Jack Simmons. London: Faber & Faber, 1957. 2nd ed. 280p. 11 maps. bibliog.

Of the eleven explorers whose works are excerpted here, several journeyed in present-day Nigeria: Mungo Park (1771–1806); Hugh Clapperton (1788–1827); Richard Lemon Lander (1804–34); and William Balfour Baikie (1825–64).

92 **Journals of the Rev. James Frederick Schön and Mr. Samuel Crowther who, with the sanction of Her Majesty's government, accompanied the expedition up the Niger in 1841 on behalf of the Church Missionary Society.**
James Frederick Schön, Samuel Crowther, introduced by J. F. Ade Ajayi. London: Hatchard & Son, 1842. Reprinted, London: Frank Cass, 1970. 2nd ed. 393p. map. (Missionary Researches and Travels, no. 18).

These journals provide personal and ethnographic accounts of efforts to establish a Model Farm at the confluence of the Niger and Benue Rivers. The mission failed

Explorers', Travellers' and Missionaries' Accounts. Twentieth century

because forty-nine of the 145 Europeans died during a two-month period, but peaceful relations were established with several groups along the river. Rev. Schön (1803–89) records events from Sierra Leone on 24 June 1841 to Fernando Po, 18 October (p. 1–254). Crowther's remarks (p. 257–344) cover 24 June 1841 to 31 October. One appendix (p. 371–85) includes Crowther's letter of 1837 to Rev. William Jowett and is a valuable autobiographical document of the later 'Bishop of the Niger'.

Twentieth century

93 African encounter: a doctor in Nigeria.
Robert Collis. New York: Charles Scribner's Sons, 1961. 211p. map.
A portrait of the country and prominent personalities, with an emphasis on health and politics, seen through the eyes of a British physician as he toured the Western, Northern and Eastern Regions of Nigeria in the late 1950s. The book includes photographs of Nigerian leaders and art. It was published first in England as *A doctor's Nigeria*. Between August 1958 and September 1959, Gwendolen M. Carter travelled widely in sub-Saharan Africa. She published her observations as *Independence for Africa* (New York: Praeger, 1960. 172p. 4 maps). She recounts her visit to Nigeria in October 1958 in the chapter 'The teeming streets of Lagos' (p. 146–60). She describes Lagos ('more like an overcrowded city in India'), Jos, Awka and Kano and comments on politics, federalism, the position of women, education and community development.

94 The voice of Africa, being an account of the travels of the German Inner African Exploration Expedition in the years 1910–1912.
Leo Frobenius. London: Hutchinson, 1913. Reprinted, New York: Benjamin Blom, 1968. 2 vols. 4 maps.
Despite Frobenius's archaic notions about Atlantis and his diffusionist perspective, this is a classic early twentieth-century travel account of the Yoruba and Nupe areas of Nigeria, rich with illustrations and details of Ife and Bida. Frobenius (1873–1938) published a four-volume version of the expedition as well, entitled *Und Afrika sprach . . . Wissenschaftlich erweiterte Ausgabe des Berichts über den Verlauf der 3. Reiseperiode der Deutsche Inner-Afrikanischen Forschungs-Expedition in den Jahren 1910 bis 1912* (And Africa spoke . . . scientific enlarged edition of the report of the third travel phase of the German Inner Africa Expedition in the years 1910 to 1912.) (Berlin: Vita, 1912–19).

95 Inside Africa.
John Gunther. New York: Harper & Brothers, 1955. 952p. 8 maps. bibliog.
During 1952 and 1953, John Gunther and his wife travelled intensively throughout Africa, covering 40,000 miles, visiting 105 cities and towns and taking notes on conversations with 1,503 people, to produce this colourful journalistic report on the continent. Three chapters concern Nigeria: 'Complexities and achievements in Nigeria' (p. 746–64); 'Nigeria – its inflammatory politics' (p. 765–75); and 'The Nigerian north' (p. 776–89). Gunther offers a capsule history of the nation and commentary on Zik,

31

Awolowo and Nigerian nationalism. He was struck by Nigeria's 'immense complexities and vitality, its color without end and high-charged, hot, multifarious development' (p. 789). The selected bibliography (p. 895–906) provides a wide range of relevant titles.

96 **Four guineas: a journey through West Africa.**
Elspeth [Jocelyn Grant] Huxley. London: Chatto & Windus, 1954.
Reprinted, Westport, Connecticut: Greenwood, 1974. 303p. 5 maps.
bibliog.
Presents Huxley's account of her travels in the Gambia (p. 2–36), Sierra Leone (p. 38–74), the Gold Coast (Ghana) (p. 76–161) and Nigeria (p. 164–295). The well-known writer visited most of the major cities and regions of Nigeria, recording her observations and visits with emirs, obas and colonial officials with clarity and sensitivity. She travelled to Lagos ('Lagos assaults you with its squalor and vitality', p. 167), Ibadan, Ife, Benin, Bida, Abuja, Kaduna, Kano, Jos, Vom, the Southern Cameroons, Calabar, Ikot Ekpene, Port Harcourt, Owerri, Enugu, Udi and Onitsha, always with a sharp eye for politics, change, tradition and local colour. Fifty-nine photographs, taken by the author, twenty-six of Nigerian subjects, are included.

97 **Through African doors: experiences and encounters in West Africa.**
Janheinz Jahn, translated by Oliver Coburn. New York: Grove, 1962.
235p. 2 maps. bibliog.
The author recorded his impressions of life in Ghana, Dahomey and especially Nigeria, where he visited Lagos, Ibadan, Jos, Kano, Onitsha, Enugu, Calabar, Benin and many rural areas. His commentary is organized in chapters on West African etiquette, modes of travel, ordinary people, kings, education, politics and religion. The volume was originally published as *Durch Afrikanische Türen* (Dusseldorf, Germany: Eugen Diederichs, 1960) and contains twelve photographs by Helmut Lander.

98 **Beyond the Niger.**
Sylvia Leith-Ross. London: Lutterworth, 1951. Reprinted, Westport,
Connecticut: Negro Universities, 1971. 124p. map.
This interesting narrative reports 'the small personal things' experienced during the author's ten-month visit to Eastern Nigeria primarily among the Igbo. 'This is a self-centered book, written for myself, to please myself, to remind myself of gay and pleasant things, of absurdities and surprises, of fanciful scenes and half-understood words, of a dark people living in a strange continent, so like us and yet so unlike' (Preface, p. 10). The small volume is illustrated with drawings by Joan Kiddell-Monroe. Mrs. Leith-Ross's talk given to the Jos Branch of the Nigerian Field Society 'A glimpse of Nigeria fifty years ago' in *The Nigerian Field*, vol. 22, no. 4 (Oct. 1957), p. 160–64, is of interest as well.

99 **In my father's country: a Nigerian journey.**
Adewole Maja-Pearce. London: Heinemann, 1987. 177p. map.
The author, a writer born in 1953 in London to an English mother and a Yoruba Nigerian father, describes his visit to Nigeria in August to September 1985, his first since a three-week visit two years earlier for his estranged father's funeral. The result is an ambivalent and often critical kaleidoscope of a complex, rapidly-changing nation with swatches of local colour and people gathered during during his trips throughout much of the country. Many of his perceptions resemble those of a visiting European:

Explorers', Travellers' and Missionaries' Accounts. Twentieth century

'The amount of patience required in Nigeria to get anything done is something that has to be experienced to be understood. . . Everything is dependent on personal contacts' (p. 174). 'Nigeria is a society divided by money, not class' (p. 129). 'Nigerians generally have a terrible reputation abroad. They are considered arrogant, aggressive and loud, and so they are. It is a source of some pride to them' (p. 3). Maja-Pearce also published *Loyalties and other stories* in the Longman African Writers Series (Harlow, England: Longman, 1986. 152p.).

100 **West African passage: a journey through Nigeria, Chad, and the Cameroons, 1931–1932.**
Margery [Freda] Perham, edited and introduced by A. H. M. Kirk-Greene. London; Boston, Massachusetts: Peter Owen, 1983. 245p. map. bibliog.

This posthumous volume of diary-letters records Dame Margery Perham's (6 September 1895-February 1982) perceptive observations of Nigeria while she was researching her landmark work *Native administration in Nigeria* (q.v.) to which it forms 'the personal complement to the necessarily impersonal book' (Introduction, p. 18). The diary was kept from her arrival in the Gold Coast in November 1931 until she returned to England in April 1932; published letters cease on 18 April when she left the French Cameroons. The superb introduction and notes by her scholarly friend Kirk-Greene add biographical context to the collection. A bibliography of the author's works from 1925 to 1983 is included (p. 237–38) as are fifteen photographs.

101 **The beach of morning: a walk in West Africa.**
Stephen Pern. London: Hodder & Stoughton, 1983. 224p. 4 maps. bibliog.

In October 1980 Pern and Waziri Amadu, his Nigerian companion, began hiking from Lake Chad along the Nigerian-Cameroon border. After crossing the Mandara Mountains to the Benue River, Pern was forced by hepatitis to abandon his goal of reaching the coast and returned to London. The account of the trip is full of pithy descriptions and observations, often humourously presented in a metaphor-rich style. Pern (1950– .) spent 1971–73 as a game preservation officer in northern Nigeria with the Voluntary Service Overseas. Twenty-one colour photographs by the author and his companion illustrate the book.

Flora and Fauna

Flora

102 **The useful plants of west tropical Africa.**
J[ohn] M[cEwen] Dalziel. London: Crown Agents, 1937. 612p.
bibliog.

A vast amount of information on plant uses in the region is contained in this 'appendix' to J. Hutchinson and Dalziel's *Flora of west tropical Africa* (q.v.). The volume contains indexes to vernacular names, common names, scientific names, and a bibliography (p. ix–xi) supplementing the one in the work's first volume (1927). Dalziel (1872–1948), a physician, collected 1,645 plants throughout Northern Nigeria during 1905–12 and also published *A Hausa botanical vocabulary* (London, 1916. 119p.). H. M. Burkill authored the second edition of this standard work (Kew, England: Royal Botanic Gardens, 1985). Of special interest also is the *Catalogue of the plants collected by Mr. & Mrs. P. A. Talbot in the Oban District, South Nigeria* (London: Trustees of the British Museum, 1913. 158p.) by A. B. Rendle, E. G. Baker, H. F. Wernham, S. Moore, and others [*sic*] which describes 1,016 species and 195 new varieties collected by the Talbots during 1909–12 and given to the British Museum.

103 **West African trees.**
D. Gledhill. London: Longman, 1972. 72p. (West African Nature Handbooks).

Sixty-four of the most striking and easily recognizable West African trees are described by Dr. Gledhill and illustrated in 121 colour and line drawings by Douglas E. Woodall. Scientific and common names are given for each and an interesting final section describes 'Some introduced trees' (p. 66–68).

104   **The useful plants of Nigeria including plants suitable for cultivation in West Africa and other tropical dependencies of the British Empire.**
John Henry Holland. London: HM Stationery Office, 1908, 1911, 1915, 1922. 963p. maps. bibliog. (*Kew Bulletin of Miscellaneous Information*, Additional Series, IX).

At the time of publication and for decades afterwards this work, one volume in four parts, was the most substantial economic botany for Nigeria. The general discussion (p. 1–46) provides a substantial overview of the colonies of Northern and Southern Nigeria in 1908. The appendix contains a 'List of books and papers of general interest for West Africa' (p. 883–97) and there is an index of English, vernacular and botanical names. Large fold-out maps of the 'Botanic gardens of Calabar, June 1907' and the Onitsha plantations are included.

105   **Flora of west tropical Africa: the British West African colonies, British Cameroons, the French and Portuguese colonies south of the Tropic of Cancer to Lake Chad and Fernando Po.**
John Hutchinson, John McEwen Dalziel. London: Crown Agents, 1927, 1928, 1931, 1936, 1937. 3 vols. maps. bibliog.

This masterful work, well-illustrated with line drawings, includes in its introduction a sketch of 'Botanical exploration in West Africa' (vol. 1, pt. 1, p. 3–9) for each colony covered, and a bibliography (p. 10–12). There is a fold-out vegetation map of West Africa (vol. 2, pt. 2). The appendix is J. M. Dalziel's *The useful plants of west tropical Africa* (1937) (q.v.). The second edition was revised and edited by R. W. J. Keay (vol. 1, pt.1 in 1954; vol. 2, pt. 2 in 1958) and by F. N. Hepper (vol. 2 in 1963; vol. 3, pt. 1 in 1968 and pt. 2 in 1972). *The ferns and fern-allies of west tropical Africa* by A. H. G. Alston (London: Crown Agents, 1959) is a supplement to the second edition. The entire original work and its revisions were prepared at the Herbarium of the Royal Botanic Gardens, Kew, England, where specimens of most plants are kept.

106   **Nigerian trees.**
R[onald] W[illiam] J[ohn] Keay, C. F. A. Onochie, D. P. Stanfield. Ibadan, Nigeria: Federal Department of Forest Research; Apapa, Lagos, Nigeria: Nigerian National, 1964. 2 vols. rev. ed.

These two substantial volumes, of 349p. and 495p. respectively, illustrated with both drawings and photographs, contain full descriptions of Nigerian trees from forty families. In addition to the keys to families and genera of Nigerian trees, it has a glossary and an account of 'Early botanical collectors in West Africa' (vol. 1, p. 5–13) by Keay, and for many of the trees described, one or more names in Nigerian languages. The work first appeared in 1960. Keay also authored *An outline of Nigerian vegetation* (Lagos: Government Printer, 1953. 2nd ed. 55p.) and Brian Hopkins and D. P. Stanfield provided *A field key to the savanna trees of Nigeria* (Ibadan, Nigeria: Ibadan University, 1966, 39p.). Important earlier works were Jas. D. Kennedy's *Forest flora of Southern Nigeria* (Lagos: Government Printer, 1936. 242p.) and H. V. Lely's *The useful trees of Northern Nigeria* (London: Crown Agents, 1925. 128p.) which describes the uses of 120 species from thirty families and provides a full-page drawing of each. L. G. Cooper describes twenty-three examples of 'Some Nigerian high forest trees' in *The Nigerian Field*, vol. 22, no. 1 (Jan. 1957), p. 21–36.

Flora and Fauna. Flora

107 **West African lilies and orchids.**
J. K. Morton. London: Longman, 1961. 71p. (West African Nature Handbooks).

This small handbook provides a synopsis of the families of wild flowers, then brief descriptions of lilies (twenty-four genera), ginger lilies (three), gladioli (two), arrowroot lilies (one), arum lilies (eight), canna lilies (one), orchids (nine), and an index. Each species is illustrated in colour by Iona Loxton, S. K. Avumatsodo and S. C. Rowles. The author was Senior Lecturer in Botany, University College of Ghana and Curator of the Ghana Herbarium at the time of publication.

108 **Nigeria's useful plants.**
Bep Oliver[-Bever]. *The Nigerian Field*, vol. 23, no. 4 (Oct. 1958), p. 147–71; vol. 24, no. 1 (Jan. 1959), p. 13–34, no. 2 (April 1959), p. 54–71, no. 3 (July 1959), p. 121–42, no. 4 (Oct. 1959), p. 160–82; vol. 25, no. 1 (Jan. 1960), p. 46–48, no. 4 (Oct. 1960), p. 174–92; vol. 26, no. 2 (April 1961), p. 70–90, no. 4 (Oct. 1961), p. 170–80. bibliog.

This extremely useful series of articles, each with a brief bibliography and well-illustrated with photographs and drawings, covers 'Plants yielding fibres, fats and oils' (Oct. 1958), 'Medicinal plants' (Jan., April, July, and Oct. 1960), 'Plants yielding essential oils' (Oct. 1960), 'Plants yielding gums, resins and rubber' (April 1961), and 'Plants yielding dyes' (Oct. 1961). Much information for this series was extracted from J. M. Dalziel's *The useful plants of west tropical Africa* (q.v.) which does not classify or index plants by their uses. The author's *Medicinal plants in Nigeria* (Ibadan, Nigeria: Nigeria College of Arts, Science and Technology, 1960. 138p.) was published separately.

109 **Medicinal plants in tropical West Africa.**
Bep Oliver-Bever, foreword by G. B. Marini Bettolo, preface by T. A. Lambo. Cambridge: Cambridge University, 1986. 375p. bibliog.

A most impressive study organized along a simplified pharmacological approach, with chapters on plants affecting the cardiovascular system, the nervous system and hormonal secretions, plants with anti-infective activity and those with oral hypoglycaemic action. The local uses, chemistry and pharmacology of each plant are described within each therapeutic group. The volume is illustrated with the author's numerous drawings of plants and contains a single botanical and general index and a very extensive set of references (p. 269–354). The author is a qualified chemical engineer, a linguist and has a consuming interest in practical botany. This study is a remarkable sequel to her earlier series in *The Nigerian Field* (q.v.) and her *Medicinal plants in Nigeria* (q.v.). Another excellent resource is Edward S. Ayensu's *Medicinal plants of West Africa* (Algonac, Michigan: Reference Publications, Aug. 1978. 330p.) which illustrates 127 of the 187 species of medicinal plants it describes and provides numerous local names, a bibliography (p. 297–300) and a detailed medicinal index subdivided by medical problems.

110 **Taxonomy of West African flowering plants.**
Omotoye Olorode. London, New York: Longman, 1984. 158p.
bibliog.

The majority of this practical illustrated volume consists of descriptions of selected angiosperm families, four chapters on dicotyledonous plants and one on monocotyledonous plants. Preliminary chapters discuss the science of taxonomy with particular emphasis on West Africa. A glossary, author citations, keys to groups of plants and an 'Index to the Nigerian names of some West African angiosperms' with Yoruba, Hausa and Fulani terms round out the book. The author is a botanist at Obafemi Awolowo University, Ile-Ife, Nigeria. Margaret Steentoft Nielsen's *Introduction to the flowering plants of West Africa* (London: University of London, 1965. 246p.) is an excellent earlier volume with descriptions of the ecology and vegetation of West Africa and of over 600 species from 128 families of plants. She was formerly a botanist at the University of Ibadan, Ibadan, Nigeria.

111 **Medicinal plants in Nigeria.**
Compiled by S[atish] C[handra] Singha. Apapa, Nigeria: Nigerian National, 1965. 82p.

This slender volume contains a 'list of one hundred medicinal plants of Nigeria – mostly collected and preserved in 1960–61 in the museum and herbarium of the agricultural research station, Umudike – incorporating a study of their pharmaceutical properties and uses' (p. 6.) Information includes common, local and botanical names, active ingredients and medicinal use. Thirty-one plants are illustrated. Singha was a botany laboratory technician at Umudike during 1959–62. J. R. Ainslie, then Chief Conservator of Forests for Nigeria, describes the uses of 366 plants in *A list of plants used in native medicine in Nigeria* (Oxford: Oxford University, Imperial Forestry Institute, Institute Paper, no. 7, 1937. 108p.). His 'Index to diseases, treatments & certain medicines' (9p.) and the 'Index to vernacular names' (7p.) are quite useful.

112 **The flora of Nigeria: grasses.**
D. P. Stanfield. Ibadan, Nigeria: Ibadan University, 1970. 2 vols.

In Nigeria grasses occur from more than ninety genera and 330 species. The author provides a systematic description of these, a glossary of terms, a brief introduction and a 'key to Nigerian grasses'. Vol. 1 (118p.) consists of the main text; vol. 2 (58p.) contains the illustrations. A second edition by Joyce Lowe is at press. *The flora of Nigeria: sedges (family Cyperaceae)* by Lowe and Stanfield (Ibadan, Nigeria: Ibadan University, 1974. 144p.) describes and illustrates the members of the sedges represented in Nigeria by 230 species belonging to twenty-three genera, four-fifths of which grow in damp environments. This volume contains thirty-eight figures and is thoroughly indexed. The *Flora of Nigeria* was jointly edited by Stanfield and Lowe until the former's death in May 1971. A. Blair Rains's 'A field key to the commoner genera of Nigerian grasses', *The Nigerian Field*, vol. 22, no. 3 (July 1957), p. 99–119; no. 4 (Oct. 1957), p. 148–59, includes drawings, notes, lists and descriptions of Nigerian grasses.

Nigerian chewing sticks.
See item no. 330.

Forestry and the Nigerian economy.
See item no. 728.

Flora and Fauna. Fauna

Forestry policy in Nigeria, 1897–1960.
See item no. 730.

Savanna. A Journal of the Environmental and Social Sciences.
See item no. 1110.

Nigeria.
See item no. 1139.

Fauna

113 **The birds of tropical West Africa with special reference to those of the Gambia, Sierra Leone, the Gold Coast and Nigeria.**
David Armitage Bannerman. London: Crown Agents for the Colonies, 1930–51. 8 vols. maps. bibliog.

This magnificent work is the most detailed account of avifauna in the region and describes 1,537 species and subspecies in the eight volumes. Vol. 1 (1930) has four maps, an ornithological history of Nigeria (p. li–lv) and a bibliography arranged geographically (p. 359–63; Nigeria, p. 360), eight colour plates and 119 figures, in addition to full descriptions for 190 types of birds, many with Hausa names included. Vol. 5 (1939) contains a large colour War Office map showing most of Nigeria and part of Chad (scale 1:2,000,000; 1932) and a smaller orographic map of Nigeria (War Office, 1928). Bannerman published a more 'portable' handbook, *The birds of West and Equatorial Africa* (Edinburgh: Oliver & Boyd, 1953. 2 vols) totalling 1,526 pages in which he omitted the technical descriptions and synonymy and condensed 'a history of birds of West Africa up to the end of 1950' (Preface, p. vii). This version contains numerous plates and figures from the larger work.

114 **West African butterflies and moths.**
John Boorman. London: Longman, 1970. 79p. bibliog. (West African Nature Handbooks).

A practical handbook with non-technical details, colour photographs and numerous drawings of about 225 of the most common butterflies and moths, grouped by family, in West Africa. A useful bibliography is included (p. 77–79). The author's 'The hawkmoths of Nigeria', in *The Nigerian Field*, vol. 25, no. 4 (Oct. 1960), p. 148–72; vol. 26, no. 1 (Jan. 1961), p. 17–42, describes eighty-nine species, shown in photographs, and provides a key to their identification. These hawkmoths are among the largest moths in Nigeria where the number of moth species 'probably well exceeds 10,000' (p. 148).

115 **The Nigerian butterflies.**
John Boorman, Patrick Roche. Ibadan, Nigeria: Ibadan University, 1957, 1959, 1961, 1965, 1973. 6 parts. bibliog.

This six-part 'atlas' of Nigerian butterflies attempts to describe with minimal text and to illustrate with a life-size black-and-white photograph every species found in Nigeria and the Cameroons. Patrick Roche offers 'Notes on Nigerian butterflies of the genus

Charaxes' in *The Nigerian Field*, vol. 21, no. 4 (Oct. 1956), p. 163–67, and 'A processionary butterfly caterpillar in Nigeria' [*Mylothris chloris*], *The Nigerian Field*, vol. 23, no. 3 (July 1958), p. 120–23.

116 **Small mammals of West Africa.**
A[ngus] H. Booth. London: Longman, 1960. 68p. map. (West African Nature Handbooks).

Descriptions of the characteristics and habitats of seventy-six small mammals include insectivora, bats, apes, monkeys and prosimians, pangolins, hares and rodents, civets and mongooses. Colour illustrations, by Clifford Lees, of each mammal enhance identification and the local names in Mende, Ewe, Twi, Dagbana, Yoruba, Igbo and Hausa for many are useful. The author was in the Zoology Department of the University College of Ghana, but died suddenly after completing the manuscript of this book.

117 **Notes on collections and observations of lizards in Nigeria.**
Joseph A. Butler. *The Nigerian Field*, vol. 51 (1986), p. 85–94. map. bibliog.

The author provides an annotated list of seventeen lizard species collected or observed in Nigeria between September 1981 and August 1982. In 'Capture au Nigeria d'un Naja noir et blanc de grande taille et notes sur les autres Najas de l'ouest africain', *Notes Africaines*, no. 176 (Oct. 1982), p. 110–11, Professor Butler reports his capture of a record 267 cm. long cobra (*Naja melanoleuca*) in January 1982 near Ibadan, Nigeria. Butler and Jon Reid describe their collection and observation of 127 snakes representing thirty-four species in 'Habitat preferences of snakes in the southern Cross River State, Nigeria' in *Studies in herpetology*, edited by Zbynek Roček (Prague: Charles University for the Societas Europaea Herpetologica, 1986, p. 483–88). In an article entitled 'Record of snakes from Nigeria', forthcoming in 1989 in *The Nigerian Field*, Butler and Reid provide a list of 513 records representing seventy-three species with a table of another thirty-three species, the most complete listing of Nigerian snakes ever compiled.

118 **West African snakes.**
G[eorge] S. Cansdale. London: Longman, 1961. 74p. (West African Nature Handbooks).

In this practical guide the author explains the frequency and social and economic importance of snakes in West Africa, gives advice on the prevention and treatment of snake bite and describes the forty-three most common snakes, grouped as the python family, harmless snakes, back-fanged snakes, cobras and mambas, and vipers. Colour illustrations of most species by John Norris Wood provide a means of easy identification. The author also wrote, in 1946, *Animals of West Africa* (London, New York: Longmans, Green, 1960, 3rd ed. 124p.) which for years was the only guide to the more common West African mammals, birds, snakes and insects.

119 **The lizards and snakes of Nigeria.**
G. T. Dunger. *The Nigerian Field*, vol. 32, no. 2 (April 1967), p. 53–74, no. 3 (July 1967), p. 117–31, no. 4 (Oct. 1967), p. 170–78; vol. 33, no. 1 (Jan. 1968), p. 18–47, no. 4 (Oct. 1968), p. 167–92; vol. 37, no. 3 (Sept. 1972), p. 99–120; vol. 38, no. 2 (June 1973), p. 54–80. bibliog.

In this seven-part series, the author describes and illustrates 'The Chameleons of Nigeria' (April 1967, seven species); 'The Lacertids of Nigeria' (July 1967, five species); 'The monitors and a plated lizard' (Oct. 1967, two species); 'The geckos of Nigeria' (Jan. 1968, fifteen species); 'The Amphisbaenids of Nigeria including a description of three new species' (Oct. 1968); 'The skinks of Nigeria' (Sept. 1972 and June 1973, fifteen species). The author describes 'The snakes of Nigeria' in a four-part article in *The Nigerian Field*, vol. 36, no. 2 (April 1971), p. 54–71; no. 4 (Oct. 1971), p. 151–63; vol. 37, no. 1 (March 1972), p. 21–38; vol. 38, no. 4 (Dec. 1973), p. 158–80. Part one describes seven species of 'The file snakes of Nigeria'; part two, 'The house snakes of Nigeria' (four species); part three, 'The harmless water and marsh snakes of Nigeria' (six species); and part four 'The harmless green snakes of Nigeria' (seven species). Of related interest is 'Uses of some reptiles by the Yoruba people of Nigeria', *Herpetological Review*, vol. 16, no. 1 (March 1985), p. 15–16 by Joseph A. Butler and Eugenia Shitu.

120 **Birds of West African town and garden.**
John H. Elgood. London: Longman, 1960. 66p. (West African Nature Handbooks).

One hundred of the most common West African birds are described and illustrated in colour paintings to facilitate identification. The author was a Visiting Professor of Zoology at the University of Lagos, Nigeria, and writes, 'inevitably the selection, being the author's own, is coloured by his own experiences, largely in southern Nigeria' (Preface, p. ix). Of related interest is F. Sander's 'A list of birds of Lagos and its environs, with brief notes on their status' in *The Nigerian Field*, vol. 21, no. 4 (Oct. 1956), p. 147–62; vol. 22, no. 1 (Jan. 1957), p. 5–17; no. 2 (April 1957), p. 55–69. Katherine A. Dobbs identified 240 birds between October 1945 and December 1954 for her article 'Some birds of Sokoto, Northern Nigeria, with brief notes on their status', *The Nigerian Field*, vol. 24, no. 3 (July 1959), p. 102–19; no. 4 (Oct. 1959), p. 185–91.

121 **Large mammals of West Africa.**
D[avid] C[hristopher] D[awber] Happold. London: Longman, 1973. 105p. map. bibliog. (West African Nature Handbooks).

This volume describes all the larger mammals found in West Africa, including smaller mammals omitted from the companion volume *Small mammals of West Africa* by A. H. Booth (q.v.). Most species are illustrated by colour photographs. In addition to comments on the conservation of large mammals, the author surveys the national parks and game reserves of eleven West African countries. For each, including Nigeria's Borgu Game Reserve and Yankari Game Reserve (p. 94–96), the survey provides a description of the park or reserve, its facilities, access, rainfall, vegetation and a list of main mammal species. At the time of publication, Dr. Happold was lecturing in Zoology at the University of Ibadan, Ibadan, Nigeria.

122 **The mammals of Nigeria.**
D. C. D. Happold. Oxford: Clarendon, 1987. 402p. maps. bibliog.
(Oxford Science Publications).

An indispensable volume describing in rich, well-illustrated detail Nigeria's 247 mammalian species. 'The book begins with a brief description of Nigerian climates and vegetation. Chapters 2–14 describe each species in detail. Finally chapters 15–19 present a much broader view of Nigerian mammals and consider the structure of mammalian communities in rainforest and savanna, the interactions of these communities with their environment, and the relationships between humans and mammals in Nigeria' (Preface). Supplementary material includes a glossary, a gazetteer, animal names in Bini, Hausa, 'Ibo', and Yoruba, a list of twenty-four species included by D. R. Rosevear in his 1953 *Checklist and atlas of Nigerian mammals* (q.v.) which are seemingly no longer present in Nigeria, a checklist showing the distribution of mammals throughout West Africa, 112 small distribution maps for Nigerian mammals and an excellent bibliography (p. 374–87). The author was formerly Reader in Zoology, University of Ibadan, Ibadan, Nigeria.

123 **West African freshwater fish.**
Michael Holden, William Reed. London: Longman, 1972. 68p.
bibliog. (West African Nature Handbooks).

The authors describe, for the non-specialist, about eighty of the most common and interesting freshwater fish of West Africa, concentrating on those of the Niger-Benue river system. Colour photographs and black-and-white drawings make this a useful book for the beginner. Brief chapters describe 'Angling and aquarium-keeping' (p. 54–60) and 'Traditional fishing gear and methods' (p. 61–64).

124 **Birds of west central and western Africa.**
C. W. Mackworth-Praed, C. H. B. Grant. London: Longman, 1970,
1973. 2 vols. maps. (African Handbook of Birds, series 3, vols. 1–2).

An extremely useful handbook, fully describing 1,371 birds of the large region. Most of the birds are portrayed in small colour paintings; each is shown in a distribution map. Both volumes are indexed and W. Serle provides a brief introduction to regional topography and climate in vol. 1 (p. vii–xxvii). Captain Grant died in January 1958, but he had already done extensive work on the taxonomy for these volumes.

125 **Checklist and atlas of Nigerian mammals, with a foreword on
vegetation.**
D[onovan] R[eginald] Rosevear. Lagos, Nigeria: Government
Printer, 1953. 131p. 240 maps. bibliog.

This excellent resource, originally prepared for publication in 1949, has been superseded only recently by D. C. D.Happold's *The mammals of Nigeria* (q.v.). Here Nigeria's Inspector-General of Forests provides a detailed checklist (p. 77–129) with scientific and English names, range, habitat, type locality and races of 239 mammalian species from thirteen orders. A distribution map is given for each and a large colour fold-out map of Nigerian vegetation (scale 1:3,000,000) is included. Forty black-and-white photographs (p. 43–75) and thirty-one general references follow the Foreword on 'Vegetation and habitats' (p. 9–37).

Flora and Fauna. Fauna

126　**The bats of West Africa.**
　　D. R. Rosevear.　London: Trustees of the British Museum (Natural
　　History), 1965. 418p. map. bibliog.

The author (1900– .) describes in detail ninety-seven named species and nine subspecies of bats belonging to thirty-one genera in West Africa. He provides a general introduction, references (p. 352–59), a fold-out map of the region (scale 1:10,000,000), two colour plates and 232 line drawings by Joanna Webb and himself. Earlier, D. C. D. Happold and M. Happold published 'The fruit bats of western Nigeria', in *The Nigerian Field*, vol. 43, pt. 1 (March 1978), p. 30–37; pt. 2 (June 1978), p. 72–77; pt. 3 (Sept. 1978) p. 121–27, which describes eleven species of fruit bats, three of which were unrecorded before, from Nigeria.

127　**The rodents of West Africa.**
　　D. R. Rosevear.　London: Trustees of the British Museum (Natural
　　History), 1969. 604p. bibliog. (Publication no. 677).

Rodents comprise the largest group of mammals both in genera and species and in actual numbers and in West Africa range from the tiny Hausa Mouse (*Leggada*) weighing less than an ounce to the Creseted Porcupine (*Hystrix*) weighing as much as 'half a hundredweight' (p. 9). The author provides elaborate descriptions, references (p. 581–90), a checklist (p. 2–8), and a general introduction (p. 9–34). The volume includes eleven colour plates by Joanna Webb and Rita Parsons, eight half-tone drawings by Rita Parsons and 248 line drawings by Joanna Webb, Patricia Wolseley, Rita Parsons and the author.

128　**The carnivores of West Africa.**
　　D. R. Rosevear.　London: Trustees of the British Museum (Natural
　　History), 1974. 548p. map. bibliog. (Publication no. 723).

This impressive formal description of the region's carnivores as far north as the eighteenth parallel of latitude includes a general account of the area and its ecology and is illustrated by eleven colour plates by Rita Parsons and 172 line drawings by Patricia Wolseley, Monika Shaffer, Rita Parsons and the author. The bibliography (p. 524–37) is extensive.

129　**A field guide to the birds of West Africa.**
　　William Serle, Gérard J. Morel.　London: Collins, 1977. 351p. map.

This most practical field guide to Nigerian birds covers 1,097 species, 'all the birds known to occur in West Africa' (p. 11), with 726 species treated fully and 371 included in brief status notes. The nomenclature used is a more modern condensed form than that used by D. A. Bannerman in *Birds of West and Equatorial Africa* (q.v.), but includes his names in the comprehensive checklist (p. 263–94). Latin, English, Spanish, French and German names are given for most species (p. 295–335) and there is a complete index of scientific names (p. 337–45) and of English names (p. 347–51). In all, 515 species are illustrated, 335 in colour, forty-eight in colour plates by Wolfgang Hartwig. The authors each spent more than twenty years in West Africa, Dr. Serle mainly in Nigeria and the Cameroons in the Colonial Medical Service, and Dr. Morel in Senegal.

Periodical

130 **The Nigerian Field.**
London: Nigerian Field Society, 1931– . quarterly.

The journal of the Nigerian Field Society publishes illustrated articles on the flora and fauna, natural history, and occasionally on the culture, history, sports and pastimes of Nigeria and other West African countries. It is currently edited by Joyce Lowe, Department of Botany, University of Ibadan, Ibadan, Nigeria. More specialized Nigerian journals include the *Nigerian Ornithologists' Society Bulletin*, published since 1964 on an irregular basis at Ahmadu Bello University, Zaria, Nigeria, and *The Nigerian Entomologists' Magazine*, begun in 1966 and superseded by *The Nigerian Journal of Entomology* in 1974. Both were and are published on an irregular basis by the Nigerian Entomological Society at the University of Ibadan, Ibadan, Nigeria.

Kemwin-kemwin: the apothecary shop in Benin City.
See item no. 560.

Nigeria Magazine
See item no. 1107.

Savanna. A Journal of the Environmental and Social Sciences.
See item no. 1110.

Nigeria.
See item no. 1139.

Game and forest reserves

131 **The vegetation of Yankari Game Reserve: its utilization and condition.**
Chris Geerling. Ibadan, Nigeria: University of Ibadan, Department of Forestry, 1973. 49p. maps. bibliog. (Bulletin 3).

This excellent study and J. Henshaw's *The ecology and management of Yankari Game Reserve* (Rome: Food & Agricultural Organization, 1975, 106p. (FAO Technical Report)) provide detailed information on the Reserve's flora and on the interaction of humans with the flora and fauna. 'Notes on the history of human influence in the Yankari Game Reserve area, Nigeria', *The Nigerian Field*, vol. 39, no. 2 (June 1974), p. 76–85, by N. M. Gadzama, S. Mustafa and M. J. Parr reports on interviews with residents of Wikki village in the centre of the reserve and on conservation issues. It is preceded in the same issue (p. 71–76) by S. S. Ajayi's 'Nigeria's progress in wildlife management', which provides a brief overview of the situation as it was in the early 1970s.

Flora and Fauna. Game and forest reserves

132 **The Olokemeji Forest Reserve.**
Brian Hopkins. *The Nigerian Field*, vol. 34, no. 3 (July 1969),
p. 115–26, no. 4 (Oct. 1969), p. 147–70; vol. 35, no. 2 (April 1970),
p. 54–78; no. 3 (July 1970), p. 123–44. maps. bibliog.

Located twenty-five miles west of Ibadan, this is one of the best-known forest reserves
in Nigeria. Part one describes the Reserve's natural history. Part two, 'The local
history' includes a fold-out aerial photograph of the Reserve; part three describes
physical features, climate, forest, and vegetation zones. Part four provides checklists of
flora, mammals, birds, other vertebrates, butterflies and other insects. Each part
contains references and photographs.

133 **The Borgu Game Reserve of northern Nigeria.**
John H. Howell. *The Nigerian Field*, vol. 33, no. 3 (July 1968),
p. 99–116, no. 4 (Oct. 1968), p. 147–65; vol. 34, no. 1 (Jan. 1969),
p. 32–35. maps.

The Borgu Game Reserve is the second and largest of the Nigerian game reserves. It
was developed during the period 1961–66 and covers 1,462 square miles. This three-
part article describes the Reserve's history, climate, geology and soils, vegetation,
fauna (with lists including the English, Latin and Hausa names of larger mammals) and
provides estimates of species numbers and their status in the Reserve. Photographs by
R. H. Kemp illustrate the article. The author was Assistant Conservator of Forests and
Provincial Forest Officer at Ilorin, Nigeria, and was responsible for much of the work
on this reserve.

134 **A guide to the Yankari Game Reserve.**
Alhaji Jibirin Jia, Philip Marshall, Humphrey Crick. Zaria, Nigeria:
Hudahuda, 1982. 32p. map.

This attractive booklet describes the history of Nigeria's Yankari Game Reserve,
whose 866 square miles officially opened to the public on 1 December 1962, and
presents brief descriptions and colour photographs of twenty-four animal species found
there. Common, scientific and Hausa names are given for each animal pictured and for
twenty-one additional animal species found at Yankari. See also S. S. Ajayi and Kevin
R. N. Milligan's illustrated *The wildlife of Nigeria: a guide to Yankari and Borgu Game
Reserves* (Ibadan: University of Ibadan, Department of Forest Resources Management,
1975. 42p.). Additional information about Yankari Game Reserve can be obtained
from The Senior Wildlife Officer, Game Preservation Unit, Forestry Division,
M.A.F.R. Bauchi, Nigeria. Letters concerning accommodation at Yankari Hotel and
current prices should be addressed to Yankari Booking Office, c/o Bauchi State
Hotels, P.M.B. 0012, Bauchi, Nigeria.

135 **A game survey of the Yankari Reserve of northern Nigeria.**
Sylvia K. Kikes. *The Nigerian Field*, vol. 29, no. 2 (April 1964),
p. 54–82, no. 3 (July 1964), p. 127–41. map. bibliog.

This survey of fauna was conducted in April 1963. The author gives a brief history of
the Reserve and descriptions of its geography, climate, habitats and soils, and notes on
the status of mammals listed alphabetically by their English names. Among the forty-
seven mammal, fifty-five bird and thirteen reptile species she offers estimates of their
populations. Lions and leopards were found to be extinct or nearly extinct, with roan
antelopes and giraffes in jeopardy; there were fewer than ten lions, about 150

elephants, 1300–1500 warthogs and about 2000 (to the nearest 500) West African buffaloes. See also Chris Geerling's 'Birds in Yankari Game Reserve', *The Nigerian Field*, vol. 41, no. 2 (June 1976), p. 64–78, which records 225 bird species, and P. J. Marshall's 'A new method of censussing elephants and a hippo census in Yankari Game Reserve' and 'An analysis of game viewing trips in Yankari Game Reserve', both in *The Nigerian Field*, vol. 50 (1985), p. 5–11 and p. 53–58, respectively.

The Nigerian Field.
See item no. 130.

Forestry and the Nigerian economy.
See item no. 728.

Forestry policy in Nigeria, 1897–1960.
See item no. 730.

Nigeria.
See item no. 1139.

Prehistory and Archaeology

136 Cross River monoliths.
Philip Allison. Lagos: Federal Republic of Nigeria, Department of Antiquities, 1968. 44p. map. bibliog.

This booklet describes the 295 stone carvings or *akwanshi* found in Ogoja Province of the middle Cross River region studied by the author in 1961. Sixty-seven photographs show the basalt carvings from Nta, Nselle, Nnam and Iyala.

137 The archaeology of Benin: excavations and other researches in and around Benin City, Nigeria.
Graham Connah, foreword by Chief A. Y. Eke. Oxford: Clarendon, 1975. 266p. maps. bibliog.

This volume provides the most comprehensive account of archaeological aspects of the Benin Empire available. The author gives a lucid description of 'Archaeological research in Benin City before 1961' (p. 7–9), his own intensive investigations in 1961–64 at the Benin Museum site, the clerk's quarters site, the Ogba Road site, the Reservation Road site, the Usama site and on the Benin City walls. Findings suggest that the thirteenth century was the earliest date of settlement of Benin. Sixteen brief specialist reports on such topics as pottery content, anthropometric observations, cowry shells, smoking-pipes, European wares, rock samples and historical implications are included, authored by, among others, D. C. D. Happold, Thurstan Shaw, and A. F. C. Ryder. Numerous plates, figures, tables and an excellent bibliography make this a most informative volume.

138 Three thousand years in Africa: man and his environment in the Lake Chad region of Nigeria.
Graham Connah. Cambridge: Cambridge University, 1981. 268p. maps. bibliog. (New Studies in Archaeology).

Periodically, from June and July 1963 to February 1969 and for three weeks in 1978, Professor Connah surveyed and excavated Nigerian sites south of Lake Chad 'in an area where virtually no other archaeological field research [had] yet been done'

(Preface, p. xv). This volume is his comprehensive report, integrating findings from numerous sites, especially Daima (800 BC–AD 1100). Dates reach back to about 2500 BC at a settlement mound near Bama. The result is a model holistic reconstruction of man-land relations in the difficult region for three millenia or more. Profusely illustrated with maps, diagrams and photographs, the book also includes an excellent bibliography (p. 255–63). Connah worked as an archaeologist in Nigeria from 1961–71; from 1971 through to the publication of this volume he was at the University of New England, Armidale, New South Wales, Australia.

139 **Archaeology and history in southern Nigeria: the ancient linear earthworks of Benin and Ishan.**

P. J. Darling. Oxford: British Archaeological Reports (BAR), 1984. 2 vols. maps. bibliog. (Cambridge Monographs in African Archaeology, 11. BAR International Series, 215).

This remarkably detailed study of the Edo earthworks skilfully combines geography, linguistics, historical analysis and archaeological surveys in the fullest treatment of the subject. Maps, diagrams and illustrations abound throughout vol. I, 'Fieldwork and background information' and vol. II, 'Ceramic and other specialist studies'. The author surveyed nearly 1,500 kilometres of linear earthworks between 1973 and 1977 out of an estimated 16,000 kilometres and obtained radiocarbon dates as early as the fourteenth century AD. 'Four to five times longer than the Great Wall of China and with over a hundred times as much material moved as the Great Pyramid of Cheops, these earthworks cover about six-and-a-half thousand square kilometers (two-and-a-half thousand square miles) of rain forest with a complicated network of enclosures' (Preface, p. 6).

140 **Nigerian archaeological literature: a classified bibliography, 1960–1983.**

Compiled by Stephen E. Ezennia. *A Current Bibliography on African Affairs*, vol. 18, no. 3 (1985–86), p. 213–29.

Using a thematic approach, the author has organized 253 unannotated references by site, culture, artefact type and notable period headings. Although he makes no claims for completeness, the listing is very useful indeed. Ezennia is a lecturer in the Department of Library Science, Anambra State College of Education, Awka, Nigeria. *A bibliography of Nigerian archaeology* compiled by Thurstan Shaw and Joel Vanderburg (Ibadan, Nigeria: Ibadan University for the Institute of African Studies, 1969. 68p.) offers 764 unannotated entries listed first by subject and then by author.

141 **Nok terracottas.**

Bernard Fagg. Lagos: Ethnographica for the National Musuem, 1977. 40p. + [85] leaves of plates. 2 maps. bibliog.

In forty pages of illustrated text Fagg describes the discovery and retrieval of the Nok terracottas, their age and manufacture, and provides an interpretation of their meaning. Eighty-five additional pages contain 153 plates, many full-page colour photographs by Harri Peccinotti, of the figures themselves. In 'The Nok sculptures of Nigeria', *Scientific American*, vol. 244, no. 2 (Feb. 1981), P. 154–66, 176, Professor Thurstan Shaw explains the discovery, excavation, dates, cultural implications and functions of the famous terracotta figures of central Nigeria. These 'oldest manifestations of Nigerian artistic excellence' (p. 154) date back 2,500 years and were first discovered in 1928 by Colonel Dent Young, a tin miner in the area. Shaw doubts earlier claims that the artefacts were produced by a single 'Nok culture' and suggests that sufficient evidence to establish this does not exist. Twelve photographs of the sculptures are included in the article.

142 **The Niger Delta, aspects of its prehistoric economy and culture.**
Nwanna Nwewunwa. Oxford: BAR, 1980. 267p. maps. bibliog.
(Cambridge Monographs in African Archaeology, 1; BAR
International Series, 75).
This detailed study consists of two parts. Part I (p. 1–78) is an introduction to the Niger Delta, its environment, ecology, patterns of human settlement and relevant theory. Part II is called 'Archaeology of the eastern Niger Delta', and describes field surveys and shell midden excavations in 1976 and 1977. An extensive bibliography (p. 249–67) is included as are numerous illustrations of the artefacts found. The monograph was originally presented as the author's 1979 Cambridge University doctoral thesis.

143 **A sourcebook for Nigerian archaeology.**
Nwanna Nzewunwa. [Lagos]: National Commission for Museums in
collaboration with the Archaeological Association of Nigeria, 1983.
140p. 14 maps. bibliog.
This practical archaeological guidebook to Nigeria contains systematic descriptions of fifty-one sites throughout the country with information on location, excavation history, finds and dating and useful references for each site. The author also discusses prehistoric research and cultural resource management in Nigeria. A list and brief description of fifty-five national monuments (p. 126–31), notes on nine national museums and a very select bibliography (p. 135–37) are included. Important Nigerian sites and finds are given regional and continental contexts in David W. Phillipson's excellent *African archaeology* (Cambridge: Cambridge University, 1985. 234p. (Cambridge World Archaeology Series)), which has a substantial list of references (p. 212–27).

144 **History and ethnoarchaeology in eastern Nigeria: a study of Igbo-Igala relations with special reference to the Anambra valley.**
Philip Adigwe Oguagha, Alex Ikechukwu Okpoko. Oxford: BAR,
1984. 298p. 12 maps. bibliog. (Cambridge Monographs in African
Archaeology 7; BAR International Series, 195).
This data-filled study of the Igbo and the Igala combines archaeological and ethnographic materials. In Part I, Okpoko analyzes the 'Archaeology and ethnoarchaeology in the Anambra Valley' (p. 1–184) using excavation data from 1976–81 in three districts (Aguleri, Idah and Ogurugu) in Anambra State. Oguagha describes 'Historical and traditional evidence' in Part II (p. 185–295). The authors integrate their findings in the Preface and Conclusions. Substantial bibliographies are included for both studies (p. 113–24 and p. 281–88). Professor Thurstan Shaw reviewed the work in 'Eastern Nigeria: excavations and interviews', *Journal of African History*, vol. 26, no. 1 (1985), p. 111–13.

45 **West African culture dynamics: archaeological and historical perspectives.**
Edited by B. K. Swartz, Jr., Raymond E. Dumett. The Hague, Paris, New York: Mouton, 1980. 636p. maps. bibliog. (World Anthropology Series).

Among the thirty papers in this volume are several of special relevance for Nigerian studies: D. G. Coursey's 'The origins and domestication of yams in Africa' (p. 67–90); Donald D. Hartle's 'Archaeology east of the Niger: a review of cultural-historical developments' (p. 195–203); John A. Rustad's 'The emergence of iron technology in West Africa, with special emphasis on the Nok culture of Nigeria' (p. 227–45); A. E. Afigbo's 'Prolegomena to the study of the culture history of the Igbo-speaking peoples of Nigeria' (p. 305–25); S. J. S. Cookey's 'An ethnohistorical reconstruction of traditional Igbo society' (p. 327–47); R. G. Armstrong's 'The dynamics and symbolism of Idoma kingship' (p. 393–411); and Jan S. Hogendorn's 'Slave acquisition and delivery in precolonial Hausaland' (p. 477–93).

146 **Igbo-Ukwu: an account of archaeological discoveries in eastern Nigeria.**
Thurstan Shaw. London: Faber & Faber; Evanston, Illinois: Northwestern University for the Institute of African Studies, University of Ibadan, Ibadan, Nigeria, 1970. 2 vols. 3 maps. bibliog.

This is the comprehensive archaeological report on the excavations in Igbo-Ukwu conducted by the author in 1959–60 and 1964. This lucid report is exemplary for its thoroughness in discussing every aspect of the excavation, its artefacts and their interpretation. Vol. I includes the full text of the analysis and interpretation of this most-famous Nigerian archaeological site which has been dated to the ninth century AD, as well as eight colour plates, forty-three figures, an extensive appendix and excellent bibliography (p. 332–37). Vol. II consists of 514 monochrome plates of all aspects of the project and its artefacts, from photographs by the author and Doig Simmonds. This entire body of research is summarized in a small, non-technical book by Professor Shaw, *Unearthing Igbo-Ukwu: archaeological discoveries in Eastern Nigeria* (Ibadan, Nigeria: Oxford University, 1977, 121p. 3 maps). The site is considered to be the burial chamber of a ruling priest or *Eze* of the nearby town of Nri.

147 **Discovering Nigeria's past.**
Edited by Thurstan Shaw. Ibadan, Nigeria: Oxford University, 1975. 130p. map. bibliog.

This well-illustrated collection of twelve short essays by the editor, Graham Connah, Doig Simmonds, Ekpo Eyo and Adebisi Sowunmi began as a series of broadcasts on NBC (the Nigerian Broadcasting Corporation). Collectively, they offer excellent coverage for the layman of archaeological discoveries, processes and contributions to the understanding of Nigeria's past. The author's earlier edited collection *Lectures on Nigerian prehistory and archaeology* (Ibadan, Nigeria: Ibadan University for the Institute of African Studies, 1969. 61p.) is well worth examination. His 'The prehistory of West Africa' in *History of West Africa*, edited by J. F. A. Ajayi and M. Crowder New York: Columbia University, 1976, 2nd ed., vol. 1, p. 33–71) is a fine summary of what is known about this broad topic.

Prehistory and Archaeology

148 **Nigeria: its archaeology and early history.**
Thurstan Shaw. London: Thames & Hudson, 1978. 216p. 9 maps.
bibliog. (Ancient Peoples and Places).

An indispensable volume on Nigerian prehistory and archaeology, covering the earlies
evidence for human occupation as well as the better known empires of souther
Nigeria. The author synthesizes widely-published materials and his own decades-lon
research. The selective bibliography (p. 195–208) is one of the best on this broad topic
the volume contains 147 photographs and line drawings. Shaw founded the
Department of Archaeology at the University of Ibadan; in addition he founded and
was editor of the *West African Journal of Archaeology* (Ibadan: Ibadan University
1971– . annual). Before 1970 this was the *West African Archaeological Newslette*
(Ibadan: Institute of African Studies, Ibadan University, nos. 1–12, Dec. 1964–Marc
1970), 'sponsored by the Universities of Ghana, Ibadan and Ife, the University College
of Cape Coast, and the Ghana National Museum' (p. 1). Shaw's Hans Wolff Memoria
Lecture, *Filling gaps in Afric maps: fifty years of archaeology in Africa* (Bloomington
Indiana: Indiana University, African Studies Program, 1984, [49]p.) devotes consider
able attention to the Nok, Igbo-Ukwu and Benin cultures of Nigeria.

149 **The stone images of Esie, Nigeria.**
Phillips Stevens, Jr. [Ibadan], Nigeria: Ibadan University and the
Nigerian Federal Department of Antiquities, 1978. 398p. 3 maps.
bibliog.

The nearly 1,000 carved soapstone figures of men, women, children and animals nea
the Igbomina Yoruba village of Esie 'constitute what is by far the largest collection o
stone carvings in Africa, and their origins are one of the continents' great mysteries'
(p. 1). Although annually worshipped in a sacred grove throughout the reigns of fifteen
successive chiefs of Esie, the images were unknown to the wider world until thei
'discovery' in 1933. Radiocarbon dating suggests an origin for them of around AD
1100. This comprehensive volume explores theories of their origins and cultura
contexts (p. 1–93) and contains a complete descriptive and photographic catalogue
(p. 95–398) of the figures. The author is presently Associate Professor of Anthropolg
at the State University of New York at Buffalo and began his work on the images while
assigned to Esie in the Peace Corps in 1965–66.

African stone scuplture.
See item no. 936.

Two thousand years Nigerian art.
See item no. 961.

Treasures of ancient Nigeria.
See item no. 962.

Guide to the Nigerian Museum, Lagos.
See item no. 1055.

Guide to the National Museum, Kaduna.
See item no. 1056.

25 years of Jos Museum
See item no. 1057.

Guide to the National Museum, Oron.
See item no. 1062.

The Benin Museum collection.
See item no. 1063.

History

General

150 **Milestones in Nigerian history.**
J[acob] F[estus] A[deniyi] Ajayi. Ibadan, Nigeria: Ibadan University,
June 1962. London: Longman, 1980. 2nd ed. 47p. map. bibliog.
This small volume contains revised versions of the radio talks given by the author in
1960. Dr. Ajayi describes the events surrounding four key dates in Nigerian history:
the Fulani *jihad* of Shehu Usuman dan Fodio in 1804; the age of Bishop Samuel Ajayi
Crowther, 1864; Lord Lugard's scheme of amalgamation of Northern and Southern
Nigeria on 1 January 1914; and the Richard's Constitution of 1947, which 'provided the
first opportunity for Nigerian politicians and Native Administration officials from
different parts of the country to meet together in a council as fellow countrymen' (p.
38). Twenty-two illustrations and a brief reading list (p. 47) supplement the text.

151 **A thousand years of West African history: a handbook for teachers and
students.**
Edited by J. F. A. Ajayi, Ian Espie, foreword by K. O. Dike. New
York: Humanities, 1972. 2nd ed. 549p. maps. bibliog.
First published in 1965 and reissued in 1969, this volume contains twenty-five essays, a
broad list of sixty topics for further study (p. 498–500) and a bibliography (p. 501–11).
While many essays are generally relevant for students of Nigeria, especially significant
are: A. A. B. Aderibigbe's 'Peoples of Southern Nigeria'; Tekena N. Tamuno's
'Peoples of the Niger-Benue confluence'; A. F. C. Ryder's 'Portuguese and Dutch in
West Africa before 1800'; C. C. Ifemesia's 'Bornu under the Shehus'; J. C. Anane's
'Benin, Niger Delta, Ibo and Ibibio peoples in the nineteenth century'; A. E. Afigbo's
'A reassessment of the historiography of the period'; and James O'Connell's 'Trends
and tasks in the independent states of West Africa'. End-paper maps show the ethnic
groups and language families of West Africa. Another valuable regional history is *A
short history of West Africa: A.D. 1000 to the present* (New York: Hill & Wang, 1973.
345p.) by T. A. Osae, S. N. Nwabara and A. T. O. Odunsi. Nigerian cultures appear
prominently throughout.

152 **History of West Africa.**
Edited by J. F. A. Ajayi, Michael Crowder. New York: Columbia
University; Harlow, England; New York; Ikeja, Nigeria: Longman,
1985, vol. 1, 3rd ed.; 1987, vol. 2, 2nd ed. maps. bibliog.
For students of West African history up to 1800, these 'lucid, scholarly and
authoritative' (Introduction, p. 1) volumes in their various editions are essential. Vol.
1 (568p.) first appeared in 1971, was revised in 1976 and again in 1985 with several new
chapters added in this third edition. Among its sixteen chapters, Murray Last's 'The
early kingdoms of the Nigerian savanna' (p. 167–224) is new as are Philip D. Curtin's
'The external trade of West Africa to 1800' (p. 624–47) and Paul Lovejoy's 'The
internal trade of West Africa to 1800'. Vol. 2 (764p.) was first published in New York
1972 and the following year in England and Nigeria. Several essays are annotated
individually in this compilation.

153 **History of Nigeria.**
Sir Alan [Cuthbert] Burns. London; Boston, Massachusetts: George
Allen & Unwin, 1978. 8th rev. ed. 366p. 8 maps. bibliog.
One of the most durable histories of Nigeria, this was first published in 1929. The
author provides a standard colonial history of the country with minimal background on
the Nigerian peoples except as they interacted with the British. Especially valuable are
the treaties, genealogies of sultans and kings, and lists of consuls, governors and high
commissioners of Nigeria reproduced in the appendices. 'The book is designed to give
to those who are interested in Nigeria, and particularly to such as are resident in the
country, whether as missionaries, traders or officials, a short account of the history of
its people and of their relations with the British Government' (Preface, 1st ed., p. 7).
A fold-out 1955 Directorate of Colonial Surveys map is bound into the volume;
however, this and portraits of distinguished Nigerians are omitted from the 1978
paperback edition. Sir Alan (1887–1980) first went to Nigeria in 1912, was acting
Governor for a few months in 1942 and attended the 1960 independence ceremony.

154 **A short history of Nigeria.**
Michael Crowder. New York: Praeger; London: Faber & Faber,
1978. 4th ed. 432p. 11 maps. bibliog.
This excellent general history, originally published in 1962, 'is an attempt to bring
together in one short volume the history of the various groups that go to make up
modern Nigeria, to trace their connexions with each other and to dispel the assumption
. . . which is still often made that before the colonial period Africans had very little
history. It is essentially a political history . . .' (Preface, 1st ed., p. 13). The fourth
edition has a new chapter dealing with events after independence. Crowder and Guda
Abdullahi published *Nigeria: an introduction to its history* (London: Longman, 1979.
216p), a richly-illustrated historical overview from Nigeria's prehistory to about 1970,
although the chapter on independent Nigeria is the least satisfactory. This history is
aimed at West African Examinations Council (WAEC) history students and teacher-
training college students and includes sixty-five sample questions as well as a brief
bibliography (p. 209–11).

History. General

155 **An economic history of Nigeria, 1860–1960.**
Richard Olufemi Ekundare, foreword by Peter Mathias. London:
Methuen; New York: Africana/Holmes & Meier, 1973. 458p. 9 maps.
bibliog.
This economic history covers roughly the period of colonial rule. In the foreword,
Professor Peter Mathias of Oxford writes, 'It is no exaggeration to claim that this book
opens a new chapter in the historiography of Africa. . . This is the first systematic
study of the general economic development of Nigeria, including its long pre-colonial
story, and, with this, it stands as the first academic economic history of any black
African country' (p. xvii). Numerous tables, a large statistical appendix (p. 403–16)
and an extensive bibliography (p. 417–440) are included in the impressive study.

156 **An outline of Nigerian history.**
M. C. English. London: Longmans, 1959. 212p. 10 maps.
A history of Nigeria from the Stone Age to 1959 intended for secondary schools and
teacher-training colleges. The volume has questions at the end of each chapter and
twenty-nine photographic plates. 'A summary of subjects of Nigeria's development in
the twentieth century' (p. 201–6) is an elementary but informative chronology. The
author was a former Principal of Government Secondary School, Owerri, Nigeria.
Wale Ademoyega's *The Federation of Nigeria, from earliest times to independence*
(London: George G. Harrap, 1962. 208p.) is a solid general history, illustrated by the
well-known artist Ben Enwonwu.

157 **Nigeria and Ghana.**
John E. Flint. Englewood Cliffs, New Jersey: Prentice-Hall, 1966.
176p. 4 maps. bibliog. (Modern Nations in Historical Perspective
Series).
The author succeeds in relating a survey history of these nations in only five chapters:
'The land, the people, and the politics of independence'; 'Origins'; 'The European
impact and the slave trade'; 'The nineteenth century'; and 'The colonial period'. The
bibliographic essay (p. 165–67) suggests important further reading. In 1963–64, Dr.
Flint was Head of the History Department at the University of Nigeria, Nsukka; later
he was Reader in History at King's College, University of London.

158 **Nigeria: a history.**
John Hatch. London: Secker & Warburg, 1970. 288p. map. bibliog.
A straightforward, popular history of Nigeria by one who visited often between 1955
and 1970, which begins with a sketch of pre-colonial cultures and concludes soon after
the end of the civil war. The American edition is entitled *Nigeria: the seeds of disaster*
(Chicago: Henry Regnery, 1970. 313p.) and lacks the epilogue of the London edition.

159 **Nigerian perspectives: an historical anthology.**
Edited by Thomas Hodgkin. London: Oxford University, 1975. 2nd
ed. 432p. 3 maps. bibliog.
An unrivalled collection of brief excerpts from the most important works concerning
the traditional cultures, emirates and empires of Nigeria. The 164 selections are
arranged in general chronological order from 'Legends of origin' to about 1900, from
'The legend of Daura' to Muhammad Al-Bukhari's 'The dilemma of the Wazir'. The

volume is particularly rich in translations of Arabic manuscripts commenting on northern Nigerian societies. The editor's extended introduction (p. 1–71) offers a synthesis and overview of the same period. The list of sources and other works (p. 399–421) is one of the most useful available. The second edition considerably expands the 1960 edition published to coincide with Nigerian independence.

160   **The shell money of the slave trade.**
Jan Hogendorn, Marion Johnson.   Cambridge: Cambridge University, 1986. 230p. 8 maps. bibliog. (African Studies Series, 49).

This highly readable and meticulously documented economic history of the cowrie, to some extent *Cypraea annulus* from East African coasts but particularly *Cypraea moneta* from the Maldives, describes the shells' uses before, during and long after the slave trade. With extensive data the authors trace the shells' international trade routes, inflation resulting from over-abundance and eventual replacement by colonial coinage. The uses of cowries in Nigerian societies are a prominent feature of the volume. The study provides a critique of the substantivist school of economic anthropology, which viewed the cowrie as a 'special purpose money'. Christopher Fyfe reviews the book in *African Affairs* vol. 86, no. 344 (July 1987), p. 446–47.

161   **An economic history of West Africa.**
A[nthony] G. Hopkins.   New York: Columbia University, 1973. 337p. 17 maps. bibliog. (Columbia Economic History of the Modern World Series).

A highly-regarded, comprehensive account of the region incorporating anthropological, economic and geographical perspectives in an effort 'to direct attention away from the adventures and triumphs of great leaders, past and present, and towards the activities of the overwhelming majority of Africans' (p. 296). Professor Hopkins describes traditional domestic economies and their encounters with external and colonial trade up to 1960, keeping to the study's central theme of 'the interaction of the various internal and external factors which have determined the structure and performance of the market economy' (p. 293). The bibliography (p. 297–326) is excellent. The author's 1964 London University doctoral dissertation was an *Economic history of Lagos, 1880–1914.*

162   **Groundwork of Nigerian history.**
Edited by Obaro Ikime.   Ibadan, Nigeria: Heinemann (Nigeria) for the Historical Society of Nigeria, 1980. 615p. 18 maps. bibliog.

This essential volume, intended by the Historical Society of Nigeria as a comprehensive history of the nation for university students, contains twenty-eight essays by specialists. The contributors' essays are grouped by topic: 'Geographical and archaeological backgrounds' (R. K. Udo, Thurstan Shaw); 'Nigeria before 1800' (E. J. Alagoa, A. E. Afigbo, O. Ikime, A. F. C. Ryder, I. A. Akinjogbin, E. A. Ayandele, Ade Obafemi, Sa'ad Abubakar, J. E. Lavers, S. A. Balogun, J. F. Ade Ajayi); 'Nigeria in the 19th century' (E. J. Alagoa, O. Ikime, I. F. Ade Ajayi, S. A. Akintoye, Sa'ad Abubakar, T. G. O. Gbadamosi); and 'Nigeria in the twentieth century' (T. M. Tamuno, A. E. Afigbo, A. I. Asiwaju, Sa'ad Abubakar, R. J. Gavin, W. Oyemakinde, G. O. Olusanya, S. O. Osoba, A. Fajana). Despite gaps in coverage the volume provides one of the best composite histories of Nigeria.

163 **A history of Nigeria.**
Elizabeth Isichei, with Peter Uche ιsichei. London, Lagos, New
York: Longman, 1983. 517p. 10 maps. bibliog.

A substantial cultural history, including but going beyond the most usual account of
rulers, battles and colonial administration. In the story of Nigeria from prehistoric
times to 1979, the author tries 'to shift the focus from the captains and the kings, the
sarakuna, the *oba*, the *alafin*, at least to some extent to the peasant farmers, the
blacksmiths, the weavers, the calabash carvers, the potters, the slaves . . .' (p. xi). She
writes about 'life and livelihood', 'social relationships and conditions', 'urban planning
and architecture', 'religion', 'varieties of literacy', 'patterns of social and economic
change', and independent Nigeria's search for identity, among many other topics. The
author's husband, physician Peter Uche Isichei, provides an article in the appendix on
'Genetic markers in Nigeria' (p. 481–87). The bibliography (p. 488–503) is excellent.
Nigeria is emphasized in Professor Elizabeth Isichei's *History of West Africa since 1800*
(London, Basingstoke: Macmillan, 1977, 380p.) which is written for students in West
Africa and has study questions for each chapter and an especially useful reading guide
(p. 356–75).

164 **Who coined the name 'Nigeria'?**
A[nthony] H[amilton] M[illard] Kirk-Greene. *West Africa*, no. 2071
(22 Dec. 1956), p. 1035. map.

Kirk-Greene reviews several older names for the territory which became Nigeria and
examines F. W. Taylor's claim that Major Mockler-Ferryman (1856–1930) first used
the term in his book *British West Africa* (London: Imperial; New York: New
Amsterdam, 1899). He then credits *The Times* with the paternity of the name in its 8
January 1897 issue, '. . . the name 'Nigeria', applying to no other portion of Africa,
may, without offence to any neighbors, be accepted as co-extensive with the territories
over which the Royal Niger Company has extended British influence, and may serve to
differentiate them equally from the British colonies of Lagos and the Niger
Protectorate on the coast, and from the French territory of the Upper Niger' (p. 1035).
The unsigned article from *The Times* is attributed to Flora Shaw, later Lady Lugard,
by Kirk-Greene in *West Africa*, no. 2078 (9 Feb. 1957), p. 132. Of interest also is C. K.
Meek's 'The Niger and the classics: the history of a name' in the *Journal of African
History*, vol. 1 (1960), p. 1–17.

165 **The horse in West African history: the role of the horse in the societies of
pre-colonial West Africa.**
Robin Law. Oxford; London; New York: Oxford University for the
International African Institute, 1980. 224p. 7 maps. bibliog.

'The real subject of this book, it should be stressed, is not the horse, but the human
societies in West Africa which made use of horses' (Preface, p. viii). This splendid
study, complete with line drawings and photographs and based on fieldwork in Nigeria,
and to a lesser extent in Ghana, in 1973 and 1975, relates the history of the horse in the
region, its maintenance, health and training, equipment, cavalry warfare and non-
military aspects, horses and society in pre-colonial societies and the decline of the
horse in twentieth-century West Africa. Nigerian groups receiving special emphasis
include the Yoruba, Benin, Nupe, Hausa, Fulani and Kanem-Borno. The bibliography
(p. 210–11) is selectively brief because each chapter has extensive notes and
references.

166 **Dictionary of African historical biography.**
Mark R. Lipschutz, R. Kent Rasmussen. Berkeley; Los Angeles:
University of California, 1986. 2nd ed. 328p. 2 maps. bibliog.
This enlarged edition of this excellent reference work advances its cut-off date for
material from 1960 to 1980. Biographical sketches of important Nigerian traditional
rulers, politicians, military figures, administrators and others are included. The
'Subject guide to entries', 'Index of variant spellings, variant names, and names of
figures cited under entries' and extensive bibliography (p. 291–316) are very helpful.
New material is included in the 'Supplement of post-1960 political leaders' (p. 258–90).

167 **L'évolution du commerce africain depuis le XIXe siècle en Afrique de
l'Ouest. The development of indigenous trade and markets in West
Africa. Studies presented and discussed at the Tenth International
African Seminar at Fourah Bay College, Freetown, December 1969.**
Edited and introduced by Claude Meillassoux, foreword by Daryll
Forde. London: Oxford University for the International African
Institute, 1971. 444p. map. bibliog.
An important collection of papers in French and English, each with a summary in the
other language, discussing principal themes of traditional trade and markets, the
adaptation of African economies and trade to nineteenth-century changes and the
impact of modern capitalism on African trade. Of particular interest for Nigerian
studies are: Abner Cohen's 'Cultural strategies in the organization of trading diasporas'
(p. 266–81); Polly Hill's 'Two types of West African house trade' (p. 303–18);
R. H. T. Smith's 'West African market-places: temporal periodicity and locational
spacing' (p. 319–46); and B. W. Hodder's 'Periodic and daily markets in West Africa'
(p. 347–58). The bibliography is extensive (p. 411–32).

168 **Eminent Nigerians of the nineteenth century.**
Nigerian Broadcasting Corporation, introduced and edited by K. O.
Dike. Cambridge: Cambridge University, 1960. 98p.
This is a series of eleven biographical studies originally broadcast by the Nigerian
Broadcasting Corporation and introduced by Professor Dike. The eminent Nigerians
are: King William Dappa Pepple, by K. O. Dike; Jaja of Opobo, by J. C. Anana;
Prince Kosoko of Lagos, Madame Tinubu and Oluyole of Ibadan, by Saburi Biobaku;
Samuel Ajayi Crowther and Oba Overami of Benin, by T. C. Eneli; Usumanu dan
Fodio, by H. F. C. Smith; El Kanemi of Bornu and Umoru and Ibrahim Nagwamatse,
by Robin Hallett; and Nanna the Itsekiri.

169 **Nigerian history and culture.**
Edited by Richard Olaniyan. Harlow, England: Longman, 1985.
360p. map. bibliog.
This rich volume offers twenty essays on Nigeria by experts from nine disciplines, and
includes: the editor's 'Introduction: the relevance of Nigerian history'; Biodun
Adediran's 'The origins of Nigerian peoples'; Nwanna Nzewunwa's 'Pre-colonial
Nigeria: east of the Niger'; I. A. Akinjogbin and Biodun Adediran's 'Pre-colonial
Nigeria: west of the Niger'; Toyin Falola and A. Adebayo's 'Pre-colonial Nigeria:
north of the Niger-Benue'; Toyin Falola's 'Nigeria's indigenous economy'; Richard
Olaniyan's 'The Atlantic slave trade'; Akin Olorunfemi's 'The Fulani Jihad and the
Sokoto Caliphate in the nineteenth century'; Fola Soremekun's 'The British

History. General

penetration and conquest'; Ibrahim A.Gambari's 'British colonial administration' Tekena N. Tamuno's 'The independence movement'; Leo Dare's 'Politics since independence'; Olajide Aluko's 'Nigeria's foreign policy'; A. A. Akiwowo and R. Olaniyan's 'Social change and stability in contemporary Nigeria'; J. O. Kayode and E. Dada Adelowo's 'Religion in Nigeria'; Sue Picton's 'The visual arts of Nigeria'; S. M. Olutomori's 'Aspects of language in Nigeria'; B. Ajuwon's 'Oral and written literature in Nigeria'; Y. Ogunbiyi's 'The performing arts in Nigerian culture'; and A. Euba', 'Music in Nigeria today'. Professor Olaniyan also edited a similar volume, *African history and culture* (Harlow, England: Longman; Lagos: Longman Nigeria, 1982, 259p) which contains, among many useful articles, Wole Soyinka's 'Theater in African traditional culture: survival patterns' (p. 237–48).

170 The Cambridge history of Africa.

General editors Roland Oliver, J. D. Fage. Cambridge: Cambridge University, 1975–86. 8 vols. maps. bibliog.

This invaluable history covers the continent from prehistoric times to 1975 and contains substantial material on West Africa and Nigeria in each volume as well as detailed maps and bibliographies. J. Desmond Clark edited vol. 1, *From the earliest times to c. 500 BC* (1982. 1157p.); J. D. Fage edited vol. 2, *From c. 500 BC to AD 1050* (1979. 700p.); Roland Oliver edited vol. 3, *From c. 1050 to c. 1600* (1977. 816p.); Richard Gray edited vol. 4, *From c. 1600 to c. 1790* (1975. 752p.); John E. Flint edited vol. 5, *From c. 1790 to c. 1870* (1977. 816p.); R. Oliver and G. N. Sanderson edited vol. 6, *From c. 1870 to c. 1905* (1985. 956p.); A. D. Roberts edited vol. 7, *From 1905 to 1940* (1986. 1063p.); and the late Michael Crowder edited vol. 8, *From c. 1940 to c. 1975* (1984. 1011p.).

171 General history of Africa.

UNESCO International Scientific Committee for the Drafting of a General History of Africa. Paris: UNESCO; London: Heinemann; London; Berkeley, California: University of California, 1981– . 8 vols. maps. bibliog.

When completed, the series will provide a comprehensive history of Africa by Africans. Inevitably, Nigerian societies and the region which became Nigeria figure prominently in numerous articles. In vol. 1, *Methodology and African prehistory* (1981. 819p.) edited by J. Ki-Zerbo is C. T. Shaw's 'The prehistory of West Africa' (p. 611–33); vol. 2, *Ancient civilizations of Africa* (1981. 804p.) edited by G. Mokhtar contains B. Wai Andah's 'West Africa before the seventh century' (p. 593–619); vol. 3, *Africa from the seventh to eleventh century* (1988. 869p.) is edited by M. El Fasi; D. T. Niane edited vol. 4, *Africa from the twelfth to the sixteenth century* (1984. 751p.); B. A. Ogot is editing vol. 5, *Africa from the sixteenth to eighteenth century*; prominent Nigerian historian J. F. Ade Ajayi is the editor for vol. 6, *The nineteenth century until 1880*; Ghanaian historian A. Adu Boahen edited vol. 7, *Africa under colonial domination, 1880–1935* (1985. 865p.) which contains A. E. Afigbo's 'The social repercussions of colonial rule: the new social structures' (p. 487–507) and Wole Soyinka's 'The arts in Africa during the period of colonial rule' (p. 539–64); vol. 8, *Africa since the Ethiopian War, 1935–1975* is being edited by A. A. Mazrui.

Periodicals

172 **The Journal of African History.**
Cambridge: Cambridge University, 1960– . three times yearly.
This is a major source for scholarly historical articles and both substantial and shorter book reviews. The editorial address is The Editors, *The Journal of African History*, School of Oriental and African Studies, University of London, London, WC1E 7HP.

173 **Journal of the Historical Society of Nigeria.**
Ibadan, Nigeria: Department of History, University of Ibadan, Dec. 1956– . biannual.
From an annual publication of limited circulation, this learned journal has grown and now has a broad national and international circulation, publishing articles on Nigerian history by European and North American scholars as well as by Nigerians. Articles of particular interest in the Silver Jubilee issue, vol. 10, no. 3 (Dec. 1980), include K. O. Dike's 'African history twenty-five years ago and today' (p. 13–22) and J. F. Ade Ajayi's 'A critique of themes preferred by Nigerian historians' (p. 33–39). *Tarikh*, an occasional journal has been published by Humanities and Longman for the Historical Society of Nigeria since 1965 and consists of thematic issues, many of which concern Nigerian history. '*Tarikh*' is the Arabic word for 'written history'. For example, vol. 3, no. 3 (1970), 'Indirect rule in British Africa' contained three articles on the subject in Nigeria: Obaro Ikime's 'The establishment of indirect rule in Northern Nigeria' (p. 1–15); J. A. Atanda's 'Indirect rule in Yorubaland' (p. 16–28); and P. A. Igbafe's 'Indirect rule in Benin' (p. 29–40).

Discovering Nigeria's past.
See item no. 147.

Nigeria: its archaeology and early history.
See item no. 148.

Africa.
See item no. 1096.

African Affairs.
See item no. 1098.

The Cambridge encyclopedia of Africa.
See item no. 1115.

Historical dictionary of Nigeria.
See item no. 1118.

Nigerian official publications, 1869–1959: a guide.
See item no. 1127.

Nigeria: a guide to official publications.
See item no. 1134.

Lagos past & present: an historical bibliography.
See item no. 1137.

The United States and Africa: guide to official documents and government-sponsored publications on Africa, 1785–1975.
See item no. 1147.

Regional history

174 **The Hausa factor in West African history.**
Mahdi Adamu. Zaria, Nigeria: Ahmadu Bello University; Ibadan, Nigeria: Oxford University (Nigeria), 1978. 224p. 7 maps. bibliog. (Ahmadu Bello University History Series).

This significant volume reconstructs social and economic relations between Hausaland and the rest of West Africa from the sixteenth century to about 1900 making the point that, 'There is no part of West Africa in which strong aspects of Hausa culture are not found' (p. 179). Supplementary materials contain brief descriptions of Hausa dress and music, lists of informants throughout the region, a Hausa glossary (p. 198–205) and a substantial bibliography (p. 206–16). This study is based on the author's doctoral thesis at the University of Birmingham, England.

175 **Power and diplomacy in Northern Nigeria 1804–1906: the Sokoto Caliphate and its enemies.**
R. A. Adelẹyẹ. New York: Humanities, 1971. 387p. 6 maps. bibliog. (Ibadan History Series).

This excellent study of the Sokoto Caliphate provides a general background and describes the impact of European penetration and the British overthrow of the Caliphate. Eight interesting historic photographs accompany the text and the appendices contain the Bornu-British and Sokoto-British treaties and five letters, notably four between Lord Lugard and Caliph 'Abd al-Raḥmān in 1901 and 1902. The bibliography (p. 360–70) is usefully organized into 'contemporary sources', including archives, and 'later works' including theses. The study in regional power relations derives from the author's University of Ibadan doctoral dissertation. Professor Adeleye's chapter 'Hausaland and Borno, 1600–1800' in the *History of West Africa*, edited by J. F. A. Ajayi and Michael Crowder (New York: Columbia University, 1976, 2nd ed., vol. 1, p. 555–601) is a lucid scholarly account of these major empires in northern Nigeria over two centuries.

176 **Evolution of political culture in Nigeria: proceedings of a national seminar organized by the Kaduna State Council for Arts and Culture.**
Edited by J. F. Ade. Ajayi, Bashir [Ahmed] Ikara. Ibadan, Nigeria: University Press and Kaduna State Council for Arts and Culture, 1985. 227p. 2 maps. bibliog.

These fourteen papers, originally presented at a national seminar in 1981, examine nearly 1,000 years of political developments in Nigeria. Essay topics and authors include: factors in the evolution of political culture (J. F. A. Ajayi); Kanem and Borno, AD 700–1900 (John E. Lavers); Kanem-Borno government (M. Nur Alkali); Sukurin eighteenth and nineteenth centuries (Bawuro Barkindo); pre-colonial Nupe

(Sa'ad Abubakar); nineteenth-century eastern Nigeria (E. J. Alagoa); nineteenth-century western Nigeria (J. A. Atanda); nineteenth-century Ibadan (Toyin Falola); nineteenth-century Kano (Abdullahi Mahadi); Kano, 1900–1960 (C. N. Ubah); 1976 local government reforms (Bashir Ahmed Ikara); the military and political engineering, 1966–79 (J. I. Eliagwu); and political prospects for the future (P. C. A. Daudu).

177 **Yoruba warfare in the nineteenth century.**
J. F. Ade. Ajayi, Robert Smith, foreword by K. Onwuka Dike.
Cambridge: Cambridge University, in association with the Institute of African Studies, University of Ibadan, 1971. 2nd ed., 172p. 6 maps. bibliog.

This volume combines two complementary studies read as papers at the Nigerian Historical Society in December 1962 and published in 1964. Robert Smith discusses 'The Yoruba wars, c. 1820–93' (p. 9–55), describing armies, weapons, tactics, strategy, major battles at Oshogbo (c. 1840), Abeokuta (1851), Ijaye (1860–62), and Ikirun (1878), casualties, captives and the wars' results. Professor Ajayi contributes 'The Ijaye War, 1860–5: a case study in Yoruba wars and politics' (p. 59–128), covering a conflict between Ibadan and the Ijaye led by Kurunmi and with their allies the Egba of Abeokuta. Appendices contain the report of Captain Arthur Trefusis Jones on the Egba army in 1861 (p. 129–40) and an essay on Lagoon warfare (p. 141–49). The bibliography (p. 159–63) is useful. Of relevance also is Toyin Falola's *The military in nineteenth century Yoruba politics* (Ile-Ife, Nigeria: University of Ife. 1984. 127p.).

178 **Revolution and power politics in Yorubaland, 1840–1893: Ibadan expansion and the rise of Ekitiparapọ.**
S[tephen] A[debanji] Akintoye. Atlantic Highlands, New Jersey: Humanities, 1971; Harlow, England: Longman, 1977. 278p. 3 maps. bibliog. (Ibadan History Series).

This study describes the growth of Ibadan as the most powerful Yoruba state and its expansion into the eastern states of Yorubaland during the 1840s. Professor Akintoye focuses on the Ekitiparapọ, a confederacy of four 'sub-ethnic divisions' (the Ekiti, Ijẹsa, Akoko, and Igbomina) which, in alliance with Ibadan's rivals, fought Ibadan for sixteen years until the British peace missions ended the wars in 1893. This book grew out of the author's 1966 PhD thesis at the University of Ibadan. The extensive oral interviews conducted in 1963–64 as well as print and archival sources are listed in the bibliography (p. 243–62). Appendices contain a list of 'Some leaders of the Ekitiparapọ in the Kiriji War', the 1886 Peace Treaty and the 'Enactment for the abolition of human sacrifices in the Ekiti countries'.

179 **The small brave city-state: a history of Nembe-Brass in the Niger Delta.**
Ebiegberi Joe Alagoa. Ibadan, Nigeria: Ibadan University; Madison, Wisconsin: University of Wisconsin, 1964. 173p. 3 maps. bibliog.

A history of the Brass or Nembe people from about the mid-fifteenth century to 1936, with a concentration on the nineteenth century and the 'Akassa War' of 1895 and a few references up to the 1960s. The people call themselves and their capital city Nembe (p. 5). 'Small' and 'brave' in the title are from the traditional praise name of the people which was beaten out on a talking drum as war canoes of Nembe approached another town or returned home. Appendices contain king lists and genealogies, fragments of the 1856 Comey treaty, the 1899 Brass Trading company agreement, the house rule proclamation and amendment, a list of 'consuls', 1849–1920, and a description of the bar as an accounting 'unit'. The selected bibliography (p. 167–68) is brief. See also Professor Alagoa's *King Boy of Brass* (London; Ibadan, Nigeria: Heinemann, 1975, 38p. (African Historical Biographies Series)) for an excellent succinct history of the powerful trader-king who escorted John Lander and Richard Lander from Aboh to the coast in 1830.

180 **A history of the Niger Delta: an historical interpretation of Ijọ oral tradition.**
Ebiegberi Joe Alagoa. Ibadan, Nigeria: Ibadan University, 1972. 231p. 9 maps. bibliog.

The leading scholar for this region provides an invaluable description of forty-three Ijọ subgroups (*ibe*) in the Delta from west to east and grouped as 'The western Delta fringe', 'The western Delta', 'The central Delta', 'The eastern Delta', 'The eastern Delta fringe', and 'The northern Delta fringe', providing an account of the Delta environment and general conclusions as well. Maps, several plates, king lists and genealogies, and an Ijọ glossary and selected bibliography (p. 217–23) enhance an already important volume. Also important are the author's articles 'Long-distance trade in the Niger Delta', *Journal of African History*, vol. 11, no. 3 (1970), p. 319–29, and 'The Niger Delta states and their neighbors, to 1800' in the *History of West Africa*, edited by J. F. A. Ajayi and Michael Crowder (New York: Columbia University, 1976, 2nd ed., vol. 1, p. 331–72).

181 **A chronicle of Grand Bonny.**
Ebiegberi J[oe] Alagoa, Adadọnye Fọmbọ. Ibadan, Nigeria: Ibadan University, 1972. 134p. map. bibliog.

In modern times Bonny is Nigeria's main oil terminal port, but for several centuries it was a major slave port and the capital of an ancient kingdom of the Niger Delta, whose people call themselves Ibani and are bilingual in Igbo and Ibani, or south-eastern Ijọ (Ijaw). This study is a reorganization and reinterpretation by Professor Alagoa of Adadonye Fọmbọ's manuscript 'Short outline history of Bonny', now in the Africana collection of the University of Ibadan library. The history concentrates on the period from the early 1800s to the mid-twentieth century but focuses on King William Dappa Pepple (1835–66) and King George Pepple (1866–88), the Houses, or major lineage corporations, and on Bonny's relations with neighbours and the Europeans. Eight plates, a list of kings and a collection of treaties and conventions (p. 90–121) make this a valuable local history.

182 **Studies in the history of Kano.**
Edited by Bawuro M. Barkindo. Ibadan, Nigeria: Heinemann for the Department of History, Bayero University, Kano, 1983. 214p. 3 maps. bibliog.

This volume presents a wide-ranging view of the city based on the papers presented at the Kano International Seminar in Kano in September 1981. The papers are: 'The gates of Kano City: a historical survey', by the editor (p. 1–30); 'The *Kano Chronicle* as history' by M. G. Smith (p. 31–56); 'The place of mosques in the history of Kano' by M. S. Zahradeen (p. 57–66); 'From sultanate to caliphate: Kano ca. 1450–1800' by Murray Last (p. 67–91); 'Approaching the study of production in rural Kano' by P. J. Shea (p. 93–115); 'Notes on taxation as a political issue in 19th century Kano' by H. K. Said (p. 117–25); 'Periphery and the centre: the 19th century trade of Kano' by M.

Johnson (p. 127–46); 'Industrial labour in Kano: historical origins, social characteristics and sources of differentiation' by Paul M. Lubeck (p. 147–69); 'Some remarks on the development of raw material production in the colony of Kano ca. 1912–1919' by S. Bello (p. 171–8); 'The London and Kano papers – an introduction' by R. Shenton (p. 187–92); '*Bara* [begging] by some *Almajirai* [students] in Kano City in the 20th century: a critical assessment' by I. A. Abba (p. 193–206); and 'A Kano anomaly: a terracotta figurine' by Murray Last (p. 207–08).

183 **The Egba and their neighbours, 1842–1872.**
Saburi O[ladeni] Biobaku. Oxford: Clarendon, 1958. 128p. 4 maps. bibliog.

Using written sources and oral histories from 1949, the author reconstructs the Egba state and its external relations from the arrival of the first missionary at Abeokuta to the departure of Commander J. H. Glover, Lieutenant-Governor and Acting Consul at Lagos. Issues discussed include: 'the impact of the transatlantic slave trade; the return of kinsmen once carried away into slavery; the advent of missionary enterprise; the installation of official British influence and, later, power at Lagos: and the groping towards the expansion of trade into the interior' (Preface, p. v). Glover's treaty with the Egba, Lagos trade statistics, lists of British consuls and governors-in-chief, and kings in and around Lagos appear in the appendices. The bibliography (p. 108–18) is strong for contemporary sources and lists those persons interviewed. The study is based on the author's 1951 University of London PhD thesis, *The Egba State and its neighbors, 1842–1872.*

184 **Nigerian panoply: arms and armour of the Northern Region.**
A. D. H. Bivar. [Lagos]: Department of Antiquities, Federal Republic of Nigeria, 1964. 68p. bibliog.

In a scholarly text illustrated with twenty-two photographs, primarily of swords and chain mail, the author provides a valuable monograph on arms and armour used in Northern Nigerian emirates.

185 **From empire to colony: Bornu in the nineteenth and twentieth centuries.**
Ronald Cohen. In: *Colonialism in Africa, 1870–1960. Vol. 3. Profiles of change: African society and colonial rule.* Edited by Victor Turner. Cambridge: Cambridge University, 1971, p. 74–126. map. bibliog.

Based on oral history accounts and documentary materials in the Provincial Office at Maiduguri, Bornu Province, Nigeria, gathered and examined by the author in 1956–57, this article provides an excellent account of the nineteenth-century Bornu Empire, its economic and administrative structure and the structural changes occurring during during the colonial period. Professor Cohen writes, 'Bornu may be viewed as a complex interaction between continuity and change' (p. 124); 'The British standards became limiting conditions within which traditional modes of behaviors have operated, and these were used as sanctions by both Kanuri and British officials to enforce discipline' (p. 122). Of considerable value also is the author's 'Incorporation in Bornu' in *From tribe to nation in Africa: studies in incorporation processes*, edited by himself and John Middleton (Scranton, Pennsylvania: Chandler, 1970. p. 150–74).

186 **Africa remembered: narratives by West Africans from the era of the
slave trade.**
Edited by Philip D. Curtin. Madison, Wisconsin: University of
Wisconsin, 1968. 363p. 16 maps. bibliog.

Ten accounts, all of which 'mirror the West African slave trade from the non-
European viewpoint' (p. 4), introduced and annotated by prominent scholars, give a
highly personal view of the lives of West Africans in the eighteenth and nineteenth
centuries. Five of the narratives are by men from what is now Nigeria: 'Olaudah
Equiano of the Niger Ibo' by G. I. Jones (p. 60–98); 'Ali Eisami Gazirmabe of Bornu'
by H. F. C. Smith, D. M. Last and Gambo Gubio (p. 199–216); 'Osifekunde of Ijebu'
by P. C. Lloyd (p. 217–88); 'Samuel Ajayi Crowther of Oyo' by J. F. Ade Ajayi
(p. 289–316); and 'Joseph Wright of the Egba' by Curtin (p. 317–33). Of related
interest is Paul E. Lovejoy's excellent *Transformations in slavery: a history of slavery in
Africa* (Cambridge: Cambridge University, 1983. 347p. (African Studies Series, 36))
which has numerous references to Nigerian groups (Hausa States, Borno, Nupe, Oyo
and Igbo) and a lengthy bibliography (p. 309–36).

187 **Trade and politics in the Niger Delta, 1830–1885: an introduction to the
economic and political history of Nigeria.**
Kenneth Onwuka Dike. Oxford: Clarendon, 1956. Reprinted,
Westport, Connecticut: Greenwood, 1981. 250p. map. bibliog.

From the author's doctoral thesis in history at the University of London emerged this
landmark in the study of Nigerian history. Using British and local historical sources,
the work examines 'the detailed process by which the existing native governments were
gradually supplanted by British consular power and following it the Crown Colony
administration' (Preface, p. v). Dike who was a professor at Ibadan University
discusses the slave and palm-oil trades, treaties, the rise of political figures such as Ja
Ja, head of the Anna Pepple House of Opobo, and the growth of the British trading
companies on the Niger River. Appendices contain copies of treaties (p. 219–23) and
there is a bibliographic essay (p. 224–30). The author's 'Origins of the Niger Mission,
1841–1891. A paper read at the centenary of the mission at Christ Church, Onitsha, on
13 November 1956' (Ibadan: Ibadan University for the CMS Niger Mission, 1957,
1962. 21p.) summarizes fifty years of missionary work along the lower Niger.

188 **The political economy of a pre-colonial African state: Ibadan,
1830–1900.**
Toyin Falola. Ile-Ife, Nigeria: University of Ife, 1984. 229p. 4 maps.
bibliog.

Using oral traditions and published sources, the author reconstructs the economic and
political systems of nineteenth-century Ibadan and describes warfare and its relation to
political economy, as well as the integration of Ibadan into the European economy.
'This study argues, among other things, that there is a recognizable African mode of
production which enables everybody in the society to be gainfully employed, that the
production and exchange system was efficient and well organized and that the
Eurocentric assumption that the economy was revitalized and developed because of
contacts with Europe was grossly misleading' (Preface, p. ix). Professor Falola also
provides a bibliography with 'a note on sources and methodology' (p. 209–25). Of
related interest is the author's 'From hospitality to hostility: Ibadan and strangers,
1830–1904' in *Journal of African History*, vol. 26, no. 1 (1985), p. 51–68, in which he
uses unpublished papers of former rulers of Ibadan.

189 **A history of Lagos, Nigeria: the shaping of an African city.**
Takiu Folami, foreword by the Oba of Lagos, Oba Adeyinka
Oyekan II. Smithtown, New York: Exposition, 1982. 175p. map.
Although not a scholarly work, this well-illustrated account provides extensive
information that is not easily available elsewhere. Part one 'Early settlements and obas
of Lagos' (p. 3–98) covers the period from before 1630 to the present. Part two
concerns 'Traditional chiefs of Lagos 1600–1980' (p. 101–33) with an account of each
chieftaincy and a photograph of each reigning modern chief. The appendix (p. 135–75)
describes the 'Birth and growth of Lagos State', providing statistics and descriptions of
local government and photographs of leading personalities and officials and lists of
colonial administrators. Valuable related articles are Robin Law's 'Trade and politics
behind the slave coast: the lagoon traffic and the rise of Lagos, 1500–1800', *Journal of
African History*, vol. 24, no. 3 (1983), p. 321–48, and his 'The career of Adele at Lagos
and Badagry, c. 1807–c. 1837', *Journal of the Historical Society of Nigeria*, vol. 9, no. 2
(1978), p. 35–39.

190 **Efik traders of Old Calabar.**
Edited by Daryll Forde. London: International African Institute,
1956. Reprinted, London: Dawsons of Pall Mall, 1968. 166p. map.
bibliog.
Following the editor's introduction to this volume on the famous trading people of the
Cross River estuary of Nigeria in the eighteenth and nineteenth centuries are: 'An
ethnographic sketch of the Efik people' by Donald C. Simmons (p. 1–26); 'The diary
of Antera Duke, being three years in the life of an Efik chief, 18th January 1785 to 31st
January 1788, in a modern English version' by A. W. Wilkie and Donald C. Simmons
(p. 27–65); 'Notes on the diary' by D. C. Simmons (p. 66–78); 'The original text of the
diary' by Antera Duke (p. 79–115); 'The political organization of Old Calabar'
(p. 116–57), and an addendum (p. 158–60), both by G. I. Jones; and a brief
bibliography (p. 161–62).

191 **The growth of Islam among the Yoruba, 1841–1908.**
T. G. O. Gbadamosi. Atlantic Highlands, New Jersey: Humanities,
1978. Harlow, England: Longman, 1979, 265p. 3 maps. bibliog.
(Ibadan History Series).
This study of the Muslim history of the Yoruba in Lagos and in Nigeria's western states
is based on diverse archival and published sources and on oral evidence collected
during 1963–65. Its focuses are the expansion and development of Islam in Yorubaland
and its relations with Christianity, traditional Yoruba society and the colonial
government. Appendices list chief *imams* in some Yoruba towns, Arabic loan words in
Yoruba and several historical documents. The bibliography (p. 235–58) is diverse and
valuable. The book is a revision of the author's 1969 doctoral thesis, *The growth of
Islam among the Yoruba, 1840–1908*, at the University of Ibadan.

192 **A chronicle of Abuja.**
Translated and arranged from the Hausa of Malam Hassan, Malam
Shuaibu, foreword by S. Barau, introduced by Frank Heath.   Ibadan,
Nigeria: Ibadan University for the Abuja Native Administration, 1952.
92p. map.

An invaluable historical account of the Emirate of Abuja, located near the geographi‹
centre of Nigeria and once part of the Kingdom of Zazzau. The chronicle is divide‹
into the history (p. 1–39) and the land and the people (p. 43–92) and contains thirtee‹
photographs. The *Chronicle* was revised and enlarged with new illustrations by Africa‹
Universities Press (Lagos, 1962, 91p.).

193 **The sword of truth: the life and times of the Shehu Usuman dan Fodio.**
Mervyn Hiskett.   New York: Oxford University, 1973. 194p. 5 maps.
bibliog.

A straightforward, lucid biography of the man who led the revolutionary Islami‹
reform movement in northern Nigeria, Shehu Usuman dan Fodio (15 Dec. 1754–2‹
April 1817). Basing his work, largely, on fieldwork in Nigeria from July 1966 to Jun‹
1967, the author uses Hausa and Arabic sources to reconstruct the man and his socio‹
cultural milieu. The important final chapter assesses the Shehu's continuing influence
in Hausa society and the nation. The selected bibliography (p. 171–75) is followed b‹
an informative bibliographic essay (p. 177–83) and exploratory notes to th‹
diagrammatic maps (p. 185–88).

194 **The emirates of Northern Nigeria: a preliminary survey of their
historical traditions.**
S[idney] J[ohn] Hogben, A. H. M. Kirk-Greene, foreword by
Abubakar T. Balewa.   London: Oxford University, 1966. 638p. 15
maps. bibliog.

This is a greatly revised and expanded version of the first author's 1930 *Muhammadar
emirates of Nigeria* (London: Humphrey Milford, Oxford University, 204p. 10 maps)
Part one (p. 3–142) provides an overview of empires throughout the Western Sudan
including Ghana, the Mandingo Empire of Mali, the Mossi states, Songhai, Bornu an‹
Kanem. Part two (p. 143–585) offers succinct histories of emirates deriving from th‹
Hausa states (Daura, Katsina, Kano, Zaria, Kebbi, Yauri, Nupe and Ilorin), from th‹
Bornu Empire (Bornu, Dikwa, Gumel, Fika and Bedde), from the Sokoto Empir‹
(Sokoto, Gwandu, Adamawa, Muri, Bauchi, Gombe, Kazaure, Katagum, Hedejia
Jama'are, Misau, Kontagora, Agaie, Lapai, Pategi, Lafiagi, Keffi, Nassarawa, Lafia
Jema'a and Wase), and those deriving independently (Abuja, Biu and Borgu)‹
Appendices (p. 586–92) contain 'Notes on European travellers in the Sudan and th
Sahara between 1795 and 1880', a list of the 'Chiefs of the Northern Region of Nigeri‹
and a bibliography (p. 593–603).

195 **Stateless societies in the history of West Africa.**
Robin Horton.   In: *History of West Africa*. Edited by J. F. A. Ajayi,
Michael Crowder.   New York: Columbia University, 1976. 2nd ed.
vol. 1, p. 72–113. bibliog.

Professor Horton describes the difficulties of writing a history of stateless societie‹
their present-day distribution and varieties of stateless social organization, the‹

religion and their relation to the nation. Prominent stateless groups from Nigeria include most of the Igbo, the Ibibio, the Ijọ, the Tiv, the Idoma, the Birom, the Angass, the Yako, the Mbembe, the Ekoi and the Fulani.

196 **Songhay, Borno and Hausaland in the sixteenth century.**
John O. Hunwick. In: *History of West Africa.* Edited by J. F. A. Ajayi, Michael Crowder. New York: Columbia University, 1976. 2nd ed. vol. 1, p. 264–301. 3 maps. bibliog.

Using sixteenth-century Arabic records, the author, then in the University of Ghana Department of History, reconstructs the history of the Songhay Empire and of the Borno, Kano, Katsina and Kebbi Empires of present-day northern Nigeria.

197 **Poverty in nineteenth-century Yorubaland.**
Joh Iliffe. *Journal of African History*, vol. 25, no. 1 (1984), p. 43–57. bibliog.

This article draws from the observations of missionaries living in Yoruba towns and demonstrates that, contrary to widespread opinion, poverty and the poor were a common feature of the social landscape. Ways by which the poor survived, especially begging, which did not arrive with Islam or Christianity, are described. The author asserts that 'the absence of poverty from pre-colonial Africa is a myth and that the subject deserves full study' (p. 57). He did just that in *The African poor* (Cambridge: Cambridge University, 1988, 387p. (African Studies Series, no. 58)) which includes extensive information on the Hausa, Igbo and Yoruba of Nigeria.

198 **Studies in the history of Plateau State, Nigeria.**
Edited by Elizabeth Isichei. London; Basingstoke, England: Macmillan, 1982. 288p. 2 maps. bibliog.

The editor, Professor of History at the University of Jos, together with Arnold Rubin, John Garah Nangel, J. Olowo Ojoade, Stephen Banfa, John Ola Agi, Ade Adefuye, A. C. Unomah, J. H. Morrison, J. J. Grace, Ricad Bruce and Daniel N. Wambudta, provide the best overview available for this complex area of Nigeria. Articles cover art history, ethnic history, proverbs, the salt industry, tin mining, the slave trade, colonialism, and religion. Fifteen photographs are included.

199 **The Fulani Empire of Sokoto.**
H[ugh] A[nthony] S[tephens] Johnston. London: Oxford University, 1967. 312. 6 maps. bibliog. (West African History Series).

An impressive history of the Fulani Sokoto Emirate up to its defeat by the British in 1903. This history provides background on Hausaland and the Fulani, but begins primarily with Shehu Usuman dan Fodio and his *jihad*. Sultan Bello's reign and the *jihad* in Nupe and Ilorin, trade and economy, the machinery of government, the Kebbi wars, the coming of the Royal Niger Company and the fall of Sokoto complete the account. Twelve photographs, useful maps and a bibliography (p. 291–95) are included. Johnston was Resident of Sokoto Province in 1952 and makes extensive use of Hausa and Arabic sources.

200 **The trading states of the oil rivers: a study of political development in eastern Nigeria.**

G. I. Jones. London; Ibadan, Nigeria: Oxford University for the International African Institute, 1963. 262p. 2 maps. bibliog.

This study of the history, politics and economy of the slave and palm-oil trading states of the Niger Delta in the eighteenth and nineteenth centuries 'was inspired by Dr Dike's *Trade and politics in the Niger Delta* [q.v.] and is an attempt to extend the trail blazed by that work' (Preface, p. v). The author concentrates on the states of New Calabar (Kalabari) and Grand Bonny (Bonny) up to 1884, but includes discussion o the broader region, from Nembe in the Delta to Old Calabar in the Cross River area He makes full use of the earliest accounts of European exploration in the region. For many years Jones was an Administrative Officer in Nigeria. In 'European and African tradition on the Rio Real', *Journal of African History*, vol. 4, no. 3 (1963), p. 391–402 he provides a fascinating analysis of two European legends, the sacrifice of a virgin in the Bonny River and 'the eating of King Amakiri's heart', and other traditions in the Delta.

201 **The Sokoto Caliphate.**

Denis Murray Last. London: Longman, 1967. 280p. 9 maps. bibliog. (Ibadan History Series).

An impressive history and historiography of Sokoto chiefly covering the nineteenth century, and up to its fall to the British in 1903. Sokoto was founded as a camp in 1809 five years after the *jihad* of the Shaikh, Usuman dan Fodio; it became the largest town in the area and in 1903 became the headquarters of a province named after it. This important work reconstructs the community of the Shaikh, its workings, and a history of a leading family of Sokoto. The study was originally done for a 1964 PhD thesis a the University of Ibadan, entitled, *Sokoto in the nineteenth century, with special reference to the vizierate*, for which the author worked in the Sokoto area during 196 and 1963, especially in the historical library of Wazirin Sokoto. The study relies heavily on Arabic sources which are critically discussed in an introductory chapter (p. xxv–lvii and are listed in the substantial bibliography (p. 236–62). In *West Africa*, no. 371 (14–20 Nov. 1988), p. 2133, D. W. [David Williams] reports on the death of Sir Siddi Abubakar III (15 March 1903–) who had been Sultan of Sokoto for fifty years 'religious leader of Nigeria's Islamic millions, and of millions elsewhere in West Africa'. Rioting greeted the appointment of Ibrahim Dasuki as the eighteenth Sultan of Sokoto. See also Peter K. Tibenderana's 1974 University of Ibadan thesis, *The administration of Sokoto, Gwandu and Argungu Emirates under British rule, 1900–1946* and his forthcoming *Sokoto Province under British rule, 1903–1939* (Zaria: Ahmadu Bello University).

202 **Old Calabar 1600–1891: the impact of the international economy upon a traditional society.**

A. J. H. Latham. Oxford: Clarendon, 1973. 193p. 6 maps. bibliog. (Oxford Studies in African Affairs).

This history describes Efik society and the port city of Old Calabar from the first recorded European contact in 1668 to 1891 when the British Consul-General' authority replaced that of the *Obong*, the Efik civil authority or king. Part one considers the impact of the slave trade on the Efik; part two examines the development of the palm-oil trade at Calabar. The brief epilogue describes the decline of Calabar' importance from 1891–1971. Appendices (p. 151–65) contain trade statistics and lists o treaties; the sources and bibliography offer complete documentation (p. 166–78). The work is based on the author's fieldwork in Nigeria in 1965–66.

203 **The Ọyọ Empire, c. 1600–c.1836: a West African imperialism in the era of the Atlantic slave trade.**
Robin Law. Oxford: Clarendon, 1977. 340p. 7 maps. bibliog. (Oxford Studies in African Affairs).

This volume is a detailed study of the Ọyọ Empire, one of the most powerful states in coastal West Africa during the seventeenth and eighteenth centuries, and the early nineteenth century until it disintegrated in civil war. Professor Law argues that Ọyọ benefitted materially from participation in the slave trade at the expense of its neighbours and that wealth from the slave trade was 'an integral factor in the success of the kingdom's imperial expansion'. In addition, the kingdom's demise was hastened by European demand for slaves when the Ọyọ themselves became victims of slave raids (Preface, p. vii). The bibliography (p. 313–25) is excellent. The book is 'the direct, if by now somewhat remote, descendant' of the author's 1971 University of Birmingham doctoral thesis. Of related interest are Law's 'A West African cavalry state: the kingdom of Oyo' in the *Journal of African History*, vol. 16 (1975), p. 1–15, and I. A. Akinjogbin's 'The expansion of Oyo and the rise of Dahomey, 1600–1800' in *History of West Africa*, edited by J. F. A. Ajayi and M. Crowder (New York: Columbia University, 1976, 2nd ed. vol. 1, p. 373–412).

204 **Caravans of kola: the Hausa kola trade, 1700–1900.**
Paul E. Lovejoy. Zaria, Nigeria: Ahmadu Bello University and University Press in association with Oxford University, 1980. 181p. 9 maps. bibliog. (Ahmadu Bello University History Series, vol. 4).

A marvellous, carefully documented study of the place of the kola nut in West African culture and society, especially among the Asante, the Volta Basin peoples, the Central Sudan and the Hausa states of present-day northern Nigeria. The work is also a history of three commercial associations which dominated the trade in the nineteenth century, Agalawa, Tokarawa, and Kambarin Beriberi, found throughout northern Nigeria. Kola nuts, primarily *Cola nitida*, are the only readily available stimulant not condemned by Islam and have one to four per cent caffeine and traces of theobromine, a skeletal muscle stimulant. This is a revised version of the author's 1973 University of Wisconsin PhD thesis, *The Hausa kola trade: 1700–1900*. The bibliography (p. 159–76) is extensive.

205 **Salt of the desert sun: a history of salt production and trade in the central Sudan.**
Paul E. Lovejoy. Cambridge: Cambridge University, 1986. 351p. 4 maps. bibliog. (African Studies Series, 46).

This excellent scholarly work describes the complexities of production, use and trade of salt and natron (a salt mixture with a high sodium carbonate content) in the broad central Sudan region. The author explains salt's history in the area, its culinary, medicinal and industrial uses and its geology and chemisty, and also the social organization of its trade and production, its politics, proprietorship and marketing networks, and estimates the volume of salt produced at perhaps 15,700 tonnes per year. Nigerian sites in the Benue valley and Borno sahel around Lake Chad feature prominently in the story. The author conducted fieldwork throughout the region between 1969 and 1975. In 'The Borno salt industry' *International Journal of African Historical Studies*, vol. 11, no. 4 (1978), p. 629–68, Professor Lovejoy describes a northern Nigerian empire which may have produced 6,000–9,500 metric tonnes of salt annually and employed perhaps 25,000 workers. He writes, 'probably more salt was traded within [Borno's] borders than anywhere else in pre-colonial Africa' (p. 629).

206   **Three Nigerian emirates: a study in oral history.**
       Victor N. Low.   Evanston, Illinois: Northwestern University, 1972.
       296p. 11 maps. bibliog.
An excellent historical study of the Gombe, Katagum and Hadejia Emirates in northeastern Nigeria from about 1800 to 1900, based on the author's eighteen months of field and archival research. Initial chapters discuss the Bornu Emirate border states, Islamic states and society, field methodology, oral testimony and 'The Nigerian Sudan to 1800'. Four fold-out maps and one figure for the region's emirates in 1900 are included separately in an envelope. A full set of Professor Low's field notes is available on microfilm at the University of Ibadan library, Ibadan, Nigeria. The author's 1968 University of California at Los Angeles doctoral dissertation was *The border emirates: a political history of three north-east Nigerian emirates, c. 1800–1902.*

207   **Palm oil and protest: an economic history of the Ngwa region, south-eastern Nigeria, 1800–1980.**
       Susan M. Martin.   Cambridge, England; New York: Cambridge
       University, 1988. 209p. 10 maps. bibliog. (African Studies Series, 59).
An important study based on archival and published materials and on oral evidence gathered in the Ngwa region in 1980–81. Topics covered include the oil-palm industry, the impacts of colonial rule, cassava and Christianity, the Women's Riot of 1929, cash cropping and economic changes, especially from 1930 to 1980. The bibliography (p. 193–203) is substantial. In a related article, Professor Martin examines 'Gender and innovation: farming, cooking and palm processing in the Ngwa region, south-eastern Nigeria, 1900–1930', *Journal of African History*, vol. 25, no. 4 (1984), p. 411–27. The subject is explored at length in her 1984 University of Birmingham PhD thesis, *The history of the oil palm industry in south-eastern Nigeria: the case of the Ngwa region, 1891–1929.*

208   **History of Itsekiri.**
       William A. Moore, introduced by P. C. Lloyd.   London: Frank Cass,
       1970. 2nd ed. 224p. bibliog. (Cass Library of African Studies. General
       Studies, no. 89).
A local history of the Itsekiri people of the western coastal Niger Delta. This study was first published in 1936 and is introduced by Dr. Lloyd who lived in Warri in the Delta in 1955–56. Moore describes history with great emphasis on the chiefs of the Itsekiri, law, taxation and native administration, religion, village organization and trade.

209 **Trade without rulers: pre-colonial economic development in south-eastern Nigeria.**
David Northrup. Oxford: Clarendon, Oxford University, 1978. 269p. 7 maps. bibliog. (Oxford Studies in African Affairs).

An economic history, primarily of the period of trans-Atlantic slavery, of the hinterlands, with particular emphasis on the Ngwa Igbo, the Aro traders of Arochukwu, the Anang and the Ibibio proper, although the rôles of many other groups are discussed. The development of trade before 1500 and the rise of the oil-palm trade in the nineteenth century are discussed extensively as well. The notes and bibliography (p. 240–58) are most useful. The author taught at Central Anang Secondary School, Ikot Ekpene, Nigeria in 1965–66 and returned to the area in 1972–73 to conduct research for his University of California at Los Angeles doctoral dissertation on which this is based.

210 **The Yoruba and Edo-speaking peoples and their neighbors before 1600.**
H. M. Ade Obayemi. In: *History of West Africa.* Edited by J[acob] F[estus] A[deniyi] Ajayi, Michael Crowder. New York: Columbia University, 1976, 2nd ed. vol. 1, p. 196–263. 2 maps. bibliog.

This scholarly article describes 'the emergence of the cultures of the Yoruba and Edo peoples and the outline of their history, with particular emphasis on the processes of state-formation' (p. 196). To a lesser extent it also deals with the neighbouring Nupe, Ebira (Igbira), Igala and Idoma peoples. For each of these groups and areas the author synthesizes a large literature on the processes of state formation, migration and interstate warfare and possible avenues for further research.

211 **Studies in southern Nigerian history.**
Edited by Boniface I. Obichere. London: Frank Cass, 1982. 265p. map. bibliog.

Ten essays by Nigerian scholars follow the editor's introduction: 'Joseph Christopher Okwudili Anene: 1918–68' by E. A. Ayandele (p. 9·19); 'Nigeria: the country of the Niger area' by C. C. Ifemesia (p. 23–37); 'Political history of the city states of Old Calabar, 1820–60' by M. Efiong Noah (p. 39–70); 'The Native Revenue Ordinance in the eastern provinces: the adventures of a colonial legislative measure' by A. E. Afigbo (p. 73–100); 'The newspaper press in Southern Nigeria, 1800–1900' by Fred I. A. Omu (p. 103–25); 'The Nigerian Union of Teachers: 1930–65' by Uga Onwuka (p. 127–53); 'The role of ethnic unions in the development of Southern Nigeria: 1916–66' by Austin M. Ahanotu (p. 155–74); 'The Nigerian civil service in the colonial era: a study of imperial reactions to changing circumstances' by G. O. Olusanya (p. 175–200); 'The British navy and 'Southern Nigeria' in the nineteenth century' by Paul M. Mbaeyi (p. 201–18); and 'An aspect of British colonial policy in Southern Nigeria: the problem of forced labour and slavery' by Walter I. Ofonagoro. A useful bibliography (p. 245–60) is included.

212 **A short history of Urhobo.**
M[ichael] P[eter] Okumagba. Nigeria: Kris & Pat, [1979]. 184p. map. bibliog.

Chief Okumagba has collected and preserved in print a wealth of information in this non-academic history and ethnography of his own people in the Niger Delta area of Bendel State. Chapters cover the origin, government and administration of Urhobo clans and various aspects of culture such as marriage and divorce, circumcision, titles, religion, festivals, industries, death and burial, slavery and the land tenure system. A glossary of Urhobo words (p. 147–58), copies of several historical documents and a fold-out copy of the Federal Survey Department's 1958 map of the Urhobo division, Delta Province, are included. The author was born in Warri in the area in 1923 and worked at the Central Bank of Nigeria until his retirement in 1974.

213 **'Tarikh 'Umara Bauchi' and its contribution to pre-colonial Ningi resistance to Sokoto Caliphate: exegesis and methodology in African oral history, ca. 1846–1902.**
Adell Patton. *A Current Bibliography on African Affairs*, vol. 18, no. 2 (1985–86), p. 105–16. bibliog.
The author translates a 1957 version of a 1912 Arabic text on the history of the Bauchi Emirate, 'the single most comprehensive reconstruction of the Ningi Chiefdom, which in the nineteenth century, was located between Bauchi and Kano Emirates' (p. 105). Of particular interest is the discussion of state formation as a response to external aggression. Among Dr. Patton's many articles on the Ningi is 'An Islamic frontier polity: the Ningi Mountains of Northern Nigeria, 1846–1902' in *The African frontier: the reproduction of traditional African societies*, edited by Igor Kopytoff (Bloomington, Indiana: Indiana University, 1987, p. 193–213).

214 **The development of an export oriented dyed cloth industry in Kano Emirate in the nineteenth century.**
Philip James Shea. PhD thesis, University of Wisconsin, Madison, Wisconsin, 1975. 314p. (Ann Arbor, Michigan: University Microfilms. Order no. 76–2506).
A fascinating history of dyed cloth, the most important single product exported from Kano Emirate in the nineteenth century. Kano was able to produce more of the shiny black, indigo-dyed cloth at lower costs than any other area. The author describes the technology and economics of the process as well as the industry's history through the 1920s when demand declined and dyers began using tinned indigo, cement pits and factory-woven cloth.

215 **Warfare in the Sokoto Caliphate: historical and sociological perspectives.**
Joseph P. Smaldone. Cambridge: Cambridge University, 1977. 228p. 3 maps. bibliog. (African Studies Series, 19).
In this detailed study of the Sokoto Caliphate up to about 1903, the author emphasizes how warfare and military organization, more so than Islam itself, functioned as 'institutions of integration' in the Caliphate's emirates (p. 159), 'predatory states organized for war' (p. 162). The volume contains illustrations of weaponry, maps, estimates of the numbers of cavalry and infantry in the seventeen emirates, glossaries of general and military terms and an extensive bibliography (p. 203–15). The study was originally prepared as the author's 1970 Northwestern University doctoral thesis.

216 **Government in Zazzau, 1800–1950.**
M[ichael] G[arfield] Smith.   London, New York: Oxford University
for the International African Institute, 1960. 371p. 3 maps. bibliog.
This is a superb historical study of the central region of northern Nigeria called
Zazzau, Zakzak, Zegzeg, or Zaria, which is also the name of its capital city. The
author, Professor Emeritus of Anthropology at Yale University, New Haven,
Connecticut, emphasizes a diachronic view of politics and government focusing on
three eras: the introduction of Islam, about 1456; the conquest of Zaria by the Fulani
leader Othman Dan Fodio [Usuman dan Fodio] in 1804; and the merger of Zaria into
the Protectorate of Northern Nigeria by Lord Lugard in 1900. Also discussed is the
Habe state of Abuja (p. 34–72), the location of the present Federal Capital Territory.

217 **The affairs of Daura: history and change in a Hausa state, 1800–1958.**
M. G. Smith.   Berkeley, California: University of California, 1978.
532p. 8 maps. bibliog.
This major study of history and change in the Muslim Hausa emirate of Daura in
Northern Nigeria from 1800–1958 integrates political, economic and social events over
more than a century and a half. This account is based 'almost entirely on oral data
collected in the field' (Preface p. xvii) during 1958–59. Extensive information is
included also on the chiefdoms of Zango and Baure. The rich text is intended as the
first monograph in a series of political histories which will include Katsina, Kano and
Sokoto in Nigeria and Maradi in Niger. The notes (p. 499–511) contain bibliographic
citations. Six photographs, maps, charts, diagrams, and genealogies are included, as
are a list of the queens and kings of Daura and other valuable historical materials.
Professor Smith has pubished several studies on the Kadara and Kagoro peoples of
Kaduna State including: 'Secondary marriage in Northern Nigeria', *Africa*, vol. 23, no.
4 (Oct. 1953), p. 298–323, which won the Wellcome Medal; 'After secondary marriage,
what?', *Ethnology*, vol. 19, no. 3 (July 1980), p. 265–77; 'Cosmology, practice and
social organisation among the Kadara and Kagoro', *Ethnology*, vol. 21, no. 1 (Jan.
1982), p. 1–20; and 'Kagoro political development', *Human Organization*, vol. 19
(1960), p. 137–49.

218 **A revolution in history: the jihad of Usman Dan Fodio.**
Ibraheem Sulaiman, foreword by Shehu Usman M. Bugaje.   London,
New York: Mansell, 1986. 189p. bibliog.
Using 'original Arabic sources written by the Sokoto jihad leaders and their
contemporaries' (Foreword, p. xi) as well as more available sources in English, the
author has written a biography of Shehu Usman Dan Fodio [or Usuman dan Fodio]
who 'recreated' the jihad and Islamic state of Mohammed with the Sokoto Caliphate in
what became northern Nigeria. Usman Dan Fodio's life (1754–1817) is set in religious,
social and political contexts. In a recent sequel, *The Islamic state and the challenge of
history: ideals, policies and operation of the Sokoto Caliphate* (London: Mansell, 1987.
162p.), the author focuses on the life and work of Muhammed Bello and continues the
Sokoto Caliphate's history up to post-independent Nigeria. For the current status of the
Sultan of Sokoto, see David Williams's 'A spiritual celebration', *West Africa*, no. 3698
4 July 1988), p. 1201, 1217.

73

219 **Cities of the savannah (a history of some towns and cities of the Nigerian savannah).**
Y. B. Usman, A. Mahadi, A. R. Augi, S. Bello, Y. T. Gella, M. Hamman, E. Oyedele, C. K. Gonyok. Lagos: Nigeria Magazine, Cultural Division, Federal Ministry of Information, [n.d.]. 125p. 6 maps. (Nigeria Magazine Special Publication, no. 5).

The authors, all members of the Department of History, Ahmadu Bello University, Zaria, Nigeria, produced this collection of outline histories of northern Nigerian cities for students in schools and colleges and for the general reader. Their intent is to present the cities as complex units, rather than to emphasize 'any lineage or group or its claims and privileges' (p. 7). Cities discussed include those of Borno, Kano, Sakkwato, Gwandu, Yawuri, Kontagora, Bida, Kaduna, Zaria, Jos, Bauchi, Yola, Wukari, Ilorin, Okene and Lokoja.

The archaeology of Benin: excavations and other researches in and around Benin City, Nigeria
See item no. 137.

Three thousand years in Africa: man and his environment in the Lake Chad region of Nigeria.
See item no. 138.

Archaeology and history in southern Nigeria: the ancient linear earthworks of Benin and Ishan.
See item no. 139.

The Niger Delta, aspects of its prehistoric economy and culture.
See item no. 142.

History and ethnoarchaeology in eastern Nigeria: a study of Igbo-Igala relations with special reference to the Anambra Valley.
See item no. 144.

West African culture dynamics: archaeological and historical perspectives.
See item no. 145.

Guide to research and reference works on sub-Saharan Africa.
See item no. 1129.

Niger Delta studies, 1627–1967: a bibliography.
See item no. 1138.

A bibliographic guide to Borno studies, 1821–1983.
See item no. 1142.

Colonial Nigeria (1851–1960)

220 **The judicial system in Southern Nigeria, 1854–1954: law and justice in a dependency.**
Omoniyi Adewoye. Harlow, England: Longman; Atlantic Highlands, New Jersey: Humanities, 1977. 331p. map. bibliog. (Ibadan History Series).
This study traces Nigerian legal history from the first 'court of equity' established at Bonny in 1854 to the beginning of a regionalized judiciary in 1954. Professor Adewoye treats the imposed English legal system as an agency of colonial control. Nine relevant photographs and an extensive bibliography (p. 306–17) are included. The author was in the history department at Ibadan University, Ibadan, Nigeria, at the time of publication. This work derives from his 1968 doctoral thesis at Columbia University, New York, entitled the *Legal profession in Southern Nigeria, 1861–1943*.

221 **The warrant chiefs: indirect rule in southeastern Nigeria, 1891–1929.**
A[diele] E[berechukwu] Afigbo. New York: Humanities, 1972; Harlow, England: Longman, 1979. 338p. 4 maps. bibliog. (Ibadan History Series).
This political history of the Igbo, Ibibio, Ijaw (Ijọ) and Ogoja peoples under colonial rule 'seeks to explain why [the British] attempt at total conquest through institutional control failed for over three decades' (Preface, p. xii). Dr. Afigbo examines both the British and indigenous peoples' sides using oral data gathered in 1963 and 1964 and official government records. Warrant chiefs were individuals given warrants of authority by the British who incorrectly believed them to be local leaders whose people would obey them without question. The first chapter of this excellent study provides an important historiography of 'The indigenous political background'. The study evolved from the author's 1964 University of Ibadan PhD thesis. See also Afigbo's 'Indirect rule in Southern Nigeria: the era of warrant chiefs, 1881–1929', *Tarikh*, vol. 4, no. 4 (1974), p. 11–24.

222 **Christian missions in Nigeria, 1841–1891: the making of a new élite.**
J. F. Ade. Ajayi, series introduced by K. Onwuka Dike. Harlow, England: Longman, 1969; Evanston, Illinois: Northwestern University, 1965. 317p. 5 maps. bibliog. (Ibadan History Series).
This study traces efforts to re-establish Christianity in what became Nigeria from the year of the 1841 Niger Expedition, which attempted to begin a model farm at Lokoja, to the death of Bishop Samuel Crowther in 1891. Professor Ajayi describes the activities and relations with Nigerians of five dominant missionary societies: 'the Anglican Church Missionary Society (CMS), many of whose missionaries were at this time Germans; the Wesleyan Methodist Missionary Society, a committee of the English Methodist Conference; the Foreign Mission Committee of the United Presbyterian Church of Scotland; the Foreign Mission Board of the Southern Baptist Convention of the United States; and the Catholic Society of African Missions (the Société des Missions Africaines, SMA) of France' (p. xiii–xiv). This revision of the author's 1958 London University PhD thesis is the first volume in the important Ibadan History Series.

History. Colonial Nigeria (1851–1960)

223 **Southern Nigeria in transition, 1885–1906: theory and practice in a colonial protectorate.**
J[oseph] C[hristopher] [Okwudili] Anene. Cambridge: Cambridge University, 1966. 360p. 3 maps. bibliog.

Using oral traditions, government papers and Intelligence Reports and other archival sources, the author reconstructs a detailed history of Britain's political and economic entrenchment and conquest of the area which became the Protectorate of Southern Nigeria (1900–06). He describes the indigenous background, the 'paper protectorate' (1885–90), the overthrow of indigenous authority (1891–1906), the 'native' court system and the consolidation of British rule (1901–06). Eleven plates from the period taken in the Niger Delta are included and the bibliography (p. 340–46) is useful. This book grew out of the author's University of London MA thesis. See E. A. Ayandele's tribute, 'Joseph Christopher Okwudili Anene: 1918–68' in B. I. Obichere's *Studies in southern Nigerian history* (q.v.).

224 **The international boundaries of Nigeria, 1885–1960: the framework of an emergent African nation.**
J. C. Anene. New York: Humanities, 1970. 331p. 16 maps. bibliog. (Ibadan History Series).

This thorough study of the eastern, western, and northern boundaries of Nigeria seeks to 'examine objectively the validity of the fashionable and generalized claims that the international boundary arrangements for Nigeria were 'mortally injurious' to the pre-existing political order' (Preface, p. xv). Professor Anene concludes that 'unqualified suggestions of arbitrariness and subjective criticisms are misleading and dangerous' (p. 288). A select bibliography (p. 300–11) is provided. This book is based on the author's 1960 doctoral thesis at the University of London. J. F. Ade Ajayi provides 'Professor J. C. Anene: a tribute' (p. ix–x) and a bibliography of his late colleague who had been Professor of History at the University of Nigeria, Nsukka up to his death in 1968.

225 **Nigeria and its British invaders, 1851–1920: a thematic documentary history.**
Johnson U. J. Asiegbu. New York; London; Enugu, Lagos, Nigeria: Nok, 1984. 377p. 21 maps. bibliog.

The author has performed a valuable service in compiling into a single volume extracts of key documents in Nigeria's colonial history. Following a general introduction (p. xiii–xxxii), the book is divided into six parts, each of which is introduced and concludes with a list of additional readings. The parts are entitled: 'The British in Lagos and Yorubaland' (p. 3–68); 'Trade rivalry and monopoly in the Niger Delta' (p. 71–156); 'The British and the Sokoto Caliphate, 1897–1903' (p. 159–232); 'The British in Igboland' (p. 235–308); 'Military campaigns on the Cross River: the surrendering and gathering of the guns' (p. 311–330); and 'Further resistance and military expeditions in Igboland' (p. 333–51).

226 **Western Yorubaland under European rule 1889–1945: a comparative analysis of French and British colonialism.**
A. I. Aṣiwaju. London: Longman, 1976. 303p. 5 maps. bibliog. (Ibadan History Series).

This is a case study of 'two colonial regimes as they operated simultaneously in a Yoruba locality of similar precolonial conditions' focused on the *souspréfectures* (now called 'districts') of Sabẹ, Ketu, Ipobẹ and Itakete in Dahomey (now the Republic of Benin) and on the Ègbado Division of Abẹokuta Province in Nigeria (p. 5). The history begins in 1889, when Western Yorubaland was partitioned between France and Britain, and ends in 1945 'because after that date the effective phase of colonial rule gradually drew to a close' (p. 6). Combining oral history and archival materials, the University of Lagos historian contributes substantially to the view emphasizing contrasts between the French and British colonial patterns. Seven photographs and an excellent bibliography (p. 279–95) are included.

227 **The new Ọyọ Empire: indirect rule and change in Western Nigeria, 1894–1934.**
J. A. Atanda. New York: Humanities, 1973; Harlow, England: Longman, 1979. 334p. 5 maps. bibliog. (Ibadan History Series).

This study examines the manner in which British Administrative Officer Captain W. A. Ross, by working with the leaders of the once vigorous Yoruba group, 'raised Oyọ from virtual political ruins to prominence during the first three decades of the twentieth century', arresting 'at a crucial moment the drift of Oyọ into political oblivion' (p. 294). Background history of the Old Oyọ Empire and descriptions of social and economic events in Oyọ during 1900–30 form significant parts of this excellent work. Included also are five maps of Oyọ, seven photographs, an appendix with Anglo-Yoruba treaties of 1886, 1888, 1893 (with the Alafin of Oyọ) and 1893 (with Ibadan) (p. 296–308) and a bibliography detailing evidence from oral interviews, and archival and published sources (p. 309–24). The study is based on the author's University of Ibadan PhD thesis.

228 **The missionary impact on modern Nigeria, 1842–1914: a political and social analysis.**
E[mmanuel] A[yankanmi] Ayandele. New York: Humanities, 1967; Harlow, England: Longman, 1977. 393p. 5 maps. bibliog. (Ibadan History Series).

This study emphasizes 'the reaction of the various sections of Nigerian community – chiefs, educated Africans, the ordinary people and slaves – to missionary activity. Mission policies and opinions at the headquarters in Europe and America have no place whatsoever, except when these affected the Nigerian peoples' (Preface, p. xvii). Themes include missionary activity and politics in Yorubaland and Southern Nigeria (1875–1900), and in Northern Nigeria (1900–14); 'Ethiopianism' or ecclesiastical African nationalism (1875–1914); missions and education; and the missionary impact on society. Photographs of leading personalities, maps and a useful bibliography (p. 347–60) are included. The author made extensive use of mission archives in London, Edinburgh and Rome. The book is a revised version of his PhD thesis at the University of London.

229 **Holy Johnson, pioneer of African nationalism, 1836–1917.**
E. A. Ayandele.   New York: Humanities, 1970. 417p. 4 maps.
bibliog.

A detailed biography of James Johnson (1835 or 1836–May 1917) known to Sierra
Leonians as 'Wonderful Johnson', to Nigerians as 'Holy Johnson' and to the
authorities of the Anglican Church Missionary Society as the 'Pope of Nigeria'.
Johnson was born in Sierra Leone to Yoruba parents, graduated from Fourah Bay
Institution in 1858 and rose quickly to prominence in the CMS's Native Pastorate,
advocating an Africanized church and increased educational opportunities for
Africans. After arriving in Lagos in 1874, 'he was to be the most respected, the most
popular, the most influential and the greatest patriot for the rest of the century'
(p. 85). From 1886 to 1894 in Lagos he became the first African clergyman to sit on the
Legislative Council in British colonial Africa. He organized the Niger Delta Pastorate
and for a time kept it exclusively in the control of Africans. He was a pioneer in his
goals of 'Pan-Africanism, political and religious independence, mental emancipation,
and cultural renaissance' (p. 369).

230 **Benin: the city of blood.**
R[eginald] H[igh] [Spencer] Bacon.   London, New York: Edward
Arnold, 1897. 151p. map.

A famous account of the British Punitive Expedition of 1897 sent to avenge the deaths
on 4 January 1897 of seven Englishmen and numerous bearers, and to subdue
Ovonramwen, King of Benin. Commander Bacon, R.N., intelligence officer for the
expedition, describes the military operation in which a force of 1,200 men was
organized and landed and succeeded in capturing the town by mid-February. Bacon
does not mention the art works taken by the British, rather he emphasizes the scene
they encountered: 'Crucifixions, human sacrifices, and every horror the eye could get
accustomed to, . . . but the smells no white man's internal economy could stand. . .
Blood was everywhere; . . .' (p. 88, 89). Appendices include lists of military
provisions, armaments and medical supplies. One of the survivors of the ambush,
Captain Alan Boisragon, offered his own lurid account in *The Benin massacre*
(London: Methuen, 1897. 190p.). Recent scholarship is more enlightening in James D.
Graham's 'The slave trade, depopulation and human sacrifice in Benin history',
Cahiers d'Etudes Africaines, vol. 5 (1965), p. 317–34; and Robin Law's 'Human
sacrifice in pre-colonial West Africa', *African Affairs*, vol. 84, no. 334 (Jan. 1985),
p. 53–88.

231 **The dialectics of colonial labour control: class struggles in the Nigerian
coal industry, 1914–1949.**
Carolyn A. Brown.   In: *Third World workers: comparative
international labour studies.* Edited by Peter C. W. Gutkind. Leiden,
Netherlands: E. J. Brill, 1988. p. 32–59. bibliog. (International Studies
in Sociology and Social Anthropology, vol. 49).

This is a case study of the labour movement at the Enugu Government Colliery from
its opening in 1914 to 1949, when twenty-one striking miners were killed. The author
develops the theme of 'the emergence of worker consciousness in a context of
overlapping ethnic and class-based affiliations and its expansion in acts of collective
and individual protest' (p. 32). The paper derives from the author's 1985 Columbia
University doctoral thesis, *A history of the development of workers' consciousness of
the coal mines at Enugu Government Colliery, Nigeria, 1914–1950.* The author is in the
Department of History of the City College of the City University of New York.

232 **Gender, culture and empire: European women in colonial Nigeria.**
Helen Callaway. London: Macmillan; Urbana; Chicago, Illinois:
University of Illinois, 1987. 278p. map. bibliog.

An original and fascinating ethnography of European women who were either
dependent wives or officers within the Colonial Serivce in Nigeria between 1900 and
1960. Nigeria was considered 'perhaps the prime example of 'a man's country'' (p. 4)
and was 'no place for a white woman' (p. 5). 'One in five of the European population
in Northern Nigeria either died or was invalided home every year' (p. 5). Professor
Callaway explains how women participated in health care, education, administration
and their husbands' careers, yet remained invisible or appeared mainly in pejorative
stereotypes, and suggests in a structural and feminist analysis that 'women contributed
to the loss of Empire by helping to gain the Empire' (p. 244). The volume's
bibliography (p. 252–66) is extensive. The author is a social anthropologist at Oxford
University.

233 **The Colonial Office and Nigeria, 1898–1914.**
John M. Carland. Stanford, California: Hoover Institution, 1985.
258p. 5 maps. bibliog.

This interesting study, based primarily on Colonial Office and Treasury records at the
Public Record Office, Kew, England, describes in detail the British policies and
personalities which lead to an amalgamated Nigeria, 'the flagship of Britian's tropical
empire' (p. 1). Following chapters on the Colonial Office and Crown Colony
government with biographical sketches of the cast of characters (p. xiii–xviii), the
author uses the case study approach to analyse 'Public expenditure and development in
Southern Nigeria, 1900–12'; 'Budgetary conflict over revenue estimates in Northern
Nigeria, 1899–1913'; the Lagos railway (1895–1911); the Baro-Kano railway (1897–1911);
and the 'Search for petroleum in Southern Nigeria, 1906–14'. Comprehensive notes
and a bibliography are included. The study evolved from the author's 1977 PhD
dissertation at the University of Toronto, entitled *Colonial Office staff and Nigeria,
1898–1914.*

234 **Nigeria and its tin fields.**
Albert F[rederick] Calvert. London: E. Stanford, 1910. Reprinted,
New York: Arno, 1977. 188p. 25 maps. (European Business: Four
Centuries of Foreign Expansion).

The author (1872–1946) describes the early years of Nigerian tin field exploitation,
providing an account of the history and setting of Northern Nigeria and detailed
reports on the 'Particulars of companies working tin properties in Northern Nigeria'
(p. 71–152) and the mining regulations of 'The minerals proclamation, 1910'
(p. 153–88). The fields were first officially recognized in the Colonial Report of 1905,
and in 1906 in the first Report on the Results of the Mineral Survey of Northern
Nigeria, 1904–05. These and later reports 'all tend to prove that in Northern Nigeria
we have one of the largest, if not the very largest of the tin-producing areas of the
world' (p. 57). Perhaps most interesting in this book are the 234 photographs of scenes
and people throughout the country and of the tin-mining activities.

235 **My Tanganyika service and some Nigeria.**
Sir Donald Cameron. London: George Allen & Unwin, 1939. 293p.

Cameron (1872–1948) was Governor of Tanganyika, 1925–31, in Nigeria in secretarial appointments from 1908–24 and Governor of Nigeria, 1931–35. This book is primarily concerned with his Tanganyika service, although Nigeria is mentioned frequently. The author describes his views on British colonial policy, Native Administration and indirect rule in Nigeria.

236 **Modern and traditional elites in the politics of Lagos.**
Patrick Cole. New York, London: Cambridge University, 1975. 297p. bibliog. (African Studies Series, 12).

A detailed treatment, focusing with insight on competing groups in Lagos and their rôles in local and national politics between about 1851 and 1949. The author traces the relations of four communities (whites; the indigenous Yoruba-Benin population; black repatriated freed slaves from Brazil; and Saros, black liberated slaves from Sierra Leone), the political rôles of Henry Rawlinson Carr (15 August 1863–6 March 1945) and Herbert Samuel Heelas Macaulay (14 November 1864–7 May 1946), and the traditional rulers of Lagos. Significantly, 'The indigenous Yoruba social system of Lagos is important in that it provided one and perhaps the most important, of the bases for the organisation of modern political parties in Lagos, which pioneered the pattern for all subsequent Southern Nigerian national parties' (p. 190). One-third of the book consists of detailed notes (p. 192–278) and a select bibliography (p. 279–90).

237 **British enterprise in Nigeria.**
Arthur Norton Cook. Philadelphia, Pennsylvania: University of Pennsylvania; London: Humphrey Milford, Oxford University, 1943. Reprinted, London: Frank Cass, 1964; New York: Barnes & Noble, 1965. 330p. bibliog.

A substantial older history of the colony by an American professor of history at Temple University, Philadelphia, Pennsylvania, based on research into archival and official documents in London and into the records of the Niger Company. He concludes, 'In the long run there is a very real possibility that Nigeria will evolve into a national state' (p. 273) and praises the system of indirect rule. The bibliography (p. 291–319) has very brief annotations and is one of the best for its time. The study is based on his 1927 University of Pennsylvania doctoral thesis.

238 **Nigeria: a critique of British colonial administration.**
Walter R. Crocker. London: G. Allen, 1936. Reprinted, Freeport, New York: Books for Libraries, 1971. 277p. map. bibliog.

Much of this interesting book consists of extracts from the author's 'Journal of an administrative officer, June 1933–June 1934' which show 'the Administrative Service in action day by day and how the English official spends his life' (p. 5). Following this he discusses colonial administration and its problems in Nigeria, particularly his concern that officials manage effectively the juxtaposition of English and Africans and that they 'show the African the example of the best way of European life' (p. 249). His great fear is 'to lose our Englishry in compromising with the standards around us' (p. 250). The introduction contains a lucid description of the organization and membership of the Administrative Service.

239 **Indirect rule – French and British style.**
Michael Crowder. *Africa*, vol. 34, no. 3 (July 1964), p. 197–205.
bibliog.

This essay was written in response to Gouverneur Hubert Deschamps' 'Et maintenant, Lord Lugard?' ('And now, Lord Lugard?') in *Africa*, vol. 33, no. 4 (Oct. 1963), p. 293–306, which tended to minimize differences between French and British 'native' administration in Africa. The late Professor Crowder uses indirect rule in Northern Nigeria as a model to demonstrate the fundamental differences in degree and kind between the two systems. The British system emphasized an advisory relationship between the political officer and the native authority while the French system made the chief entirely subordinate to the political officer. Chiefs in Francophone areas 'retained no traditional judicial authority', as their counterparts in British West Africa did (p. 200). British officers stayed in the same territory for longer periods and were apt to learn local languages. The British excluded Nigerians from senior service posts and tended to discourage formation of a class of Europeanized Africans. See also Obaro Ikime's 'Reconsidering the indirect rule: the Nigerian example', *Journal of the Historical Society of Nigeria*, vol. 4, no. 3 (Dec. 1968), p. 421–39; and Peter K. Tibenderana's 'The irony of indirect rule in Sokoto Emirate, Nigeria, 1903–1944', *African Studies Review*, vol. 31, no. 1 (April 1988), p. 67–92.

240 **West African resistance: the military response to colonial occupation.**
Edited by Michael Crowder. New York: Africana, 1971. 314p. 15 maps. bibliog.

An introduction and nine case studies, each 'concerned with the opposition to the European forces by an organised army of a centralised state' (p. 5), and set in Ghana, Mali, Senegambia, Guinea, Dahomey, Sierra Leone and Nigeria. The Nigerian studies are 'Nigeria–Ijebu' by Robert Smith (p. 170–204), an analysis of the British campaign against Ijebu in southern Yorubaland in 1892; 'Nigeria–Ebrohimi' by Obaro Ikime (p. 205–32), an account of the British expedition in the western Delta and the battle against Nana Olomu, the Itsikiri leader at Ebrohimi in 1894; and 'Nigeria–Sokoto Caliphate' by D. J. M. Muffett (p. 268–99), a history of the last great West African state to fall to European invaders, during 1900–03. Each article has excellent maps and references.

241 **Revolt in Bussa: a study of British 'native administration' in Nigerian Borgu, 1902–1935.**
Michael Crowder. Evanston, Illinois: Northwestern University, 1973. 273p. 8 maps. bibliog.

A case study of the hitherto little-known rebellion in Borgu Province of Northern Nigeria, the events which preceded it and its aftermath. On about 14 June 1915 (the date is uncertain) 600 armed warriors led by Sabukki, prince of Bussa, occupied Bussa and killed 'half the members of the Native Administration who had only three months before taken over' and took over its government from King Kitoro Gani, Sabuki's half-brother (p. 17). This book shows how the British administration provoked 'a people generally regarded as peaceful into armed rebellion . . . [and how] the British, in order to govern these once 'docile' people, were forced to undo the administrative reforms initiated immediately before the rebellion of which they were one of the major causes' (p. 18). Appendices list the relevant British officials and the kings of Bussa, and include the petition by the peoples of Yawuri and Boussa. The sources and notes (p. 243–66) are extensive. A brief overview of these events is offered by Professor Crowder's 'The Borgu revolts of 1915–17', *Tarikh*, vol. 5, no. 3 (1977), p. 18–30.

242 **Colonial West Africa: collected essays.**
Michael Crowder. London: Frank Cass, 1978. 341p. bibliog.
Fifteen of the late author's essays, published between 1956 and 1975, are collected
here, covering extensive geographic and historical ground. Nigeria appears throughout
many, especially 'The white chiefs of tropical Africa' (1970); 'West African chiefs'
(1970, with Obaro Ikime); 'West Africa 1919–1939: the colonial situation' (1974, with
J. F. Ade Ajayi); 'The imposition of the Native Authority System in Bussa: the
rebellion of 1915' (1974); and 'Indirect rule – French and British style' (1964) (q.v.). A
recent essay by the author, 'Lugard and colonial Nigeria: towards an identity?' in
History Today, vol. 36 (Feb. 1986), p. 23–29, provides a fascinating view of political
relations between Sir Frederick Lugard and the administrator of Lagos Colony and
Protectorate, Sir William MacGregor, and Consul-General of Southern Nigeria, Sir
Ralph Moor. The ultimate partial amalgamation of these regions may have had
consequences for the Nigerian civil war fifty years later, argues Professor Crowder.
The author, one of the most esteemed African historians, died in August 1988, aged 54.

243 **West African chiefs: their changing status under colonial rule and
independence.**
Edited by Michael Crowder, Obaro Ikimẹ. Ile-Ife, Nigeria:
University of Ife; New York: Africana, 1970. 453p. 3 maps. bibliog.
In this compilation of nineteen articles, from an international seminar of the same title
held at the University of Ife in 1968, are nine concerning chieftaincy in Nigeria. These
are: 'The relationship of the British political officer to his chief in Northern Nigeria' by
John Smith (p. 14–22); 'Aspects of emirship in Kano' by John N. Paden (p. 162–86);
'The kingship in Bornu' by Ronald Cohan (p. 187–210); 'The changing status of the
Alafin of Oyo under colonial rule and independence' by J. A. Atanda (p. 212–30);
'The changing position of the Awujales of Ijebuland under colonial rule' by E. A.
Ayandele (p. 231–54); 'Obas of the Ekiti confederacy since the advent of the British'
by S. A. Akintoye (p. 255–70); 'The changing status of the Obas of Benin under
colonial rule and since independence' by Philip A. Igbafe (p. 272–88); 'The changing
status of chiefs among the Itsẹkiri' by Obaro Ikimẹ (p. 289–311); and 'Chieftaincy in
the former Eastern Region of Nigeria' by G. I. Jones (p. 312–24). The editors provide
an informative overview of West African chiefs and indirect rule in their introduction
(p. vii–xxix).

244 **100 years of British rule in Nigeria, 1851–1951.**
K. Onwuka Dike. Lagos, Nigeria: Federal Information Service and
the Nigerian Broadcasting Corporation, 1958. 49p.
In these 1956 Lugard Lectures the author interprets the main features of British rule in
Nigeria from before the occupation of Lagos in 1851 to the inauguration of the
'Macpherson' Constitution in 1951, which marked the beginning of the gradual
withdrawal of British control from the country. The six lectures are: 'The origins of
British power' (up to 1851); 'Rise of consular power' (1851–85); 'Development of
inland trade' (1788–1885); 'Subjugation and pacification, 1885–1914'; 'Christianity,
nationalism and constitutional development' (1843–1922); and 'Freedom and independence' (1922–54). Period photographs accompany the text. A second edition (1960.
52p.) contains several more illustrations.

245   **The conquest of Northern Nigeria.**
Richard H. Dusgate.   London: Frank Cass, 1985. 305p. map. bibliog.

A lucid, straightforward history of the British penetration into and conquest of
Northern Nigeria from the late-nineteenth century to 1906. After establishing the
earlier history of trade and settlement and the rôle of Sir George Goldie in the colony,
the author concentrates on the Niger Sudan Campaign of 1897 at Kabba, Bida and
Ilorin, the rôle of the West African Frontier Force, the Bauchi-Borno expedition of
1902, the Hausaland campaigns of 1903 against Kano and Sokoto, the battles of Bormi,
the subjugation of the pagans, 1903–06, and the final defeat of the rebels in 1906 in
Munshi, Satiru, and Hadejia. Documentation is ample. F. P. Crozier provides a first-
hand account of the battles for Sokoto and Kano, vivid descriptions of military action
and camp life and sixteen photographs in *Five years hard, being an account of the fall
of the Fulani Empire and a picture of the daily life of a regimental officer among the
peoples of the Western Sudan* (London, New York: Jonathan Cape & Robert Ballou,
[1932]. 221p.).

246   **Victorian Lagos: aspects of nineteenth century Lagos life.**
Michael J. C. Echeruo.   London; Basingstoke, England: Macmillan
Education, 1977. 124p.

The author skilfully combines and comments on extensive excerpts from editorials,
news reports and correspondence columns of Lagos newspapers during 1863–1900, 'to
reconstruct the patterns of life and thought' in Lagos (p. 1). Eight pages of period
photographs are a valuable addition. The resulting study probably provides a more
accurate idea of the mood and atmosphere of nineteenth-century Lagos than do official
reports and academic histories.

247   **Britain and Nigeria: exploitation or development?**
Edited by Toyin Falola.   London; Atlantic Highlands, New Jersey:
Zed, 1987. 250p. bibliog.

The editor and nine contributors analyse from a 'progressive' perspective the various
ways in which Britain exploited Nigeria. Essays by Falola, J. Ihonvbere, L. I. Izuakor,
S. A. Olanrewaju, J. O. Ahazuem, A. G. Adebayo, O. N. Njoku, D. C. Obadike,
A. A. Lawal and S. O. Osoba discuss historical, economic, agricultural and industrial
issues, trade, labour and economic development. The editor teaches history at
Obafemi Awolowo University and is editor of *Odu: A Journal of West African Studies*
(q.v.).

248   **Sir George Goldie and the making of Nigeria.**
John E. Flint.   London: Oxford University, 1960. 340p. 6 maps.
bibliog. (West African History Series).

This is the first formal biography of George Dashwood Goldie Taubman (1846–1925),
better known as Sir George Goldie, who founded the Royal Niger Company and built
a private empire on the Niger. Goldie played a major rôle in creating the boundaries of
the territory which became Nigeria, in expanding British influence on the Niger, and in
fending off French and German ambitions. In addition to a select bibliography
(p. 321–24), the author includes 'The financial history of the Niger Company' and the
'Royal charter granted to the National African Company, later called the Royal Niger
Company'. Goldie destroyed all his papers before he died, but Professor Flint uses
British official correspondence with Goldie, first made available in 1952. The resulting

study is far superior to Dorothy Wellesley's 1934 work *Sir George Goldie, Founder of Nigeria* (London: Macmillan. Reprinted, New York: Arno, 1977. 195p. (European Business Series)).

249 **Nigeria: the colonial experience from 1880 to 1914.**
John E. Flint. In: *Colonialism in Africa, 1870–1960. Vol. 1, The history and politics of colonialism, 1870–1914.* Edited by L. H. Gann, Peter Duignan. Cambridge: Cambridge University, 1969, p. 220–60. map. bibliog.

Offers one of the most informative succinct accounts of the extension of colonial rule in the region which became Nigeria in 1914. The author describes British motives in the 1880s as pragmatic, and 'meant only to prevent France from obtaining control of the British palm-oil trade on the Niger and in its delta' (p. 224). He also considers the rôle of educated Africans in the 1880s and 1890s; the relations with King Ja Ja, 'the greatest African middleman of all time' (p. 233); and the growth of indirect rule. Northern Nigeria is described as a failure 'whether judged in terms of administrative efficiency or of economic development . . . In reality the British had done little more than make themselves the overlords of an existing feudal system' (p. 250).

250 **Lugard and the Abeokuta uprising: the demise of Egba independence.**
Harry A. Gailey. London: Frank Cass, 1982. 138p. map. bibliog.

This study critically examines an episode in the career of Sir Frederick Lugard and provides a history of the Egba, a Yoruba-speaking people of Abeokuta and its vicinity, from pre-1865 to about 1918. It focuses on the confrontations in August 1914 and June–July 1918 when thirty-eight and 600 Egba respectively were killed by British troops. Using British colonial records as well as research in Nigeria, the author suggests that 'Lugard, although a tireless worker, was only a mediocre administrator, consistently ignoring his most able assistants and failing to build an adequate structure of government for Nigeria' (Preface, p. ix), and that 'Lugard should certainly be condemned for his lack of understanding of the Egba situation if one accepts his explanation for the disturbances' (p. 85).

251 **The strong brown god: the story of the Niger River.**
Sanche de Gramont. Boston: Houghton Mifflin, 1976. 350p. 7 maps. bibliog.

A captivating history of the European search for and exploration of West Africa's greatest river, one-third of which flows through Nigeria. The author recounts the river's vital rôle in the region and the cultures which live along it as he describes the efforts of explorers from Mungo Park in 1795 to Heinrich Barth in 1849 and William Balfour Baikie in 1854, concluding with the commercial ventures of Frederick Lugard and Sir George Goldie. In researching this book the author and his wife spent three months following the river's 2,600-mile course from its source to its mouth in the Niger Delta. Thirty-two pages of photographs are included.

252 **The white man in Nigeria.**
George Douglas Hazzledine. London: Edward Arnold, 1904. Reprinted, New York: Negro Universities, 1969. 228p. map.

An account of British and Hausa-Fulani relations and prospects, written soon after the British conquest of Northern Nigeria. The author writes about slavery, health, empire-

uilding, Kano, cotton and 'ju-ju'. He is enthusiastic about the trade prospects offered
y the new territory, saying, 'We can provide the Hausas with clothes cheaper than
iey have ever known them before' (p. 138). He states that, 'These chapters have been
ritten in the hope they may be useful to the men who will go out to the magnificent
ork for civilization waiting to be done in Northern Nigeria, and also in the hope of
iowing those at home who take interest in such things that the control of the country
, well worth retaining, even at an apparent financial loss for a few years' (Preface,
. vii).

53 **The British in Northern Nigeria.**
Robert Heussler. London: Oxford University, 1968. 210p. map.
bibliog.

n intelligent, study, displaying much insight, of the British colonial administration of
Jorthern Nigeria, 'the most populous British-ruled unit in sub-Saharan Africa' (p. 6),
uring roughly the first half of the twentieth century. The author makes full use of the
rivate letters and diaries of administrators as well as their public papers and reports
nd the Nigerian National Archives in Kaduna, as he discusses the formation of Anglo-
\frican government, policies, power, District Officers (D.O.s), chiefs and touring.
Jltimately, writes the author, 'the British did two things above all others: they faced
ne facts of local culture, and they gradually altered those facts' (p. 189). In addition to
ne list of sources (p. 192–97), the biographical information provided for the 'List of
fficers' (p. xiii–xxi) is especially useful.

54 **Nigerian groundnut exports: origins and early development.**
Jan S. Hagendorn. Zaria; Ibadan, Nigeria: Ahmadu Bello University
and Oxford University, 1978. 173p. 3 maps. bibliog. (Ahmadu Bello
University History Series).

n excellent illustrated economic history of the groundnut (*Arachis hypogaea*) as an
xport crop in northern Nigeria, based on extended fieldwork by the author in 1965
nd 1975. The history focuses primarily on the 'sudden' emergence of Nigerian
;roundnut exports earlier in this century and in so doing examines Kano in 1907 and
fterwards, construction of the railway from Kano to Lagos, competition with the
3ritish Cotton Growing Association in Nigeria and the structure of the groundnut
rade itself. The author takes a formalist economic stance; he highlights the economic
nitiative and adaptability of Hausa traders and farmers in 1912–14 and argues that the
ll-too-general tendency to minimize indigenous entrepreneurial efficiency may lead to
ash prediction and bad policy (p. 2). The detailed bibliography (p. 155–67) contains a
st of relevant unpublished theses. The author's 1966 London University thesis was
The origins of the groundnut trade in Northern Nigeria.

?55 **City of Blood revisited: a new look at the Benin expedition of 1897.**
Robert Home. London: Rex Collings, 1982. 141p. 3 maps. bibliog.

\ critical re-examination of the British Punitive Expedition of 1897 which has usually
)een portrayed as being morally justified in avenging the deaths of seven British
nembers on a peaceful mission to Benin City. For this study the author retraced the
xpedition's route, spoke with men who remembered the incidents, interviewed the
ast four surviving naval officers of the expedition, and uncovered private papers and
nemoirs as well as official dispatches in British archives. Twenty-two photographs are
ncluded. In Home's view, 'The Benin expedition was less a war of righteous revenge,
nuscular Christianity triumphing over barbarous paganism, than part of a sombre and
:omplex game of political chess, and in that game the eventual winners and losers were
iot who they might at first appear' (Preface, p. xii).

85

256 **Benin under British administration: the impact of colonial rule on an African kingdom, 1897–1938.**
Philip Aigbona Igbafe. Harlow, England: Longman; Atlantic Highlands, New Jersey: Humanities, 1979. 432p. 6 maps. bibliog. (Ibadan History Series).

'This study examines . . . the administrative, social and economic consequences fc Benin of its capture by the British, the measures and changes to Benin institutior brought about by colonial rule. It explores the political manoeuvres among the chie and all those who found themselves at the seat of power after the removal of the Ob from the political scene' (Preface, p. xiii). The emergence of a new educational élit and the shifting balance of power from traditional rulers is described in detail. Th final chapter 'Developments after 1938' brings the history up to the 1950s. The map ten plates, various lists, historical data in the appendices and the bibliograph (p. 410–19) all add to the value of the work. This volume evolved from the author 1968 University of Ibadan doctoral thesis. The author is Professor of History at th University of Benin, Benin City, Nigeria.

257 **Niger Delta rivalry: Itsẹkiri-Urhobo relations and the European presence, 1884–1936.**
Obaro Ikimẹ. New York: Humanities, 1969. 301p. 4 maps. bibliog. (Ibadan History Series).

This study examines the relations between the Itsẹkiri, fisher-people and traders of th, coastal belt, and the Urhobo, a 'hinterland, agricultural' people of the Delta Province in the Midwestern State (now Bendel State) of southern Nigeria. The themes of coas versus hinterland, of the influence of geography on social relations, and of th importance of British colonial rule from 1884 are developed. The author emphasize the régime of Chief Nana, 1884–94, and the native court system and the career of Chie Dogho, 1900–25. Research for this study, which grew out of the author's University o Ibadan doctoral thesis, was conducted in the Delta area itself, at the Nigerian Nationa Archives, Ibadan, and at London archives. The bibliography (p. 285–90) lists bot manuscript and published sources. Professor Ikimẹ has also published number ten i the African Historical Biographies Series entitled, *Chief Dogho of Warri* (London Heinemann, 1976, 48p.), a brief biography of Ọmadọghọgbọnẹ Numa (early 1860s t 24 Sept. 1932) and 'Chief Dogho' in the *Journal of the Historical Society of Nigeria* vol. 3, no. 2 (Dec. 1965), p. 313–33.

258 **Merchant Prince of the Niger Delta: the rise & fall of Nana Olomu, last governor of the Benin River.**
Obaro Ikimẹ. New York: Africana, 1969. 218p. 5 maps. bibliog.

The prolific University of Ibadan historian has written a biography of Nana the Itsẹkir (1858–1916), which is not a biography in the technical sense but rather 'a detailed stud of the life of Nana Olomu in the period beginning in 1884, the year he was appointe 'Governor of the River' by the Itsẹkiri elders, and ending with his death in 1916, te years after his return from the exile to which the British condemned him in 1894 (Preface, p. vii). This excellent account of British-Itsẹkiri relations in the Niger Delt also contains copies of seven key documents, including treaties, exhibits and comment from Nana's trial and Nana's last petition. Younger readers will find Ikimẹ's *Nana o the Niger Delta*, (London: Heinemann, 1972. 40p. (African Historical Biographie Series, no. 3)) a highly readable history of the Itsẹkiri of this time.

259   **The fall of Nigeria: the British conquest.**
        Obaro Ikimẹ.   London: Heinemann, 1977. 232p. 13 maps. bibliog.
This excellent study is primarily intended as a synthesis of existing works, designed to
provide Nigerian university students with a one-volume account of the British
conquest. The author omits footnotes, but provides brief bibliographic notes at the end
of each chapter, a bibliography (p. 224–26), copies of three treaties in the appendices
and twenty-two illustrations.

260   **The principles of native administration in Nigeria: selected documents,**
        1900–1947.
        Edited and introduced by A. H. M. Kirk-Greene, foreword by
        Margery Perham.   London: Oxford University, 1965. 248p. bibliog.
The editor has performed a valuable service for African scholars by compiling excerpts
from ten critical documents 'that illustrate the historical evolution of native
administration from 1900 to 1947; in brief, its origins and its spirit. Thus genesis and
genius comprise the philosophy and policy of Lugard's indirect rule . . .; its
liberalization and restatement as Cameron's indirect administration; and its cullmination
in the emergence of the Colonial Office emphasis on local government as a prerequisite
for ultimate self-determination' (p. 3–4). The documents are introduced and their
significance explained in the introduction (p. 1–42). Included are: '1903: the speech at
Sokoto'; '1914: the amalgamation report'; '1918: Temple's political testimony'; '1918:
Lugard's political memoranda'; '1922: Lugard's political testimony'; '1922: the Clifford
minute'; '1928: two secretariat directives'; 1934: Cameron's policy of indirect
administration'; '1939: the Bourdillon minute'; and '1947: the local government
despatch'.

261   **Lugard and the amalgamation of Nigeria: a documentary record, being**
        a reprint of the report by Sir F. D. Lugard on the amalgamation of
        Northern and Southern Nigeria and administration, 1912–1919, together
        with supplementary unpublished amalgamation reports, and other
        relevant documents.
        Compiled and introduced by A. H. M. Kirk-Greene.   London: Frank
        Cass, 1968. 281p. 8 maps. bibliog.
Most of this volume consists of F. D. Lugard's amalgamation report (p. 49–208), a
crucial document in Nigeria's history. In addition, six other important documents are
included: Lugard's 'strictly confidential' memorandum on the administration of Nigeria
from May 1905; C. L. Temple's 'Confidential minute' on his scheme for the
amalgamation of Nigeria, February 1913; Lugard's 'Confidential' proposals on
amalgamation, May 1913; 'Financial and staff proposals for the first unified estimates
of Nigeria, 1913'; Lugard's speech on Amalgamation Day, 1 January 1914; and two
1919 editorials from *The Lagos Weekly Record*. These are all set in 'politico-
administrative' context in Kirk-Greene's scholarly introduction (p. 1–44).

262   **Gazetteers of the northern provinces of Nigeria.**
        Edited and introduced by A. H. M. Kirk-Greene.   London: Frank
        Cass by arrangement with the Federal Government of Nigeria, 1972. 4
        vols. maps. bibliog.
An invaluable series of historical synopses compiled originally by officers of the
Nigerian Administrative Service in the 1920s (and one in 1934), with each volume

clearly introduced and provided with a bibliography by Kirk-Greene. Vol. one 'The Hausa emirates' contains Bauchi Province compiled by F. B. Gall (1920); Sokoto Province and Zaria Province, both compiled by E. J. Arnett (1920); and Kano Province, compiled by W. F. Gowers (1921). Vol. two, 'The eastern kingdoms' contains Muri Province, edited by J. M. Fremantle (1920); Yola Province, compiled by C. O. Migeod (1927); and Bornu Province, compiled by H. R. Palmer and revised by J. B. Welman (1929). Vol. three, 'The central kingdoms', has Kontagora Province compiled by E. C. Duff, revised by Major W. Hamilton-Browne (1920); Nassarawa Province, compiled by J. C. Sciortino (1920); Nupe Province, by E. G. M. Dupign (1920); and Ilorin Province, by K. V. Elphinstone (1921). Vol. four, 'The highland chieftaincies' contains Plateau Province, by C. G. Ames (1934).

263   **A biographical dictionary of the British colonial governor. Vol. 1: Africa.**

A. H. M. Kirk-Greene, foreword by Peter Duignan.   Brighton, England: Harvester; Stanford, California: Hoover Institution, 1980. 320p. bibliog. (Hoover Press Bibliographical Series, 61).

Full biographical notes on Africa's British governors describe their education, careers, governorships, honours, clubs, and recreations, and contain other facts. A scholarly introduction (p. 3–58) describes the project and its sources and draws conclusions. The appendix contains 'A chronology of the British Governors of tropical Africa, c 1875–1968' (p. 299–320). This valuable volume places a wealth of information, laid ou with concise clarity, at a researcher's fingertips. An interesting article on 'the paradigm of colonial despotism' (p. 25) is Felix K. Ekechi's 'Portrait of a colonizer: H. M Douglas in colonial Nigeria, 1897–1920', in *African Studies Review*, vol. 26, no. ﹒ (March 1983), p. 25–50.

264   **Imperial administration and the athletic imperative: the case of the district officer in Africa.**

A. H. M. Kirk-Greene.   In: *Sport in Africa: essays in social history*. Edited by William J. Baker, James A. Mangan. New York, London: Africana, 1987, p. 81–113. bibliog.

This article demonstrates, convincingly, that in the minds of those selecting the British corps of colonial administrators for Africa 'there was a professional rationalization of the linkage not only between public schoolboy and potential proconsul but also between athletic excellence and likely administrative success. . . The qualities held to be indispensable in the making of the district officer included many of those proved to be inseparable from the making of the school prefect and captain of the college team (p. 106). Numerous examples in support of this are offered from the Sudan and Nigeria. Passing references to Nigerian sports appear throughout the volume. A complementary essay is the author's 'The merit principle in an African bureaucracy Northern Nigeria' in *Nations by design*, edited by Arnold Rivkin (New York Doubleday, 1968. p. 253–332) and also 'Bureaucratic cadres in a traditional milieu' in J. S. Coleman, *Educational and political development* (q.v.) (p. 372–407).

265 **Letters & sketches from Northern Nigeria.**
Martin S. Kisch, introduced by Sir Percy Girouard. London: Chatto
& Windus, 1910. 232p. map. bibliog.
This interesting volume contains the letters written home by an Assistant Resident in
Northern Nigeria, dated from his London departure 3 October 1908 to 18 February
1909, a few weeks before his death in Sokoto of diphtheria. The appendices
(p. 175–232) contain historical notes from other sources and a bibliography (p. 227–32).

266 **A preface to modern Nigeria: the 'Sierra Leonians' in Yoruba,
1830–1890.**
Jean Herskovits Kopytoff. Madison, Wisconsin: University of
Wisconsin, 1965. 402p. 3 maps. bibliog.
This study examines the rôles and accomplishments of Yoruba Africans liberated from
captured slave ships or repatriated from the New World to Sierra Leone, who then
returned to their homeland in the region later known as Western Nigeria. In three
parts the author describes 'the emigrants' experiences in Sierra Leone and their return
to Yoruba country', 1800–45; 'the penetration of British influence around Lagos
through the consular period', 1845–61; and the place of the emigrants in Lagos and the
hinterland in trade and politics during 1861–86 (Preface, p. vii). The study, which
evolved from the author's 1960 Oxford University doctoral thesis *Liberated Africans
and the history of Lagos Colony to 1886*, uses both archival data and fieldwork data
gathered in 1958. The bibliography (p. 372–83) is extensive. A substantial extract from
this volume appeared as 'The Sierra Leoneans of Yorubaland' in *Africa & the West:
intellectual responses to European culture*, edited by Philip D. Curtin (Madison,
Wisconsin: University of Wisconsin, 1972, p. 75–98).

267 **Stepping-stones: memoirs of colonial Nigeria, 1907–1960.**
Sylvia Leith-Ross, edited and introduced by Michael Crowder.
London; Boston, Massachusetts: Peter Owen, 1983. 191p. 4 maps.
Sylvia Ruxton (30 Sept. 1883–13 Feb. 1980) married Arthur Leith-Ross in 1907 and
went with him to Zungeru in Northern Nigeria where she was the third British wife
allowed to join her husband. He died in 1908 of blackwater fever and she continued
living on and off in Nigeria until June 1968. This volume contains a sensitive
biographical portrait by Crowder and Leith-Ross's own accounts of Nigeria in 1907–08;
1910–13, when she stayed with her brother Upton Fitzherbert Ruxton, a Resident in
Northern Nigeria and later Lieutenant-Governor of the Southern Provinces; 1925–31;
1934–37; 1941–43; 1951–55; 1956–60; and a brief postscript written in 1971. This
remarkable woman also wrote *Practical West African cookery* with Geneviève Ruxton,
(Zungeru, 1908; Ibi, 1910) which was later reissued as *West African cookery book;
Fulani grammar* (Lagos, [1920]); *African women* (London, 1939) (q.v.); *African
conversation piece* (London, 1943); *Cocks in the dawn* (London, 1944); *Beyond the
Niger* (London, 1951) (q.v.); and *Nigerian pottery* (Ibadan, 1970) (q.v.).

268 **A tropical dependency: an outline of the ancient history of the Western Sudan with an account of the modern settlement of Northern Nigeria.**
Lady Lugard (née Flora L. Shaw).   London: James Nisbet, 1906.
Reprinted, London: Frank Cass, 1964; New York: Barnes & Noble, 1965. 508p.

About half of this book by the wife of Sir Frederick D. Lugard concerns the history of the Hausa, Fulani and Bornu states of Northern Nigeria, the conquest of Bornu, Sokoto and Kano by the British and British rule of the territory. The history and account of indirect rule are written with a self-conscious view that the British Empire was at its pinnacle. The author coined the name 'Nigeria' in 1897 in a newspaper article and here writes: 'Nigeria – as we call our latest expression – is not properly a name. It cannot be found upon a map that is ten years old. It is only an English expression which has been made to comprehend a number of native states covering about 500,000 square miles of territory in that part of the world which we call the Western Sudan' (p. 7).

269 **The dual mandate in British tropical Africa.**
Lord Lugard [Sir Frederick D. Lugard], introduced by Margery Perham.   London: Frank Cass, 1965. 5th ed. 643p. bibliog.

This is the authoritative work on British indirect rule, first published in 1922, by the man who conceived and applied the approach in Nigeria. Lord Lugard (1858–1945) describes the acquisition of the British African tropics and the workings of the British Colonial Office. Most important are his chapters on 'Methods of ruling native races', taxation, land tenure and transfer, slavery, labour, education, transport, trade, economic development and legal matters. In the concluding chapter, 'The value of British rule in the tropics to the British democracy and to the native races', he justifies British colonial efforts. The 'dual mandate' refers to the mutual benefits responsible rule should bring to both rulers and ruled. The introduction to the fifth edition (p. xxvii–xlix) by Lugard's biographer, provides an informative context for the volume and a succinct sketch of the man himself.

270 **The red book of West Africa: historical and descriptive, commercial and industrial facts, figures, & resources.**
Compiled and edited by Allister Macmillan.   London: W. H. & L. Collingridge, 1920. Reprinted, London: Frank Cass, 1968. 312p.

With eighty-four brief biographies of prominent Nigerian and British individuals, numerous business histories for Lagos and Calabar, lists of officials, trade statistics, historical descriptions of the colony and dozens of photographs (p. 18–137), this volume offers a valuable portrait of Nigeria during the first two decades of this century. Similar information appears for the Gold Coast, Sierra Leone and the Gambia. The quantities and values of exports of palm-oil, palm kernels, mahogany logs, rubber, hides and skins, cotton seed, ground nuts, maize, cotton lint, benneseed, cocoa, shea products, and tin between 1900 and 1918 are included (p. 43–46).

271 **Marrying well: marriage, status and social change among the educated elite in colonial Lagos.**
Kristin Mann. Cambridge: Cambridge University, 1985. 194p. 2 maps. bibliog. (African Studies Series, 47).
This book examines the history of marriage among the educated African élite of Lagos between 1880 and 1915. It contrasts Yoruba and Christian marriages in detail and concludes 'that marriage played a fundamental part in the consolidation of elite status, and that changes in the political economy of Lagos deeply affected marriage and the relationship between the sexes' (p. 2). Ironically, the author stresses, adopting European customs brought African women material comforts, legal rights and prestige, but it also undermined their autonomy. This excellent study is based on Professor Mann's 1977 Stanford University doctoral dissertation, *A social history of the new African elite in Lagos Colony, 1880–1913*. The author, a historian at Emory University, Atlanta, Georgia, conducted numerous interviews and examined both public and private records in 1973–74 and 1980. Of related interest are the author's 'The dangers of dependence: Christian marriage among elite women in Lagos Colony, 1880–1915' in *Journal of African History*, vol. 24, no. 1 (1983), p. 37–56, and 'Marriage choices among the educated African elite in Lagos Colony, 1880–1915' in *International Journal of African Historical Studies*, vol. 14, no. 2 (1981), p. 201–28.

272 **Nigerian women mobilized: women's political activity in Southern Nigeria, 1900–1965.**
Nina Emma Mba. Berkeley, California: University of California, Institute of International Studies, 1982. 344p. 3 maps. bibliog. (Research Series, no. 48).
This important study covers several major facets of women's political activity: their situation before 1900 and the effects of colonialism; the women's war of 1929; mass protests in Eastern Nigeria from 1932–65; women's actions in Abeokuta; women's organizations; women in Lagos politics, 1900–65; and women in political parties, 1951–65. An appendix (p. 306–11) lists the large number of people interviewed in the mid-1970s. The bibliography (p. 315–36) lists archival and secondary sources used. Dr. Mba encourages women to mobilize in order to 'regain their solidarity and use it to achieve political power' (p. 304). The author is Principal Lecturer in History at the Institute of Management and Technology, Enugu, Nigeria. See also Judith van Allen's article ''Aba riots' or Igbo 'women's war'? Ideology, stratification,and the invisibility of women', in *Women in Africa: studies in social and economic change*, edited by Nancy J. Hafkin and Edna G. Bay (Stanford, California: Stanford University, 1976, p. 59–86, 287–90).

273 **Government and the decline of the Nigerian oil-palm export industry, 1919–1939.**
David Meredith. *Journal of African History*, vol. 25, no. 3 (1984), p. 311–29. bibliog.
This article examines the economic consequences of the British policy excluding expatriate owned plantations from West Africa in favour of a policy of 'trusteeship'. After the palm oil share of Nigeria's domestic exports fell from ninety-two per cent in 1909–13 to fifty-seven per cent in 1922, European expatriate investment was encouraged in every stage of oil-palm production except cultivation. This effort failed, too, and the Nigerian palm-oil export industry lost its place in the world market. The

author judges that the failure to secure expatriate capital for direct agricultural production and the reluctance to substitute state enterprize were major obstacles to the development of the industry.

274 **Nigeria: its peoples and its problems.**
E[dmund] D[ene] Morel, introduced by Kenneth Dike Nworah.
London: Frank Cass, 1968. 3rd ed. 264p. maps. (Cass Library of
African Studies, no. 73).

Morel (1873–1924), critic, journalist, editor of the *African Mail*, and author, visited Nigeria and West Africa from November 1910 to March 1911. This book, a revised compilation of his articles from *The Times* in 1911 and originally published in 1911 (London: Smith, Elder; London: Smith, Elder & J. Murray, 1912, 2nd ed.), is his attempt to paint 'a picture of Nigeria as it is today; to portray the life of its people, the difficulties and tasks of its British governors, and the Imperial responsibilities the nation has contracted in assuming control over this vast region' (Author's Introduction, p. xxxi). Following a series of 'pen-and-ink sketches' he describes Southern Nigeria, Northern Nigeria, and discusses Islam, cotton growing and the liquor traffic. Forty-eight photographs provide turn-of-the-century views of the people and the country. The introduction by Nworah (p. vii–xx) provides background on the author.

275 **Nigerian kaleidoscope: memoirs of a colonial servant.**
Sir Rex Niven. London: C Hurst; Hamden, Connecticut: Archon,
1982. 278p. map.

This book covers the years 1921–61 when the author served in various ranks of the Nigerian Administrative Service, from the Secretariate in Lagos to the Speaker of the Northern House of Assembly. The book is full of the genial memories of a man dedicated to service in the Empire. He describes the beginning of his Nigerian affair: 'No one would employ me in the United Kingdom at a salary above £200 a year, so, after taking a three-month course in 'colonial' subjects in London, I went to Nigeria. The salary that started when the mail-boat left Liverpool was a princely £500 a year, with an advance of £60 to pay for essential equipment' (Preface, p. vii). On the early-1956 visit of the Queen and the Duke of Edinburgh he writes, 'The entire visit cost about £2,000,000 – of Nigerian money – but no one begrudged it' (p. 259). And finally, he ends, 'It had been a happy service' (p. 272).

276 **From wealthy entrepreneurs to petty traders: the decline of African middlemen in Eastern Nigeria, 1900–1950.**
Anthony I. Nwabughuogu. *Journal of African History*, vol. 23, no. 3
(1982), p. 365–79. bibliog.

This article traces the impact of British colonial rule on indigenous traders in Eastern Nigeria. During 1900–05, the middlemen lost only political control of their areas but benefitted comercially. From 1905–16, foreign firms moved inland and created a new group of smaller, dependent middlemen. With the opening of the eastern railway in 1916 and the construction of roads, the firms gained complete control of their markets. The introduction of produce inspection in 1928 and the collapse in 1930 of the system of trust created by the African middleman combined to leave most middlemen as petty traders with little capital and only marginal profits.

277 **The making of Northern Nigeria.**
Sir Charles [William James] Orr, introduced by A. H. M. Kirk-Greene. London: Macmillan, 1911. Reprinted, London: Frank Cass, 1965. 2nd ed. 306p. 3 maps. bibliog.

Kirk-Greene provides an informative biography of Charles Orr (20 Sept. 1870–18 April 1945) in his lengthy introduction (p. xi–xxxviii) to the new edition. Orr's volume is both a history of Northern Nigeria and an account, based 'mainly on the Annual Reports submitted by the High Commissioner to the Secretary of State for the Colonies' (Preface, p. v) of the details of British administration while he was in the Colonial Service in Nigeria from 1903–10 as 'one of the ablest and most trusted of Lugard's inner circle' (p. xx). Orr describes the occupation of Bauchi and Bornu in 1902, of Kano and Sokoto in 1903, taxation problems, railway construction, slavery, commerce and trade, British and native courts of justice, land tenure, religion, and education. Of interest are the maps, two of which are from the early-nineteenth century; the third is a fold-out map of Nigeria in 1911.

278 **Nigeria in the First World War.**
Akinjide Osuntokun. London: Longman, 1979. 336p. maps. bibliog. (Ibadan History Series).

This study looks at Nigerian involvement in the 'Great War' and the impact of it on Nigeria. Themes receiving emphasis include Nigerian trade and economy; views of the élite; disaffection and revolts in Southern Nigeria and the spectre of revolt in the north; the war in the German Cameroons, 1914–16; Nigeria's rôle in East Africa, 1916–18; and Lugard's reluctance to commit Nigerian troops in the war effort. 'Altogether, Nigeria during the war provided 17,000 combatants, 1,800 gun carriers, 35,000 transport carriers, 350 motor drivers, 800 inland water transport men, 500 railway men, postmen, policemen and artisans' (p. 269). The war had pervasive effects on Nigeria. 'Economically it was almost ruinous, politically it was upsetting; to some extent it was socially destructive, and in terms of the morale and discipline of the administrative staff, it was a disaster. . . It ushered in an era of political liberalisation in the country' (p. 291). This book developed from the author's 1970 doctoral thesis of the same title at Dalhousie University, Halifax, Nova Scotia. Of additional interest are Professor Osuntokun's 'West African armed revolts during the First World War', *Tarikh*, vol. 5, no. 3 (1977), p. 6–17 and Captain W. D. Downes's *With the Nigerians in German East Africa* (London: Methuen, 1919).

279 **Borrioboola-Gha: the story of Lokoja, the first British settlement in Nigeria.**
Howard J. Pedraza. London; Ibadan, Nigeria: Oxford University, 1960. 118p. 2 maps. bibliog.

A history of early British ventures in Nigeria focusing on the town of Lokoja, founded in 1860 at the confluence of River Niger and River Benue. 'Lokoja was the germ of Nigeria; as Nigeria's importance increased, so Lokoja's diminished until now it is a backwater, but its history is a significant thread in the larger history' (Prologue, p. ix). 'Borrioboola-Gha' is the name given by Charles Dickens in *Bleak house* to a settlement on the Niger, a site of 'misplaced and even perverted zeal' (p. x), based on the 'philanthropic experiment' to establish a Model Farm described by W. Allen and T. R. H. Thomson in *A narrative of the expedition sent by Her Majesty's government to the River Niger in 1841* (q.v.). The book emphasizes the works of W. B. Baikie

History. Colonial Nigeria (1851–1960)

(p. 37–65) and George Taubman Goldie (p. 76–88), brings the history up to the 1950s, and includes a plan for Lokoja in 1960, seven plates of photographs and a useful bibliography (p. 113–15).

280 **Native administration in Nigeria.**
Margery Perham. London: Oxford University, 1937. Reprinted, 1962. 404p. bibliog.

An important study of the history and workings of Native Administration or indirect rule, based on the author's nine months' visit to Nigeria. The author discusses the development of Native Administration, surveys widely the situations in the northern and southern provinces and examines issues and problems of administration. A separate chapter describes 'The governorship of Sir Donald Cameron'. The appendix (p. 365–93) includes the 1933 ordinances on native courts and native authority. A basic bibliography (p. 394–98) provides details of the works referred to in the text and a 'short reading list'. 'The introduction to the second impression' (p. ix–xii) provides thoughtful comments on the issues between 1937 and independence. See also A. H. M. Kirk-Greene's *Principles of native administration in Nigeria* (q.v.). Perham's edited work *Ten Africans* (London: Faber & Faber; Evanston, Illinois: Northwestern University, 1936; 1963, 2nd ed. 356p.) contains two biographies of Nigerians from the 1930s: 'The story of Udo Akpabio of the Anang tribe, Southern Nigeria, recorded by Rev. W. Groves' (p. 41–61), and 'The story of Kofoworola Aina Moore, of the Yoruba tribe, Nigeria, written by herself' (p. 323–43).

281 **Lugard: the years of adventure, 1858–1898; Lugard: the years of authority, 1898–1945. The life of Frederick Dealtry Lugard later Lord Lugard of Abinger, P.C.,G.C.M.G. C.B., D.S.O..**
Margery Perham. London: Collins, 1956, 1960. 2 vols. 25 maps. bibliog.

Represents the definitive biography of the principal architect of colonial Nigeria by one who knew him well for the last seventeen years of his life. Vol. one (750p.) traces Lugard's life from his birth in India in 1958 through his youth to East Africa (Lake Nyasa, 1887–89 and Uganda, 1889–94), the Niger region (1894–95 and 1897–98) and the Kalahari (1895–97). Vol. two (748p.) recounts his years in Northern Nigeria (1898–1906), Hong Kong (1907–12), Nigeria again (1912–18) and his years following retirement from the Colonial Service in 1919 until his death on 11 April 1945, aged eighty-seven. The author describes his life as dominated by the themes of 'order' and 'constancy' in her study of the 'actions and the character of this great imperialist'. 'He was all of a piece, sincere in the real meaning of the word, solid marble with no faking mixture of wax' (vol. II, p. 709, 712). Each volume is fully indexed, well-illustrated, contains a chronology of Lugard's life, a list of sources, and in vol. two, a list of Lugard's own publications.

282 **Concerning brave captains, being a history of the British occupation of Kano and Sokoto and of the last stand of the Fulani forces.**
D. J. M. Muffett, foreword by Alhaji Sir Ahmadu Bello. London: André Deutsch, 1964. 224p. 4 maps. bibliog.

Muffett has woven together extensive original information from official reports, dispatches, letters and archival sources to trace the events surrounding the British invasion and conquest of northern Nigeria from about 1900 to the final battle at Burmi

(27 July 1903) in the conquest of Sokoto. In addition he includes a glossary of Hausa terms, genealogies of the Sultans of Sokoto and the Emirs of Kano, biographical notes on thirty-four men in the story, a chronological reconstruction of events and dates subsequent to the battle and seventeen period illustrations or photographs of documents. Brigadier F. P. Crozier (1879–1937) who was also present at the Kano-Sokoto campaign recounts his experiences in *Five years hard* (London: Jonathan Cape, 1932).

283 **Politics and society in south-eastern Nigeria, 1841–1906: a study of power, diplomacy and commerce in Old Calabar.**
Kannan K. Nair. London: Frank Cass, 1972. 324p. 4 maps. bilbog.
(Cass Library of African Studies. General Studies, no. 128).

Basing his work on archival and oral evidence gathered in 1964–67, the author, a historian at the University of Malaya, describes in detail the history of the Efik people of Calabar and the changes brought about by European contact and colonization. Appendices add information on Efik genealogy, names, communities, trade statistics, towns, and British officials. The bibliography (p. 297–310) is extensive.

284 **Trade and imperialism in Southern Nigeria, 1881–1921.**
W. Ibekwe Ofonagoro. New York, London, Lagos: Nok, 1979.
429p. 13 maps. bibliog.

This critical study begins where K. O. Dike's *Trade and politics in the Niger Delta, 1830–1885* (q.v.) ends and emphasizes the economic motivations behind British conquest of Nigeria. In his conclusion the author analyses the costs and advantages of colonialism to the area, describing the 'paltry benefits' of colonialism as 'crumbs from the master's table, or bones for dogs after a repast' (p. 407). The detailed bibliography (p. 409–19) is useful.

285 **Benin and the Europeans, 1485–1897.**
A[lan] F. C. Ryder. London: Longman, 1969. 372p. 3 maps. bibliog.
(Ibadan History Series).

An in-depth historical account of Portuguese, English, Dutch, French, Spanish and Italian relations with a single West African kingdom over four centuries. A major product of the Benin History Scheme begun by K. O. Dike at Ibadan University in 1956, this study combines oral traditions and archival research in Lisbon, Rome, the Hague and the Public Record Office, London, to produce the finest history of the Benin Empire available. Nine historical documents from 1522–1892 are reproduced in the appendices. The bibliography (p. 349–58) lists both manuscript and printed sources. See also the author's excellent article 'A reconsideration of the Ife-Benin relationship' in the *Journal of African History*, vol. 6, no. 1 (1965), p. 25–37.

286 **The development of capitalism in Northern Nigeria.**
Robert William Shenton. London: James Currey; Toronto: University of Toronto, 1986. 169p. bibliog.

Presents a study of the way in which Northern Nigeria was incorporated into the world capitalist system during the first forty years of this century. Particularly interesting is the chapter describing the linkage between European soap and margarine manufacture and Nigerian groundnut production in the 1920s. The author argues convincingly that 'the development of capitalism, fostered by the hothouse of colonial rule, transformed

History. Colonial Nigeria (1851–1960)

Northern Nigerian society from top to bottom . . . while preserving a facade of changelessness' (p. 139). He uses this argument to explain the agrarian crisis currently facing northern Nigeria. This volume is based on the author's 1981 PhD thesis in history at the University of Toronto, entitled *Studies in the development of capitalism in Northern Nigeria*, and contains an excellent bibliography of archival and published sources (p. 142–64).

287 **Recollections of British administration in the Cameroons and Northern Nigeria, 1921–1957: 'But always as friends'.**
Sir Bryan Sharwood Smith. Durham, North Carolina: Duke University, 1969. 460p. 5 maps. bibliog.

The former Lieutenant Governor and Governor of the Northern Region (1952–57) of Nigeria (1899– .) provides a wealth of detail in this personal account of his work. Appendices (p. 415–41) include useful diagrams of the administrative structure, a glossary of personal and place names, and notes on personalities and education in Northern Nigeria. An epilogue (p. 387–404) brings coverage from 1958 to 1965. The volume was published simultaneously in Britain as *But always as friends* (London: Allen & Unwin, 1969. 460p.). That phrase is taken from the independence day speech by Sir Abubakar Tafawa Balewa, on 1 October 1960.

288 **Colonial cadet in Nigeria.**
John Smith. Durham, North Carolina: Duke University for the Duke University Commonwealth Studies Center, 1968. 202p. 3 maps. bibliog. (Commonwealth Studies Center Series, no. 34).

This book recalls the first five years in Northern Nigeria of John Smith, appointed as a cadet to the Nigerian Administrative Service in 1951. Using diaries, correspondence, and official reports he wrote, Smith attempts 'to show the kind of men we were and the type of work the majority of us, at the broad base of the administrative pyramid, did, and how we did it' (Author's note, p. v). Smith served as a Touring Officer in Kano Division and as Assistant District Officer, Zaria Division during this time and includes some of his touring reports. This volume is of especial value because so little has been published about the civil service in this time period in contrast to earlier years.

289 **The Lagos consulate, 1851–1861.**
Robert S. Smith. Berkeley; Los Angeles: University of California, 1979. 188p. 3 maps. bibliog.

A study of the British consulate for the Bight of Benin from the end of 1851 to the annexation of Lagos as a colony in 1861, based primarily on British government and missionary society archives. This decade of transition from independence under Kosoko and Dosunmu, obas (kings) of Lagos, to colonial rule is a critical phase in Nigerian history. An important figure in the story is Benjamin Campbell, a long-time resident of West Africa, who served as consul at Lagos from July 1853 until his death from dysentery on 17 April 1859. The author not only treats complex political and economic events within the consulate, but also sets them in the context of broader events along the coast. Appendices contain copies of the 'Treaty between Great Britain and Lagos, 1 January 1852', 'The treaty of Epe, 28 September 1854' and 'The treaty of cession, 6 August 1861'. A bibliography (p. 177–81) and four illustrations from the period are included.

290 **Nigeria and elective representation, 1923–1947.**
Tekena N[itonye] Tamuno. London; Ibadan, Nigeria: Heinemann,
1966. 136p. bibliog.
This is a study of Nigeria's use of the franchise at legislative council elections during
the years 1923–47, emphasizing the themes of the origins of the franchise, details of the
elections and the issue of Nigerian 'indifference' to the franchise. Appendices list
candidates for Legislative Council Elections 1923–47 with polling figures.

291 **The police in modern Nigeria, 1861–1965: origins, development and role.**
Tekena N. Tamuno. Ibadan, Nigeria: Ibadan University, 1970. 332p.
map. bibliog.
A thorough history of the Nigerian police from its establishment by W. McCoskry,
Acting Governor of Lagos, in October 1861, to its rôles and functions in 1967.
Appendices show the organization of the force in 1965–66 and the distribution of its
20,291 members. A number of photographs are included.

292 **The evolution of the Nigerian state: the southern phase, 1898–1914.**
T. N. Tamuno. London: Longman, 1972. 422p. 5 maps. bibliog.
(Ibadan History Series).
An important contribution to Nigeria's administrative history, based on sources in
Nigerian and British archives. The detailed study begins with recommendations made
in August 1898 by the Niger Committee for the amalgamation of the 'Niger territories'
or 'Districts' and ends with the further implementation of these proposals in January
1914. Fourteen photographs show important individuals of the period. This book
developed from the author's 1962 London University doctoral thesis, *The rise and
development of British administrative control of Southern Nigeria, 1900–1912: a study in
the administration of Sir Ralph Moor, Sir William MacGregor and Sir Walter Egerton.*

293 **Herbert Macaulay, Nigerian patriot.**
Tekena N. Tamuno. London; Ibadan, Nigeria: Heinemann, 1975.
48p. 2 maps. bibliog. (African Historical Biographies, no. 7).
Gives a short biography of Herbert Samuel Heelas Macaulay (14 Nov. 1864–7 May
1946). Macaulay, 'H.M.' became the first professional Nigerian civil engineer in 1893.
After thirteen years he resigned from the civil service and devoted himself to a life
seeking justice for Nigerians. He was a prolific journalist in Lagos and a critic of
government. In 1923 'H.M.' helped form the first Nigerian National Democratic Party
(NNDP), 'the first well-organized political party in Commonwealth West Africa'
(p. 35). The multifaceted 'Grand Old Man', 'the apostle of Nigerian unity' was also
known as 'the Champion and Defender of Native Rights and Liberties', the 'Gandhi of
West Africa', and because of his abilities with the violin, 'the Musical Wizard of
Kirsten Hall' (p. 8).

294 **Native races and their rulers: sketches and studies of official life and administrative problems in Nigeria.**
C[harles] L[indsay] Temple. Capetown, South Africa: Argus, 1918. Reprinted, Chicago: Afro-Am, 1969; London: Frank Cass, 1968. 2nd ed. 252p.
An unusual volume of observations and reflections by an important British administrator with a long career as Resident in Baushi, Sokoto, Kano (1901–13) and as Lieutenant-Governor of Northern Nigeria (1914–17). About one-third of the book consists of the author's 'ponderations' on indirect rule which he helped Sir Frederick Lugard create. Other chapters are his sketches and musings on 'The Resident's dilemma', 'The anatomy of lying', and various topics including land tenure, drink, justice, taxation, missionaries, education and slavery. The author's drawings appear throughout the book. M. Hiskett provides an introduction to Temple and to 'The historical background to Lugard's occupation of Northern Nigeria' (p. vii–xxxix) in the second edition.

295 **The role of the British administration in the appointment of the emirs of Northern Nigeria, 1903–31: the case of Sokoto Province.**
Peter Kazenga Tibenderana. *Journal of African History*, vol. 28, no. 2 (1987), p. 231–57. bibliog.
This well-documented article argues that, at least for Sokoto Province during 1903–30, emirs who were appointed, although they had traditional claims to their position, were chosen by the British and not by the kingmakers. This policy was dictated by the British fears of Mahdism. By 1931, because unpopular chiefs had been more of a liability than an asset, the British restored the kingmakers' right to select emirs without interference. Two other excellent articles by the author describe education in Northern Nigeria during the colonial years: 'The emirs and the spread of western education in Northern Nigeria, 1910–1946', *Journal of African History*, vol. 24, no. 4 (1983), p. 517–34, and 'The beginnings of girls' education in the native administration schools in Northern Nigeria, 1930–1945', *Journal of African History*, vol. 26, no. 1 (1985), p. 93–109. The author wrote his 1974 University of Ibadan thesis on *The administration of Sokoto, Gwandu and Argungu Emirates under British rule, 1900–1946*.

296 **Figures in ebony: past and present in a West African city.**
Raymond Tong. London: Cassell, 1958. 131p. bibliog.
The author worked in the Colonial Education Service in Benin Province from 1949 to 1953. Here he recounts his experiences with the Edo people and the history and culture of Benin City. Initially wondering whether they had erred, the author and his wife grew to appreciate the city and its environs. Six illustrations show Benin art, a map of West Africa in 1705 and paintings by Maurice Fiévet of Benin chiefs and the Oba.

297 **Central administration in Nigeria, 1914–1948: the problem of polarity.**
Jeremy White, foreword by Adebayo Adediji. Dublin: Irish Academic; London: Frank Cass, 1981. 369p. maps. bibliog.
In this thorough study the author concludes that 'the British never really faced up to the problem of the political unification of the country they had created in 1914' and focused more on the development of native administration than on the development of

central government (p. 292). Appendices contain lists of officials and biographical notes on major figures. Part of this study appeared as the author's University of Ibadan doctoral thesis in history. Another significant study of the period is I. F. Nicolson's *The administration of Nigeria, 1900 to 1960: men, methods and myths* (Oxford: Oxford University, 1969. 336p.).

298 **Dan Bana: the memoirs of a Nigerian official.**
Stanhope White. London: Cassell, 1961. 268p. map.

This personal account of a 'Bush D.O.'s' eighteen years in the Colonial Administrative Service in Northern Nigeria (1936–54) contains a mixture of history and first-hand experiences, but above all gives a fascinating record of events from the remote administrative officer's point of view. The author's postings in Bornu, Benue, Kano, Birnin Kebbi and Idoma from 1936 to 1954 are described and the volume is flavoured by White's anger at the assassination of his friend Abubakar Tafawa Balewa who was to have written the book's foreword. Twenty-five photographs are included. White translates 'Dan Bana', his Hausa name, as 'he who is up to date'. Another substantial account of eighteen years in Northern Nigeria (1906–24), 'written without spread-eagleism, devoid of bombast, and without the cheap expression of opinion of the average globe-trotter' (Introduction, p. 11) is A. C. G. Hastings' *Nigerian days* (London: Jonathan Cape, 1925. Reprinted : The Traveller's Library, 1930. 285p.).

Silent violence: food, famine & peasantry in northern Nigeria.
See item no. 537.

Nigerian pioneers of modern medicine: selected writings.
See item no. 539.

African pioneers of modern medicine: Nigerian doctors of the nineteenth century.
See item no. 540.

A history of the Nigerian health services.
See item no. 568.

Forestry policy in Nigeria, 1897–1960.
See item no. 730.

The history of tin mining in Nigeria.
See item no. 731.

The Nigerian oil palm industry (government policy and export production, 1906–1965.
See item no. 733.

History of the Nigerian Broadcasting Corporation.
See item no. 1083.

Press and politics in Nigeria, 1880–1937.
See item no. 1085.

Guide to research and reference works on sub-Saharan Africa.
See item no. 1129.

Colonialism in Africa, 1870–1960. Volume 5. A bibliographical guide to colonialism in sub-Saharan Africa.
See item no. 1130.

Africa since 1914: a historical bibliography.
See item no. 1141.

Independent Nigeria (1960–present)

299 **Proceedings of the national conference on Nigeria since independence. Zaria, March, 1983. Vol. 1, Political development. Vol. II, The economic and social development of Nigeria.**
Edited by J. A. Atanda, A. Y. Aliyu, M. O. Kayode, Y. B. Usman, preface by T. N. Tamuno, Chariman. Zaria, Nigeria: Nigeria since Independence History Project, 1985. 2 vols. bibliog.
These two volumes are cornucopias of information and statistical data on Nigeria since 1960, presented in dozens of essays by prominent Nigerian scholars. Vol. one contains twenty-three papers discussing government and public policy, public administration, international relations, constitutional development, party politics and elections. Vol. two has thirty-one papers on the economy, education, culture, religion, social stratification and change. Significant contributions include papers by I. Gambari (on foreign policy), Pius Okigbo (on economic planning), J. Osuntokun (on university expansion) and L. E. N. Ekwueme (on Nigerian music).

300 **'Stay by your radios': documentation for a study of military government in tropical Africa.**
A. H. M. Kirk-Greene. Leiden, Netherlands: Afrika-Studiencentrum; Cambridge: African Studies Centre, 1981. 156p. bibliog. (African Social Research Documents, vol. 12).
Presents a compilation of basic documents for the entry and exit of military governments in Africa, with chronologies of coups by year and by country. The Nigerian coups of 15 January 1966, 29 July 1966, 29 July 1975 and 13 February 1976 are included. Ruth First's study *Power in Africa: political power in Africa and the coup d'etat* (Harmondsworth, England; Baltimore, Maryland: Penguin, 1972. (Penguin African Library, AP 33)) uses official documents and personal interviews to describe the Nigerian coups of 1966 (p. 144–69, 278–362). She also provides a 'coup inventory' and 'scoreboard' for the continent's coups.

301 **The Nigerian military: a sociological analysis of authority & revolt, 1960–67.**
A. Robin Luckham. Cambridge: Cambridge University, 1971. 376p. map. bibliog. (African Studies Series, no. 4).
Offers a detailed look at the Nigerian military as a social system, at its relations with civilian government and as a government itself after the coups of 15 January and 29 July 1966. Appendices (p. 341–55) show 'Origins, training and promotions up to 1966

of officers in 1944 to 1961 cohorts' and 'Extracts from documents concerning meeting of the Nigerian military leaders held at Peduase Lodge, Aburi, Ghana 4th and 5th January 1967'. The book was first written as a 1969 PhD dissertation at the University of Chicago, *The Nigerian military: a case study in institutional breakdown* and was based on data collected during 1963–65 and January 1967–January 1968 while the author taught at a Nigerian university.

302 **Military leadership in Nigeria, 1966–1979.**
Major General James J. Oluleye. Ibadan, Nigeria: University Press, 1985. 260p. 6 maps. bibliog.
A personal account of the army's rôle in Nigeria in which there is emphasis (about one hundred pages) on the civil war. The author (1930– .) received military training in England and India and commanded the 2nd Infantry Division of the Nigerian army during 1970–75, and participated in the UN peace-keeping rôles in Zaire (then the Belgian Congo) and on the India-Pakistan border. Between 1975 and his retirement in 1979, he was a member of the Supreme Military Council. The volume contains numerous photographs, appendices of relevant documents (p. 233–44), and a brief bibliography (p. 245–46). Adewale Ademoyega's *Why we struck: the story of the first Nigerian coup* (Ibadan, Nigeria: Evans, 1981. 194p.) is a vivid account of the 15 January 1966 coup by one of its planners.

Armies and parties in Nigeria.
See item no. 587.

Political conflict and economic change in Nigeria.
See item no. 588.

Yukubu Gowon: faith in a united Nigeria.
See item no. 589.

Class, ethnicity, and the democratic state: Nigeria, 1950–1966.
See item no. 592.

Nigeria in search of democracy.
See item no. 594.

Nigeria between dictatorship and democracy.
See item no. 596.

Class, ethnicity and democracy in Nigeria: the failure of the First Republic.
See item no. 597.

An introduction to Nigerian government and politics.
See item no. 601.

The rise & fall of Nigeria's Second Republic, 1979–84.
See item no. 603.

African revolutionary: the life and times of Nigeria's Aminu Kano.
See item no. 604.

Nigeria: power and democracy in Africa.
See item no. 605.

Democracy and prebendal politics in Nigeria: the rise and fall of the Second Republic.
See item no. 607.

West Africa: Nigeria and Ghana.
See item no. 609.

Nigeria since 1970: a political and economic study.
See item no. 610.

Nigerian government and politics: prelude to the revolution.
See item no. 613.

Nigeria: modernization and the politics of communalism.
See item no. 614.

Shehu Shagari: the biography of Nigeria's first executive president.
See item no. 620.

Nigerian government and politics under military rule, 1966–79.
See item no. 622.

Democratic experiment in Nigeria: interpretative essays.
See item no. 625.

Soldiers and oil: the political transformation of Nigeria.
See item no. 627.

Nigeria: the tribes, the nation, or the race – the politics of independence.
See item no. 630.

Nigeria.
See item no. 637.

The political economy of Nigeria.
See item no. 640.

Nigerian foreign policy: alternative perceptions and projections.
See item no. 676.

Political economy of Nigeria.
See item no. 687.

Multinationals, the state, and control of the Nigerian economy.
See item no. 691.

Soldiers and power: the development of the Nigerian military regime.
See item no. 703.

Nigerian capitalism.
See item no. 708.

Nigeria: economy and society.
See item no. 717.

The civil war

303 **Nigerian civil war, 1967–70: an annotated bibliography.**
Compiled by Christian Chukwunedu Aguolu. Boston, Massachusetts:
G. K. Hall, 1973. 181p. bibliog.
This well-organized comprehensive compilation contains pertinent references from
numerous international publications as well as a large selection of background volumes
on Nigeria and the war. In addition to the briefly annotated items, the bibliography
contains a 'Chronology of important events related to Nigeria from pre-European
arrival to the end of the Civil War, January 15, 1970' (p. xi–xvii); biographical sketches
of 'some key personalities directly or indirectly connected with the war'; population
statistics; 'Excerpts of the controversial decree of May 24, 1966'; the 'Text for
broadcast by Major-General Yakubu Gawon'; a list of major relief agencies; the text
of the Biafran surrender; the National Anthem; and an author index. Of interest also is
Chidi Amuta's 'A selected checklist of [ninety] primary and critical sources on Nigerian
Civil War literature' in *Research in African Literatures*, vol. 13, no. 1 (1982), p. 68–72.

304 **The struggle for secession, 1966–1970: a personal account of the
Nigerian civil war.**
Ntieyong U. Akpan. London: Frank Cass, 1972. 225p. 2 maps.
During 1966–70, Akpan was Chief Secretary to the Government and Head of the Civil
Service of Eastern Nigeria, the territory which declared itself 'Biafra' in 1967. This
personal record, written nine months after the war ended, describes events leading up
to the war, the war itself and Biafra's collapse. The appendix contain the concluding
parts of Governor Ojukwu's Ahiara Declaration given on 1 June 1969.

305 **The tragic years: Nigeria in crisis, 1966–1970.**
Ola Balogun. Benin City, Nigeria: Ethiope, 1973. 125p. 3 maps.
bibliog.
The author, Press Attaché of the Nigerian Embassy in Paris during part of the civil
war, provides his analysis of the major factors leading to the war and dictating its
course. He writes from the point of view of one who believes firmly in Nigerian unity
and who opposed Biafran secession. The book includes nine photographs and a brief
bibliography (p. 125).

306 **The making of an African legend: the Biafra story.**
Frederick Forsyth. Harmondsworth, England; Penguin, 1977. 2nd ed.
286p. Reprinted, London: Seven House, 1983. 281p. 2 maps.
A sympathetic, and in some respects controversial, account 'told from the Biafran
standpoint' of the Nigerian civil war. The book recounts 'The road to partition' and the
events of the war up to December 1969. According to Forsyth, 'it remains the only
contemporary narrative of Biafra from start to finish, written at the time and inside the
Biafran enclave by a European eye-witness' (p. 8). The famous author was a war
correspondent in Biafra from 10 July–10 September 1967 and from 18 February 1968 to
late January 1969. First published in June 1969 as *The Biafra story* (Harmondsworth,
England; Baltimore, Maryland: Penguin, 1969. 236p.), most of the original edition was
written in January 1969 while the war was still in progress. For the second, revised,

edition, a brief prologue and an epilogue were added. See also Biafran leader Chukwuemeka Odumegwu Ojukwu's account *Biafra: selected speeches and random thoughts on C. Odumegwu Ojukwu, with diaries of events* (New York: Harper & Row, 1969, 2 vols.).

307 The brutality of nations.
Dan Jacobs. New York: Knopf, 1987. 383p. bibliog.

The author was a consultant with UNICEF from July–December 1968 as 'the person at the United Nations authorized to talk with the press about humanitarian assistance to victims of the Nigerian-Biafran conflict' (Notes about the Author'); he was also Executive Director of the Committee for Nigeria-Biafra Relief. Dissatisfied with Secretary General Thant's curtailment of UNICEF's relief efforts he founded a citizens' group and during 1969 and early 1970 was executive director of the Committee for Nigerian-Biafra Relief. This book, based on interviews, personal experience and research on printed sources, is his indictment of the way the relief effort was frustrated by the UN, Britain, the United States and the Federal Government of Nigeria during and after the war.

308 Crisis and conflict in Nigeria: a documentary sourcebook, 1966–1970.
A. H. M. Kirk-Greene. London: Oxford University, 1971. 2 vols. 2 maps. bibliog.

This is an essential work for anyone interested in the Nigerian civil war. Kirk-Greene has reproduced 227 documents of all types written, issued and delivered by the major personages of the conflict and has introduced them with essays displaying much insight. Vol. one contains the essays 'January 1966: the political prologue' and 'Coups and aftermath: January 1966–July 1970' and documents from January 1966 to July 1967. Vol. two has 'War and peace: July 1967–January 1970' and documents for the same period. Also included are an epilogue, 'An outline calendar of events', from 15 January 1966 to 15 January 1970 and one of the best bibliographies available on the subject (p. 482–518).

309 The genesis of the Nigerian civil war and the theory of fear.
A. H. M. Kirk-Greene. Uppsala, Sweden: Scandinavian Institute of African Studies, 1975. 27p. bibliog. (Research Report, no. 27).

The author argues that, more than any other factor, the pressure of fear, or *angst*, contributed to the civil war. He outlines five sources of conflict – politics, economics, society, élites and history – and their rôles in the psychological fear of discrimination and dominance. He sees the creation of more states as an effective way to reduce the fear. See also Kirk-Greene's article 'The peoples of Nigeria: cultural background to the crisis', *African Affairs*, vol. 66, no. 1 (1967), p. 3–12.

310 The economics of political instability: the Nigerian-Biafran war.
E. Wayne Nafziger. Boulder, Colorado: Westview, 1983. 251p. 3 maps. bibliog. (A Westview Replica Edition).

This study offers an economic approach to internal political instability, focusing on the Nigerian civil war and concluding with a case study comparison with Pakistan. The author examines in detail the economic factors contributing to the war (p. 25–116), the Biafran economy and the diverse economic impacts of the devastating war. The penultimate chapter is an essay on 'Reconstruction, reconciliation, and reorientation in postwar Nigeria' (p. 173–96). The volume is replete with data presented in tables and figures, notes and a useful bibliography (p. 223–36). Dr. Nafziger researched this book and other publications on Nigeria while at the Economic Development Institute, University of Nigeria, Enugu (1964–65), Ahmadu Bello University, Zaria (1969, 1970) and the University of Ibadan (1976). He is Professor of Economics at Kansas State University.

311 **The war of Nigerian unity, 1967–1970.**
Sir Rex Niven, preface by Chief Anthony Enahoro. Ibadan, Nigeria; London: Evans Bros. (Nigeria), 1970. 175p. 9 maps.

As an administrator in Nigeria for forty years, Niven is able to offer this popular account of the civil war's background and its major events. The book was written before the war ended and makes extensive use of materials from the Nigerian Federal Ministry of Information. In a recent article, 'The Biafran crisis and the Midwest', *African Affairs*, vol. 86, no. 344 (July 1987), p. 367–83, S. E. Orobator examines 'the situation in the Midwest before the invasion, the motives for the invasion and the administration of the Region by the invaders' (p. 367) during the period 8 August to 20 September 1967. He uses press releases, radio programmes and personal observations and includes a chronology of events from 30 May to 20–23 September 1967.

312 **My command: an account of the Nigerian civil war, 1967–1970.**
General Olusegun Obasanjo. London: Heinemann, 1981. 178p. 8 maps. (African Writers Series, no. 249).

General Obasanjo (5 March 1937– .) was Commander of the Second Area Command of the Nigerian Army, Commander of the Second Division (Rear) Ibadan and Commander, Ibadan Garrison during 1967–69. In May 1969 he became General Officer Commanding 3 Marine Commando Division of the Nigeria Army. Eventually he became Head of State and Commander-in-Chief of the Armed Forces (1976–79) before handing over power to the elected President, Alhaji Shehu Shagari. Here he describes 'the background to the Nigerian crisis, the military operations up to May 1969, and how within a space of six months I turned a situation of low morale, desertion and distrust within my divisions and within the Army into one of high morale, confidence, co-operation and success for my division and for the Army' (Prologue, p. xii–xiii). The book, with its twelve photographs and useful maps, provides an able account of the war by one of its major participants. Professor M. A. Onwuejeogwu, an Igbo social anthropologist, published *The Biafran army: a study in military sociology* (Enugu, Nigeria: Fourth Dimension, 1986. 250p. (Issues in Nigerian Development, 5)), a thorough examination of the army.

313 **Nigerian civil war: index to foreign periodical articles.**
Compiled by A. Olu Olafioye. Lagos: National Library of Nigeria, 1972. 68p.

An unannotated listing of 550 articles published by thirty-eight African, Asian, European and North American journals between March 1967 and July 1970. The articles are arranged alphabetically by title and indexed by author. Nearly all the journals listed are available at the National Library of Nigeria in Lagos. Of significance also is George B. Affia's *Nigerian crisis 1966–1970: a preliminary bibliography* (Lagos: Yakubu Gowon Library, University of Lagos, 1970. 24 leaves). This unannotated listing covers 'books and pamphlets . . . published by governments and their agencies, trade unions and individuals about the crisis' (Introduction, p. i).

314 **Nigerian politics and military rule: prelude to civil war.**
Edited by S. K. Panter-Brick. London: University of London for the
Institute of Commonwealth Studies, 1970. 276p. 3 maps. bibliog.
(Commonwealth Papers).

A compilation of seven essays whose authors have extensive experience in Nigeria, and
important documents from 1966 and 1967. The essays include: 'The ethnic background
to the Nigerian crisis' by P. C. Lloyd (p. 1–13); 'From military coup to civil war,
January 1966 to May 1967' by the editor (p. 14–57); 'The Nigerian military:
disintegration or integration?' by A. R. Luckham (p. 58–77); 'The military and the
politicians' by M. J. Dent (p. 78–93); 'Western Nigeria and the Nigerian crisis' by B. J.
Dudley (p. 94–110); 'Enugu: the psychology of secession, 29 July 1966 to 30 May 1967'
by K. Whiteman (p. 111–27); and 'The creation of new states in the north' by the
editor and P. F. Dawson (p. 128–38).

315 **The Nigerian civil war.**
John de St. Jorre. London: Hodder & Stoughton, 1972. 437p. 6 maps.
bibliog.

This is a highly readable 'story' of the war intended neither as 'pure history nor pure
journalism' (p. 17). The author covered the war for the London *Observer* and gives an
informed, balanced account, illustrated with sixty photographs. The writer believes
600,000 people died in the conflict (p. 412). The bibliography (p. 416–24) is
substantial. This book was published in Boston, Massachusetts as *The brothers' war:
Biafra and Nigeria* (Houghton Mifflin, 1972).

316 **The international politics of the Nigerian civil war, 1967–1970.**
John J. Stremlau. Princeton, New Jersey: Princeton University, 1977.
425p. 6 maps. bibliog.

A significant history of Nigerian and Biafran foreign relations during 1967–70. The
author discusses, among many other topics: Nigerian pre-war foreign policy; the
involvement of the Organization of African Unity (OAU); Biafra's international
public relations efforts; peace conferences; diplomacy; and the war itself. Included are
a 'Chronology of important events in the Nigerian Civil War' (p. xv–xix); a 'Schedule
of Nigerian interests in other countries' (p. 391–98); 'Aid to African countries
1960–1965' (p. 399–401); and a discussion of sources and a list of works cited
(p. 413–18). The author was a research associate at the Nigerian Institute of
International Affairs in Lagos 1969–71, travelled extensively in eastern Nigeria after
January 1970 and conducted interviews with dozens of prominent individuals, listed on
p. 409–12.

317 **Reflections on the Nigerian civil war: facing the future.**
Raph Uwechue, forewords by Nnamdi Azikiwe and Léopold Sédar
Senghor. New York: Africana, 1971. 206p. 4 maps. rev. ed.

The author, an Igbo from the former Mid-West region who supported Biafra in the
war, examines the factors which led to war and pleads for a peaceful 'confederate
arrangement' or 'elastic federal union'. Useful appendices contain 'Minutes of the
Supreme Military Council held in Ghana on 4th and 5th January 1967', 'Decree no. 8
which implemented the Aburi agreements'; and 'Portraits of the principal figures in the
Nigerian conflict' (p. 188–99). This is a revised and expanded version of *Reflections on
the Nigerian civil war: a call for realism* (London: OITH International, 1969).

Ethics in Nigerian culture.
See item no. 1.

Nigeria: a history.
See item no. 158.

Military leadership in Nigeria, 1966–1979.
See item no. 302.

Girls at war, and other stories.
See item no. 862.

Christmas in Biafra, and other poems.
See item no. 863.

Restless city and Christmas gold, with other stories.
See item no. 869.

The anonymity of sacrifice.
See item no. 890.

Forty-eight guns for the general.
See item no. 900.

Behind the rising sun.
See item no. 901.

Labyrinths, with Path of thunder.
See item no. 907.

Monkey on the tree.
See item no. 912.

Population

Demography and migration

318 **Population growth and socioeconomic change in West Africa.**
Edited by John C. Caldwell, with N. O. Addo, S. K. Gaisie, A. Igun,
P. O. Olusanya. New York; London: Columbia University for the
Population Council, New York, 1975. 763p. maps. bibliog.
In this important volume of thirty-seven commissioned papers, a large section of
seven chapters (p. 187–336) is devoted to Nigeria: Robert W. Morgan, P. O. Ohadike,
'Fertility levels and fertility change' (p. 187–235); Jean Trevor, 'Family change in
Sokoto: a traditional Moslem Fulani/Hausa city' (p. 236–53); P. O. Olusanya,
'Population growth and its components: the nature and direction of population'
(p. 254–74); Francis Olu Okediji, 'Socioeconomic status and attitudes to public health
problems in the Western State: a case study . . . Ibadan' (p. 275–97); Reuben K. Udo
'Migration and urbanization in Nigeria' (p. 298–307); Charles N. Ejiogu, 'Metropoli-
tanization: the growth of Lagos' (p. 308–20); and A. D. Goddard, M. J. Mortimore,
D. W. Norman, 'Some social and economic implications of population growth in rural
Hausaland' (p. 321–36). Among the eight chapters giving a regional analysis is Akin L
Mabogunje's 'Migration and urbanization' (p. 153–68).

319 **Custom and politics in urban Africa: a study of Hausa migrants in**
Yoruba towns.
Abner Cohen. Berkeley, California: University of California, 1969.
252p. map. bibliog.
A detailed study conducted in 1962–63 of the Hausa community living in the Sabo
(Sabon Gida) section of Ibadan in western Nigeria. Professor Cohen provides a
combination of community study and social history to illustrate the migratory process
and how Hausas establish and maintain their ethnic polity outside Hausaland. The
Hausa trading network and the kola nut trade receive special emphasis. 'Numerical
abstracts' (p. 215–19) provide demographic details on the 4,147 Hausa of Sabo; the

bibliography (p. 231–38) is a useful one. An important and well-known article is William Bascom's 'Some aspects of Yoruba urbanism' in *American Anthropologist*, vol. 64 (1962), p. 699–709.

320 **Nigerian population and urbanization, 1911–1974: a bibliography.**
Compiled by Herbert O. Emezi. Los Angeles: University of California, African Studies Center, July 1975. 145p. (Occasional Paper, no. 10).
Represents an important source for works on Nigerian demography and urbanization. The 1,628 unannotated entries are grouped under headings for urbanization, urban administration and infrastructure, settlement, labour and employment, housing, élite, economic and social implications of urbanization, migration, census, population, population density and distribution, marriage, fertility and mortality, and family planning. The materials listed include conference papers, unpublished doctoral dissertations and masters' theses as well as undergraduate research essays, books and journal articles. This work includes the 231 books and articles in Emezi's earlier 'Nigerian population studies: a partial bibliography of periodical literature, 1950–1970' in *A Current Bibliography of African Affairs*, vol. 6, no. 3 (summer 1973), p. 333–44. Another important resource is *A survey of Nigerian population literature* compiled by David Lucas and John McWilliam (Lagos: University of Lagos, Human Resources Research Unit, 1976. 143p. (Monograph no. 4)) which offers extensively annotated (but unnumbered) entries arranged by topic and indexed by author.

321 **The Nigerian student movement in the United States, 1949–1967.**
Jacob U. Gordon. *A Current Bibliography on African Affairs*, vol. 10, no. 2 (1977–78), p. 119–46. bibliog.
This historical study of a Nigerian overseas population traces the beginnings and organization of Nigerian (and other African) students in the United States, which were especially due to Nnamdi Azikiwe's education at Lincoln University in 1929–33. In 1949 the Union of Nigerian and Cameroonian Students in America was formed to represent 250 students in American schools. The author describes the rôle of the Nigerian Student Union in Nigerian nationalism throughout the 1950s and its involvement in Nigerian domestic political issues in the 1960s up to its demise in 1967. On another major overseas population, Obinna Anyadike reports in 'Second-class settlers', *West Africa*, no. 3713 (10–16 Oct. 1988), p. 1876–77 on 'probably the largest concentration of Nigerians abroad', primarily Hausas, living in the Sudan.

322 **Population densities and agriculture in Northern Nigeria.**
A. T. Grove. In: *Essays on African population*. Edited by K. M. Barbour, R. M. Prothero. New York: Praeger, 1962. p. 115–36. 6 maps. bibliog.
Grove describes, and illustrates with maps, settlement patterns, population density and farming patterns in several areas of Northern Nigeria, namely south-west Bornu; north-east Zaria; northern Katsina; and Kano City. The author was a lecturer in geography, University of Cambridge at the the time of publication and had published several earlier studies on Nigerian land use, population and soil conservation.

Population. Demography and migration

323 **Internal migration and rural development in Nigeria: lessons from Bendel State.**
Paulina Kofoworola Makinwa. Ibadan, Nigeria: Heinemann, 1981.
226p. 3 maps. bibliog.

Three separate rural-urban and rural-rural migration studies carried out in 1976–78 are presented here with the objectives of studying the rôle of the extended family in migration as well as the characteristics of migrants and the determinants and consequences of both types of migration. The study contains extensive data on the fertility and family characteristics of the migrants and an excellent bibliography (p. 174–87) on Nigerian migration. Appendices contain the survey instrument used and a copy of the interviewers' instructions. Of related interest is the author's 'Population dynamics and rural development: a study of six Edo villages', *Nigerian Behavioral Sciences Journal*, vol. 1, nos. 3, 4 (1978), p. 131–39, which reports on interview results from all heads of families in 283 houses with 1,218 inhabitants conducted between January and June 1977 near Benin City, Nigeria. Another important work of fourteen studies, edited by Pins O. Sada and Animam B. Osirike is *Case studies in migration and urbanization in Nigeria: perspectives in policy issues* (Benin City, Nigeria: Department of Geography and Regional Planning, University of Benin, in collaboration with the Research Triangle Institute, North Carolina, 6 June 1984. 195p.).

324 **Nigerian fertility survey, 1981–1982.**
National Population Commission. Lagos: National Population Commission, Federal Republic of Nigeria; London: World Fertility Survey, March 1983. 49p.

This important, careful survey was conducted throughout the country in two stages in 1981 and 1982 and is based on 9,757 interviews with women in 8,664 households. Results cover general background characteristics, nuptiality, fertility, and contraceptive use. Eighty per cent of the women were currently married; the oldest cohort (age 45–49) had 5.8 children, which 'appears low for the country and may reflect omission of children' (p. 25); about nineteen per cent of children born to these women had died by the time of the interview; the crude birth rate was fifty-two per 1,000; eighty-four per cent want to have more children; and only fourteen per cent had ever used any type of contraception including abstinence. The full report was issued by the National Population Bureau in 1984.

325 **Sex roles, population and development in West Africa: policy-related studies on work and demographic issues.**
Edited by Christine Oppong. London: James Currey; Portsmouth, New Hampshire: Heinemann, 1987. 242p. bibliog.

Among the thirteen essays in this volume are seven pertaining directly to Nigeria, five of which concern 'Fertility, parenthood and development: Yoruba experiences (p. 75–132). In addition, Renée Pittin discusses 'Documentation of women's work ir Nigeria: problems and solutions' (p. 25–44), and Eleanor R. Fapohunda writes or 'Urban women's roles and Nigerian government development strategies' (p. 203–12).

Censuses

326   How many Nigerians? An analysis of Nigeria's census problems, 1901–63.
S. A. Aluko.   *Journal of Modern African Studies*, vol. 3, no. 3 (Oct. 1965), p. 371–92. bibliog.

Professor Aluko gives an excellent description of census efforts from 1901 to 1953 and describes the controversies surrounding the censuses of 1962 and 1963. Tables summarize the growth of the Nigerian population, 1901–63, and provide samples of historical events of national, regional and local importance since 1900 used to aid individuals in calculating their age. 'There has been suspicion and criticism in Nigeria since regular census counts began in 1911' (p. 371). Significant related articles, by Chukwudum Uche, include 'The study of mortality' in *Social development in Nigeria: a survey of policy and research* edited by E. O. Akeredolu-Ale (Ibadan, Nigeria: Nigerian Institute of Social and Economic Research (NISER) 1982, p. 117–46); and 'The contexts of mortality in Nigeria', *Genus*, vol. 37, no. 1–2 (1981), p. 123–35.

327   The handbook of national population censuses: Africa and Asia.
Eliane Domschke, Doreen S. Goyer.   New York: Greenwood, 1986. 1,032p. map. bibliog.

This large volume contains a succinct description of each census conducted in both continents surveyed. Censuses described for Nigeria (p. 334–41) are 1901, 1911, 1921, 1931, 1950, 1952–53, 5 November 1963 and 1973. For the 1963 census the authors write that no final report was issued, but that results are compiled in three mimeographed volumes. Appendices contain international population and topic charts.

328   The 1963 Nigerian census: a critical appraisal.
I. Ekanem, foreword by Colonel S. O. Ogbemudia.   Benin City, Nigeria: Ethiope, 1972. 217p. map. bibliog.

The main purpose of this book is to determine the extent and nature of errors in the 1963 census of Nigeria' (p. 4). This controversial census reported a total population of 55,670,000 and was widely rejected for government use. Following a discussion of census data in developing countries, and a history of Nigeria's demographic problems, the author provides a detailed comparison with the 1952–53 census and an analysis of every aspect of the 1963 census. The University of Ife lecturer in demography and statistics concludes, 'Thus we have indicated the relative uselessness of the 1963 Nigerian census data. The total population was unduly inflated especially in the West; the reported ages were grossly distorted especially in the North (the female ages in particular); the total population for the urban areas derived from different tabulations on the same census do not agree; there is evidence of considerable inflation of the population by religion especially in the North' (p. 203). Numerous tables and figures display the census data.

The northern tribes of Nigeria: an ethnographic account of the northern provinces of Nigeria together with a report on the 1921 decennial census.
See item no. 433.

Population. Censuses

The peoples of Southern Nigeria: a sketch of their history, ethnology and languages with an abstract of the 1921 census.
See item no. 442.

The Nigerian general elections, 1959 and 1979 and the aftermath.
See item no. 611.

Ethnic Groups

General

29 **Continuity and change in African cultures.**
Edited by William R. Bascom, Melville J. Herskovits. Chicago:
University of Chicago, 1959; Phoenix Edition, 1962. 309p. 3 maps.
bibliog.

A respected collection of fifteen essays examining the continent as a whole as well as
individual cultures. Articles on African languages, art and music by Joseph Greenberg,
. M. Cordwell and A. P. Merriam, respectively, mention Nigeria in their broad
overviews. Specific Nigerian ethnic groups are discussed in 'Ibo receptivity to change',
y Simon Ottenberg (p. 130–43); 'The changing economic position of women among
the Afikpo Ibo', by Phoebe V. Ottenberg (p. 205–23); and 'Religious acculturation
among the Anang Ibibio', by John C. Messenger, Jr. (p. 279–99).

30 **Nigerian chewing sticks.**
M. A. Isawumi. *Nigerian Field*, vol. 43, pt. 2 (June 1978), p. 50–58;
pt. 3 (Sept. 1978), p. 111–21; pt. 4 (Dec. 1978), p. 161–70. bibliog.

This interesting article provides details on the commonest chewing sticks used by
ethnic groups all over the country. The sticks are from twenty-three species belonging
) fourteen families. The author describes not only the botanical aspects of the species,
ach illustrated in a full-page drawing by Joan Bacon, but also the custom itself and its
possible health benefits.

31 **Bibliography of Nigeria: a survey of anthropological and linguistic
writings from the earliest times to 1966.**
Compiled by Nduntuei O[tu] Ita. London: Frank Cass, 1971. 273p.

An invaluable compilation of 5,411 sources, numbered serially and frequently given
brief annotations. The work is divided into two parts. Part one, 'Nigeria – general'
. 3–76), includes 1,519 references on physical anthropology and archaeology, social

Ethnic Groups. General

and cultural anthropology, ethnography and linguistics. Part two, 'Nigeria – ethnic divisions' (p. 79–245), contains general, ethnographic and linguistic studies on sixty one ethnic groups. The largest groups receive more extensive coverage with work grouped into numerous sub-categories. Framing the compilation are a brief preface and author, ethnic and Islamic studies indexes. The librarian author (22 Nov. 1936– . was born in Oron, now Akwa Ibom State.

332 **Africa: its peoples and their culture history.**
George Peter Murdock. New York: McGraw-Hill, 1959. 456p. 17 maps. bibliog.

This remarkable standard reference work by a scholar who spent less than a month i Africa surveys the major groupings of peoples throughout the continent and provides select bibliography for each group. Nigerian ethnic groups described are: 'Negroes c the Sudan fringe' (p. 133–48); 'Southern Nigerians' (p. 242–51); 'Fulani' (p. 413–21) and 'Plateau Nigerians' (p. 89–100). A large, separate fold-out 'Tribal map of Africa locates each group.

333 **Cultural atlas of Africa.**
Edited by Jocelyn Murray. New York: Facts on File, 1981. 240p. maps. bibliog.

An attractive and useful atlas for the continent, divided into 'The physical background', 'The cultural background', and brief individual descriptions and country maps of 'The nations of Africa'. Not only is Nigeria considered in the several general maps and discussions of Africa, and individually (p. 147–48), but also in special featur sections are 'Yoruba traditional religion' (p. 38–39) and 'Nigerian bronzes' (p. 86–87 A gazetteer and index afford access to the maps and materials.

334 **The physical anthropology of Southern Nigeria: a biometric study in statistical method.**
P[ercy] Amaury Talbot, H. Mulhall, preface by J. C. Trevor.
Cambridge: Cambridge University, 1962. 127p. 3 maps. bibliog.

This study is a posthumous analysis of the anthropometric data collected by Talbot (1877–1945) mostly in 1922–23 while he was Resident of Southern Nigeria. 'It is likely that he produced one of the largest bodies of measurements on living subjects eve made by a single observer' (Introduction, p. xii). The data on nearly 7,000 person representing around 100 ethnic groups and sub-groups are subjected to sophisticate statistical analysis here by Mulhall, the Senior Lecturer in Mathematical Statistic University of Sydney. The resulting work is not only a study of the physical relations c numerous gourps, but an application of modern statistical procedures to physica anthropology. The bibliography (p. 15–27) is a practical one for the topics covered.

335 **Handbook of ethnic units in Nigeria.**
Renate Wente-Lukas, with the assistance of Adam Jones. Wiesbaden GFR: Franz Steiner, 1985. 466p. map. bibliog. (Studien zur Kulturkunde of the Frobenius Institute, Frankfurt University, vol. 74)

This invaluable volume is a handbook of ethnic units, not of languages, 'a sort c dictionary' covering from A to Z all known ethnic units of Nigeria, listed under the 'principal name' with the materials derived from printed sources (Introduction, p. 1 In the introduction (p. 1–6) the author describes 'ethnogenesis', the parameters fc defining an ethnic unit and the organization of the material. Most of the 550 unnumbered entries contain the primary name, autonym, synonyms, variants, subgroups, present location, previous location, population estimate, language affiliation, name of language and literature for each unit. The bibliography (p. 365–401) is excellent. The detailed index (p. 402–66) was compiled by Theda Schumann. A lengthy review of the volume with additional useful references by Conrad Max Benedict Brann appears in *Africa*, vol. 57, no. 3 (1987), p. 391–96.

336 **Nigerian geophagical clay: a traditional antidiarrheal pharmaceutical.**
Donald E. Vermeer, Ray E. Ferrell, Jr. *Science*, vol. 227, no. 4687
(8 Feb. 1985), p. 634–46. map. bibliog.

A discussion of the clay, *eko*, dug near the village of Uzalla, Bendel State, Nigeria, distributed throughout West African markets as far away as Ghana and Togo, and commonly eaten by pregnant women. The clay is used in several medicinal preparations and to 'ease stomach and dysenteric ailments'. Minerological analysis hows the Uzalla clay is strikingly similar to clay used in the commercial pharmaceutical Kaopectate. Professor Vermeer is in the Department of Geography and Anthropology, Louisiana State University, Baton Rouge, Louisiana and has written elsewhere on clay-eating in Nigeria: 'Geophagy among the Tiv of Nigeria' *Annals of the Association of American Geographers*, vol. 56 (June 1966), p. 197–207; and 'A note on geophagy among the Afenmai and adjacent peoples of Bendel State, Nigeria', *African Notes* (Ibadan), vol. 8, no. 1 (1979), p. 13–14.

337 **Africa counts: number and pattern in African culture.**
Claudia Zaslavsky. Westport, Connecticut: Lawrence Hill, 1973.
Reprinted, 1979. 328p. 7 maps. bibliog.

An original synthesis of information from sub-Saharan Africa on 'How Africans count', 'Numbers in daily life', time, money, number games, magic squares, geometry in architecture and regional studies of East Africa and southwest Nigeria (the Yoruba and Bini cultures). Other Nigerian cultures discussed include the Igbo, Efik, Hausa, Kanuri, Fulani, Ijo, Jaba, Nupe and Tiv. The book is well illustrated with figures and photographs and the bibliography (p. 311–17) is excellent.

Edo (Bini)

38 **The Benin Kingdom and the Edo-speaking peoples of south-western Nigeria.**
R[ay] E. Bradbury, with P. C. Lloyd. London: International African
Institute, 2nd ed. 1970. 215p. 2 maps. bibliog. (Ethnographic Survey of
Africa. Western Africa, part XIII).

First published in 1957 and reprinted with an updated bibliography (p. 211–15) in 1970, Bradbury's report is the most comprehensive ethnographic survey of the region of the Benin Kingdom, the Ishan, the Northern Edo, the Urhobo and Isoko of the Niger Delta. In addition, Lloyd surveys 'The Itsekiri' (p. 172–205). Each author provides an excellent bibliography (p. 165–71 and 203–05) and professional descriptions of each

Ethnic Groups. Edo (Bini)

group's history, political and social organization, economy and life-cycle. Tw
excellent fold-out maps, 'The Edo-speaking peoples of south-western Nigeria' and 'Th
Itsekiri', are included.

339 **Benin studies.**
R. E. Bradbury, edited and introduced by Peter Morton-Williams,
foreword by Daryll Forde. London; New York; Ibadan, Nigeria:
Oxford University for the International African Institute, 1973. 293p.
map. bibliog.

An indispensible volume for the study of the Benin Kingdom, consisting of nin
detailed articles and edited sections of the author's 1956 University of London PhI
thesis, *The social structure of Benin, with special reference to the politico-ritua
organisation (the village community)*. Bradbury was fluent in Bini due to his fieldwor
in Benin during 1952–54 and 1956–60. This collection of the highest qualit
ethnographic writings was prompted by his premature death in December 1969 at th
age of forty. Forde's foreword (p. ix–xii) provides an appreciation of Bradbury's work
Morton-Williams' introduction (p. xiii–xxi) elaborates on the intellectual developmen
of the scholar and on his papers in this collection. There is a general bibliograph
(p. 283–86) and one of Bradbury's writings (p. 287–88) as well as four plates, nin
figures and an index.

340 **A short history of Benin.**
Jacob U[wadie] Egharevba, foreword by R. E. Bradbury. Ibadan,
Nigeria: Ibadan University, 1968. 4th ed. 100p.

A valuable and respected account of the kingdom's history by a prolific local scholar
This history is especially important because Chief Egharevba (27 Jan. 1893–[1971]
'collected his material thirty years or more ago from well-selected informants who ha
grown to maturity before 1897' (Foreword, p. ix). In addition to the chronologica
history (p. 1–69), there are information-packed appendices containing, among othe
topics, a list of Benin sovereigns, descriptions of Bini titles, morning salutations, a lis
of district heads, Benin Division, and a 'Chronological table of events' (p. 90–95)
Four plates and 'Biographical notes on the author' (p. vii–viii) are included as well
The first edition appeared in 1934 (Lagos: CMS Bookshop), the second in 1953 (Beni
City: The Author) and the third in 1960 (Ibadan: Ibadan University). Anothe
important publication is Egharevba's *Benin law and custom* (Port Harcourt, Nigeria
CMS Niger, 1949, 3rd ed. 120p.) which was first published in 1946.

341 **[Twelve works on Benin]**
Jacob U. Egharevba. Nendeln, Liechtenstein: Kraus Reprint, 1973.
(Black Experience Series, 142).

This volume reprints twelve valuable booklets on Bini culture by the Bini historia
Chief Egharevba: *Concise lives of the famous Iyases of Benin* (1947. 2nd ed. 48p.)
Benin games and sports (1951. 2nd ed. 27p.); *Who does not speak his mother tongue*
lost (1956. 40p.); *Bini titles* (1956. 46p.); *The murder of Imaguero and tragedy of Ida
war* (1959. 3rd ed. 35p.); *Marriage of the princesses of Benin* (1962. 24p.); *The origin c
Benin* (1964. 2nd ed. 30p.); *Chronicle of events in Benin* (1965. 45p.); *Fusion of tribe
(1966. 15p.); *Brief autobiography* (1968. 75p.); *Some prominent Bini people* (196!
96p.); and *Descriptive catalogue of the Benin Museum* (1969. 56p.). Kraus al:
reprinted four works in a similar volume (Nendeln, Liechtenstein, 1971): *The city c

Benin (1952. 27p.); *Benin law and custom* (1949. 120p.); *Some stories of ancient Benin* (1951. 57p.); and *Some tribal gods of Southern Nigeria* (1951. 59p.).

342 **Benin.**
Kit Elliott. Cambridge, England: Cambridge University, 1973. 48p. 3 maps. (Cambridge Introduction to the History of Mankind, Topic Book).

This booklet tells the story of the Benin Kingdom 'as it was when Europeans saw it for the first time' (p. 3). By combining historical accounts and interpretations with abundant photographs of contemporary Benin City, surrounding areas, Benin art work and drawings by Gareth Floyd, the author conveys extensive information about the ancient kingdom. S. B. Omoregie's *Emotan and the kings of Benin* (Harlow, England: Longman, 1972. 51p.), in the Makers of African History Series, tells the story of the Edo heroine Emotan who saved the life of Prince Ogun, later Oba Ewuare. Consequently, she has been honoured by every succeeding Oba. In 1951 Oba Akenzua II called her 'a saint, a prophetess and the soul of the Bini nation' (Introduction, p. iv).

343 **Divine kingship in Africa.**
William Fagg. London: British Museum Publications for the Trustees of the British Museum, 1978. 2nd ed. 64p. bibliog.

This booklet was first published in 1970 as a guide to the British Museum's first exhibition of its complete collection of Benin art, the largest in existence. The volume presents a brief account of Great Benin and the Benin Exhibition and describes the objects in the exhibition chronologically or by type; commentary on 'Divine kingship elsewhere in Africa' concludes the text. Thirty-five photographs of the art are included as well as several scenes of Benin rituals taken by Fagg and by the late anthropologist R. E. Bradbury, to whom the guide is dedicated.

344 **Kingship succession rituals in Benin.**
Joseph Nevadomsky. *African Arts*, pt. 1, vol. 17, no. 1 (Nov. 1983), p. 47–54, 87; pt. 2, vol. 17, no. 2 (Feb. 1984), p. 41–47, 90–91; pt. 3, vol. 17, no. 3 (May 1984), p. 48–57, 91. bibliog.

An informative ethnographic account, in three parts, of the 1978–79 ceremonies marking the accession of the thirty-eighth Oba of Benin, Omo N'Oba N'Edo, Uku Akpolokpolo, Erediauwa. These rituals 'reaffirmed the synchronic solidarity of the community and the diachronic solidarity of the kingdom' (p. 47). Part one, 'Becoming a crown prince' is by Nevadomsky with field research and co-authorship by Daniel E. Inneh. Part two (by Nevadomsky), 'The big things', explains the second burial rites for the Edaiken's father Oba Akenzua II. Part three (by Nevadomsky), 'The coronation of the Oba', concludes the account with the accession ceremonies themselves. This unique documentary series is illustrated throughout with numerous photographs. Inneh is head of Public Relations for the Oba of Benin. Dr. Nevadomsky, resident in Benin City for more than a decade, has also published 'A note on the Benin bronze horseman', *African Arts*, vol. 17, no. 4 Aug. 1984), p. 10, 12–13, and 'The Benin bronze horseman as the Ata of Idah', *African Arts*, vol. 19, no. 4 (Aug. 1986), p. 40–47, 85.

Ethnic Groups. Edo (Bini)

345 **Edo studies: a preliminary bibliography.**
Thompson Omoerha. Benin City, Nigeria: Benin University Library, 1975. 65p.

This bibliography surveys Benin (the Bini, the Edo people) history, ethnology, linguistics and art. The author lists 785 numbered sources, which are arranged in the following categories: bibliographies; exploration; description and travel; historical studies; archaeology; ethnography, social and cultural anthropology; politics, government and administration; religion; economy (agriculture and trade); art and sculpture; and literary and linguistic studies. There is an author and name index and a selected list of bibliographic sources consulted.

346 **Great Benin: its customs, art and horrors.**
H. Ling Roth. Halifax, England: F. King, 1903. Reprinted, Northbrook, Illinois: Metro Books, 1972. 234p.

A classic, turn-of-the-century history and ethnography of Benin City and the Benin Kingdom, published six years after the city and its king were conquered by British troops. Roth synthesizes accounts by earlier explorers and describes segments of the life-cycle, customs, beliefs, 'character', material culture, architecture and art of the Bini (Edo). The appendices (p. i–xxiv) include: 'The treaty between the King of Benin and Capt. Callway, D.S.O.'; 'A diary of a surgeon with the Benin Punitive Expedition by F. N. Roth, M.R.C.S.' (H. Ling Roth's brother); 'The surrender and trial of the King'; 'On the British loss of antique works of art from Benin'; and 'Land tenure and inheritance in Yoruba, by Cyril Punch', (a trader who first visited Benin in 1889 and supplied Roth with valuable information and photographs of the city). The volume contains 275 illustrations of the culture and its art works.

347 **Anthropological report on the Edo-speaking peoples of Nigeria.**
Northcote W. Thomas. London: Harrison & Sons, 1910. Reprinted, New York: Negro Universities, 1969. 2 vols. map.

Represents one of the earliest ethnographic reports published on the Edo peoples of Southern Nigeria. Vol. one 'Law and custom', (163p.), describes language, religion and magic, marriage and birth, inheritance, adoption and property, law and kinship. Vol. two 'Linguistics' (251p.), contains texts in both Edo and English of numerous narratives, an Edo grammar, a 'Contemporary dictionary of selected words in the Edo languages' (p. 151–86) and an Edo dictionary (p. 187–251). The author collected the extensive materials while he was Government Anthropologist in the area in 1909–10 and published several other brief reports on the Edo in *Man*: 'Decorative art among the Edo-speaking peoples of Nigeria', no. 37 (1910), p. 65–66; 'Pottery-making . . .', no. 53 (1910), p. 97–98; 'Nigeria: ritual', nos. 74–75 (Sept. 1918), p. 138–42; 'Nigerian notes. Twins', nos. 86–87 (Nov. 1919), p. 173–74; 'Nigerian notes. Astronomy', nos. 91–92 (Dec. 1919), p. 179–83; and 'West Africa. The Edo week', nos. 72–73 (Oct. 1920), p. 152–53.

The archaeology of Benin: excavations and other researches in and around Benin City, Nigeria.
See item no. 137.

Archaeology and history in southern Nigeria: the ancient linear earthworks of Benin and Ishan.
See item no. 139.

The Yoruba and Edo-speaking peoples and their neighbors before 1600.
See item no. 210.

Benin: the city of blood.
See item no. 230.

City of Blood revisited: a new look at the Benin expedition of 1897.
See item no. 255.

Benin under British administration: the impact of colonial rule on an African kingdom, 1897–1938.
See item no. 256.

Benin and the Europeans, 1485–1897.
See item no. 285.

Figures in ebony: past and present in a West African city.
See item no. 296.

An Ẹdo-English dictionary.
See item no. 452.

A concise dictionary of the Bini language of Southern Nigeria.
See item no. 453.

An introduction to Bini.
See item no. 454.

Kemwin-kemwin: the apothecary shop in Benin City.
See item no. 560.

Poems in Bini.
See item no. 909.

African mud sculpture.
See item no. 939.

The art of Benin.
See item no. 941.

The art of power, the power of art: studies in Benin iconography.
See item no. 942.

Art as statecraft: a king's justification in ivory, a carved tusk from Benin.
See item no. 944.

An introduction to Benin art and technology.
See item no. 953.

An illustrated catalogue of Benin art.
See item no. 954.

Two thousand years Nigerian art.
See item no. 961.

Treasures of ancient Nigeria.
See item no. 962.

Benin art.
See item no. 965.

Royal Benin art in the collection of the National Museum of African Art.
See item no. 966.

Images of power: art of the royal court of Benin.
See item no. 970.

Antique works of art from Benin.
See item no. 977.

Antiquities from the city of Benin and from other parts of West Africa in the British Musuem.
See item no. 980.

Sweet words: storytelling events in Benin.
See item no. 1024.

Stories of the Benin Empire.
See item no. 1030.

The Benin Museum collection
See item no. 1063.

Fulani

348 **Pastoralists of the West African savanna: selected studies presented and discussed at the fifteenth International African Seminar, held at Ahmadu Bello University, Nigeria, July 1979.**
Edited by Mahdi Adamu, A. H. M. Kirk-Greene, foreword by J. F. Ade Ajayi.   Manchester, England: Manchester University Press in association with International African Institute, 1986. 359p. map. bibliog. (International African Seminars, New Series, no. 2).

Twenty-one papers, eleven in French, by scholars from throughout West Africa provide historical, linguistic, literary, social and economic insights on the Fulani pastoralists. Among several relevant for the Fulani of Nigeria are: Kyari Tijani's 'The Shuwa Arabs' (p. 62–73); Agnes Wedderbum's 'The Koyam' (p. 74–83); D. W. Arnott's 'Fula language studies: present position and future prospects' (p. 87–100); and M. O. Awogbade's 'The Fulani of the Jos Plateau' (p. 214–24). The bibliography (p. 327–51) is an important source of material on the Fulani. Mahdi Adamu is Vice-Chancellor of the University of Sokoto, Sokoto, Nigeria.

349 **The pastoral Fulbe family in Gwandu.**
C. Edward Hopen, foreword by Daryll Forde. London: Oxford
University for the International African Institute, 1958. 165p. 2 maps.
bibliog.

Based on the author's fieldwork in 1952–53 and 1953–55. Hopen provides an historical
and ethnographic account of Fulani pastoralism in the Gwandu Emirate of what is now
Sokoto State in northern Nigeria. He sets his study of the complexities of family life
and the interdependence of the family and cattle in the contexts of inter-family and
clan relations, ecology and the historical rôle of the Fulani in the politics of the region.
Included are a quantitative analysis of households and herds (p. 61–76) and six
photographs of daily life. The study was reprinted in 1970. An illustrated study by
Cornelius O. Adepegba, *Decorative arts of the Fulani nomads* (Ibadan, Nigeria: Ibadan
University, 1986. 48p.) provides rare documentation of the aesthetic aspects of Fulani
life.

350 **Adamawa past and present: an historical approach to the development
of a northern Cameroons province.**
A. H. M. Kirk-Greene, foreword by Daryll Forde. London: Oxford
University for the International African Institute, 1958. Reprinted,
London: Dawsons, 1969. 230p. 5 maps. bibliog.

Adamawa Province, in today's Gongola State, in north-eastern Nigeria, was created in
1926, and is larger than Scotland. The author, who served in the Nigerian
Administrative Service there, provides a history covering the previous 150 years, a
general description of the area and its peoples, and ethnological notes. In short,
everything factual that an officer posted to the province might desire in a handbook. A
note on the Fulani language, Fufulde, is provided as Adamawa is the only Northern
Nigerian province where it is still used as the *lingua franca* (p. 206–7). An 'Adamawa
bibliography' is included (p. 194–97), as is a large fold-out map of the Province. 'The
Mba ceremony of the Marghi' is reprinted in the volume with the author's photographs
from *The Nigerian Field*, vol. 24, no. 2 (April 1959), p. 80–87.

351 **Savannah nomads: a study of the Woɗaaɓe pastoral Fulani of
western
Bornu Province, Northern Region, Nigeria.**
Derrick J. Stenning, foreword by Daryll Forde. London: Oxford
University for the International African Institute, 1959. 266p. 4 maps.
bibliog.

An important study of the pastoral Fulani, based on the author's (d. 1964) fieldwork in
Northern Nigeria, 1951–53. Following part one, an historical account of the Woɗaaɓe
up to 1931, part two describes 'the Woɗaaɓe today' including: 'founding a family and a
herd'; marriage; 'fertility of women and cattle'; divorce; clans; movements; and
headships. Photographs, maps and a 'General bibliography of Fulani studies'
(p. 249–53) contribute to this detailed work. Part of the book is based on the author's
Cambridge University doctoral thesis. The author's 'The pastoral Fulani of Northern
Nigeria' in *People of Africa* (New York: Holt, Rinehart & Winston, 1965, p. 361–401)
edited by James L. Gibbs, Jr., is the finest succinct description of these people. An
excellent recent study is Tukur Abu-Jalal Muhammad-Baba's doctoral dissertation,
The pastoral Ful'be, economy and society in contemporary Nigeria: the political

economy of agricultural and livestock development policy programs, at the University of Missouri at Columbia, Missouri (Ann Arbor, Michigan: University Microfilms 1987. 401 leaves).

352 **The red men of Nigeria: an account of a lengthy residence among the Fulani, or 'Red Men', and other pagan tribes of central Nigeria, with a description of their headhunting, pastoral and other customs, habits and religion.**
J. R. Wilson-Haffenden, foreword by Bronislaw Malinowski.
Philadelphia: Lippincott, 1930. Reprinted, London: Frank Cass, 1967. 318p. map. bibliog. (Cass Library of African Studies, no. 38).
During the 1920s Captain Wilson-Haffenden served as a government anthropologis throughout parts of Northern Nigeria, spending five years in Nasarawa (and late Benue) Province, especially in the Lafia and Keffi Divisions. This book is hi functionalist ethnography and personal account of observations of the peoples of the Keffi and Nasarawa Emirates. According to the author, the root of the word 'Fulani' i the Berber, 'ful' or 'pul', meaning 'the red men' (p. 7, 93–94). The book contain twenty-two photographs, a small fold-out map of northern and western Africa and a index.

Power and diplomacy in Northern Nigeria, 1804–1906: the Sokoto Caliphat and its enemies.
See item no. 175.

The sword of truth: the life and times of the Shehu Usuman dan Fodio.
See item no. 193.

The emirates of Northern Nigeria: a preliminary survey of their historica traditions.
See item no. 194.

The Fulani Empire of Sokoto.
See item no. 199.

The Sokoto Caliphate.
See item no. 201.

Warfare in the Sokoto Caliphate: historical and sociological perspectives.
See item no. 215.

A revolution in history: the jihad of Usman Dan Fodio.
See item no. 218.

The conquest of Northern Nigeria.
See item no. 245.

The white man in Nigeria.
See item no. 252.

The British in Northern Nigeria.
See item no. 253.

Gazetteers of the northern provinces of Nigeria.
See item no. 262.

Letters & sketches from Northern Nigeria.
See item no. 265.

A tropical dependency: an outline of the ancient history of the Western Sudan with an account of the modern settlement of Northern Nigeria.
See item no. 268.

The making of Northern Nigeria.
See item no. 277.

Concerning brave captains, being a history of the British occupation of Kano and Sokoto and of the last stand of the Fulani forces.
See item no. 282.

The role of the British administration in the appointment of the emirs of Northern Nigeria, 1903–31: the case of Sokoto Province.
See item no. 295.

Bibliography of Nigeria: a survey of anthropological and linguistic writings from the earliest times to 1966.
See item no. 331.

Handbook of ethnic units in Nigeria.
See item no. 335.

Dictionaire élémentaire fulfulde-français-english-elementary dictionary.
See item no. 482.

A reference grammar of Adamawa Fulani.
See item no. 483.

The development of Islam in West Africa.
See item no. 490.

Islam in West Africa.
See item no. 491.

Northern Nigeria.
See item no. 502.

My life.
See item no. 576.

The politics of tradition: continuity and change in Northern Nigeria, 1946–1966.
See item no. 584.

Shehu Shagari: the biography of Nigeria's first executive president.
See item no. 620.

Ahmadu Bello, Sardauna of Sokoto: values and leadership in Nigeria.
See item no. 626.

Ethnic Groups. Hausa

Burning grass: a story of the Fulani of Northern Nigeria.
See item no. 867.

Nigerian weaving.
See item no. 1001.

Nigeria Magazine.
See item no. 1107.

Savanna. A Journal of the Environmental and Social Sciences.
See item no. 1110.

Hausa

353 **Horses, musicians, & gods: the Hausa cult of possession-trance.**
Fremont E. Besmer, foreword by Willard Rhodes. South Hadley,
Massachusetts: Bergin & Garvey, 1983. 290p. bibliog.

A remarkable scholarly study of the Hausa *bori* cult of spirit-possession or possession-
trance, as practiced in Kano, northern Nigeria, which is based on data gathered in
1972–73 while the author was a research fellow at Ahmadu Bello University in Zaria.
In this healing cult of the mostly urban, non-Muslim Hausa, the 'horses' are the cult-
adepts who see themselves as mounts for the spirits, the musicians are non-initiates
who invoke the spirits with their special songs, and the gods are divine horsemen, the
residents of the invisible city of Jangare who cause illness but then also cure it.
Professor Besmer provides a full analysis of the participants, their beliefs and social
context, as well as a Hausa glossary and index, detailed genealogies of the houses of
Jangare, twenty-seven musical transcriptions, photographs and a bibliography
(p. 277–80).

354 **Muslim Hausa women in Nigeria: tradition and change.**
Barbara J. Callaway, foreword by Enid Schildkrout. Syracuse, New
York: Syracuse University, 1987. 242p. bibliog.

An excellent, wide-ranging and sensitive account of Muslim Hausa women in Kano
society. Callaway provides historical and cultural depth to her contemporary study of
women at all levels of society. She analyses data from hundreds of interviews and from
questionnaires given to teachers at girls' secondary schools, students, their mothers and
fathers, village women and university students, focusing on 'the norms by which Hausa
women defined their roles . . . their expectations for and ideas about changing roles
for their daughters and themselves . . . and their actual behavior in response to
expanding educational opportunities and political exhortations' (Preface, p. xix). Her
final essay, on Islam, Hausa women and change, places her findings in broader
perspective and adds a feminist theoretical dimension. Photographs by Enid
Schildkrout, a Hausa glossary and a useful bibliography (p. 223–34) are included. The
author was a Fulbright Professor at Bayero University in Kano, 1981–83. Larry
Diamond offers additional perspective in his review of the book, in *Journal of Modern
African Studies*, vol. 25, no. 4 (Dec. 1987), p. 692–94.

355 **Rural Hausa: a village and a setting.**
Polly Hill. Cambridge: Cambridge University, 1972. 368p. 8 maps.
bibliog.

The major part of this important work is the analysis of the socio-economic affairs of a single village, Batagarawa, located six miles south of Katsina in the present Katsina State. Using her fieldwork data from the late 1960s and that gathered by M. S. Nuhu, the author provides a lucid account of farming patterns and social relations in this village, relentlessly examining the theme of economic inequality. The final chapter describes nine 'causes' of general poverty, but concludes that 'the mystery is not poverty, but how such splendid and proud communities can flourish in such unpropitious circumstances' (p. 198). Valuable features of the book are its extensive alphabetical commentary and Hausa glossary (p. 201–337). The bibliography (p. 338–49) is excellent; thirty-five photographs contribute substantially to the volume.

356 **Population, prosperity and poverty: rural Kano, 1900 and 1970.**
Polly Hill. Cambridge University, 1977. 240p. 7 maps. bibliog.

In this companion volume to *Rural Hausa: a village and a setting* (q.v.), the author compares and contrasts Dorayi, 'an extremely densely populated farming area of dispersed settlement near Kano City' (p. xi), with the village studied earlier, providing an historical perspective on Dorayi 'by examining socio-economic conditions in rural Kano generally in immediately pre-colonial and early colonial times' (Preface, p. xi). The author describes the historical prosperity of Dorayi and traces its transition to its present-day status as a 'stagnating, impoverished, long-established, overcrowded rural community' (p. 95). Other topics include a discussion of the economic relationship between city and countryside in 1900; 'indirect rule as rural non-rule'; 'the attitude to farmland'; 'the failure to migrate'; 'the married son'; 'the big house'; and farm-slavery in Dorayi. Each chapter has detailed appendices; the final bibliography (p. 223–28) is useful.

357 *Mutumin kirkii:* **the concept of the good man in Hausa.**
A. H. M. Kirk-Greene. Bloomington, Indiana: African Studies
Program, Indiana University, 1974. 41p. bibliog.

This fascinating, scholarly essay, originally delivered as the third Annual Hans Wolff Memorial Lecture, 11 April 1973, at Indiana University, fleshes out the dimensions of the 'good man' in Hausa culture. His characteristics include (but go beyond): trustworthiness, generosity, patience, integrity, good sense, a proper sense of propriety, good manners, wisdom, scrupulous behaviour, and a fear of God. A 'Select bibliography of A. H. M. Kirk-Greene's publications on Hausa history, politics and language' (p. 40–41), a Hausa-English 'Glossary for a study of *mutumin kirki*' (p. 38–39) and extensive notes are included.

358 **Religion and political culture in Kano.**
John N. Paden. Berkeley; Los Angeles; London: University
California, 1973. 461p. 9 maps. bibliog.

A brilliant case-study of religion and politics in Kano, based on the author's residence there from June 1964 to September 1965 and for six months in 1970. Part one, 'Patterns of religious authority and community' and part two, 'Patterns of political authority and community' describe their themes thoroughly for Kano and anchor them in historical perspective, in the broader unit of Hausa culture, in Kano State and in the nation. The bibliography (p. 436–42) is a listing of Hausa sources; glossary one

contains 'Hausa terms used in text (with Arabic and English equivalents)' (p. 423–28).
This study derives from the author's 1968 Harvard University doctoral dissertation,
*The influence of religious elites on political culture and community integration in Kano,
Nigeria.* Of additional interest is Dr. Paden's 'Urban pluralism, integration, and
adaptation of communal identity in Kano, Nigeria' in *From Tribe to nation in Africa:
studies in incorporation processes* (Scrinton, Pennsylvania: Chandler, 1970, p.
242–70), edited by Ronald Cohen and John Middleton.

359 **Hausa studies: a selected bibliography of B.A., M.A., and Ph.D. papers
available in Northern Nigerian universities.**
Compiled by Edward L. Powe. [Kano, Nigeria: Bayero University],
1983. rev. ed. 29p.

The compiler, a lecturer in the Department of Nigerian languages, Bayero University,
Kano, lists 330 papers from the University of Sokoto, the University of Maiduguri,
Ahmadu Bello University and Bayero University, completed as of July 1983 (except
for 1983 B.A. papers for the univeristy of Maiduguri and 1983 M.A. papers from all
institutions). The unannotated references are arranged in eleven categories: Hausa
society and customs; education and attitudes concerning education; games and
celebrations; history; language and linguistics; marriage and divorce; occupations; oral
literature; religion, beliefs and medicine; royalty and nobility; and written literature.
There is an author index.

360 **The Hausa people: a bibliography.**
Compiled by Frank A. Salamone, with the assistance of James A.
McCain. New Haven, Connecticut: Human Relations Area Files,
1983. 2 vols. (HRAFlex Books, MS12-001, Bibliography Series).

An excellent, and easy-to-use alphabetical listing of 1,271 selected references to the
Hausa, up to 1980. Each item is coded to identify the time period covered by the
document, the geographic location, the language if other than English, ethnic
subgroups, and especially important works. In place of an index, the author offers a
'Data quality control bibliography' (vol. II, p. 241–95) in which each item is grouped
topically and coded systematically for analysis in *Worldwide theory testing* by R.
Naroll, G. L. Michik and F. Naroll (HRAF, 1976. 139p.). The informative
introduction (vol. l, leaves 1–47) is a revision of the essay in the author's 'A Hausa
bibliography' , *Africana Journal*, vol. 6, no. 2 (summer 1975), p. 99–163, which also
has a large number of references.

361 **Young traders of northern Nigeria.**
Enid Schildkrout. *Natural History*, vol. 90, no. 6 (June 1981),
p. 44–53, 82–83. bibliog.

An account, supplemented with colour photographs, of the activities of children in
Muslim Hausa households. The author shows the importance of the trading activities
of two young girls, especially to their secluded mothers and describes the economic
value of children for the household, for their future marriage expenses, and also for
the 'children's economy' of things they buy and sell for themselves. The theme is
elaborated in the author's 'The employment of children in Kano' in *Child work,
poverty and underdevelopment*, edited by Gerry Rodgers and Guy Standing (Geneva:
International Labour Office, 1981, p. 81–112) and in 'Age and gender in Hausa
society: socio-economic roles of children in urban Kano' in *Sex and age as principles of*

social differentiation, edited by J. S. Fontaine (London: Academic, 1978, p. 109–37 (A.S.A. Monograph, 17)).

362 **Baba of Karo: a woman of the Muslim Hausa.**
Mary F[elice] Smith, introduction and notes by M[ichael] G[arfield] Smith, foreword by Hilda Kuper. London: Faber & Faber, 1954. Reprinted, New Haven, Connecticut; London: Yale University, 1981. 299p.

The most famous autobiography in the anthropological literature. Mary Smith (1924– .) recorded Baba's life history in Hausa between November 1949 and January 1950 at Giwa and Zaria City in Zaria Province, Northern Nigeria. Baba (1877–1951) skilfully tells of life before the British arrived, of her barrenness and four marriages, and of life in general for women in Muslim Hausa society. The introduction and notes by Smith add broader context to the story. Eight photographs depict Baba in her world. Two excellent biographies of northern Nigerian women appear in *Life histories of African women*, edited by Patricia W. Ramero (London; Atlantic Highlands, New Jersey: Ashfield, 1988. 200p.). These are 'Hajiya Ma'daki: a royal Hausa woman', by Beverly Mack (p. 47–77); and 'Hajiya Husaina: notes on the life history of a Hausa woman', by Enid Schildkrout (p. 78–98).

363 **The Hausa of Northern Nigeria.**
M. G. Smith. In: *Peoples of Africa*. Edited by James L. Gibbs, Jr. New York: Holt, Rinehart & Winston, 1965, p. 119–55. map. bibliog.

This excellent ethnographic account delineates the main features of life for the Muslim Hausa of northern Nigeria. Topics described briefly for this enormous, complex group include ecology, agriculture, occupations and crafts, material culture, exchange and markets, the Hausa compound, political organization including the concept of office, clientship and political structure under the British, ethos, kinship organization, matrimonial relations, the life-cycle, friendship, Islam and social change. Professor Smith researched several Hausa groups in Nigeria and Niger during 1949–50 and 1958–59. Other significant publications by the prolific author include *The economy of Hausa communities of Zaria* (London: HM Stationery Office, 1955. (Colonial Research Studies, no. 16)) and 'The Hausa system of social status', *Africa*, vol. 29, no. 3 (1959), p. 239–52.

Dreams and deeds: achievement motivation in Nigeria.
See item no. 18.

Barth's travels in Nigeria: extracts from the journal of Heinrich Barth's travels in Nigeria, 1850–1855.
See item no. 88.

West African travels and adventures: two autobiographical narratives from Northern Nigeria.
See item no. 89.

The Hausa factor in West African history.
See item no. 174.

Ethnic Groups. Hausa

Power and diplomacy in Northern Nigeria, 1804–1906: the Sokoto Caliphate and its enemies.
See item no. 175.

Evolution of political culture in Nigeria: proceedings of a national seminar organized by the Kaduna State Council for Arts and Culture.
See item no. 176.

Studies in the history of Kano.
See item no. 182.

Nigerian panoply: arms and armour of the Northern Region.
See item no. 184.

The emirates of Northern Nigeria: a preliminary survey of their historical traditions.
See item no. 194.

Songhay, Borno and Hausaland in the sixteenth century.
See item no. 196.

Caravans of kola: the Hausa kola trade, 1700–1900.
See item no. 204.

The development of an export oriented dyed cloth industry in Kano Emirate in the nineteenth century.
See item no. 214.

Government in Zazzau, 1800–1950.
See item no. 216.

The affairs of Daura: history and change in a Hausa state, 1800–1958.
See item no. 217.

Cities of the savannah (a history of some towns and cities of the Nigerian savannah).
See item no. 219.

Indirect rule – French and British style.
See item no. 239.

West African chiefs: their changing status under colonial rule and independence.
See item no. 243.

The conquest of Northern Nigeria.
See item no. 245.

The British in Northern Nigeria.
See item no. 253.

Nigerian groundnut exports: origins and early development.
See item no. 254.

Gazetteers of the northern provinces of Nigeria.
See item no. 262.

Letters & sketches from Northern Nigeria.
See item no. 265.

A tropical dependency: an outline of the ancient history of the Western sudan with an account of the modern settlement of Northern Nigeria.
See item no. 268.

The making of Northern Nigeria.
See item no. 277.

Concerning brave captains, being a history of the British occupation of Kano and Sokoto and of the last stand of the Fulani forces.
See item no. 282.

The development of capitalism in Northern Nigeria.
See item no. 286.

Recollections of British Administration in the Cameroons and Northern Nigeria, 1921–1957.
See item no. 287.

Colonial cadet in Nigeria.
See item no. 288.

Native races and their rulers: sketches and studies of official life and administrative problems in Nigeria.
See item no. 294.

Dan Bana: the memoirs of a Nigerian official.
See item no. 298.

Bibliography of Nigeria: a survey of anthropolgical and linguistic writings from the earliest times to 1966.
See item no. 331.

Handbook of ethnic units in Nigeria.
See item no. 335.

The early study of Nigerian languages: essays and bibliographies.
See item no. 449.

Dictionary of the Hausa language.
See item no. 456.

Manual of Hausa idioms.
See item no. 457.

A Hausa-English dictionary and English-Hausa vocabulary compiled for the governemnt of Nigeria with some notes on the Hausa people and their language by Professor D. Westermann.
See item no. 458.

Spoken Hausa.
See item no. 459.

Ethnic Groups. Hausa

Neologisms in Hausa: a sociological approach.
See item no. 460.

Hausa.
See item no. 461.

Introductory Hausa.
See item no. 462.

Studies in Hausa language and linguisitcs, in honour of F. W. Parson.
See item no. 463.

An anthology of Hausa literature in translation.
See item no. 464.

The development of Islam in West Africa.
See item no. 490.

Islam in West Africa.
See item no. 491.

Religion, legitimacy and conflict in Nigeria.
See item no. 498.

The influence of Islam on a Sudanese religion.
See item no. 500.

New religious movements in Nigeria.
See item no. 501.

Northern Nigeria.
See item no. 502.

Child-rearing practices in Northern Nigeria.
See item no. 511.

Islam and urban labor in northern Nigeria: the making of a Muslim working class.
See item no. 523.

Perspective on drought and famine in Nigeria.
See item no. 529.

Ambiguous consequences of the socialization and seclusion of Hausa women.
See item no. 530.

Silent violence: food, famine & peasantry in northern Nigeria.
See item no. 537.

Hausa medicine: illness and well-being in a West African culture.
See item no. 570.

The politics of tradition: continuity and change in Northern Nigeria, 1946–1966.
See item no. 584.

Parties and politics in Northern Nigeria.
See item no. 599.

African revolutionary: the life and times of Nigeria's Aminu Kano.
See item no. 604.

Elections in Nigeria: a grass roots perspective.
See item no. 615.

Universal primary education in Nigeria: a study of Kano State.
See item no. 776.

A history of Hausa Islamic verse.
See item no. 842.

Shaihu Umar.
See item no. 891.

The arts of the Hausa: an aspect of Islamic culture in Northern Nigeria.
See item no. 967.

Nigeria's traditional crafts.
See item no. 998.

Hausa tales and traditions: an English translation of Tatsuniyoyi na Hausa, originally compiled by Frank Edgar.
See item no. 1026.

Hausa folk-lore, customs, proverbs, etc., collected and transliterated with English translation and notes.
See item no. 1028.

Magana Hausa. Native literature, or proverbs, tales, fables and histroical fragments in the Hausa language to which is added a translation in English.
See item no. 1029.

Hausa superstitions and customs: an introduction to the folk-lore and the folk.
See item no. 1031.

The history and performance of durbar in northern Nigeria.
See item no. 1035.

Hausa architecture.
See item no. 1040.

A guide to the Gidan Makama Museum, Kano.
See item no. 1060.

Nigeria Magazine.
See item no. 1107.

Savanna. A Journal of the Environment and Social Science.
See item no. 1110.

Igbo (Ibo)

364 **Ropes of sand: studies in Igbo history and culture.**
A. E. Afigbo. Ibadan, Nigeria: University Press in association with Oxford University, 1981. 387p. 2 maps. bibliog.

The author, a distinguished historian at the University of Nigeria, Nsukka, using or and printed sources, attempts a reconstruction of Igbo history, a task as difficult a making ropes out of grains of sand. His account includes discussions of the holy city Nri, Nsukka before 1916, Aro society, the Igbo under colonialism and colonialism impact on the Igbo language. Dr. Afigbo has published in *Tarikh* 'The indigenou political systems of the Igbo', vol. 4, no. 2 (1972), p. 13–23; and 'Patterns of Igb resistance to British conquest', vol. 4, no. 3 (1973), p. 14–23. More recently he ha published a historical study, *The Igbo and their neighbors: inter-group relations Southeastern Nigeria to 1953* (Ibadan, Nigeria: University Press, 1987, 189p.).

365 **Male daughters, female husbands: gender and sex in an African society.**
Ifi Amadiume. London; Atlantic Highlands, New Jersey: Zed, 1987. 223p. 2 maps. bibliog.

This study of gender in the nineteenth and twentieth centuries was conducted in th author's home area of Nnobi, near Onitsha between 1980 and 1982 for her Universit of London doctoral thesis. The author argues that the colonial period undermined th status of women. The book contains five photographs, a bibliography (p. 211–16) an an Igbo-English glossary (p. 217–20). Of related interest is Kamene Okonjo's 'Th dual-sex political system in operation: Igbo women and community politics i Midwestern Nigeria' in *Women in Africa: studies in social and economic chang* (Stanford, California: Stanford University, 1976, p. 45–58, 287), edited by Nancy J Hafkin and Edna G. Bay. The author describes how the colonial period saw a declin in the dual-sex system in which 'each sex manages its own affairs, and women's interest are represented at all levels' (p. 45), but that in independent Nigeria there has been resurgence of traditional values.

366 **The Ibo-speaking peoples of southern Nigeria: a selected annotated list o writings, 1627–1970.**
Compiled by Joseph C[hike] [Anthony] Anafulu. Munich, West Germany: Kraus International, 1981. 321p. map.

This excellent bibliography of 3,063 entries for books, pamphlets, periodical articles conference papers, theses and a number of unpublished Nigerian government reports i organized according to twenty broad topics. These include: biography, history population, health, economy, education, archaeology, art and crafts, music, dance an theatre, linguistics, literature, politics and government, religion, social organization unpublished government reports, periodicals and newspapers published in Iboland an in Biafra. For some references very brief remarks are added. The author (1939– .) i on the staff of Nnamdi Azikiwe Library, University of Nigeria, Nsukka, Nigeria. H also published a briefly annotated compilation of 162 items as 'Igbo life & art; Igb languáge & literature: selected bibliographies' in *The Conch*, vol. 3, no. 2 (1971) p. 181–203.

367 **Among the Ibos of Nigeria: an account of the curious & interesting habits, customs & beliefs of a little known African people by one who has for many years lived amongst them on close & intimate terms.**
G[eorge] T[homas] Basden. London: Seeley, Service; Philadelphia: J. B. Lippincott, 1921. Reprinted, Frank Cass, 1966. 315p. map. bibliog.

Presents an account of the Igbo as seen by CMS missionary Basden (1873–1944) who lived in Onitsha from September 1900 until 1935. Despite his biases, '[The black man] is not controlled by logic: he is the victim of circumstance, and his policy is very largely one of drift' (p. 9.), the author presents a broad and generally informed view of Igbo culture. Topics covered include, *inter alia*: the life-cycle, slavery, sports and dance, arts, music, war, religion chiefs, etiquette, fables, folklore, proverbs, and the competition between Islam and Christianity for the Igbos. Thirty-seven photographs from the period are included. The new edition has a bibliographic note by John Ralph Willis. Basden first wrote on the Igbo in 'Notes on the Ibo country and the Ibo people, southern Nigeria' in the *Geographical Journal*, vol. 39 (1912), p. 241–47.

368 **Niger Ibos: a description of the primitive life, customs and animistic beliefs, etc., of the Ibo people of Nigeria by one who, for thirty-five years, enjoyed the privilege of their intimate confidence and friendship.**
G. T. Basden, forewords by Walter Buchanan-Smith, A. C. Onyeabo, V. N. Umunna. London: Seeley, Service, 1938. Reprinted, London: Frank Cass; New York: Barnes & Noble, 1966. 456p. map. bibliog.

A fact-filled volume with seventy illustrations about nearly all aspects of Igbo life and culture, compiled during the author's thirty-five years' residence in Igbo territory. In the penultimate chapter the Rev. Basden discusses 'Some similarities between the Israelites & the Ibos'. A useful bibliographical note has been added to the 1966 edition by John Ralph Willis (p. 439–45). Basden, known as the 'Archdeacon of the Niger' was a missionary in Nigeria from 1900 to 1935.

369 **The Igbo: a bibliographic essay.**
Mark W. DeLancey. *Africana Library Journal*, vol. 2, no. 4 (winter 1972), p. 3–30.

An informative introductory essay (p. 3–16) discusses major groupings of works (basic data, language, technology and economics, education, the arts, literature, religion, social structure, government) and is followed by an alphabetical listing of 691 items. Herbert O. Emezi published an important listing of European, North American and Nigerian dissertations on the Igbo as 'Igbo studies: a bibliography of doctoral dissertations in the humanities and social sciences, 1930–1980' in *A Current Bibliography on African Affairs*, vol. 14, no. 4 (1981–82), p. 319–30.

370 **The Ibo and Ibibio-speaking peoples of south-eastern Nigeria.**
Daryll Forde, G. I. Jones. London: International African Institute, 1967. 98p. map. bibliog. (Ethnographic Survey of Africa. Western Africa, part III).

For both of these peoples, who, in the main, live east of the Niger River, the authors describe language, physical environment, the economy, social and political organization, distinctive cultural features and religion. Much of the account is concerned with differentiating the numerous sub-groupings of the Igbo and Ibibio. Originally published in 1950, the volume has a substantial bibliography (p. 61–65, 93–94) supplemented in the new printing by an updated listing compiled by Mark W DeLancey (p. [95–98]).

371 Igbo village affairs, chiefly with reference to the village of Umueke Agbaja.

M. M. Green. London: Frank Cass, 1964. 2nd ed. 2 maps. bibliog.

First published in 1947 and based on a total of two years' fieldwork completed between 1934 and 1937, this is a study of the social organization of a small village in eastern Nigeria. The author describes in detail the economy, social structure and customary aspects of village life, the system of exogamy and 'women's organization'. In the appendix she attempts to define the rôle of 'temperament', providing a brief cultural and psychological profile of the people. A fold-out map of Nigeria in 1935 is included.

372 The king in every man: evolutionary trends in Onitsha Ibo society and culture.

Richard N. Henderson. London; New Haven, Connecticut: Yale University, 1972. 576p. 6 maps bibliog.

This massive study of pre-colonial Onitsha Igbo society uses early written accounts oral traditions and fieldwork conducted from September 1960 to July 1962 to reconstruct not only the area's history from c. 1500–1880, but also the social system kinship patterns and the 'dynamics of power, wealth, solidarity and prestige' (chapter 13). He analyses Onitsha society as a segmentary lineage system. The title refers to the potential in every man to become king. A substantial listing of works on southern Nigeria appears in the bibliography (p. 549–63). *Groundwork of the history and culture of Onitsha* (Nigeria: [n.p., n.d.] 224p. map. bibliog.) by S. I. Bosah is a valuable non academic, local history of the major market city on the Niger River. The well illustrated book includes 340 proverbs in Igbo and English (p. 175–95), a chronology of events in Onitsha, a list of Onitsha sovereigns, chieftaincy grades and copies of several treaties between the British and the king and chiefs of Onitsha.

373 The Ibo people and the Europeans: the genesis of a relationship – to 1906.

Elizabeth Isichei. New York: St. Martin's, 1973. 207p. 7 maps. bibliog.

This is the first volume of a trilogy on the Igbo people, based on archival research in England, Germany, France, Italy and Nigeria and oral traditions collected in Asaba and western Igboland. The author traces the history of the Igbo people from prehistoric times but concentrates on the period from 1830, when Richard Lander and John Lander journeyed down the River Niger, to 1906, when the British colonial and missionary presence was well established. In the epilogue to this excellent illustrated history, Professor Isichei ventures a 'colonial balance sheet' noting both the creative and destructive impacts of colonialism. Full documentation appears throughout; notes on archival sources (p. 187–91) and the list of books cited (p. 193–99) are very useful.

374 **A history of the Igbo people.**
Elizabeth Isichei. London; Basingstoke, England: Macmillan, 1976. 303p. 12 maps. bibliog.

An outstanding, lucid history of the Igbo people up to about 1973. The author divides the history into 'The first phase'; 'The middle years of Igbo history'; 'The nineteenth century'; 'The colonial experience'; and 'The uses of autonomy'. The volume has a bibliography (p. 285–92) and includes eight plates. This is part two of the author's trilogy on the Igbo, which began with *The Ibo people and the Europeans; the genesis of a relationship – to 1906* (q.v.).

375 **Ibgo worlds: an anthology of oral histories and historical descriptions.**
[Edited by] Elizabeth Isichei. Philadelphia: Institute for the Study of Human Issues, 1978. 355p. bibliog.

A vast amount of information and diverse perspectives on the Igbo are contained in this the third volume in the trilogy, presenting an anthology of excerpts from the works of foreign travellers, nineteenth-century visitors and Igbo historians, ethnographers and religious men. The editor provides bibliographic notes for all selections, a postscript offering 'Some guidelines for the amateur historian' (p. 300–08) and a glossary of Igbo terms (p. 333–50).

376 **African women: a study of the Ibo of Nigeria.**
Sylvia Leith-Ross, foreword by Lord Lugard. New York: Frederick A. Praeger, 1965. 367p. 2 maps.

A study of Igbo women in Owerri Province of eastern Nigeria (now Imo State) originally conducted in 1936–38. Igbo women are studied in four settings ranging from a highly traditional and rural to a westernized, urban centre (from the village of Nneato, to Nguru, to Owerri Town, to Port Harcourt). The author considers the Igbo to be 'the most numerous, the most adaptable, the most go-ahead, the most virile, and at the same time the most primitive' (p. 19). The Aba Riots of 1929, the rôles of education, and urbanization are among the many topics discussed. She concludes with a call for the creation of a post of 'Woman Secretary of Women's Affairs'. The brief glossary (p. 359–61) is helpful, as are the eleven photographs.

377 **Law and authority in a Nigerian tribe: a study in indirect rule.**
C. K. Meek, foreword by Lord Lugard. Oxford: Oxford University, 1937. New York: Barnes & Noble, 1970. 372p. 2 maps. bibliog.

Following the 1929 women's riots in the south-eastern provinces of Nigeria, the author, who had worked in the northern provinces for eighteen years, was assigned to study the Igbo area and the complexities of the British system of indirect rule. This study is the product of two years' research and emphasizes Igbo religion, social and political structure, titles, kingship, age-grades, and native law. The final chapter 'Practical conclusions' describes the complexities of indirect rule among 'one of the largest and most progressive tribes in Africa' (p. 365). The author, government anthropologist in the Nigerian Administrative Service, was responsible for compiling the 1921 census of Nigeria. Maps of 'Ibo sub-tribes' and 'The Southern Provinces of Nigeria' are included.

378 **Igbo political culture.**
Mazi Elechukwu Nnadibuagha Njaka. Evanston, Illinois:
Northwestern University, 1974. 173p. map. bibliog. (Studies in Political
Culture and National Integration).

The author, an Igbo, Western-educated academic, describes and analyses Igbo culture
'as it shapes and is in turn conditioned by *oha*, a sovereign abstract entity with political
power structured for social control' (Preface, p. xi, xii). He describes Igbo religion,
'Ofoism' as an aspect of politics, political values and organizations, and counter
balancing systems in the Igbo polity. A brief statement on orthography, Igbo numbers
and a glossary are included, as is a substantial bibliography (p. 159–73). The study
focuses on 'the culture of central Igbo country' in the provinces of Oka, Okigwe,
Onicha (outside the city, Onitsha) and Olu.

379 **An Igbo civilization: Nri Kingdom & hegemony.**
M. Angulu Onwuejeogwu. London: Ethnographica; Benin City,
Nigeria: Ethiope, 1981. 204p. 12 maps. bibliog.

The author uses historical accounts, archaeology, oral tradition and data gathered
during fieldwork in 1966–68 and 1970–72 to provide a diachronic and synchronic
reconstruction of Nri culture. Thirty-nine plates, thirteen figures, forty-eight tables and
a bibliography (p. 198–200) contribute to this impressive study. Professor Onwuejeogwu
is Chairman, Department of Sociology and Anthropology, University of Benin, Benin
City, Nigeria.

380 **The Afikpo Ibo of Eastern Nigeria.**
Phoebe Ottenberg. In: *Peoples of Africa*. Edited by James L. Gibbs,
Jr. New York: Holt, Rinehart & Winston, 1965. p. 3–39. bibliog.

The author's description of Afikpo culture and society as it existed in the early 1950s is
based on her fieldwork in 1951–53 and 1959–60. She delineates Afikpo village-group
values; economy; division of labour; social organization including patrilineages,
matriclans, (female-headed clans), age-grades, and social stratification; marriage
patterns and the life-cycle; political organization; law; religion; folklore; and social
change in this excellent survey.

381 **Double descent in an African society: the Afikpo village group.**
Simon Ottenberg. London; Seattle, Washington: University of
Washington, 1968. 284p. 4 maps. bibliog. (American Ethnological
Society Monograph, 47).

Professor Ottenberg examines in detail an unusual form of social organization, as it
appears in the Afikpo twenty-two village group of the eastern Igbo area. Double
unilineal descent, which stresses both maternal and paternal ties, is rare both in
Nigeria and in other world societies. The author describes matrilineal and patrilineal
groupings, and explains the system from the vantage points of both individuals and
from the group itself. Nine photographs, a glossary (p. 266–70) and a bibliography
(p. 271–78) are included. This study received the 1968 P. Amaury Talbot Prize for the
best book on West Africa.

82 **Leadership and authority in an African society: the Afikpo village-group.**

Simon Ottenberg. London; Seattle, Washington: University of Washington, 1971. 336p. 4 maps. bibliog. (American Ethnological Society Monograph, 52).

This study, based on the author's fieldwork in south-eastern Nigeria in 1951–53 and 959–60, is an analysis of individual leadership, patterns of authority and organizational orms of twenty-two closely related villages on or near the Cross River. Professor Ottenberg recounts Afikpo history and describes the four main types of village tructues and the double unilineal descent system found there. In addition to lineage, ompound, ward and village structures he describes age sets and grades and secret ocieties. The glossary (p. 319–22) and the bibliography (p. 323–28) are helpful. The uthor's 1957 doctoral dissertation at Northwestern University was *The system of uthority of the Afikpo Ibo of southeastern Nigeria*.

83 **Ibo politics: the role of ethnic unions in Eastern Nigeria.**

Audrey C. Smock. Cambridge, Massachusetts: Harvard University, 1971. 274p. map. bibliog.

Using data gathered during the first half of 1966, the author focuses on political systems of two Igbo groups in what was then Eastern Nigeria: 'Abiriba, a large village-group or town in Bende Division, and Mbaise, a populous county council area in Owerri Division, during the period from 1941 until 1966' (p. 3). She describes ethnic unions in a rural environment, in the urban context of Port Harcourt, and considers local 'micropolitical systems and their effect on local political development', demonstrating that ethnic associations preceded organization efforts of both political parties and the colonial administration and 'contributed greatly to the rapid economic and educational development of the Ibo people' (p. 3). The author rejects claims that Igbo tribalism resulted in the civil war '. . . Ibo unity rarely existed on any political ssue. Consequently, unless the definition of tribalism is severely qualified, it becomes difficult to attribute Biafran secession to Ibo ethnicity' (p. 4).

384 **Anthropological report on the Ibo-speaking peoples of Nigeria.**

Northcote W. Thomas. London: Harrison & Sons, 1913. Reprinted, New York: Negro Universities, 1969. 4 vols. 3 maps.

The government anthropologist compiled a wealth of material on the Igbo living to the east and west of the large market town of Onitsha. Vol. one concerns 'Law and custom of the Ibo of the Awka neighborhood, S. Nigeria', has details of the author's census of the area and is illustrated by twenty photographs; vol. two is an English-Ibo and Ibo-English dictionary; vol. three contains 'Proverbs, narratives, vocabularies and grammar' with comparisons between the Awka and Onitsha dialects; and vol. four reports on 'Law and custom of the Ibo of the Asaba District, S. Nigeria' and has nineteen photographs.

Ethnic Groups. Igbo (Ibo)

385 **The Igbo of southeast Nigeria.**
Victor C[hikezie] Uchendu. New York: Holt, Rinehart & Winston, 1965. 111p. map. bibliog. (Case Studies in Cultural Anthropology).
An ethnographic study of his own people by an Igbo anthropologist, who shows muc insight. The author presents an authoritative account of the Igbo worldview, villag life-styles and life-cycles, family relations, kinship, government, hospitality, status an religion. Several photographs, a map, a brief bibliography and a reading lis (p. 109–11) are included.

Dreams and deeds: achievement motivation in Nigeria.
See item no. 18.

Eastern Nigeria: a geographical review.
See item no. 37.

A geography of the eastern provinces of Nigeria.
See item no. 39.

Equiano's travels, his autobiography: the interesting narrative of the life o Olaudah Equiano, or Gustavus Vassa the African.
See item no. 82.

Beyond the Niger.
See item no. 98.

History and ethnoarchaeology in eastern Nigeria: a study of Igbo-Igala realtions with special reference to the Anambra Valley.
See item no. 144.

Igbo-Ukwu: an account ot archaeological discoveries in eastern Nigeria.
See item no. 146.

History of West Africa.
See item no. 152.

A history of Nigeria.
See item no. 163.

Africa remembered: narratives of West Africans from the ear of the slave trade.
See item no. 186.

Stateless societies in the history of West Africa.
See item no. 195.

Trade without rulers: pre-colonial economic development in south-eastern Nigeria.
See item no. 209.

Studies in southern Nigerian history.
See item no. 211.

The warrant chiefs: indirect rule in southeastern Nigeria, 1891–1929.
See item no. 221.

Christian missions in Nigeria, 1841–1891: the making of a new élite.
See item no. 222.

Nigeria and its British invaders, 1851–1920: a thematic documentary history.
See item no. 225.

Nigerian civil war, 1967–70: an annotated bibliogaphy.
See item no. 303.

The making of an African legend: the Biafra story.
See item no. 306.

Bibliography of Nigeria: a survey of anthropological and linguistic writings from the earliest times to 1966.
See item no. 331.

Handbook of ethnic units in Nigeria.
See item no. 335.

The early study of Nigerian languages: essays and bibliographies.
See item no. 449.

Igbo: a learner's dictionary.
See item no. 467.

Igbo-English dictionary based on the Onitsha dialect.
See item no. 468.

Sacrifice in Ibo religion.
See item no. 493.

Socio-ethical issues in Nigeria.
See item no. 534.

Zik: a selection from the speeches of Nnamdi Azikiwe, Governor-General of the Federation of Nigeria.
See item no. 573.

My odyssey: an autobiography.
See item no. 574.

Cultural and political aspects of rural transformation: a case study of Eastern Nigeria.
See item no. 712.

Conflict and control in an African trade union: a study of the Nigerian Coal Miners' Union.
See item no. 766.

Morning yet on creation day.
See item no. 792.

The rise of the Igbo novel.
See item no. 800.

Ethnic Groups. Igbo (Ibo)

Critical perspectives on Chinua Achebe.
See item no. 804.

Critical perspectives on Christopher Okigbo.
See item no. 821.

Onitsha market literature.
See item no. 822.

An African popular literature: a study of Onitsha Market literature.
See item no. 823.

Achebe's world: the historical and cultural context of the novels of Chinua Achebe.
See item no. 833.

Things fall apart.
See item no. 857.

Arrow of god.
See item no. 859.

Popular arts in Africa.
See item no. 913.

African images: essays in African iconology.
See item no. 923.

Ikenga figures among the north-east Igbo and the Igala.
See item no. 940.

Mbari: art and life among the Owerri Igbo.
See item no. 950.

I am not myself: the art of African masquerade.
See item no. 951.

Igbo arts: community and cosmos.
See item no. 952.

The art of eastern Nigeria.
See item no. 969.

Masked rituals of Afikpo: the context of an African art.
See item no. 975.

Mbari: art as sacrifice.
See item no. 976.

Traditional Igbo art: 1966. An exhibition of wood sculpture carved in 1965–66 from the Frank Starkweather collection.
See item no. 983.

Akwete weaving: a study of change in response to the palm oil trade in the nineteenth century.
See item no. 991.

140

Tales of land of death.
See item no. 1027.

The way we lived.
See item no. 1032.

Words are sweet: Igbo stories and storytelling.
See item no. 1033.

Igbo architecture: a study of forms, functions and typology.
See item no. 1037.

Ikenga. A Journal of African Studies.
See item no. 1106.

Tiv

386 **The Tiv people.**
Captain R[oy] [Clive] Abraham. London: Crown Agents for the
Government of Nigeria, 1940. 2nd ed. 177p. Reprinted, Farnsworth,
England: Gregg, 1968. 239p. 3 maps. bibliog.
One of the outstanding ethnographies written by an officer of the Nigerian
Administrative Service and based on one year's field research. The study describes the
Tiv's worldview, religion, social organization, folklore and social life; it includes forty-
nine photographic plates and an index of Tiv words.

387 **Akiga's story: the Tiv tribe as seen by one of its members.**
Akiga, translated and annotated by Rupert M. East, preface by D.
Westermann. London: Oxford University for the International
Institute of African Languages & Cultures, 1939. 436p. map. bibliog.
This is a remarkable account of Tiv Society by a Tiv, 'the first of his tribe to come
directly under European influence' (p. 1). Akiga ('more correctly A-kighir-ga') was the
lame and half-blind son of Sai, a prominent Tiv ritual specialist and blacksmith, with
whom he had an especially close relationship. Akiga describes Tiv history and customs,
households, farming, marriage and tribal organization, magical and ritual beliefs,
diseases and their treatment, chiefs and colonial administration of the Tiv. The volume
is organized, well annotated and indexed by East. Twenty-four excellent photographs
provide views of Tiv life.

388 **Shakespeare in the bush.**
Laura Bohannan. *Natural History*, vol. 75, no. 7 (Aug.–Sept. 1966),
p. 28–33.
This essay, many times reprinted, describes the author's attempt to tell the story of
Hamlet to a group of Tiv elders. During the telling, the elders translated the tragedy
into Tiv cultural categories and in so doing taught the anthropologist much about Tiv
kinship, politics and beliefs about the supernatural. Of special interest is Laura
Bohannan's novel about her fieldwork among the unnamed and fictionalized Tiv

published under her pen name Eleanor Smith Bowen, *Return to laughter: a anthropological novel* (New York: Harper, 1954). In the foreword to the Doubleda Anchor edition (Garden City, New York, 1964) David Riesman offers a more explic Nigerian context.

389　**The Tiv of central Nigeria.**
Laura Bohannan, Paul Bohannan. London: International African Institute, 1969. 103p. map. bibliog. (Ethnographic Survey of Africa. Western Africa, part VIII).

This excellent survey was originally published in 1953 and is based on the author fieldwork in 1949–52 among the Tiv, who numbered then some 800,000 and remai one of Nigeria's largest ethnic groups. In the 1969 reprint, a supplementar bibliography (p. 94–99) has been added to accompany the descriptions of Tiv history social and political organization, economy, migration, kinship, life-cycle and religion The Bohannans published eight volumes on the Tiv in the Human Relations Area File HRAFlex Ethnography Series, published in New Haven, Connecticut: *Tiv history an political organization* (1966, no. FF57-001); *Tiv subsistence, technology and economic* (1966, no. FF57-002); *Tiv life cycle* (1966, FF57-003); and *Tiv religion* (1969, 5 vols. FF57-004-008). The result is one of the most complete and accessible ethnographies o an African culture. Recently, a *Tiv bibliography* was compiled by Gabriel A. Gund and Heinz Jockers (Makurdi, Nigeria: Government Printer, 1985. 72p.).

390　**Justice and judgment among the Tiv.**
Paul Bohannan. New York, London: Oxford University for the International African Institute, 1957. 221p. bibliog.

The purpose of this exceptional legal anthropological study is 'to elicit the systematization of jural phenomena in the folk system of the Tiv, and to give a sociological explanation, in more general terms, which will serve as an analytica system for comparing Tiv jural institutions with those of other societies' (p. 208) Professor Bohannan explains the concept of *jir* meaning 'native court', moot o tribunal and case and describes in detail the structure of the *jir* as well as marriage debt, 'criminal', market and age-set *jir*. The author lived among the Tiv for twenty-six months and spoke Tiv fluently. A glossary of Tiv terms is included (p. 215–17), as are eight photographs.

391　**The Tiv of Nigeria.**
Paul Bohannan. In: *Peoples of Africa*. Edited by James L. Gibbs, Jr. New York: Holt, Rinehart & Winston, 1965, p. 513–46. 2 maps. bibliog.

A clear, concise, illustrated overview of the 'largest pagan group in the Norther Region of Nigeria' (p. 515). The author describes Tiv agricultural patterns, markets social organization, child training and socialization, political organization and religion He explains the functions of patrilineal organization as well as the beliefs in *akombo* supernatural forces central to the Tiv religion, and includes a brief bibliography. A poignant article about Dago'om, 'A man apart', *Natural History*, vol. 77, no. 8 (Oct 1968), p. 8–16, 66–69, contrasts madness, marginality and death in Tiv society wit western society.

392   Tiv economy.
Paul Bohannan, Laura Bohannan.   Evanston, Illinois: Northwestern
University, 1968. 265p. maps. bibliog. (Northwestern University
African Studies, no. 20).

An important volume in the Bohannans' unparalleled series of studies on the Tiv, parts
of which amplify other publications, notably their *Three source notebooks in Tiv
ethnography* (New Haven, Connecticut: HRAF, 1958). The authors describe and
analyse Tiv compounds and farms, resources, animal husbandry, hunting and
gathering, and domestic economy and offer extensive discussion of the dynamics and
structure of the market place. A chapter entitled, 'The principles of Tiv economy'
provides an analysis of the complex exchange system of which market exchange is but
one form.

393   Sex roles in the Nigerian Tiv farm household.
Mary E. Burfisher, Nadine R. Horenstein.   West Hartford,
Connecticut: Kumarian, 1985. 62p. map. bibliog. (Women's Roles &
Gender Differences in Development).

This study examines the 'division of labor, income and financial obligations . . . and
the implications of these divisions for the ability and incentives of each sex to adopt
technologies introduced by the agricultural development project' (p. xiii). With
quantitative measures of labour for each sex and each crop produced on a Tiv farm,
the authors are able to clearly establish the differential impact of development projects
on men and women. Tables, charts, diagrams, data-rich appendices and a bibliography
(p. 59–62) make this monograph a valuable resource for agricultural project planners.
The authors' article 'Sex roles and development effects on the Nigerian Tiv farm
household', *Rural Africana*, no. 21 (winter 1985), p. 31–49, summarizes these same
findings. The authors are, respectively, in the US Department of Agriculture, Africa
and Middle East Branch, and in the US Agency for International Development,
Women in Development Program.

394   Tiv song.
Charles Keil.   Chicago; London: University of Chicago, 1979. 301p.
bibliog.

This study is based on field research from November 1965–September 1966 and
May–June 1967; the author presents a profound and thorough analysis of Tiv
ethnomusicology. He discusses Tiv music, composers, songs, techniques and style,
placing all in the context of Tiv culture and developing a theory of Tiv expression using
metaphors of circles and angles. The book includes a bibliography (p. 285–89), an
index of Tiv terms (p. 291–95), twenty-two photographic plates and nineteen figures.

A dictionary of the Tiv language.
See item no. 475.

The arts of the Benue: to the roots of tradition.
See item no. 973.

Yoruba

395 **Rituals of power: the politics of *orisa* worship in Yoruba society.**
Andrew Herman Apter. PhD thesis, Yale University, New Haven,
Connecticut, 1987. 315 leaves. bibliog. (Available from University
Microfilms, Ann Arbor, Michigan, 1988).

'Based on 26 months of fieldwork among the Ekiti Yoruba of Nigeria, the study
analyzes *orisa* cult organization, ritual performances and religious cosmology from two
complementary perspectives'. This political interpretation of Yoruba religion offers an
'external' view which 'identifies the corporate bases of collective action in Yoruba
political and ritual systems' and an 'internal' or dialectical view which 'explicates the
language and symbolism of religious experience'. Together they show 'how symbolic
idioms of revitalization and renewal, including muted expressions of deposition and
fission, sublimate the contested distribution of political power between Yoruba kings
and their chiefs' (author's abstract). Apter's 'The historiography of Yoruba myth and
ritual' in *History in Africa* (Los Angeles), vol. 14 (1987), p. 1–25, provides an excellent
survey on the subject.

396 **An introduction to Yoruba history.**
J. A. Atanda. Ibadan, Nigeria: Ibadan University, 1980. 77p. bibliog.

This small book is an expanded version of 'Talks on Yoruba history' given on Radio
Nigeria between January and April 1974. Here the author intends to 'present an
outline picture of the Yoruba people – their origin, their political, cultural and
intellectual development' (Preface). The book complements more detailed studies, by
Samuel Johnson, entitled, *The history of the Yorubas from the earliest times to the
beginning of the British Protectorate* (r.v.) and Robert S. Smith, entitled *Kingdoms of
the Yoruba* (q.v.). Included among the fifteen photographs are portraits of several
Yoruba leaders. The author is in the Department of History at the University of
Ibadan, Ibadan, Nigeria.

397 **Yoruba beliefs and sacrificial rites.**
Joseph Ọmọṣade Awolalu, foreword by Geoffrey Parrinder. London:
Longman, 1979. 203p. bibliog.

This examination of Yoruba traditional religion is divided into two parts. Part one
'Beliefs', describes beliefs in the Supreme Being Olodumare, in divinities and spirits, in
the ancestors and in mysterious powers including medicine and witchcraft. Part two
'Sacrificial rites', considers elements of worship, divination and the complexities of
sacrifice. Finally, the author addresses the effects of Islam, Christianity and education
on traditional rites. Sixteen photographs are included. This work is a revision of the
author's 1971 University of Ibadan doctoral thesis, *Sacrifice in the religion of the
Yoruba*. The author is in the University of Ibadan Department of Religious Studies,
Ibadan, Nigeria.

398   **The Yoruba of southwestern Nigeria: an indexed bibliography.**
Compiled by David E. Baldwin, Charlene M. Baldwin. Boston,
Massachusetts: G. K. Hall, 1976. 269p.
An unannotated alphabetical listing of 3,488 articles, books, some government
publications and theses on the Yoruba. The authors explain their methodology and the
'truly comprehensive nature' of their bibliography in the introduction (p. vii–xiii) and
emphasize their special concerns with anthropology, history, linguistics, sociology,
economics and Yoruba authored literature. A listing of bibliographies and periodicals
consulted precedes the main references. A detailed subject index (p. 257–69) provides
access to the material. The Baldwins were resident in Lalupon near Ibadan during
1966–68. Janet L. Stanley provides an informative critique of the volume in 'Review
essay: Yoruba bibliography', *Journal of African Studies*, vol. 4, no. 4 (winter 1977–78),
p. 474–83, in which she concludes that the work is 'an unfinished product whose utility
and authority must be questioned' (p. 483). Despite flaws, this work contains a wealth
of material on one of Nigeria's largest and most studied groups.

399   **The rise and fall of an African utopia: a wealthy theocracy in
comparative perspective.**
Stanley R. Barrett.   Waterloo, Ontario: Wilfred Laurier University,
1977. 251p. 2 maps. bibliog. (Development Perspectives, 1).
This is a study of the Yoruba utopian community of Olowo, located on the coast of
Nigeria. The community was founded in 1947, thrived for twenty years and then
suddenly declined. The author contrasts Olowo with a nearby village, Talika, and
similar movements in Africa and elsewhere. Based on dissertation fieldwork from July
1969 to July 1970 and one month in 1972, the methodology for the study is described in
an appendix. The book contains a brief Yoruba and Arabic glossary and a bibliography
(p. 241–46).

400   **The Yoruba of southeastern Nigeria.**
William Bascom.   New York: Holt, Rinehart & Winston, 1969. (Case
Studies in Cultural Anthropology). Reprinted, Prospect Heights,
Illinois: Waveland, 1984. 118p. map. bibliog.
This is perhaps the best introduction to one of Africa's largest and most highly
urbanized ethnic groups. The author, whose years of fieldwork date back to 1937–38,
here largely confines his ethnographic account to the Yoruba of Ife, an artistic and
ritual centre for the entire culture. An enormous amount of information is condensed
into the subject areas of origins and history, economics, government, social structure,
the life-cycle, the spiritual cycle, deities, aesthetics and a brief postscript. A useful
map, several photographs, a bibliography and a reading list with brief annotations
(p. 116–18) are included.

401   **Sources of Yoruba history.**
Edited by S[aburi] O. Biobaku.   Oxford: Clarendon, 1973. 268p.
bibliog. (Oxford Studies in African Affairs).
An invaluable collection of articles on the Yoruba: 'Contemporary written sources' and
'Traditional history' by Robin Law; 'The literature of the Ifa cult' by Wándé
Abímbólá; 'Oriki' [praise-names] by Chief J. A. Ayorinde; 'Proverbs, songs, and
poems' by Chief I. O. Delano; 'Ceremonies' by Oyin Ogunba; 'Archaeology' by Frank
Willett; 'Art in metal' by Denis Williams; 'Art in wood' by Father K. F. Carroll; 'The

Yoruba language in Yoruba history' by Abiọdun Adetugbo; 'Political and social structure' by P. C. Lloyd; and 'Yoruba warfare and weapons' by Robert Smith. The topical bibliography (p. 250–62) is excellent. The editor was director of the Yoruba Historical Research Scheme in 1956 and Vice-Chancellor of the University of Lagos in 1972.

402 **The soul of Nigeria.**
    Isaac O. Delano. London: T. W. Laurie, 1937. Reprinted, Nendeln,
    Liechtenstein: Kraus Reprint, 1973. 251p; New York: AMS Press,
    1978. 251p.
An interesting, personal and wide-ranging, view of Yoruba society in the 1920s and 1930s. The author describes religion, history, language, medicine men, trade and industry, government, and native games, as well as many other topics. He writes, 'On train, canoe and lorry I gathered my information from the rank and file of Nigerians, much of which I had to sift very carefully to avoid repetition, uncertainty and irrelevancy' (p. 7). There are forty-five leaves of plates; twenty-three photographs from the period contribute to his text.

403 **Nigerian studies, or the religious and political system of the Yoruba.**
    R. E. Dennett. London: Macmillan, 1910. Reprinted, London: Frank
    Cass, 1968. 235p. map. (Cass Library of African Studies, General
    Studies, no. 48).
Despite the prejudices and 'primitive' ideas of a European writing early in this century, Dennett has compiled extensive information about the Yoruba belief system, gods, government and land laws, drawing often on the work of Colonel A. B. Ellis, Bishop S. Johnson and the *Nigerian Chronicle*. The addendum contains an account from the *Nigerian Chronicle* of 25 February 1910 concerning 'The smallpox god. How its priests and priestesses ply their inhuman trade' and the fold-out map shows Nigeria in 1910. Fifteen photographs are included.

404 **The Yoruba today.**
    J. S. Eades. Cambridge: Cambridge University, 1980. 188p. 5 maps.
    bibliog. (Changing Cultures Series).
This is the best available overview of the history, economy, urbanism, political organization, belief systems, kinship systems and social stratification of Nigeria's second largest ethnic group, with an estimated population of fifteen million. Very useful maps, ten photographs and a bibliography (p. 169–81) are provided. At the time of publication, the author was Lecturer in Social Anthropology, University of Kent, Canterbury, and had written extensively on the Yoruba migrants in northern Ghana.

405 **The Yoruba-speaking peoples of the Slave Coast of West Africa, their**
    religion, manners, customs, laws, languages, etc., with an appendix
    containing a comparison of the Tshi, Gã, Ewe, and Yoruba languages.
    A[lfred] B[urdon] Ellis. London: Chapman & Hall, 1894. Reprinted,
    Oosterhout N.B., The Netherlands: Anthropological Publications,
    1966; London: Curzon Press, 1974. 402p. 2 maps.
The author (1852–94) describes the peoples situated between Badagry and the Benin river in what is now Nigeria. In particular, he provides an early account of gods

religious beliefs and rituals; measurements of time; ceremonies at birth, marriage and death; systems of government; laws and customs; and language. Colonel Ellis, with his systematic account of rituals and myths, dominated the field of Yoruba studies for fifty years; however, according to N. A. Fadipe, in his book *The Sociology of the Yoruba* (p. 282) (q.v.), his work was flawed by his incomplete knowledge of the Yoruba language. The volume contains a selection of 250 Yoruba proverbs, sixteen aphorisms, five riddles and six folktales. The appendix has 'A comparison of the Tshi (or Oji), Gã, Ewe, and Yoruba languages' (p. 305–402).

406 **The sociology of the Yoruba.**
Nathaniel Akinremi Fadipẹ, edited by Francis Olu. Okediji, Ọladẹjọ O. Okediji. Ibadan, Nigeria: Ibadan University, 1970. 354p. map. bibliog.
This macro-sociological study of the Yoruba was extracted from the 1,000 page, 1939 doctoral thesis of Fadipẹ (1839–1944) at the University of London. Fadipẹ's work covers ethnic history, language, marital process, family and kinship, economic and political organization, associations, religion and morals, social psychology, social control, and socio-cultural change. A glossary of Yoruba words and phrases is included and the editors, sociologists at the Universities of Ibadan and Lagos, add a selected bibliography and references (p. 335–48), as well as an informative introduction (p. 1–20). In their view, Fadipẹ's 'monumental work . . . qualifies him as the foremost expert on Yoruba studies. There is hardly any scholarly work of note on the Yoruba in the second half of this century which has not used Fadipẹ's manuscript as the baseline for self information or selected some aspects of his work as points of departure' (p. 19).

407 **The Yoruba-speaking peoples of south-western Nigeria.**
Daryll Forde. London: International African Institute, 1969. 103p. map. bibliog. (Ethnographic Survey of Africa. Western Africa, part IV).
This ethnographic account of the Yoruba, originally published in 1951, describes their language, environment, economy, political structure, social organization and distinctive cultural features. Nine geographic sub-units of the Yoruba are examined as well. The 1969 reprint includes a bibliography (p. 84–100), revised and updated by Peter Morton-Williams and E. C. Rowlands. There is a large fold-out map of the Yoruba area.

408 **Orisha: the gods of Yorubaland.**
Judith [Illsley] Gleason. New York: Atheneum, 1971. 122p.
A creative effort attempting to describe the powers and mythology of thirteen best-known *orisha* or gods of the traditional Yoruba. Eshu, Oba, Obatala, Oduduwa, Ogun, Oranyan, Schun, Oya, Shango, Obaluaiye, Yemonja, Ifa and Orunmila are presented through poems, first-person accounts, or stories. A brief afterword and supplementary notes offer a broader context for understanding the *orisha*. Art by Aduni Olorisa, a Yoruba priestess, appears throughout the book. The author explores Yoruba religion further in *Oya: in praise of the goddess* (Boston, Massachusetts: Shambhala, 1987. 304p.) and, with Awotunde Aworinde and John Olaniyi Ogundipe, in *A recitation of Ifa, oracle of the Yoruba* (New York: Grossman, 1973. 338p.)

147

409 **The history of the Yorubas from the earliest times to the beginning of the British Protectorate.**
Rev. Samuel Johnson, edited by Obadiah Johnson. London: Routledge & Kegan Paul, 1921. Reprinted, Westport, Connecticut: Negro Universities Press, 1970. 684p. map.

The manuscript of this impressive history was completed and sent to an English publisher in 1899, who 'misplaced' it. It was finally located, but the author had died in 1901; his brother, the editor, finished rewriting it in 1916 but its publication was delayed by the war until 1921, a year after Obadiah Johnson's death. In this lengthy volume, the author and editor provide a sketch of the Yoruba language (p. xxiii–lv), and a discussion of religion, government, names, towns and villages, land law, manners and customs (p. 1–140). The bulk of the book consists of Yoruba history from its mythological origins to the establishment of the British Protectorate in August, 1893. In the appendices are twelve treaties and agreements and lists of kings and notable events. The volume has a brief index and a fold-out 'map of the Yoruba country'.

410 **Yoruba towns and cities: an enquiry into the nature of urban social phenomena.**
Eva Krapf-Askari. Oxford: Clarendon, 1969. 195p. 3 maps. bibliog.

The author provides an informative description of Yoruba settlement patterns, their layout and appearance and the important rôle of kinship and descent in structuring neighbourhoods. In addition she discusses the rôles of interest groups, associations, and social stratification. Six town plans (of Ife, Ilesha, Ado Ekiti the places of Abeokuta, the palace in Qwo and of Ondo) are included as well as three maps. The bibliography (p. 165–76) is extensive. Much of this book derives from the author's 1964 bachelor's thesis at Oxford University and from her fieldwork in 1964–66.

411 **Yoruba land law.**
P. C. Lloyd. London; New York; Ibadan, Nigeria: Oxford University for the Nigerian Institute of Social and Economic Research, 1962. 378p. 11 maps. bibliog.

This volume is the author's classic report on customary land law conducted during 1956–59 when he was Land Research Officer in the Ministry of Lands and Labour of the Western Region of Nigeria. In it he describes customary law, Yoruba towns, legal concepts, and land rights in the kingdoms of Ondo, Kjebu, Ado Ekiti and Egba, and then discusses the problems of succession, land and credit, land sales, equity and local government.

412 **The Yoruba of Nigeria.**
P. C. Lloyd. In: *Peoples of Africa.* Edited by James L. Gibbs, Jr. New York: Holt, Rinehart & Winston, 1965. p. 547–82. map. bibliog.

An excellent, illustrated summary of Yoruba culture and society, describing history, urbanism, agricultural practices, crafts, markets, lineage organization, age-grades and sets, marriages, child training and socialization, political organization, religion and social change. The author is careful to emphasize the diversity of this huge ethnic group about which he generalizes. The term 'Yoruba' then applied to some 6,000,000 people, divided into fifty kingdoms, but was originally used only for the people of the Oyo kingdom. 'One could, I think, write a textbook on comparative political systems, drawing almost all one's examples from the Yoruba!' (p. 551). Lloyd carried out fieldwork from 1949 to 1959 and was head of the Department of Sociology at the University of Ibadan in Nigeria before joining the Centre for West African Studies at the University of Birmingham, England.

413 **The cult of Ifá among the Yoruba. Vol. 1: folk practice and the art.**
E[lizabeth] M. McClelland.   London: Ethnographica, 1982. 125p.
map. bibliog.

'The purpose of this work is to record in permanent form, and so preserve, some of the important body of Yoruba oral literature known as the Odù Corpus and to describe and analyze the system which derives from it' (Foreword, p. 5). The material presented here was collected during 1958–67 in Western Nigeria. The divining and healing cult and its oral literature containing its history, mythology and philosophy are of enormous importance in traditional Yoruba culture. In six chapters the author explains: 'What is the Ifá cult?'; 'The divination system'; The Odù corpus'; 'The Ifa priest or *babaláwo*'; 'Medical practice'; and 'Effect on the cult of wider contacts'. An appendix lists the prohibitions associated with the Odù and a bibliography lists relevant literature. Christoph Staewen and Friderun Schoenberg's *Ifa: das Wort der Götter* (Ifa: the word of the gods) (Wiesbaden, GFR: Franz Steiner, 1982. 235p.) is another recent study of this major Yoruba belief system.

414 **Esu Elegbara, the Yoruba god of chance and uncertainty: a study in Yoruba mythology.**
Ayodele Ogundipe.   PhD thesis, Indiana University, Bloomington, Indiana, 1978. 475 leaves. 2 vols. bibliog. (Available from University Microfilms, Ann Arbor, Michigan, 1979. Order no. 7900410).

The author investigates Esu, variously called a trickster god, the Devil and a phallic god, as a mythological personage in Yoruba belief. Based on fieldwork in Nigeria from 1966 to 1969 and using a phenomenological approach, this work examines myths, folksongs and praise poetry in which Esu appears. The study argues that Esu is the personification of the principle of chance and uncertainty deriving from Yoruba notions of impermanence and change and the balancing ideas of fate and destiny. Esu as he appears in Dahomey (Republic of Benin) and in Brazil is also discussed. Esu is discussed at length in Robert D. Pelton's *The trickster in West Africa: a study of mythic irony and sacred delight* (Berkeley, California: University of California, 1980 Hermeneutics: Studies in the History of Religions)).

415 **Ijeshas and Nigerians: the incorporation of a Yoruba kingdom, 1890s–1970s.**
J. D. Y. Peel.   Cambridge: Cambridge University, 1983. 346p.
9 maps. bibliog. (African Studies Series, no. 39).

While lecturing at the University of Ife from September 1973 to August 1975 and again during July–August 1979, Peel researched the history and social relations of the nearby Yoruba town of Ilesha (population about 180,000) and its inhabitants, the Ijeshas. This historical sociological study demonstrates how 'it is communities, rather than classes, which are able to generate powerful enduring identities and so to dominate the pattern in which interests are pursued in the public sphere' (p. 262). The author used extensive interviews, oral traditions and lengthy questionnaire surveys, plus archival and published materials, to provide a full account of the pre-colonial kingdom and the

149

social, economic and political changes during the twentieth-century incorporation of the kingdom into the modern state of Nigeria. Peel is Charles Booth Professor of Sociology at the University of Liverpool, England.

416 **Yoruba religion and medicine in Ibadan.**
George E. Simpson. Ibadan, Nigeria: Ibadan University, 1980. 195p. bibliog.

This is a detailed study of magic, witchcraft, religion and medicine in Ibadan in 1964 based on the data collected by the author from 272 'rank-and-file' informants and thirty-five 'persons who were reputed to be especially well informed about traditional Yoruba religion, or medicine, or both' (Preface, p. xi). The author provides substantial descriptions of the major *orisa* or deities, traditional medical practices, and of changes in both medicine and religion resulting from the influences of Islam, Christianity and modern medicine. Appendices contain copies of the interview forms and demographic information on the 272 informants. The bibliography (p. 194–95) is brief but useful and twenty-six rather faded photographs are included.

417 **Kingdoms of the Yoruba.**
Robert S. Smith. London: James Curry; Madison, Wisconsin: University of Wisconsin Press, 1988. 3rd ed. 174p. (Studies in African History, 2).

A 'minor classic' and a fine introduction to Yoruba history up to the end of the nineteenth century. Smith discusses in particular the Oyo Kingdom for which he proposes a chronology from 1774 to 1838. Following a description of 'the primacy of Ife', he describes the kingdoms of the east (Ijesha, Ekiti, Igbomina, Owo and Ondo), the west (Ketu, Shabe and Dassa), the south (Ijebu, Egba, Egbado and Lagos), traditions, war and relationships between the *oba* and his people. The bibliography is succinct and practical. The first edition was published in 1969, and the second in 1976. Smith has been Senior Lecturer and Professor of History at Lagos, Ife and Ibadan Universities in Nigeria.

418 **Ife, the holy city of the Yoruba: an annotated bibliography.**
Compiled by Janet Stanley, Richard Olaniyan, with contributions from Depo Adenle. Ile-Ife, Nigeria: University of Ife, 1982. 228p.

This excellent annotated compilation of 706 references on the important Yoruba city covers all relevant sources including archival records, seminar papers and student essays, and German and French publications, and is not limited by any time period. Entries are grouped by topic: history, religion, art, archaeology, sociology and demography, and miscellany. The author index (p. 195–228) lists each publication after its author. Stanley was a reference librarian and Olaniyan is a historian at the University of Ife (now Obafemi Awolowo University).

Dreams and deeds: achievement motivation in Nigeria.
See item no. 18.

Abeokuta and the Cameroons mountains: an exploration.
See item no. 77.

Journal of a second expedition into the interior of Africa for the Bight of benin to Soccatoo to which is added the journal of Richard Lander from Kano to the sea-coast, partly by a more eastern route.
See item no. 78.

Travels and explorations in Yorubaland, 1854–1858.
See item no. 79.

Journal of an expedition up the Niger and Tshadda Rivers undertaken by Macgregor Laird in connection with the British government in 1854.
See item no. 80.

Search for a place: black separatism and Africa, 1860.
See item no. 81.

The Niger journal of Richard and John Lander.
See item no. 83.

Seventeen years in the Yoruba country. Memorials of Anna Hinderer, wife of the Rev. David Hinderer, C.M.S. missionary in western Africa, gathered from her journals and letters.
See item no. 85.

The voice of Africa, being an account of the travels of the German Inner African Exploration Expedition in the years 1910–1912.
See item no. 94.

In my father's country: a Nigerian journey.
See item no. 99.

Yoruba warfare in the nineteenth century.
See item no. 177.

Revolution and power politics in Yorubaland, 1840–1893: Ibadan expansion and the rise of Ekitiparapo.
See item no. 178.

The Egba and their neighbors, 1842–1872.
See item no. 183.

Africa remembered: narratives by West Africans from the era of the slave trade.
See item no. 186.

The political economy of a pre-colonial African state, 1830–1900.
See item no. 188.

A history of Lagos, Nigeria: the shaping of an African city.
See item no. 189.

The growth of Islam among the Yoruba, 1841–1908.
See item no. 191.

Poverty in nineteenth-century Yorubaland.
See item no. 197.

Ethnic Groups. Yoruba

The Oyo Empire, c. 1600–c. 1836: a West African imperialism in the era of the Atlantic slave trade.
See item no. 203.

The Yoruba and Edo-speaking peoples and their neighbors before 1600.
See item no. 210.

Western Yoruba land under European rule 1889–1945: a comparative analysis of French and British colonialism.
See item no. 226.

The new Oyo Empire: indirect rule and change in Western Nigeria, 1894–1934.
See item no. 227.

Holy Johnson, pioneer of African nationalism, 1836–1917.
See item no. 229.

West African resistance: the military response to colonial occupation.
See item no. 240.

Colonial West Africa: collected essays.
See item no. 242.

West African chiefs: their changing status under colonial rule and independence.
See item no. 243.

Victorian Lagos: aspects of nineteenth century Lagos life.
See item no. 246.

Lugard and the Abeokuta uprising: the demise of Egba independence.
See item no. 250.

A preface to modern Nigeria: the 'Sierra Leoneans' in Yoruba, 1830–1890.
See item no. 266.

Marrying well: marriage, status and social change among the educated elite in colonial Lagos.
See item no. 271.

Nigerian women mobilized: women's political activity in Southern Nigeria, 1900–1965.
See item no. 272.

The Lagos consulate, 1851–1861.
See item no. 289.

Herbert Macaulay, Nigerian patriot.
See item no. 293.

Bibliography of Nigeria: a survey of anthropological and linguistic writings from the earliest times to 1966.
See item no. 331.

Handbook of ethnic units in Nigeria.
See item no. 335.

Professional associations, ethnic and discipline among Yoruba traditional healers of Nigeria.
See item no. 565.

Awo: the autobiography of Chief Obafemi Awolowo.
See item no. 572.

Patrons and power: creating a political community in metropolitan Lagos.
See item no. 586.

Hegemony and culture: politics and religion change among the Yoruba.
See item no. 612.

Nigerian politics: the ordeal of Chief Awolowo, 1960–65.
See item. no. 632.

Cocoa, custom, and socio-economic change in rural Western Nigeria.
See item no. 689.

Nigerian cocoa families: an economic survey of Yoruba cocoa farming families.
See item no. 696.

The politics of transporting.
See item no. 757.

A writer and his gods: a study of the importance of Yoruba myths and religious ideas to the writing of Wole Soyinka.
See item no. 810.

Myth, literature and the African world.
See item no. 830.

Yoruba oral tradition: poetry in music, dance and drama.
See item no. 838.

Hubert Ogunde: the making of Nigerian theatre.
See item no. 841.

The Yoruba popular travelling theatre of Nigeria.
See item no. 843.

Features of Yorùbá oral poetry.
See item no. 847.

Yoruba poetry: an anthology of traditional poems.
See item no. 849.

African art in cultural perspective: an introduction.
See item no. 914.

African art in motion: icon and act.
See item no. 931.

Flash of the spirit: African and Afro-American art and philosophy.
See item no. 932.

African art: an introduction.
See item no. 934.

William Bascom: in memoriam.
See item no. 937.

Contemporary art in Nigeria.
See item no. 940.

Yoruba religious carving: pagan & religious sculpture in Nigeria and Dahomey.
See item no. 948.

The arts of the Egungun among Yoruba peoples.
See item no. 956.

African artistry: technique and aesthetics in Yoruba scuplture.
See item no. 957.

Gèdèlé: art and female power among the Yoruba.
See item no. 958.

The living arts and crafts of Ile-Ife.
See item no. 960.

Yoruba sculpture of West Africa.
See item no. 964.

Ibeji: Zwillingsfiguren der Yoruba/Twin figures of the Yoruba.
See item no. 984.

Black gods and kings: Yoruba art at UCLA.
See item no. 985.

The sculpture of Western Nigeria.
See item no. 987.

Ife in the history of West African sculpture.
See item no. 988.

Adire cloth in Nigeria: the preparation and dyeing of indigo patterned cloth among the Yoruba.
See item no. 992.

Yoruba beaded crowns: sacred regalia of the Olokuku of Okuku.
See item no. 993.

Yoruba beadwork: art of Nigeria.
See item no. 997.

Yoruba hairstyles: a selection of hairstyles in southern Nigeria.
See item no. 999.

Crafts and cooperation in Western Nigeria: a sociological contribution to indigenous economics.
See item no. 1000.

155

Other groups

419· **The Kanuri of Bornu.**
Ronald Cohen. New York: Holt, Rinehart & Winston, 1967. (Case Studies in Cultural Anthropology). Reprinted, Prospect Heights, Illinois: Waveland, 1986. 125p. map. bibliog.

An ethnographic case study of the Kanuri, the largest ethnic group in north-eastern Nigeria, based on the author's twenty-six months of fieldwork in 1956–57, 1964 and 1965 and his 1960 University of Wisconsin doctoral thesis, *The structure of Kanuri society.* Following a discussion of the setting and history of the Kanem-Bornu Empire and the Kingdom of Bornu, the author shows 'how each of the major sectors of Kanuri social life, the family, the household, the individual life experience, the political, and economic systems, are related to one another, through their use of the household organization and its modes of behavior' (p. 11). Through the household 'a building block . . . upon which the rest of the complicated activities of the Bornu society rests' are carried out the organized activities making possible the 'maintenance, continuity, and evolution' of Kanuri society (p. 11). The new edition contains 'Epilogue, 1986' summarizing the events of the previous twenty-five years. The author is Professor of Anthropology at the University of Florida, Gainesville, Florida.

420 **The Anaguta of Nigeria: suburban primitives.**
Stanley Diamond. In: *Three African tribes in transition.* Edited by Julian H. Steward. Urbana, Illinois: University of Illinois, 1967. vol. 1, p. 360–505. 9 maps. bibliog. (Contemporary Change in Traditional Societies).

This ethnography describes a 'virtually unknown Nigerian people, whose culture is vanishing' (p. 363), these being a traditional 'pagan' group of the Jos Plateau of central Nigeria. It also discusses the peoples of the 'Middle Belt' in general, including 'the Plateau pagans'; the colonial economy of the region especially Unilever and the United Africa Company of Nigeria; the growth of Jos; ethnic relations; and the complex process of change confronting a small group of people. Numerous photographs by Olga Diamond are included, as is a useful bibliography (p. 501–05). The study is based on fieldwork done in the late 1950s.

421 **A bibliography of Efik-Ibibio-speaking peoples of the Old Calabar Province of Nigeria, 1668–1964.**
Compiled by A. N. Ekpiken. Ibadan, Nigeria: Ibadan University, 1970. 96p. map. (Ibadan University Library Bibliographical Series).

The compiler lists, and for some items annotates, 1,513 source materials on the Efik and Ibibio of south-eastern Nigeria. The twenty topical categories include intelligence reports, district and provincial reports and works in local languages as well as the more usual subjects. The volume is well indexed. Of interest also is Daniel A. Offiong's article 'Witchcraft among the Ibibio of Nigeria', *African Studies Review*, vol. 26, no. 1 (March 1983), p. 107–24, in which he analyses the Akpan Ekwong witch-purge crusade in Cross River State in 1978–79.

422 **Marriage and family among the Yakö in south-eastern Nigeria.**
Daryll Forde. London: International African Institute, 1951. 121p. 2nd ed. map. bibliog.

This ethnography of the Yakö, then a group of about 20,000 people living east of the Cross River in Eastern Nigeria, was carried out in 1935 and 1939 and is 'aimed primarily at analysis of the social values and institutions involved in the establishment and maintenance of marital relationships' (p. 1). The first edition was published in 1941 (London School of Economics and Political Science Series of Monographs on Social Anthropology, no. 5). The Yakö are one of the few societies practising double unilineal descent. Professor Forde's numerous publications on the Yakö include *Yakö studies* (London: Oxford University for the International African Institute, 1964. 288p.).

Ethnic Groups. Other groups

423 **Peoples of the Niger-Benue confluence: the Nupe, the Igbira, the Igala, the Idoma-speaking peoples.**
Daryll Forde, Paula Brown, Robert G[elston] Armstrong. London: International African Institute, 1970. rev. ed. 162p. maps. bibliog. (Ethnographic Survey of Africa. Western Africa, part X).
Presents four excellent ethnographic surveys, each with a bibliography and a supplementary bibliography (p. 156–57) in the 1970 edition. These are: the Nupe (p. 17–52) by Forde; the Igbira (p. 55–74) by Brown; the Igala (p. 77–90) and the Idoma-speaking peoples (p. 91–155) by Armstrong. The volume was originally published in 1955 and contains a fold-out ethnographic map of the area.

424 **Peoples of the plateau area of Northern Nigeria.**
Harold D. Gunn. London: International African Institute, 1953. 111p. map. bibliog. (Ethnographic Survey of Africa. Western Africa, part VII).
Offers a synthesis of existing fragmentary ethnographic information on an ethnically complex area of central northern Nigeria. The peoples whose demography, social and political organization, economy, and distinctive cultural features are described here are: the Jerawa group of Bauchi, Plateau and Zaria Provinces; the Chawai of Zaria Province; the Afusare (Hill Jarawa) and related peoples of Bauchi and Plateau Provinces; the Birom, Aten and Irigwe; the Aten (Ganawuri, Jal); the Irigwe; and 'some unclassified communities of Bauchi and Plateau Provinces: the Pyem ofk Gindiri District, the peoples of south-western Lere District' (p. 101–09). As in all volumes of this valuable series, an excellent fold-out map of the area is included.

425 **Pagan peoples of the central area of Northern Nigeria.**
Harold D. Gunn. London: International African Institute, 1956. 146p. map. bibliog. (Ethnographic Survey of Africa. Western Africa, part XII).
This is a survey of an ethnically complex and little described region comprizing more than fifty named communities classified by the author into six larger groupings in what were then the provinces of Bauchi, Benue, Kano, Niger, Plateau and Zaria. Population, social structure, religion, life-cycle and dress are described for the peoples of the Bauchi-Kano borderland (the Butawa, Kudawa, Ningawa, Warkawa and others) and some communities of central and eastern Zaria Province (the Kurama, the hill peoples of Lere and Kauru Districts, Zaria Emirate, the Katab group of tribes), and the Kajuru, Kadara and Kuturmi. The bibliography (p. 138–41) is useful, as is the fold-out map of the region.

426 **Peoples of the middle Niger region, Northern Nigeria.**
Harold D. Gunn, F. P. Conant. London: International African Institute, 1960. 138p. map. bibliog. (Ethnographic Survey of Africa. Western Africa, part XV).
Based on fieldwork by Gunn in 1949–51 and Dr. Conant in 1953–54 and 1957–59, this volume of the invaluable Ethnographic Survey of Africa contains profiles of peoples of what were then the Ilorin, Sokoto, Zaria, Niger, Kabba and Benue Provinces of Northern Nigeria, numbering around 500,000. These include: the riverine peoples of Yauri and Borgu (Gungawa, Yaurawa, Bakarawa, Lopawa, Larawa); peoples of

Kontagora and Zuru (Kambari, Dakakari, Dukawa); and peoples of the north-eastern hinterland of the middle Niger (Achipawa, Kamuku, Bassa, Gwari and Koro). The bibliography (p. 128–36) is characteristically detailed and a large map of the region is included.

427 **The Sobo of the Niger Delta: a work dealing with the history and languages of the people inhabiting the Sobo (Urhobo) Division, Warri Province, Southern Nigeria, and the geography of their land.**
John Waddington Hubbard, foreword by G. B.Stooke. Zaria, Nigeria: Gaskiya Corporation, [1948]. 369p. 5 maps.
Hubbard worked for years in the Niger Delta as a missionary of the Church Missionary Society, and spoke Isoko. Here he presents extensive ethnographic and linguistic material on the Urhobos, the Western Ijaw and the Aboh-Igbo peoples of the delta region. Twenty-five photographs are included. The foreword is dated 10 June 1948.

428 **The kingdom of Sukur: a Northern Nigerian Ichabod.**
Anthony H. M. Kirk-Greene. *The Nigerian Field*, vol. 25, no. 2 (April 1960), p. 67–96. bibliog.
This description of a little-known group of 5,033 people (in 1953) in Adamawa Province is based on both the author's observations, made when he toured the Madagali District as District Officer, Mubi, in 1954, and on notes made thirty years earlier by F. H. MacBride and H. S. Kulp. Kirk-Greene recounts Sukur history, and describes their views of divine kingship and their chief, the Llidi, the courtiers and smithing guilds, and annual ceremonies. Fourteen photographs taken while on tour are included.

429 **Enculturation and socialization in an Ijaw village.**
Philip E. Leis. New York: Holt, Rinehart & Winston, 1972. (Case Studies in Cultural Anthropology). Reprinted, New York: Irvington, 1984. 112p. map. bibliog.
This illustrated study of Ijaw patterns of enculturation and socialization is based on the author's fieldwork between 1957 and 1959 in the western Niger Delta, especially in the isolated village of Ebiama. He describes the village itself, beliefs regarding pregnancy and parturition, childhood, and adolescence, demonstrating the influence of childhood learning on cultural and social change. A short list of Ijaw words is included in the glossary (p. 109–10). In addition to his doctoral thesis at Northwestern University, Evanston, Illinois, on which this volume is based, Professor Leis has published 'Ijaw enculturation, a reexamination of the early learning hypothesis' in *Southwestern Journal of Anthropology*, vol. 20 (1964), p. 32–42 and other works on the Ijaw. With Marida Hollos, Leis has authored *Becoming Nigerian in Ijo society* (New Brunswick, New Jersey: Rutgers University, 1989. 167p. (Adolescents in a Changing World Series)).

Ethnic Groups. Other groups

430 **The lower Niger and its tribes.**
Arthur Glyn Leonard, preface by A. C. Haddon. London:
Macmillan, 1906. Reprinted, London: Frank Cass, 1968. 564p. map.
(Cass Library of African Studies, no. 67).

Major Leonard, following a decade of study, attempts to generalize about religion and
language among the ethnic groups of Southern Nigeria from the Niger Delta to
Calabar, including the hinterlands and focusing especially on the Igbo people. His
analysis is concerned with 'the philosophy of the people as expressed in words, names,
proverbs, and fables'; 'natural religion' and 'naturism'; 'spiritualism'; 'emblemism, or
the embodiment of the spirit'; 'ceremonials'; and 'demonology' or witchcraft.
Appendices (p. 503–59) detail comparative grammatical constructions and 'the
primitive philosophy of words'.

431 **Hill farmers of Nigeria: cultural ecology of the Kofyar of the Jos
Plateau.**
Robert McC. Netting. Seattle, Washington: University of
Washington, 1968. 259p. 4 maps. bibliog. (American Ethnological
Society Monograph, no. 46).

This study of the Kofyar peoples, who numbered about 70,000 in 1963, living near the
geographic centre of Nigeria examines their intensive hill agriculture, population and
settlement patterns, attitudes and ideology and migratory farming. The author explains
'the distribution and cooperative organization of people as adaptations to the demands
of the agricultural system' (p. 225–26). Based on eighteen months' fieldwork in
1960–62, this study includes eighteen photographs and a useful bibliography on the
region (p. 236–46). An earlier version of the work was the author's 1963 University of
Chicago doctoral thesis, *Kofyar agriculture: a study in the cultural ecology of a West
African people*. Professor Netting published in the Human Relations Area Files
HRAFlex Ethnocentrism Series two volumes on the *Kofyar of Nigeria* (New Haven,
Connecticut, 1972, nos. FF6-001, FF6-002) and, among other publications, authored a
popular article entitled 'Heritage of survival', *Natural History*, vol. 74, no. 3 (1965),
p. 14–21.

432 **Foundations of the Bida Kingdom.**
Michael Mason. Zaria, Nigeria: Ahmadu Bello University, 1981.
201p. 9 maps. bibliog. (Ahmadu Bello University History Series).

This detailed historical study of the Bida Kingdom in the nineteenth century is based
on the author's fieldwork in Nupe during 1966–67, 1969, 1970 and 1971, archival
research, and materials gathered from about 100 villages by Abel Yisa in 1971–72. The
result is a lucid account of the Bida Emirate's rise, stressing the rôle of class relations.
Included are king and title lists, a guide to the kings of Nupe, a Nupe glossary and a
bibliography (p. 185–96). The volume derives from Professor Mason's 1970 Birmingham
University doctoral thesis, *The Nupe kingdoms in the nineteenth century: a political
history*.

160

433 **The northern tribes of Nigeria: an ethnographic account of the northern provinces of Nigeria together with a report on the 1921 decennial census.**
C[harles] K[ingsley] Meek, preface by Sir Hugh Clifford. London: Oxford University, 1925. Reprinted, New York: Negro Universities,, 1969. 2 vols. 3 maps.

A rich source of early-twentieth century information on northern Nigerian ethnic groups by the Government Anthropologist, District Officer and Census Commissioner. The two volumes consist of nine chapters divided into ethnographic categories: general description; ethnic types; history and tradition; economic life and industries; social organization; government and law; religion, language and lore; and ethnological conclusions. The 1921 census, the first detailed census of the Northern Provinces, is analysed (vol. II, p. 169–263) according to: area, population, density and race relations; age and sex; occupations, civil condition; religious statistics; and education. Data on these topics are displayed in fifty-eight tables. One hundred and twenty-two black-and-white illustrations are interspersed with the text.

434 **A Sudanese kingdom: an ethnological study of the Jukun-speaking peoples of Nigeria.**
C. K. Meek, introduction by H. R. Palmer. London: Kegan Paul, 1931. Reprinted, New York; Negro Universities Press, 1969. 548p. 2 maps. bibliog.

Meek conducted fieldwork for less than five months in the 1920s among the Jukun-speaking peoples located on either side of the Benue River in eastern Nigeria. The result is, nevertheless, an impressive ethnography containing 147 illustrations and covering the culture remarkably well. The introduction by the former Lieutenant-Governor of Northern Nigeria (p. xiii–xxxiii) provides historical background to the region. There is an appendix, 'Schedules of words and phrases of the various Jukun dialects' (p. 499–535).

435 **Tribal studies in Northern Nigeria.**
C. K. Meek. London: Kegan Paul, Trench, Trubner, 1931. Reprinted, Millwood, New York: Kraus Reprint, 1976. 2 vols. 3 maps. bibliog.

This ethnographic encyclopaedia of some fifty non-Muslim peoples of the Northern Provinces embodies 'a collection of tribal reports submitted by [C. K. Meek] to the Nigerian Government at various times' over the period 1926–31 (Preface, p. v). The volumes consist of sixteen chapters containing accounts of social and political organization, religious practices, vocabulary lists and such customs as Meek could record during visits of varying lengths. Included are studies of: vol. I, 'The Bachama and Mbula'; 'The Bata-speaking peoples of the Adamawa Emirate'; 'The Bura and Pabir tribes'; 'The Kilba and Margi of Adamawa'; 'Some mandated tribes'; 'The Chamba'; 'The Verre'; 'The Mumuye and neighboring tribes'; 'The Mambila mandated territory)'; vol. II, 'The Katab and their neighbors'; 'Some tribes of Zaria Province'; 'some tribes of Bornu Province'; 'Some tribes of Adamawa Province'; 'The Yungur-speaking peoples'; 'Divine kings'; and 'Some tribes of the Cameroons'. The author includes 108 plates, providing a valuable visual record of the cultures.

436 **A black Byzantium: the Kingdom of Nupe in Nigeria.**
S[iegfried] F[erdinand]. Nadel, foreword by Lord Lugard. London,
New York: Oxford University for the International African Institute,
1942. Reprinted, 1973, 420p. 2 maps. bibliog.

A major ethnography by a well-known Austrian-born social anthropologist, who spent two years conducting research in Bida and other Nupe towns in 1934 and 1935–36. In this sophisticated study of one of Nigeria's largest ethnic groups, the author emphasizes the political organization and political history of the village, the Nupe kingdom and 'government in modern Nupe', as well as agriculture and economy. Thirty-four photographs and maps of Bida City and the Nupe tribal area are included. Professor Nadel published an important sequel, *Nupe religion: traditional beliefs and the influence of Islam in a West African chiefdom* (London: Routledge & Kegan Paul; Glencoe, Illinois: Free Press, 1954. 288p. Reprinted, New York: Schocken, 1970. 288p.), which contains a full discussion of divination, ritual, medicine, witchcraft and Islam in Nupe and has thirty-one photographs.

437 **Ishan native laws and customs.**
Christopher Gbelokoto Okojie. Yaba, Nigeria: John Okwesa, 1960.
338p. 3 maps.

This informative history and ethnography gives a full account of the Ishan, or Esan, an important group of northern Bendel State. The author describes laws and customs, social and political organization, justice, land tenure, main cultural features, and twenty-seven sub-groups of the Esan. Fifty-two illustrations supplement the text. Okojie was a prominent physician and had been appointed a member of the NBC (Nigerian Broadcasting Corporation) in 1959.

438 **Gods and goods in Africa: persistence and change in ethnic and religious identity in Yauri Emirate, North-Western State, Nigeria.**
Frank A. Salamone. New Haven, Connecticut: Human Relations
Area Files, 1974. 2 vols. 307 leaves. 3 maps. bibliog. (HRAFlex Books,
Ethnography Series, no. FF36-001).

This ethnography, conducted in the early 1970s in present day Sokoto State, of the Dukawa and Gungawa and of their relations with the ruling Hausa seeks 'to establish the chief mechanisms through which groups maintain or modify religious and ethnic identities' (p. 2). The author presents historical material on the Yauri Emirate but mainly concentrates on the period from 1960 to 1972, and describes the rôles of cultural, social, ecological, ideological and political factors in establishing or maintaining traditional ethnic boundaries and interethnic relations. Professor Salamone has also written on games in the area: 'Gungawa wrestling', *Sport Sociology Bulletin*, vol. 3 (1975), p. 1–12; 'Nigerian children's games and ethnic identity', *Review of Sport and Leisure*, vol. 1 (1976), p. 62–92; and 'Children's games as mechanisms for easing ethnic interaction in ethnically heterogenous communities – a Nigerian case', *Ethnicity* vol. 5 (1978), p. 203–12.

439 **Woman's mysteries of a primitive people: the Ibibios of Southern Nigeria.**

D. Amaury Talbot. London, New York: Cassell, 1915. Reprinted, London: Frank Cass, 1968. 252p. (Cass Library of African Studies, no. 57).

An attempt by the author (1871–1916), wife of government anthropologist Percy Amaury Talbot (1877–1945), and her sister, both resident in Nigeria for many years, to provide ethnographic detail on the cultural life of women, from 'the woman's point of view'. This study is based on ten months' travel and study among the Ibibio of south-eastern Nigeria. The result is a fascinating, if dated, description of women's customs, the life-cycle, secret societies, widowhood and burial customs, which is valuable despite the author's contention that, 'Saving the more civilised Efiks, it is indisputable that the Ibibios occupy a low rung on the ladder of culture, and are perhaps as blood thirsty as any people throughout the length and breadth of the Dark continent' (p. 4). Forty-four illustrations are included.

440 **In the shadow of the bush.**

P. Amaury Talbot. London: William Heinemann; New York: George H. Doran, 1912. 500p. map.

A study of the Ekoi people of the Oban District of south-eastern Nigeria, 'most of whom were untouched by white influence on my arrival among them in 1907' (Foreword, p. vii), which is profusely illustrated with photographs and drawings. Appendices contain information on anthropometry, languages, flora and fauna and minerology. Talbot also published 'The land of the Ekoi, Southern Nigeria', in the *Geographical Journal*, vol. 36, no. 6 (1910), p. 637–57, and a shorter version, 'Notes on the Ekoi', in *National Geographic Magazine*, vol. 23, no. 1 (Jan. 1912), p. 32–38.

441 **Life in Southern Nigeria: the magic, beliefs and customs of the Ibibio tribe.**

P. Amaury Talbot. London: Macmillan, 1923. Reprinted, London: Frank Cass, 1967. 356p. map. (Cass Library of African Studies, no. 31).

A description, written in 1914, of the beliefs and practices of the Ibibio of Eket District in south-eastern Nigeria (now Cross River State). Talbot details the Ibibios' 'jujus', witchcraft, deities, divination practices, mortuary custom, secret societies, marriage customs and social organization. Fifty-one photographs of the people, their activities and material culture are reproduced as is a large fold-out map of the Eket District in 1913. Talbot acknowledges not only his wife and her sister who aided his ethnographic work, but also W. W. Eakin of the 'Kwa Ibo Mission' and especially Chief Daniel Henshaw, 'Native Political Agent for the District' for his invaluable help in working through Sir James Frazer's 'exhaustive list of questions'.

442 **The peoples of Southern Nigeria: a sketch of their history, ethnology and languages with an abstract of the 1921 census.**

P. Amaury Talbot. London: Oxford University, H. Milford, 1926. Reprinted, London: Frank Cass, 1969. 4 vols. 35 maps. bibliog.

Presents a remarkable compendium of information on the Lagos Colony, the ten provinces of Southern Nigeria and the mandated area of the Cameroons by Talbot, government anthropologist in the region at the time. Vol. one contains 'Historical notes' on the region and on each division; vols. two and three, 'Ethnology' cover in thirty-eight chapters nearly every aspect of social life among the diverse ethnic groups; vol. four 'Linguistics and statistics' provides a detailed analysis of the 1921 census of the region's more than eight million people by ethnic and linguistic group. Throughout the volumes appear 251 illustrations and 145 tables, many of them of the fold-out variety, making this early study an invaluable encyclopaedia for Southern Nigeria at the time.

443 **Some Nigerian fertility cults.**
P. Amaury Talbot. London: Oxford University, 1927. Reprinted, London: Frank Cass, 1967. 140p. (Cass Library of African Studies. General Studies, no. 33).

This monograph deals with the religion of Ijaw and Igbo peoples in the Degama Division of the Niger Delta to which Talbot was posted as government anthropologist in June, 1914. In one of the earliest attempts to analyse the substance and context of traditional Nigerian religions, the author describes the great Ikuru drum to which sacrifices were made, Igbo *mbari* or shrine houses, the Sky God and Earth Goddess, ibudu and eku, phallic cults, the yam cult and Ale and the ancestors. Forty-seven line drawings and photographs appear throughout the volume.

444 **The tribes of the Niger Delta: their religions and customs.**
P. Amaury Talbot. London: Sheldon; New York: Macmillan, 1932. Reprinted, London: Frank Cass; New York: Barnes & Noble, 1967. 350p. map.

A substantial compilation of ethnographic detail, particularly on the southern and western Igbo, the Ijaw and the Kalabari of Degama Division, collected primarily during 1914–16 by the author, government ethnologist for the area. Religion, magic, witchcraft and the life-cycle are featured but there is also information on tribal organization, slavery, secret societies and folklore. Sixty-five photographs from the period are included.

445 **Notes on the tribes, provinces, emirates and states of the northern provinces of Nigeria, compiled from official reports.**
O[live Susan Miranda] Temple, edited by C. L. Temple. Lagos: CMS (Nigeria) Bookshops, 1922, 2nd ed. Reprinted, London: Frank Cass, 1965; New York: Barnes & Noble, 1967. 595p. bibliog.

An encyclopaedic compilation of information collected up to October 1916 on scores of tribes listed alphabetically (p. 1–408) and on the provinces with their emirates (p. 409–577). A brief bibliographic note has been added to the 1965 edition (p. 5–6). The first edition appeared in 1919. Sir Charles L. Temple (1871–1921) was a Resident in Northern Nigeria (1901) and in Bauchi (1903), Chief Secretary of Northern Nigeria (1910–13) and Lieutenant-Governor of Northern Nigeria (1914–17).

Evolution of political culture in Nigeria: proceedings of a national seminar organized by the Kaduna State Council for Arts and Culture.
See item no. 176.

The small brave city-state: a history of Nembe-Brass in the Niger Delta.
See item no. 179.

A history of the Niger Delta: an historical interpretation of Ijo oral tradition.
See item no. 180.

A chronicle of Grand Bonny.
See item no. 181.

From empire to colony: Bornu in the nineteenth and twentieth centuries.
See item no. 185.

Trade and politics in the Niger Delta, 1830–1885: an introduction to the economic and political history of Nigeria.
See item no. 187.

Efik traders of Old Calabar.
See item no. 190.

A chronicle of Abuja.
See item no. 192.

The emirates of Northern Nigeria: a preliminary survey of their historical traditions.
See item no. 194.

Stateless societies in the history of West Africa.
See item no. 195.

Songhay, Borno and Hausaland in the sixteenth century.
See item no. 196.

Studies in the history of Plateau State, Nigeria.
See item no. 198.

The trading states of the oil rivers: a study of political development in eastern Nigeria.
See item no. 200.

Old Calabar, 1600–1891: the impact of the international economy upon a traditional society.
See item no. 202.

Salt of the desert sun: a history of salt production and trade in the central Sudan.
See item no. 205.

Three Nigerian emirates: a study in oral history.
See item no. 206.

History of Itsekiri.
See item no. 208.

A short history of Urhobo.
See item no. 212.

Ethnic Groups. Other groups

'Tarikh 'Umara Bauchi' and its contribution to pre-colonial Ningi resistance to Sokoto Caliphate: exegesis and methodology in African oral history, ca. 1846–1902.
See item no. 213.

Niger Delta rivalry: Itsekiri-Urhobo relations and the European presence, 1884–1936.
See item no. 257.

Merchant prince of the Niger Delta: the rise & fall of Nana Olomu, last governor of the Benin River.
See item no. 258.

Gazetteers of the northern provinces of Nigeria.
See item no. 262.

Bibliography of Nigeria: a survey of anthropological and linguistic writings from the earliest times to 1966.
See item no. 331.

Handbook of ethnic units in Nigeria.
See item no. 335.

The traditional artist in African societies.
See item no. 916.

The living arts of Nigeria.
See item no. 918.

African art in motion: icon and act.
See item no. 931.

Flash of the spirit: African and Afro-American art and philosophy.
See item no. 932.

African Arts.
See item no.935.

African stone sculpture.
See item no. 936.

The essential gourd: art and history in northeastern Nigeria.
See item no. 943.

Decorated gourds in north-eastern Nigeria.
See item no. 949.

Two thousand years Nigerian art.
See item no. 961.

Treasures of ancient Nigeria.
See item no. 962.

Kalabari sculpture.
See item no. 968.

Ethnic Groups. Other groups

Folk pottery of Nigeria.
See item no. 1044.

Nigerian pottery: a catalogue.
See item no. 1045.

Pottery in Nigeria.
See item no. 1047.

Guide to the Nigerian Musuem, Lagos.
See item no. 1055.

Guide to the National Musuem, Kaduna.
See item no. 1956.

25 years of Jos Museum.
See item no. 1057.

The story of Old Calabar: a guide to the National Museum at the Old Residency, Calabar.
See item no. 1061.

Guide to the National Museum, Oron.
See item no. 1062.

Annals of Borno.
See item no. 1103.

Nigeria Magazine.
See item no. 1107.

Savanna. A Journal of the Environmental and Social Sciences.
See item no. 1110.

Niger Delta studies, 1627–1967: a bibliography.
See item no. 1138.

A bibliographic guide to Borno studies, 1821–1983.
See item no. 1142.

Nigerian women: a bibliographic essay.
See item no. 1146.

Languages and Dialects

General

446 **Nigerian slangs: a dictionary of slangs and unconventional English used in Nigeria.**
C. N. C. Asomugha. Onitsha, Nigeria: ABIC, 1981. 2nd ed. 82p.
An interesting and informative dictionary of colloquial Nigerian speech, from 'aaron' meaning 'to lose in a bargain', to 'yabis' meaning 'an insulting statement'. First published as *A pocket dictionary of selected Nigerian student slangs*, the second edition is enlarged and may be of use in much of English-speaking West Africa. A few popular words and phrases coined from several Nigerian languages are included. The publisher's address is ABIC Publishers, P.O. Box 3120, Onitsha, Nigeria. The volume is reviewed in *West Africa*, no. 3527 (1 April 1985), p. 623.

447 **Language in education and society in Nigeria: a comprehensive bibliography and research guide.**
Compiled by C. M. B. Brann, preface by W. F. Mackey. Quebec: International Center for Research on Bilingualism, 1975. 233p. map. (Publication B-52).
This complex bibliography contains works, in particular from the decade 1960–70, concerned with aspects of language education, broadly defined. An important area concerns the influences of Christian missions on Nigerian languages and on English use in Nigeria. References are primarily to Nigerian, English and North American sources. The bibliography has five parts: an alphabetical list of unnumbered and unannotated citations by author; an analytical index; a list of journals; a list of collections; and a list of relevant conferences. Of interest also is 'Bimpe Aboyade's 'A preliminary bibliography of Nigerian languages', *African Notes* (Ibadan), vol. 5, no. 1 (1968), p. i–xxvi.

Languages and Dialects. General

448 **The languages of Africa.**
Joseph H[arold] Greenberg. Bloomington, Indiana: Indiana
University, 1970. 3rd ed. 180p. 5 maps. bibliog. (Research Center for
the Language Sciences, Indiana University, pub. 25).
This volume contains a 'complete genetic classification of the languages of Africa'
(p. 1). The author (1915– .), in a major revision of his own earlier work and D
Westermann's *Languages of Africa* (q.v.), classified 730 languages into the language
groups: Niger-Congo, Afroasiatic, Khosian, Chari-Nile, Nilo-Saharan, and Niger-
Kordofanian. An index of languages (p. 163–71) is supplied. Professor Greenberg
studied languages in Northern Nigeria in 1954–55. One map and an enlargement show
the locations of Nigerian languages. The study was originally published as Part II of the
International Journal of American Linguistics, vol. 29, no. 1 (1963), with the second
edition appearing in 1966. Of related interest is *A thesaurus of African languages: a
classified and annotated inventory of the spoken languages of Africa, with an appendix
on their orthographic representation*, edited by Michael Mann and David Dalby
(Munich: K. G. Saur/Hans Zell, 1987. 325p.) which provides an annotated inventory
of 2,550 African languages, a country-by-country survey, and an extensive bibliography
of 1,450 titles.

449 **The early study of Nigerian languages: essays and bibliographies.**
P. E. H. Hair. London: Cambridge University in association with the
West African Languages Survey and the Institute of African Studies,
Ibadan, 1967. 110p. map. bibliog. (West African Language Monograph
Series, no. 7).
A marvellous study describing the nineteenth-century works on nine major Nigerian
languages. Three separate essays, each followed by a bibliography for the languages
concerned, provide lucid histories of the particluar languages or language area and
their study by both foreigners and native speakers, with emphasis on the work of
missionary societies. The essays are: 'The early study of Yoruba, 1825–1850'; 'The
early study of Hausa and Kanuri, 1840–1890'; and 'The early study of the languages of
the lower Niger and Benue, 1840–1890' (with bibliographies of Nupe, Igala, Igbira
Igbo and Ijaw).

450 **Languages of West Africa.**
Diedrich Westermann, M. A. Bryan. Folkestone, England: Dawsons
of Pall Mall for the International African Institute, 1970. rev. ed. 277p.
map. bibliog.
This important volume surveying languages in the broad region of West Africa was first
published in 1952 and includes a large fold-out map showing language locations. The
revised edition has an extensive bibliography by D. W. Arnott (p. 203–63
supplementing the original (p. 178–201). Each language is described, located and its
number of speakers estimated. *An introduction to West African pidgin English* (East
Lansing: Michigan State University, African Studies Center, 1966. (African Monograph
Series)) by David Dwyer provides a careful examination of this important variety of
English.

**Bibliography of Nigeria: a survey of anthropological and linguistic writing
from the earliest times to 1966.**
See item no. 331.

170

Handbook of ethnic units in Nigeria.
See item no. 335.

Periodical

51   **Journal of West African Languages.**
Ibadan, Nigeria: Cambridge University in association with the Institute of African Languages, University of Ibadan, Nigeria, January 1964– . biannual.
This important journal is currently published by the West African Linguistic Society. Its editorial address is The Editor, Summer Institute of Linguistics, 1700 W. Camp Wisdona Road, Dallas, Texas 75236. Vol. 17, no. 2 (Nov. 1987) was a special issue in honour of Robert G. Armstong (1917–87) who published extensively on Nigerian language, culture and art. His publications are noted elsewhere in this bibliography.

Edo (Bini)

452   **An Edo-English dictionary.**
City, Nigeria: Ethiope, 1986. 169p. bibliog. Compiled by
Rebecca N. Agheyisi.   Benin
Represents the only modern dictionary of the Edo language, spoken by more than a million people in south-central Nigeria. The introduction (p. iii–xxiv) discusses the language, the extent of the speaking population, Edo's affinity with other Nigerian languages, the present work, orthography, consonants and grammar. The volume contains approximately 4,000 entries. The author is professor in the Department of Linguistics and African Languages, at the University of Benin, Benin City, Nigeria.

453   **An introduction to Bini.**
Ernest F. Dunn, assisted by Rebecca N. Agheyisi. [East Lansing, Michigan]: African Studies Center, Michigan State University, 1968. 224p. 2 maps. (African Monographs, no. 9).
A practical introduction to the Bini (Edo) language of Bendel State, southern Nigeria, designed especially for American Peace Corps volunteers. In addition to providing instruction in the essential aspects of spoken Bini through drills and texts, the author includes cultural information and: proverbs (p. 150–51), model conversations (154–64); four folktales in both Bini and English (165–81); a glossary (p. 185–94); and a brief but useful reference grammar (p. 195–224). Of interest also are 'Bini proverbs' by M. E. Omijeh in *Nigeria Magazine*, no. 96 (March–May 1968), p. 40–44, and Emmanuel Akponmwosa Aigbe's *Itan Edo na zedu ere ye ebo. 1040 Edo proverbs with their English translation* (Lagos: The Author, 1960. 57p.) in which the proverbs are printed in parallel columns of Edo and English.

454 **A concise dictionary of the Bini language of Southern Nigeria.**
Compiled by Hans [J.] Melzian. London: Kegan Paul, Trench,
Trubner, 1937. 233p.

A masterful dictionary, with full definitions, which are often ethnographicall
informative. Most of the material was collected with the help of H. G. Amadasu c
Benin City from November 1933 to July 1934 and checked during a second visit i
1935. Additional items and information were obtained from Jacob U. Egharevba, J. E
Edegba and from H. L. M. Butcher's *An elementary dictionary of the Bini languag*
(Benin City, Nigeria: CMS, 1936). The author's other major publication on Bini, th
central Edoid language, is *Vergleichende Charakteristik des verbums im Bir
(Südnigerien)* (Comparative characteristics of verbs in Bini (Southern Nigeria)
(Berlin: Institut für Lautforschung an der Universität Berlin, 1942. 123p.) whic
contains a detailed description of tones and verb forms. At one time Dr. Melzian was
Lecturer in African Phonetics and Linguistics at the School of Oriental Studies
University of London.

455 **Ẹdo grammar for school and colleges.**
Osaren S. B. Ọmọregie. Lagos: Thomas Nelson (Nigeria), 1983.
107p.

This pragmatic introduction to the Ẹdo language, spoken by the Bini, Esan, Etsakc
Ivbiosakon (Owan) and Akoko-Edo of Bendel State, uses a 'grammatical approach'
Chapters, initially with explanations in English, concern: the sentence, parts of speec
and the counting system. At the time of publication, Dr. Ọmọregie was Chie
Educational Planning officer, Ministry of Education, Benin City, Nigeria.

An initial orthography and lexicon for Emai: an Edoid language of Nigeria.
See item no. 480.

Kemwin-kemwin: the apothecary shop in Benin City.
See item no. 560.

Poems in Bini.
See item no. 909.

Sweet words: storytelling events in Benin.
See item no. 1024.

Hausa

456 **Dictionary of the Hausa language.**
Compiled by R[oy] C[live] Abraham, Malam Mai Kano. London:
Crown Agents, 1949. 992p.

This work which has a brief preface, an introduction and a verb table (p. xi–xxvii)
recognized as an unsurpassed rendering of Hausa to English and is the product
Major Abraham's (1890–1963) twenty-three years devoted to the study of Haus
Compiled especially for Nigerian secondary and post-secondary school students is th

Modern Hausa-English dictionary. Sabon kamus na Hausa zuwa turanci (Oxford: Oxford University, 1977. Reprinted with corrections, Ibadan: University Press, 1979, 1985. 153p.) by Paul Newman and Roxane Ma Newman, assisted by Ibrahim Yaro Yahaya and Linda Dresel and the Centre for the Study of Nigerian Languages, Bayero University College, Kano, Nigeria. The preface is in both English and Hausa.

457 **Manual of Hausa idioms.**
Dauda M. Bagari, William R. Leben, Faye McNair Knox.
Bloomington, Indiana: Indiana University Linguistics Club, July 1979.
2nd ed. 233p.

This book consists of twenty-two lessons, each with a story or selection of writing, followed by drills, exercises and grammatical discussion emphasizing idiomatic usage. It is intended as a supplementary text for intermediate and advanced students of Hausa. The first edition was published in September 1976 by Stanford University, NDEA Center for African Language and Area Studies.

458 **A Hausa-English dictionary and English-Hausa vocabulary compiled for the Government of Nigeria with some notes on the Hausa people and their language by Professor D. Westermann.**
Compiled by Rev. G. P. Bargery. London: Oxford University, 1934.
Reprinted, 1951. 1,226p.

Following Westermann's notes (p. ix–xix) and the compiler's introduction (p. xxi–xlviii) are the Hausa-English dictionary (p. 1–1,151) and the English-Hausa vocabualry (p. 1,154–226). Bargery's work is considered to be superior to the *Dictionary of the Hausa language* by Charles Henry Robinson (Cambridge: Cambridge University, 1925, 4th ed. 2 vols. Reprinted, Amersham, England: Gregg International, 1969.) who lectured in Hausa at Cambridge University. The first edition appeared in 1899 and comprised: vol. one, Hausa-English, 475p.; vol. two, English-Hausa, 289p.

459 **Spoken Hausa.**
J. Ronayne Cowan, Russel G. Schuh. Ithaca, New York: Spoken Language Service, 1976. 378p. bibliog.

This volume is intended as a basic textbook for both beginning and intermediate courses in Hausa at university level and is accompanied by a set of tapes integrated with the text. In twenty-five units the authors cover Hausa fundamentals and provide numerous drills for review. A brief bibliography (p. 3–4) directs students to the most useful published works on Hausa. The book and tapes can be obtained from Spoken Language Services, P.O. Box 783, Ithaca, New York 14850. The *Hausa basic course* by Carleton T. Hodge and Ibrahim Umaru (Washington, DC: Department of State, Foreign Service Institute, 1963. 399p.) contains thirty drills, conversations, translations and a Hausa-English vocabulary (p. 377–99).

460 **Neologisms in Hausa: a sociological approach.**
A. H. M. Kirk-Greene. *Africa*, vol. 33, no. 1 (Jan. 1963), p. 25–44.
bibliog.

Offers an informative analysis of new words and idioms in black Africa's most widely spoken language. The author examines Hausa vocabulary – 'the words used, their forms, and their syntactical modification or assimilation' (p. 27); their provenance; and

Languages and Dialects. Hausa

social and cultural idiomatic influences on the language. Included with the numerous examples are a discussion of *malamanci*, an idiomatic speech form mixing English and Hausa, a passage of 'modern' Hausa with an 'orthodox' Hausa translation and a passage of 'ultra-modern Hausa slang' (p. 44). An interesting complementary article is Kirk-Greene's 'The vocabulary and determinants of schoolboy slang in Northern Nigeria', *Journal of African Languages*, vol. 5, no. 1 (1966), p. 7–33. See also his survey, 'The linguistic statistics of Northern Nigeria: a tentative presentation', in *African Language Review (The African Language Journal of Fourah Bay College)*, vol. 6 (1967), p. 75–101.

461 **Hausa.**
Charles H. Kraft, in association with A. H. M. Kirk-Greene. London: English Universities, 1973. 394p. bibliog. (Teach Yourself Books).

An excellent, carefully-produced and very usable treatment of the language. The authors describe pronunciation and grammar in detail, as well as providing discussions of greetings, numbers, time, money and marketing, family and kinship terms and pronouns. Supplementary materials include letter writing, proverbs and riddles, conversations and texts, a bibliography of grammars (p. 289–99), dictionaries, reading materials, and specialized and technical studies of Hausa. Appendices include both Hausa-English and English-Hausa vocabularies.

462 **Introductory Hausa.**
Charles H. Kraft, Marguerite G. Kraft. Berkeley, California: University of California, 1973. 408p.

Contains: a guide to Hausa pronunciation; twenty practical lessons with suggestions for testing; a synopsis of Hausa grammar; a glossary of technical terminology; Hausa-English vocabulary and English-Hausa vocabulary; an index of Hausa names; and an index of grammar. Professor Kraft collected and edited *A Hausa reader: cultural materials with help for use in teaching intermediate and advanced Hausa* (Berkeley, California: University of California, 1973. 510p.) which contains a lengthy text (p. 1–330) of diverse exercises including fables and customs entirely in Hausa and a workbook in Hausa and English. He has also published *A study of Hausa syntax* (Hartford, Connecticut: Department of Linguistics, Hartford Seminary Foundation, 1963. 3 vols; (Hartford Studies in Linguistics, no. 8)) as part of his PhD thesis. A. H. M. Kirk-Greene and Yahaya Aliyu published *A modern Hausa reader* (London: University of London, 1966. 143p.) containing Hausa speeches and newspaper articles.

463 **Studies in Hausa language and linguistics, in honour of F. W. Parsons.**
Edited by Graham Furniss, Philip J. Jaggar. London, New York: Kegan Paul in association with the International African Institute, 1988. 282p. bibliog.

Among this important volume's eighteen essays on Hausa linguistics and literature are A. H. M. Kirk-Greene's 'Examinees, examiners and examinations: the Hausa language requirement of the Northern Nigerian government, 1902–62' (p. 1–14) and Nicholas Awde's 'A Hausa language and linguistics bibliography 1976–86, (including supplementary material for other years)' (p. 253–78). This updates Sergio Baldi's extensive but hard to obtain *Systematic Hausa bibliography* (Rome: Istituto Italo-Africano, 1977 (Collana di Studi Africani, 3)). Other significant papers are by J. Carnochan, Claude Gouffé, Philip J. Jaggar, H. J. Mayr, J. A. McIntyre, Pau

Newman, Roxana Ma Newman, N. Pilszczikowa-Chodak, L. Tuller, D. W. Arnott, Dauda Muhammad Bagari, Graham Furniss, Stanislaw Pilaszewicz, Russell G. Schuh, Neil Skinner and Ibrahim Yaro Yahaya. The volume is a *Festschrift* for Frederick William Parsons (1908– .) who spent thirteen years as a District Officer in Northern Nigeria (1931–44) and taught Hausa at the School of Oriental and African Studies, University of London.

464 **An anthology of Hausa literature in translation.**
Edited by Neil Skinner. Madison, Wisconsin: University of Wisconsin, African Studies Program, 1977. 189p. bibliog. (Occasional Paper, no. 7).

A wide range of Hausa literature is discussed and translated into English in this volume, including tales (*tatsuniyas*), drama, proverbs, poetry and modern prose. Most are drawn from other published sources, including the editor's *Hausa tales and traditions* (q.v.). Professor Skinner's *Hausa language course* (Madison, Wisconsin: University of Wisconsin, Department of African Language and Literature, 1973. 4th ed. 125 leaves) contains thirty practical lessons illustrating Hausa basics, a short vocabulary index (1. 93–105) and appendices with numerals, weekdays, pronoun forms, verb patterns, parts of speech and a short list of books for further reading (1. 113).

A history of Hausa Islamic verse.
See item no. 842.

Hausa tales and traditions: an English translation of Tatsuniyoyi Na Hausa, originally compiled by Frank Edgar.
See item no. 1026.

Hausa folk-lore, customs, proverbs, etc., collected and transliterated with English translation and notes.
See item no. 1028.

Magana Hausa. Native literature, or proverbs, tales, fables and historical fragments in the Hausa language to which is added a translation in English.
See item no. 1029.

Hausa superstitions and customs: an introduction to the folk-lore and the folk.
See item no. 1031.

Igbo (Ibo)

465 A descriptive grammar of Igbo.
M. M. Green, G. E. Igwe. London: Oxford University; Berlin: Akademie-Verlag, 1963. 235p. bibliog.

This formal study of Igbo is 'an essay in descriptive linguistics at the grammatical level' (Introduction, p. xi) and contains a lengthy analysis of the Igbo grammatical system (p. 11–196), a series of texts printed in parallel columns of Igbo and English (p. 198–221), including proverbs and riddles and an Igbo-English vocabulary (p. 222–35) of about 900 entries.

466 Igbo basic course.
L. B. Swift, A. Ahaghotu, E. Ugorji. Washington, DC: Department of State, US Foreign Service Institute, 1962. 498p.

This course is based on the 'Central Igbo' spoken between Owerri and Umuahia in Imo State. The course materials include seventy-five exercises on tone distinctions (p. 1–41); twenty-four units containing dialogues, notes and drills (p. 43–415); six units with dialogues and short narratives (p. 416–61); and a basic Igbo-English vocabulary (p. 462–98). A related volume is Richard A. Williams' an *Igbo basic course*, tested at the Morehouse-Spelman Peace Corps project (Xenia, Ohio: ABC, 1966. 172p.).

467 Igbo: a learner's dictionary.
Compiled by Beatrice F. Welmers, William E. Welmers. Los Angeles: University of California, African Studies Center, 1968. 397p.

This dictionary is intended for those English speakers who have a minimum competence in speaking Igbo and who know the major structural patterns of the language. It contains both Igbo-English and English-Igbo sections. The two-volume product of four refresher courses for post-primary Igbo language teachers, *Igbo language and culture*, edited by F. Chidozie Ogbalu and E. Nolue Emenanjo (Ibadan, Nigeria: Oxford University, 1975. 1982) covers history, art, poetry, literature, proverbs, dress, religion and music as well as grammar, tones, spelling and verbs. Notable essays by A. E. Afigbo, M. A. Onwuejeogwu and M. J. C. Echeruo are included.

468 Igbo-English dictionary based on the Onitsha dialect.
Edited by Kay Williamson. Benin City, Nigeria: Ethiope, 1972. 568p. bibliog.

This dictionary is a product of the author's study of Igbo in the 1960s and, with the assistance of C. N. and E. I. Madunagu, her reworking and enlarging of an unpublished compilation by G. W. Pearman. In the lengthy introduction (p. v–lxx), Dr. Williamson provides a survey of other works on Igbo, 'strangely neglected by lexicographers' probably, she feels, because of dialectical variations (p. v). She explains the development of the present work, its intricacies and includes a substantial bibliography (p. lxvi–lxx). Her *Practical orthography in Nigeria* (Ibadan: Heinemann, 1984. 70p.) is also an important contribution to the study of Nigerian languages.

Tales of land of death.
See item no. 1027.

The way we lived: Ibo customs and stories.
See item no. 1032.

Words are sweet: Igbo stories and storytelling.
See item no. 1033.

Yoruba

469 **Essentials of Yoruba grammar.**
Ọladele Awobuluyi. Oxford; London: Oxford University, 1978;
Ibadan, Nigeria: University Press, 1979. 158p.

This volume is intended as a 'simple, straightforward, comprehensive, and scientific
book on Yoruba grammar for use in Grammar Schools, Colleges, and introductory
courses for undergraduates' (Introduction, p. xiii). In ten chapters the author explains,
using numerous subcategories and examples: parts of speech, nouns, qualifiers, verbs,
modifiers, introducers, conjunctions and disjunctions, sentences, sounds and combinations of sounds. Following each chapter are questions to test comprehension and
exercises to reinforce the lessons.

470 **Dictionary of modern Yoruba.**
R. C. Abraham. London: Hodder & Stoughton, 1962. 2nd ed. 776p.
bibliog.

This authoritative, encyclopaedic work is the product of many years of research
sponsored by the Nigerian Government and by the Nigerian Institute for Social and
Economic Research (NISER), Ibadan. It is the first African dictionary to be illustrated
and the first to mark tone throughout the key-words and examples. This *magnum opus*
contains an introduction describing the tone system, sounds, tenses, numerals,
grammar and many subtleties of the language. Illustrations provide the Yoruba for
many plants, birds, mammals, reptiles and traditional art forms. The dictionary is a
Yoruba-English listing (but not also English-Yoruba). Of related interest are Oyekan
Owomoyela's *A ki ī: Yoruba proscriptive and prescriptive proverbs* (Lanham,
Maryland: University Press of America, 1988. 398p.) and Modupẹ Oduyọye's *Yoruba
names: their structure and meaning* (London: Karnak, 1982. 108p.).

471 **A short Yoruba grammar.**
Ayọ Bamgboṣe. Ibadan, Nigeria: Heinemann, 1974. 2nd ed. 63p.

The essential points of Yoruba grammar are extracted from the author's more
technical *A grammar of Yoruba* (Cambridge: Cambridge University, 1966. 175p.) and
presented here. Chapters cover 'Consonants, vowels and tones'; 'The nominal group'
(nouns, pronouns, pronomials, qualifiers, compound nomial groups); 'The verbal
group' (verbs, verb-nominal combinations, tenses); 'Adverbs and adverbials'; 'Clauses';
'Sentences'; and 'Assimilation and contraction'. Several exercises and keys to the
exercises conclude the book, which is intended for use in secondary schools and

technical colleges. The author, a linguist in the Department of Linguistics and Nigerian Languages, Ibadan University at the time of publication, has also published the oft-reprinted *Yoruba orthography* (Ibadan, Nigeria: Ibadan University, 1965. 33p.).

472 **Yorùbá dùn ún sọ (book one): a beginner's course in Yoruba.**
Karin Barber. New Haven, Connecticut; London: Yale University, 1985. 144p. (Yale Language Series).
This text was created and illustrated by the author while she taught Yoruba at the University of Ife (now Obafemi Awolowo University), Ile-Ife, Nigeria. The volume is based on dialogue between the teacher and student, with each lesson presenting a new grammatical construction and new vocabulary. The aim of the book is to stimulate oral participation. Aside from the brief foreword and the word list, it is entirely in Yoruba. The title, *Yorùbá dùn ún so* translated is 'Yoruba is pleasant to speak'.

473 **Yoruba proverbs: translation and annotation.**
Bernth Lindfors, Oyekan Owomoyela. Athens, Ohio: Ohio University Center for International Studies, Africa Program, 1973. 77 leaves. (Papers in International Studies African Series, no. 17).
Each of the 150 proverbs in this volume is recorded in Yoruba, translated literally into English and then translated creatively with an explanation of its meaning and sometimes its context. Cross-references are frequently given to A. B. Ellis's volume *The Yoruba-speaking peoples of the slave coast of West Africa* . . . (q.v.) and to Isaac O. Delanọ's *Òwo l'ẹsin ọrọ: Yoruba proverbs – their meaning and usage* (Ibadan: Oxford University, 1966, 154p.) which contains 504 proverbs in Yoruba and English and a short story using proverbs. Raphael Odekunle Areje's *Yoruba proverbs* (Ibadan, Nigeria: Daystar, 1985. 119p.) is also a useful compilation.

474 **Yoruba: a complete working course.**
E. C. Rowlands. New York: David McKay; London: Hodder & Stoughton, 1969. 276p. (Teach Yourself Books).
A thorough introduction to the language of more than ten million people of western Nigeria. Instruction is organized into thirty-nine topics based on parts of speech, and special and useful basic constructions. The course includes passages for translation and a limited vocabulary (p. 257–76). H. David McClure and John O. Oyewale's *Yoruba: intermediate texts* (Washington, DC: Department of State, Foreign Service Institute, 1967. 254p.) was produced especially for Peace Corps Volunteers in Nigeria. It contains a series of practical monologues, presented in several different ways with minor variations, and followed by questions in Yoruba to emphasize vocabulary and oral fluency. No glossary appears in this volume.

The Yoruba-speaking peoples of the Slave Coast of West Africa, their religion, manners, customs, laws, languages, etc., with an appendix contain a comparison of the Yshi, Ga, Ewe, and Yoruba languages.
See item no. 405.

Features of Yorùbá poetry.
See item no. 847.

Yoruba myths.
See item no. 1023.

Tales of Yoruba gods and heroes.
See item no. 1025.

Nigerian folktales as told by Olawale Idewu and Omotayo Adu.
See item no. 1034.

Other languages

475 **A dictionary of the Tiv language.**
Compiled by R. C. Abraham. London: Crown Agents, 1940.
Reprinted, Farnborough, England: Gregg International, 1968. 331p.
Following a brief preface and 'instructions for the use of the dictionary' is the author's
Tiv-English (but not English-Tiv) dictionary. Captain (later Major) Abraham
(1890–1963) was formerly Anthropological Officer, Northern Provinces, Nigeria, and
in the Nigerian Administrative Service, seconded for language research.

476 **Twelve Nigerian languages: a handbook on their sound systems for
teachers of English.**
Edited by Elizabeth Dunstan, foreword by David Abercrombie. New
York: Africana; London: Longmans, Green, 1969. 185p. bibliog.
This book presents the structure and sound systems of English and twelve major
Nigerian languages. Included are systematic descriptions for each language of
consonants, vowels, syllable structure, tone, intonation, and stress and a select
bibliography. The languages and their contributors are: Fula and Tiv (D. W. Arnott);
Yoruba (Ayo Bamgbose); Efik (T. L. Cook); Hausa (Carl Hoffmann, Paul Schachter);
Urhobo (John Kelly); Etsako (J. D. M. Laver); Isoko (Bernard Mafeni); Itsekiri
(A. E. Opubor); Nupe (N. V. Smith); Igbo and Ijo (Kay Williamson). The book is
intended as background for teachers of English as a second language. Dr. Dunstan
(1932– .) was formerly in the Department of Linguisitcs and Nigerian Languages at
Ibadan University, Ibadan, Nigeria.

477 **Dictionary of the Efik language in two parts. I. Efik and English. II.
English and Efik.**
Compiled by Rev. Hugh Goldie. Glasgow, 1862. Reprinted,
Amersham, England: Demand Reprints, Gregg International, 1983.
643p. & 42p.
The author of this well-known work was a missionary from the United Presbyterian
Church, Scotland, to Old Calabar. He provides a detailed introduction to Efik
grammatical constructions and commentary on other African languages (p. iii–li).

478 **A reference grammar of the Kanuri language.**
John P. Hutchison, foreword by A. Neil Skinner. Madison,
Wisconsin: University of Wisconsin, African Studies Program; Boston,
Massachusetts: Boston University, African Studies Center, 1981. 363p.
map. bibliog. (US Office of Education, Foreign Language and Area
Research Program, document no. 02-G008002123).

This study describes the intricacies of Kanuri, one of the three major languages spoken
in Islamic northern Nigeria. The author draws on his study of Kanuri and the related
language Kanembu from his Peace Corps service to the present, including his research
and work as a lecturer in the universities of Kano and Maiduguri (1974–78). The
volume includes a discussion of Kanuri, covering dialects, sound system and written
Kanuri, word formation, verbs, phrases and sentence construction. The bibliography
(p. 361–63) lists numerous other references to Kanuri.

479 **Ibibio dictionary.**
Compiled by Elaine Marlowe Kaufman. Leiden, Netherlands: Cross
River State University and Ibibio Language Board, Nigeria, in
cooperation with the African Studies Centre, Leiden, 1985. 617p.

This valuable work is easily the most comprehensive dictionary for the Ibibio-Efik
cluster since the Rev. Hugh Goldie's *Dictionary of the Efik language* (q.v.). It contains
an introduction (p. i–xiv), corrections, the dictionary (p. 1–466), personal and tribal
names (p. 467–76), addenda (p. 477–82), a glossary of Nigerian English words used in
the dictionary (p. 483–84) and an English index (p. 485–617). Copies are available
from the African Studies Centre, Stationsplein 12, 2312 AK Leiden, the Netherlands.
The dictionary began during the author's preparation of an Ibibio grammar for her
1968 doctoral thesis at the University of California, Berkeley. *Ibibio names: their
structure and meaning* (Ibadan: Daystar, 1986. 94p.) by Okon E. Essien provides
interesting linguistic information as well.

480 **An initial orthography and lexicon for Emai: an Edoid language of
Nigeria.**
Ronald P. Schaefer. Bloomington, Indiana: Indiana University
Linguistics Club, Aug. 1987. 132p. bibliog. (Studies in African
Grammatical Systems, no. 5).

An introduction (p. 1–21) describes the orthography of Emai, an Edoid language
spoken in Afuze, in northern Bendel State. This is followed by an Emai-English
lexicon (p. 22–132) based on the author's fieldwork during 1981–85 and 1987. Professor
Schaefer has published numerous technical articles on Emai and is at Southern Illinois
University, Edwardsville, Illinois. Other Nigerian volumes in this series are Nicholas
Faraclas's *A grammar of Obolo* (Sept. 1984, 122p. (SAGS, no. 1)) covering a language
of Rivers State, and E. Nwanolue Emenanjo's *Auxiliaries in Igbo Syntax: a
comparative study* (June 1985, 231p. SAGS, no. 2)).

81 **A Jukun grammar.**
Kiyoshi Shimizu. Vienna: Institut für Afrikanistik und Agyptologie der Universität Wien, 1980. 319p. bibliog. (Beiträge zur Afrikanistik, vol. 9, 11).

he author provides a systematic description of the phonology, morphology, noun and rb phrases and sentences of the language of the Jukun people, one of the largest oups living in Gongola State. His 1971 dissertation at the University of Ibadan, *omparative Jukunoid*, was published in 1980 (Vienna: Afro-Pub, 2 vols.). His was the rst doctorate awarded by the University of Ibadan's Department of Linguisitcs and frican Languages. Dr. Shimizu studied Jukun during his ten years in Nigeria 967–77); since 1978 he has taught Hausa and African linguistics at the University of ienna.

82 **Dictionaire élémentaire fulfulde-français-english elementary dictionary.**
[Elementary dictionary of Fulani in French and English]
Edited and introduced by Alfâ Ibrâhîm Sow. Niamey, Niger:
CRDTO, 1971. 166p.

ollowing work at the Regional Documentation Centre for Oral Tradition in Niamey, iger, this very practical trilingual dictionary was compiled for Fulani, an important nguage of northern Nigeria and of much of the Francophone Western Sudan. Copies n be obtained from CRDTO (Centre Régional de documentation pour la Tradition rale), B.P. 369, Niamey, Niger. Much more detailed is Paul Kazuhisa Eguchi's *An nglish-Fufulde dictionary*, (Tokyo: Institute for the Study of Languages and ultures of Asia and Africa, 1986. 372p. (African Languages and Ethnography Series, ol. 21)).

83 **A reference grammar of Adamawa Fulani.**
Leslie H[erman] Stennes. East Lansing, Michigan: Michigan State University, African Studies Center, 1967. 285p. bibliog.

he author describes Fulani phonemics, morphophonemics, morphology, verbs, dverbs, expletives, time words and interrogatives as well as syntax, clauses and iscourses. Appendices contain six folktales printed in Fulani and English; the selected ibliography (p. 269–78) provides an excellent listing of sources on Fulani. See also . W. Taylor's *A Fulani-English dictionary* (Oxford: Clarendon, 1932. 242p.). Taylor as also authored *A Fulani-English phrase book* (Oxford: Clarendon, 1926. 158p.) lthough the *Fula basic course* by Lloyd B. Swift, Kalilu Tambadu and Paul G. Imhoff Washington, DC: Department of State, Foreign Service Institute, 1965. 489p.) is ased on the Firdu Fulbe of the Senegambia dialect of Fula, it is also useful for igerian Fulani.

84 **A grammar of the Kolokuma dialect of Ịjọ.**
Kay Williamson. Cambridge: Cambridge University in association with the West African Languages Survey and the Institute of African Studies, Ibadan, 1965. 127p. bibliog. (West African Language Monographs, 2).

his revision of the author's 1963 Yale University doctoral thesis is a generative-ansformational grammar of North Central Ijọ (Ijaw) as spoken in Kaiama of the iger Delta. Using data collected in 1957, 1959 and 1962–63, the author describes the nguage's phonology, phrase-structure rules, verb phrase, noun phrase and sentence

181

transformations as well as non-tonal, tonal and elision morphophonemics. Of mor
general interest is the introduction describing the various Ijo dialects, earlier studie
and the present study. Dr. Williamson (1935– .), perhaps the outstanding student c
languages southern Nigeria, wrote the foreward and introduction to M. H. I. Kaliai
Nembe-English dictionary (Ibadan, Nigeria: University of Ibadan, Institute of Africa
Studies, 1964, 1966. 2 vols.), which considers a variety of Eastern Ijo.

485   **The Benue-Congo languages and Ijo.**
   Kay Williamson.   In: *Current trends in linguistics, vol. 7. Linguistics ir
   sub-Saharan Africa.* Edited by Thomas A. Sebeok. The Hague, Paris:
   Mouton, 1971, p. 245–306. bibliog.

Provides an important survey of Benue-Congo languages and Ijo (Ijaw), a large diale
cluster spoken in the Niger Delta. Dr. Williamson classifies the numerous language
supplies an excellent bibliography (p. 286–99) and an alphabetical list of names c
Benue-Congo languages and groups (p. 299–306). In the same volume, John M
Stewart discusses 'Niger-Congo, Kwa languages' (Akan and Yoruba, p. 179–212) an
Willaim J. Samarin describes 'Adamawa-Eastern' (p. 213–44).

Religion

General

86   Emerging themes in Nigerian and West African religious history.
J. F. Ade Ajayi, E. A. Ayandele. *Journal of African Studies*, vol. 1
(1974), p. 1–39. bibliog.

In addition to an especially useful and thoughtful survey of the literature already
produced on African religions, Islam and Christianity, the authors identify several
broad themes and enough issues in need of study to provide thesis topics for graduate
students for many years. Several Nigerian groups are among the many mentioned in
John S. Mbiti's well-known *African religions & philosophy* (New York: Praeger, 1969.
290p.) and the more general *Introduction to African religion* (New York: Praeger,
1975. 211p.). Benjamin C. Ray's *African religions: symbol, ritual, and community*
(Englewook Cliffs, New Jersey: Prentice-Hall, 1976. 238p.) includes the Yoruba, the
jihad of Shehu Usuman dan Fodio, the Hausa Tijaniyya of Ibadan and the Aladura
Church of the Lord among several featured religious groups. Historian Elizabeth
Isichei edited *Varieties of Christian experience in Nigeria* (London: Macmillan, 1982.
211p.).

487   West African traditional religion.
J. Omosade Awolalu, P. Adelumo Dopamu.   Ibadan, Nigeria:
Onibonoje, 1979. 310p. map. bibliog.

In their analysis of the religious beliefs of thirteen West African ethnic groups, the
authors discuss the Yoruba, Igbo, Edo, Nupe, Ijo, Tiv and Ibibio of Nigeria. A brief
bibliography (p. 292–95) is included. G[eoffrey] E[dward] Parrinder's *West African
religion: a study of the beliefs and practices of Akan, Ewe, Yoruba, Ibo and kindred
peoples* (London: Epworth, 1969, 3rd ed. 203p.) has become the standard work by a
European on the subject. Bini, Ibibio and Nupe religious practices are described as
well as those of the groups in the title. Professor Parrinder was the first lecturer in the
University of Ibadan Department of Religious Studies and for many years taught the
course entitled 'Indigenous religious beliefs of West Africa', and also authored

Religion in an African City (q.v.). More recently, T. N. O. Quarcoopome's illustra*
West African traditional religion (Ibadan, Nigeria: African Universities Press, 19*
200p.) has been published. It contains questions at the end of each chapter and ai*
'to satisfy the demands of the G.C.E. 'A' Level Religious Studies paper III' (Prefa*
p. [iii]).

488 **A select periodical bibliography on African traditional religion, with
special emphasis on Nigeria, 1900–1970.**
Herbert O. Emezi. *A Current Bibliography on African Affairs*,
vol. 12, no. 3 (1979–80), p. 329–39.

An unannotated listing, organized alphabetically by author, of 208 items, mos*
articles, focusing on Nigerian traditional religion. Some useful materials publish*
after 1970 are included as well. The list cites numerous articles from Nigeri*
periodicals such as *Nigeria Magazine* (q.v.), *Nigerian Field* (q.v.), and W*
African Religion (q.v.). The author was at the Alvan Ikoku College of Educatio*
Owerri, Nigeria, at the time of publication.

489 **Oedipus and Job in West African religion.**
Meyer Fortes, with an essay by Robin Horton, introduced by Jack
Goody. Cambridge: Cambridge University, 1983. 92p. bibliog.
(Cambridge Sutdies in Social Anthropology, no. 48).

The title of this volume refers to anthropologist Fortes' famous essay, original*
delivered as a Frazer Lecture in 1957 and published in 1959, which was concerned on*
with the Tallensi of Ghana (p. 1–40). To Fortes, Oedipal ideas refer to 'Fate*
Destiny' and Jobian ideas refer to 'Supernatural Justice'. In this reprinting his essay*
accompanied by Horton's comparison of a set of concepts found in different forn*
among the Tallensi and Ashanti of Ghana and the Yoruba and Kalabari of southe*
Nigeria. In 'Social psychologies: African and western' (p. 41–82), Horton shows th*
although the Tallensi may be an extreme example, West African cosmologies a*
'above all means of explaining, predicting and attempting to control the relationsh*
between the individual and his or her society – i.e. 'social psychologies'' (p. 43*
Horton is Professor of Philosophy at the University of Port Harcourt, Port Harcou*
Nigeria.

490 **The development of Islam in West Africa.**
Mervyn Hiskett. London, New York: Longman, 1984. 353p. 13 map*
bibliog.

A superb scholarly synthesis of the current materials on the complex history of Islam*
spread in West Africa, with emphasis on the west and central Sudan. Major them*
concern the processes of conversion to Islam, the formation of states, and literacy. Th*
author concludes, 'The fact is, there is no pattern; but there is a single, unbroke*
thread. It is that the history of Islam in the west and central Sudan, from its beginnin*
until now, has been a triumph for the power of literate ideas' (p. 39). Students c*
northern Nigeria will find much useful information here on the Kanem, Born*
Hausaland and the Sokoto Caliphate, as well as on the attitudes of the British towar*
Islam in the region, and the relations between them. An invaluable resource volume *
J. F. P. Hopkins' and N. Levtzion's *Corpus of Early Arabic sources for West Africa*
history* (Cambridge: Cambridge University, 1981. 492p. bibliog).

491 **Islam in West Africa.**
J. Spencer Trimingham. Oxford: Clarendon, 1964. 262p. map. bibliog.

Using scholarly sources and observations made during a 1952 survey throughout West Africa, sponsored by the Church Missionary Society and the Methodist Missionary Society, Rev. Trimingham describes the impact of Islam on the peoples of the region. In particular, he discusses the process of cultural change, institutional Islam, the influence of Islam on ideas concerning the supernatural and the social structure, the life-cycle, economics and material culture. Several northern Nigerian peoples, especially the Nupe, Fulani and Hausa have important places in this study. The 'Glossary-index of Arabic and African terms' (p. 235–49) is very useful as is the fold-out map of religious distributions in West Africa. The historical background is described in the author's *A history of Islam in West Africa* (London: Oxford, 1962, 262p.) which covers about ten centuries and contains chronological tables of important dates and events in the central Sudan. Trimingham was formerly Professor of History at the American University of Beirut.

Nigerian

492 **Sixteen great poems of Ifá.**
Wande Abimbọla. Zaria, Nigeria: Gaskiya, 1975. 468p. bibliog.

A lengthy, lucid account of the most pre-eminent religious divination system of the Yoruba people. The book is divided into an explanation of the cult of Ifá (or Orúnmilà) and its paraphernalia (p. 1–42) and the sixteen lengthy poems comprising the Ifá literary corpus, 'by far the most important of the numerous genres of Yoruba oral literature . . . The Yoruba people themselves regard Ifá as the great authority on their mythology, history and philosophy. Indeed, Ifá can be regarded as the unwritten text-book of Yoruba culture in its true historical and philosophical perspective' (Preface, p. iii). Each poem is presented in Yoruba and English, is preceded by a thematic analysis and contains explanatory end-notes. The appendix provides a traditional interpretation for each poem as offered by the Ifá priests who supplied the poems. This work derives from the author's 1969 University of Lagos dissertation, *An exposition of Ifá literary corpus*. Dr. Abimbọla was at the University of Lagos, Lagos, Nigeria at the time of publication.

493 **Sacrifice in Ibo religion.**
Francis A. Arinze, edited by J. S. Boston. Ibadan, Nigeria: Ibadan University, 1970. 129p. bibliog.

Using the ethnographic present tense, the author gives a thorough account of 'the question of sacrifice in the religion which was prevalent in Iboland before the arrival of Christianity' (Preface), describing in detail the objects and ends of Igbo sacrifice. The functions of the *dibia*, the diviner, and especially the *eze-alusi*, the shrine or cult priest, the associated rituals, and the types of sacrifices, ranging from foods and animals to humans, are discussed. The appendix lists sixty-one proverbs with English translations. This book is the first part of the author's 1960 doctoral thesis written in Rome, entitled *Ibo sacrifice as an introduction to the Catechesis of Holy Mass*. At the time of

publication, the author was Catholic Archbishop of Onitsha. Christopher I. Ejizu':
Ọfọ: Igbo ritual symbol (Enugu, Nigeria: Fourth Dimension, 1986. 190p.) provides a
useful, illustrated analysis as well.

494 **How man makes god in West Africa: Yoruba attitudes towards the òrìṣà.**
Karin Barber. *Africa*, vol. 51, no. 3 (1981), p. 724–45. bibliog.

The author examines *òrìṣà* creation and maintenance in a small Yoruba town in Oyo
State, stating that 'The *òrìṣà* are said to have been people living on earth who on their
departure from it were deified' (p. 729). She sees human-*òrìṣà* relations as 'in some
sense a projection of relations between people in society', suggesting 'that if the
Yoruba see the *òrìṣà's* power as being maintained and augmented by human attention
this is because they live in a kind of society where it is very clear that the *human*
individual's power depends in the long run on the attention and acknowledgement of
his fellow-men' (p. 724). Barber lived in the Yoruba town of Òkukù for three years
while researching oral poetry. Her 1979 doctoral thesis at the University of Ife was
Oriki in Òkukù: relationships between verbal and social structures.

495 **Ogun: an old god for a new age.**
Sandra T. Barnes. Philadelphia, Pennsylvania: Institute for the Study
of Human Issues (ISHI), 1980. 64p. 2 maps. bibliog. (ISHI Occasional
Papers in Social Change, no. 3).

The author examines the Yoruba cult of Ogun, the god of iron, a cult which seems to
be thriving rather than disappearing in the face of rapid social change. She places the
Ogun cult in a broader African 'sacred iron complex' characterized by the 'belief that
iron or related items are sacred, that Ogun has a marginal status, and that the smithy is
a sanctuary' (p. 7). Applying intellectualist, formalist and functionalist and adaptive
explanations, Professor Barnes concludes that no other figure lends itself as well to
being a symbol of civil unrest and revolt. 'Thus the cult of Ogun flourishes because it
addresses itself to a universal human problem: the fact that man creates the means to
destroy himself' (p. 44). Her research on the Ogun cult was conducted in 1971–72.

496 **Ifá divination: communication between gods and men in West Africa.**
William Bascom. Bloomington, Indiana; London: Indiana University,
1969. 575p. bibliog.

Represents a masterful study of Ifa, 'the most respected, in many ways the most
interesting, system of divination of five to ten million Yoruba in Nigeria and millions
more of their African neighbors and their descendants in the New World' (Preface,
p. ix). Based largely on data gathered in 1937–38, but supplemented by visits in
1950–51, 1960 and 1965, the study gives a full description of Ifa divination (p. 3–137).
The remainder of the book consists of the verses of Ifa, transcribed in Yoruba and
translated into English with explanatory notes and a useful bibliography (p. 565–75).
Figures, tables and twenty-four black-and-white plates taken of divination paraphernalia
and a divination ceremony in 1937 add to the comprehensiveness of the volume.

497 **Sixteen cowries: Yoruba divination from Africa to the New World.**
William Bascom. Bloomington, Indiana; London: Indiana University,
1980. 790p. bibliog.

' "Sixteen cowries" . . . is a form of divination employed by the Yoruba of Nigeria and
by their descendants in the New World. It is simpler than Ifa divination and is held in

less esteem in Nigeria, but in the Americas it is more important than Ifa because it is more widely known and more frequently employed' (p. 3). Dr. Bascom (1912–82) tape-recorded the lengthy divination verses presented here in Yoruba and English during 1950–51 and conducted additional research during visits in 1960 and 1965. In the relatively brief first part (p. 3–52) he describes the belief system and its rituals as it exists in Nigeria, Cuba and Brazil. Part two (p. 54–773) consists of the seventeen verses of the system, one for each of the sixteen numbers of cowries and one for zero cowries. An appendix with the various names of the seventeen cowrie figures in different locations and a brief bibliography (p. 787–90) conclude this distinguished work.

498 **Religion, legitimacy and conflict in Nigeria.**
Henry Bienen. *Annals of the American Academy of Political and Social Science*, vol. 483 (Jan. 1986), p. 50–60. bibliog.

The author examines the rôle of religion, especially Islam which has been an 'unofficial state religion' in the north (p. 60), in recent Nigerian history. The Maitatsine movement which Professor Bienen mentions is treated more fully by Raymond Hickey's 'The 1982 Maitatsine uprising in Nigeria: a note' in *African Affairs*, vol. 83, no. 331 (April 1984), p. 251–56, and by Mervyn Hiskett's 'The Maitatsine riots in Kano, 1980: an assessment' in *Journal of Religion in Africa*, vol. 17, no. 3 (1987), p. 209–23, which shows much insight. *The Maitatsine riots in Nigeria, 1980–1984*, an annotated bibliography of 343 entries from eighteen daily and weekly publications, by Moses A. Omoniwa and John A. Abu (Zaria, Nigeria: Kashim Ibrahim Library, Ahmadu Bello University, Sept. 1986. 47p.) is also an important source of information.

499 **Ifẹ shrines.**
M. A. Fabunmi. Ibadan, Nigeria: University of Ife, 1969. 28p. map.

This guide to twenty-two shrines and thirteen other points of interest in Ile-Ife, the most sacred city of the Yoruba, was prepared from notes the author made when he took the University of Ife Women's Group on tour in 1968. In this 'introduction to the city' he describes much of Ife's religious heritage and lore. A map locating the shrines and other sites is included. Chief Fabunmi was Honorary Research Associate of the Institute of African Studies, University of Ife. Frank Speed photographed fifteen shrines and sacred objects for the booklet. Of related interest is the illustrated *Guide to the Museum of the Institute of African Studies, University of Ife* (Ile-Ife: University of Ife Press, 1969. 13p.) published by the University Museum.

500 **The influence of Islam on a Sudanese religion.**
Joseph [H.] Greenberg. Seattle, Washington; London: University of Washington, 1966. 73p. map. bibliog. (Monographs of the American Ethnological Society, no. 10).

Originally published in 1946 and based on fieldwork from October 1938 to August 1939, this study describes the impact of Islam on the religion of the Maguzawa (a Hausa term for all Hausa-speaking 'pagans') of Kano and its environs in northern Nigeria. The distinguished author examines historical contacts between Kano and Islamic culture, the non-Islamic Hausa and primarily 'Maguzawa religion' (p. 27–63). The bibliography (p. 71–73) is useful.

501 **New religious movements in Nigeria.**
Edited by Rosalind I. J. Hackett, foreword by Harold W. Turner.
Lewiston, New York; Queenston, Ontario: Edwin Mellen, 1987. 245p.
map. bibliog. (African Studies, vol. 5).

Among the twelve essays on diverse religious movements, the following are of particular interest: 'Introduction: variations on a theme', (p. 1–18), a study of the Celestial Church of Christ, 'Thirty years of growth and change in a West African independent church: a sociological perspective' (p. 161–78); 'Women as leaders and participants in the spiritual churches' (p. 191–208); and 'Conclusion: religious innovation and self-determination: the continuing quest' (p. 237–42), all by the editor, and Peter B. Clarke's 'The Maitatsine movement in northern Nigeria in historical and current perspective' (p. 93–115). Other contributors include E. Samson Akama, J. K. Olupona, G. I. S. Amadi, Daniel I. Ilega, Essien A. Offiong, and Friday M. Mbon. The editor lectured in religious studies at the University of Calabar (1979–83) and at the time of publication was at the University of Tennessee, Knoxville, Tennessee. She has also published *Religion in Calabar: the religious life and history of a Nigerian town* (Berlin, New York: Mouton de Gruyter, 1989. 481p.) and *The Celestial Church of Christ* (Ibadan, Nigeria: Ibadan University) which is in press.

502 **Northern Nigeria.**
Mervyn Hiskett. In: *Islam in Africa.* Edited by James Kritzeck,
William H. Lewis. New York: Van Nostrand-Reinhold, 1969,
p. 287–300. bibliog.

The author discusses the spread of Islam in Hausaland from the mid-fourteenth century through to the Fulani *jihad* of the early-nineteenth century, including the broader consequences of the *jihad.* Useful, too, are the author's discussions of the sources of this history, 'The Kano Chronicle' (English translation by Sir Richmond Palmer. In: *Sudanese memories*, Lagos, 1928, vol. III), described by Hiskett in 'The Kano Chronicle', *Journal of The Royal Asiatic Society*, no. 1–2 (April 1957), p. 79–81; and the 'History of Katsina', an unpublished work recorded from oral tradition by F de F. Daniel, available only as a typescript in a limited private edition; one copy is available in the library of the School for Arabic Studies, Kano in Nigeria. *Wakar Bagauda*, an account in Hausa verse, is translated and described by Hiskett in 'The "Song of Bagauda": a Hausa king list and homily in verse', *Bulletin of the School of Oriental and African Studies*, part I, vol. 27, no. 3 (1964), p. 540–67; part II, vol. 28, no. 1 (1965), p. 112–35; part III, vol. 28, no. 2 (1965), p. 363–85, and represents an important source. See also his criticisms of M. G. Smith's article 'Historical and cultural conditions of political corruption among the Hausa' in *Comparative Studies in Society and History*, vol. 6, no. 2 (Jan. 1964), p. 164–9.

503 **A hundred years of change in Kalabari religion.**
Robin Horton. In: *Black Africa: its peoples and their cultures today.*
Edited by John Middleton. London: Macmillan, 1970, p. 192–211.
bibliog.

The author outlines the traditional Niger Delta Kalabari concept of a supreme being and sketches the effects of a century of Christian mission activity on this idea. He explains the ready identification of the Christina God with the Kalabari *tamuno*, emphasizing an 'essential continuity' between the two belief systems rather than a 'conversion' from one to the other.

04 **Olódùmarè: god in Yoruba belief.**
E. Bọlaji Idowu. New York: Praeger, 1963. 222p. map. bibliog.
Not only does this oft-cited volume explain in detail the diverse dimensions of the
Yoruba supreme god Olódùmarè – his attributes, status, ministers, priesthood and
values – but it also provides extensive material on Yoruba beliefs and culture in
general. Seventeen photographic plates of the god's social context in Yoruba religion
are included. The book is based on the author's 1955 doctoral thesis presented to the
faculty of theology at the University of London. In *African traditional religion: a
definition* (Mary Knoll, New York: Orbis, 1975. 228p.), Professor Idowu explores the
study, nature and structure of, and prospects for African traditional religions and
provides a complex definition of religion.

05 **Of God and maxim guns: Presbyterianism in Nigeria, 1846–1966.**
Geoffrey Johnston. Waterloo, Ontario: Wilfrid Laurier University for
the Canadian Corporation for Studies in Religion, 1988. 322p. map.
bibliog. (Editions in the Study of Religion (EdSR), 8).
This history traces Presbyterian mission activities, particularly among Efiks of the
Calabar area, from 1846 to the national crises of 1966. It emphasizes the church's
educational mission and the evolution of its intimate relationship with colonial and
post-colonial developments. By 1960 the Presbyterian Church of Nigeria operated a
school system with 60,000 students and 2,000 teachers, four hospitals, a bookshop and
the Hope Waddell Training Institution, as well as cooperative efforts with other
churches. The author was Presbyterian tutor at Trinity College, Umuahia, Nigeria.

06 **Religion in an African city.**
Geoffrey Parrinder. London: Oxford University. Reprinted,
Westport, Connecticut: Negro Universities Press, 1974. 211p. bibliog.
A famous account, based on field research in 1949–51, of traditional religion, Islam
and Christianity in Ibadan. Appendices provide lists of temples and shrines, Chief
Imams of Ibadan, statistics of mission churches and separatist sects, and religious
mottoes on lorries, taxis and shops.

07 **Aladura: a religious movement among the Yoruba.**
J[ohn] D[avid] Y[eadon] Peel. London: Oxford University for the
International African Institute, 1968. 338p. 2 maps. bibliog.
Professor Peel investigates two independent churches, the Christ Apostolic Church and
the Cherubim and Seraphim, among the Yoruba of Western Nigeria. These are the
two largest Aladura ('praying') Churches, and are part of a movement which has
spread from Calabar to Freetown, Sierra Leone, over the fifty years preceding the
study. Data based on interviews and surveys, genealogies, a brief glossary of Yoruba
words and phrases, and an extensive bibliography (p. 316–31) accompany the full
sociological study of the churches' histories, beliefs and doctrines, activities,
organizations and rôles within society. This book is a revision of the author's
University of London doctoral thesis and is based on research conducted in Nigeria
during 1964–65. A related article on the Aladura churches is the author's 'Syncretism
and religious change' in *Comparative Studies in Society and History*, vol. 10, no. 2 (Jan.
1968), p. 121–41.

Periodical

508 **Journal of Religion in Africa.**
Leiden, Netherlands: E. J. Brill, 1967– . three times yearly.

Extensive material on Nigeria appears regularly in this scholarly journal. For example vol. 18, no. 1 (Feb. 1988), contains five articles on aspects of religion among the Yoruba, the Igbo and in central Nigeria, as well as numerous book reviews. The editorial address is: Professor Adrian Hastings, Department of Theology and Religious Studies, the University, Leeds, LS2 9JT, England.

The sword of truth: the life and times of the Shehu Usuman dan Fodio.
See item no. 193.

A revolution in history: the jihad of Usman Dan Fodio.
See item no. 218.

Hegemony and culture: political and religious change among the Yoruba.
See item no. 612.

Society and Social Conditions

General

509 **Nigerian children: developmental perspectives.**
Edited by H. Valerie Curran. London; Boston, Massachusetts: Routledge & Kegan Paul, 1984. 237p. bibliog.
An unusual collection of eight articles on the psychological and social development of Nigerian children, comprising: Introduction (p. 1–11) and 'Developmental perspectives on memory' (p. 118–55) by the editor; 'Looking strategies in Nigerian infants: a cross-cultural study' by R. Bunday and A. Mundy-Castle (p. 12–33); 'The educational experiences of Nigerian infants' by A. Whiten and P. Milner (p. 34–73); 'Cognitive and affective aspects of infant development' by I. Agiobu-Kemmer (p. 74–117); 'Home and school: effects of micro-ecology on children's educational achievement' by A. I. Oyewole (p. 156–73); 'Traditional child-rearing practices of the Oje Market women of Ibadan' by B. Meldrum (p. 174–97); and 'Handicapped children: an epidemiological study in Plateau State' by Charles A. Saunders (p. 197–234).

510 **Regional rivalry, party politics, and ethnic identity in Nigeria – 1979–1983.**
Elizabeth A. Eames. *Cultural Survival Quarterly*, vol. 9, no. 3 (1985), p. 12–15.
The author, who lived in the Yoruba town of Ondo from 1981–84, describes the relationships between Yoruba ethnic consciousness and party rivalries up to the coup of August 1985 in a broader national context. She analyses current events in another recent article, entitled, 'Why the women went to war: women and wealth in Ondo Town 1985' in *Traders versus the state: anthropological approaches to unofficial economies*, edited by Gracia Clark (Boulder, Colorado: Westview, 1988, p. 81–97).

Society and Social Conditions. General

511 **Child-rearing practices in Northern Nigeria.**
James M. Hake, preface by S. A. Olawuyi.   Ibadan, Nigeria: Ibadan
University, 1972. 141p. 2 maps. bibliog.
This study is based on data collected during 1968–70 from 108 males and sixty-seve
females, with average ages of twenty-five and twenty-three, respectively. The subjec
were from fifty-one different ethnic groups and answered questions seeking t
determine patterns of parent-child relations, concerning: learning; moral training an
punishment; joys and fears; play activities; diet and foods; and sex training. About ha
of the book consists of the questionnaire itself and the details of the responses. Eigl
photographs are included. The author was a member of an Ohio University, Unite
States Agency for International Development (USAID) team of educational exper
and taught educational psychology at the Advanced Teachers College, Kano, Nigeriz

512 **Urbanization in Nigeria.**
Akin L. Mabogunje.   New York: Africana, 1969. 353p. maps. bibliog
This impressive study combines substantial descriptions of pre-European Nigeria
urbanization in the north and in Yoruba towns with a detailed history and analysis c
urbanization in Ibadan 'the apogee of pre-European urbanization' and Lagos, 'th
metropolitan creation of the colonial era' (p. 27). Unfortunately, 1952 data are th
most recent used in the analyses because of disputes over the 1963 census. The volum
has twenty-nine photographs, forty-eight figures, many of Ibadan and Lagos, and fift
four tables of data, and derives in part from the author's doctoral thesis at Universit
College, London. M.Y.I. Salami describes the problems of Lagos's rapid growth i
'Nigeria's booming capital', *World Health*, (July 1983), p. 8–10.

513 **Yoruba towns.**
A. L. Mabogunje.   Ibadan, Nigeria: Ibadan University, 1962. 22p.
8 maps. bibliog.
This booklet is based on the author's lecture 'Problems of a pre-industrial urbanizatio
in West Africa' delivered in April 1961. He surveys the problems of pre-colonia
colonial, and post-colonial urban growth among the Yoruba, one of the continent
most urbanized traditional cultures, and offers suggestions for urban reconstructior
Several Yoruba town plans, tables and photographs accompany the discussion. /
recent exploration of Yoruba urbanization, particularly in Mushin, a suburb of Lago
and Ibadan is Sandra T. Barnes's 'The political dynamics of the urban frontier' in *Th
African frontier: the reproduction of traditional African societies*, edited by Ige
Kopytoff (Bloomington, Indiana: Indiana Univeristy, 1987, p. 255–81).

514 **Nigerian cultural nationalism.**
Victor O. Olorunsola.   In: *Race and ethnicity in Africa.* Edited by
Pierre L. van den Berghe. Nairobi, Kenya: East African Publishing
House, 1975, p. 166–78. bibliog.
A discussion of 'political culture' in Nigeria where politics 'is largely ethnic an
regional, not national' with a description of Yoruba, Hausa and Igbo political culture
seen largely as 'the politics of regional and ethnic security' (p. 167). Bolstering h
account is a quote from 'Peter Pan' (pseud. of Peter Enahoro), who wrote of ethni
affiliation being an 'identikit' defining one's social, political, economic and persona
outlook in 'How to be a Nigerian', *Daily Times* (Lagos), 9 May 1965. The article
reprinted from *African Forum*, vol. 3 (1967).

192

15   **Housing in Nigeria (a book of readings).**
      Edited by Poju Onibokun, foreword by Akin Mabogunje. Ibadan,
      Nigeria: Nigerian Institute of Social and Economic Research (NISER),
      1985. 446p. bibliog.

his most comprehensive study of Nigerian housing yet published contains twenty-
ven artilces (five by the editor) organized around seven themes: housing problems
ad needs; housing policy and programmes; housing finance; housing design
nstruction and technology; housing: redevelopment options; human implications of
using; and housing administration and management. Professor Mabogunje contributed
a introductory essay entitled 'Towards an urban policy in Nigeria' (p. 19–35). The
litor is Professor of Urban and Regional Planning, NISER, Ibadan. He has also
ablished *Issues in Nigerian housing: a bibliographic review* (Ibadan: NISER, 1983)
ad, with Ajit Atwal and George Rich, *Housing need: an annotated bibliography*
Monticello, Illinois: Council of Planning Librarians, 1973. 42p.). See also A. O. Ozo's
'ublic housing policies and the urban poor in the Third World: a case study from
igeria', *Third World Planning Review*, vol. 8, no. 1 (Feb. 1986), p. 51–67, for an
nalysis of housing in Benin City.

16   **Strangers to the city: urban man in Jos, Nigeria.**
      Leonard Plotnicov.   Pittsburgh, Pennsylvania: University of
      Pittsburgh, 1967. 320p. 2 maps. bibliog.

The object of this study is to describe and analyze the adjustments individuals make to
modern conditions of urban development in a West African community' (p. 3). Based
n fieldwork from November 1960 to August 1962, it presents detailed chapters on
ur migrants to the city and shorter accounts of four other migrants. This life history
nalysis reveals the background and urban adaptive efforts of Yoruba, Ijaw, Tiv, Efik,
Iausa, Igbo, Kagoro and Birom men. Plotnicov, Professor of Anthropology at the
Jniversity of Pittsburg, concludes that urban life is complex but not disorganized, that
rban behaviour is logical and appropriate from the individual's viewpoint and that
everal factors prevent urban immigrants from returning home after occupational
etirement.

17   **Urbanization processes and problems in Nigeria.**
      Edited by P[ius] O[gheneruhowho] Sada, J. S. Oguntoyinbo.   Ibadan,
      Nigeria: Ibadan University, 1978. 202p. maps. bibliog.

'his is a selection of sixteen papers from the Nigerian Geographical Association's
onference on 'Urban Systems and the Process of Development' held at the University
f Lagos in 1973. Papers by seventeen Nigerians concern the themes of urban policy in
Jigeria, urbanization and development and the urban physical environment. Notable
apers include Akin L. Mabogunje's 'Towards an urban policy in Nigeria' (p. 7–20);
'. E. B. Inyang's 'Environmental pollution in some Nigerian towns' (p. 169–77); and
The research frontiers of urban geography' (p. 181–93) by the editors. The editors are
oncerned that while Nigeria's population is estimated to be growing at more than
hree per cent each year, urban growth is a 'startling' eleven per cent (Preface, p. iii).

518 **The WIN document: conditions of women in Nigeria and policy
recommendations to 2,000 AD.** [*sic*]
Women in Nigeria. Edited by Ayesha Imam, Nema Ngur-Adi, Joy
Mukubwa-Hendrickson, introduced by Molara Ogundipe-Leslie.
Samaru, Zaria, Nigeria: Women in Nigeria, 1985. 195p. bibliog.

This document describes the status and rôles of women in Nigeria. Specialists descri
in nine chapters: women and work in rural areas; women and work in the urban are;
women and education; women and the law; women's associations and network
women and the mass media of communication; women and the family; women a
religion; and women and health. The excellent bibliography contains citations for mo
than 155 authors. The volume is available from Women in Nigeria, P. O. Box 25
Samaru, Zaria, Nigeria.

519 **Women in Nigeria today.**
Edited by S. Bappa, J. Ibrahim, A. M. Imam, F. J. A. Kamara, H.
Mahdi, M. A. Modibbo, A. S. Mohammed, H. Mohammed, A. R.
Mustapha, N. Perchonock, R. I. Pittin (Editorial Committee, Women
in Nigeria). London: Zed, 1985. 257p. bibliog.

A collection of thirty essays and rapporteur's comments, compiled by the Editori
Committee of Women in Nigeria, discussing theoretical perspectives, women
Nigerian history, women in production, contemporary perspectives and futu
prospects. Essayists include Molara Ogundipe-Leslie, John Haynes, E. Madanag
Rachael Agheyisi and others as well as the editors. The papers comprise t
proceedings of the first seminar on women in Nigeria, held at Ahmadu Be
University, Zaria, in May 1982.

Ethics in Nigerian culture.
See item no. 1

Nigeria: twenty years of independence.
See item no. 6.

Katsina: profile of a Nigerian city.
See item no. 8.

How to be a Nigerian.
See item no. 10.

Nigeria struggles with boom times.
See item no. 11.

The Africans.
See item no. 17.

Nigeria: a country study.
See item no. 21.

Nigerian life and culture: a book of readings.
See item no. 23.

Nigeria.
See item no. 25.

Friends, Nigerians, countrymen.
See item no. 26.

Nigeria: the land and its peoples.
See item no. 28.

Social structure

520 **Fathers work for their sons: accumulation, mobility and class formation in an extended Yorubà community.**
Sara S. Berry. Berkeley, California: University of California, 1985. 225p. bibliog.
An informative study of the transformation of the political economy of Western Nigeria, and in particular of the cocoa-producing sector near Ife in Oyo State in the 1970s, which is based on fieldwork conducted in 1970–71 and 1978–79. The author uses a Marxist approach to analyse how individuals have developed strategies 'in the general competition for wealth and influence [which] have exacerbated inequality and promoted unproductive patterns of accumulation and resource use and management' (p. 192). She describes, in addition to cocoa growers, school teachers and motor mechanics, two other groups created by and during colonialism. She considers community development, demonstrating that 'townspeople's collective efforts to improve the material conditions of their community have engendered competition and political conflict, which in turn have absorbed the surplus collected for local improvements' (p. 189). Books, articles, theses and archive materials are listed in the bibliography (p. 207–19). The volume was reviewed by Susan Martin in *African Affairs*, vol. 86, no. 343 (April 1987), p. 279–81.

521 **Social stratification in Bornu.**
Ronald Cohen. In: *Social stratification in Africa.* Edited by Arthur Tuden and Leonard Plotnicov. New York: Free Press; London:Collier-Macmillan, 1970, p. 225–67. bibliog.
An informative analysis of social structure and stratification among the Kanuri of north-eastern Nigeria, based on fieldwork conducted in 1955–57, 1964, 1965 and 1966. Professor Cohen describes the evolution of Kanuri social and political structure, status distinctions, age, sex and rural or urban residence factors, class and mobility. Occupations are discussed, with a table ranking fifty-five occupations by Maiduguri secondary-school boys. The rôle of praise-singers is discussed in terms of status anxiety and the author describes 'the Kanuri theory of success and its relation to stratifiction' (p. 264–65).

522 **African social studies: a radical reader.**
Edited by Peter C. W. Gutkind, Peter Waterman. New York: Monthly Review; London: Heinemann, 1977. 481p. bibliog.
Among the forty-three articles in this volume are several on Nigeria: Philip Ehrensaft's 'The rise of a proto-bourgeoisie in Yorubaland' (p. 116–24); Peter Gutkind's 'Social organization of the unemployed in Lagos and Nairobi' (p. 251–62); Gavin Williams's

195

Society and Social Conditions. Social structure

'Class relations in a neo-colony: the case of Nigeria' (p. 284–94); Otonti Nduka's 'The nationality of the rich in Nigeria' (p. 343–50); and Segun Osoba's 'The Nigerian power elite, 1952–65' (p. 368–82). Christopher Allen's 'Radical themes in African social studies: a bibliographical guide' (p. 424–62) contains a useful essay and numerous references.

523 **Islam and urban labor in northern Nigeria: the making of a Muslim working class.**
Paul M. Lubeck. Cambridge: Cambridge University, 1986. 362p. 5 maps. bibliog. (African Studies Series, 52).

Lubeck explains 'the complex process of working-class formation among Muslims residing in the northern Nigerian city of Kano during the period 1966–80' (p. 1). Combining comparative-historical methods, a 1971 survey of 3,075 workers from the five largest employers of industrial labour, and field research which included residence in Tudun Wada, the oldest working-class area of Kano and visits to Nigeria during 1970–72, 1975, 1978, 1980 and 1981, he presents a thorough analysis of the impact of the civil war, the petroleum boom and the consequent social change affecting workers in Kano. The author is Professor of Sociology, Merrill College, University of California, Santa Cruz, California.

524 **The African bourgeoisie: capitalist development in Nigeria, Kenya, and the Ivory Coast.**
Edited by Paul M. Lubeck. Boulder, Colorado: Lynne Rienner, 1987. 414p. bibliog.

This collection of papers which 'developed from research first presented at the Dakar Conference on the African Bourgeoisie in December 1980' (p. ix), emphasizes the rise of the indigenous bourgeoisie and the primacy of internal microlevel factors such as capitalist class formation and conflict within and between classes in the relatively successful African states. Four articles concern Nigeria: 'Peasantry, merchant capital, and the colonial state: class in Northern Nigeria, 1900–1945' by Michael J. Watts (p. 59–96); 'Green capitalism in Nigeria' by Okello Oculi (p. 167–84); 'Indigenization and the Nigerian bourgeoisie: dependent development in an African context' by Thomas J. Biersteker (p. 249–80); and 'State capital, capitalist development, and class formation in Nigeria' by Tom Forrest (p. 307–42). The general bibliography (p. 385–401) is very useful.

525 **The modern African elite of Jos, Nigeria.**
Leonard Plotnicov. In: *Social stratification in Africa.* Edited by Arthur Tuden, Leonard Plotnicov. New York: Free Press; London: Collier-Macmillan, 1970, p. 269–302. bibliog.

A theoretical article on social class formation in Africa using Jos, a mid-sized city in central Nigeria, as a case study. The author describes the general characteristics of Jos and its social stratification; differentiates traditional, modern and ambiguous élites; and discusses the community-integrative activities of the modern élite as well as 'upper stratum crystallization and incipient middle class development' (p. 292–96). Professor Plotnicov concludes that Nigeria 'will develop a class system as it undergoes modernization of its economy, and now that a modern elite upper stratum has formed we can expect the crystallization of a middle class. The general mass, as a residual category will continue to form the base of the pyramid' (p. 300).

526 **The rise of a new elite amongst the women of Nigeria.**
S[ylvia] Leith-Ross. In: *Africa: social problems of change and conflict.*
Edited by Pierre L. van den Berghe. San Francisco, California:
Chandler, 1965, p. 221–29.

The editor reprinted this interesting article about Nigerian women in the mid-1950s
from the *International Social Sciences Bulletin*, vol. 8 (1956), p. 481–88. Leith-Ross
discusses women in southern Nigeria, their place in society, the impact of Western
education and their relations with men. She identifies three high status groups: the
traditional élite; 'big' women traders; and the new 'industrial elite'.

527 **The new Nigerian elite.**
Hugh H. Smythe, Mabel M. Smythe. Stanford, California: Stanford
University, 1960. 196p. map. bibliog.

Presents a study of 'the class of persons who [were] in positions of leadership, power,
and influence' (Preface, p. viii) in Nigeria on the verge of independence. The authors
estimate that the country had about 20,000 élite when the study was conducted in
1957–58 and that of these, 1,500–3,000 are 'upper-level elite'. The book analyses the
history and political development of the élite and factors favouring the growth of the
new élite. A detailed survey of 156 of the élite enables a discussion of their
characteristics and their relations with the British. The chapter 'How the elite live'
(p. 137–53) describes their housing, servants, dining patterns, dress, work and rest
habits and leisure-time activities. The chapter notes (p. 175–91) also provide a
comprehensive bibliography on the subject at the time.

Social problems

528 **The trouble with Nigeria.**
Chinua Achebe. Enugu, Nigeria: Fourth Dimension, 1983; London:
Heinemann, 1984. 68p.

Nigeria's acclaimed author turns his attention to contemporary political and social
issues in this impassioned essay. In brief chapters he examines: 'Where the problem
lies', 'Tribalism', 'False image of ourselves', 'Leadership', 'Nigerian style', 'Patriotism',
'Social injustice and the cult of mediocrity', 'Indiscipline', 'Corruption', 'The Igbo
problem' and 'The example of Aminu Kano'. Writes Achebe, 'The trouble with
Nigeria is simply and squarely a failure of leadership' (p. 1). 'I can see no rational
answer to the drastic jumble of tragic and tragi-comical problems we have unleashed
on ourselves in the past twenty-five years, but the example of [the late] Aminu Kano –
a selfless commitment to the common people of our own land whom we daily deprive
and dispossess and whose plight we treat so callously and frivolously' (p. 62).

529 **Perspectives on drought and famine in Nigeria.**
G. Jan Van Apeldoorn. London: Allen & Unwin, 1981. 184p.
5 maps. bibliog.

This book analyses the origins, causes and significance of the drought and famine
experience in Nigeria during the 1970s. Against the background 'of a deteriorating

Society and Social Conditions. Social problems

food situation in the 1980s, it shows how the outcome of current Nigerian rural-development policy will be increased vulnerability of the poor to disasters' (p. 1) and proposes an alternative policy orientation to increase self-reliance. Following a description of the geographical and historical contexts of Nigerian drought and famine, the author examines the 1972–74 disaster in detail. He describes the impact of the colonial economy on traditional Hausa systems for coping with drought and stresses the need for policy makers to understand local conditions in order to create an effective early-warning system. The bibliography (p. 170–78) is substantial. The author was Senior Research Fellow at the Reformed University of Amsterdam. This book evolved from his 1978 research report *Drought in Nigeria* written for the Centre for Social and Economic Research at Ahmadu Bello University, Zaria, Nigeria. Michael J. Mortimore's *Adapting to drought: farmers, famines, and desertification in West Africa* (Cambridge; New York: Cambridge University, 1988) is also an important contribution to studies of northern Nigeria.

530   **Ambiguous consequences of the socialization and seclusion of Hausa women.**
       Barbara J. Callaway.   *Journal of Modern African Studies*, vol. 22, no. 3 (Sept. 1984), p. 429–50. bibliog.

This article, based on 150 interviews in the Muslim city of Kano, Nigeria, a survey of 300 rural women in Kano State, and questionnaires given to 800 university students, describes the situation of Hausa women and 'speculates upon the possibilities for changes in their status and life options' (p. 429). Professor Callaway describes 'growing up female in Hausaland' and persuasively argues that, paradoxically, the seclusion of women may give them 'the kind of foundation for real emotional self-sufficiency and independence only recently achieved in western societies' (p. 433). Though outwardly subordinate, Hausa women in seclusion develop a 'hidden muted autonomy [which] may provide the foundation for change in the social structure. . .' (p. 449). The author was resident in Kano during 1981–83 when she was Visiting Fulbright Senior Lecturer in Political Science at Bayero University. Currently, she is Associate Professor of Political Science, Rutgers University, New Brunswick, New Jersey.

531   **Theft and social protest among the tin miners of northern Nigeria.**
       William Freund.   In: *Banditry, rebellion and social protest in Africa.*
       Edited by Donald Crummey. London: Currey; Portsmouth, New Hampshire: Heinemann, 1986, p. 49–63. map. bibliog.

The author discusses theft or 'direct appropriation' as a form of social protest in the twentieth century, up to the 1970s, in central Nigeria, especially among the Birom tin miners. Illicit tin mining is a means of capital accumulation for petty entrepreneurs. 'Theft continues to form the basis of an alternative economy for the Birom (and indeed much of the Nigerian labour force generally) and, as such, reflects the resistance of Nigerian countrymen and women with rights in land-subsistence production and without total recourse to the market. But it also reflects the continued importance of petty commodity production and exchange' (p. 60). This chapter was originally published in *Radical History Review*, no. 26 (Oct. 1982), p. 68–86. Freund has taught at Ahmadu Bello University in Nigeria and is currently Professor of Economic History at the University of Natal, Durban, South Africa.

532 **Ethnic groups in conflict.**
Donald L. Horowitz. Berkeley; Los Angeles: University of
California, 1985. 697p. bibliog.
Presents a major theoretical study of ethnic conflict in global perspective. The work
consists of five parts: 'Ethnic relations and ethnic affiliations'; 'The theory of ethnic
conflict'; 'Party politics and ethnic conflict'; 'Military politics and ethnic conflict'; and
'Strategies of conflict reduction'. Nigeria provides one of the important cases
considered throughout with emphasis on events in the First and Second Republics
(1960–66 and 1979–83) and the structural techniques developed to reduce ethnic
conflict. One of the tables provides results from the Nigerian elections of 1959, 1979
and 1983. The author concludes that 'the Nigerian coup [of 31 December 1983] was a
blow to democratic institutions, but not necessarily an apt test of their durability in a
severely divided society' (p. 683). A review essay by Larry Diamond, 'Ethnicity and
ethnic conflict' in the *Journal of Modern African Studies*, vol. 25, no. 1 (1987),
p. 117–28, addresses in particular the issues that are relevant for Nigeria in Horowitz's
book.

533 **Postwar ethnic relations in Nigeria.**
Stephen O. Imoagene. In: *Race and ethnicity in Africa*. Edited by
Pierre L. van den Berghe. Nairobi, Kenya: East African Publishing
House, 1975, p. 151–65. bibliog.
Explores the thesis 'that a major cause of the Nigerian crisis can be traced to faults in
the patterns of recruitment to the new and increasing positions in the society' (p. 152).
The author describes the system of recruitment through three historical periods from
about 1940 to about 1970 and offers several suggestions for post-war reconstruction: a
multi-party system with seats in parliament distributed on a quota basis; a 'severe
restriction' of the activities of large, tribally-centred associations; establishment of an
'employment ombudsman' who would monitor merit-based recruitment in the public
and private sectors; and routine inter-state secondments.

534 **Socio-ethical issues in Nigeria.**
Nwachukwuike Sonde Sylvanus Iwe. New York; Bern, Switzerland;
Frankfurt, Main, Germany: Peter Lang, 1987. 276p. bibliog.
Iwe analyses Nigeria's social and political ills, describing the constraints on effective
civic education, obstacles to local government efficiency, the pre-requisites for a
successful presidential system, capital punishment, and the right to life. Iwe, who is
himself an Igbo, holds out 'the spirit of Igbo culture' and a generally Christian ethical
orientation as models for the good citizen. The author is Associate Professor at the
University of Calabar and read history, theology, law and education at the Universities
of London, Rome and Cambridge.

535 **Policing Nigeria: control and autonomy in the exercise of coercion.**
Otwin Marenin. *African Studies Review*, vol. 28, no. 1 (March 1985),
p. 73–93. bibliog.
Analyses the position and power of police in Nigeria with respect to the dominant
political party and classes. The author offers both theory and history in describing a
model of policing, patterns of routine policing, and factional struggles over control of
the police, concluding that 'the evidence supports the argument that no faction
consistently controls this coercive agency of the state. The police are used, yet they are

Society and Social Conditions. Social problems

useless in times of threat, when it counts, when the ruling faction needs protection against other factions. The police seem quite willing, and they have the autonomy, to shift sides when their own interests dictate' (p. 88). Detailed notes and a substantial bibliogaphy on the Nigerian police make this a particularly useful article. More recently, the author published 'The Anini saga: armed robbery and the reproduction of ideology in Nigeria', *Journal of Modern African Studies*, vol. 25, no. 2 (June 1987), p. 259–81, using Lawrence Anini, the 'outlaw king of Benin' to describe Nigerian ideology and political culture of 1986.

536 **Ethnic relations in Nigeria: problems and prospects.**
Edited by Akinade Olumuyiwa Sanda. Ibadan, Nigeria: Department of Sociology, University of Ibadan; Canberra, Australia: Department of Demography, Australian National University, 1976. 216p. bibliog.

Fourteen articles, most reprinted from journals, on ethnic relations, ethnic identity, politics and ethnicity, non-ethnic determinants of ethnic relations and ethnic relations and change comprise this volume. Among the most important included are: Onigu Otite's 'On the concept of a Nigerian society'; A. A. Akiwowo's 'The sociology of Nigerian tribalism'; Isaac George's 'Linguistic aspects of ethnic relations'; Hans Wolff's 'Language, ethnic identity and social change in southern Nigeria'; the editor's 'Ethnicity and students politics in a Nigerian university' [University of Ibadan] and 'The ethnic factor in urban social relations'; Richard L. Sklar's 'Ethnicity and social class', *Journal of Modern African Studies*, vol. 5, no. 1 (1967), p. 1–11; H. D. Seibel's 'Some aspects of inter-ethnic relations in Nigeria'; and Frank A. Salamone's 'Becoming Hausa: ethnic identity change and its implications for the study of ethnic pluralism and stratification', *Africa*, vol. 45, no. 4 (1975), p. 410–23. The editor's 1974 University of California at Los Angeles doctoral thesis was *The dynamics of ethnicity among the Yoruba*.

537 **Silent violence: food, famine & peasantry in northern Nigeria.**
Michael Watts. Berkeley; Los Angeles: University of California, 1983. 687p. 6 maps. bibliog.

In this exceptional study of Hausaland and the Sokoto Caliphate, especially with respect to the history of famine and agricultural patterns, the author analyses the political economy of food production in the nineteenth century and up through the oil boom of the 1970s. The splendid volume contains a glossary of Hausa words (p. xv–xix), an appendix of 'Hausa verse pertaining to famine' (p. 515–20), notes (p. 521–84), and an extensive bibliography (p. 585–663). On contemporary food production patterns, he concludes 'There is every reason to expect that the rural development projects serve only to marginalize further the small holders, who are most vulnerable to climatic perturbations . . .' (p. 512). The study grew from the author's 1979 doctoral thesis at the University of Michigan, entitled *A silent revolution: the changing character of food production and the nature of famine in northern Nigeria*.

Ethics in Nigerian culture.
See item no. 1.

The most African country: a survey of Nigeria.
See item no. 12.

The political history of Nigeria's new capital.
See item no. 616.

Health

538 **Some aspects of the sociology and epidemiology of abortion.**
Lola V. Adekunle. *Nigerian Behavioral Sciences Journal*, vol. 1, no. 2 (1978), p. 104–11. bibliog.
Discusses the sociology and epidemiology of abortion in Africa generally and most usefully provides statistics on abortions, abortion rates and subsequent death rates at Ibadan's University College Hospital, Lagos Teaching Hospital and Lagos Island Maternity Hosptial, 1965–73. Comparisons with rates in other countries conclude the article. The author, a lecturer in the Department of Preventive and Social Medicine, University College Hospital, Ibadan, urges a 'new look at our abortion laws' (p. 111). Dr. O. A. Ladipo's article 'Abortion among Nigerian youth',· *Nigerian Behavioral Sciences Journal*, vol. 1, no. 2 (1978), p. 112–16, asserts that induced abortion, illegal in Nigeria, has reached 'epidemic proportions'. He describes its incidence, socio-cultural characteristics of women obtaining abortions, and reasons for and sequelae of abortions, and he too pleads for the liberalization of Nigeria's abortion law.

539 **Nigerian pioneers of modern medicine: selected writings.**
Edited by Adelola Adeloye. Ibadan, Nigeria: Ibadan University, 1977. 299p. bibliog.
This valuable collection of MD theses and other writings by early Nigerian physicians is introduced and provided with biographical sketches and commentary by the editor. The theses of James Africanus Beale Horton (1835–83), Obadiah Johnson (1849–1920), and Sodeinde Akinsiku Leigh-Sodipe (1865–1901) are included as are a report on smallpox in Yourba areas, by Oguntola Odunbaku Sapara (1861–1935) 'Cancer in West Africa' by W. Renner and John Randle (1855–1928) and J. A. B. Horton's writings on fevers, diseases of the spleen, chronic rheumatism and guinea worm. The 'Index of West African plants' (p. 287–89) mentioned by the authors is useful. Both the original handwritten and the typeset texts of Obadiah Johnson's *An essay on West African therapeutics*, introduced by Philip Singer and prefaced by Elizabeth A. Titus (Owerri, Nigeria: Buffalo, New York: Trado-Medic Books, Conch Magazine, 1982. 110p. (Traditional Healing Series, no. 7)), is available.

Health

540   **African pioneers of modern medicine: Nigerian doctors of the nineteenth century.**
Adelola Adeloye.   Ibadan, Nigeria: University Press, 1985. 253p. bibliog.

Dr. Adeloye, Professor of Neurological Surgery at the University College Hospital, Ibadan, Nigeria, describes the beginnings of modern medicine and the early colonial medical service in Nigeria and provides the biographies of nine prominent physicians: William Broughton Davies (1833–1906); James Africanus Beale Horton (1835–83); Nathaniel King (1847–84); Obadiah Johnson (1849–1920); John Randle (1855–1928); Charles Jenkins Lumpkin (1851–1919); Sodeinde Akinsiku Leigh-Sodipe (1865–1901); Oguntola Odunbaku Sapapa (1861–1935); and Orisadipe Obasa (1863–1940). Thirteen illustrations portray the physicians and pages of their relevant reports.

541   **African therapeutic systems.**
Edited by Z. A. Ademuwagun, John A. A. Ayoade, Ira E. Harrison, Dennis M. Warren.   Waltham, Massachusetts: Crossroads Press, African Studies Association, 1979. 273p. bibliog.

With forty-one articles, most reprinted from other sources, a filmography (p. 259–61) and 'Sources for further study' (p. 257–58), this is easily the best anthology on traditional African medicine and its interaction with western medicine. Twelve articles concern Nigeria: D. R. Price-Williams's 'A case study of ideas concerning disease among the Tiv'; John A. A. Ayoade's 'The concept of inner essence in Yoruba traditional medicine'; Ira E. Harrison's 'Traditional healers as a source of traditional and contemporary powers' and 'Traditional healers: a neglected source of health manpower'; R. Prince's 'Symbols and psychotherapy: the example of Yoruba sacrificial ritual'; N. H. Wolff's 'Concepts of causation and treatment in the Yoruba medical system: the special case of barrenness'; Z. A. Ademuwagun's 'The relevance of Yoruba medicine men in public health practice in Nigeria', 'Problem and prospect of legitimatizing and integrating aspects of traditional health care systems and methods with modern medical therapy: the Igbo-Ora experience' and 'The challenge of the co-existence of orthodox and traditional medicine in Nigeria'; Tolani Asuni's 'Modern medicine and traditional medicine' (Yoruba); Rita Braito and T. Asuni's, 'Traditional healers in Abeokuta'; and Catherine M. Una Maclean's 'Traditional healers and their female clients: an aspect of Nigerian sickness behavior'.

542   **Yoruba medicine.**
Anthony D. Buckley.   New York: Clarendon, Oxford University, 1985. 275p. bibliog.

In a brilliant structural analysis the author decodes symbols and metaphors of three Yoruba herbalists studied during two years of fieldwork begun in 1969. Professor Buckley uses images offered by his informants to define a paradigm in which they organize their encyclopaedic knowledge, suggesting that 'underlying the diversity of Yoruba medicinal knowledge . . . is a simple framework of structured concepts' (p. 24). The study was presented originally as the author's doctoral thesis at the University of Birmingham in 1982 and won the 1985 Amaury Talbot Prize for African Anthropology. In his critical review, John M. Janzen calls the book 'an elegant but decontextualized portrayal of Yoruba medical knowledge', *American Ethnologist*, vol. 15, no. 1 (Feb. 1988), p. 175.

543 **Bilharziasis (schistosomiasis) in Nigeria.**
S. G. Cowper. *Tropical and Geographical Medicine*, vol. 25 (1973), p. 105–18. bibliog.

This review article condenses findings from a large literature to give an overview of this health problem. It states that 'Nigeria is one of the most serious affected countries and the disease is hyperendemic over large areas' (p. 105). The author documents the disease in Nigeria from at least 1881, and describes the extent of the problem, the intermediate hosts, a chronology of clinical aspects and pathology, treatment and chemotherapy, procedures for prevention, control and eradication and the disease as a military medical problem in Nigeria. A lengthy 'Bibliography of bilharziasis in Nigeria including Cameroon Province' (p. 115–18) concludes the article. The author was at the School of Tropical Medicine, Liverpool, England, at the time of publication.

544 **Three decades of medical research at the College of Medicine, Ibadan, Nigeria, 1948–1980: a list of the papers published by members of the College of Medicine of the University of Ibadan from its foundation through 1980.**
Compiled by Freya D. DeCola, Patricia H. Shoyinka. Ibadan, Nigeria: Ibadan University for the E. Latunde Odeku Medical Library, 1984. 208p. (Ibadan Tropical Medicine Series, no. 4).

This bibliogaphy of medical research at the oldest and most prestigious university in Nigeria includes 3,788 items published over a period of thirty-two years. The items are arranged by department as the College of Medicine existed in 1980, with author and subject indexes providing ready access to the compilation. The volume includes articles in Nigerian and other African journals not indexed by *Index Medicus*, the standard international medical reference work. This compilation updates and improves the earlier *25 years of medical research: a list of papers published by past and present members of the Faculty of Medicine of the University of Ibadan from its foundation to Nov. 1973*, compiled by O. Soyinka, M. Amosu, E. O. Osunlana (Ibadan: Medical Library, Univeristy of Ibadan, 1973, 184p.). In the first twenty-five years there were 1,500 entries, whereas nearly 2,300 entries appear for the succeeding seven years. A significant compilation of some seventy-five papers appears in *Fifty years of medical research in Nigeria*, the proceedings of the First Medical Research Seminar 1 Feb.–4 Feb. 1972, Yaba, Lagos, sponsored by the West African Council for Medical Research (Yaba, Lagos, Nigeria: WACMR (Nigeria), [1972], 276p.).

545 **Needs of dentistry today and tomorrow in Nigeria.**
A. A. Adele Doherty. *Quarterly of the Nigerian Dental Association*, vol. 39, no. 3 (April 1981), p. 135–41.

Dr. Doherty reviews dentistry in Nigeria, covering: reasons for establishing a directorate of dental health at the national level, the state of dental centres and dental schools in the country, gum disease and projections of dental needs. The first Nigerian dental school opened in 1966 with the first dentists graduating in 1971. When the article was written, there were four dental schools (at Ibadan, Lagos, Ife, and Benin City) and about 200 dentists practising in Nigeria.

Health

546 **Scientific insights into Yoruba traditional medicine.**
James I. Durodola, foreword by Adelola Adeloye. Owerri, Nigeria;
New York; London: Trado-Medic Books, Conch Magazine, 1986. 92p.
bibliog. (Traditional Healing Series, no. 8).

This slender volume offers several tantalizing perspectives on Yoruba traditiona
medicine. The author asserts that 'the greatest achievement of traditional medicine i
in the realm of mental illness and psychosomatic problems' (p. 85), but demonstrate
the efficacy of traditional remedies, two anti-bacterial and one anti-tumour. It i
important, he writes, for traditional healers to recognize their limitations and to allow
their patients to use scientific medicine when appropriate. Dr. Durodola, son of a
traditional Yoruba healer and trained in western medicine is uniquely poised to
investigate the topic. His 1972 doctoral thesis at the University of Ibadan was *Studie
on certain Nigerian medical plants with potential antineoplastic activity*; he is a lecture
in oncology in the Department of Surgery, University College Hospital, Ibadan
Nigeria.

547 **An overview of health manpower in three states of Nigeria.**
J. A. Ebigbola, F. A. Ilori. *Nigerian Behavioral Sciences Journal*,
vol. 1, no. 1 (1978), p. 17–25. bibliog.

The authors, both demographers at the University of Ife (now Obafemi Awolowc
University), Ile-Ife, Nigeria, describe health manpower and facilities in Oyo, Ondo,
and Ogun States of western Nigeria between 1969 and 1973. The article includes data
on medical and para-medical staff and patients in hospitals and nursing homes,
maternity centres, rural health centres and dispensaries during these years. See also
Dennis A. Ityavyar's 'The state, class and health services in Nigeria' in *Afrika
Spectrum*, vol. 22, no. 3 (1987), p. 285–314, for a discussion of the politics of health
services. The author's 1985 PhD thesis at the University of Toronto was *The
development of health services in Nigeria, 1960–1985.*

548 **Strategy for medical research in Nigeria: proceedings of 1980
symposium.**
Edited by C. O. Enwonwu, N. I. Onyezili, G. C. Ejezie. Ibadan,
Nigeria: Ibadan University, 1984. 305p. bibliog.

Papers on twenty-two topics ranging from 'Research in traditional medicine', 'Major
paediatric problems in Nigeria', and 'Status of oral health of Nigerians', to 'Training
for medical research in Nigeria' and 'Funding of medical research', some general and
theoretical and others with useful data analysis, are in this volume. A broad overview
of the history, issues and future prospects of medical research is offered in Babatunde
Kwaku Adadevoh's *Medical research in Nigeria: a tribute with historical and perspective
considerations* (Ikoyi Falomo, Nigeria: Educational Professional & Scientific, 1983.
93p.). Dr. Adadevoh describes the West African Council for Medical Research, the
Medical Research Council of Nigeria, university medical research, pharmaceutica
research, future trends and ethics in research.

549 **Nigerian perspectives on medical sociology.**
Edited by Olayiwola A. Erinosho. *Studies in Third World Societies*,
no. 19 (March 1982), 135p. bibliog.

A collection of eight articles on Nigerian health issues from sociological, geographica
and anthropological perspectives. Included are: 'Medical sociology in perspective' by

the editor; 'Traditional Ibo ideas about disease and its treatment' by N. Ezeabasili; 'The supernatural aspect of disease and therapeutics among the Igala' by J. S. Boston; 'Social epidemiology' by Adewale Oke; 'Models of health-seeking behaviour' by U. A. Igun; 'Spatial location and utilization of health facilities' by S. I. Okafor; 'Traditional medicine and social change in the West African subregion' by S. Kofi Bonsi; and 'Medical systems and the Nigerian society' by Tola Olu Pearce. The articles by Ezeabasili and Boston are reprinted from *The traditional background to medical practice in Nigeria*, edited by Robert G. Armstrong (Ibadan: Institute of African Studies, 1971 (Occasional publication, no. 25)).

550 **Mental health in Africa.**
Edited by Olayiwola A. Erinosho, Norman W. Bell. Ibadan, Nigeria: Ibadan University and the Research Committee on the Sociology of Mental Health, 1982. 266p. bibliog. (Tropical Medicine Series, no. 3).

This volume contains thirty-two papers selected from the sixty papers presented at the first regional conference of the Research Committee on the Sociology of Mental Health (of the International Sociological Association) held at Ibadan University in December 1980. The papers are organized in five categories (evolution and concept of mental health, epidemiological issues, perspectives on mental health services, attitude to mental illness and 'other research reports'). Although several concern case studies or issues in other African nations, the overwhelming majority deal with mental health in Nigeria. The bibliography (p. 248–62) is quite useful for this broad topic.

551 **The health of Nigerians, 1983/84. Health and nutrition status survey. (A module of the National Integrated Survey of Households (NISH) April, 1983–March, 1984).**
Federal Office of Statistics. Lagos, Nigeria: Federal Office of Statistics, September 1985. 76p. 2 maps. bibliog.

This important survey is the follow-up to the pilot survey of 226 households carried out in Kano, Borno, Cross River and Lagos States and reported in *The health of Nigerians. Results from a pilot survey in four states in September 1982. Interim Report* (Lagos: Federal Office of Statistics, March 1983. 45p.). This carefully-designed survey of 40,721 people of all ages in 8,392 rural and urban households in, at that time, all nineteen states presents the best available data for Nigeria on recent illness and injury prevalence, mortality estimates, breastfeeding, nutritional status, and episodes of recent diarrhoea, with much of the data focused on children under five years of age. The infant mortality rate was 127 per 1,000 births in rural areas and fifty-five per 1,000 in urban sites. The rural child mortality rate was 193 per 1,000, more than double the ninety-four per 1,000 urban rate. The study found that twenty-one per cent of urban children under five and twenty per cent of rural children were moderately or severely malnourished. Extensive data and discussion of data quality-control are included in the report.

552 **Adolescent fertility in Nigeria.**
Benjamin Gyepi-Garbrah. Boston, Massachusetts; Nairobi: Pathfinder Fund, 1985. 69p. (Adolescent Fertility in Sub-Saharan Africa Series).

Like other studies on Kenya, Liberia and Sierra Leone in this series of resource volumes for policy makers and programmers, this study synthesizes most of the statistical data available on the socio-economic characteristics of adolescents reproductive health behaviour, and implications of adolescent fertility for the country The bibliography (p. 59–69) is extensive and the summary of fertility-related programmes in Nigeria in 1979–80 is useful. A separate six-page 'Executive Summary is included. The preliminary report of the Nigerian Fertility Survey 1981–82 (Lagos National Population Commission, Federal Republic of Nigeria; London: World Fertility Survey, March 1983. 49p.) describes the results of interviews with 9,81 women throughout the country.

553 **Source of drinking water supply and transmission of guinea worm disease in Nigeria.**
V. A. Ilegbodu, B. L. Christensen, R. A. Wise, A. E. Ilegbodu, O. O. Kale. *Annals of Tropical Medicine and Parasitology*, vol. 81, no. 6 (1987), p. 713–18. bibliog.

An investigation, in 1982, of ecological issues in the rural community of Idere in Oyo State showed that the drinking water supply was less than one-tenth that recommended by the World Health Organization and was a major source of the guinea worm infections among one-third of the residents. The authors present data on the distribution of pathological organisms in Idere ponds and discuss the need for potable water supplies. In related articles, L. D. Edungbola, S. J. Watts, T. O. Alabi, and A. O. Bello discuss 'The impact of a UNICEF-assisted rural water project on the prevalence of guinea worm disease in Asa, Kwara State, Nigeria', *Journal of the American Society of Tropical Medicine and Hygiene*, vol. 39 (1988), p. 79–85, and J. K. Udonsi describes 'Dracontiasis in the Igwun River Basin, Nigeria: its distribution, epidemiology and transmission dynamics', *Tropical Medicine and Parasitology*, vol. 38, no. 4 (1987), p. 304–08.

554 **The professionalisation of African medicine.**
Edited by Murray Last, G. L. Chavunduka. Manchester, England: Manchester University in association with the International African Institute, 1986. 293p. bibliog. (International African Seminar Studies, vol. 1).

From the seminar by the same title held at the University of Botswana, Gaborone, in September 1983, came the twelve informative papers published here. Each is concerned with traditional medical systems in Africa, with the articulation of these systems and a national health care plan, or with the development of professional associations. In addition to the thoughtful introduction by Professor Last (p. 1–19) and the concluding survey by both editors (p. 259–69), two papers directly concern Nigeria. Dr. D. D. O. Oyebola's 'National medical politics in Nigeria' (p. 221–36) provides an excellent synopsis of the history and difficulties of the relations between traditional medical associations and the government up to 1983. In 'Professional interests and the creation of medical knowledge in Nigeria' (p. 237–58), medical sociologist Tola Olu

Pearce compares the production and dissemination of medical knowledge within the indigenous and western systems emphasizing the need to understand the rôle of emotions in disease and recovery, so central to the work of traditional healers.

555 **Psychiatric disorder among the Yoruba: a report from the Cornell-Aro Mental Health Research Project in the Western Region, Nigeria.**
Alexander H. Leighton, T. Adeoye Lambo, Charles C. Hughes, Dorothea C. Leighton, Jane M. Murphy, David B. Macklin. New York: Cornell University, 1963. 413p. map. bibliog.

A model cross-cultural psychiatric survey which attempts to estimate the types and prevalence of psychiatric disorder among a group of Egba Yoruba. The study is based on 416 interviews from Abeokuta and nearby villages, from the Aro Hospital for Nervous Diseases and other relevant places in 1961. Chapter III 'The Yoruba world' defines strongly-held Yoruba sentiments. The volume provides complete discussion of the material and conclusions, plus appendices on Abeokuta, methodology and the survey instruments used. The bibliography (p. 395–403) cites literature on the Egba Yoruba and on psychiatry in sub-Saharan Africa.

556 **Medicine and medical education in Nigeria.**
Lawrence D. Longo. *New England Journal of Medicine*, vol. 268, no. 19 (9 May 1963), p. 1,044–55. 2 maps. bibliog.

This article provides brief background on geography, ethnography, economy, history and demography, and surveys health problems, traditional medicine, professional medical practice, health facilities, paramedical personnel, and medical education. Ample data on mortality, manpower and facilities are included. The author notes the need for emphasis on preventive medicine and for increased development funds. At the time, Dr. Longo was in the Department of Obstetrics and Gynaecology at the University of California, Los Angeles, and had worked at hospitals in Ibadan and Ile-Ife, Nigeria. Of related interest is the recent article by U. D. Anyanwu, entitled 'Health services in a Nigerian area (Imo State, 1914–1966)' in *Nigeria Magazine*, vol. 54, no. 1 (Jan.–March 1986), p. 92–101.

557 **Magical medicine: a Nigerian case study.**
Una Maclean. Harmondsworth, England: Penguin, 1971. 167p. bibliog. (Pelican Books).

A study of traditional medical beliefs and healers in Ibadan, Nigeria, and of the underlying reasons for the tenacity of Yoruba medicine in the face of western medicine. Here the author's broad enquiry covers the problems faced by patients, Yoruba religious and magical beliefs, modern and traditional health resources in Ibadan, data from 100 Ibadan herbalists and diviners, Yoruba medical literature, a variety of cures and a comparison of health behaviour in lower-class and élite Ibadan families. The bibliography (p. 157–67) is divided into general, 'Nigerian' and 'other African' sections. Dr. Maclean spent seven years in Western Nigeria engaged in cancer and sociological research.

207

Health

558   **Traditional medicine in Nigeria.**
Joseph Ojo Mume.   Agbarho, Nigeria: Jom Nature Cure Centre,
[1973]. 112p.

Dr. Mume (1929– .), a well-known traditional doctor or 'tradomedical naturopathic physician' in southern Bendel State, describes his philosophy and principles of healing. In addition he provides a succinct account of eight traditional therapies (herbalism, hydrotherapy, massage, cupping, faith-healing, fasting, surgery and heat therapy) as well as traditional psychiatry, diet and preventive medicine. The first chapter, 'How I acquired the knowledge of traditional medicine' (p. 9–26) was published in *Conch*, vol. 8, no. 1–2 (1976), p. 136–57. In the booklet *The confession of the wizard of Igbinse* (Agbarho: Jom Nature Cure Centre, [n.d.] 71p.), he explains the 'science of witchcraft' and details thirty-four concoctions used for magical purposes. His longer *Tradomedicalism: what it is* (Agbarho: Jom Nature Cure Centre, [post-Feb. 1982], 186p.) explores the subject with extensive Nigerian medical information and clinical reports.

559   **Circumcision: its nature and practice among some ethnic groups in southern Nigeria.**
Robert A. Myers, Francisca I. Omorodion, Anthony E. Isenalumhe,
Gregory I. Akenzua.   *Social Science & Medicine*, vol. 21, no. 5 (1985),
p. 581–88. 2 maps. bibliog.

This questionnaire survey of 280 adults (and their 1,417 children) in five rural communities in Bendel State, Nigeria, documents the degree and range of male and female circumcision practices among Bini, Esan, Etsako, Ijaw and Ukwuani (Western Igbo) ethnic groups. Nearly all males and most females in these groups are circumcised or excised, although the timing of the procedure varies widely. Data are presented on prevalence, reasons for the operations, age at circumcision, decision-makers and type of surgeon for each group and sex. The complication rate appears low; three of every 100 males and two of every 100 females experienced a complication, usually excessive bleeding or infection. Data on these groups plus the Urhobo are analysed further in 'Female and male perceptions of male genital operations in six southern Nigerian ethnic groups' by Myers (East Lansing, Michigan: Michigan State University, Women in International Development, August 1986. 21p. (WID Forum 86-IX)).

560   **Kemwin-kemwin: the apothecary shop in Benin City.**
Joseph Nevadomsky.   *African Arts*, vol. 22, no. 1 (Nov. 1988),
p. 72–83, 100. bibliog.

This exceptionally detailed cultural analysis of *kemwin-kemwin*, 'anything and everything', 'local drugstores' especially petty traders' stalls at markets, explains many health concepts of the Bini people, the largest group of Bendel State. It looks at animal motifs in some of their art and uses of many wild animals. Included is a poem in Bini and English by poet Ikponmwosa Osemwegie commissioned for the article. Dr. Nevadomsky has also published several articles on drug use in Nigeria, among them, 'Self-reported drug use among secondary school students in two rapidly developing Nigerian towns', *Bulletin on Narcotics* (United Nations), vol. 34, nos. 3, 4 (1982), p. 21–32, and 'Drug use among Nigerian university students: prevalence of self-reported use and attitudes to use', *Bulletin on Narcotics* (United Nations), vol. 37, nos. 2, 3 (1985), p. 31–42.

561 **The public health significance of trypanosomiasis (sleeping sickness) in Nigeria.**
Okey. C. Nwanyanwu, James H. Steele, Samuel O. Osueke, Donna J. Carpenter. *International Journal of Zoonoses*, vol. 12, no. 1 (March 1985), p. 28–34. bibliog.

The authors review the history, epidemiology, control methods and socio-economic consequences of trypanosomiasis in humans and animals in Nigeria. First documented in Nigeria in 1903, parts of Northern Nigeria in the 1930s had infection rates as high as twenty per cent. Rates in animals and humans in recent years are unavailable for bureaucratic reasons. Although no large-scale economic impact study has been done in Nigeria, the authors conclude, 'If one would take into account all the direct and indirect losses that are, and can be attributed to trypanosomiasis . . . in Nigeria, unquestionably, the amount would involve hundreds of millions of dollars annually' (p. 33).

562 **Policy and practice: the case of medical facilities in Nigeria.**
S. I. Okafor. *Social Science & Medicine*, vol. 16 (1982), p. 1,971–77. map. bibliog.

The author, a geographer at the University of Ibadan in Nigeria, uses 1977 data to examine the distribution of health manpower and facilities in Bendel State in southern Nigeria. Out of 253 doctors in the state in 1976–77, 221 were attached to government hospitals, while only thirty-two worked at private hospitals, only one of which was in a rural area. He estimates a doctor-to-population ratio for the state of 1:10,023, but an actual range in local government area ratios of from 1:1,626 to 1:86,140, reflecting urban and rural differences. The review of government health programmes and analysis of the 'basic problems of the system' (p. 1,975–76) is very informative. Other significant articles from *Social Science & Medicine* include Folorunso Abudu's 'Planning priorities and health care in Nigeria' vol. 17, no. 24 (1983), p. 1,995–2,002, and T. O. Fadayomi and O. Y. Oyeneye's 'The demographic factor in the provision of health facilities in developing countries: the case of Nigeria', vol. 19, no. 8 (1984), p. 793–97.

563 **Use of contraceptives for birth spacing in a Nigerian city.**
Gbolaham A. Oni, James McCarthy. *Studies in Family Planning*, vol. 17, no. 4 (July–Aug. 1986), p. 165–71. bibliog.

This article examines the use of contraceptives among women aged fifteen to thirty five years in Ilorin, Kwara State in 1983–84. About nineteen per cent of ever-married women in 932 households surveyed had used contraceptives at some time and about six per cent were using them at the time of the survey. Most women reported wanting seven or more children. In the same issue a survey of 681 Nigerian physicians is reported by Deborah L. Covington, E. O. Otolorin, Barbara Janowitz, Deborah S. Gates, Peter Lamptey and O. A. Ladipo in 'Physician attitudes and family planning in Nigeria' (p. 172–80). Also of direct relevance are Eric O. Udjo's 'Obstacles to successful fertility control in Nigeria', *Social Science & Medicine*, vol. 19, no. 11 (1984), p. 1,167–71, and 'The evolution of family planning in an African city: Ibadan, Nigeria', *Population Studies*, vol. 31, no. 3 (Nov. 1977), p. 487–507.

Health

564 **Kaposi's sarcoma and HTLV-III: a study in Nigerian adult males.**
A. A. Otu. *Journal of the Royal Society of Medicine*, vol. 79, no. 9
(Sept. 1986), p. 510–14.

This study reports on the examination of sera from thirty-seven adult Nigerian men
with Kaposi's sarcoma (KS), thirty controls with primary cell carcinoma of the liver,
and 150 healthy individuals, for the AIDS virus HTLV-III/LAV, between January
1978 and December 1982 at the University of Calabar Teaching Hospital and nearby
areas. The results 'clearly show that Nigerian KS is not associated with infection by
HTLV-III' (p. 513). The author suggests that 'tropical African KS and epidemic
AIDS-linked KS seem to be two different diseases with possibly different aetiological
agents' (p. 513). In her article, 'Kaposi's sarcoma in Nigeria', *British Journal of
Cancer*, vol. 17, no. 2 (June 1963), p. 195–205, based on research on sixty-eight cases
of KS twenty years earlier, Catherine M. U. Maclean reviews the literature for skin
malignancies in Africa and elsewhere and calls attention to the over-representation of
KS in southern Nigeria. A brief, recent article by C. K. O. Williams describes 'AIDS
and cancer in Nigerians', *The Lancet*, vol. 1, no. 8,471 (1986), p. 36–37.

565 **Professional associations, ethics and discipline among Yoruba traditional
healers of Nigeria.**
D. D. O. Oyebola. *Social Science & Medicine*, vol. 15B, no. 2 (April
1981), p. 87–105. bibliog.

This study reports on four Yoruba healers' views of their professional associations and
on the results of a 'semi-structured' questionnaire given to 165 healers on their ethics
and the discipline of erring members. Photographs of healers' signboards are included.
Of special value are the critical responses (p. 93–102) to the article by leaders in this
field, followed by Professor Oyebola's response (p. 105–07). Other significant articles
by the author include 'Traditional medicine and its practitioners among the Yoruba of
Nigeria: a classification', *Social Science & Medicine*, vol. 14A, no. 1 (Jan. 1980),
p. 23–29; 'Some aspects of Yoruba traditional healers and their practice', *Transactions
of the Royal Society of Tropical Medicine and Hygiene*, vol. 74, no. 3 (1980),
p. 318–325; and 'Yoruba traditional bonesetters: the practice of orthopaedics in a
primitive setting in Nigeria', *Journal of Trauma*, vol. 20, no. 4 (April 1980), p. 312–22.
Oyebola's 1977 MD thesis at the University of Ibadan was *Studies on the traditional
medical care among the Yoruba of Nigeria*. He is in the Department of Physiology,
College of Medicine, University of Ibadan, Ibadan, Nigeria.

566 **Principles of medicine in Africa.**
Edited by E. H. O. Parry, foreword by Lambo. Oxford; Nairobi:
Oxford University, 1984. 2nd ed. 1,119p. maps. bibliog.

Forty-five contributors (at least thirteen of whom are Nigerian or have recently worked
in Nigeria) wrote the twenty-seven chapters of this compendium. References to Nigeria
appear throughout the volume. Articles include broad overviews such as 'Climate and
disease', 'People and disease' and 'Animals and disease', as well as organ system and
disease specific topics. Dr. Lambo, author of the brief foreword, is Deputy Director-
General, World Health Organization (WHO), Geneva.

567   Political and economic changes in Nigeria and the organisation of
      medical care.
      Tola Olu Pearce.   Social Science & Medicine, vol. 14B, no. 2 (May
      1980), p. 91–98. bibliog.

This informative article documents how 'the structure and effectiveness of medical
services reflect changes in the political and economic changes of a nation' (p.
97) by examining pre-colonial, colonial, and post-colonial medical care in Nigeria.
Among many publications by the author, a member of the Department of Sociology and
Anthropology, Obafemi Awolowo University, Ile-Ife, Nigeria, are 'Integrating
Western orthodox and indigenous medicine: professional interests and attitudes among
university-trained Nigerian physicians', Social Science & Medicine, vol. 16, (1982),
p. 1,611–17, 'Social change and the 'modernization' of the medical sector' in Social
change in Nigeria, (q.v.) (ch. 7, p. 158–75), and 'Producing medical knowledge in
pluralistic systems: the contribution of laymen' in Analysis in medical anthropology
edited by S. Lindenbaum and M. Lock (Reidel, forthcoming 1989). All provide both
theoretical insights and specifics about health behaviour in Nigeria.

568   A history of the Nigerian health services.
      Ralph Schram, introduced by Sir Samuel Manuwa.   Ibadan, Nigeria:
      Ibadan University, 1971. 480p. 7 maps. bibliog.

Presents an impressive history of health care in Nigeria from 1460 to 1960. The volume
is divided into four chronological parts: 'Reaching frontiers, 1460–1850'; 'Established
work, 1850–1900'; 'Colonial growth, 1900–1960'; and 'Towards independence,
1940–1960'. With tables, graphs, plates of medical notables and data-laden appendices
to supplement the detailed text, the author's efforts have not yet been equalled on the
subject. The bibliography (p. 437–58) is extensive. This book is a condensed version of
the author's Cambridge University thesis for the doctor of medicine degree. Dr.
Schram spent nine years practising medicine in Nigeria, several of them at Ibadan
University. In 1970 he became Reader in Community Medicine at Ahmadu Bello
University, Zaria, Nigeria. The present status of medicine in Nigeria (Ibadan: Ibadan
Univeristy, Nov. 1971. 41p.) by O. O. Akinkugbe, then Dean of the University of
Ibadan Faculty of Medicine, offers six illustrated essays on 'burning but 'trendy'
medical issues' (Preface, p. v), including medical education, medical manpower and
medical research.

569   Cancer in Nigeria: Proceedings of the Nigerian Cancer Society
      Conference, December, 1979.
      Edited by T. F. Solanke, B. O. Osunkoya, C. K. O. Williams,
      O. O. Agboola.   Ibadan, Nigeria: Ibadan University for the Nigerian
      Cancer Society, 1982. 267p. bibliog. (Tropical Medicine Series).

This important collection of thirty papers contains an enormous amount of data on
diverse types of cancer in Nigeria. Following a discussion of World Health
Organization Cancer Programmes in Africa by T. A. Lambo, the papers are grouped
in eight sections: 'Environmental factors and epidemiology' (covering plant-based
chemicals, environmental chemicals, palm-wine drinking and cancer, and cigarette
smoking trends in Nigeria); 'Tumours of genito-urinary system'; 'Haemopoietic
tumours' (Hodgkin's disease); 'Tumours of the respiratory, skeletal and central
nervous system'; 'Care of the cancer patient'; 'Problems of cancer management';
'Cancer patterns in East and West Africa' (Uganda and Nigeria); and 'Experimental
cancer research'.

Health. Periodical

570 **Hausa medicine: illness and well-being in a West African culture.**
L. Lewis Wall. Durham, North Carolina: Duke University, 1988.
3 maps. bibliog.
Much more than a thorough study of Hausa medicine, this volume provides an
excellent introduction to Hausa society. In this medical ethnography of Malumfashi, a
northern Nigerian town, the author describes rural Hausa society, the life-cycle, the
Islamic basis of life, and, in particular, Hausa concepts of illness, stressing the concept
lafiya or 'health'. He includes lucid descriptions of the various practitioners: medicine
sellers, barber-surgeons, bonesetters, midwives, Koranic scholars, the *bori* or cult of
spirits, and herbalists or *bokaye*. His important chapter 'The logic of Hausa medicine'
is a superb overview of the themes and presuppositions permeating Hausa medicine.
The study is the result of Dr. Wall's fifteen months' fieldwork during 1976–77, and
derives partially from his Oxford University doctoral thesis. Of related interest is
Murray Last's article on the medical 'non-system' of Malumfashi, entitled 'The
importance of knowing about not knowing', *Social Science and Medicine*, vol. 15B, no.
3 (July 1981), p. 387–92. Robert Stock describes both prophetic and herbal remedies,
basing the essay on interviews with eighty healers and some 5,000 patients in Kano
State, in 'Islamic medicine in rural Hausaland', in *African healing strategies*, edited by
Brian M. du Toit and Ismail H. Abdalla (Owerri, Nigeria; New York; London: Trado-
Medical Books, 1985, p. 29–46).

Periodical

571 **Nigerian Medical Journal.**
Lagos; Ibadan, Nigeria: Nigerian Medical Association, Jan. 1971– .
quarterly.
This journal contains original articles, review articles, case reports, book reviews, a
general practice forum, notes and news. In January 1980, the editorial address moved
to Ibadan. The *West African Journal of Medicine* (Yaba; Lagos, Nigeria: West African
College of Physicians & West African College of Surgeons, 1981– . quarterly)
publishes articles in English and occasionally in French, original papers, case reports,
notices, and information on current practice. In 1987 the editorial address was Prof.
A. O. Odejide, Editor-in-Chief, Department of Psychiatry, University College
Hospital, Ibadan. The *West African Medical Journal* (Ibadan: Directors of Medical
Services of Nigeria, Gold Coast, Sierra Leone and Gambia, 1927–38, 1952–66) became
the *West African Medical Journal and Nigerian Practitioner* in 1967 and then the *West
African Medical Journal and Nigerian Medical & Dental Practitioner* in 1972.

**Land and people in Nigeria: the human geography of Nigeria and its
environmental background.**
See item no. 36.

The useful plants of west tropical 'Africa.
See item no. 102.

Nigeria's useful plants.
See item no. 108.

Medicinal plants in tropical West Africa.
See item no. 109.

Medicinal plants in Nigeria.
See item no. 111.

Nigerian fertility survey, 1981–1982: preliminary report.
See item no. 324.

Nigerian chewing sticks.
See item no. 330.

Yoruba religion and medicine in Ibadan.
See item no. 416.

Nigerian children: developmental perspectives.
See item no. 509.

Child-rearing practices in Northern Nigeria.
See item no. 511.

The WIN document:conditions of women in Nigeria and policy recommendations to 2,000 AD. [*sic*]
See item no. 518.

Silent violence: food, famine & peasantry in northern Nigeria.
See item no. 537.

Nutrition and food policy in Nigeria.
See item no. 741.

Nigeria's foods and feeding stuffs: their chemistry and nutritive value.
See item no. 749.

Efficient resource use for tropical nutrition: Nigeria.
See item no. 750.

Nigerian women in development: a research bibliography.
See item no. 1126.

Politics

Pre-independence
(pre-1 October 1960)

572 **Awo: the autobiography of Chief Obafemi Awolowo.**
Obafemi Awolowo. Cambridge: Cambridge University, 1960. 316p.

Chief Obafemi Awolowo (6 March 1909–9 May 1987) tells his story from before he was born in the village of Ikenne in Ijebu Remo Administrative Division of present day Ogun State, and through his schooling and education at Wesley College, Ibadan, his journalist work, his involvement in the Nigerian Youth Movement, his political development and his eight years in office in the 1950s, including office as the first Premier of the Western Region beginning in 1954. He began the book in July 1957 but wrote most of it from February–June 1960 after he lost the 1959 federal elections for the House of Representatives. Among his many publications are *Path to Nigerian freedom*, originally published in 1947 with a thoughtful foreword by Margery Perham (London: Faber & Faber, 1966. 137p.), in which he refered to Nigeria as a 'geographical expression' and not a nation, and *Path to Nigerian greatness* (Enugu Nigeria: Fourth Dimension, 1981. 225p.) which discusses the political situation c 1978–80.

573 **Zik: a selection from the speeches of Nnamdi Azikiwe, Governor-General of the Federation of Nigeria, formerly President of the Nigerian State, formerly Premier of the Eastern Region of Nigeria.**
Compiled by Philip Harris, with a preface by Nnamdi Azikiwe.
Cambridge: Cambridge University, 1961. 344p.

A collection of excerpts from speeches delivered in Nigeria and abroad between 192 and 1960, selected and arranged by Harris. Azikiwe (16 November 1904– .) provides brief autobiographical sketch in the preface (p. vii–viii). The selections are arranged in topical chapters covering 'America', 'Education', 'Liberty', 'Africa'

Politics. Pre-independence (pre-1 October 1960)

'Natural rulers', 'Democracy', 'Nigerian constitutional development', 'The colour bar', 'Colonialism', 'The NCNC (National Council of Nigeria and the Cameroons)', 'Finance and banking', 'The press and broadcasting', 'The 'Ibo' people', 'Moral rearmament', 'Local government', 'The University of Nigeria', 'The development of political parties in Nigeria', and 'The Church Missionary Society'.

574 **My odyssey: an autobiography.**
Nnamdi Azikiwe. New York: Praeger, 1970. 452p.

The author's story from his ancestry and birth, 16 November 1904, through the 1960s. The account of the 1940s and later focuses on the Zik Group of newspapers, legal confrontations, publishing efforts and sports, with the major political events of his life reserved for a subsequent volume. Azikiwe, one of Nigeria's most important leaders in the twentieth century, describes 'the sociological realities [he] had to grapple with during [his] formative years' (p. 17), his schooling in Nigeria, his college and graduate school days in the United States, his time in London and the Gold Coast, and his return to Nigeria, where he became active as a newspaper editor and publisher. The volume contains eight photographs, Zik's genealogy, a glossary of names, a list of 'Members of the Zik Group' and a list of prominent alumni of the Zik Group.

575 **Urbanization and political change: the politics of Lagos, 1917–1967.**
Pauline H. Baker. Berkeley; Los Angeles; London: University of California, 1974. 384p. 2 maps. bibliog.

This study provides a socio-political examination of fifty years of the growth of Lagos, from the formation of a local town council in 1917 to the creation of Lagos State in May 1967. The author describes the city's history, its major constituents, government structure, the rôles of traditional rulers and the influence of market women, as well as its constitutional status. Appendices include socio-economic and political profiles of Lagos Councillors from 1920 to 1966 and a chronology of important political events from 1849 to 1967. Spencer H. Brown's 1964 doctoral thesis at Northwestern University, *A history of the people of Lagos, 1852–1886* charts the earlier history of Lagos.

576 **My life.**
Alhaji Sir Ahmadu Bello. Cambridge: Cambridge University, 1962. 246p. 2 maps.

This informative autobiography by the Sardauna of Sokoto and the first Premier of the Northern Region of Nigeria contains a genealogy of the House of Fodio, the lineage from Shehu Usuman dan Fodio, Ahmadu Bello's great-great-grandfather, to the Holy Prophet, and numerous photographs. The Sardauna (12 June 1910–15 January 1966) was born near Sokoto in Rabbah. Here he describes his growth as a politician and administrator, crises in Lagos and Kaduna, the London conferences leading to independence and Nigeria's general progress toward independence. He was assassinated in the coup of 15 January 1966. Ahmadu Bello University, the first in northern Nigeria, was named in his honour.

Politics. Pre-independence (pre-1 October 1960)

577 **Nigeria: background to nationalism.**
James S[moot] Coleman. Berkeley; Los Angeles: University of
California, 1965. 510p. 15 maps. bibliog.
This exemplary political history is one of the most important and most frequently cited
works on Nigerian politics. The author (1919–87) provides a case study of the rise of
nationalism with its full social and historical background in four parts: 'The cultural
and historical setting'; 'The western impact and the roots of nationalism'; 'The rise of
the Nigerian nationalist movement'; and 'Postwar developments in the nationalist
movement'. Maps, tables, detailed notes, and an excellent bibliography (p. 481–96)
amplify the text. The author spent 1951–52 in Nigeria doing field research for the study
which is detailed up to 1952 and only briefly surveys events after that date.

578 **The Nigerian federal election of 1959: politics and administration in a
developing political system.**
K[enneth] W. J. Post. London: Oxford University for the Nigerian
Institute of Social and Economic Research, 1963. 518p. 6 maps. bibliog.
Based on eighteen months'research in Nigeria during 1958–60, this examines in
exhaustive detail the Nigerian political system on the eve of independence, using the
federal election of 12 December 1959 as a focal point. The appendices cover the aims
and objectives for many constituencies in the country and a list of registration numbers
and voting results for each of the country's 320 constituencies, and are followed by a
substantial bibliography (p. 475–86).

579 **The price of liberty: personality and politics in colonial Nigeria.**
Kenneth W. J. Post, George D. Jenkins. Cambridge: Cambridge
University, 1973. 494p. 3 maps. bibliog. (African Studies Series, no. 7).
'This is a biography of Adegoke Adelabu, whose political career spanned all levels of
Nigerian politics during the crucial last years of colonial rule' (p. 1). Alhaji Gbadomosi
Adegoke Oduola Adelabu Akande, a Muslim Yoruba of Ibadan (1914/15–25 March
1958), rose to high office in the National Council of Nigeria and Cameroons (NCNC).
Elected to the Federal House of Representatives, he became the Minister of Natural
Resources and Social Services in the national government. In 1957 he led the Western
Nigeria NCNC to the Constitutional Conference in London but was killed in a motor
accident in 1958, causing riots and death when Action Group members were blamed,
wrongly, for his death. The authors made extensive use of Adelabu's personal papers
and interviews in writing his biography. Five photographs of Adelabu are included.

580 **The contribution of tribalism to nationalism in Western Nigeria.**
Richard L. Sklar. *Journal of Human Relations*, vol. 8, nos. 3,4
(spring, summer 1960), p. 407–15. bibliog.
This seminal article differentiates between 'pantribalism', defined as 'the destructive
expression of ethnic group activity for the most politically conscious members of a new
and rising class' (p. 407), and 'communal partisanship' which affirms traditional values
and stresses their positive rôles in Nigerian nationalism. Professor Sklar describes
communal partisanship in two societies – in Benin City (the Edo) and in Ibadan (the
Yoruba). In another important article, Professor Sklar analyses 'Contradictions in the
Nigerian political system', *Journal of Modern African Studies*, vol. 3, no. 2 (1965)
p. 201–13, identifying three basic weaknesses in the distribution of power and the
machinery of government.

581 **Nigerian political parties: power in an emergent African nation.**
Richard L. Sklar. Princeton, New Jersey: Princeton University, 1963.
578p. 2 maps. bibliog. Reprinted, New York; Enugu, Nigeria: NOK,
1983.

This impressive study is 'concerned with the development of the Nigerian party system
during the final decade of British colonial rule' which reveals 'the interplay of three
converging social forces, namely, the thrust of nationalism, the persistence of cultural
particularlism, and the crystallization of emergent class interests' (Preface, p. v). Part
one describes the rise of political parties; part two 'Studies in power and conflict'
focuses on the National Council of Nigeria and the Cameroons (NCNC), the Action
Group, and party politics in Ibadan and Northern Nigeria. Part three analyses 'Party
structure and social structure'. The appendices provide comprehensive lists of
executive members and national officers of the parties in 1957 and 1958. The
bibliography (p. 535–59) is excellent. Professor Sklar taught at the University of
Ibadan, Ibadan, Nigeria. The volume is based on his 1961 Princeton University
doctoral thesis, *Nigerian political parties*. The reprint of this valuable study contains a
new introduction (p. xiii–xxi) written in 1980.

582 **Nigeria.**
Richard L. Sklar, C. S. Whitaker, Jr. In: *Political parties and
national integration in tropical Africa.* Edited by James S. Coleman,
Carl G. Rosberg, Jr. Berkeley; Los Angeles: University of California,
1964, p. 597–651. bibliog.

Presents an admirable discussion of the major political parties of Nigeria during the
1950s and up to 1962 with an added brief postscript describing events in 1963. Tables
show the attitudes of the parties on important issues, communal and class bases of
party support and election results between 1951 and 1960, as well as ethnic, religious
and occupational affiliations of party leaders.

583 **The Nigerian political scene.**
Edited by Robert O. Tilman, Taylor Cole. Durham, North Carolina:
Duke University; London: Cambridge University for the Duke
University Commonwealth Studies Center, 1962. 340p. bibliog. (Duke
University Commonwealth Studies Center Publication, no. 17).

Twelve essays written in 1960 and 1961 describe Nigeria's traditional background,
politics and government, economic development, political future and research on the
country. These are George P. Murdock's 'The traditional socio-political systems of
Nigeria: an introductory survey' (p. 3–16); W. B. Hamilton's 'The evolution of British
policy toward Nigeria' (p. 17–41); Taylor Cole's 'Emergent federalism in Nigeria'
(p. 45–62), 'The independence constitution of Federal Nigeria' (p. 63–88), and
'Bureaucracy in transition' (p. 89–114); L. Gray Cowan's 'Nigerian foreign policy'
(p. 115–43); Joseph J. Spengler's 'Population movements and economic development
in Nigeria' (p. 147–97); Frederick Harbison's 'Human resources and economic
development' (p. 198–219); Archibald Callaway's 'Schoolleavers and the developing
economy of Nigeria' (p. 220–38); Pendleton Herring's 'The future for democracy in
Nigeria' (p. 241–70); Francis X. Sutton's 'Authority and authoritarianism in the new
Africa' (p. 271–84); and James O'Connell's 'A survey of selected social science
research on Nigeria since the end of 1957' (p. 287–327).

Politics. Post-independence (1 October 1960– .)

584 **The politics of tradition: continuity and change in Northern Nigeria, 1946–1966.**
C. S. Whitaker, Jr.   Princeton, New Jersey: Princeton University for the Center of International Studies, 1970. 563p. bibliog.

The author presents a comprehensive examination of Northern Nigeria as a type of 'confrontation society', 'in which aspects of institutions of different historical origins actually coexist and interact' (p. 14). The volume contains an extended discussion and analysis of traditional political structures, reforms, regional politics and political parties, concluding that the phrase 'stable symbiosis' appropriately describes the challenge of modernization for traditional society. Particularly informative among the appendices is 'A selected biographical directory of Northern Nigerian political leaders' (p. 471–97) which provides data on 188 individuals; the bibliography (p. 509–46) is impressive.

Post-independence (1 October 1960– .)

585 **Nigeria elects '83: a brief guide to 1983 general elections in Nigeria for the foreign observer.**
African Bibliographic Center.   Washington, DC: ABC, 1982. 345p.
(Current Reading List Series, vol. 14, no. 1. Habari Special Report).

This 'selected bibliographic survey of recent political developments in Nigeria' contains 1,940 briefly annotated entries grouped into seventeen headings covering everything from administration to corruption, strikes and unrest.

586 **Patrons and power: creating a political community in metropolitan Lagos.**
Sandra T[heis] Barnes.   Manchester, England: Manchester University; Bloomington, Indiana: Indiana University in association with the International African Institute, 1986. 272p. 4 maps. bibliog.

A remarkable book about the two million residents, mostly Yoruba, of Mushin, a densely-populated, low-income suburb of Lagos where the author did fieldwork in 1971–72 and three months of 1975. 'This book is about power – getting it, wielding it, and perpetuating it', and about people 'who began at the bottom of their society's structure of power, acquired resources, and developed political skills' (p. 1). The volume covers the colonial history of Mushin and its development as a polity up to mid-1975, land and housing as sources of power, community leadership, market conflicts and the institutionalization of power. This volume received the 1986 Amaury Talbot Prize of the International African Institute. The author's 1974 University of Wisconsin at Madison doctoral thesis, *Becoming a Lagosian* (Ann Arbor, Michigan: University Microfilms, 1975. 274 leaves. Order no. 75-9966) is a valuable preliminary work.

Politics. Post-independence (1 October 1960– .)

587 **Armies and parties in Africa.**
Henry Bienen. New York, London: Africana, 1978. 278p. bibliog.
In this volume essays and articles written and published between 1966 and 1977 have been edited and slightly altered (but not revised) and new introductions have been added. Several essays offer a view of the military throughout the continent; others are about the military in Kenya, Uganda, Tanzania and Tanganyika. Nearly one-third of the book examines politics, civil servants, military rule and the transition from military rule in Nigeria, which in 1977 had Africa's largest army with 221,000 members (p. 13).

588 **Political conflict and economic change in Nigeria.**
Henry Bienen. London: Frank Cass, 1985. 180p. 6 maps. bibliog.
This book is based on four articles written between 1978 and 1983; they were published elsewhere and are introduced and edited, but not revised. Each of the essays is a rich source of political and economic data for events in Nigeria during the late 1970s and early 1980s. They are entitled: 'Oil revenues and policy choice in Nigeria' (p. 8–63); 'The politics of income distribution: institutions, class and ethnicity' (p. 64–115); 'Religion and economic change in Nigeria' (p. 116–32); and 'The 1979 Nigerian elections' (p. 133–80). The author is Professor of Politics and International Affairs, Woodrow Wilson School, Princeton University, Princeton, New Jersey. Of interest also is William D. Graf's *The Nigerian state: political economy, state class and political system in the post-colonial era* (Portsmouth, New Hampshire: Heinemann; London: James Currey, 1988. 281p.).

589 **Yakubu Gowon: faith in a united Nigeria.**
John D. Clarke. London: Frank Cass, 1987. 150p. 6 maps. bibliog.
This biography profiles Yakubu Gowon (19 Oct. 1934- .) who became Head of State in Nigeria after a military coup of late July 1966, commanded the armed forces during the civil war and was himself deposed on 29 July 1975 while attending a conference in Kampala, Uganda. The author concentrates on Gowon's military career and term of office, but makes brief mention of Gowon's exile in England where he earned a PhD in the School of Politics at Warwick University in 1984. Clarke served in Nigeria during 1926–52, for a time as Education Officer on the Bauchi Plateau near Gowon's birthplace. More detail is provided by J. Isawa Elaigwu in *Gowon: the biography of a soldier-statesman* (Ibadan, Nigeria: West, 1985. 306p.) which contains sixteen pages of plates and a bibliography.

590 **Nigeria: a bibliography of politics, government, administration, and international relations.**
Compiled by Mark W. DeLancey, Elizabeth L. Normandy. Los Angeles: Crossroads, 1983. 188p. (Archival and Bibliographic Series).
The compilers bring together, in a single source, 2,207 references on government politics and international relations from 1960 to the end of 1980. Some government documents and doctoral dissertations are included. About half the items have brief annotations which often include references to book reviews. The items are arranged in seven sections: 'Bibliography'; 'General works'; 'Local, regional and state government and politics'; 'National government and politics'; 'Foreign relations'; 'The civil war: foreign relations'; and 'The civil war: domestic politics'. Subject and personal name indexes provide easy access to the items.

Politics. Post-independence (1 October 1960– .)

591 **Cleavage, conflict, and anxiety in the second Nigerian republic.**
Larry [Jay] Diamond. *Journal of Modern African Studies*, vol. 20,
no. 4 (1982), p. 629–68. bibliog.

Diamond, a Senior Research Fellow at the Hoover Institution, Stanford University,
Stanford, California brings insight to this article describing the social changes of the
1970s and their impact on the political scene in 1979 and the early 1980s. He suggests
that these changes 'predict a more prominent role for class in political conflict' (p.
632) and a diminished rôle for ethnicity. He describes the increasingly diverse social bases
of the major political parties and cleavage alignments in the 1979 elections and in post-
election conflicts, including resource allocation conflicts, the split in the Peoples
Redemption Party, the impeachment of Balarabe Musa, the P.R.P. Governor of
Kaduna State, and the riot against the Kano State government in July 1981. While
recognizing the profound basis of ethnicity in Nigeria, he feels that cultural pluralism
does not pose a threat to the Second Republic. Most important, the Shagari
government must reduce 'the pervasive state presence in economic life' and develop 'a
genuinely pluralistic economic structure' (p. 668). In 'Shagari's first two years', *Africa
Report*, vol. 27, no. 1 (Jan.–Feb. 1982), p. 4–10, Diamond evaluates the first half of
the Second Republic.

592 **Class, ethnicity, and the democratic state: Nigeria, 1950–1966.**
Larry Diamond. *Comparative Studies in Society and History*, vol. 25,
no. 3 (July 1983), p. 457–89. bibliog.

Discusses the relationships among class, ethnicity and politics in pre- and post-
independent Nigeria. In Professor Diamond's analysis, 'state power is the engine of
class formation; the competition for it and the manipulation of it represent
fundamentally class, not ethnic action. Hence, the failure of Nigeria's first attempt at
liberal democracy must be understood in light of the distinctive interaction among
ethnicity, in an ethnically plural and modernizing society; class action, in a dependent
and highly underdeveloped economy; and political competition, in a democratic polity
in which elite competition required mass mobilization' (p. 460).

593 **The coup and the future.**
Larry Diamond. *Africa Report*, vol. 29, no. 2 (March–April 1984),
p. 9–15. map.

An informative overview of the failure of the Second Republic, the widespread
corruption, the 1983 elections and the new government of Major General Muhammed
Buhari. Diamond accurately describes the country, its people and their problems:
'Nigerians are dreamers, in the best sense of the word. They are ambitious and highly
expectant people' (p. 9); 'Beneath a surface that is once again calm, there persists a
dangerous level of anger and discontent over the injustice of gross inequalities, the
arrogance of extravagant wealth, and the simple, terrible pain of poverty and declining
standards of life' (p. 15). In an interesting collection of articles from *West Africa* (q.v.)
and *Africa Now* (q.v.), entitled *Agbada to khaki: reporting a change of government in
Nigeria* (Enugu, Nigeria: Fourth Dimension, 1985. 89p.), a Jamaican-born journalist
resident in Nigeria, Lindsay Barrett, describes the events of 1983 and 1984 and gives an
interview with Major General M. Buhari.

594 **Nigeria in search of democracy.**
Larry Diamond. *Foreign Affairs*, vol. 62, no. 4 (spring 1984),
p. 905–27. bibliog.

A thoughtful essay on the collapse of Nigeria's Second Republic (1979–83), the re-emergence of military rule and the prospects for democracy in Nigeria. The military coup was brought about, he asserts, by 'staggering corruption, crippling economic waste and mismanagement, and the vitiating of the electoral process through violence and fraud' (p. 905). The author describes the positive rôle the military has played in Nigeria in its ability to span 'deep ethnic cleavages' and argues that it continues 'to show a sensitivity to basic liberal concerns' (p. 914). Professor Diamond proposes several structural and political reforms and urges flexibility and support of Nigeria as it 'struggles to establish the legacy of justice that is a precondition of accountability' (p. 927). Another excellent, important essay is Diamond's 'Nigeria: pluralism, statism, and the struggle for democracy' in *Democracy in developing countries: vol. 2, Africa*, which Diamond edited with Juan J. Linz and Seymour Martin Lipset (Boulder, Colorado: Lynne Rienner, 1988, p. 33–91).

595 **Nigeria update.**
Larry Diamond. *Foreign Affairs*, vol. 64, no. 2 (winter 1985/86),
p. 326–36.

Analyses the overthrow of the M. Buhari–T. Idiagbon military government by their third-ranking member Major-General Ibrahim Babangida. Diamond asserts the need for a diarchy of shared rule between civilians and the military and urges the US to 'take the lead in helping Nigeria to restructure its international obligations' (p. 336). He states that Buhari had arrogantly overstepped his popular mandate; his 'fall from grace was due primarily to his anti-democratic behavior; regionalism, factionalism and economic woes also contributed to his demise' (p. 327). In 'High stakes for Babangida', *Africa Report*, vol. 30, no. 6 (Nov.–Dec. 1985), p. 54–57, he also describes the causes of the coup of 27 August 1985. Chief among these were 'the need to strike a deal with the IMF and the desire to make the Nigerian government more accountable to its citizenry' (p. 54).

596 **Nigeria between dictatorship and democracy.**
Larry Diamond. *Current History*, vol. 86, no. 520 (May 1987),
p. 201–4, 222–24. bibliog.

A timely and forward-looking analysis of the 27 August 1985 coup and the issues confronting Major General Ibrahim Babangida. The author discusses the debate over an IMF loan, the economic adjustments of the Second-tier Foreign Exchange Market (SFEM), the killing of students at Ahmadu Bello University, Zaria, by police in May 1986, and the assassination of Dele Giwa, editor of *Newswatch* magazine in October 1986. Richard A. Joseph's 'Principles and practices of Nigerian military government' in *The military in Africa*, edited by John W. Harbesson (New York: Praeger, 1987. p. 67–91) gives an especially lucid overview of military governments from the Yakubu Gowon era to Babangida's régime. A significant analysis of the contemporary Nigerian situation is offered by Otwin Marenin in 'The Nigerian state as process and manager: a conceptualization', *Comparative Politics*, vol. 20, no. 2 (Jan. 1988), p. 215–32, in which he presents a model of the state, which is 'an expression of interests and retains a concern for the structural as well as individual determinants of social action' (p. 228).

Politics. Post-independence (1 October 1960– .)

597 **Class, ethnicity and democracy in Nigeria: the failure of the First Republic.**
Larry Diamond. Syracuse, New York: Syracuse University; Basingstoke, England: Macmillan, 1988. 376p. map. bibliog.
A mature study of Nigeria from 1960 to 1965. Professor Diamond develops a 'theory of crosscutting cleavages', with class as the most destructive cleavage, writing, 'At the root of democratic failure . . . were the processes of class formation and class action' (p. 298). In explaining the 'web of causation' leading to the First Republic's failure, the author provides a detailed analysis of five major conflicts: the 1962 split in the Action Group; the bitter 1963–64 census crisis; the 1964 general strike; the 1964 federal election crisis; and the 1965 Western Regional election crisis. The bibliography (p. 342–55) is a rich source of theoretical and Nigerian-specific sources. This study originated in the author's 1980 Stanford University PhD thesis *The social foundations of democracy: the case of Nigeria.* The important rôle of class is further explored in 'Class formation in the swollen African state', *Journal of Modern African Studies,* vol. 25, no. 4 (Dec. 1987), p. 567–96.

598 **Nigeria: model of a colonial failure.**
Stanley Diamond. New York: American Committee on Africa, 1967. 89p. map.
This slender volume is a collection of eight essays by anthropologist Stanley Diamond first published in *Africa Today* between 1962 and 1966. They include critical responses by Simon Obi Anekwe and Chief F. U. Anyiam, with Diamond's reply; an essay by Akintunde Emiola and a longer response by Diamond; an essay by Diamond 'Accra & Lagos: chiaroscuro' (p. 66–77) from *Dissent* (spring 1963) with a critical response by William McCord; and, finally, Diamond's reply 'The moral colonialists' (p. 82–88). These articles present 'a subtly detailed analysis of a fundamental Nigerian dynamic which culminated in the January [1966] coup and subsequent violence' (p. vi).

599 **Parties and politics in Northern Nigeria.**
Billy J. Dudley. London: Frank Cass, 1968. 352p. 2 maps. bibliog.
This fact-filled analysis, written during the civil war, begins with a political and social history of Northern Nigeria, and traces the emergence of political parties in the 1940s. It covers the Northern Elements Progressive Union (NEPU) in 1950, the Northern Peoples Congress (NPC) in 1951, and the United Middle Belt congress (UMBC) in 1955. Political processes, grass-roots politics and Nigerian Federalism in the north are other major themes of the book. The author urges the creation of more states in Nigeria to reduce bloc-voting in existing regions and to restructure Nigerian society to make the Federal Republic less fragile. Appendices (p. 301–34) contain *inter alia* 'The Northern Peoples Congress Constitution' and a fold-out map showing the constituencies of Northern Nigeria. Thirty tables display numerous data; the bibliography (p. 335–44) is useful and documentary notes are copious.

600 **Instability and political order: politics and crisis in Nigeria.**
B[illy] J. Dudley. Ibadan, Nigeria: Ibadan University, 1973. 265p. map. bibliog. (Ibadan Political and Administrative Studies).
In this important work, Professor Dudley examines the nature of Nigeria's political instability using game theory. He describes the inherent instability of a three participant game and shows that political instability can have redeeming features. He

Politics. Post-independence (1 October 1960– .)

writes, 'Instability should be seen as a necessary and inescapable condition in the creation of political order and is thus intimately bound up with the process of modernization and political development' (p. 13–14). Of interest also is *Nigeria 1965: crisis and criticism, selections from Nigerian Opinion*, edited by B. J. Oritsetsaninomi Dudley (Ibadan, Nigeria: Ibadan University, 1966. 130p.), which contains sixty brief editorials and essays from the monthly *Nigerian Opinion* concerning recent political and social issues. Other contributors include Richard L. Harris, T. N. Tamuno, Akin L. Mabogunje, Howard Wolpe, Sayre P. Schatz, J. O'Connell, and M. E. Obasi.

601 **An introduction to Nigerian government and politics.**
Billy Dudley, edited and introduced by A. D. Yahaya, preface by Dennis Austin. Bloomington, Indiana: Indiana University, 1982. 367p. bibliog.

The early death of the author cut short the career of one of the most productive and perceptive scholars of the Nigerian political scene. This volume lacks a chapter on political behaviour and the conclusion, planned for inclusion, but otherwise covers the relationship between societal values and political will. From this perspective, Professor Dudley discusses the First and Second Republics, the military and politics, the 1979 elections, the economy, and external relations. The volume contains a useful select bibliography compiled by Chris Allen. The introduction by Yahaya (p. 1–12), which was written in July 1981, reviews Dudley's political analyses and defines the political issue at hand as not being national unity but rather the distribution of wealth between the élite and the producers. Dudley published an analysis entitled 'The Nigerian elections of 1979: the voting decision' in *Journal of Commonwealth and Comparative Politics*, vol. 19, no. 3 (1981), p. 276–98, which contains detailed notes and election data.

602 **West African states, failure and promise: a study in comparative politics.**
Edited by John Dunn. Cambridge; London; New York: Cambridge University, 1978. 259p. map. bibliog. (African Studies Series, no. 23).

This volume examines political development in seven coastal West African states (Ghana, Guinea, Ivory Coast, Liberia, Nigeria, Senegal and Sierra Leone), attempting to explain their diversity and their post-independence political problems. In 'Nigeria' (p. 132–72, 240–45), Gavin Williams and Terisa Turner analyse the political economy, the politics of resource allocation, public policy, and class relations, covering first the period 1939–66 followed by 1967–75. Finally, they discuss 'The 1975 coup and the politics of capitalism', concluding that 'civilian rule is thus likely to repeat the 'failure of politics', and hence to invite in its turn a fresh demonstration from the military of the 'failure of administration'' (p. 172). The introductory essay by the editor, 'Comparing West African states' (p. 1–21) and his 'Conclusion' (p. 211–16) are also enlightening. The detailed notes and reading lists (p. 217–52) are important for Nigerian scholars. Plans for a sequel volume, with essays on Nigeria by John Paden and Richard Joseph, are reported by Kaye Whiteman in *West Africa*, no. 3,648 (13 July 1987), p. 1,349.

Politics. Post-independence (1 October 1960– .)

603 **The rise & rall of Nigeria's Second Republic, 1979–84.**
Toyin Falola, Julius Ihonvbere. London: Zed Books, 1985. 290p.
bibliog. (Third World Books).

A Marxist analysis which seeks to 'document in a correct (dialectical) manner, the dynamics and conditions of Nigeria's Second Republic' (Preface, p. ix). It emphasizes class relations; Nigeria's place in the world capitalist system; the bourgeois nature of the 1979 constitution; and the poverty of Nigerian social science. The authors describe the military and the transition to civilian rule (1975–79); the presidential constitution, the economy; agriculture and the food crisis; labour and strikes; external relations; the 1983 elections; and the coup of 31 December 1983. The authors are, respectively, a historian and a political economist at Obafemi Awolowo University, Ile-Ife, Nigeria.

604 **African revolutionary: the life and times of Nigeria's Aminu Kano.**
Alan Feinstein, foreword by John N. Paden. Boulder, Colorado;
London: Lynne Rienner, 1987. rev. ed. 387p. 2 maps. bibliog.

Mallam Aminu Kano (9 Aug. 1920–17 April 1983) was a widely respected northern Nigerian political leader who died prematurely as a result of a stroke following a bout of malaria (p. 331). He had founded the Northern Element Progressive Union (NEPU) and later ran for president, as the candidate of the People's Redemption Party (PRP) which he had founded in 1978. He was Federal Commissioner for Communication (1967–71) and for Health (1971–74) and was a member of the Constituent Assembly (1977–78), among his numerous political offices. 'He was a Kano man, a man of the north, a man for all Nigeria, and a world class leader, who was as much at home in the corridors of the United Nations as in the back streets of Sudawa ward . . .' (Foreword, p. ix). The author was Kano's friend from 1960–83; for this authorized biography, he had full access to Kano's papers and had spent extensive time in Nigeria. The volume was first published in 1973 and has eleven photographs by the author's son.

605 **Nigeria: power and democracy in Africa.**
Jean Herskovits. New York: Foreign Policy Association, 1982, 72p.
map. bibliog. (Headline Series, no. 257).

A lucid overview of Nigerian history with the focus on post-independence political events and relations between Nigeria and the United States. A brief chronology of 'Milestones in Nigeria's history' (p. 31) and a reading list (p. 71) are included Informative essays on related topics are the author's 'Nigeria: Africa's new power' *Foreign Affairs*, vol. 53, no. 2 (1975), p. 314–33, 'Dateline Nigeria: a black power' *Foreign Policy*, no. 29 (winter 1977–78), p. 167–81, 'Democracy in Nigeria', *Foreign Affairs*, vol. 58, no. 2 (1979), p. 314–35, and 'Dateline Nigeria: democracy down but not out', *Foreign Policy*, no. 54 (spring 1984), p. 171–90. Herskovits is Professor of History at the State University of New York (SUNY), Purchase, has been a frequent visitor to Nigeria since 1958 and was in Nigeria for the 1983 elections and the coup which followed on 31 December 1983.

606 **The overthrow of Nigeria's Second Republic.**
Richard A. Joseph. *Current History*, vol. 83, no. 491 (March 1984),
p. 122–24, 138. bibliog.

This brief article examines both the political and economic problems which led to the 31 December 1983 coup which ended the government of President Shehu Shagari and the dilemmas posed for the new Buhari military government. Joseph suggests 'perhaps it is time to try the military-civilian diarchy which the country's first President, Nnamdi Azikiwe, has long proposed as the only temporary solution to Nigeria's ruinous political cycles' (p. 138). Related themes are explored in his 'Class, state and prebendal politics in Nigeria', *Journal of Commonwealth and Comparative Politics*, vol. 21, no. 3 (Nov. 1983), p. 21–38, and 'Affluence and underdevelopment: the Nigerian experience' *Journal of Modern African Studies*, vol. 16, no. 2 (1978), p. 221–40. Dr. Joseph is Associate Professor of Government, Dartmouth College, Hanover, New Hampshire.

607 **Democracy and prebendal politics in Nigeria: the rise and fall of the Second Republic.**
Richard A. Jospeh. Cambridge; New York: Cambridge University, 1987. 237p. 2 maps. bibliog. (African Studies Series, 56).

This political sociology of democratic Nigeria from 1979–83 traces Nigerian social dynamics and military rule and the return to tripartism in the Second Republic. Professor Joseph argues that 'the requisite social terrain for competitive party politics did not exist in Nigeria' (p. 170) and that 'prebendal politics, and especially its major features involving the mobilization of sectional support groups, the exploitation of public office, and the resulting encouragement of corrupt practices' embody 'a political rationality or logic which is ill-suited to the creation of the national political order . . .' (p. 198). The select bibliography (p. 224–32) contains useful lists of printed materials and of the individuals who were formally interviewed. The author lectured at the University of Ibadan from February 1976 to August 1979. Among many other papers on Nigeria is his 'Political parties and ideology in Nigeria', *Review of African Political Economy*, no. 13 (1979), p. 78–90.

608 **Ethnic engineering and the 'federal character' of Nigeria: boon of contentment or bone of contention?**
A. H. M. Kirk-Greene. *Ethnic and Racial Studies*, vol. 6, no. 4 (Oct. 1983), p. 457–76. bibliog.

An informative critique of the Nigerian tendency to create ever more states as a way of dealing with ethnic rivalries, with particular reference to the goals and implications of the 1979 constitution. The author concludes, 'although loyalty may be a shared commodity, there cannot be a multiplicity of equal loyalties. . . Nigeria has long indulged in a national capacity for infinite regression. Patriotism must in the end take precedence over parochialism and particularism. The whole must remain greater than the parts; to reverse the priority was the fatal flaw of Nigeria's First Republic' (p. 473). See also Kirk-Greene's "A sense of belonging': the Nigerian Constitution of 1979 and the promotion of national loyalty', *Journal of Commonwealth and Comparative Politics*, vol. 26, no. 2 (July 1988), p. 158–72.

609 **West Africa: Nigeria and Ghana.**
A. H. M. Kirk-Greene. In: *Politics & government in African states, 1960–1985*. Edited by Peter Duignan, Robert H. Jackson. London: Croom Helm; Stanford, California: Hoover Institution, 1986, p. 30–77. bibliog. (Hoover Press Publication, 348).

This frank, informative article, containing twelve tables and generous notes, is 'less a synchronic political or economic comparison of Ghana and Nigeria than a diachronic comparison of the history of the two countries since independence' (p. 33). The author remarks that because African scholars are now able to offer objective accounts of independent Africa's "dismal record' . . . [he] overcame [his] own initial reluctance to undertake the writing of this pessimistic and personally painful critique of the performance of a country with which [he has] been closely and happily associated for thirty-five years' (p. 76).

610 **Nigeria since 1970: a political and economic outline.**
Anthony Kirk-Greene, Douglas Rimmer. London: Hodder & Stoughton, 1981. 161p. map. bibliog.

This detailed study is divided into three parts and covers the political and economic events in Nigeria during the 1970s. Part one, 'The making of the Second Republic' (p. 1–58) by Kirk-Greene describes the military régimes of Y. Gowon, Murtala Mohammed and Olusegun Obasanjo, and the new constitution of 1979, and analyses the general elections of 1979. Brief accounts of foreign policy, education and the armed forces are added. Part two, 'The economy since 1970' (p. 59–150) by Rimmer provides a broad look at major sectors and institutions, these being: agriculture; petroleum; industrialization; infrastructure; public finance; external trade and payments; and development planning. Part three offers brief conclusions (p. 153–56). The 'Guide to further reading' (p. 157–61) and 'An outline chronology of Nigeria from 1960 [to August 1980]' (p. x–xii) are very useful.

611 **The Nigerian general elections, 1959 and 1979 and the aftermath.**
Amadu Kurfi. Lagos; Ibadan, Nigeria: Macmillan Nigeria, 1983. 291p. 4 maps.

This interesting personal account by a career civil servant describes the elections of 1959 and 1979, the censuses of 1962, 1963, and 1973, and the major political events from 1959 to 1980; it also offers proposals for electoral reform. The appendix contains extensive voting data from the 1979 elections (p. 266–91). The author was Executive Secretary of the Federal Electoral Commission (FEDECO) from 1976–81 and was a senior administrator in the Ministry of Defence, 1960–66.

612 **Hegemony and culture: politics and religious change among the Yoruba.**
David D. Laitin. Chicago: University of Chicago, 1986. 252p. 2 maps bibliog.

A lucid theoretical study based on the author's fieldwork in Ile-Ife in 1977 and 1979–80. After exploring and ultimately rejecting the social and cultural systems theory of Clifford Geertz and the rational choice theory of Abner Cohan, Professor Laitin develops a 'state-centered' (p. 19, 180–82) theory of hegemony from the work of Antonio Gramsci to explain why religious differences between Moslem and Christian Yorubas have not caused deep political divisions. This fascinating analysis of the politics of culture relates both modern and nineteenth-century political history in Yorubaland and particularly in Ile-Ife. Research methodology, which included formal survey of thirty-five Christians and thirty-five Muslims, is described in the final chapter. The author is Professor of Political Science at the University of California, San Diego.

226

Politics. Post-independence (1 October 1960– .)

613 Nigerian government and politics: prelude to the revolution.
John P. Mackintosh. Evanston, Illinois: Northwestern University,
1966. 651p. 12 maps. bibliog.

A massive study of the workings of Nigerian political and governmental institutions
focusing on the years just before and after independence. Regional and federal
elections from 1957 through to the 1964 federal election in the North are examined in
great detail. Five important chapters were contributed by others: 'The machinery of
the Federal and Regional governments' by I. Nicolson; 'Local government' by R. E.
Wraith; 'The Northern People's Congress' by B. J. Dudley; 'The National Council of
Nigeria and the Cameroons,the decision of December 1959' by K. W. Post; and 'A
minority party in the United Middle Belt Congress' by M. J. Dent. The author taught
politics and government at the University of Ibadan from 1961 to 1963 and conducted a
study in Nigeria in January 1965, following the general election. The bibliography
(p. 627–41) is excellent.

614 Nigeria: modernization and the politics of communalism.
Edited by Robert Melson, Howard Wolpe. East Lansing, Michigan:
Michigan State University, 1971. 680p. bibliog.

This mammoth volume contains twenty-five substantive essays, eight of which are
published for the first time. It emphasizes, as a general theme, that 'it is probably more
accurate to suggest that political conflict produces 'tribalism' than to argue that
'tribalism' is the cause of conflict' (Preface, p. vii). Among the many important essays
are: Richard L. Sklar's 'Nigerian politics in perspective', 'The contribution of tribalism
to nationalism in Western Nigeria', and 'Contradictions in the Nigerian political
system'; James S. Coleman's 'The Ibo and Yoruba strands in Nigerian nationalism';
Abner Cohen's 'The social organization of credit in a West African cattle market [in
Ibadan]' and 'Politics of the kola trade'; John N. Paden's 'Communal competition,
conflict and violence in Kano'; 'The military and politics: a study of the relation
between the army and political process in Nigeria' and 'Tarka and the Tiv: a
perspective on Nigerian federation' by M. J. Dent; Ronald Cohen's 'Bornu and
Nigeria: 'political kingdom' in a troubled nation'; and C. S. Whitaker, Jr.'s 'Three
perspectives on hierarchy' [A. Bello, A. T. Balewa, and Aminu Kano]. Other authors
are John R. Harris and Mary P. Rowe, Robert A. LeVine, R. N. Henderson, Ulf
Himmelstrand, Audrey C. Smock, Alvin Magid, David B. Abernathy, Alan Peshkin,
Leonard Plotnicov, James O'Connell and the editors.

615 Elections in Nigeria: a grass roots perspective.
William F. S. Miles. London; Boulder, Colorado: Lynne Rienner,
1988. 168p. 2 maps. bibliog.

This fascinating study describes what the August 1983 Nigerian elections were 'really'
like in the northern border village of Yardaji. The account combines political and
social historical background with a unique description of local Hausa culture in this
village of about 3,000 in the former emirate of Daura. One theme emphasized by the
author is that 'Yardaji-ites came not only to take a negative attitude toward civilian
politics as a process but also to assume a jaded view of electoral democracy as an idea'
(p. 20). The volume contains photographs by the author, a sample ballot, tables
showing the results of the 1979 and 1983 elections, campaign songs, a glossary of
Hausa political terminology, notes and a bibliography (p. 162–65). Related articles by
the author include 'Partitioned royalty: the evolution of Hausa chiefs in Nigeria and
Niger', *Journal of Modern African Studies*, vol. 25, no. 2 (June 1987), p. 233–58, and
'Self-identity, ethnic affinity, and national consciousness: an example from rural

227

Politics. Post-independence (1 October 1960– .)

Hausaland', *Ethnic and Racial Studies*, vol. 9, no. 4 (Oct. 1986), p. 427–44. Ar excellent 'grass roots perspective' from southern Nigeria is provided by Andrew Apter in 'Things fell apart: Yoruba responses to the 1983 elections in Ondo State, Nigeria' *Journal of Modern African Studies*, vol. 25, no. 3 (Sept. 1987), p. 489–503.

616 **The political history of Nigeria's new capital.**
Jonathan Moore. *Journal of Modern African Studies*, vol. 22, no. 1 (March 1984), p. 167–75. bibliog.

This article traces the history of the attempts to relocate Nigeria's capital, from the early ideas of Sir Frederick Lugard in 1912 to the Shagari administration's hurried efforts to complete the Federal Capital Territory at Abuja in 1982 and 1983. One result has been that 'Abuja is widely perceived today as a Northern, not a Nigerian capital. . . Abuja threatens to become a symbol of North-South discord, and this may well become perilous to the stability and growth of a united Nigeria' (p. 175). The author is an Associate of the Center for International Affairs at Harvard University Cambridge, Massachusetts.

617 **Path to Nigerian development.**
Edited by Okwudiba Nnoli. Dakar, Senegal: Codesria, 1981. 264p.

This volume contains eleven articles by four Nigerians seeking new avenues for Nigerian social, political and economic development. The articles are: 'Introduction the intellectual aspects of the struggle for Nigerian development', 'Development underdevelopment: is Nigeria developing?', 'A short history of Nigerian underdevelop ment', 'Progress versus reaction in Nigerian development', and 'Path to Nigerian development: conclusion', by the editor; 'Indigenization for lumpen-bourgeois development in Nigeria' by Inyang Eteng; 'Imperialism and Nigerian development' 'Planning for underdevelopment in Nigeria' and 'Class struggle as a reality of Nigeriar development' by Bade Onimode; and 'The poverty of ideology in Nigerian development' by Uzodinma Nwala. The editor is Professor of Political Science at the University of Nigeria, Nsukka. The volume was sponsored by the Council for the Development of Economic and Social Research in Africa (Codesria), B. P. 3304 Dakar, Senegal.

618 **Political integration: the Nigerian case.**
James O'Connell. In: *African integration and disintegration: case studies in economic and political union.* Edited by Arthur Hazlewood. London: Oxford University under the auspices of the Oxford University Institute of Economics and Statistics and the Royal Institute of International Affairs, 1967, p. 129–84, 399. map. bibliog.

This essay provides a remarkably informative overview of political patterns both before and after independence, up to the end of 1966. O'Connell's concern is the problem of political integration at the state level. The author had been in Nigeria since 1957 and was a Professor of Political Science at the University of Ibadan at the time of publication.

Politics. Post-independence (1 October 1960– .)

619   **Military politics in Nigeria: economic development and political stability.**
Theophilus Olatunde Odetola.   New Brunswick, New Jersey:
Transaction, 1978. 179p. 3 maps. bibliog.

In this revision of his 1973 Rutgers University doctoral thesis, concerning events in the
decade up to early 1973, the author examines the nature of military rule in Nigeria and
the characteristics which enabled the military to govern, effectively, the complex
nation. Several topics receive special attention: military organization and ideology;
political development and stability; resource allocation and power structure; and
military effectiveness in economic development. A postscript (p. 159–62) updates the
study to early 1976. Appendices describe the author's methodology and list Nigerian
military personnel and hardware and ethnic distributions.

620   **Shehu Shagari: the biography of Nigeria's first executive president.**
Okion Ojigbo, foreword by Shehu Shagari.   Lagos: Tokion (Nigeria),
1982. 629p. 5 maps. bibliog.

A large formal biography of the President, with numerous colour and black-and-white
photographs, a family genealogy and statistics from the 1979 federal election. In
President and power in Nigeria: the life of Shehu Shagari (London: Frank Cass, 1982,
276p.), Kurt Waldheim provides a foreword, and the author, David Williams, presents
Alhaji Shehu Usman Aliyu Shagari (25 February 1925– .) as an 'individual who has
had a long and varied public career; not as a representative of a party, of a class, or of
an ethnic group' (Preface, p. xiii). About one-third of this well-illustrated, informative
biography covers his return to politics in 1977 and rôle as President from 1979 to 1982.
The author, who made extensive use of personal interviews with Shagari and had
access to his personal papers, has known Nigeria well since 1949 when he became
editor of *West Africa*. A volume entitled *Shehu Shagari: my vision of Nigeria*, edited by
Aminu Tijjani and David Williams (London: Frank Cass, 1981. 424p.) contains
selected speeches by Shagari which were delivered in 1979 and 1980, organized by
broad topic.

621   **Nigerian politics.**
John M. Ostheimer.   New York: Harper & Row, 1973. 200p. 5 maps.
bibliog. (Harper's Comparative Government Series).

The author provides a clearly written and reasonably thorough analysis of Nigerian
politics, frequently comparing and contrasting the Nigerian political situation with
those in the United States and Europe. He reviews constitutional developments, the
collapse of the First Republic, the military government, political attitudes, pressure
groups, political parties, development plans and policy dilemmas, and foreign policy.
A select bibliography (p. 186–93) lists key sources.

622   **Nigerian government and politics under military rule, 1966–79.**
Edited by Oyeleye Oyediran.   New York: St. Martin's Press, 1979.
319p. bibliog.

Fourteen articles examine Nigerian military rule between the first two republics.
Included are: 'Background to military rule' and 'Civilian rule for how long?' by the
editor; 'The civil war' by Turi Mohammadu and Mohammed Haruna; 'The military
and the economy' by Akin Iwayemi; 'The civil service: an insider's view' by P. Chiedo
Asiodu; 'The civil service: an outsider's view' by Stephen O. Olugbemi; 'The press and
military rule' by Lateef Kayode Jakande; 'Foreign policy and military rule' by Ray
Ofoegbu; 'Mohammed/Obasanjo foreign policy' by A. Bolaji Akinyemi; 'Local

Politics. Post-independence (1 October 1960– .)

government and administration' by O. Oyediran and E. Alex Gboyega; 'The military and the politics of revenue allocation' by O. Oyediran and Olatunji Olagunju; 'Dilemma of military disengagement' by J. 'Bayo Adekson; 'The making of the Nigerian constitution' by E. A. Gboyega; and 'The struggle for power in Nigeria, 1966–79' by A. D. Yahaya. A select bibliography (p. 307–10) is given. The editor was Senior Lecturer in the Department of Political Science, University of Ibadan, at the time of publication. He has also published *Survey of Nigerian affairs 1975* (Ibadan: Oxford University, 1978. 347p.), and *Survey of Nigerian affairs 1976–77* (Lagos: Macmillan Nigeria and Nigerian Institute of International Affairs, 1981. 312p.).

623 **The Nigerian 1979 elections.**
Edited by Oyeleye Oyediran. Lagos; Ibadan, Nigeria: Macmillan Nigeria, 1981. 193p. 4 maps. bibliog.

An excellent survey of the 1979 elections by political scientists from the Universities of Lagos, Ife and Ibadan and a sociologist (O. Arowolo) from the University of Ibadan. The articles include: the editor's 'The road to the 1979 elections', 'Political parties: formation and candidate selection', 'Voting behaviour', and 'Presidential election result controversy'; L. Adele Jinadu's 'The Federal Election Commission'; Adeoye Akinsanya's 'The Nigerian press and the 1979 general elections'; O. Oyediran and O. Arowolo's 'In defense of the Nigerian electorate'; and Alex E. Gboyega's 'Choosing a new cabinet'. Two important bibliographies for this period are: Michael Afolabi's *Nigeria in transition, 1978–79: an annotated bibliography of party politics, elections and the return to civil rule* (Zaria: Department of Library Science, Ahmadu Bello University, 1980, 350p.) which offers 1,651 detailed entries from the *Daily Times* and the *New Nigerian* newspapers; and Moses Adekunle Omoniwa's *Party politics and the transition from military to civilian rule in Nigeria: a bibliographical index* (Sanaru-Zaria: Kashim Ibrahim Library, Ahmadu Bello University, 1981, 559p.) with 3,245 items culled from nineteen Nigerian newspapers and journals between September 1978 and December 1979.

624 **Federalism in Nigeria: a study in the development of the Nigerian state.**
Sam Egite Oyovbaire. New York: St. Martin's Press, 1985. 306p. 3 maps. bibliog.

This valuable book examines the changing nature of Nigerian federalism particularly during the fourteen years of military rule (1966–79) and the first two years of the Second Republic (1980–81). The constitutional and social contexts of federalism under military rule are set against an explanation of Nigeria's earlier experiences with federalism. Fiscal federalism and development planning are discussed at length. The select bibliography (p. 285–94) is excellent. This volume is a revision of Professor Oyovbaire's 1976 doctoral thesis at the University of Manchester. In an interesting related article, C. O. Ikporukpo discusses 'Politics and regional policies: the issue of state creation in Nigeria', *Political Geography Quarterly*, vol. 5 (April 1986), p. 127–39. The political history of the Midwest Region (now Bendel State) is used to demonstrate that economic development did occur as a result of its creation, but that state creation can itself create new problems. See also the work edited by A. B. Akinyemi, P. D. Cole and Walter Ofonagoro, entitled *Readings on federalism* (Lagos: Nigerian Institute of International Affairs, 1979. 444p.), which includes papers presented at the International Conference on Federalism, May 1976, in Lagos, Nigeria.

625 **Democratic experiment in Nigeria: interpretative essays.**
Edited by Sam Egite Oyovbaire.   Benin City, Nigeria: Omega, 1987.
194p. bibliog.

The editor, one of Nigeria's most prominent political scientists and Chair of the
Department of Political Science at the University of Benin, Benin City, presents ten
essays by political scientists which explore aspects of democracy in Nigeria. The essays
are: 'The context of democracy in Nigeria' and 'Democratisation of the political
process – the sword of Damocles' by the editor; 'Failure of the first experiment – a
viewpoint' by Anthony Oyewole; 'Transition to the second experiment – some political
issues' by Tunji Olagunju; 'Federalism and democracy – debate and its lessons' by A.
Adele Jinadu; 'Ethnic pluralism and democratic stability – the basis of conflict and
consensus' by Y. R. Barongo; 'Class structure and democracy in Nigeria' by Otwin
Marenin; 'Democratic values and limitations of local government reforms' by Akase P.
Sorkoa; 'Local priorities and attitudes – governance in Benin' by Mae C. King; and
'Military rule, democracy and the post-military state' by Olatunde J. B. Ojo.

626 **Ahmadu Bello, Sardauna of Sokoto: values and leadership in Nigeria.**
John N. Paden.   London: Hodder & Stoughton, 1986. 799p. 22 maps.
bibliog.

A thorough study of Ahmadu Bello (June 1909–15 January 1966) which goes beyond
the limitations of traditional biography to set the man in the ethnic, religious and
political contexts of Sokoto, Northern Nigeria, and the new Nigerian nation. The study
is divided into four parts: 'Early life and career (1909–49)'; 'Transition to
independence (1949–60)'; 'Early independence (1960–66)'; and 'Crisis and reconstruction'. Appendices contain a valuable essay 'The Nigerian legacy: bibliographic
background' (p. 729–60) and 'Hausa poetry and songs cited in text' (p. 761–85). Dr.
Paden is Professor of International Studies and Political Science at Northwestern
University, Evanston, Illinois, and has had extensive experience at both Ahmadu Bello
University, Zaria, and Bayero University, Kano.

627 **Soldiers and oil: the political transformation of Nigeria.**
Edited by Keith Panter-Brick.   London: Frank Cass, 1978. 375p.
3 maps. bibliog. (Studies in Commonwealth Politics and History, no.
5).

An especially informative volume, by Nigerian, American, Australian and British
experts, which focuses, in the main, on the period 1966–78. There are twelve chapters,
divided among the four parts, entitled 'The military in office'; 'Political economy';
'Federal reform'; and 'Local government reform'. The chapters are: 'Back to the
barracks: a decade of marking time' by Valerie P. Bennett and A. H. M. Kirk-Greene;
'Soldiers, politicians and civil servants' by Henry Bienen with Martin Fitton; 'Army
reorganisation and military withdrawal' by Ian Campbell; 'Corrective government:
military rule in perspective' by Martin Dent; 'Elements of the political economy' by
Douglas Rimmer; 'Commercial capitalism and the 1975 coup' by Terisa Turner; 'The
creation of states' by Ali D. Yahaya; 'The politics of revenue allocation' by Sam Egite
Oyovbaire; 'Introduction' [to local government reform] and 'The constitution drafting
committee' by the editor; 'A view from Ibadan' by Alex E. Gboyega and Oyeleye
Oyediran; and 'As seen in Kaduna' by Abubakar Yaya Aliyu. Maps show the states
created in 1967 and 1976 and the oil and gas fields. The bibliography (p. 361–66) is
brief but its entries are of relevance.

Politics. Post-independence (1 October 1960– .)

628 **Nigerian politics: the people's view.**
Margaret Peil. London: Cassell, 1976. 209p. 2 maps. bibliog.

This book reports the results of interviews, in 1971–72, with 841 members of the general public including market traders, university students, farmers, craftsmen, clerical workers and housewives. Conducted throughout Nigeria, they demonstrate 'that Nigerian public opinion is informed, pragmatic and rational; that it is concerned about and able to influence national, state and local governments and that it deserves to be heard when changes in government structure are being made' (p. 185). These Civilian Rule Survey results allow the author to offer critiques of earlier studies of Nigerian political élites and to comment on the people's views on military versus civilian government, corruption, constitutional questions, political efficiency and participation in politics. The author was Senior Lecturer in Sociology at the Centre of West African Studies at Birmingham University at the time of publication and has taught at Lagos University.

629 **Structure and conflict in Nigeria, 1960–1966.**
Kenneth Post, Michael Vickers. Madison, Wisconsin: University of Wisconsin, 1973. 248p. map. bibliog.

In their study of the failure of Nigeria's First Republic, the authors use models of Nigeria as a 'conglomerate society' with a constitutional and institutional 'structural frame' and a 'system of rewards'. This analysis of social and political events focuses especially on the federal elections of 1964 and the Western Region election of October 1965, which did nothing to resolve the high tensions among major cultural groups. In 1973 Kenneth Post was Professor of Political Science, Institute of Social Studies at The Hague, the Netherlands, and Michael Vickers was an Assistant Professor in the Political Science Division, St. Thomas Univeristy, Fredericton, Canada. For an excellent and more general study, see Post's *The new states of West Africa* (Harmondsworth, England; Baltimore, Maryland: Penguin, 1964. 206p. (Penguin African Library, AP 14)), which grew out of his 1962–63 lectures at the University of Ibadan.

630 **Nigeria: the tribes, the nation, or the race – the politics of independence.**
Frederick A. O. Schwarz, Jr. Cambridge, Massachusetts, London: M.I.T.Press, 1965. 316p. 3 maps. bibliog.

Setting his discussion in historical and sociological context, the author writes about the growth of Nigerian politics and government, the 1959 and 1964 elections, prospects for democracy, federalism, and foreign policy. The book suggests that Nigeria 'will hold together because of economic reality, her federal system, the prestige of being big, and hope of becoming part of a still larger political community. . . The book is also in large measure about democracy in Nigeria and the forces that support and undercut democratic practices and ideals' (Preface, p. vii, viii). The bibliographic essay (p. 271–302) is especially informative. Dr. Schwarz was Assistant Commissioner for Law Revision in the Attorney-General's office in Northern Nigeria for a year in 1961–62.

Politics. Post-independence (1 October 1960– .)

631 **A bibliography for the study of African politics.**
Compiled by Eric R. Siegel. Los Angeles: University of California,
African Studies Association, Crossroads Press, 1983. vol. 3. 348p.
(Archival and Bibliographical Series).

This updates two earlier volumes; among the 5,721 unannotated entries for the
relevant literature of 1976–80, are about 350 for Nigeria (p. 147–64, entries no.
2,630–979), more than for any other African country. In the second volume (Waltham,
Massachusetts: Brandeis University, Crossroads Press, 1977. 193p.) compiled by Alan
C. Solomon and covering 1971–75 are 235 entries for Nigeria (p. 62–72). In the original
volume, compiled by Robert B. Shaw and Richard L. Sklar, (Los Angeles: University
of California, African Studies Association, June 1973. Reprinted, Waltham,
Massachusetts, Crossroads, 1977. 206p.) there are 270 useful works on Nigeria
(p. 72–84) among the 3,951 thoroughly indexed entries. In each volume other relevant
publications appear under numerous topical headings.

632 **Nigerian politics: the ordeal of Chief Awolowo, 1960–65.**
Richard L. Sklar. In: *Politics in Africa: 7 cases.* Edited by Gwendolen
M. Carter. New York: Harcourt, Brace & World, 1965, p. 119–65. 2
maps. bibliog. (Harbrace Casebook in Political Science).

This excellent article examines both the trials for treason of Chief Obafemi Awolowo,
former Premier of Western Nigeria, in 1962–63 and that of his Action Group second
vice-president Chief Anthony Enahoro in 1963. Both were convicted and sent to prison
in September 1963. These events are examined and set in the context of conflict with
Chief Samuel Ladoke Akintola and the political evolution of independent Nigeria. The
author regards this case study as an addendum to his major study *Nigerian political
parties* (q.v.). See also his 'Contradictions in the Nigerian political system', *Journal of
Modern African Studies*, vol. 3, no. 2 (Aug. 1965), p. 201–13.

633 **The colonial imprint on African political thought.**
Richard L. Sklar. In: *African independence: the first twenty-five years.*
Edited by Gwendolen M. Carter, Patrick O'Meara. Bloomington,
Indiana: Indiana University; London: Hutchinson, 1985, p. 1–30.
bibliog.

In this wide-ranging essay, considering trends toward 'colonial freedom' and 'post-
colonial freedom', the author includes 'autochthony in British Africa: the case of
Nigeria' (p. 5–10) and favourable discussion of Nigerian political scientist Peter P.
Ekeh's critique of the study of colonialism. In Professor Sklar's view, 'The colonial
imprint is indelible, but it need not be pervasive and should be allowed to fade without
misguided enhancement' (p. 25). Among other stimulating articles in this important
volume is Hans Panofsky's 'Bibliographic essay: a twenty-five year perspective'
(p. 339–54) in which he offers a list of studies of enduring value.

Politics. Post-independence (1 October 1960– .)

634 The Federal Republic of Nigeria.

Richard L. Sklar, C. S. Whitaker, Jr. In: *National unity and regionalism in eight African states: Nigeria, Niger, The Congo, Gabon, Central African Republic, Chad, Uganda, Ethiopia.* Edited by Gwendolen M. Carter. Ithaca, New York: Cornell University, 1966, p. 7–150. 2 maps. bibliog.

In one of the best survey articles available for the time, the authors describe the political culture of a plural society; nationalism and constitutional development; political structures and processes; the sources and uses of power in Nigerian society; and Nigerian foreign policy. The bibliography (p. 137–50) is particularly useful.

635 Nigeria: imperialism, oil technology and the comprador state.

Terisa Turner. In: *Oil and class struggle.* Edited by Petter Nore, Terisa Turner. London: Zed, 1980, p. 199–223. bibliog.

The author describes political issues in the transfer of modern oil technology to Nigeria in the mid- and late-1970s, characterizing the country as governed by a 'neo-colonial comprador state' (p. 221). *Comprador* is Portuguese for 'buyer'. 'Compradors are state officials who use their public offices for personal gain', or 'professional intermediaries who organise the access of foreign traders to the local market' (p. 204). This article appeared earlier as 'The transfer of oil technology and the Nigerian state' *Development and Change*, vol. 7 (1976)). The author has also published *Two refineries: a comparative study of technology transfer to the Nigerian refining industry* (The Hague: Institute of Social Studies, March 1977. 40p., (ISS Occasional Papers, no. 62)), which compares the 1965 Port Harcourt refinery, Nigeria's first, with the 1977 Warri refinery, Nigeria's second; and *Soldiers and oil: the 1983 coup in Nigeria*, with Arnold Baker (Montreal, Quebec: Centre for Developing Area Studies, March 1985. 31p. (CDAS Discussion Paper, no. 28)).

636 Perspectives on the Second Republic of Nigeria.

Edited by C. S. Whitaker, Jr. Waltham, Massachusetts: Crossroads, 1981. 50p. bibliog.

A collection of eight short essays on some of the diverse political aspects of Nigeria's second effort at democratic government which began on 1 October 1979. The articles are: 'Second beginnings: the new political framework' by the editor (p. 2–13); 'Democracy for the Second Republic' by R. L. Sklar (p. 14–16); 'The ethnic trap: notes on the Nigerian campaign and elections, 1978–79' by Richard A. Joseph (p. 17–23); 'Islamic political culture and constitutional change in Nigeria' by John N. Paden (p. 24–28); 'Prospects for the administration of justice in Nigeria: courts, police and politics' by Helen Marshall Carter (p. 29–34); 'Nigeria's petro-political fluctuation' by Sayre P. Schatz (p. 35–40); 'Nigerian foreign policy and southern Africa: a choice for the West' by Nicholas J. Spiliotes (p. 41–45); and 'The fundamentals of Nigerian foreign policy' by John S. Stremlau (p. 46–50). The collection is dedicated to Billy J. Dudley (1931–23 December 1980) and first appeared as a special issue of *Issue: a Quarterly Journal of Africanist Opinion*, vol. 11, nos. 1/2 (spring/summer 1981.) 50p.

Politics. Post-independence (1 October 1960– .)

637 Nigeria.
Edited by Gavin Williams (et al.), ROAPE Editorial Working Group. *Review of African Political Economy* , no. 13 (May–Aug. 1978), 107p. bibliog.

The eight articles and the introductory editorial by Williams, in this special issue, critically examine Nigerian developments in the midst of the oil-boom years. The articles are: 'The incorporation of Northern Nigeria into the world capitalist economy' by Bob Shenton and Bill Freund (p. 8–20); 'Hausa women on strike' by Sam Jackson (p. 21–36); 'Labour in Kano since the petroleum boom' by Paul M. Lubeck (p. 37–46); 'Consciousness, organisation and action amongst Lagos portworkers' by Peter Waterman (p. 47–62); 'The deepening crisis of the Nigerian national bourgeoisie' by Segun Osoba (p. 63–77); 'Political parties and ideology in Nigeria' by Richard Joseph (p. 78–90); 'Oil boom and crisis in contemporary Nigeria' by Bill Freund (p. 91–100); and 'The World Bank and Nigeria' by John Peter Olinger (p. 101–07).

638 Oil, debts and democracy: Nigeria.
Edited by Gavin Williams (et al.), ROAPE Editorial Working Group. *Review of African Political Economy*, no. 37 (Dec. 1986), 120p. bibliog.

This special issue of the journal contains several essays which examine Nigerian issues from leftist viewpoints: 'The outlook for Nigerian oil: four senarios' by Bright Erakpoweri Okogu (p. 11–23); 'Structural adjustment and the political question' by Yusuf Bangura (p. 24–37); 'The political debate and the struggle for democracy in Nigeria' by Jibrin Ibrahim (p. 38–48); 'The military as revolutionary vanguard: a critique' by Bjorn Beckman (p. 50–62); 'The national question and radical politics in Nigeria' by Abdul Raufu Mustapha (p. 81–96); 'The aftermath of the Ahmadu Bello University students' crisis of May 1986' by A. S. Mohammed (p. 97–103); and 'WIN: a militant approach to the mobilisation of women' by Altine Mohammed and Bene Madunagu (p. 103–05). The lead editorial, 'Editorial: Nigeria: oil, debts and democracy' (p. 6–10) is by Williams, Tajudeen Abdulraheem, A. Olukoshi and A. R. Mustapha.

639 Urban politics in Nigeria: a study of Port Harcourt.
Howard Wolpe. Berkeley; Los Angeles: University of California, 1974. 314p. 4 maps. bibliog.

Based on research conducted in Nigeria from April 1963 to February 1965, this study provides a full account of Port Harcourt's physical, economic, social, cultural and regional setting, as background to a political history of this growing port city. Case studies, of electoral politics, labour-management conflict, religious confrontation, and ethnic tensions between Igbos and non-Igbos over the creation of a separate Ijaw-dominated, Port Harcourt-centred Rivers State, comprise most of the volume. Appendices describe methodology and data and list parliamentarians and municipal councillors from 1945–66. Extensive notes and a bibliography (p. 287–303) complete this study. Of interest also is the author's 'Port Harcourt: Ibo politics in microcosm' in *Journal of Modern African Studies*, vol. 7, no. 3 (1969), p. 469–93. Port Harcourt was created after the 1909 discovery of coal in Eastern Nigeria's Udi Division, to provide a seaport and railway terminus for its distribution. The port was named after Lewis Harcourt (later Viscount Harcourt) who served as Secretary of State for the Colonies from November 1910 to May 1915 (p. 14–15).

Politics. Post-independence (1 October 1960– .)

640 **The political economy of Nigeria.**
Edited by I. William Zartman. New York: Praeger, 1983. 283p. map.
bibliog. (SAIS Study on Africa).

One of the most informative collections of essays on Nigeria's political economy during
the 1970s and up to 1983. The seven articles are: 'Introduction' by I. William Zartman
with Sayre Schatz (p. 1–24); 'Social change and political conflict in Nigeria's Second
Republic' by Larry Diamond (p. 25–84); 'Income distribution and politics in Nigeria'
by Henry Bienen (p. 85–104); 'The popular classes and the oil boom: a political
economy of rural and urban poverty' by Michael Watts and Paul Lubeck (p. 105–44);
'State strategies toward Nigerian and foreign business' by Adeoye A. Akinsanya
(p. 145–84); 'Indigenization in Nigeria: renationalization or denationalization?' by
Thomas J. Biersteker (p. 185–206); and 'Nigeria in the international system' by
Timothy M. Shaw (p. 207–36). Concluding the volume are an excellent list with brief
annotations by Robert Mandersheid 'Current works on Nigeria and sources: a
bibliography' (p. 237–72) and a detailed index. The editor is Professor of International
Studies and Director of African Studies at The Johns Hopkins University School of
Advanced International Studies (SAIS), Baltimore, Maryland.

Constitution and Legal and Judicial Systems

641 **The law of evidence in Nigeria.**
T. Akinola Aguda. London: Sweet & Maxwell, 1974. 2nd ed. 416p.
Aguda, Chief Justice of Botswana, and former Judge of the High Court of Western Nigeria, describes proper legal procedure regarding evidence – relevancy, proof, documents, production and effect of evidence and witnesses – for Nigerian law. He provides full technical references with a table of cases and citation of Nigerian statutes and subsidiary legislation.

642 **Issues in the constitutional design of a third Nigerian republic.**
Larry Diamond. *African Affairs*, vol. 86, no. 343 (April 1987), p. 209–26. bibliog.
This article was 'intended as the start of an academic debate on the role of constitutions and their relationship to social and economic factors in contemporary Africa' (Editor's note, p. 209). The author discusses federalism, the quest for ethnic balance, decentralization, checks and balances, staggered elections and the transition to democracy, all vital issues that must be resolved before Nigeria can again have a democratic government. Dr. Diamond recommends the establishment of a fourth branch of government 'to oversee the appointment, funding and operation of crucial procedural institutions' (p. 217) and proposes seven regulatory institutions for this branch. He argues that a permanent diarchy between the military and civilian office-holders would be 'inherently ill conceived and likely to prove counterproductive' (p. 219).

Constitution and Legal and Judicial Systems

643 **Constitutional developments in Nigeria: an analytical study of Nigeria's constitution-making developments and the historical and political factors that affected constitutional change.**
Kalu Ezera. Cambridge: Cambridge University, 1960. 274p. 2 maps. bibliog.

A political history of the several constitutions leading to Nigeria's independence: the Richards Constitution of 1946; the Macpherson Constitution of 1951; the revised Constitution of 1954; and the constitutional conference of 1957. A useful bibliography (p. 262–70) is included. In 1960 the author was a lecturer in government at University College, Ibadan, Nigeria.

644 **Bibliography on the constitutions of Nigeria.**
Compiled by Oluremi Jegede. London, New York: Oceana, 1981. 72p.

This compendium of books, articles and theses covers the constitutions of: 1946 (the Richards Constitution); 1951 (the Macpherson Constitution); 1954 (the Lyttleton Constitution); 1960 (the Independence Constitution); 1963 (the Republic Constitution); the constitutional conference of 1966–67; and the Constitution of 1979. The unannotated items are organized to cover each constitution, and to give general commentaries on: constitution and administrative law, federalism, the judiciary, civil rights, minority problems and status of persons including women and aliens, citizenship, and extradition. The author is a librarian at the Nigerian Institute of Advanced Legal Studies in Lagos.

645 **Nigerian legal bibliography: a classified list of materials related to Nigeria.**
Compiled by Oluremi Jegede, foreword by T. Akinola Aguda. Dobbs Ferry, New York: Oceana for the Nigerian Institute of Advanced Legal Studies, 1983. 2nd ed. 332p.

This bibliography provides the fullest coverage available, up to 1981, for all Nigerian legal topics. Subjects include primary materials, general legal literature and history, law of persons, property law and conveyancing, contract and tort, company law, commercial law and business transactions, taxation and finance, banks and banking, labour and industrial laws, social laws and social security, transportation, communication, education, minerals and mining laws, pollution, international law, constitutional and administrative law, politics and government, legislature, executive, local government, revolution and civil war, criminal law and procedure, practice and procedure, and trials and courts administration. The work is fully indexed. The first edition was published in 1975 by Harvard Law School Library. Of value also is Jill Cottrell's 'A bibliography of materials on Nigerian law published in Nigeria', *African Law Studies*, no. 9 (1973), p. 1–37.

646 **The presidential constitution of Nigeria.**
Ben O[bi] Nwabueze. London: C. Hurst; New York: St. Martin's, 1982. 558p. bibliog.

A detailed description and analysis of the 1979 Constitution of Nigeria, which is based on the US Constitution and abandons the Westminister system. The new Constitution modifies the executive powers of the American system making the Nigerian presidency a more consultative office. The author discusses the presidency, executive powers and constitutional restraints, the national assembly, the judicative and judicial review, as well as public service, citizenship, personal liberty and several freedoms guaranteed under the document. He concludes with an examination of the prospects for a national ethic, which he also defines.

647 **Federalism in Nigeria under the Presidential constitution.**
B. O. Nwabueze. London: Sweet & Maxwell, 1983. 413p. bibliog.

This book presents a detailed analysis of the 1979 constitutional division of powers between the federal and state governments in several areas, including public safety and essential services, the police, local government, land and revenue allocation. The author questions the balance of the federal system and discusses its problems. Appendices reproduce relevant parts of the Constitution. The prolific author has also published *A constitutional history of Nigeria* (London: Hurst; Harlow: Longman, 1982. 272p.), *Constitutional law of the Nigerian Republic* (London: Butterworths, 1964. 484p.) amongst others.

648 **The development of the executive under the Nigerian constitutions, 1960–81.**
J. D. Ojo. Ibadan, Nigeria: University Press, 1985. 189p. bibliog.

This work offers an examination of the office of the executive in the 1960, 1963 and 1979 Nigerian constitutions with discussion current up to January 1983, before the August elections and the 31 December coup. Not only does it discuss the constitutional weaknesses of the Westminster model which contributed to the military takeover in 1966, but it warns of serious problems: '. . . if the present can be taken as a sign of what is to come, then the future looks gloomy, and if the country is not careful, the new experiment in Presidential democracy could collapse' (p. 164). Also discussed are the state executive and the emergency provisions in the constitutions. The author is a lawyer, an administrator and a part-time lecturer in law at the University of Ibadan.

649 **Nigerian legal studies: a bibliographical discussion of the sources and resources.**
Akinola Oluwakuyide. *A Current Bibliography on African Affairs*, vol. 8, no. 2 (1975), p. 127–33. bibliog.

This informative bibliographical essay surveys the development of Nigerian legal studies and directs the reader to numerous publications and theses on diverse legal topics. The author is Africana Librarian, University of Ife (now Obafemi Awolowo University), Ile-Ife, Nigeria. Other important recent volumes on legislation are Akintunde Emiola's *Nigerian labour law* (Ibadan, Nigeria: Ibadan University, 1982. 2nd ed. 559p.); Martin M. Olisa's *Nigerian petroleum law and practice* (Ibadan, Nigeria: Fountain Books, 1987. 261p.); and Gani Fawehinmi's *Nigerian law of habeas corpus* (Lagos: Nigerian Law Publications, 1986. 457p.).

650 **Fundamental rights under the Nigerian constitution, 1960–1965.**
Paul O. Proehl. Los Angeles: African Studies Center, University of California, 1970. 41p. bibliog.

In his examination of numerous cases concerning human rights, with reference to the 1960 Independence Constitution, the author stresses that 'so far as human liberty is concerned, Nigeria essentially was and is a product of its own culture' and 'that the idea of individual liberty was rather generally implanted in the Nigerian spirit' (p. 1).

Constitution and Legal and Judicial Systems

He 'relates constitutional statements of rights to the structure of power in the society, differentiating between decentralized agrarian societies, and urbanized, technologically developed societies with centralized structures of power' (Preface, p. [i]). The author was Professor of Law and Director of the African Studies Center at the University of California, Los Angeles. Of interest also is S. S. Richardson's 'Social legal reform' in *Islam in Africa*, edited by James Kritzeck and William H. Lewis (New York: Van Nostrand-Reinhold, 1969, p. 110–26). Richardson discusses the legal issues and reforms in Moslem law in Northern Nigeria both preceding and after independence, praising the reforms as 'unique in Africa' and as having achieved national and international acceptance (p. 111).

651 **The Nigerian Legislative Council.**
Joan Wheare, introduced by Margery Perham. London: Faber & Faber, 1950. 265p. map. bibliog. (Studies in Colonial Legislatures, vol. IV).

The author discusses in detail the 'working of the Nigerian Legislative Council from 1923 to 1946' (p. 2), established by the constitution of 1922. The new constitution of 2 August 1946 which came into operation in March 1947 is described briefly but is not the focus of the study. Appendices (p. 183–252) contain the (Legislative Council) Orders in Council for 1922 and 1946 which established new constitutions as well as other key documents and tables showing membership of the legislative councils.

Yoruba land law.
See item no. 411.

Administration and Local Government

652 **Local government and the traditional rulers in Nigeria.**
Edited by Oladimeji Aborisade. Ile-Ife, Nigeria: University of Ife,
1985. 369p. bibliog.
This volume contains an introduction, twenty-seven papers and three special addresses,
presented at the national conference to consider the roles of traditional rulers, at the
University of Ife, 25 April 1983. The range of issues discussed includes traditional,
historical, financial, constitutional and local governmental aspects of governance. Most
of the thirty contributors are from southern and western Nigeria. Of particular interest
is the address by the Oba of Benin, 'The roles of traditional rulers in local government'
(p. v–xxiii).

653 **Politics and administration in Nigeria.**
Ladipo Adamolekun. Ibadan, Nigeria: Spectrum in association with
Hutchinson of London, 1986. 203p. bibliog. (Hutchinson University
Library for Africa).
This study of the relationship between politicians and administrators in Nigeria
between 1914 and 1983 assesses how both groups in the policy process 'have been
affected by the regime types, the doctrines of public accountability and the idea of a
career civil service' (p. 9). The historical view is presented from colonial government
to pre- and post-independence parliamentary government, military rule and presidential
government. Most of the book was written before the coup of 31 December 1983. The
author is Professor of Public Administration, Obafemi Awolowo University, Ile-Ife,
Nigeria.

654 **The expulsion of illegal aliens from Nigeria: a study of Nigeria's
decision-making.**
Olajide Aluko. *African Affairs*, vol. 84, no. 337 (Oct. 1985),
p. 539–60. bibliog.
Professor Aluko examines the internal and external forces which led to the 'quit' order
which caused the exodus of approximately three million aliens. The policy was

Administration and Local Government

primarily a product of President Shehu Shagari and Internal Affairs Minister Alhaji Al
Baba, using a decision-making process that was 'perhaps even more autocratic under
the Shagari government than under the previous military regime in Nigeria. . . All in
all, the quit order was a policy shambles that has damaged the standing of Nigeria as a
human society' (p. 560). Two other articles in the same issue discuss the topic. Roger
Gravil's 'The Nigerian Aliens Expulsion Order of 1983' (p. 523–37) examines the
methods and motives of the expulsion of undocumented aliens which was announced
without warning on 17 January, 25 January, and 14 February 1983. Gravil was on the
staff of the University of Lagos from 1978 to 1984 and calls the effort 'woefully
ignorant and carelessly presented' (p. 524). Lynne Brydon discusses 'Ghanaian
responses to the Nigerian expulsions of 1983' (p. 561–85). Officially, between 900,000
and 1,200,000 Ghanaians left, but many had returned to Nigeria by 1984. 'Exodus of
the unwanted' by Marguerite Johnson in *Time Magazine* (14 Feb. 1983, p. 22–23) and
'Nigeria's outcasts: the cruel exodus' by James LeMoyne in *Newsweek* (14 Feb. 1983
p. 20–22) contain dramatic photographs of the exodus.

655 **Intergovernmental relations in Nigeria.**
J. A. A. Ayoade. *A Current Bibliography on African Affairs*, vol. 14,
no. 1 (1981–82), p. 13–25. bibliog.

An analysis of the theory and history of domestic intergovernmental relations (IGR) in
Nigeria. The author delineates six contemporary levels of IGR (National-state
national-state-local; national-local; inter-state; state-local; and inter-local), examine
hypotheses concerning the types and formations of IGR, and outlines the emergence of
IGR over the country's twentieth-century history, concluding with suggestions fo
improved IGR. The author is in the Department of Political Science at the Univeristy
of Ibadan, Ibadan, Nigeria.

656 **Administration for development in Nigeria: introduction and readings.**
Edited by Paul Collins. Lagos, Nigeria: African Education Press,
1980. 337p. bibliog.

Sixteen essays provide insights into public administration at the federal, state and local
levels, dealing with such diverse topics as development planning, parastatals, farmers
co-operatives, economic indigenization, agricultural and community development and
administrative reform. Of particular interest are: 'The history of planning in Nigeria
by Gordon Idang (p. 34–52); 'Political constraints on planning: the Second National
Development Plan' by James O'Connell (p. 53–71); 'The preparation of the Third
National Development Plan' by Adebayo Adedeji (p. 72–77); 'Nigerian public
enterprises as an organizational dilemma' by Ojetunji Aboyade (p. 83–98); 'The
working of the Nigerian National Oil Corporation' by Terisa Turner (p. 99–134); 'The
reorganization of local government under military rule in Nigeria, 1966–74' by Bell
Harris (p. 208–21); 'New dimensions in the administration of agriculture in Nigeria' b
S. O. Olayide, E. O. Idusogie and Dupe Olatunbosun (p. 275–286); and 'Current
issues of administrative reform in the Nigerian public services: the case of the Udo
Review Commission' by the editor (p. 310–28). A useful bibliography is include
(p. 329–37).

657 **Bureaucratic cadres in a traditional milieu.**
Anthony H[amilton] M[illard] Kirk-Greene. In: *Education and political development.* Edited by James S. Coleman. Princeton, New Jersey: Princeton University, 1965, p. 372–407. bibliog. (Studies in Political Development, 4).

In this informative article the author examines the impact of new leadership cadres on the highly structured traditional Hausa-Fulani societies in Northern Nigeria. He describes the social and administrative structure of Hausa society, the rôle of the government administrator and the present and likely future relations between the new leadership cadres and the traditional system. An idealized emirate administrative structure is shown in a useful diagram and a table compares selected attributes of administrative leadership cadres in Northern Nigeria with trainees in East Africa (p. 384–85). Kirk-Greene joined the Nigerian Administrative Service in 1950, spent seven years as a DO in the field and then was selected to organize the first Administrative Service training course for African civil servants.

658 **Studies in Nigerian administration.**
Edited by D. J. Murray, preface by Adebayo Adedeji. London: Hutchinson, 1978. 2nd ed. 342p. bibliog. (Hutchinson University Library for Africa).

Each of these eight studies depicts an aspect of Nigerian public administration during the 1960s: 'High level ministerial organization in Nigeria and the Ivory Coast' by Ladipo Adamolekun (p. 11–42); 'Accountability and public control of public corporations – the experience of Western Nigeria' by R. O. Teriba (p. 43–89); 'Nigerian field administration: a comparative analysis' by D. J. Murray (p. 90–139); 'The executive class in Nigeria: introduction, problems, prospects' by F. J. Fletcher (p. 140–76); 'The Nigerian public service commissions' by O. Nwanwene (p. 177–208); 'Work and motivation: a study of village level agricultural extension workers in the Western State of Nigeria' by R. K. Harrison (p. 209–58); 'Personal income tax administration' by G. M. Walker, Jr. (p. 259–82); and 'The role of higher public servants in Nigeria: as perceived by the western-educated élite' by R. L. Harris (p. 283–309). A postscript by Ladipo Adamolekun (p. 310–27) updates developments in Nigerian administration since the essays appeared in 1970.

659 **Local administration in Nigeria.**
Robert F. Ola. London; Boston, Massachusetts: Kegan Paul, 1984. 185p. bibliog.

This volume examines local government's structure and functions during the pre-colonial, colonial, self-governing and military periods of Nigerian history. The author is Director of the Institute of Public Administration, University of Benin, Benin City, and was deeply involved in the 1975–76 nationwide local government reform. Of considerable value also is M. J. Balogun's *Public administration in Nigeria: a developmental approach* (London: Macmillan Nigeria, 1983. 308p.).

660 **Local government in Nigeria: the changing scene.**
   G. Oka Orewa, J. B. Adewumi. Benin City, Nigeria: Ethiope, 1983.
   314p. bibliog.

The authors examine 'the various facets of local government in the country against the background of the colonial and post-colonial eras, with a view to assessing the extent to which structural, functional, financial, leadership, and staffing problems have impaired the progressive development of local government during the last quarter of a century' (Preface, p. vii). A significant portion of the book offers a comprehensive review of the 1976 local government reforms.

Periodical

661 **The Quarterly Journal of Administration.**
   Ile-Ife, Nigeria: University of Ife, Faculty of Administration, 1966– .
   quarterly.

This valuable journal publishes articles on all aspects of administration and management. The editor in 1983 was Pat Oribabor, Faculty of Administration, University of Ife (now Obafemi Awolowo University), Ile-Ife, Nigeria, and in 1988 was O. Adamolekun.

Foreign Relations

662 **Readings and documents on ECOWAS: selected papers and discussions from the 1976 Economic Community of West African States Conference.**
Edited by A. B. Akinyemi, S. B. Falegan, I. A. Aluko. Lagos: Nigerian Institute of International Affairs with Macmillan Nigeria, 1984. 779p. bibliog.

An extremely full discussion of the Economic Community of West African States (ECOWAS) by thirty contributors. Topics covered include: the basic concept of ECOWAS; economic issues; industrial development; customs and trade; agricultural and natural resources; transport; labour migration and basic socio-political problems. There are a number of specific and general recommendations (p. 656–63). The text and related protocols of the treaty of ECOWAS are included (p. 669–766).

663 **Essays on Nigerian foreign policy.**
Olajide Aluko. London: George Allen & Unwin, 1981. 288p. bibliog.

The author, Professor of International Relations at Obafemi Awolowo Univeristy, Ile-Ife, Nigeria, describes Nigeria's post-1960 foreign policy in seventeen essays. Among the topics covered are Nigeria's initiative in ECOWAS and in the Organization of African Unity (OAU); its relations with Israel, the United States, and the Soviet Union; Ghana; the civil war; the foreign service; and the making of foreign policy and post-Gowon foreign policy. Finally, Aluko projects options for Nigerian foreign policy in the 1980s. He is also the author of the substantive work *Ghana and Nigeria, 1957–70: a study in inter-African discord* (New York: Barnes & Noble, 1976. 275p).

664 **Decolonization and dependence: the development of Nigerian–U.S. relations, 1960–1984.**
Bassey E. Ate. Boulder, Colorado; London: Westview, 1987. 282p. bibliog. (Westview Special Studies on Africa).

In this lucid history and analysis, the author explains how, after 1960, US influence replaced British, preserving in many ways the very colonial order Africans sought to transform. Part of this relationship has been based on oil: from 1973 to 1979, Nigeria sold the United States 'about 38–56 per cent of its total oil exports (compared to 11 per cent in 1965), and this accounted for about 18–26 per cent of the total US crude imports' (p. 2). Topics covered include the Congo crisis (1960–64), relations with Ghana and Togo, the Rhodesian conflict (1971–73), the Angola crisis (1975–76), relations between General Obasanjo and President Carter, and between President Shehu Shagari and President Reagan. Appendices list US firms in Nigeria financed by USAID in 1966 and US companies in the oil and gas industry in Nigeria in 1976. The initial work for this study was done for a doctoral thesis at Columbia University. The author is Senior Research Fellow at the Nigerian Institute of International Affaris, Lagos.

665 **Selected bibliography on the foreign policy of Nigeria, 1970–1977.**
Compiled by Orobola Fasehun. *A Current Bibliography on African Affairs*, vol. 14, no. 2 (1981–82), p. 98–101. bibliog.

Following a brief introduction, the compiler presents a list of forty-three items grouped under the headings 'National level of analysis', 'Regional level of analysis' and 'Global level of analysis'. Dr. Fasehun is in the Department of International Relations, Obafemi Awolowo University, Ile-Ife, Nigeria. This article also appeared earlier in this journal in vol. 12, no. 2 (1979–80), p. 166–69.

666 **Nigeria and Cameroun: an annotated bibliography.**
Compiled by Modupe Irele. Lagos, Nigeria: Libriservice, 1984. 67p. 4 maps.

This informative bibliography contains 286 references, briefly annotated, covering relations between Nigeria and Cameroon (Cameroun) from 1960 to September 1983. Entries are grouped into 'African boundaries', 'Cameroun: politics and government', 'Nigeria: politics and government', and 'Nigeria-Cameroun relations'. Oscar O. B. Ede contributes an essay 'The relations between Nigeria and Cameroun: fluctuating cooperation and tensions' (p. 3–10) and there is a list of agreements between the two nations (p. viii) as well as an index. The compiler is Senior Librarian at the Nigerian Institute of International Affairs, Lagos, and is fluent in French.

667 **Sub-regional security and Nigerian foreign policy.**
Emeka Nwokedi. *African Affairs*, vol. 84, no. 335 (April 1985), p. 195–209. bibliog.

An analysis of Nigerian foreign relations with the francophone West African states, especially of Nigeria's rôle in ECOWAS and relations with the Communauté Economique de l'Afrique de la Ouest (CEAO). Nigeria refused to enter a defence treaty with the Republic of Benin and generally prefers multilateral to bilateral agreements. CEAO–French ties undermine Nigeria's ECOWAS objectives, but the author argues that 'the extra-African accords, should they reinforce regime stability and the process of national integration in the sub-region, are to Nigeria's advantage' (p. 209). Dr. Nwokedi is a Lecturer in International Relations, Obafemi Awolowo University, Ile-Ife, Nigeria.

668 **Nigerian participation at the U.N.**
George A. Obiozor. Enugu, Nigeria: Fourth Dimension, 1985. 249p.
bibliog.

This study is a history and analytical record of Nigeria's participation at the United
Nations since 1960. It provides a complete voting record for Nigeria from 1960–80. The
volume is subdivided into 'Decolonization & self-determination', 'Economic development & trade matters', 'Apartheid & racial discrimination', 'The Middle-East crisis',
'Disarmament', 'China representation', 'UN peace-keeping operations', and 'Human
rights'. The bibliography (p. 184–86) is brief. The author was a Ralph Bunche Fellow
at the UN in 1977–78 when he researched this study and is currently Senior Research
Fellow at the Nigerian Institute of International Affairs, Lagos. An informative, well-
illustrated publication is *Nigeria at the United Nations, 1975/76* by the Permanent
Mission of Nigeria to the United Nations (New York, [1976. 68]p.) which contains
numerous speeches made by Nigerian officials (including Gen. M. Muhammed, J. N.
Garba, L. O. Harriman, Olu Adeniji, E. Olu Sanu, and B. Akporode Clark) at the
UN General Assembly, and elsewhere, articulating Nigeria's position on various
issues.

669 **Nigerian-Soviet relations, 1960–87.**
Oye Ogunbadejo. *African Affairs*, vol. 87, no. 346 (Jan. 1988),
p. 83–104. bibliog.

This article reviews the relationship between the Soviet Union and each Nigerian
régime since 1960, from that of Prime Minister A. T. Balewa to General Babangida's.
The Soviets have maintained 'fraternal' relations with Nigerian leaders, supplied the
federalists with arms in the civil war, are building the iron and steel complex at
Ajaokuta and maintain a modest level of trade. 'In sum, the Soviet interest in Nigeria
has been persistent', yet nothing has 'provided a politically congenial base for the
protection of Soviet military power' and 'successive rulers in Lagos have been more
pro- than anti-Western' and are likely to remain so (p. 104). Professor Ogunbadejo is
Head of the Department of Political Science at Obafemi Awolowo University, Ile-Ife,
Nigeria.

670 **Nigeria and the UN mission to the Democratic Republic of the Congo: a
case study of the formative stages of Nigeria's foreign policy.**
Festus Ugboaja Ohaegbulam. Tampa, Florida: University Presses of
Florida, 1982. 190p. 4 maps. bibliog.

This study examines the rôle of Nigeria in the resolution of the Congo crisis
(1960–June 1964). 'It is both a case study in the international mediation of a national
conflict and an attempt to ascertain what effective use Nigeria made of the United
Nations as an instrument of its maiden foreign policy' (p. 7). This was Nigeria's 'first
major involvement in complex international politics' (p. 146) and was used by Nigeria
to express its orderly and co-operative entry into the world community of nations. The
'selected references' (p. 171–83) include UN and Nigerian government publications,
doctoral theses, books and articles.

Foreign Relations

671 **Nigeria's external relations: the first twenty-five years.**
Edited by G. O. Olusanya, R. A. Akindele, foreword by G. O.
Olusnaya. Ibadan, Nigeria: University Press, 1986. 577p. bibliog.

A comprehensive study by twenty-six contributors, comprising twenty-nine articles, followed by fifteen appendices, most of which are major foreign policy statements issued between 1960 and 1985. The first three articles provide general overviews of foreign policy; the others discuss Nigeria and various international organizations (the UN, OAU, EEC, OPEC, ECOWAS and others), individual countries and groups of countries. R. T. Okotore compiled 'Twenty-five years of Nigerian foreign policy: a select bibliography' (p. 477–504), some entries of which are briefly annotated. These papers were presented at a 1985 conference organized by the Nigerian Institute of International Affairs. An interesting, wide-ranging interview is Margaret A. Novicki's with 'Bolaji Akinyemi, Minister of External Affairs' in *Africa Report*, vol. 31, no. 4 (July–Aug. 1986), p. 26–30.

672 **African development: the OAU/ECA Lagos Plan of Action and beyond.**
Edited by Ralph I. Onwuka, 'Layi Abegurin, Dhanjoo N. Ghista,
foreword by Ibrahim Gambari. Lawrenceville, Virginia: Brunswick
for the Department of International Relations, University of Ife,
Ile-Ife, Nigeria, 1985. 241p. bibliog.

This collection of sixteen papers emerged from a conference sponsored by the Ford Foundation at the University of Ife (now Obafemi Awolowo University) in March 1984. All of the essays discuss theoretical background, problems of implementation, regionalism and related issues concerning Nigeria indirectly. Amechi Okolo's 'Nigeria and the IMF loan' (p. 198–219) and A. O. Okore's 'The dilemma of socioeconomic development in Africa with Nigeria as an example' (p. 40–52) relate specifically to the country.

673 **Lagos Plan of Action for the economic development of Africa,
1980–2000.**
Organisation of African Unity. Geneva: International Institute for
Labour Studies, 1981. 132p.

An important strategy for develoment adopted by the Heads of State and Government of the OAU summit meeting at Lagos, 28–29 April 1980, which stressed cooperative, internal and inter-African approaches to development, considering 'sectoral integration at the continental level, and particularly in the fields of agriculture, food transport and communication, industry, and energy' (p. 128). For an excellent follow-up, see the workshop proceedings edited by David Fashole Luke and Timothy M. Shaw, entitled *Continental crisis: the Lagos Plan of Action and Africa's future* (Lanham, Maryland; New York: University Press of America, and Dalhousie University Centre for African Studies, 1984. 231p.).

674 **A problematic power: the debate about Nigerian foreign policy in the
1980s.**
Timothy M. Shaw. *Millennium: Journal of International Studies*, vol.
12, no. 2 (summer 1983), p. 127–48. bibliog.

A first-rate overview and analysis of the 'rise and fall' (p. 130–32) and 'continuity and change' (p. 132–35) of Nigerian foreign policy at the national, regional and continental levels. Professor Shaw examines Nigeria's claim to be a 'middle power' and a 'newly

influential country or newly industralising country' and draws upon Peter Evans'
Dependent development: the alliance of multi-national, state and local capital in Brazil
(Princeton, New Jersey: Princeton University Press, 1979. 362p.) describing Nigeria as
the 'Brazil of Africa' as well as other positions he describes as realist, idealist and
radical. He suggests that 'Nigeria's foreign policy is likely to be constrained and
contradictory in the mid-term future as it wrestles with both rapid, yet uneven and
uncertain growth and with the apparently growing gap between aspirations and
capabilities' (p. 130).

675 **Nigeria restrained: foreign policy under changing political and
petroleum regimes.**
Timothy M. Shaw. *Annals of the American Academy of Political and
Social Science*, vol. 489 (Jan. 1987), p. 40–50. bibliog.

The author presents a thoughtful review and analysis of Nigeria's foreign policy goals
in light of the loss of oil revenues, and 'the meteoric rise and fall in its foreign policy
status and success' (p. 41). New economic and foreign policy realism may enable
Nigeria to re-emerge as a significant African leader. 'If Nigeria can take its own
medicine – economic and political, social and psychological – then it may yet be able to
lay the foundation for a successful post-petroleum period' (p. 47). Dr. Shaw is
Professor of Political Science and Director of the Centre for African Studies at
Dalhousie University in Nova Scotia, Canada.

676 **Nigerian foreign policy: alternative perceptions and projections.**
Edited by Timothy M. Shaw, Olajide Aluko. London; Basingstoke:
Macmillan, 1983. 257p. 2 maps. bibliog.

The editors and seven other political scientists and international relations experts
describe diverse perceptions of Nigerian foreign policy as well as scenarios it may
follow in the 1980s and 1990s. Several of the chapters were presented in draft form at
the 1980 African Studies Association conference. Included are: 'Introduction: Nigeria
as Africa's major power' (p. 1–20) and 'Nigeria in world politics: contemporary
calculations and constraints' (p. 23–24) by Timothy Shaw; 'Nigerian-American
relations: converging interests and power relations' by Daniel C. Bach (p. 35–55); 'The
administration of Nigeria's foreign service, 1960–80' by Sola Ojo (p. 56–76);
'Bureaucratic politics and foreign policy decision-making in Nigeria' by O. Aluko
(p. 77–92); 'Nigerian foreign policy: a case of dominance or dependence?' by Stephen
Wright (p. 93–121); 'Indigenisation in Nigeria: renationalisation or denationalisation?'
by Thomas J. Biersteker (p. 125–46); 'Nigeria's development strategy in global
perspective' by Sonni Tyoden (p. 147–63); 'Nigeria: foreign policy alternatives' by
Mark W. DeLancey (p. 164–90); 'Nigerian foreign policy in the year 2000' by O.
Aluko (p. 191–204); and 'Nigeria in the world system: alternative approaches,
explanations and projections' by Timothy Shaw and Orobola Fasehun (p. 205–35).
Fasehun and Shaw present a very useful bibliography on Nigerian foreign policy
(p. 236–46).

Periodical

677 **Nigeria: Bulletin on Foreign Affairs.**
Lagos, Nigeria: Nigerian Institute of International Affairs, 1971– .
quarterly.

The Nigerian Institute of International Affairs (P.O. Box 1727, Lagos, Nigeria) was
established in 1961 as an independent, non-official, non-political organization. In 1971
the Institute was taken over by the Nigerian Government, yet it remains independent
and non-political. The *Bulletin on Foreign Affairs* contains three sections: 'Documents',
'Events' and 'Commentaries', each of which provides information on diplomatic and
economic-technical relations. The Institute also produces *Nigerian Forum* (1981– .
monthly), which contains articles covering diverse international topics, usually
organized around a special theme. For example, there was an issue on the 'UN
International Year of Peace', vol. 5, nos. 11, 12 (Nov.–Dec. 1985). The preceding issue
was on 'Women'. The *Nigerian Journal of International Affairs* (1975– . quarterly) also
published by the Institute, covers Nigeria's rôle in the international community. A
recent issue, vol. 12, nos. 1, 2, (1986), contained articles on future foreign policy,
Nigeria and France, international borders, defence, minerals, Latin America, South
Africa and the Nigerian Foreign Service.

Economy

Regional

678 **Accelerated development in sub-Saharan Africa: an agenda for action.**
Elliot Berg, K. Y. Amoako, Rolf Güsten, Jacob Meerman, Gene
Tidrick. Washington, DC: World Bank, 1981. 198p. map. bibliog.
This report by the World Bank African Strategy Review Group, headed by Berg,
'highlights the severity and complexity of the problems facing many of the countries of
Sub-Saharan Africa in their efforts to raise the living standards of their people'
(Foreword, p. v). Accepting the goals of the *Lagos Plan of Action* (q.v.), the report
emphasizes that scarce resources must be more efficiently used and that African
governments should rely more on the private sector. Several suggestions for improving
incentives and institutional supports, especially in agriculture, are made. The analysis
is provided in nine clearly-written chapters: 'Introduction'; 'Basic constraints';
'External factors'; 'Policy and administrative framework'; 'Policies and priorities in
agriculture'; 'Human resources'; 'Other productive sectors'; 'Longer-term issues'; and
'External assistance in the 1980s', each laced with tables and special topic boxes. In the
'Statistical annex' (p. 134–98) are forty-three tables presenting a wealth of data on each
of the thirty-nine countries covered in the report. Extensive material on Nigeria is
provided.

679 **Economic transition in Africa.**
Edited by Melville J. Herskovits, Mitchell Harwitz. Evanston,
Illinois: Northwestern University, 1964. 444p. bibliog. (Northwestern
University African Studies, no. 12).
Nineteen papers presented at a Conference on Indigenous and Induced Elements in
the Economies of Subsaharan Africa held at Northwestern Univeristy in November
1961 are collected here. Nigeria and Nigerian ethnic groups are mentioned throughout
the volume. Particularly relevant essays include: 'Land use, land tenure and land
reform' by Paul J. Bohannan (p. 133–49) on the Tiv and Yoruba of Nigeria and the
Kikuyu of Kenya; 'The role of the small entrepreneur' by Margaret Katzin (p. 179–98)

Economy. Regional

covering Ghana and Nigeria; 'Real income trends in West Africa, 1939–1960' by Elliot J. Berg (p. 199–238) focusing on Nigeria, Ghana and French West Africa; and 'Independence and the problem of economic growth' by Pius N. C. Okigbo (p. 323–35), and 'Economic growth and political reorientation' by James S. Coleman (p. 377–96) both of which are important to Nigerian studies. A lengthy bibliography (p. 409–25) is included.

680 **The emergence of African capitalism.**
John Iliffe. Minneapolis, Minnesota: University of Minnesota, 1983. 113p. bibliog.

This book is an expanded version of the Anstey Memorial Lectures given in the University of Kent at Canterbury, England, in May 1982. In it the author surveys the growth of African capitalism south of the Sahara, focusing on the emergence of farmers, merchants and free wage labourers in industry. African societies were exposed to a distinctive kind of capitalism: 'a very late capitalism, large in scale, sophisticated in technology, and already threatened by the rival force of socialism' (p. 86). He argues that capitalism does not necessarily either develop or underdevelop African countries but that the response is highly individualized by forces in the country itself. Nigeria is prominent in this analysis, and there is extensive information about Hausa, Igbo and Yoruba peoples. In 1978 Dr. Iliffe was a Research Associate at Bayero University, Kano, Nigeria. He has taught in Uganda, Tanzania and Malawi as well as at Cambridge University.

681 **Toward sustained development in sub-Saharan Africa: a joint program of action.**
Stanley Please, Ramgopal Agarwala, Robert Liebenthal, Satish Mannan, Principal Editor, Rupert Pennant-Rea. Washington, DC: World Bank, 1984. 102p. map. bibliog.

The World Bank team led by Please which prepared this report organized its analysis in five chapters: 'The deepening crisis';. 'The roots of the problem'; 'Long-term constraints'; 'Managing policy reform'; and 'Supporting policy reform'. The statistical annex (p. 49–100) contains thirty-two tables with technical notes on production, trade, aid, debt and capital flows, agriculture, social indicators and fiscal data, providing valuable information on the thirty-nine countries of sub-Saharan Africa. A brief bibliography (p. 101–02) lists the data sources. The report is positive and constructive regarding the continent's 'acute economic difficulties' and reiterates 'the need for domestic policy reforms to accelerate growth'. Unlike earlier reports, it 'places more emphasis on donor assistance strategy', 'stresses that better use of investment – both domestic and foreign – is the key issue', 'analyses the growing debt servicing burden', and 'draws attention to the long-term constraints on development' (p. 1).

682 **The economies of West Africa.**
Douglas Rimmer. New York: St. Martin's, 1984. 308p. map. bibliog.

An examination of the economies of the sixteen sovereign members of ECOWAS, with a concentration on Nigeria, Ghana and the Ivory Coast which in 1979 were estimated to have seventy per cent of the region's population and eighty-five per cent of its economic production. The author focuses on the period from 1960 (and in some cases earlier) to the early 1980s in his examination of economic structures, population and labour force, external trade, policy instruments, and development policies. He concludes that economic growth and social amelioration in West Africa have been considerable, but that many policies have been ineffective, especially in development programmes and as 'levers of economic progress' (p. 259). Dr. Rimmer is Director of the Centre of West African Studies, University of Birmingham, Birmingham, England.

683 **Dependency and underdevelopment in West Africa.**
Edited by Victor C. Uchendu. Leiden, Netherlands: E. J. Brill, 1980. 136p. bibliog. (International Studies in Sociology and Social Anthropology, vol. 29).

An excellent collection of varied articles concerning historical, economic, cultural and institutional aspects of the title's subject. Most articles pertain directly to Nigeria, including: 'Dependency and the development process: an introduction' by V. C. Uchendu (p. 3–16); 'Colonialism and the process of underdevelopment in Nigeria: a review' by S. J. S. Cookey (p. 19–31); 'Structural dependency: the Nigerian economy as a case study' by B. C. Sullivan (p. 44–55); 'Ideological dependency and the problem of autonomy in Nigeria' by Uzodinma Nwala (p. 59–66); 'Dependency theory: problems of cultural autonomy and cultural convergence' by V. C. Uchendu (p. 78–96); 'The 'received' Nigerian law and the challenge of legal independence' by S. N. Nwabara (p. 99–108); 'ECOWAS: is it a countervailing power for economic independence?' by J. C. Aghaji (p. 109–20); and 'The indigenisation of 'imported religions': how independent are our religious ideas?' (p. 121–28). A selected bibliography (p. 129–31), and author and subject indexes conclude the useful volume.

684 **Readings in the applied economics of Africa.**
Edited by Edith H. Whetham, Jean I. Currie. Cambridge: Cambridge University, 1967. 2 vols. bibliog.

This collection of articles is intended to supplement economics courses in African universities. Volume one, on micro-economics, considers the use of resources by the firm or the farm; volume two, on macro-economics, offers papers on the framing and implementation of economic policy. Several articles pertain to Nigeria in both volumes; in volume one these are: C. Davis Fogg's 'Economic and social factors affecting the development of small holder agriculture in Eastern Nigeria' (p. 25–31); R. S. May's 'Direct overseas investment in Nigeria 1953–63' (p. 72–92); Sayre P. Schatz's 'The capital shortage illusion: government lending in Nigeria' (p. 93–101); S. U. Ugoh's 'The Nigerian cement industry' (p. 102–113); S. Williams's 'Start-up of a textile industry' (p. 114–125); T. M. Yesufu's 'The shortage of skilled labour' (p. 126–32); A. Cohen's 'Politics of the kola trade' (p. 153–63); P. Kilby's 'Competition in the Nigerian bread industry' (p. 164–72); O. Olakanpo's 'Distributive trade – a critique of government policy (p. 193–204); and H. A. Oluwasanmi's 'Agriculture in a developing economy' (p. 205–16). In volume two are: P. N. C. Okigbo's 'Nigerian national accounts 1950–7' (p. 1–20) and 'The fiscal system and the growth in national income' (p. 126–40); R. H. Green's 'Four African development plans: Ghana, Kenya, Nigeria and Tanzania' (p. 21–32); and G. K. Helleiner's, 'The fiscal role of the marketing boards in Nigerian economic development 1947–61' (p. 70–93). The editors were economists at Ahmadu Bello University, Zaria, Nigeria, at the time of publication.

An economic history of West Africa.
See item no. 161.

Nigerian

685 **Foundations of an African economy: a study of investment and growth in Nigeria.**
Ojetunji Aboyade. New York, London: Praeger, 1966. 366p. bibliog. (Praeger Special Studies in International Economics and Development).

Following a background chapter providing an historical view of Nigeria in the world economy, the author discusses: capital formation, development theory investment, the national planning effort, the decision-making process and institutional peculiarities of the planning, and possible new directions for planning. In addition to the extensive data and analysis presented, of particular interest are the author's comments on the First National Development Plan of 1962–68. The volume's bibliography (p. 291–366) is extensive. In 1962–63, Dr. Aboyade was an adviser to the Federal Economic Planning Unit in Lagos; at the time of publication, he was Editor of the *Nigerian Journal of Economic and Social Studies* (q.v.) and an economist at the University of Ibadan.

686 **The dynamics of foreign private investment in Nigeria.**
M. O. Ajuogu. *A Current Bibliography on African Affairs*, vol. 16, no. 2 (1983–84), p. 85–103. bibliog.

An examination of the patterns of foreign trade and investment in Nigeria; particular emphasis is given to American private investment, and data abounds. The author, who is at the University of Calabar, Calabar, Nigeria, discusses the failure of private American business ventures relative to the opportunities, the characteristics of investment in Nigeria in the 1960s and 1970s, the investments in various manufacturing sectors, and Nigerian oil production, and gives detailed data for exports in February 1979. He emphasizes the need for investment in agriculture that would sustain meaningful economic growth and use available labour.

687 **Political economy of Nigeria.**
Edited by Claude Ake. New York, London, Lagos: Longman, 1985. 207p. bibliog.

A valuable volume about the 'general logic by which the Nigerian state and social formation proceed. . . The whole book is really making one point – at any rate one argument – about how the Nigerian state is constituted and what the implication of this 'constitution' must be' (Introduction, p. xi). The editor and six colleagues approach the issue from several directions in nine chapters: 'The Nigerian state: antinomies of a periphery formation' and 'Indigenization: problems of transformation in a neo-colonial economy' by the editor; 'Nigeria's evolving class structure' by Mark Anikpo; 'State and economic development in Nigeria' by Eme N. Ekekwe; 'Public policy and rural-urban distribution of income in Nigeria' by Willie Okowa; 'The structure of state capitalism in the Nigerian petroleum industry' by Cliff Edogun; 'Oil companies and environmental pollution in Nigeria' by Eboe Hutchful; and 'Self-reliance as a development strategy' by Olatunde Ojo. All are from the Faculty of Social Sciences, University of Port Harcourt, Nigeria. Professor Ake has also published *A political economy of Africa* (Harlow, England: Longman, 1981. 196p.).

688 **The entrepreneur as culture hero: preadaptations in Nigerian economic development.**
Bernard I. Belasco. New York: Praeger, 1980. 239p. bibliog. (Praeger Special Studies).

A study based on published materials and data gathered from 'a group of Yoruba informants studying in the United States' (Preface, p. xii). It is primarily concerned with trade, marketing and entrepreneurship in pre-colonial Yoruba society. The author links these aspects intimately with Yoruba deities, especially Ajé the goddess of trade, describes the history of the important trading family of Ayorinde Ajé of Kuta in the Osun District of central Yorubaland and the links of the Yoruba states to the larger global markets. This work is 'shaped' by the author's twenty-year business career and extends his PhD at the New School for Social Research, New York, entitled *Ethnomarketing and entrepreneurs: the apotheosis of trade in Nigeria* (Ann Arbor, Michigan: University Microfilms, 1977. 359 leaves. bibliog.).

689 **Cocoa, custom, and socio-economic change in rural Western Nigeria.**
Sara S. Berry. Oxford: Clarendon, 1975. 240p. 5 maps. bibliog. (Oxford Studies in African Affairs).

Professor Berry presents an impressive analysis of the historical and geographical contexts of the spread of cocoa planting in Western Nigeria, from the late-nineteenth century through to the 1960s, 'as a process of capital formation in a land surplus economy'. She shows how farmers incorporated the new crop and how cocoa cultivation affected the region's economy. Details of cocoa production and social organization, migration, settlement patterns and land tenure are presented from her studies of villages near Ibadan, Ife and Ondo in Nigeria's cocoa belt. Appendices contain 'Biographical note on some early cocoa planters', 'Case studies of migration from Savannah communities' and cocoa statistics from 1886 to 1970. The author's 1967 University of Michigan doctoral thesis was *Cocoa in Western Nigeria: a study of an innovation in a developing economy*.

690 **Inequality and development in Nigeria.**
Edited by Henry Bienen, V. P. Diejomaoh. New York, London: Holmes & Meier, 1981. 364p. bibliog. (Political Economy of Income Distribution in Developing Countries Series).

For this paperback volume, eight chapters were chosen from the longer *Political economy of income distribution in Nigeria* (New York: Holmes & Meier, 1981. 520p.) to which was added a new introduction by Bienen (p. 1–16). The chapters that comprise this volume are: 'Development in Nigeria: an overview' by Douglas Rimmer (p. 17–75); 'The structure of income inequality in Nigeria: a macro analysis' by V. P. Diejomaoh and E. C. Anusionwu (p. 77–113); 'The politics of income distribution: institutions, class, and ethnicity' by Bienen (p. 115–59); 'Special aspects of urbanization and effects on the distribution of income in Nigeria' by Bola Ayeni (p. 161–69); 'Aspects of income distribution in the Nigerian urban sector' by Olufemi Fajana (p. 193–236); 'Income distribution in the rural sector' by O. O. Ladipo and A. A. Adesimi (p. 237–59); 'The structure of production and rural incomes in northern Nigeria; results of three village case studies' by Peter Matlon (p. 261–310); and 'Education and income distribution in Nigeria' by V. P. Diejomaoh and E. C. Anusionwu.

691 **Multinationals, the state, and control of the Nigerian economy.**
Thomas J. Biersteker. Princeton, New Jersey: Princeton University,
1987. 344p. bibliog.

Synthesizing a wide range of data including that from 157 formal interviews conducted
in Nigeria, the US and the UK in 1979, 1981 and 1982, the author critically examines
the issues and policies determining control of the Nigerian economy. Central to this is
his analysis of the first (1972) and second (1977) indigenization decrees and their
effects for the business and financial communities. Regarding the issue of control,
Professor Biersteker writes, 'Are Nigerians in greater control of enterprises, sectors of
their economy, or their national economy as a whole because of the indeginization
program? In short, the answer is yes, but not much' (p. 298). Appendices explain the
author's research methods, provide a 'Chronology of economic nationalism in Nigeria'
from 1946 to 1982 (p. 324–26) and a bibliography (p. 327–35).

692 **The economic development of Nigeria: report of a mission organized by
the International Bank for Reconstruction and Development at the
request of the Governments of Nigeria and the United Kingdom.**
A. Broches, Chief of Mission. Baltimore, Maryland: Johns Hopkins
University for the International Bank for Reconstruction &
Development (IBRD) 1955. 686p. 15 maps. bibliog.

Ten full-time and five part-time members of an IBRD mission visited Nigeria from
late-September until mid-December 1953, 'to assess the resources available for future
development, to study the possibilities for development in the major sectors of the
economy and to make recommendations for practical steps to be taken . . .' (Preface,
p. vii). The result is this compendium containing a vast amount of data and analysis
organized into two parts. Part I, 'The general report' (p. 3–125), summarizes the
mission's findings. Part II, 'The technical reports', contains twenty-one detailed studies
of segments of the national infrastructure and economy. Among these are trade,
banking, marketing boards, agriculture, crops, livestock and fisheries, co-operatives,
forestry, water resources, industry, mining, electric power, air, rail, road and water
transport, communications and education. The volume is an invaluable resource for
understanding Nigeria in the mid-1950s.

693 **IMF and Nigeria: a selected bibliography, 1960–1985.**
Q. F. Coker. Lagos: Nigerian Institute of International Affairs, 1985.
94p.

This selective bibliography contains unnumbered, briefly annotated entries arranged
alphabetically in two parts: 'IMF-general' (p. 2–28) and 'IMF and Nigeria' (p. 29–75).
There is an author and title index. Most of the entries in the second section are drawn
from Nigerian newspapers and magazines. In the brief introduction is a list of fourteen
IMF (International Monetary Fund) conditions already fulfilled and one of three
conditions Nigeria had not met as of the time of going to press, October 1985.

94 Nigeria and the evolution of money.
Ekpo Eyo. Lagos, Nigeria: Central Bank of Nigeria in association
with the Federal Department of Antiquities, 1979. 117p. bibliog.

This book is the catalogue for a major exhibition at Nigeria's National Museum held in
conjunction with the twentieth anniversary of the founding of the Central Bank of
Nigeria. The profusely illustrated volume is useful as a source book on the evolution of
money, particularly for: 'African pre-coinage currencies' (p. 31–48); 'Pre-coinage
currencies of Nigeria' (p. 49–70); 'The standardisation of West African currency: the
emergence of commercial banking insittutions' (p. 91–100); and 'The birth of the
Central Bank of Nigeria' (p. 101–07). The author is the former Director of the
Nigerian Museum, Lagos. Of related interest is Walter Ibekwe Ofonagoro's *The
currency revolution in Southern Nigeria, 1880–1948* (Los Angeles: University of
California, African Studies Center, July 1976, 32p. (Occasional Paper, no. 14)) which
describes the replacement of pre-exisitng currencies with British currency.

95 Nigeria and the international capitalist system.
Edited by Toyin Falola, Julius O[mozuanvbo] Ihonvberé. Boulder,
Colorado: Lynne Rienner, 1988. 154p. bibliog. (GSIS Monograph
Series in World Affairs, University of Denver).

Seven essays analyse Nigerian economy and foreign policy since independence. The
editors contributed 'Domestic economy and foreign policy'; 'The economy, the civilar,
and Nigeria's foreign policy, 1967–1970'; and 'Shagari: oil and foreign policy in the
second Republic, 1979–1983'. Segun O. Osoba wrote 'The economic background of
Balewa's foreign policy, 1960–1965'; Akanmu Gafaru Adebayo provides 'Postwar
economy and foreign policy: Gowon and the oil boom, 1970–1975' and 'Oil and the
Murtala/Obasanjo foreign policy'; Ihonvbere concludes with 'The economy and foreign
policy since 1984'. The selected bibliography (p. 129–48) is particularly useful since it
includes numerous dissertations. A review by Ayo Oluktun appears in *West Africa*,
no. 3709 (12–18 Sept. 1988) p. 1   . Timothy Shaw and Ihonvbere's *Towards a
political economy of Nigeria: petroleum and politics at the (semi)-periphery* (Aldershot,
England: Avebury; Brookfield, Vermont: Gower, 1988. 213p. bibliog.) has been
published recently.

**96 Nigerian cocoa farmers: an economic survey of Yoruba cocoa farming
families.**
R. Calletti, K. D. S. Baldwin, I. O. Dina. London: Oxford University
for the Nigerian Cocoa Marketing Board, 1956. 744p. 5 maps. bibliog.

This exhaustive survey of nearly 7,000 Yoruba cocoa growers was conducted between
March 1951 and March 1953 for the Nigerian Cocoa Marketing Board, to record in
detail 'how the cocoa farmer and his family lived, worked, and secured their livelihood'
'Preface, p. vi). The study includes data on the rural environment, the commercial
organization, the property of the families and their pattern of consumption, social
structure, public institutions and finance, land rights, inheritance and indebtedness.
Nigeria's cocoa production peaked in 1941–42 at 106,000 tonnes, 18.5 per cent of world
production, and declined to 14.2 per cent in 1950–51. The study recommends several
ways to increase production. The massive volume contains 309 tables and thirty-three
charts interspersed with the text, another sixty tables in the appendix (p. 623–724), a
select bibliography (p. 725–27), an index and five fold-out maps of the cocoa producing
areas.

257

Economy. Nigerian

697   **The future of development in Nigeria and the Sahel: projections from th**
      World Integrated Model (WIM).
      Barry B. Hughes, Patricia A. Strauch. In: *Alternative futures for*
      Africa. Edited by Timothy M. Shaw. Boulder, Colorado: Westview,
      1982, p. 179–99. bibliog.
This article describes a computer simulation run, in 1978, of several scenarios fc
Nigeria and the Sahel, two extremes of development opportunity, for the yea▮
1975–2001. Projections consider population, per capita income, Gross Nation▮
Product (GNP), malnourished population, calories per day, cumulative paymen▮
balance, food import bill and oil revenues. They compare the Sahel and Nigeria an▮
place their development scenarios in global context.

698   **Survey of African economies. Vol. 6: The Gambia, Ghana, Liberia,**
      Nigeria, and Sierra Leone.
      International Monetary Fund, edited by O. Mary Price, prepared unde▮
      the direction of Rattan J. Batia. Washington, DC: International
      Monetary Fund, 1975. 480p. 5 maps.
This volume offers an excellent overview of the Nigerian economy (p. 281–380) whic▮
includes descriptions of the structure of the economy, economic development an▮
planning, prices, wages, employment, government finance, money and bankin▮
balance of payments and the exchange and trade control system. The text ▮
supplemented by thirty-one tables of data, primarily from 1969 to 1973.

699   **Nigeria: impact of the oil economy.**
      Edited by Tilden J. LeMelle, George W. Shepherd, Jr.   *Africa Today*
      vol. 24, no. 4 (Oct.–Dec. 1977), 112p. map. bibliog.
This thematic issue of *Africa Today* contains four articles on Nigerian economic
political, and development topics (p. 5–58). 'Nigeria: a political economy' by Pa▮
Lubeck surveys regional and state economics (p. 5–10, reprinted from *Africa News*
vol. 9, no. 20, 14 Nov. 1977). Ademola T. Salau discusses Abuja and the Feder▮
Capital Territory in 'A new capital for Nigeria: planning, problems and prospect▮
(p. 11–22). Humphrey N. Nwosu offers a critique entitled 'Nigeria's Third Nation▮
Development Plan, 1975–80: major problems to implementation' (p. 23–38). Politic▮
scientist Gemuh E. Akuchu provides a case study of the Nigeria-Biafran conflict ▮
'Peaceful settlement of disputes: unsolved problem for the OAU' (p. 39–58). The issu▮
also contains book reviews (p. 61–98) and an index (p. 107–12).

700   **African Capitalism: a case study in Nigerian entrepreneurship.**
      E. Wayne Nafziger.   Stanford, California: Stanford Univeristy,
      Hoover Institution, 1977. 293p. map. bibliog.
This significant study focuses on the footwear industry as a means for elaborating o▮
broader themes. Professor Nafziger studied firms of different sizes and collected dat▮
throughout Nigeria from December 1964 to December 1965, and researched th▮
context of entrepreneurship during visits in 1967, 1970 and 1976. He offers suggestio▮
for ways to stimulate indigenous entrepreneurial activity. In the appendix, he discuss▮
David McClelland's need-achievement hypothesis; the bibliography (p. 265–84) ▮
extensive, as are the author's other publications on the Nigerian economy. His 196▮
University of Illinois doctoral thesis was *Nigerian entrepreneurship: a study ▮
indigenous businessmen in the footwear industry.*

258

701 **Structure of the Nigerian economy.**
F. A. Olaloku, A. Adejugbe, F. O. Fajana, E. R. Fapohunda,
S. Tomori, R. E. Ubogu, I. I. Ukpong, J. Umo. New York: St.
Martin's, 1979. 270p. bibliog.

This volume, by members of the Economics Department at the University of Lagos,
provides a profile of the Nigerian economy, with chapters devoted to major economic
sectors. Other substantial studies include Ishrat Husain's *Perspectives on the Nigerian
economy* (Lagos: Nigerian Institute of International Affairs, 1987, 157p.) and Chu
S. P. Okungwu's *The Nigerian economy: anatomy of a traumatised economy with some
proposals for stabilisation* (Enugu, Nigeria: Fourth Dimension, 1986. 462p. (Issues in
Nigerian Development, 2)).

702 **Petroleum and structural change in a developing country: the case of
Nigeria.**
Peter O. Olayiwola. New York: Praeger, 1987. 206p. map. bibliog.

During his research for this book, the goal of which is 'to provide a comprehensive
analysis of the political economy of Nigeria from 1860 to 1985' the author came to
realize that Nigeria's lack of development could be traced not to a failure of leadership
but to a 'structural condition of underdevelopment' (Preface, p. vii). The author
discusses the failure of neoclassical development theory and favours critical
development theory as applied to Nigeria, offering several recommendations for the
achievement of economic self-reliance. Extensive data appear throughout and the
bibliography (p. 177–97) is substantial. This study is essentially the author's 1985
University of Delaware at Newark, Delaware, PhD thesis. The author is a Lecturer in
the Department of Government at the University of Ilorin, Ilorin, Nigeria.

703 **Soldiers and power: the development performance of the Nigerian
military regime.**
Victor A. Olorunsola. Stanford, California: Hoover Institution, 1977.
168p. bibliog. (Hoover Institution Publication, 168).

This study examines the economic and developmental accomplishments of the Y.
Gowon military government, primarily during the first half of the 1970s. Following an
analysis of economic statistics, the author examines perceptions of the military's
development performance by students, university lecturers, farmers, traders, the press,
labour and by the military régime itself. A postscript written after the coup of 1975
demonstrates 'our contention that the citizenry (particularly relative to economic
development) was very low indeed' (p. 128). The bibliography (p. 165–68) is brief but
useful. At the time of publication, the author was a Professor of Political Science at
Iowa State University.

704 **The Nigerian oil economy: from prosperity to glut.**
J. K. Onoh. London, Canberra: Croom Helm; New York: St.
Martin's, 1983. 159p. map. bibliog.

This small book provides an informative account of the effects of oil on the Nigerian
economy from 1958 to early 1982, as well as on the position of Nigeria in OPEC. The
author describes also the formation and structure of the Nigerian National Petroleum
Corporation (NNPC) and argues for the benefits of Nigeria remaining in OPEC.
Tables of data are abundant and references are ample. In the well-illustrated *Oil glut
and the Nigerian economy* (Ikoyi, Nigeria: Nigerian National Petroleum Corporation,
1982], 29p.), L. A. O. Amu, Managing Director of the NNPC, discusses the problems

of the world oil glut for Nigeria and suggests that the present situation is a 'disguise(
blessing' (p. 17). The booklet includes petroleum statistics from the 1970s up to 198(
and 1981.

705　**Petroleum and the Nigerian economy.**
　　Scott R. Pearson.　Stanford, California: Stanford University, 1970.
　　235p. 3 maps. bibliog.
An early study of the recent and likely future impacts on the Nigerian economy of th(
flow of petroleum related investment into Nigeria (p. 2). In this revision of his doctora
thesis, the author examines the economic effects of direct foreign investment, an(
specifically the rôle of foreign petroleum corporations in Nigeria. Numerous statistic
are included, as is a bibliography (p. 221–26). The author worked in Nigeria in 1961–6.
in the Peace Corps and later for the United States Agency for Internationa
Development (USAID).

706　**The economics of a tropical dependency.**
　　Edited by Margery Perham.　London: Faber & Faber, under the
　　auspices of Nuffield College, Oxford University, 1946, 1948. 2 vols.
　　6 maps. bibliog.
An important data-rich account of Nigeria in the 1930s and early 1940s. Volume one
The native economies of Nigeria, contains: a general introduction by the editor an(
Daryll Forde; 'The rural economies', covering the south, the Hausa, Fulani and othe
groups, by Daryll Forde (p. 29–215); and 'Production for trade' focusing on palm
products, groundnuts, cocoa and livestock, by Richenda Scott (p. 217–91). Volum
two, *Mining, commerce, and finance in Nigeria*, consists of seven essays: 'The minin
industry' by Penelope A. Bower (p. 1–42); 'Extra-territorial enterprises' by J. Mar
(p. 43–136); 'The policy governing external trade' by Charlotte Leubuscher (p. 137–75)
'The monetary and banking system and loan market of Nigeria' by J. Mar
(p. 177–224); 'Public finance' by Sir Alan Pim (p. 225–79); 'The balance of payment
in 1936' by P. A. Bower (p. 281–326); and 'Conclusion: economic problems of
tropical dependency' by A. J. Brown (p. 327–48). The bibliographies (p. 349–57) ar
quite useful, as are the maps.

707　**The overvalued currency and over-administered economy of Nigeria.**
　　Douglas Rimmer.　*African Affairs*, vol. 84, no. 336 (July 1985),
　　p. 435–48. bibliog.
Examines Nigerian economic trends during the 1980s, especially trends in oil revenue
and external debts. The author discusses and prescribes devaluation of the naira
establishment of a realistic exchange rate and removal of government subsidies a
remedies for economic problems. He supposes that the magnitude of direct foreig
business investment in Nigeria has increased, but finds that data are lacking. Maj(
problems are 'gross government', 'fiscal indiscipline' and the 'ineptitude of Nigeri(
administration' (p. 446). 'In good times as bad, Nigeria is administered excessivel
inefficiently, corruptly, and often ineffectively' (p. 445). Professor Rimmer is Direct(
of the Centre for West African Studies at the University of Birmingham, England.

708 **Nigerian capitalism.**
Sayre P. Schatz. Berkeley; Los Angeles: University of California,
1977. 294p. bibliog.

An important, detailed analysis of Nigeria's economic development strategy, which the author terms 'nurture-capitalism'. The book is divided into four parts. Part one examines the period of early nurture-capitalism from 1949–66, but emphasizes the post-civil war period and the impact of oil wealth. Part two studies indigenous private enterprize. Part three looks at the business-assistance measures in the period up to the civil war, particularly in construction, focusing on the Approved Manufacturers Scheme, Yaba Industrial Estate and loans programmes. Finally, in his 'Conclusion' the author discusses broader issues of African development strategy and makes several suggestions. Professor Schatz has studied Nigerian economic issues since 1958, spent 1961–65 at the Nigerian Institute of Social and Economic Research and worked during 1974–75 as an economic advisor to the Nigerian government. Lucid prose and comprehensive documentation make this study one of the best of the Nigerian economy.

709 **The Nigerian economy since the great oil price increases of 1973–74.**
Sayre P. Schatz. *Africa Today*, vol. 29, no. 3 (1982), p. 33–42.
bibliog.

This overview of the economy from 1973–74 to c. 1981 describes the enormous impact of oil which, ironically, created a series of federal budget deficits as well as rapid economic growth. The author surveys and critically evaluates the slight increase in living standards, 'spasmodic' structural changes, lagging agriculture, persistent inflation, recurring economic fluctuation, runaway urbanisation and Nigeria's 'limping nurture-capitalism'. He concludes that 'indigenous private enterprise has hardly been an important engine of growth' (p. 42). He urges caution in the use of Nigerian data stating that, 'It remains as true as ever that data estimates for Nigeria are surely at the low end of the international reliability spectrum' (p. 42).

710 **Pirate capitalism and the inert economy of Nigeria.**
Sayre P. Schatz. *Journal of Modern African Studies*, vol. 22, no. 1
(March 1984), p. 45–57. bibliog.

The author, a prolific analyst of the Nigerian economy, argues that since the oil revenue-rich economy of 1973–74, the Nigerian economy has been inert, i.e. has moved from one with 'a weak engine of growth to one with virtually no engine at all' (p. 54). To make matters worse, he argues, the market economy has been replaced by 'pirate capitalism' in which 'manipulation of government, the most attractive route to fortune, has diverted effort into unproductive channels' (p. 56).

711 **The Nigerian economy: critical issues.**
Edited by George W. Shepherd, Jr., Tilden J. LeMelle. *Africa
Today*, vol. 33, no. 4 (1986), p. 3–69. bibliog.

Several articles in this special issue explore economic and political dimensions of contemporary Nigeria. The editor, Shepherd, offers 'Transition to democracy in Nigeria: an editorial' (p. 3–5); Olatunde Ojo and Peter Koehn assess the Second-tier Foreign Exchange Market (SFEM) in 'Nigeria's foreign exchange controls: an alternative to IMF conditions and dependency?' (p. 7–32); Terisa E. Turner, a Canadian energy economist, examines 'Oil workers and the oil bust in Nigeria'

Economy. Nigerian

(p. 33–50); Chibuzo N. Nwoke, Research Fellow at the Nigerian Institute of International Affairs, analyses the failure of economic nationalism in 'Towards authentic economic nationalism in Nigeria' (p. 51–69). In addition, four current books on Nigerian topics are reviewed in the issue.

712 **Cultural and political aspects of rural transformation: a case study of Eastern Nigeria.**
David R. Smock, Audrey C. Smock. New York: Praeger, 1972. 387p. 2 maps. bibliog. (Praeger Special Studies in International Economics and Development).

An analysis of cultural and political aspects of socio-economic development in rural Eastern Nigeria based on data gathered by the authors between 1962 and 1966. This study: examines traditions affecting agriculture, land tenure, community plantations, and resettlement schemes; develops an instrument to predict success in rural development projects; measures attitudes toward development based on a sample of 280 adults in twenty-four villages and compares Igbo and non-Igbo attitudes; finally, it describes strategies for more effective development. A useful bibliography (p. 369–87) is included as is a copy of the 'Rural development attitude survey questionnaire' (p. 353–66).

713 **Planning without facts: lessons in resource allocation from Nigeria's development.**
Wolfgang F. Stolper, foreword by Chief S. O. Adebo. Cambridge, Massachusetts: Harvard University, 1966. 348p. bibliog.

This is a 'book on the economics of development, with Nigeria providing a particularly interesting case in point' (Preface, p. xv). In lucid prose the author describes the problems and complexities of planning without reliable data, and considers national accounting and investment criteria, and economic policies on money, taxes, balance of payments, government and business, all from a planning standpoint. Sixteen tables provide extensive economic data from the period 1950–64. The appendix contains 'An input-output analysis of the Nigerian economy, 1959–60' by Nicholas G. Carter (p. 323–37), and tables of data on the Nigerian gross domestic product, 1959–60, investment and other economic indicators. The author served as Head of the Economic Planning Unit in the Federal Ministry of Economic Development in Lagos in 1960 and in 1966 was at the Center for Research on Economic Development, University of Michigan, Ann Arbor, Michigan. The brief foreword is by the Nigerian Ambassador to the United Nations. An informative overview of the 'sleeping giant of Africa' and an examination of the 'overly ambitious' First National Development Plan of 1962–68 can be found in Professor Stolper's article 'The development of Nigeria', *Scientific American*, vol. 209, no. 3 (Sept. 1963), p. 168–84, 308.

714 **Domestic policies, external constraints and economic development in Nigeria since 1950.**
Francis Teal. *African Affairs*, vol. 87, no. 346 (Jan. 1988), p. 69–81. bibliog.

In this study of the Nigerian economy from 1950–77, the author argues that the *pattern* of growth was largely determined by the raising of urban wages relative to rural prices while the growth *rate* 'has depended on the economic rents available either from agriculture or from oil' (p. 70). He asserts that very low growth rates in the 1970s were caused by the government's inefficient policy of 'rapid urban based expansion of manufacturing industries and public sector activities'. Sustained rural-urban migration resulted in more costly food prices. 'The conclusion of this study is that domestic policy has been the cause of Nigeria's economic problems' and that the current situation 'offers the best opportunity since independence for essential policy reform' (p. 81).

715   **Nigeria: options for long-term development. Report of a mission sent to Nigeria by the World Bank.**
Wouter Tims.   Baltimore, Maryland; London: Johns Hopkins University, 1974. 256p. 4 maps. bibliog. (A World Bank Country Economic Report).

Tims was Chief of Mission in this 1971 study, and co-ordinating author for this report, which also draws on reports by World Bank agriculture and transport sectors review missions and a UNESCO Project Identification mission. 'This report reviews briefly the major trends and policies that have characterized the country's economic development to date and examines in more detail the current position of the economy, its prospects during the remaining period of the Second National Development Plan (1972/73–1973/74) and the longer-term outlook through the early 1980s. The report also includes a detailed description of the petroleum industry (Chapter 6) and a brief discussion of education, agriculture, manufacturing and infrastructure (Chapter 7)' (p. 1). Data, presented in eighty-two tables and in a statistical annex (p. 199–252), are legion.

716   **Debts and falling oil prices: a case study of Nigeria.**
Franklin Vivekananda, Julius O. Ihonvbere.   *Scandinavian Journal of Development Alternatives*, vol. 6 (Dec. 1987), p. 164–85. bibliog.

This article examines 'Nigeria's debt problems within the context of falling oil prices . . . [arguing] that the excessive dependence on oil rents and the gross mismanagement of the rents within the context of the contradictions of neo colonial growth and development have combined to plunge Nigeria into its present problems' (p. 177). The authors provide extensive data in support of their position and urge that 'the only solution to the problem of fluctuating oil prices is a diversified economic base, a mobilised populace and the struggle for self-reliance' (p. 177).

717   **Nigeria: economy and society.**
Edited by Gavin Williams.   London: Rex Collings, 1976. 226p. 3 maps. bibliog.

Ten scholars contributed nine articles and an introduction to this informative volume. The introduction is by the editor. The articles are: Williams' 'Nigeria: a policital economy'; R. K. Home's 'Urban growth and urban government: contradictions in the colonial political economy'; J. I. Tseago's 'The emirate system and Tiv reaction to 'pagan' status in northern Nigeria'; Otonti Nduka's 'Colonial education and Nigerian society'; E. O. Akeredolu-Ale's 'Private foreign investment and the underdevelopment of indigenous entrepreneurship in Nigeria'; Dorothy Remy's 'Underdevelopment and the experience of women: a Nigerian case study'; C. E. F. Beer and Williams' 'The politics of the Ibadan peasantry'; Peter Waterman's 'Conservatism amongst the Nigerian workers'; Paul Collins, Terisa Turner, and Williams' 'Capitalism and the coup'. The editor lectured in politics and sociology at St. Peter's College, Oxford, at the time of publication and had been in Nigeria during 1970–71 and in 1975.

Periodicals

718 **African Business.**
London: IC Publications, 1966– . monthly.
Formerly published as *African Development,* this monthly magazine of business and economic news provides broad continent-wide coverage. Reports on Nigeria are conspicuous in nearly every issue. Special 'Nigeria surveys' were published in March and August 1987 (nos. 103 and 108), and in April 1988 (no. 116).

719 **Country Report: Nigeria.**
London: Economist Intelligence Unit, 1986. quarterly. (Report no. 59).
This excellent, up-to-date publication gives an overview of important political and economic events and includes information on energy, agriculture and industry, foreign trade and investments and statistical appendices. In addition an invaluable annual *Country Profile* is published. The most recent, *Country Profile: Nigeria 1988–89* (April 1988, 53p.), contains a detailed survey of every economic sector, two maps, statistical data and a brief bibliography (p. 53). Steven Wright's *Nigeria, the dilemmas ahead: a political risk analysis* (London: EIU, Nov. 1986 (EIU Political Risk Series, Special Report, no. 1072)) offers three scenarios for Nigerian political evolution and their economic consequences. The quarterly *Country Report: Nigeria* (1986– .) replaced the *Quarterly Economic Review of Nigeria* (1976–86) which superseded the *Quarterly Economic Review: Nigeria* (1968–76), itself preceded by *Quarterly Economic Review (of) Ghana, Nigeria, Sierra Leone, Gambia* (1953–67). Christopher Stevens provides a lucid, highly informative survey in *The political economy of Nigeria* (London: The Economist; New York: Cambridge University, 1984). This thirty-two-page report contains succinct analyses, extensive data, maps and a reading list.

720 **Nigerian Journal of Economic and Social Studies.**
Ibadan, Nigeria: Nigerian Economic Society, 1959– . irregular.
Published by the Nigerian Economic Society at the Department of Economics, University of Ibadan, Ibadan, Nigeria, this journal includes articles on current economic topics. Vol. 28, no. 1 (March 1986), for example, was a special issue on the Second-tier Foreign Exchange Market (SFEM). The *Nigerian Economist* began publication in Lagos in October 1987.

The most African country: a survey of Nigeria.
See item no. 12.

Nigeria: a country study.
See item no. 21.

Nigeria: the political and economic background.
See item no. 30.

Annual Report on Nigeria.
See item no. 33.

The Nigeria Handbook.
See item no. 34.

An economic history of Nigeria, 1860–1960.
See item no. 155.

Nigerian groundnut exports: origins and early development.
See item no. 254.

Government and the decline of the Nigerian oil-palm export industry, 1919–1939.
See item no. 273.

From wealthy entrepreneurs to petty traders: the decline of African middlemen in Eastern Nigeria, 1909–1950.
See item no. 276.

Proceedings of the national conference on Nigeria since independence. Zaria, March, 1983. Vol. I, Political development. Vol. II, The economic and social development.
See item no. 299.

The economics of political instability: the Nigerian-Biafran war.
See item no. 310.

Political conflict and economic change in Nigeria.
See item no. 588.

Nigeria since 1970: a political and economic outline.
See item no. 610.

Military politics in Nigeria: economic development and political stability.
See item no. 619.

Soldiers and oil: the political transformation of Nigeria.
See item no. 627.

Oil, debts and democracy: Nigeria.
See item no. 638.

Forestry and the Nigerian economy.
See item no. 728.

The Nigerian petroleum industry: a guide.
See item no. 735.

The wheat trap: bread and underdevelopment in Nigeria.
See item no. 739.

Private foreign investment in Nigerian agriculture.
See item no. 746.

Agriculture and Nigerian economic development.
See item no. 748.

Finance and Banking

721 **The AED African financial directory, 1987.**
Africa Economic Digest. London: Middle East Economic Digest
(MEED), 1987. 289p.

The first edition of this directory draws on the expertise of the staff of the *Africa Economic Digest* (London: Africa Economic Digest, 1980– . weekly) to compile data on banks and financial institutions in the fifty-two member countries of the Organization of African Unity, and briefly cover head offices in fifty other countries. In the very short introductions experts describe: 'International banks in Africa and financial flows to the continent'; 'International financial institutions in Africa'; 'Banking systems in Africa'; 'The franc zone'; and the 'African Development Bank'. For each African country, general information on banking hours, currency, and exchange rates is presented, followed by basic data on the Central Bank authority and all other banks and financial institutions. For Nigeria (p. 149–60), in addition to the Central Bank, seventy-five financial institutions are listed, many with information on finances, shareholders and the members of their boards of directors. AED also published *Nigeria: an AED special report, the first of AED's authoritative special reports on business in OAU member countries*, edited by Richard Synge (London: MEED, 1982. 96p.) and *Nigeria: an AED special report* (London: MEED, 1986. 48p.).

722 **Government and banking in Western Nigeria: a case study in economic policy.**
Charles V. Brown. Ibadan; Lagos: Oxford University for the Nigerian
Institute of Social & Economic Research, 1964. 141p. bibliog. (Nigerian
Social and Economic Studies, no. 5).

This monograph is a case study in the implementation of the economic policy of the Western Nigeria government aimed at aiding indigenous banks. The problems of the administration of the policy to the Agbonmagbe Bank and the Merchants Bank, including the complexities of communication among politicians, civil servants and public corporations, are analysed. Several conclusions and recommendations regarding policy formation, execution and bank operation are made. The appendices (p. 51–140) contain the banks' balance sheets and correspondence. The study was taken from the author's University of London thesis, *The development of monetary and credit institutions in Nigeria.*

723   **The Nigerian banking system.**
Charles V. Brown.   Evanston, Illinois: Northwestern University, 1966. 214p. map. bibliog.

'This study describes and analyses developments in the Nigerian banking system from 1950 to the end of 1963' (p. 9). The author examines commercial expatriate, indigenous and mixed banks in detail. He also covers the changing structure of banking, the Central Bank of Nigeria, and the development of a money market, and provides recommendations for both commercial banks and the Central Bank. Numerous data are presented in tables and figures. This study is a revised form of the author's doctoral thesis.

724   **Nigeria's financial system.**
Pius Nwabufo C. Okigbo.   Harlow, England: Longman, 1981. 288p. bibliog.

This important study explains how the Nigerian financial system evolved, how it works and why it works the way it does. In thirteen chapters the author analyses the financial institutions and system of Nigeria. The first three chapters introduce the subject by outlining trends in the economy, in prices, in banking and in monetary policies (1960–79). Other chapters discuss and analyse interest rates, commercial banking (1894–1978), merchant banking (1970–78), development banking, savings institutions, the financial public sector, the capital market, the Central Bank of Nigeria and prospects for the future. Professor Okigbo is one of Nigeria's most prolific and well-known economists and is also the senior brother of the late poet Christopher Okigbo whose works appear elsewhere in this volume. His *Nigerian national accounts, 1950–57* (Enugu, Nigeria: Federal Ministry of Economic Development, 1962. 206p.) was hailed in its foreword, by Waziri Ibrahim, as 'a milestone in the development of a firm statistical basis for economic planning'.

Trade and Commerce

725 The Nigerian business environment: an introduction to business and society in an African economy.
Efiong J. Etuk. London; Basingstoke: Macmillan, 1985. 278p. bibliog. (Macmillan International College Edition).

This book, intended for both students of business administation and management and for those wishing to operate a business successfully in Nigeria, describes the various business environments (socio-cultural, political, legal, economic, moral and behavioural) and issues, problems, and management decision-making, in the Nigerian context. The appendix contains the Nigerian Enterprise Promotion Act of 1977 and the select bibliography (p. 268–70) contains several useful references. The author is a lecturer in the Department of Management Studies at the University of Calabar, Calabar, Nigeria. Of related interest is Titus A. Oshagbemi's *Small business management in Nigeria* (London, Lagos: Longman, 1983. 129p.) and *Nigeria into the 1990s – a CRIS country study* (London: Control Risk Information Services, 1987. 22p.) by Control Risk Information Services (CRIS). This report is designed for suppliers or potential investors in Nigeria and assesses risks to businesses from political instability, violence, and political change. It offers scenarios developed for short-, medium- and long-term consequences. The report is available from CRIS, 83 Victoria Street, London SW1H OHW, or from CRIS, 4330 East West Highway, Suite 320, Bethesda, Maryland, 20814 USA.

726 Interregional trade and money flows in Nigeria, 1964.
Alan M. Hay, Robert H. T. Smith. Ibadan, Nigeria: Oxford University for the Nigerian Institute of Social & Economic Research, 1970. 245p. bibliog.

'The purpose of this study is to estimate the volume and value of interregional trade in Nigeria in 1964' (p. v), and despite the study's age, it remains an exemplary work of this type. In their analysis of trade among the North, West, East and Midwest Regions and Lagos, the authors provide extensive economic data on foodstuffs and livestock as well as on timber, minerals and manufactured items. The bases of the trade, the rôle of major towns, road traffic surveys, 'derivation of the estimates of interregional payments' (Appendix, p. 167–239) and the authors' methodology are all discussed at length. Hay was in Nigeria from September 1963 to July 1965 and Smith from September 1964 to July 1965 to gather the data presented here.

727 **Nigeria: a survey of U.S. export opportunities.**
Karl P. Magyar. Washington, DC: US Department of Commerce, International Trade Administration, Nov. 1981. 104p. map. bibliog.
(US Government Printing Office: 1981, 0-358-320/71.74).

This survey document was produced as part of an effort to increase US exports to Nigeria and to reduce a large US trade imbalance. Most of the data presented are for the period 1977–80. The study discusses US trade in Africa and gives an economic profile of Nigeria with a description of the Third and Fourth National Development Plans (1975–80 and 1981–85). Each of the eight chapters focuses on a major market, describing its highlights, structure and growth prospects, marketing environment, supplier universe and marketing considerations. The markets considered are: electric power; education; health care; construction and public works; manufacturing industries, agriculture; food processing; and other markets (tourism, hotels, office equipment, communications, and textiles). An earlier version was published as *Nigeria: a survey of U.S. business opportunities* (Washington, DC: Bureau of International Commerce, 1976. 190p. (International Marketing Information Series: Country Market/Sectoral Surveys)). The chapter 'Doing business with Africans' (p. 479–95) in Philip R. Harris and Robert T. Moran's *Managing cultural differences* (Houston, Texas: Gulf, 1987, 2nd ed., 609p.) provides excellent advice and focuses on Nigeria.

Annual Report on Nigeria.
See item no. 33.

The Nigeria Handbook.
See item no. 34.

Nigerian groundnut exports: origins and early development.
See item no. 254.

Government and the decline of the Nigerian oil-palm export industry, 1919–1939.
See item no. 273.

The wheat trap: bread and underdevelopment in Nigeria.
See item no. 739.

Nigeria: an export market profile.
See item no. 745.

Private foreign investment in Nigerian agriculture.
See item no. 746.

Industry

General

728 **Forestry and the Nigerian economy.**
S. Kolade Adeyoju. Ibadan, Nigeria: Ibadan University, 1975. 308p.
bibliog.

This study analyses thoroughly the forestry sector of the Nigerian economy, providing extensive data for the 1950s and 1960s, up to 1971, and offering projections from 1972 up to 1980. The author describes: British colonial policy and its legacies, economic aspects of forest management, timber markets and marketing, the importance of wood-based industries, social benefits of forestry and forestry revenue and financial commitments and contemporary forestry policy. This book derives in part from the author's 1968 thesis for a Diploma in Forestry at Oxford's Commonwealth Forestry Institute, *Forestry in the national economy of Nigeria* (242 leaves) and follows his 1966 doctoral thesis at the London School of Economics and Political Science, *The development of the timber industry in the Western and Mid-Western Regions of Nigeria*. In 1975 the author was Senior Lecturer in Forestry at the University of Ibadan, Ibadan, Nigeria.

729 **Industrialisation policies in Nigeria.**
Manfred Berger, J. A. Oyelabi, translated by G. Fulton-Smith.
Munich: Weltforum, 1975. 333p. 3 maps. bibliog. (IFO-Institut für Wirtschaftsforschung München, Afrika-Studien no. 88; Nigerian Institute of Social and Economic Research, Ibadan).

This study is based on the author's research in Nigeria during the twenty months he was a Research Fellow at NISER, Ibadan, and critically examines Nigerian industrialization policies in light of objectives set by the Second National Development Plan, 1970–74. Principal among these objectives were rapid industrial growth and diversification, Nigerianization, even regional distribution and increased employment and income. The author evaluates these areas thoroughly, supplying data in thirty-two tables. J. A. Oyelabi contributed 'Tariffs, domestic prices, effective protection and the structure of foreign trade in Nigeria' (p. 275–333), a technical analysis of foreign trade problems written shortly before he died in a car accident in 1973. The study was originally in German and was translated to English for this edition.

730 **Forestry policy in Nigeria, 1897–1960.**
Edmund O[nyemeke] Egboh. Nsukka, Nigeria: University of Nigeria, Department of History, 1985. 246p. 3 maps. bibliog.

This excellent inter-disciplinary study is a history of forestry, the forest reserves, and timber and forest product exports during Nigeria's colonial period. It examines: forestry policy and legal aspects of control over the forests, timber processing and supply, overseas demand for timber and the development of the rubber industry and rubber export trade. Statistical data on all aspects of forestry, forest products and exports are supplied and nineteen illustrations are included.

731 **The history of tin mining in Nigeria.**
Federal Department of Antiquities. Jos, Nigeria: Federal Department of Antiquities, National Musuem, Jos, 1979. 27p.

'This booklet is a catalogue to the permanent exhibition at the National Museum, Jos, illustrating the history of tin mining in Nigeria' (p. 3). Tin ore was mined in central Nigeria as long ago as the sixteenth century and its modern exploitation by the British was begun in 1902. Since 1961 all Nigerian tin ore has been processed by the Makeri Smelting Company. Because of the tin mining, Nigeria's oldest culture, the Nok, was discovered and its artefacts preserved in the Jos Museum, which opened in 1952 and was 'the first of its kind in Africa' (p. 16).

732 **Industrial development in Nigeria: patterns, problems and prospects.**
Edited by O. Teriba, M. O. Kayode. Ibadan, Nigeria: Ibadan University, 1977. 402p. bibliog.

This is an important collection of twenty-eight papers, many published previously in the *Nigerian Journal of Economic and Social Studies* (q.v.) and elsewhere, which give a comprehensive view of Nigerian industrialization in the 1960s and early 1970s. The articles are grouped in five parts: introduction, the industrial environment, industrial patterns, government industrial policies and strategies, and 'The way ahead'. Among the most important contributors are the editors, Sayre P. Schatz (three articles), Eno J. Usoro (two articles), John R. Harris, O. Aboyade, A. O. Phillips (three articles), P. C. Asiodu (two articles) and T. A. Oyejide (two articles). Topics include policy analysis, the petroleum industry, the cement, sawmilling and printing industries, the Yaba Industrial Estate and future developments. Each article has its own bibliography and there is also a 'select bibliography' (p. 389–93). The volume contains more than 100 tables of data.

733 **The Nigerian oil palm industry (government policy and export production, 1906–1965).**
Eno J. Usoro. Ibadan, Nigeria: Ibadan University, 1974. 153p. bibliog. (Ibadan Social Science Series, no. 4).

This data-filled analysis examines production, distribution and marketing of oil-palm products during three periods (1906–38, 1939–54, and 1955–65), and makes suggestions for ways to increase production and earnings in the future. 'Nigeria was the main source of palm products important in the world market in the period 1924–38 – the only period when comprehensive statistics of production from the main producing countries are available' (p. 22). The study is based on the author's University of London doctoral thesis.

734 **Studies in industrialisation: Nigeria and the Cameroons.**
F. A. Wells, W. A. Warmington. London: Oxford University for the
Nigerian Institute of Social & Economic Research, 1962. 266p. 2 maps.
bibliog.

This interesting study examines two production systems: the rapidly changing
production systems of Nigeria, where groundnuts, cocoa, palm produce and rubber,
the four most important export crops, are produced primarily by small-scale peasant
cultivators, and the system of the Southern Cameroons, where large plantations
account for most exports. The Nigerian study by Wells (p. 25–124) is the result of his
investigations, during April and May 1959, of African Timber and Plywood Ltd, of
Sapele, Southern Nigeria and four groundnut crushing mills at Kano. He describes
factors in efficiency in the Sapele timber industry, labour policy, labour conditions in
Kano and industrial development in the Northern Region. Warmington studied the
Southern Cameroons during 1953–59, when that region was administered as part of
Nigeria. Among their many conclusions is a plea for a 'co-ordinated policy, involving
agriculture and manufacture, transport and marketing facilities' (p. 258).

Petroleum industry

735 **The Nigerian petroleum industry: a guide.**
Compiled by Beverly Ann Gray. Washington, DC: Library of
Congress, 1978. 66p. (Maktaba Afrikana Series).

In 400 useful citations, most of which are annotated, 'this bibliography presents a
selection of government and quasi-governmental publications, books, periodical
articles, and dissertations on the Nigerian petroleum industry from the early 1900s
through 1976' (Preface, p. v). The entries are arranged by broad topics (general, civil
war, development and production, economic impact, government oil policies, and
natural gas) and derive mainly from the holdings of the Library of Congress and of
'other libraries reporting to the *National Union Catalogue* and to *New Serial Titles*'. A
combined author, subject and title index provides easy access to the entries. The
compiler is the head of the African Section, African and Middle Eastern Division,
Library of Congress. Less easily available, but more comprehensive, is Stephen A
Amune's *Petroleum industry in Nigeria: a selective annotated bibliography* (Zaria,
Nigeria: Kashim Ibrahim Library, Ahmadu Bello University, 1979. 284p.) which lists
1,552 citations from the early 1900s to August 1979 in twenty topical sections.

736 **The oil industry in Nigeria: an annotated bibliography.**
Compiled by Julius O[mozuanvbo] Ihonvbere. Montreal, Quebec:
Centre for Developing-Area Studies, McGill University, Sept. 1983.
85p. (Bibliography Series, no. 11).

An invaluable compilation of 592 briefly annotated references, arranged by subject and
introduced by the compiler (p. 1–3). There is an author index. Topics covered are: 'Oil
law and regulations'; 'History of the Nigerian oil industry: impact of the civil war';
'Foreign capital, exploration and drilling'; 'State participation, marketing, mationaliza-
tion and indigenization'; 'The Nigerian National Petroleum Corporation'; 'Petrochemical

nd natural gas development: pipelines and transport'; 'Refining and technology
ransfer'; 'Nigeria in OPEC and foreign policy'; 'Labour and manpower development';
Class formation, class relations and internal politics'; and 'Impact of the oil industry
n the Nigerian economy: revenue, profits and economic development'.

37 **Fuelling the Nigerian economy: NNPC's 10th anniversary.**
   Tunji Oseni. *OPEC Bulletin*, no. 18 (May 1987), p. 38–43, 76–77.
Offers a description of the Nigerian National Petroleum Corporation's first decade of
organization and accomplishment. The NNPC's function is to guide Nigeria's
development of its oil resources. The 1977 Decree Number thirty-three charged it with
exploring, prospecting for, working, winning, or otherwise acquiring, possessing and
disposing of petroleum' and with 'refining, treating, processing and generally engaging
in the handling of petroleum' and its products and by-products. Between 1977 and
986, sixty-three wells were drilled, of which thirty were 'discovery wells' in the Niger
Delta. The NNPC's board chairman is the Minister of Petroleum Resources, Alhaji
Rilwanu Lukman, leader of the Nigerian delegation to and (in 1987 and 1988)
President of the OPEC Conference.

Energy in Nigeria.
See item no. 53.

Nigeria: impact of the oil economy.
See item no. 699.

Petroleum and structural change in a developing country: the case of Nigeria.
See item no. 702.

The Nigerian oil economy: from prosperity to glut.
See item no. 704.

Petroleum and the Nigerian economy.
See item no. 705.

Debts and falling oil prices: a case study of Nigeria.
See item no. 716.

African Business.
See item no. 718.

Agriculture, Food Policy and Nutrition

738　**An agricultural atlas of Nigeria.**

S. A. Agboola.　Oxford; London: Oxford University, 1979. 248p. bibliog.

In some eighty-five maps and diagrams and thirty tables, the author provides systematic analysis of Nigeria's physical environment, root crops, cereals and pulse tree crops, oil seeds, industrial crops, livestock, modern agricalatural development and patterns of land use. His primary concern is 'space utilization in Nigeria agriculture and the problems of increased productions' (Preface, p. v). Th bibliography (p. 211–30) is extensive.

739　**The wheat trap: bread and underdevelopment in Nigeria.**

Gunilla Andrae, Björn Beckman.　London: Zed, in association with the Scandinavian Institute of African Studies, 1985. 180p. 4 maps. bibliog.

Presents an astute analysis of how 'Nigeria is trapped between the growing dependenc on North American wheat on the one hand and the illusory policy of impor substitution on the other' (p. 139). The authors show how Nigerian wheat import increased eighteen times from the 1960s to the 1980s (from an average of 75,000 tonne per annum in the early 1960s to an average of 1,350,000 tonnes per annum in the earl 1980s). They explain the foreign policy relations with the US from which ninety pe cent of the wheat comes and analyse three wheat-growing projects in northern Nigeri (the Bakolori, Kano River and South Chad projects). Also discussed are the rôle played by rural bakers, millers, wheat traders and foreign agribusiness. It is shown how they link the village with the world market and ways to disengage from the trap and t achieve food self-sufficiency are suggested. A review of the book by U. M. Igbozurik appears in *Africa*, vol. 57, no. 3 (1987), p. 390–91.

740 **Achieving self-sufficiency in African agricultural food production: the case of Nigeria.**
Mark Anikpo. *Africa Today*, vol. 32, no. 4 (1985), p. 29–38. bibliog.
The author, Head of the Sociology Department at the University of Port Harcourt, Port Harcourt, Nigeria, argues that efforts at 'achieving long-term food self-sufficiency n Africa have failed . . . because African agriculture lacks an appropriate organizational base to mobilize the predominantly peasant producers into an efficient and more productive work force' (p. 30). He describes the characteristics of peasant agriculture and the turnaround in Nigerian food production, providing data on the value of food imports from 1962 to 1980, and the ongoing Nigerian failure in agriculture through the Buhari government of 1985. The subject was also explored in his 'The peasantry and the dilemma of underdevelopment in Nigeria', *Pan-African Social Science Review*, no. 1 (Oct. 1984), p. 27–47.

741 **Nutrition and food policy in Nigeria.**
Edited by Tola Atinmo, Laolu Akinyele. Kuru; Jos, Nigeria:
National Institute for Policy & Strategic Studies, 1983. 447p. bibliog.
This book includes forty-two papers presented at the National Conference on Food and Nutrition Policy for Nigeria held at the University of Ibadan, 27–31 May 1979. The papers, full of raw data and statistics and with references, are grouped in eight sections: 'Health and nutrition interface'; 'Food production and distribution in Nigeria'; 'Agro-forestry and food supplies in Nigeria'; 'Nutrition and food production interface'; 'Food technology and production strategies in Nigeria'; 'Nigerian food industries and policy formulation'; 'Socio-economic aspects of a food and nutrition policy'; and 'Problems of formulation and implementation of a food and nutrition policy'. There are subject and author indexes to this cornucopia of information. See also S. Olajuwon Olayide's *Food and nutrition crisis in Nigeria* (Ibadan, Nigeria: Ibadan University, 1982. 179p.) which contains eighty tables of data from government surveys and farm population statistics.

742 **Agriculture and economic development in Nigeria: a prescription for the Nigerian green revolution.**
Adekunle Folayan. New York: Vantage, 1983. 276p. 2 maps. bibliog.
In his analysis of various problems confronting Nigerian agriculture, the author, a doctoral candidate at Howard University in Washington, DC, calls for greater diversion of Nigeria's oil revenue to the rural poor. The author provides extensive statistical data on agricure. David A. Iyegha's recent *Agricultural crisis in Africa: the Nigerian experience* (Lanham, Maryland: Univeristy Press of America, 1988. 246p.) is also a significant analysis of the major issues.

743 **Agricultural development in Nigeria, 1965–1980.**
Food and Agriculture Organization of the UN. Rome: FAO 1966.
512p. 7 maps. bibliog.
This extremely data-rich volume is a FAO report to the government of Nigeria made in 1965. The report contains statistics, projections, analyses and recommendations for nearly every aspect of Nigerian agriculture, but especially for cocoa, rubber, oil-palm, groundnuts and cotton, as well as for water resources, livestock, forestry and fisheries. Three colour soil maps are included, as is a brief bibliography (p. 511–12).

744 **Land resources of central Nigeria: agricultural development possibliities.**
LRDC Central Nigeria Project Team. Surbiton, England: Land
Resources Development Centre, Overseas Development
Administration, 1981. 7 vols. bibliog.

Six volumes of this Land Resources Development Centre (LRDC) project report
contain large-scale maps covering *The Bauchi Plains*, *The Jos Plateau*, *The Jema's
Platform*, *The Benue Valley*, *The Kaduna Plains* and *The Kano Plains*. Volume seven
An atlas of resource maps, contains nineteen excellent large maps (scale 1:1,500,000)
summarizing the project's findings. It also has a complete list of the numerous reports
of the Central Nigerian Project published from 1971–78, which cover topics including
landforms, soils, livestock, tin mining, climate and vegetation, farming systems, and
animal production in Kano State. Two of the most important of these reports are J. G
Bennett's *Environmental aspects of the Kano Plains* (Land Resource Report, vol. 20
1978. 3 vols.) and P. N. Gosden's *Peasant farming systems* (Land Resource Report
vol. 17, 1978. 3 vols.).

745 **Nigeria: an export market profile.**
Carl Mabbs-Zeno. Washington, DC: International Economics
Division, Economic Research Service, United States Department of
Agriculture, April 1986. 54p. map. bibliog. (Foreign Agricultural
Economic Report, no. 218).

This report surveys the basic factors underlying agricultural supply and demand
includes an overview of the agricultural production system, presents long-run
projections of food and agricultural trade and suggests opportunities for expanding US
agricultural exports to Nigeria. At the time of going to press, about one-quarter of
Nigeria's substantial agricultural imports, especially corn and wheat, came from the
United States. Three alternative production scenarios are used to project Nigerian
agricultural imports through to 1990. A substantial bibliography is included (p. 42–47).

746 **Private foreign investment in Nigerian agriculture.**
Carl Mabbs-Zeno. Washington, DC: International Economics
Division, Economic Research Service, United States Department of
Agriculture, Oct. 1986. 20p. bibliog. (Economic Research Service. Staff
Report, AGES860918).

This report discusses investment and agricultural policy in Nigeria by placing these in
the perspective of worldwide patterns of private foreign investment, and by tracing the
foreign investment policy history of Nigeria. From an examination of the policies
rationales and impacts of the Babangida government, privatization of firms in June
1986, import licences issued and multinational agribusiness firms, the conclusion is
drawn that 'the hypothesis that private foreign investment is not improving national
agricultural performance in Nigeria is tentatively supported by the evidence although
more experience with new programs is needed before a full evaluation is possible'
(p. 16).

747 **Farming systems in the Nigerian savanna: research and strategies for development.**
David W. Norman, Emmy B. Simmons, Henry M. Hays. Boulder, Colorado: Westview, 1982. 275p. 3 maps. bibliog. (Westview Replica Edition).

At the heart of this book on agricultural development in northern Nigeria is a study of farming patterns from 1965–73 in three villages (Dan Mahawayi, Doka and Hanwa) near Zaria. The authors place this in the context of descriptions of the agroecology of the Nigerian savanna, farming communities and institutional arrangements. All this is followed by a systematic account of a 'farming systems' approach which aims to enhance agricultural productivity. Extensive data appear in tables and the bibliography (p. 247–66) is an important listing of relevant works.

748 **Agriculture and Nigerian economic development.**
H. A. Oluwasanmi. Ibadan, Nigeria: Oxford University, 1966. 240p. bibliog.

This book examines the many facets of agriculture, 'the most important sector of the Nigerian economy' (Preface, p. v.). It describes, with ample statistical data, land use, population, resources, capital and investment, patterns of production, marketing, agricultural development and industrialization. The author, who was then Professor of Agricultural Economics at the University of Ibadan, discusses the 'conditions under which the Nigerian peasant carries out his productive functions', 'the place of Nigerian in the national economy' and 'undertakes to propose remedial measures and emphases' for improving the agricultural situation (Preface, p. v.).

749 **Nigeria's foods and feeding stuffs: their chemistry and nutritive value.**
V. A. Oyenuga. Ibadan, Nigeria: Ibadan University, 1968. 3rd ed. 99p. bibliog.

This analysis of the chemical constituents of the human foods and animal feeding-stuffs in common use in Nigeria contains descriptions of and tabular data on: common roots; tubers and green leaves (cassava, yam, sugar cane, sweet potato,); concentrates (acha grain, locust bean tree, groundnut, blood meal, coconut seed, cocoa bean, cottonseed, soya sunflower, and water melon); and various dried leaves, hays and tusks. Nutritional values and chemical components are identified for each food item. The volume was published originally and as a second edition as *Faculty of Agriculture Technical Bulletin*, no. 1, March 1959. 65p. The author was Professor and Head of the Department of Animal Science, and Dean, Faculty of Agriculture, Forestry and Veterinary Science, Univeristy of Ibadan.

750 **Efficient resource use for tropical nutrition: Nigeria.**
Victor E. Smith. East Lansing, Michigan: Michigan State University, Graduate School of Business Administration, Division of Research, 1975. 375p. 3 maps. bibliog. (MSU International Business and Economics Studies).

This detailed study integrates extensive nutritional, agricultural and economic data from Nigeria in the 1960s to suggest 'an agricultural production pattern that is efficient in nutritional terms (not simply in market terms), to discover which crops or which techniques of cultivation are most efficient nutritionally, and to identify changes in the production pattern that would lower the cost of obtaining adequate nutrition (Introduction, p. xxiv). The author is Professor of Economics, Michigan State Univeristy, East Lansing, Michigan. See also Jacques May's study *The ecology of malnutrition in middle Africa (Ghana, Nigeria, Republic of the Congo, Rwanda, Burundi, and the former French Equatorial Africa)* (New York: Hafner, 1965. 255p. (Studies in Medical Geography, vol. 5)) for a discussion of the relation between economic development and malnutrition in Nigeria.

751 **The challenge of food: Nigeria's approach to agriculture, 1975–80.**
Tina Wallace. *Canadian Journal of African Studies*, vol. 15 no. 2 (1981), p. 239–58. bibliog.

A review and critique of strategies promoted in the Third Development Plan (1975–80) which included large scale irrigation projects, World Bank projects, the National Accelerated Food Production Programme, Operation Feed the Nation and the provision of credit through banks. Central to the author's criticism is that all these strategies are either based on imported technology, or favour the large-scale farmer, or both. The small farmers who comprise the vast majority of agriculturalists are ignored by the plans. 'In fact present strategies are actually weakening the position of many farmers, forcing some off the land altogether, pushing others on to smaller, less fertile plots' (p. 258). In the recent volume *Satisfying Africa's food needs: food production and commercialization in African agriculture*, edited by Ronald Cohen (Boulder, Colorado: Lynne Rienner, 1988. 244p. (Carter Studies on Africa, vol. 1)) are two relevant articles: Akin Mabogunje's 'Coping with structural adjustment: the Nigerian case' (p. 191–208) and the editor's 'Adversity and transformation: the Nigerian light at the end of the tunnel' (p. 209–37).

752 **State, oil, and agriculture in Nigeria.**
Edited by Michael Watts. Berkeley, California: University of California, Institute of International Studies, 1987. 327p. 3 maps. bibliog. (Research Series, no. 66).

Between the editor's introduction and postscript appear ten substantial and thoughtful articles analysing the impact of the oil boom-and-bust cycle on Nigerian agriculture. These are: Robert Shenton's, 'Nigerian agriculture in historical perspective: development and crisis, 1900–60' (p. 34–57); M. Watts' 'Agriculture and oil-based accumulation: stagnation or transformation?'; Alan Richards' 'Oil booms and agricultural development: Nigeria in comparative perspective' (p. 85–109); Bjorn Beckman's 'Public investment and agrarian transformation in Northern Nigeria' (p. 110–37); Richard Palmer-Jones' on 'Irrigation and the politics of agricultural development in Nigeria' (p. 138–67); Paul Clough and Gavin Williams' 'Decoding Berg: the World Bank in rural northern Nigeria' (p. 168–201); Sara S. Berry's 'Oil and the disappearing peasantry . . .' (p. 202–22); Paul J. Ross' on 'Land as a right to membership . . .' (p. 223–47); Louise Lennihan's on 'Agricultural wage labor in Northern Nigeria' (p. 248–67); and Paul M. Lubeck's 'Islamic protest and oil-based capitalism: agriculture, rural linkages, andurban popular movements in northern Nigeria' (p. 268–90). A lengthy bibliography (p. 297–317) is included.

753 **Crisis and change in African agriculture: a comparative study of the Ivory Coast and Nigeria.**
Michael J. Watts, Thomas J. Bassett. *African Studies Review*, vol 28, no. 4 (Dec. 1985), p. 3–27. bibliog.

This informative, analytical article, with extensive notes and references, examines the colonial and recent past of agricultural programmes in the Ivory Coast and Nigeria, and rejects common simplistic conclusions about the agrarian crisis in Africa. Instead, the authors conclude that there is no single explanation for African food deficits and 'no *one* cheap food policy or, alternatively, one path of agrarian transition associated with peripheral capitalist development' (p. 6). 'The Nigerian case shows clearly that reference to agrarian stagnation may obfuscate more than it clarifies. . . . The new attempts to encourage large scale corporate investment in agriculture are probably too immature to be assessed' (p. 21).

754 **Rural development in Nigeria.**
S. K. Taiwo Williams. Ile-Ife, Nigeria: University of Ife, 1978. 129p. map. bibliog.

Dr. Williams analyses the problems and strategies for rural development and for agricultural extension work in Nigeria. He uses as a case study the University of Ife's Isoya Rural Development Project, begun in 1972 and including nine villages with a total population of nearly 2,000 people. The author is Professor and Head of the Department of Agricultural Extension Services, University of Ibadan. The study is illustrated with photographs. Gavin Williams' 'Taking the part of peasants: rural development in Nigeria and Tanzania', in *The political economy of contemporary Africa* edited by Peter C. W. Gutkind and Immanuel Wallerstein (Beverly Hills, California; London: Sage, 1976, p. 131–54), describes the historic and contemporary views of governments of these two countries towards rural cultivation, and their largely unsuccessful efforts to increase peasant productivity. Increased food production, 'cannot be achieved by state direction of peasant producers, but only by encouraging peasant initiative based on their own experience and improving their own material well-being' (p. 152).

Rural Hausa: a village and a setting.
See item no. 355.

Population, prosperity and poverty: rural Kano, 1900 and 1970.
See item no. 356.

Sex roles in the Nigerian Tiv farm household.
See item no. 393.

Fathers work for their sons: accumulation, mobility and class formation in an extended Yorubà community.
See item no. 520.

Perspectives on drought and famine in Nigeria.
See item no. 529.

Silent violence: food, famine & peasantry in northern Nigeria.
See item no. 537.

Agriculture, Food Policy and Nutrition

The health of Nigerians, 1983/84. Health and nutrition status survey. (A module of the National Integrated Survey of Households (NISH) April 1983–March, 1984).
See item no. 551.

Cocoa, custom, and socio-economic change in rural Western Nigeria.
See item no. 689.

Nigerian cocoa farmers: an economic survey of Yoruba cocoa farming families.
See item no. 696.

Nigeria.
See item no. 1139.

Transport

755 Transport systems in Nigeria.
Edited by Toyin Falola, S. A. Olanrewaju. Syracuse, New York: Syracuse University, Maxwell School of Citizenship and Public Affairs, 1986. 175p. 9 maps. bibliog. (Foreign and Comparative Studies/African Series, XLII).

Nine essays by the editors, and other contributors, G. O. Ogunremi, A. A. Ogunsnaya, M. O. Filani, Iz. Osayimwese, O. Aloba and S. A. Musisi-Nkambwe cover traditional, rail road, and air transport systems, port development, and rural and urban transportation issues. The bibliography (p. 163–72) is very useful. Professor Ogunremi has also published *Counting the camels: the economics of transportation in pre-industrial Nigeria* (New York, Lagos: Nok, 1982. 238p.). Nigeria's railway system which began in 1912 with 29,000 employees is examined by a 'Special correspondent' in 'Railways at the junction', *West Africa*, no. 3713 (10–16 Oct. 1988), p. 1879–80.

756 Transportation in Nigeria: a bibliography.
Compiled by Abimbola Oyemakinde. Lagos, Nigeria: National Library, 1975. 57p. (National Library Publication, no. 35).

This very thorough unannotated listing covers air, railway, river and road transport as well as transportation in general, including bridges, highways and the economics of motor transport. Appendices include extracts from the first, second and third National Development Plans, 1962–80. Official publications, archival materials, theses, articles and books are included. It is indexed by author. Of use also is Adepoju G. Onibokun's *Socio-economic impact of highways and commuter rail systems on land use and activity patterns: an annotated bibliography* (Monticello, Illinois: Council of Planning Librarians, 1975. 35p.).

757 The politics of transporting.
Adrian Peace. *Africa*, vol. 58, no. 1 (1988), p. 14–28. bibliog.

This interesting paper describes the economics, social hierarchy and political organization of transporting in Agege, a town on the northern egdge of Lagos. In the

Transport

same issue, Olatunde Bayo Lawuyi's 'The world of the Yoruba taxi driver: an interpretative approach to vehicle slogans' (p. 1–13), analyses the slogans on taxis in Ile-Ife as expressions of social stratification. Of related interest is A. B. Cozens's 'Lorry names in Southern Nigeria', in the *Nigerian Field*, vol. 26, no. 4 (Oct. 1961), p. 158–62. The author compiled some 170 lorry names and grouped them by religious motif, motto or proverb motif, road jargon, title or nickname with some 'unclassified'. However, their significance is not interpreted. A shorter list of thirty-two names was published by Catherine Wareham the *Nigerian Field*, vol. 21, no. 2 (April 1956), p. 91 and a note by H. Spottiswoode in the following issue, (July 1956) p. 139, adds two more.

Employment and
Manpower

758 **Country labor profile: Nigeria.**
Donald S. Harris, Badru I. O. Rabin. Washington, DC: US
Department of Labor, Bureau of International Labor Affairs, Office of
Foreign Labor Affairs, 1980. 8p. map. bibliog.
This succinct pamphlet provides a useful summary of Nigerian government, resources,
labour force, industrial relations, and labour standards.

759 **Occupational status of women in Nigeria: a comparison of two urban
centres.**
Linda Lacey, Cathy M. DiDomenico. *Africana Marburgensia*, vol. 10,
no. 2 (1977), p. 62–79. bibliog.
The authors examine participation in both the modern and traditional economic sectors
of Kano and Ibadan. Statistical data on age, ethnicity, education, employment,
occupation, and labour force participation are presented. The data are based on
questionnaires given to 1,076 males and 1,086 females in Ibadan and 699 males and 777
females in Kano as part of the Internal Migration Project at the University of Ibadan.
Discussion of the literature and data on the rôles of women in Nigerian society is
included. The paper was reprinted in *Working Papers in Planning*, no. 27 (July 1979),
17p., by the Department of City and Regional Planning, Program in Urban and
Regional Studies, Cornell University, Ithaca, New York.

760 **Bureaucratic elites and public-sector wage bargaining in Nigeria.**
Dafe Otobo. *Journal of Modern African Studies*, vol. 24, no. 1
(March 1986), p. 101–26. bibliog.
This article briefly reviews the history of independent wage commissions in Nigeria and
provides an analysis of their dynamics from their establishment in 1931 to the
Adamolekun Commission Report of 1985. Following a discussion of their organizational
politics, the author makes several specific policy proposals to reduce the need for wage
commissions. However, he concludes that 'it is likely that this method of fixing

remuneration will persist so long as little emphasis is placed on the performance of various parastatals and the main civil service, and so long as positions are regarded primarily as opportunities for dramatically altering one's economic standing' (p. 125). Dr. Otobo is Senior Lecturer, Department of Industrial Relations and Personnel Management, University of Lagos, Yaba, Nigeria.

761 **Bibliography on labour force participation in Nigeria, 1970–1976.**
Compiled by Janet L. Stanley. Montreal, Quebec: McGill University, Centre for Developing-Area Studies, February 1978. 28p.
(Bibliography Series, no. 9).

A very useful listing of 181 sources on the Nigerian labour force, which was then estimated at more than twenty-five million. The entries are organized alphabetically into 'Retrospective studies' (five items), 'Official publications' (twenty-six items), 'International organizations' (five items), and 'General studies' (145 items) and are accessed by a comprehensive subject index. Topics covered by the references include unemployment, economic planning, urbanization and demography. This compilation extends the 890 references in Oluronke O. Orimalade's *Bibliography on labour in Nigeria, 1910–1970* (Lagos: National Library of Nigeria, 1974. 267p. (National Library Publication no. 29)), which includes a list of labour newspapers and a directory of registered trade unions, as of December 1970.

Labour Movement and Trade Unions

762   Labour and politics in Nigeria.
Robin Cohen.   London: Heinemann, 1981. 2nd ed. 304p. bibliog.
This study is a history of the rôle of organized labour in the politics of Nigeria, from the General Strike of 1945 to 1971. The author, Professor of Sociology at the University of Warwick, examines Nigerian political economy, the labour force, the major labour organizations, and trade union leadership and membership, as well as the unions' political and economic rôles and their response to military rule. A final chapter places the Nigerian situation in broader African context. The bibliography (p. 274–91) is extensive. The volume was first published in 1974 (New York: Africana; London: Heinemann, 302p.); this second impression has a new introduction. From 1967 to 1969, Cohen lectured at the Univeristy of Ibadan, Ibadan, Nigeria.

763   Capital and labour in the Nigerian tin mines.
Bill Freund.   Atlantic Highlands, New Jersey: Humanities; London: Longman, 1981. 266p. 3 maps. bibliog. (Ibadan History Series).
Professor Freund examines the history of Nigerian tin mines in the Jos Plateau from the early 1900s to 1979 from a Marxist viewpoint. He seeks to 'marry social history and economic history' (p. 2) as he traces the dissolution of social relations caused by the development of the tin industry. Extensive data on the Birom ethnic group and statistics on the tin mining labour force, production and prices and a full bibliography (p. 236–57) are included. Most of the research for this volume was done while the author was lecturing at Ahmadu Bello University, Zaria, Nigeria, during the 1970s.

764   Foreign interests and Nigerian trade unions.
Dafe Otobo.   Ibadan, Nigeria: Heinemann, 1986; Oxford: Malthouse, 1987. 198p. bibliog. (Malthouse Overseas Monographs).
Professor Otobo places the growth of Nigerian unions and central labour organizations in the context of the country's colonial labour history and the ongoing 'cold war' between Western and communist powers. In addition he presents a detailed examination of the activities and internal workings of the labour unions, usually against

a background of external interests. A longer version of this study formed the author
D.Phil. thesis at Oxford. Otobo also published *Role of trade unions in Nigeria
industrial relations* (Oxford: Malthouse, 1987. 170p.) and with M. Omole edite
Readings in industrial relations in Nigeria (Oxford: Malthouse, 1987. 292p.).

765 **Choice, class and conflict: a study of southern Nigerian factory workers.**
Adrian J. Peace. Brighton: Harvest Press; Atlantic Highlands, New
Jersey: Humanities, 1979. 204p. map. bibliog. (Humanities Studies in
African Political Economy, 1).

The author, an anthropologist at the University of Adelaide, studied the social an
political organization and economic aspects of factory workers employed on the Ikej
Industrial Estate and living in Agege near Lagos during 1970 and 1971. The result is a
informative, straightforward ethnography contributing also to the study of Nigeria
labour unions and worker conditions. A bibliography (p. 193–98) is included.

766 **Conflict and control in an African trade union: a study of the Nigerian
Coal Miners' Union.**
David R. Smock. Stanford, California: Stanford University, Hoover
Institution, 1969. 170p. map. bibliog. (Hoover Institution Studies, 23).

Based on fieldwork in Enugu during 1962–63 and 1964–66 which included numerou
interviews, attendance at union meetings and study of the records of the Nigerian Coa
Miners' Union (NCMU), Professor Smock's account is concerned with NCMU'
history, its structure and internal struggles, union-management relations and attitude
of rank-and-file members. Autobiographical statements of two union leaders ar
included, as is a helpful bibliography (p. 165–70). The coal miners of Enugu ar
ninety-nine per cent Igbo; the mines were closed in September 1967 when captured b
federal forces during the civil war. The author's 1964 doctoral thesis at Corne
University, Ithaca, New York, was *From village to trade union in Africa*.

Statistics

767 **The Nigerian statistical system: retrospect and prospect.**
S. O. Adamu, foreword by R. G. D. Allen.   Ibadan, Nigeria: Ibadan
University, 1978. 221p. bibliog.
The author, a member of the Department of Statistics at the University of Ibadan,
covers official statistical activities in Nigeria to the end of 1975, assesses the Nigerian
statistical system, highlights its main problems and suggests ways to overcome them.
He describes the structure of the national statistical system, the organization of
statistical data – its compilation, processing and publication – and manpower training.
Appendix III lists statistical publications (p. 178–210) and the bibliography lists useful
references (p. 211–14). Also of interest is the *Journal of the Nigerian Statistical
Association*, (Lagos: Nigerian Statistical Association, 1978– . irregular).

768 **Digest of statistics**
Federal Office of Statistics.   Lagos: Federal Office of Statistics, Dec.
1985. 81p.
An excellent compendium of statistical data, which is updated periodically. Data are
presented in twelve categories: population, national accounts, employment, production,
consumption, prices, external trade, balance of payments, transport, public finance,
banking, and social statistics (prison and police reports). The *Annual Abstract of
Statistics 1986 Edition* (Lagos: Federal Office of Statistics, [1988]. 202p.) is an
impressive, invaluable volume of data, most of it current through to 1984 or 1985, on:
area and climate, population and migration, health, manpower and disease, prisons,
crime, employment, education, agriculture, fishing, livestock, mining, production,
transportation and communication, economic conditions, trade, and banking. It has
been published since 1960 in Lagos, often appearing two or three years after the latest
year covered. Both publications are available from the Federal Office of Statistics,
Publications Section, P.M.B. 12528, Lagos, Nigeria.

Statistics

769 **Production and uses of statistics in Nigeria.**
Edited by Badamas Ademola Muhammed. Ibadan, Nigeria: Nigerian Institute of Social and Economic Research; Lagos: Federal Office of Statistics, 1983. 264p. bibliog.
Twenty-seven papers examine aspects of the production of statistics for local government areas, for the Federal Office of Statistics. They examine transport planning, from voters' lists and general sample surveys, methodological problems and strategies, and the various ways in which statistics are used at the local, state and federal levels.

770 **Fourth National Development Plan 1981–85.**
National Planning Office (Federal Ministry of Planning).
Lagos: National Planning Office (Federal Ministry of Planning), Jan. 1981. 2 vols.
The National Development Plans are excellent sources of statistics for all sectors of government and the economy, reviewing past levels of development and projecting national goals. In the Fourth Plan, volume one explains the economic, social and administrative sectors in extensive detail. Volume two consists of a comprehensive list of approved projects by sector and by levels of government with targets and allocations described. The first *National Development Plan 1962–68* (Lagos: Federal Ministry of Economic Development, 1962. 362p.) aimed to 'give a sense of direction to the economy, a sense of priorities and urgency and to enlist the support and co-operation of all sections of the community to work for a better future – their own future' (Chapter I, p. 5). Because of the civil war, the plan was extended to cover 1969–70. For the *Second National Development Plan, 1970–74: programme of post-war reconstruction and development* (Lagos: Federal Ministry of Information, Printing Division, 1970. 344p.) progress reports were published in Lagos in 1972 (312p.) and 1974 (342p.). The *Third National Development Plan, 1975–1980* was published in two volumes in Lagos in 1975.

First things first: meeting the basic needs of the people of Nigeria. Report to the Government of Nigeria by a JASPA basic needs mission.
See item no. 14.

Annual Report on Nigeria.
See item no. 33.

The Nigeria Handbook.
See item no. 34.

Energy in Nigeria.
See item no. 53.

An economic history of Nigeria, 1860–1960.
See item no. 155.

The red book of West Africa: historical and descriptive, commercial and industrial facts, figures, & resources.
See item no. 270.

Nigerian fertility survey, 1981–1982. Preliminary report.
See item no. 324.

288

The 1963 Nigerian census: a critical appraisal.
See item no. 328.

The health of Nigerians, 1983/84. Health and nutrition status survey. (A module of the National Integrated Survey of Households (NISH) April, 1983–March, 1984).
See item no. 551.

Adolesecent fertility in Nigeria.
See item no. 552.

Parties and politics in Northern Nigeria.
See item no. 599.

Nigeria's financial system.
See item no. 724.

Interregional trade and money flows in NIgeria, 1964.
See item no. 726.

Forestry policy in Nigeria, 1897–1960.
See item no. 730.

The Nigerian oil palm industry (government policy and export production, 1906–1965).
See item no. 733.

Nigeria: an export market profile.
See item no. 745.

Africa South of the Sahara 1989.
See item no. 1111.

Environment and Rural and Urban Planning

771 **The economics of afforestation: a case study in Africa.**
Dennis Anderson. Baltimore, Maryland; London: Johns Hopkins
University for the World Bank, 1987. 86p. map. bibliog. (World Bank
Occasional Papers, New Series, no. 1).

Following a general discussion of the problem of deforestation in Africa, the autho
presents a case study of a broad area of northern Nigeria, based on a field trip in Ma
and June 1985. The aim was to assess both previous afforestation programmes in th
region and the prospects for future programmes. He shows that technical solutions t
the ecological problems are well known and, using cost-benefit analysis, he conclude
that 'afforestation programs have low costs per hectare of farmland protected' (p. 3
He urges a positive commitment to rural afforestation and to improving soil and far
management practices. An appendix provides the mathematical background for th
analysis; the bibliography (p. 83–86) is useful.

772 **Urban planning and urban problems in Nigeria.**
Bola Ayeni. *Nigerian Behavioral Sciences Journal*, vol. 1, no. 2
(1978), p. 61–74. bibliog.

The author, a lecturer in the Department of Geography at the University of Ibada
provides insights 'into metropolitan area planning in Nigeria against a background c
planning modes and concepts', arguing that the 'conventional master plan approach
a failure' (p. 72). He discusses the complex needs of Nigerian cities, includes data o
144,164 vehicles registered in Nigeria during the period 1969–72, and provides
framework for urban planning in Nigeria which incorporates a flexible, feed-bac
based programme. Dr. Pius Ogheneruhowho Sada, Professor of Urban Geography a
the University of Benin, Benin City, published *The Nigerian city, its land-use structur
management issues and economic performance: a bibliographic review* (Kuru, Nigeri
National Institute for Policy & Strategic Studies, 1984, 50p. (Urban Studies Serie
Occasional Publication no. 3)) which contains a valuable discussion and extensiv
bibliography (p. 36–50). With C. N. Nwankwo, he edited *1976–77 seminar papers vc
1* (Benin City: Center for Social, Cultural, Environmental Studies, University

3enin, June 1978. 145p.) which contains research reports on: housing in Benin City (by
ada); internal migration (by P. K. Makinwa); population policy (by C. Uche); family
linic use (by A. C. Emovon); and new farming practices (by P. O. Agbonifo).

73   Abuja: the new federal capital of Nigeria, a selected list of references.
Compiled by Beverly Ann Gray.   Washington, DC: Library of
Congress, African Section, African and Middle Eastern Division,
March 1983. 13p. map. (Africana Directions).

This select, annotated list of eighty-nine entries, primarily based on the holdings of the
Library of Congress, provides excellent information on the new federal capital in
Abuja, an 8,000 square kilometre area in the centre of the country. The transfer of the
capital from Lagos to Abuja began with the 1 October 1982 independence celebrations
which were held there. One of the major documents describing the planning for Abuja
is *Nigeria's new federal capital study* by members of the Department of Architecture,
Faculty of Environmental Design, Ahmadu Bello University, Zaria, Nigeria (1976.
28p. maps).

74   The city of Ibadan.
Edited by P. C. Lloyd, A. L. Mabogunje, Bolanle Awe, foreword by
K. O. Dike.   Cambridge: Cambridge University in association with
the Institute of African Studies, University of Ibadan, 1967. 280p.
7 maps. bibliog.

A rich collection of papers presented at a seminar at the Institute of African Studies at
the University of Ibadan in 1964, concerning diverse aspects of 'the largest *inland*
African city south of the Sahara' (Foreword, p. viii). The sixteen papers are organized
under the headings: 'The city', 'Its people', 'Life and work' and 'The future'. The
papers are: 'Introduction' by P. C. Lloyd (p. 3–10); 'Ibadan, its early beginnings' by B.
Awe (p. 11–25); 'The agricultural environment' by H. A. Oluwasanmi (p. 27–33); 'The
morphology of Ibadan' by A. L. Mabogunje (p. 35–56); 'Indigenous Ibadan' by
Barbara B. Lloyd (p. 59–83); 'The Ijebu' by A. L. Mabogunje (p. 85–95); 'The
Western Ibo', by C. Okonjo (p. 97–116); 'The Hausa' by A. Cohen (p. 117–27); 'The
élite' by P. C. Lloyd p. 129–50); 'From traditional crafts to modern industries' by
Archibald Callaway (p. 153–71); 'The markets of Ibadan' by B. W. Hodder
p. 173–90); 'Education expansion and the rise of youth unemployment' by Archibald
Callaway (p. 191–211); 'Government and politics in Ibadan' by G. Jenkins (p. 213–33);
'Traditional religion and Christianity' by E. B. Idowu (p. 235–47); 'Islam' by F. H. El-
Masri (p. 249–57); and 'The problems of a metropolis' by A. L. Mabogunje
p. 261–71).

Urbanization in Nigeria.
See item no. 512.

Yoruba towns.
See item no. 513.

Housing in Nigeria (a book of readings).
See item no. 515.

Urbanization processes and problems in Nigeria.
See item no. 517.

Environment and Rural and Urban Planning

The political history of Nigeria's new capital.
See item no. 616.

Nigeria.
See item no. 1139.

Education

General

775 **Education in Nigeria: a selected and annotated introductory bibliographical survey of current resources.**
Compiled by Adedeji Adelabu. *A Current Bibliography on African Affairs*, vol. 4, no. 2 (March 1971), p. 78–87.
Offers a useful descriptive guide to selected works on education from the author's more comprehensive work in progress, *Literature of education in Nigeria, 1842–1970*. This listing focuses on more recent sources and includes the addresses of serials and periodicals frequently cited. Adelabu was on the staff of the Library at the University of Ife (now Obafemi Awolowo University), Ile-Ife, Nigeria, at the time of publication.

776 **Universal Primary Education in Nigeria: a study of Kano State.**
[Thomas] Mark Bray, foreword by Timo A. F. Afolayan. London; Henley-on-Thames, England; Boston, Massachusetts: Routledge & Kegan Paul, 1981. 212p. 7 maps. bibliog.
In this study, the author examines the achievements, problems and trends of Universal Primary Education (UPE), the free, public education programme begun by the governemnt of Nigeria in 1976. His focus is Kano State, the most populous in Nigeria, for which he provides a history of educational development (1900–76). Other topics include UPE and employment, UPE's social impact, the system's internal quality, and its efficiency. Ample data are presented to support the author's findings; the bibliography (p. 195–209) is extensive. Dr. Bray taught in Kano during 1976–77 and returned for follow-up studies in 1978 and 1980. This work is based on his 1980 PhD thesis at the University of Edinburgh, *The implementation of universal primary education in Kano State, Nigeria: some economic and social implications.*

Education. General

777 **Universal primary education in Nigeria: its problems and implications.**
Mary Csapo. *African Studies Review*, vol. 26, no. 1 (March 1983),
p. 91–106. bibliog.
This informative article uses Nigerian government data to discuss the problems of
underestimation of enrolment, inadequate financing, teacher shortages, the implications
of problems for post-primary institutions and for employment, curriculum, dropouts
and particular educational difficulties of the northern states. The author is a Professor
of Special Education at the University of British Columbia.

778 **History of education in Nigeria.**
Aliu Babs Fafunwa. London: George Allen & Unwin, 1974. 264p.
bibliog.
This informative history describes: 'Traditional African education'; 'Past and present
Muslim education in Nigeria'; 'Early missionary education'; 'The beginnings of modern
education (1882–1929)'; 'Educational expansion (1930–1950)'; 'The era of self-
determination in education (1951–1970)'; 'The Nigerian educational system'; and
several major issues of the early 1960s. Useful appendices (p. 211–50) contain not only
statistics on education but also extracts from important reports on education including
the 'Recommendations of the 1969 National Curriculum Conference'. The bibliography
(p. 251–54) is select, but valuable. The author, who was Dean of the Faculty of
Education, University of Ife, Ile-Ife, at the time of publication, has also published *A
history of Nigerian higher education* (London; Lagos, Nigeria: Macmillan, 1971.
363p.). Ayo Ogunsheye's 'Nigeria' in *Education and political development* (Edited by
James S. Coleman, Princeton, New Jersey: Princeton University, 1965, p. 123–43)
surveys the educational system up to about 1960 with a focus on the relationship
between education and political socialization and the creation of a Nigerian élite.

779 **Society, schools and progress in Nigeria.**
L. John Lewis. Oxford; London; New York: Pergamon, 1965. 160p.
bibliog. (Commonwealth and International Library. Society, Schools
and Progress Series).
This book examines Nigerian education 'with reference to the historical, social and
economic factors and in the context of a policy of development which has as its main
objective the attainment of self-sustaining social and economic growth for the nation'
(p. 3). The volume surveys the history of Nigerian education (1571–1960), its content
and methodology, ancillary education services and university and teacher education. It
constituted a basic text for post-secondary and postgraduate teacher training courses in
Nigeria. Professor Lewis was at the University of London Institute of Education at the
time of publication and was formerly Education Secretary, CMS Yoruba Mission and
Headmaster CMS Grammar School, Lagos, Nigeria. Festus C. Okafor's *Nigeria
teacher education: a search for a new direction* (Enugu, Nigeria: Fourth Dimension,
1988. 173p.) offers an historical overview and practical recommendations.

780 **Nigerian education: a classified bibliography of doctoral dissertations,
1946–1976.**
Compiled by E. S. Muogilim. *A Current Bibliography on African
Affairs*, vol. 14, no. 3 (1981–82), p. 235–50. bibliog.
Offers a very useful listing of 239 American, European and Nigerian dissertations,
grouped under the headings: 'General'; 'Educational administration'; 'Adult education';

'Curriculum and instruction'; 'Guidance and counselling (personnel service in education)'; 'Health and physical education'; 'Higher education'; 'History'; 'Primary'; 'Psychology (including tests and measurement)'; 'Science education'; 'Teaching and teacher education'; 'Theory and practice'; 'Special education'; 'Vocational and business education'; and 'Language and languages'. The author is Principal Librarian, Anambra State College of Education, Awka, Nigeria.

781 **Theses and dissertations on Nigerian education up to 1980.**
Compiled by H. A. Odetoyinbo, E. A. Popoola. Lagos: Libriservice, 1983. 195p.

This excellent listing of 1,718 theses and dissertations is subdivided into numerous categories, and contains a brief introduction, a list of sources consulted and author and institution indexes. *Education in Nigeria: a bibliographic guide* ([Yaba; Lagos]: [n.p.], 1972. 452p.) compiled by N. R. Olu Oshin and H. A. Odetoyinbo contains 2,302 entries alphabetically arranged in ninety categories. There is a brief introduction and an author and title index.

782 **Education & politics in tropical Africa.**
Edited and introduced by Victor C. Uchendu. Owerri, Nigeria; New York; London: Conch Magazine, 1979. 301p. bibliog.

The editor and fifteen contributors present ten essays with comments in the categories: 'The political context of education, unemployment, and ethnicity'; 'Education, politicization and national development'; and 'The politics of educational change'. Although there are essays on Kenya, Tanzania, Mali, Ivory Coast and on Cameroun, most of the studies concern Nigerian educational issues directly or indirectly. Especially useful are: 'Education and ethnic politics in Nigeria' by Okwudiba Nnoli with comment by Ronald Cohen (p. 63–86); 'Urban youth on the margins of Nigerian society: research and theoretical perspectives on the school-leavers' by Albert J. McQueen, with comment by J. Gus Liebenow (p. 87–123); 'Financing Nigerian universities: some current issues' by L. Gray Cowan (p. 217–46); and other essays by William John Hanna, Robert D. Gray, Joel D. Barkam and the editor.

Higher education

783 **The University of Ibadan, 1948–73: a history of the first twenty-five years.**
Edited by J[acob] F[estus] Ade Ajayi, Tekena N. Tamuno. Ibadan, Nigeria: Ibadan University, 1973. 436p. 2 maps.

In thirteen essays, leaders and scholars of the University of Ibadan present a comprehensive story of the development of Nigeria's flagship university. Articles examine the university from historical and from disciplinary perspectives. The articles include: 'The formative years, 1947–56' by Tekena N. Tamuno (p. 22–48); 'The making of the University of Ibadan, 1957–62' by John O. O. Abiri (p. 49–68); 'The university library and related fields' by B. O. Aboyade (p. 127–50); 'The humanities and the social sciences' by A. L. Mabogunje (p. 168–90); 'The basic and applied

sciences' by D. E. U. Ekong (p. 191–214); 'The development of medical education' by
O. O. Akinkugbe (p. 215–36); 'Problems of student welfare' by Obaro Ikime
(p. 237–65); and 'New trends and future prospects' by E. A. Ayandele and T. Ajibol
Taylor (p. 266–81). The appendices (p. 282–427) contain detailed lists of officers,
council members and graduates for each year. Another important account, illustrated
with twenty photographs, is *The birth of Nigeria's university* (London: Methuen, 1958.
263p.) by Kenneth Mellanby, the first Principal of University College, Ibadan,
1947–53.

784 **Commonwealth universities yearbook.**
Association of Commonwealth Universities.   London: Association of
Commonwealth Universities, 1914– . annual.

An excellent, impressively up-to-date annual source for information on universities in
the Commonwealth. For example, one volume, edited by A. Christodoulou and T.
Craig, contains a location map, lists of faculty and administrators and detailed
information on Nigeria's twenty-four federal universities and universities of technology
(vol. 3, 1984. 60th ed. p. 1,987–2,100). The valuable introductory overview
(p. 1,989–92) was contributed by Professor J. F. Ade Ajayi, a leading Nigerian
historian.

785 **The educated elite in the Nigerian society.**
E[mmanuel] A. Ayandele, foreword by H. O. Thomas.   Ibadan,
Nigeria: Ibadan University, 1974. 177p. bibliog.

This book consists of a series of university lectures delivered by Professor Ayandele for
the twenty-fifth anniversary celebrations of the University of Ibadan in 1973. The
stimulating essays are 'Deluded hybrids', covering the pre-colonial period; 'Collabor-
ators', on the colonial period; and 'Windsowers', focusing on the period when the
educated élite began to govern, and a new final chapter 'New Nigerians?', looking at
1966–73.

786 **A critique of technical education in Nigeria.**
Sydney E. Mgbejiofor.   *A Current Bibliography on African Affairs*,
vol. 10, no. 4 (1977–78), p. 301–8. bibliog.

This article criticizes the education provided by trade schools, technical institutes,
colleges of technology and universities, especially for ignoring the 'realities of the labor
market in Nigeria' and for not being 'employment-oriented' (p. 301). Most education
emphasizes preparation for higher levels of schooling and encourages rural-urban
migration. The author makes nine specific recommendations to remedy the situation.
The article derives from his doctoral dissertation *The development of technical
education in Nigeria, 1896–1966* at Walden University, Florida, in 1973.

87   Obafemi Awolowo University, Ile-Ife, Nigeria: decades of service to the
     nation.
     Richard Olaniyan.   Ile-Ife: Obafemi Awolowo University, 1987. 52p.
     map.
A colourful booklet describing the history of the development of the university from its
founding as the University of Ife in 1962 to its rechristening as Obafemi Awolowo
University on 12 May 1987. Eighty-nine colour photographs show the history, buildings
and grounds and personalities associated with the university. Chief Obafemi Awolowo
served as the University's Chancellor, 1967–75. The author is a prominent historian at
the University.

88   Ibadan voices: Ibadan University in transition.
     Edited by T[ekena] N. Tamuno.   Ibadan, Nigeria: Ibadan University,
     1981. 409p.
A valuable collection of seventeen personal accounts with an introduction by the editor
covering experiences and events at Nigeria's premier university from the 1950s to 1980.
The prominent authors include F. J. Ellah, J. D. Omer-Cooper, Adeniyi Williams,
Saburi Biobaku, S. J. Okudu, Emmanuel A. Ayandele, S. O. Adenyemi, and S. O.
Olayide. In addition to thirty pages of plates, the volume's appendices (p. 305–400)
contain notable addresses delivered between 1948 and 1980, and lists of university
officers and members of the council 1973–81 as well as a list of 'Members of the
students' Union Executive, 1948–80' and a table of university financial statistics.
Emmanuel Obiechina, Chukwuemeka Ike and John Anenechukwu Umeh edited *The
University of Nigeria, 1960–1985: an experiment in higher education* (Nsukka, Nigeria:
University of Nigeria, 1986. 657p.) which contains sixteen pages of plates and useful
bibliographies.

89   **Power and privilege at an African university.**
     Pierre L. van den Berghe, with the assistance of Paul Alabi, Catherine
     M. Nuttney, Peter Olori, A. K. Sonaike.   Cambridge, Massachusetts:
     Schenkman, 1973. 273p. bibliog.
This unique work, based on research conducted from July 1968 to June 1969 is 'the first
comprehensive sociological study of an African university' (p. 1), and analyses the
structure and functioning of the 'University of Ilosho' (UI), a pseudonym for the
University of Ibadan, Nigeria's first university. Following his critical examination of
senior and junior staff, students, the rôles of Islam and Christianity and of race and
ethnicity, the African-born author concludes, 'The dynamics of Nigeria, after a decade
of political independence, are still basically the dynamics of a colonial society'. UI, a
late colonial creation, as a 'neo-colonial mandarinate is, not surprisingly, a creditable
intellectual replica of its mentors' (p. 268). Although the bibliography (p. 269–73)
omits sources using the real name of the 'University of Ilosho', it is nevertheless useful.

**What science? Problems of teaching and research in science in Nigerian
universities.**
See item no. 791.

Science and Technology

790 **Scientific research and the Nigerian economy.**
S. Olajuwon Olayide. Ibadan, Nigeria: Ibadan University, 1981.
247p. map. bibliog.

This significant volume examines Nigerian research goals and planning; research in the context of the Nigerian economy; research structures; resources; and types of research in several sectors, these being agriculture, industry, technology, food, medicine and socio-economic research. In addition, the author describes the problems and constraints of research, the framework of research policy, quantitative tests of research policy and each of Nigeria's ten major research institutes. 'This book is an attempt to examine the historical development of scientific and technological research in a rapidly developing economy using the Nigerian situation as a model, and to present an organisational arrangement which would enable scientific and technological research to make the desired impact on the Nigerian socio-economic development process' (Preface, p. v). A. O. Anya's essay *Scientific research and public policy* (Lagos: Nigerian Institute of International Affairs, 1986. 33p. (Lecture Series, 38)) is also an important statement on the topic.

791 **What science? Problems of teaching and research in science in Nigerian universities.**
Edited by F. M. A. Ukoli, Frank Mene Adede-Misinwaye. Ibadan, Nigeria: Heinemann and Ibadan University, 1985. 321p. bibliog.

Twenty essays by Nigerian scientists present a forthright examination of the impacts of the shortage of funds, facilities and manpower on the sciences in Nigerian universities. The papers are grouped into: 'Fundamental issues'; 'Development structure and support services'; 'Case studies' (biology, archaeology, medical sciences and agriculture) and 'Training, assessment, recognition'. Ukoli provides the introduction and a 'Profile of the Nigerian scientist'. Numerous statistics on the science departments and enrolments of thirteen federal universities are presented. The editor is a parasitologist in the Department of Zoology, University of Ibadan, a past President of the Science Association of Nigeria and a Fellow of the Nigerian Academy of Science.

Literature

Literary history and criticism

92   Morning yet on creation day.
Chinua Achebe.   Garden City, New York: Anchor/Doubleday, 1975.
175p.

Here the novelist and poet has compiled fifteen essays written between 1961 and 1975, nine about African writers and writing and six about more personal topics. Part one contains: 'Colonialist criticism'; 'Africa and her writers'; 'Language and the destiny of man'; 'What do African intellectuals read?'; 'The novelist as teacher'; 'Where angels fear to tread'; 'Thoughts on the African novel'; 'The African writer and the English language'; and 'Publishing in Africa: a writers view'. Part two consists of: 'Named for Victoria, Queen of England'; 'Tanganyika – jottings of a tourist'; 'The African writer and the Biafran cause'; 'Dear Tai Solarin'; 'Onitsha, gift of the Niger'; and 'Chi in Igbo cosmology'. Five of these plus ten new essays appear in Achebe's recent *Hopes and Impediments* (London: Heinemann, 1988. 130p.) which is reviewed by Chris Dunton in *West Africa*, no. 3709 (12–18 Sept. 1988), p. 1675.

93   Christopher Okigbo: creative rhetoric.
Sunday O. Anozie.   New York: Africana, 1972. 203p. bibliog.
(Modern African Writers).

This critical study of the poetry of Christopher Ifeanyichukwu Okigbo (16 August 1932–August 1967) was written between 1956 and 1966 by a literary critic who knew the poet well in the early 1960s. Following a biographical sketch and description of Okigbo's literary and intellectual background, the author discusses *Four Canzones: 1957–1961* (q.v.) and the poetry of *Labyrinths* (q.v.) which form 'one single religious epic' (p. 2), 'a complete fusion of sense, sound, structure and vision' (p. 3).

794 **Nigerian literature: a bibliography of criticism, 1952–1976.**
Compiled by Claudia Baldwin. Boston, Massachusetts: G. K. Hall,
1980. 147p. (Bibliographies and Guides in African Studies).

Using the resources of the University Research Library at the University of Californ
at Los Angeles, and the Melville J. Herskovits Library of African Studies
Northwestern University, Evanston, Illinois, the author compiled 1,510 critical iten
on 148 titles by fifty-one Nigerian authors. The compilation begins with the publicatic
in English of Amos Tutuola's novel *The palm-wine drinkard* (q.v.) and Denr
Osadebay's volume of poetry, *Africa sings*. (Ilfracombe, England: A. H. Stockwe
1952. 104p.) The largely unannotated volume includes book reviews, reviews
performances and critical analyses written in French and English, but it does n
include the authors' creative works or any biographical information.

795 **Bibliography of African women writers and journalists (ancient Egypt-
1984).**
Brenda F. Berrian. Washington, DC: Three Continents, 1985. 279p.
bibliog.

This volume provides an enormous amount of useful information about 913 works
European languages and fifty-two works in African languages by 386 authors
folklore and creative literary work, and seventy-four journalists from throughout th
continent. Categories of work covered are: autobiography and biography, fictio
drama, poetry, folklore, miscellaneous prose, journalistic essays, broadcast literatu
and interviews. Other sections provide lists of criticism of the authors' works ar
sources of biographical information. Among the forty-three Nigerian women include
are: Christie Chinwe Achebe, Buchi Emecheta, Flora Nwapa, Dorothy Obi, Omola
Ogundipe-Leslie, Juliet Okonkwo, Mabel Imoukhuede Jolaosa Segun, Zulu Sofola ar
Uwa Udensi.

796 **Writers and politics in Nigeria.**
James Booth. London: Hodder & Stoughton, 1981. 192p. bibliog.

Analyses the political dimensions of the works of Amos Tutuola, Gabriel Okar
Chinua Achebe, T. M. Aluko (notably *One man, one matchet*, London: Heineman
1964. 196p.) and especially of Wole Soyinka (p. 114–70). A recent related maj
publication is *Perspectives on Nigerian literature*, edited by Yemi Ogunbiyi (Lago
Guardian Books, 1988) which collects 100 critical and historical articles from th
Nigerian *Guardian* into two volumes. A review of this by Chris Dunton appears as 'A
impressive roll-call' in *West Africa*, no. 3713 (10–16 Oct. 1988), p. 1894.

797 **Chinua Achebe.**
David Carroll. New York: Twayne, 1970. 156p. bibliog. (Twayne's
World Author Series, no. 101).

This lucid study contains informative essays on Achebe's first four novels, following a
introduction describing the general West African Nigerian and Igbo backgroun
against which he wrote. The notes, references and bibliography (p. 149–53) are bri
but useful. See also G. D. Killam's• *The novels of Chinua Achebe* (New Yor
Africana, 1969. 106p.) which has a similar format.

798   **African literature: a critical view.**
David Cook.   London: Longman, 1977. 240p. bibliog.
Represents a collection of thirteen critical essays on African literature and poetry.
Four concern Nigerian writers: 'The centre holds: a study of Chinua Achebe's *Things fall apart*' (p. 65–81); 'Men fall apart: a study of Chinua Achebe's *No longer at ease*' (p. 82–94); 'Of the strong breed: a study of Wole Soyinka's *Three plays*' (p. 113–27); and 'A good bad heroine: a study of Cyprian Ekwensi's *Jagua Nana*' (p. 144–57). The editor was Professor of English at the University of Ilorin, Nigeria, at the time of publication and had spent fifteen years at Makerere University, Kampala, Uganda.

799   **Ngambika: studies of women in African literature.**
Edited by Carole Boyce Davies, Anne Adams Graves.   Trenton, New Jersey: Africa World, 1986. 298p. bibliog.
Nineteen essays explore various aspects of women in literature and literature by male and female writers from North Africa, Senegal, Kenya, Ghana, and Nigeria. The articles of particular relevance for Nigerian literature are: 'Maidens, mistresses and matrons: feminine images in selected Soyinka works' by Boyce Davies (p. 75–88); 'African womanhood: the contrasting perspectives of Flora Nwapa's *Efuru* and Elechi Amadi's *The concubine*' by Naana Banyiwa-Horne (p. 119–30); 'Reintegration with the lost self: a study of Buchi Emecheta's *Double yoke*' by Marie Linton Umeh (p. 173–80); 'Songs from silence: Hausa women's poetry' by Beverly Mock (p. 181–90); 'Okigbo's *Labyrinths* and the context of Igbo attitudes to the female principle' by Elaine Savory Fido (p. 223–40); and 'Motherhood in the works of male and female Igbo writers: Achebe, Emecheta, Nwapa and Nzekwu' by Boyce Davies (p. 241–56). The Tshiluba phrase *ngambika* means roughly 'help me to balance/carry this load' (p. v).

800   **The rise of the Igbo novel.**
Ernest N. Emenyonu.   Ibadan, Nigeria: Oxford University, 1978. 212p. bibliog.
The author describes Igbo literary origins, the missionary influence, pioneer Igbo writers, and the work of Cyprian Ekwensi and that of Chinua Achebe, focusing on the latter. There is a brief bibliography (p. 199–202). The study is based largely on the author's 1972 University of Wisconsin doctoral dissertation *The development of modern Igbo fiction: 1857–1966*.

801   **Chinua Achebe: bio-bibliography and recent criticism, 1970–75.**
Victoria K. Evalds.   *A Current bibliography on African Affairs*, vol. 10, no. 1 (1977–78), p. 67–87. bibliog.
A biographical and bibliographical essay on Achebe covering the years 1970–75. Evalds summarizes and briefly reviews the famous author's recent works, provides biographical information based on interviews, and discusses the books, monographs and articles analysing Achebe's fiction, poetry and essays. The bibliography lists ninety-four items, fifteen of which are Achebe's own works.

802 **Critical perspectives on Wole Soyinka.**
Edited by James Gibbs. Washington, DC: Three Continents, 1980.
274p. bibliog. (Critical Perspectives, no. 5).

An important and very useful collection of literary criticism of Soyinka's plays, poetry
and prose. The editor's 'Introduction' (p. 3–16), Bernth Lindfors' 'The early writings
of Wole Soyinka' (p. 19–44) and 'Tradition and the Yoruba writer: D. O. Fagunwa,
Amos Tutuola and Wole Soyinka' by Abiola Irele (p. 45–68) provide broad overviews
of the writer. Shorter essays include, amongst others, those by D. S. Izevbaye, Gerald
Moore, D. I. Nwoga, C. Tighe, Omolara Ogundipe-Leslie, Robin Graham and Peter
Enahoro. The selected bibliography (p. 253–72) is an excellent listing of Soyinka's
works, biographical studies, reviews and literary criticism. Dapo Adelugba has edited a
collection of sixteen informative essays by friends and colleagues in *Before our very
eyes: tribute to Wole Soyinka, winner of the Nobel Prize for Literature* (Ibadan,
Nigeria: Spectrum, 1987. 213p.).

803 **Wole Soyinka: a bibliography of primary and secondary sources.**
Compiled by James Gibbs, Ketu H. Katrak, Henry Louis Gates, Jr.
Westport, Connecticut; London: Greenwood, 1986. 107p.
(Bibliographies and Indexes in Afro-American and African Studies,
no. 7).

Following separate prefaces by each compiler are 1,769 unannotated sources (248
primary, 1,521 secondary) arranged by year. Also notable are Malcolm Page's
compilation *Wole Soyinka: bibliography, biography, playography* (London: TQ
Publications, 1979. 17p.) and Greta Margaret Kay Coger's *Index of subjects, proverbs,
and themes in the writings of Wole Soyinka* (New York: Greenwood, 1988. 311p.).

804 **Critical perspectives on Chinua Achebe.**
Edited by Catherine Lynette Innes, Bernth Lindfors. Washington,
DC: Three Continents, 1978. 315p. bibliog. (Critical Perspectives,
no. 4).

Twenty-one essays by twenty scholars offer a detailed examination of Achebe's career
and creative writings. Five are general essays on his work and one is devoted to his
poetry; the remainder focus on his first four novels.

805 **The writing of Wole Soyinka.**
Eldred Durosimi Jones. Portsmouth, New Hampshire: Heinemann,
1988. 3rd ed. 238p. bibliog.

The third edition of Professor Jones' study of Soyinka brings his analysis up to
Soyinka's post-Nobel period and provides commentary on *Aké* (q.v.) and each of his
major works, an updated bibliography and a chronology. The first edition appeared in
1973 as *Wole Soyinka* (London: Heinemann, 183p.) and as no. 256 in Twayne's
World Authors Series (New York: Twayne, 1973. 183p.).

806 **A world of everlasting conflict: Joyce Cary's view of man and society.**
S. H. Kanu. Ibadan, Nigeria: Ibadan University, 1974. 300p. bibliog.
This study examines twelve novels by Joyce Cary, emphasizing the ways in which he expresses his artistic and philosophical views of 'a world in everlasting conflict between the new idea and the old allegiances, new arts and new inventions against the old establishment' (Cary, quoted in Preface, p. ix). Of special interest is Kanu's discussion of the Nigerian novels, *Aissa saved* (q.v.), *The African witch* (q.v.), *An American visitor* (q.v.), and *Mister Johnson* (q.v.) (p. 1–92).

807 **African writers on African writing.**
Edited and introduced by G. D. Killam. Evanston, Illinois:
Northwestern University, 1973. 172p.
Presents critical essays by twenty prominent African writers. Nigerian writers and their articles included are: Chinua Achebe, 'The novelist as teacher', 'Where angels fear to tread' and 'The role of the writer in a new nation'; J. P. Clark, 'Aspects of Nigerian drama'; S. Okechukwu Mezu, 'Poetry and revolution in modern Africa'; and Gabriel Okara, 'African speech . . . English words'. The editor's introduction is very brief, but the notes on contributors (p. 165–67) are useful.

808 **Introduction to Nigerian literature.**
Edited and introduced by Bruce [Alvin] King. London: Evans, 1971;
Lagos: University of Lagos, 1971; New York: Africana, 1972. 216p.
bibliog.
An introduction by the editor and thirteen essays cover a broad spectrum of Nigerian literature in this very useful volume; Yoruba, Hausa and Edo oral poetry are discussed by Wándé Abímbólá, D. Muhammad and E. Ogieiriaixi, respectively. Included are: Ola Rotimi, 'Traditional Nigerian drama' (p. 36–49); Adeboye Babalolá, 'A survey of modern literature in the Yoruba, Efik and Hausa languages' (p. 50–63); O. R. Dathorne, 'Amos Tutuola: the nightmare of the tribe' (p. 64–76); Douglas Killam 'Cyprian Ekwensi' (p. 77–96); John Povey, 'The novels of Chinua Achebe' (p. 97–112); Eldred D. Jones's, 'The essential Soyinka' (p. 113–34); Paul Theroux 'Christopher Okigbo' (p. 135–51); Dan Izevbaye, 'The poetry and drama of John Pepper Clark' (p. 152–73); Abiodun Adetugbo 'Form and style' (p. 173–92); and Clive Wake, 'Nigeria, Africa and the Caribbean: a bird's eye view' (p. 193–208). The volume lacks a comprehensive bibliography and notes on authors, although individual articles have their own bibliographies.

809 **African literatures in the 20th century: a guide.**
Leonard S. Klein, general editor. New York: Ungar, 1986. 245p.
bibliog.
This excellent guide covering most of the continent contains extracts from the *Encyclopedia of world literature in the 20th century* (New York: Ungar, 1984, rev. ed. 5 vols.). Thirty-eight national surveys including northern Africa and forty-three individual articles on major writers and on the concept of *négritude* are included, each with a spartan bibliography. Bernth Lindfors authored the Nigerian literature section (p. 119–41) which describes writing in Hausa, Yoruba and English and the works of writers Chinua Achebe, John Pepper Clark, Cyprian Ekwensi, Gabriel Okara, Christopher Okigbo, Wole Soyinka and Amos Tutuola. Nancy J. Schmidt's thorough analysis of *Children's fiction about Africa in English* (Owerri, Nigeria; New York:

Conch Magazine, 1981, 248p.) identifies that Nigeria is more frequently the geographic setting for the stories than any other locale (p. 61) and contains an excellent bibliography of children's books (p. 225–48).

810 **A writer and his gods: a study of the importance of Yoruba myths and religious ideas to the writing of Wole Soyinka.**
Stephan Larsen. Stockholm: University of Stockholm, Department of the History of Literature, 1983. 239p. bibliog.

Following a biographical essay on Akinwande Oluwole Soyinka (13 July 1934– .) born near Abeokuta in Isara, Ijebu Remo, and a description of Yoruba religion and mythology, the author examines Soyinka's dramatic works, poetry and narrative prose for Yoruba influences. He finds that the god Ogun appears most often, that Soyinka 'regards myth as a means for channelling the power of people into constructive courses' (p. 183), and that mythical figures represent a positive attitude to life since they are largely absent from his most pessimistic works (p. 186–87). The bibliography (p. 217–37) is extensive.

811 **Folklore in Nigerian literature.**
Bernth Lindfors. New York: Africana, 1973. 178p. biblog.

In this 'loose grab bag of ideas' (p. 4), of ten essays written over a six-year period, the author attempts 'to examine the artistic functions of native folklore in modern Nigerian literature in English' (p. 2–3). He asserts that 'each essay was written to prove a particular point, but together they tend to affirm that much African writing, even when done in a foreign language and a Western literary form, remains indelibly African in cultural orientation and style' (p. 4). The essays offer critical perspectives on African folklore and oral tradition; two each discuss Amos Tutuola and Chinua Achebe; one each examines Wole Soyinka and Cyprian Ekwensi; the ninth is 'Heroes and hero-worship in Nigerian chapbooks' and the final describes 'Characteristics of Yoruba and Ibo prose styles in English'. Each essay is self-contained with its own notes and references.

812 **Dem-say: interviews with eight Nigerian writers.**
Edited by Bernth Lindfors. Austin, Texas: University of Texas, African and Afro-American Studies and Research Center, Occasional Publication, 1974. 79p.

Offers very informative, high-content interviews recorded at the authors' homes or at Nigerian universities between December 1972 and May 1973. The authors interviewed were: Michael J. C. Echeruo, Obi Egbuna, Cyprian Ekwensi, John Munonye, Gabriel Okara, Kole Omotoso, Ola Rotimi and Kalu Uka.

813 **A bibliography of literary contributions to Nigerian periodicals, 1946–1972.**
Compiled by Bernth Lindfors. Ibadan, Nigeria: Ibadan University, 1975. 231p. (Ibadan University Library Bibliographical Series, III).

Professor Lindfors compiled 4,137 citations grouped according to subject, poetry, fiction, and drama. He included reviews of stage performances (and Yoruba operas) and articles on radio, television and film, literary criticism, interviews, book reviews, reports on conferences and festivals and miscellaneous essays. This invaluable

Literature. Literary history and criticism

reference work has both author and subject indexes. The research for it was carried out at the Ibadan University Library which was the legal depository for Nigerian publications from 1950–70. Additional items were added from other collections.

814 **Critical perspectives on Amos Tutuola.**
Edited by Bernth Lindfors. Washington, DC: Three Continents, 1975. 318p. bibliog. (Critical Perspectives Series, no. 1). London: Heinemann, 1980. 274p.

The volume is packed with critical assessments of Nigeria's first literary phenomenon, grouped into 'Early reviews', 'Early criticism', 'Later reviews', 'Reappraisals', 'Recent criticism' and concluded by 'Amos Tutuola: a checklist of works, reviews and criticism' (p. 307–18). Reviewers of Tutuola's works include Dylan Thomas, Selden Rodman, Kingsley Amis, Cyprian Ekwensi, Ulli Beier, V. S. Naipaul and Ola Balogun. Notable critical essays include: Gerald Moore's 'Amos Tutuola: a Nigerian visionary' (p. 49–57); Omolara Ogundipe-Leslie's '*The palm-wine drinkard*: a reassessment of Amos Tutuola' (p. 145–53); Charles R. Larson's 'Time, space and description: the Tutuolan world' (p. 171–81); Robert P. Armstrong's 'The narrative and intensive continuity: *The palm-wine drinkard*' (p. 209–35); Sunday O. Anozie's 'Amos Tutuola: literature and folklore, or the problem of synthesis' (p. 237–53); and Lindfors' 'Amos Tutuola: debts and assets' (p. 275–306).

815 **Critical perspectives on Nigerian literatures.**
Edited by Bernth Lindfors. Washington, DC: Three Continents, 1976. 286p. bibliog. (Critical Perspectives Series, no. 3).

This volume's fourteen essays provide a wealth of information on Yoruba, Hausa and Igbo vernacular literatures and on literatures in English, as well as a bibliography by the editor (p. 277–86). Included are: 'Iwi Egungun chants–an introduction' by Oludare Olajubu (p. 3–25); 'Folklore and Yoruba theater' by Oyekan Owomoyela (p. 27–40); 'Trends in the content and form of the 'Opening Glee' in Yoruba drama' by J. A. Adedeji (p. 41–57); '*Wakar Bushiya*: a Hausa satirical poem by Isa Hashim' by Neil Skinner, Tom Allen and Charles N. Davis (p. 59–73); 'The dramatic limits of Igbo ritual' by Michael J. C. Echeruo (p. 75–85); 'Early fiction in Igbo' by Ernest Emenyonu (p. 87–100); 'The narrative and intensive continuity: *The palm-wine drinkard*' by Robert P. Armstrong (p. 103–29); 'Cultural norms and modes of perception in Achebe's fiction' by Lloyd W. Brown (p. 131–45); 'From Hausa to English: a study in paraphrase' by Neil Skinner (p. 147–58); 'Plagiarism and authentic creativity in West Africa' by Donatus I. Nwoga (p. 159–67); 'The early writings of Wole Soyinka' by the editor (p. 169–94); 'The role of the publisher in Onitsha market literature' by Don Dodson (p. 195–213); '*The Horn*: what it was and what it did' by W. H. Stevenson (p. 215–41); and 'The 'communalistic' African and the 'individualistic' Westerner: some comments on misleading generalizations in Western criticisms of Soyinka and Achebe' by J. Z. Kronenfeld (p. 243–70).

816 **Early Nigerian literature.**
Bernth Lindfors. New York, London: Africana, 1982. 198p. bibliog.

Eleven lucid essays reveal the earliest thought and work of several of Nigeria's best-known authors, including: Daniel Olorunfemi Fagunwa; Amos Tutuola; C. O. D. Ekwensi; Onuora Nzekwe; Chinua Achebe; Wole Soyinka; and Christopher Okigbo. In addition, other essays discuss 'Popular literature for an African elite' (p. 75–90) and 'Ladies and gentlemen at Ibadan' (p. 107–10). Meticulous notes accompany each essay,

Literature. Literary history and criticism

some of which first appeared in various journals. More recently, Professor Lindfors has published *Nigeria's first novelists* (Mysore, India: Centre for Commonwealth Literature and Research, University of Mysore, 1986. 157p.) and *The blindmen and the elephant, and other essays in biographical criticism* (Adelaide, Australia: Centre for Research in the New Literature in English, Flinders University of South Australia, 1987. 121p.).

817 **Joyce Cary's Africa.**
M[olly] M[aureen] Mahood. Cambridge: Riverside; Boston, Massachusetts: Houghton Mifflin, 1965. 206p. map. bibliog.

Cary was, at twenty-five, one of six men, out of sixty-four, selected for the Northern Nigerian Political Service in 1913. He served in Bauchi, Gombe and Nafada of Bauchi Province and in Kalama of Borgu division, Kontagora Province, from 1914 continuously until late 1919 or early 1920, except for leaves home. He only visited Nigeria again in 1943. 'Fact' (p. 3–81) provides a reconstruction of Cary's African experiences and 'Fiction' (p. 85–196) analyses Cary's writing and African novels. These are: *Daventry* (unpublished); *Aissa saved* (q.v.); *An American visitor* (New York: Harper, 1961. 247p.); *The African witch* (New York: Harper, 1962. 313p.); *Castle corner* (New York: Harper, 1963. 424p.), and *Mister Johnson* (q.v.). Mahood writes: 'Because it is a world apart, Joyce Cary's Africa . . . is Joyce Cary's Africa and no one else's. It certainly is not the Nigeria of 1915 or 1936 as it might be recalled by the average expatriate of either date. Still less is it a Nigerian's Nigeria . . .' (p. 188). The author was a Professor of English at the University of Ibadan for nine years and made extensive use of Cary's letters and papers in the Bodleian Library at Oxford.

818 **Nigerian writing: Nigeria as seen by her own writers as well as by German authors.**
Edited by A. G. S. Momodu, Ulla Schild. Benin City, Nigeria: Bendel Book Depot; Tübingen, GFR: Horst Erdmann Verlag, 1976. 310p.

This volume includes a wide range of Nigerian writing, offering prose by, among others, C. Ekwensi, Mabel Segun, T. M. Aluko, Amos Tutuola, Chinua Achebe; poetry by Kalu Uka, Pious Oleghe, Wole Soyinka and J. P. Clark; a radio play, *The chewing stick*, by Fela Davies; essays by O. Taiwo, Kalu Uka and Demas Nwoko; and biographical notes. The German contributions are brief accounts by H. Barth, Janheinz Jahn, Ulli Beier, and Ulla Schild, and there is an appendix by K. P. Roos, entitled 'The resonance of the African culture in the work of the Goethe Institute Lagos'.

819 **Wole Soyinka.**
Gerald Moore. New York: Africana, 1971. 114p. bibliog.

The author provides a brief biography and critical analysis of Nigeria's leading playwright, trying to preserve the intimate association of Soyinka's life and work, 'relating each work to the author's total activity in the theater and in society at the time of its conception' (p. 4). Moore describes Soyinka's life from his birth near Abeokuta in 1934 to his twenty-six months in prison between August 1967 and October 1969, and gives special attention to *A dance of the forests* (q.v.), *The interpreters* (q.v.) and to later poetry. The volume contains a selected bibliography (p. 103–04), and four photographs from four different productions. Soyinka and Chinua Achebe are among those discussed in Moore's *Twelve African writers* (Bloomington, Indiana: Indiana University, 1980. 328p.).

820 **In person: Achebe, Awoonor, and Soyinka at the Univerisity of Washington.**
Edited by Karen L. Morell. Seattle, Washington: African Studies Program, Institute for Comparative and Foreign Area Studies, University of Washington, 1975. 163p.

An unusual volume containing the lectures, and discussions in class and on television of three African writers, two Nigerians and a Ghanaian, from a tape recorded at the University of Washington, Seattle, in 1973. Chinua Achebe's lecture 'Africa and her writers' (p. 5–19) appeared later in his *Morning yet on creation day* (q.v.). Wole Soyinka discussed 'Drama and the revolutionary ideal' (p. 61–88) and Kofi Awoonor lectured on 'Tradition and continuity in African literature' (p. 133–45). The work, although edited, preserves the flavour of writers interacting with their audiences. 'Their statements are not revealed truth but are a reflection of their minds in motion at a particular time, with a particular group of people' (Introduction, p. ix).

821 **Critical perspectives on Christopher Okigbo.**
Compiled and edited by Donatus Ibe Nwoga. Washington, DC: Three Continents, 1984. 367p. map. bibliog. (Critical Perspectives Series, no. 21).

A volume combining reviews, critical and memorial essays, interviews, bibliographies and sketches on Nigeria's greatest poet, Christopher Okigbo (1932–67). Following essays by Chinua Achebe and the editor are twenty-one reviews and studies (by Ulli Beier, D. Williams, S. O. Anozie, N. J. Udoeyop, D. S. Izevbaye, Obiora Udechukwu, O. R. Dathorne, M. Ruykeyser, J. A. Adedeji, D. I. Nwoga, R. N. Egudu, N. J. Udoeyup and I. Ikiddeh) of Okigbo's main works (*Heavensgate, Limits*, 'Silences', 'Distances', *Path of thunder*, and *Labyrinths* (q.v.)). In addition, four interviews with Okigbo and seven general essays by Paul Theroux, O. R. Dathorne, Gerald Moore, Omolara Ogundipe-Leslie, D. S. Izevbaye, A. Nazombe and R. Egudu are included. The bibliographies by J. C. Anafulu and Bernth Lindfors (p. 349–64) are excellent. See also Ali Mazrui's *The trial of Christopher Okigbo* (London: Heinemann, 1971. 145p. (AWS 97)).

822 **Onitsha market literature.**
Edited by Emmanuel N[wanonye] Obiechina. London; Ibadan, Nigeria: Heinemann, 1972. 182p. bibliog. (African Writers Series, no. 109).

This useful volume contains an informative introduction (p. 3–30) discussing the background, authorship, readership, content and influences on the popular chapbooks published in hundreds of titles in Onitsha since 1947. The majority of the book (p. 33–174) consists of selections from twenth-three different texts, including, for example Ogali A. Ogali's 'Veronica makes up her own mind' from *Veronica my daughter*, (Enugu, Nigeria, 1956. 40p.), A. Onwudiwe, pseud. Speedy Eric's 'Mabel the sweet honey that poured away' from *Mabel* (Onitsha, Nigeria: A. Onwudiwe, [n.d.] 72p.), and Highbred Maxwell's 'Love is a walking shadow' from *Public opinion on lovers* (Onitsha, Nigeria: [n.p.] 1962. 46p.). Dr. Obiechina (1933– .) wrote his doctoral dissertation at Cambridge University on *Cultural change and the novel in English in West Africa* and has been Associate Editor for the literary journals *Okike* (n.v.) and *Conch* (q.v.).

Literature. Literary history and criticism

823 **An African popular literature: a study of Onitsha market pamphlets.**
Emmanuel Obiechina, foreword by Chinua Achebe. Cambridge:
Cambridge University, 1973. 246p. bibliog.

About half of this volume consists of an extended examination of the appearance,
themes and influences of the remarkable Nigerian pamphlet literature which first
appeared in 1947 in the market town of Onitsha with the publication of two booklets
by Cyprian Ekwensi, *Ikolo the wrestler and other Ibo tales* (Onitsha, Nigeria: Tabansi
Bookshop, 1947.) and *When love whispers* (Onitsha, Nigeria: Tabansi Bookshop, 1947.
44p.). In addition, the appendix contain three typical pamphlets in facsimile, *Our
modern ladies characters towards boys* by Highbred Maxwell (Onitsha, Nigeria:
Students Own Bookshop, 1959. 23p.); *Elizabeth, my lover* by Okenwa Olisah
(Onitsha, Nigeria: A. Onwudire, 1940 [n.p.]) and *What women are thinking about men*
by J. O. Nnandozie (Onitsha, Nigeria: J.C. Brothers Bookshop, [n.d.] 39p.). 'A
bibliography of the pamphlet literature' (p. 237–44) and index conclude the volume.
An earlier version of this work was published as *Literature for the masses – a study of
Onitsha market literature* (Enugu, Nigeria: Nwank wo-Ifejika, 1971. 84p.). The author
was Lecturer in English, University of Nigeria, Nsukka, at the time of publication.

824 **Culture, tradition and society in the West African novel.**
Emmanuel Obiechina. Cambridge: Cambridge University, 1975.
296p. bibliog. (African Studies Series, 14).

The author provides a detailed study of the relationship between society and literature
beginning with the general background to the West African novel and examining oral
and literary traditions, nature, music and art, characterization, space and time, setting,
language, culture contact and culture conflict. Most of the books analysed are by
Nigerians, including Chinua Achebe,T. M. Aluko, Elechi Amadi, Cyprian Ekwensi,
Ndem Nwankwo, Onuorah Nzekwu, Gabriel Okara and Wole Soyinka. This book is a
variation of the author's Cambridge University doctoral thesis entitled *Cultural change
and the novel in English in West Africa*. An earlier valuable study is Margaret
Laurence's *Long drums and cannons: Nigerian dramatists and novelists 1952–1966*
(London: Macmillan, 1968. 209p.) in which she examines the works of Wole Soyinka,
J. P. Clark, Chinua Achebe, Amos Tutuola, Cyprian Ekwensi, T. M. Aluko, Elechi
Amadi, Nkem Nwankwo, Flora Nwapa, Onuora Nzekwu and Gabriel Okara.

825 **New African literature and the arts.**
Edited by Joseph [Ohiomogben] Okpaku. New York: Crowell, in
association with Third Press, 1970, 1973. 3 vols. bibliog.

Each volume compiles critical essays on the arts, poetry, short stories and drama, by a
wide range of African authors, originally published in the *Journal of the New African
Literature and the Arts* (1966– . irreg.) and contains notes on the contributors. Many of
the authors and the works discussed are Nigerian. Examples include: volume one,
'Changing themes in the Nigerian novel' by John F. Povey (p. 27–41); and 'The hole in
the dark' (p. 170–76) and 'Born astride the grave' (p. 237–74) by the editor; volume
two, 'The writer in politics – Christopher Okigbo, Wole Soyinka and the Nigerian
crisis' (p. 3–24) by the editor; 'Achebe's Christ-figure' by Donald J. Weinstock
(p. 56–65); and 'Caesar crosses the Niger: Shakespeare and Onitsha market
chapbooks' by Gene Ulansky (p. 66–71); volume three, 'The battle for cultural
freedom' by Ben Enwonwu (p. 45–48); and 'The development of theatre in Nigeria
1960–67' by Ernest Ekom (p. 265–83). The editor has been an engineer, playwright,
novelist and publisher; among his other works is included *Nigeria: dilemma of
nationhood* (Westport, Connecticut: Greenwood, 1972).

826 **A dance of masks: Senghor, Achebe, Soyinka.**
Jonathan A. Peters. Washington, DC: Three Continents, 1978. 270p.
bibliog.

This critical study of Léopold Sédar Senghor of Senegal and the most famous writers of
Nigeria, Chinua Achebe and Wole Soyinka, emphasizes each writer's 'vision of culture
and society in relation to history' (p. 11), drawing upon the cultural and metaphysical
theme of the mask wherever each writer uses it. Achebe's first four novels and four of
Soyinka's plays (*A dance of the forests*, *The road*, *Kongi's harvest*, and *Madmen and
specialists* (q.v.)) are analysed in detail. 'A dance of masks' is used by the author to
mean 'the dynamic interplay of mask and masker in a dance of celebration' (Preface,
p. ix), an idea evoked by scenes the author witnessed as a child in Freetown, Sierra
Leone. An analysis of time, character, narrative structure and symbols guide Bonnie
Jo Barthold's 1975 doctoral thesis in English at the University of Arizona, *Three West
African novelists: Chinua Achebe, Wole Soyinka, and Ayi Kwei Armah* (Available
from University Microfilms, Ann Arbor, Michigan, 1976. Order no. 76-1598).

827 **African writers talking: a collection of radio interviews.**
Edited by Cosmo Pieterse, Dennis Duerden. New York: Africana,
1972. 195p.

A collection of interviews with sixteen writers which were conducted in the 1960s,
primarily at the Transcription Centre in London. Interviews with Nigerian writers
include: Chinua Achebe, interviewed by Lewis Nkosi in 1962, by Donatus Nwoga in
1964, by Duerden in 1965, and by Robert Serumaga in 1966; J. P. Clark, interviewed
by Nkosi in 1962, and by Andrew Salkey in 1964; Cyprian Ekwensi, interviewed by
Nkosi in 1962 and by Duerden in 1964; Christopher Okigbo, interviewed by Nkosi
in 1962, by Duerden in 1963, and by Serumaga in 1965; and Wole Soyinka, interviewed
by Ezekiel Mphahlele in 1962, by Nkosi in 1962, and by Duerden in 1963. A
photograph and brief biographical notes are included for each author.

828 **Mother is gold: a study in West African literature.**
Adrian A. Rosco. London: Cambridge Univeristy, 1971. 273p.
bibliog.

Although the author refers to Ghanaian, Sierra Leonian, Gambian and Francophone
works, this is primarily a study of Nigerian literature, including children's literature,
Onitsha Market pamphlets, journalism and political writing. In particular he discusses
poets Wole Soyinka, J. P. Clark, Michael Echeruo, Gabriel Okara, Christopher
Okigbo and Dennis Osadebay; dramatists Wole Soyinka, J. P. Clark, Obatunde
Ijimere, Duro Ladipo, and Hubert Ogunde; prose writers Chinua Achebe and Cyprian
Ekwensi; political writers Sir Ahmadu Bello, Nnamdi Azikiwe and Tai Solarin; and
finally, Amos Tutuola, 'the unselfconscious eccentric who refuses to fit neatly into
traditional categories' (p. 98).

829 **An anthropological analysis of Nigerian fiction.**
Nancy Jeanne Schmidt. PhD thesis, Northwestern University,
Evanston, Illinois, 1965. 398 leaves. bibliog. (Available from University
Microfilms, Ann Arbor, Michigan, 1966. Order no. 66-2740).

The author analyses 226 works of Nigerian prose fiction (novels, short stories, plays
and chapbooks) and considers their sociocultural milieu to establish an ethnographic
view of Nigerian society. Dr. Schmidt discusses anthropological methods of studying

Literature. Literary history and criticism

literature; the context in which the works were written, including characteristics of the authors; and the fiction itself, especially its relation to oral traditions, naming, proverb and the influence of kinship bonds in the stories. Plot summaries, author data and a full bibliography for the works are included. Other publications by the prolific author include two brief articles: 'Nigeria: fiction for the average man', *Africa Report*, vol. 10 no. 8 (Aug. 1965), p. 39–41, and 'Nigerian fiction and the African oral tradition' *Journal of the New African Literature and the Arts*, vol. 5–6 (1968), p. 10–19. Schmid is African Studies Area Specialist at the Indiana University Library, Bloomington Indiana.

830   **Myth, literature and the African world.**
Wole Soyinka. London; Cambridge: Cambridge University, 1976. 168p bibliog.
This volume contains Soyinka's four lectures on literature and society delivered to the Department of Social Anthropology at Cambridge University: 'Morality and aesthetic in the ritual archetype' (considering the Yoruba deities Ogun, Obatala and Shango in myth and drama); 'Drama and the African world-view'; 'Ideology and the social vision (1): the religious factor'; and 'Ideology and the social vision (2): the secular ideal'. The appendix, 'The fourth stage: through the mysteries of Ogun to the origin of Yoruba tragedy' was published earlier in *The morality of art*, edited by D. W. Jefferson (London: Routledge & Kegan Paul, 1969, p. 119–34). Recently Soyinka published *Art dialogue and outrage: essays on literature and culture* (Ibadan: New Horn, 1988. 344p.) The collection is described by Kole Omotaso in *West Africa*, no. 3719 (21–27 Nov 1988), p. 2191, and is exclusively distributed by Hans Zell Associates, P.O. Box 56 Oxford OX1 3EL.

831   **Culture and the Nigerian novel.**
Oladede Taiwo.   New York: St. Martin's, 1976. 235p. bibliog.
This valuable study examines how Nigerian novelists have linked indigenous culture with modern experience. 'The Nigerian novel is seen in this book as an attempt to transliterate traditional customs, beliefs and attitudes into an entirely new context, that of the twentieth century, employing a language to which the modern reader can respond' (Preface, p. xiii). The author assesses the works of Amos Tutuola, Chinua Achebe, T.M. Aluko and Onuora Nzekwu at length and more briefly selected novels of Tafawa Balewa, Obi Egbuna, Adaora Ulasi, Nkem Nwankwo, Gabriel Okara and Elechi Amadi. In 'Historical and cultural influences on the Nigerian novelist' he describes two novels by Joyce Cary, *The African witch* (q.v.) and *Mister Johnson* (q.v.). Precise notes and the bibliography (p. 225–30) are very helpful. The author was at the University of Lagos at the time of publication.

832   **Three Nigerian poets: a critical study of the poetry of Soyinka, Clark and Okigbo.**
Nyong J. Udoeyop.   Ibadan, Nigeria: Ibadan University, 1973. 166p. bibliog.
Provides both useful biographical information and thoughtful analyses for each poet discussed. Part of the book came from the author's 1970 MA dissertation at York University, Toronto.

833 **Achebe's world: the historical and cultural context of the novels of Chinua Achebe.**
Robert M. Wren. Washington, DC: Three Continents, 1980; Harlow, England: Longman, 1981. 166p. map. biblog. (Longman Studies in African Literature).

A rich source of detailed information on the novelist (16 November 1930– .), his works and his culture. Following notes on texts, names, money and pidgin English, the author offers a biography, a social and religious history of the Igbo area east of Onitsha and chapters on Achebe's first four novels. Very useful are the extensive glossary (p. 119–39), general bibliography (p. 140–44) and 'Bibliography of publications by and about Chinua Achebe' (p. 145–59). Dr. Wren is Professor of English at the University of Houston in Texas, spent three years as Visiting Senior Lecturer at the University of Lagos, and has published several other articles on Achebe, notably 'Achebe's revisions of *Arrow of Gold*' in *Research in African Literatures*, vol. 7 (1976), p. 53–58.

834 **J. P. Clark.**
Robert M. Wren. Boston: Twayne, 1984; Lagos: University of Lagos, 1985. 181p. bibliog. (Twayne's World Authors Series 734. African Literature).

The first full-length study of John Pepper Clark (6 April 1935– .) from Kiagbodo, Warri Province, Bendel State, contains a biography and analysis of his works, a chronology of Clark's life and a useful bibliography (p. 171–75). Professor Wren taught at the University of Lagos, 1972–75, in the English Department which was headed then by Clark.

Periodicals

835 **Black Orpheus. A Journal of the Arts in Africa.**
Lagos, Nigeria: University of Lagos, Department of English, 1957– . biannual.

While publishing articles 'creative or critical, on any topic in literature, music, painting, sculpture and other art forms' (publisher's note), *Black Orpheus* has published the work of many of Nigeria's, and indeed Africa's, best-known writers and artists. Presently edited by Theo Vincent, its editorial address is c/o Department of English, Faculty of Arts, University of Lagos, Lagos, Nigeria. A lengthy essay by Peter Benson, "Border operators' : *Black Orpheus* and the genesis of modern African art and literature', *Research in African Literatures*, vol. 14, no. 4 (winter 1983), p. 431–73, describes the founding of 'Nigeria's pioneer cultural journal' by Ulli Beier and its evolution under Abiola Irele and J. P. Clark.

836 **Okike. An African Journal of New Writing.**
Nsukka, Nigeria: Okike Magazine, 1971– . three times yearly.

Edited by Chinua Achebe, a typical issue of this literary journal contains poetry, fiction, essays, an interview with an African writer, 'controversy and commentary' and reviews.

311

Literature. Performing arts (theatre, dance and oral arts)

837 **Research in African Literatures.**
Austin, Texas: University of Texas, 1970– . quarterly.
Represents an excellent source of critical essays, bibliographies and reviews of works in literature and the arts as well as periodic lists of relevant dissertations. Nigerian materials are in nearly every issue. A 'Special issue on Wole Soyinka', edited by James Gibbs, appeared in vol. 14, no. 1 (spring 1983). Recent articles on Nigerian literature include J. O. J. Nwachukwu-Agbada's 'A bibliography [with abstracts] of PhD dissertations on Africa, Caribbean, and Afro-American literatures completed in the English Department, University of Ibadan, Nigeria, 1968–86', vol. 18, no. 3 (autumn 1987), p. 343–47; and Craig W. McLuckie's 'A preliminary checklist of primary and secondary sources on Nigerian Civil War/Biafran War literature', vol. 18, no. 4 (winter 1987), p. 510–27.

Performing arts (theatre, dance and oral arts)

838 **Yoruba oral tradition: poetry in music, dance and drama.**
Edited by Wande Abimbola. Ile-Ife, Nigeria: Department of African Languages and Literatures, University of Ife, 1975. 1,093p. map. bibliog. (Ife African Languages and Literatures Series, no. 1).
This volume contains twenty-six selections from a seminar of the same title, held at the Institute of African Studies, University of Ife, in January 1974. The papers cover archaeology and oral history, urbanization and oral history, traditional education, thought, music, oral literature, oral poetry, folktales, two early poets, and folk theatre. Among the contributors are Richard Olaniyan, Robert G. Armstrong, Adeboye Babalola, Ayo Bamgbose and Val Olayemi.

839 **Essays on African literature.**
Edited by W. L. Ballard, Mary Twining. Atlanta, Georgia: School of Arts and Sciences, Georgia State University, June 1973. 195p. bibliog. (Spectrum. Monograph Series in the Arts and Sciences, vol. III).
A collection of essays, all but one of which are Nigerian in focus, on traditional oral literature and its transition to written, Westernized forms. The essays include: Olatunde Olatunji, 'Yoruba oral poetry: the feature types'; Adeboye Babalola 'Yoruba poetic language: transition from oral to written forms'; Joel 'Yinka Adedeji 'The literature of the Yoruba opera'; Bernth Lindfors, 'Wole Soyinka and the horses of speech'; Neil Skinner and Kabir Galadanci, 'Wakar soja ['song for the soldiers'] – a Hausa poem of the civil war'; Mervyn Hiskett, 'The origin, sources, and form of Hausa Islamic verse'; Ayo Banjo, 'Aspects of Tutuola's use of English'; and Susan M Greenstein, 'Cyprian Ekwensi and Onitsha market literature'.

Literature. Performing arts (theatre, dance and oral arts)

840   **African theatre today.**
Martin Banham, Clive Wake.   London: Pitman, 1976. 103p. bibliog.
(Theatre Today Series).

Gives an introduction to the major playwrights of East and West Africa who write in English, French and Yoruba. After a short introduction, Nigerian theatre (p. 8–50) receives the most coverage in this small volume, because 'there is a richness and a variety not to be found elsewhere in the continent' (p. 8). Nigerian writers critically discussed are Hubert Ogunde, Kola Ogunmola (d. 1972), Duro Ladipo, Ola Rotimi, J. P. Clark, Wole Soyinka, James Ene Henshaw and Obi B. Egbuna. The playlist (p. 93–99) contains a wide range of published plays in English and French.

841   **Hubert Ogunde: the making of Nigerian theatre.**
Ebun Clark.   London: Oxford University, 1979. 170p. bibliog.

This historical study, based more on newspaper articles than oral evidence, surveys the professional theatre of Hubert Ogunde from 1944 to 1977. Ogunde (1916– .), the 'doyen of Nigerian theatre', produced some fifty-one plays and operas in English and Yoruba, all premiering at Glover Hall in Lagos, until 1968. The study stresses Ogunde's cultural nationalism and important rôle in the movement toward Nigerian independence; it also analyses the theatre's evolving form and content over thirty years. Included are fourteen photographs; appendices, one with his canon of plays; and a brief bibliography (p. 163–66). This is a revision of the author's 1974 University of Leeds M.Phil. thesis; she is now Senior Lecturer in English at the University of Lagos and is married to John Pepper Clark a writer whose works appear elsewhere in this bibliography. She has also published 'The Nigerian theatre and the nationalist movement' in *Nigeria Magazine*, nos. 115–16 (1975), p. 24–33.

842   **A history of Hausa Islamic verse.**
Mervyn Hiskett.   London: School of Oriental and African Studies, University of London, 1975. 274p. bibliog.

This essay in literary history aims 'to describe the development of Hausa Islamic verse in its various genres, and the ideas and attitudes that gave rise to it'. The author describes and analyses admonitory verse, prophetic panegyric and biography, legal and theological versification, mystical verse, the verse of political and social protest, astrological and numerological verse, Hausa verse chronicling, the Islamic tradition in modern Hausa verse, poetic techniques, standards of criticism and appreciation and the place and function of Islamic verse in Hausa society. Hausa texts are appended (p. 197–256) and there is a brief glossary of recurrent Arabic and Hausa words. The selected bibliography (p. 259–62) contains Arabic works, Hausa works and more general works. The author's 1969 London PhD thesis was *Hausa Islamic verse: its sources and development prior to 1920.*

843   **The Yoruba popular travelling theatre of Nigeria.**
'Biodun Jeyifo.   Lagos: Department of Culture, Federal Ministry of Social Development, Youth, Sports and Culture, 1984. 213p. bibliog.
(A Nigeria Magazine Publication).

A fascinating illustrated description and critical study of the Yoruba Travelling Theatre by a member of the Literature in English Department of the University of Ife. In late 1981 when the book was written there were well over 100 theatre troupes in the

Literature. Performing arts (theatre, dance and oral arts)

Yoruba Travelling Theatre movement. Appendices contain interviews with three actor-managers; three representative scenarios and a list of 115 troupes. The bibliography (p. 204–10) is extensive for the topic.

844 **Theatre in Africa.**
Edited by Oyin Ogunba, Abiola Irele. Ibadan, Nigeria: Ibadan University, 1978. 224p. bibliog.

In an introduction by Ogunba (p. ix–xv) and ten essays, African drama and theatre from Nigeria, Ghana, Francophone Africa, East Africa, South Africa and Arabic drama in North Africa are discussed. Five articles concern Nigerian performances: 'Traditional African festival drama' by Oyin Ogunba (p. 3–26); ''Alarinjo': the traditional Yoruba travelling theatre' by Joel Adedeji (p. 27–51); 'Tiger on stage: Wole soyinka and Nigerian theatre' by Femi Osofisan (p. 151–76); 'J. P. Clark: his significance as dramatist' by Albert Olu Ashaolu (p. 177–200); and 'Wale Ogunyemi, 'Zulu Sofola and Ola Rotimi: three dramatists in search of a language' by Dapo Adelugba (p. 201–20). The senior editor (Ogunba) is Professor and Head of the Department of Literature in English, Obafemi Awolowo University, Ile-Ife, Nigeria.

845 **Drama and theatre in Nigeria: a critical sourcebook.**
Edited by Yemi Ogunbiyi. Lagos: Nigerian Magazine, Department of Culture, Federal Ministry of Social Development Youth, Sports and Culture, 1981. 522p. bibliog. (A Nigeria Magazine Publication).

A *smorgasbord* of thirty articles, some original, most reprinted from varied sources, especially *Nigeria Magazine*, emphasizing traditional theatre, Yoruba travelling theatre, the literary tradition in theatre and television drama and theatre management, organization and production. Articles concern the Yoruba, Bornu, Hausa, Igbo, Kalabari and Urhobo cultures. Selected titles include: J. P. Clark, 'Aspects of Nigerian drama' (p. 57–76); Ola Rotimi, 'The drama in African ritual display' (p. 77–80); Robin Horton, 'The gods as guests: an aspect of Kalabari religious life' (p. 81–113); E. O. Kofoworola,'Traditional forms of Hausa drama' (p. 164–80); Ulli Beier, 'E. K. Ogunmola: a personal memoir' (p. 321–32); Wole Soyinka, 'Towards a true theatre' (p. 457–61); and nine others. Other authors include Yemi Ogunbiyi, James Amankular, Onuora Nzekwu, M. J. C. Echeruo, Ossie Enekwe, Andrew Horn, Dapo Adelugba, J. A. Adediji, Edith Enem, R. T. E. Ellison, C. G. B. Gidley and Ebun Clark. The bibliography (p. 519–22) lists dissertations and theses as well as books and articles. The editor teaches literature and drama at Obafemi Awolowo University, Ile-Ife, Nigeria.

846 **The Ozidi saga, collected and translated from the Ijǫ of Ǫkabou Ojobolo.**
J. P. Clark. Ibadan, Nigeria: Ibadan University and Oxford University, 1977. 408p.

A remarkable epic from the Niger Delta, published in parallel columns of Ijǫ and English. In the lengthy critical introduction (p. xv–xxxvii), Clark explains the linguistic difficulties with the original text presented to him by Thomas Onduku and Kay Williamson, and describes the Ijǫ language and Ozidi myth. The generations-old saga is a seven-night-long performance about Ozidi 'a supreme warrior who has to perform a number of seemingly impossible feats to reach a destined end' (p. xx). Clark and

Frank Speed made a film version of the saga, *Tides of the Delta* (distributed by Colour Film Services, London) and *Songs from 'The Ozidi saga'*, an album of three long-playing records, was released by EMI for the Institute of African Studies, University of Ibadan, Ibadan, Nigeria.

847 **Features of Yorùbá oral poetry.**
Olatunde O. Ọlatunji. Ibadan, Nigeria: University Press, 1984. 267p. bibliog.

This excellent volume seeks to establish objective criteria for the criticism of Yorùbá poetry. The author describes general features of oral poetry including repetition, word play, metaphors and rhythm, and considers five categories of oral expression: 'Oríkì: Yorùbá praise poetry'; 'Ese ifá: ifá divination poetry'; 'Ọfọ: Yorùbá incantations'; 'Òwe: proverbial expressions of the Yorùbá'; and 'Alóàpamò: Yorùbá riddles'. A useful bibliography (p. 247–61) is provided as are notes and extensive examples in both Yorùbá and English. This study was originally the author's 1970 doctoral thesis at the University of Ibadan, entitled *Characteristic features of Yorùbá oral poetry*. Olatunji is Head of the Department of Linguistics and Nigerian Languages at the University of Ibadan.

Anthologies

848 **Political spider: an anthology of stories from *Black Orpheus*.**
Edited by Ulli Beier. New York: Africana; London: Heinemann, 1969. 118p. (African Writers Series, no. 58).

Offers seventeen stories which appeared in the literary magazine *Black Orpheus* between 1963 and 1966. 'Nigeria has the largest share in this anthology – simply because more good stories were submitted to the magazine from this country than from elsewhere' (Introduction, p. vii). The stories of three Yoruba writers are included: D. O. Fagunwa's story 'Kako', translated by Wole Soyinka; 'Ajaiyi and the witch doctor' by Amos Tutuola; and 'The mouth that commits an offence' by Bakare Gbadamosi. In addition, there are two stories by Chinua Achebe, 'The voter' and 'Uncle Ben's choice'. The title is taken from Caribbean writer Andrew Salkey's story 'Political spider'.

849 **Yoruba poetry: an anthology of traditional poems.**
Compiled and edited by Ulli Beier, illustrated by Susanne Wenger.
Cambridge: Cambridge University, 1970. 126p. bibliog.

Presents a marvellous collection of Yoruba poetry and twenty-one riddles. Translations to English were made by the editor, Bakare Gbadamosi, Bolaji Idowu, Duro Ladipo, Laoye I, Timi of Ede, Ademola Onibon-Okuta and Pierre 'Fatumbi' Verger. The poetry is grouped around topics: gods, kings and towns, the oracle, magic formulae, medicinal herbs, funerals, marriage, 'comments', animals and plants, ballads, children, and riddles. Beier also introduced and provided notes for *Three Nigerian plays* (Harlow, England: Longmans, 1967. 89p.). The plays were: *Moremi* by Duro Ladipo; *The scheme* by Wale Ogunyemi; and *Born with fire on his head* by Obotunde Ijimere. Beier adapted to English *Three Yoruba plays* (Ibadan, Nigeria: Mbari, 1964. 75p.) by Duro Ladipo, the plays being *Oba Koso*, *Oba Moro*, and *Oba Waja*.

850 **Poems from black Africa.**
Edited by Langston Hughes. Bloomington, Indiana; London: Indiana
University, 1963. 160p.

Among the poetry from fifteen sub-Saharan African countries collected here is a
sampling of Nigerian verse in English (p. 82–104). Francesca Yetunde Pereira, Frank
Aig-Imoukhuede, John Pepper Clark, Christopher Okigbo, Chuba Nweke, Dennis C.
Osadebay, Adebayo Faleti and Wole Soyinka are included, as are translations by Ulli
Beier of several traditional Yoruba poems and an Igbo poem. Brief biographical notes
appear at the volume's end (p. 151–58).

851 **The word is here: poetry from modern Africa.**
Edited by Keorapetse Kgositsile. Garden City, New York:
Anchor/Doubleday, 1973. 173p. bibliog.

This selection of the work of twenty-three poets from throughout the continent,
includes Nigerians J. P. Clark (1935–.), Ifeanyi Menkiti (1940–.), Gabriel Okara
(1921–.), Christopher Okigbo (1932–67) and Wole Soyinka (1934–.). Brief
biographical notes are supplied.

852 **Plays from black Africa.**
Edited and introduced by Fredric M. Litto. New York: Hill & Wang,
1968. 316p.

Two of the six plays in this volume are by Nigerians. John Pepper Clark's well-known
Song of a goat (p. 73–127) concerns the themes of barrenness, impotence and love
among members of a family in a Niger Delta village. James Ene Henshaw's *The jewels
of the shrine* (p. 273–93) is about the supposed treasure two greedy, disrespectful
grandsons think their grandfather will leave them. Other plays are by Lewis Nkosi
(South Africa), Alfred Hutchinson (South Africa), Efua T. Sutherland (Ghana) and
Henry Ofori (Ghana). The editor supplies an informative introduction (p. vii–xvii) and
biographical notes.

853 **The Penguin book of modern African poetry.**
Edited by Gerald Moore, Ulli Beier. Harmondsworth, England:
Penguin, 1984. 3rd ed. 315p. bibliog.

The third edition of this well-known anthology offers more than 200 poems by sixty-
seven poets in twenty-three countries. More poets from Nigeria are represented than
from any other country: Gabriel Okara; Christopher Okigbo; Wole Soyinka; John
Pepper Clark; Frank Aig-Imoukhuede (1935–.); Okogbule Wonodi (1936–.);
Michael Echeruo (1937–.); Pol N. Ndu (1940–78); Onwuchekwa Jemie (1940–.);
Aig Higo (1942–.); Molara Ogundipe-Leslie (c. 1940–.); Niyi Osundare (1947–.);
Odia Ofeimun (1950–.); and Funso Aiyejina (1950–.). The volume also includes
brief notes on the authors, sources of the poems and an index of first lines. Earlier
editions were published as *Modern poetry from Africa* (1963, 1968).

854 **African writing today.**
Edited by Ezekiel Mphahlele. Harmondsworth, England: Penguin,
1967. 347p.

Poems, short stories and extracts from longer works by forty-two writers from sixteen
sub-Saharan nations are included in this anthology which is 'intended to give the

ntelligent reader a map of themes and styles of African writing in the metropolitan anguages – English, French, and Portuguese' (Introduction, p. 11). Representing Nigerian writers are Chinua Achebe, Cyprian Ekwensi, Wole Soyinka, Amos Tutuola, (whose works appear elsewhere in this bibliography) and Onuora Nzekwu (author of *Wand of the noble wood*, (London: Heinemann, 1971. 207p. (AWS)) and *Blade among the boys* (London: Heinemann, 1972. 192p. (AWS, no. 91)). An introduction (p. 11–13) and 'Biographical notes on the authors' (p. 339–47) begin and end the volume.

855 **Ten one-act plays.**
Edited by Cosmo Pieterse. London: Heinemann, 1968. 309p.
(African Writers Series, no. 34).

Of the ten plays from Nigeria, South Africa, Kenya and Ghana printed here, there are two by Nigerian authors, which were broadcast in the BBC African Service series, African Theatre. *The game* (p. 83–107) by Femi Euba is described in the play notes as a 'light, amoral little play . . . carried forward by its vital gusto in life and the energy of its expansiveness' (p. 297). Its hero is a 'big-hearted scoundrel' in the picaresque tradition. *Blind cyclops* (p. 109–33) by Ime Ikiddeh (1938– .) is a 'swift-moving, fluid, Brechtian satire [that] exposes social evils ranging from election-trickery and rent-racketeering, to bribery and corruption and hypocrisy' (p. 298).

856 **Poems of black Africa.**
Edited and introduced by Wole Soyinka. New York: Hill & Wang, 1975; London, Secker & Warburg, 1975. 378p.

An important anthology of 241 African poems by more than sixty-six poets. Nigerian poets included are: J. P. Clark; Mbella Sonne Dipoko; Ifeanyi Menkiti; Gabriel Okara; Christopher Okigbo; Isaac Rammopo; Wole Soyinka; Kalu Uka; and Okogbule Wanodi. Soyinka's short introduction (p. 13–15) explains the thematic organization of the volume as his effort to capture 'the experience of black Africa in the idiom of the poem' (p. 15). Brief notes on the poets are included throughout.

Chinua Achebe

857 **Things fall apart.**
Chinua Achebe. London: Heinemann, 1958; New York:
Astor-House, 1959; Greenwich, Connecticut: Fawcett, 1969. 192p.
(African Writers Series, no. 1).

The most famous African novel, the title of which, taken from William Butler Yeats's poem 'The second coming', refers to the major theme of the destruction of traditional life by colonialism. The novel is set in an Igbo village in eastern Nigeria at the turn of the century and tells the tragic story of its hero Okonwko.

858 **No longer at ease.**

Chinua Achebe. London: Heinemann, 1960; New York: Obolensky, 1961; Greenwich, Connecticut: Fawcett, 1969. 170p. (African Writers Series, no. 3).

The theme of conflict and change is continued in Achebe's second novel, whose title comes from T. S. Eliot's 'The journey of the magi'. Obi Okonkwo, the idealistic grandson of the hero of *Things fall apart* (q.v.), returns to Nigeria in the late 1950s after his education abroad. Initially, he hopes to reform the civil service in Lagos where he works, but he falls in love with Clara, a woman unacceptable to his own people, and eventually becomes enmeshed in the corruption of the rapidly changing city.

859 **Arrow of god.**

Chinua Achebe. London: Heinemann, 1964; New York: John Day, 1967; Garden City, New York: Doubleday Anchor, 1969; London: Heinemann, 1974. rev. ed. 230p. (African Writers Series, no. 16).

This novel, again dealing with the impacts of the early decades of colonization, is the story of Ezeulu, Chief Priest of Ulu, an important god of the Umuaro people. Ezeulu attempts to blunt the impact of the Europeans through compromise, but in so doing, his authority is undermined and his people turn to the religion of the European missionaries. In his brief preface to second edition, Achebe explains that he removed 'certain structural weaknesses' and that this 'is the novel which I am most likely to be caught sitting down to read again'. The Doubleday Anchor edition has an informative introduction by Ken Post.

860 **Chike and the river.**

Chinua Achebe. Cambridge; London; New York: Cambridge University, 1966. 64p.

This entertaining children's story tells how eleven-year old Chike Anene moved from a village in Eastern Nigeria to his uncle's house in the large market town of Onitsha. There he adapts to new friends and school life and becomes fascinated with the idea of crossing the River Niger. Eventually he succeeds in this and, after missing the return boat, becomes a hero when he helps capture a gang of thieves. The clever story is illustrated with drawings by Prue Theobalds. Other children's stories Achebe wrote include: *The drum* (Enugu, Nigeria: Fourth Dimension, 1977. 31p.), a folktale of Mbe, the ancestor of all tortoises who finds a magical drum in the land of spirits; *The flute: a children's story* (Enugu: Fourth Dimension, 1977. 24p.); and *How the leopard got his claws* (Enugu: Nwamife, 1972; New York: The Third Press, 1973. 35p.), illustrated by Per Christiansen, which explains how claws became necessary after a selfish dog brought violence to the animal world.

361 **A man of the people.**
Chinua Achebe. London: Heinemann, 1966 (African Writers Series, no. 31); New York: John Day, 1966; Garden City, New York: Doubleday Anchor, 1967. 141p.

In Achebe's fourth novel, Odili Samalu, the intellectual narrator, tells a story of conflict in 1964 between himself and a former teacher, Chief the Honorable (*sic*) M. A. Nanga, MP, Minister of Culture. The character of Chief Nanga, the 'man of the people', represents a brilliant portrayal of the corrupt politicians of independent Nigeria. K. W. J. Post's introduction (p. v–xvii) to the Doubleday Anchor edition outlines the novel's larger themes and places it in a broader context.

362 **Girls at war, and other stories.**
Chinua Achebe. London: Heinemann, 1972. (African Writers Series, no. 100); Garden City, New York: Doubleday Anchor, 1973. 129p.
New York: Fawcett, 1974; Ballantine, 1987. 120p. (A Fawcett Premier Book).

This collection includes the stories published in *The sacrificial egg, and other stories* Onitsha, Nigeria: Etudo, 1962. 32p.). Of the dozen stories here, ten were published previously between 1952 and 1971, mostly in journals. The older stories with their dates of publication are: 'The madman' (1971); 'The voter' (1965); 'Marriage is a private affair' (1952); 'Akueke' (1962); 'Chike's school days' (1960); 'The sacrificial egg' (1960); 'Vengeful creditor' (1971); 'Dead men's path' (1953); 'Uncle Ben's choice' 1966); and 'Civil peace' (1971). 'Sugar baby' and 'Girls at war' are new. Achebe also edited *The insider: stories of war and peace from Nigeria* (Enugu, Nigeria: Nwankwo-Ifejika, 1971. 124p.).

363 **Christmas in Biafra and other poems.**
Chinua Achebe. Garden City, New York: Doubleday Anchor, 1973. 92p.

Achebe's first volume of poetry, *Beware, soul brother: poems* contained twenty-three poems (Enugu, Nigeria: Nwankwo-Ifejika 1971). Those poems are republished here, some in revised form, 'a few re-written completely and one given a brand new name' p. 9). Seven new poems are added and the entire work is grouped into five sections; Prologue', 'Poems about war', 'Poems not about war', 'Gods, men and others', and Epilogue', with explanatory notes (p. 87–92). His powerful poetry covers a wide range of topics, including the Biafran War, love, misunderstanding, and Igbo traditions, among others. In Nigeria, *Beware soul brother: poems* was revised and enlarged as for *Christmas in Biafra* . . . and reissued with the same title (Enugu, Nigeria: Nwamife, 1973. 68p.).

364 **Anthills of the savannah.**
Chinua Achebe. London: Heinemann; Garden City, New York: Doubleday Anchor, 1987. 216p.

Achebe's fifth novel, the first after a break of twenty-one years, is a story of contemporary politics in the West African state of Kangan in which three friends from Lord Lugard College have become prominent: Sam is President; Chris is the Commissioner of Information; and Ikem is editor of the government-owned newspaper. The conflicts and confrontations of these men, their friends and lovers are

319

used to create a familiar world displaying the author's unsurpassed skills in the field of African fiction. See also Nadine Gordimer's review 'A tyranny of clowns' in the New York Times Book Review. 21 Feb. 1988, p. 1, 26.

Cyprian Ekwensi

865   People of the city.
Cyprian Ekwensi.   London: Heinemann, 1963. rev. ed. 120p. (African Writers Series, no. 5).

When originally published in 1954 (London: Andrew Dakers, 237p.; Greenwich Connecticut: Fawcett, 159p.), this was the first major novel in English by a West African to be read widely throughout the English-speaking world. The author (2 September 1921– .) was born in Minna, Northern Nigeria, trained as a pharmacist in London and worked for the Nigerian Broadcasting Corporation. He became Director of Information of the Ministry of Information in Lagos and, during the civil war, moved to Enugu and was Managing Director of *The Star* newspaper group. To date the prolific author has written nine novels and thirteen books for young people and has four short story collections. Before *People of the city*, Ekwensi published *When love whispers* (Onitsha: Tanbansi Press, 1947. 44p.) and *The leopard's claw* (London: Longmans, Green, 1960. 90p.). *People of the city* is the story of Amusa Sango, a crime reporter and dance band leader, Beatrice the First, a beautiful woman destroyed by the city, and Beatrice the Second, a calm, simple woman who saves Sango. Through these and others, Ekwensi describes a famous but unnamed West African city and 'How the city attracts all types and how the unwary must suffer from ignorance of its ways' (p. 1).

866   Jagua Nana.
Cyprian Ekwensi.   London: Heinemann, 1975. 192p. (African Writers Series, no. 146).

First published in 1961 (London: Hutchinson) Ekwensi's second and most famous novel tells the story of the beautiful Jagua Nana, an Igbo living in Lagos and working as a prostitute. Jagua becomes involved with politicians, and two characters named Uncle Taiwo and Freddie Namme, and must eventually return to her village Ogabu. She matures but remains childless until she is forty-five; her baby dies two days after he is born and Jagua resolves to go to 'Onisha' to become a 'merchant princess'. The story continues in *Jagua Nana's daughter* (Ibadan, Nigeria: Spectrum, 1986. 247p.).

867   Burning grass: a story of the Fulani of Northern Nigeria.
Cyprian Ekwensi, illustrated by A. Folarin.   London: Heinemann, 1962. 150p. map. (African Writers Series, no. 2).

In his third published novel (which was written before the other two novels), Ekwensi writes of Mai Sunsaye, a nomadic Fulani cattleherder, and his family as they grapple with inter-tribal raids and changing ways of life, and as his children come of age, love and marry. 'Burning grass' refers to the cooler season, the Harmattan, when grass must be burned by agriculturalists and the cattle must be moved south to the River Niger.

8 Lokotown and other stories.
Cyprian Ekwensi. London: Heinemann, 1966. 152p. (African Writers
Series, no. 19).

seven short stories and two novellas – 'Lokotown' (p. 1–44) and 'Glittering city'
. 107–52) – Ekwensi creates a fascinating cast of characters including Charlie the
ain Driver, Diamond Jim, Fussy Joe and Iya Mai-Mai, who struggle through the
rists and turns of life in urban Nigeria. In *Beautiful feathers* (London: Heinemann,
'71. 160p. (AWS, no. 84)), the young pan-Africanist, Wilson Iyari, must deal with
roblems at home as well as in politics. A more recent collection is
stless city and Christmas gold, with other stories. (London: Heinemann, 1975. 100p.
WS, no. 172)) which offers fifteen short stories of city life. The first story, 'Restless
ty' (p. 1–6), is from an unpublished novel and is about Sokoni, trying to re-adjust to
igeria with his white wife after living a sophisticated life in London. Five of the
ories concern Christmas in the city. Ekwensi's novel *Survive the peace* (London:
einemann, 1976. 181p. (AWS, no. 185)) describes the trauma which befalls James
dugo and his family after the civil war ends. The war was again the theme in *Divided
e stand* (Enugu, Nigeria: Fourth Dimension, 1980. 235p.), and its aftermath provided
e setting in the children's novella, *Coal Camp boy* (Ibadan, Nigeria: Longman
igeria, 1973. 66p.).

Wole Soyinka

9 The lion and the jewel.
Wole Soyinka. Oxford; London: Oxford University, 1963. 64p.
(A Three Crowns Book).

rst produced in 1959 in Ibadan, *The lion and the jewel* is Soyinka's second play. This
oald comedy incorporating many rural traditions is set in the Yoruba village of
ajinle, where Baroka (the Lion), the crafty village Bale (or chief), stalks Sidi (the
wel), 'the village belle'. Other main characters include Lakunle, a westernized school
acher who also desires Sidi, and Sadiku, Baroka's senior wife. Wole Soyinka,
igeria's Nobel Laureate in Literature, was born 13 July 1934, near Abeokuta.

0 The interpreters.
Wole Soyinka, introduced by Eldred Jones. London: André Deutsch,
1965. London: Heinemann, 1970. 260p. (African Writers Series,
no. 76).

challenging novel, Soyinka's first, through which he provides a critical view of
odern Nigeria, in a non-chronological style. The story centres on five friends trying to
ad full social and professional lives yet who are frustrated by the corruption and
ypocrisy of the society around them. That the novel was written by a poet is seen in
ie creative language and imagery throughout. *The interpreters* has been described as
ne most complex narrative work yet written by an African' and compared to works by
imes Joyce and William Faulkner by Bernth Lindfors in *African literatures in the 20th
ntury: a guide* (q.v.). Jones describes the novel as an 'extended metaphor' which
akes a critical look at the human situation in modern Nigeria' (p. 6), in the novel's
seful introduction (p. 1–6).

Literature. Wole Soyinka

871 **Idanre & other poems.**
Wole Soyinka. London: Methuen, 1967; New York: Hill & Wang,
1968. 88p.

The first collection of Soyinka's poems, which were selected by the author himse
Among the thirty-seven included is his longest poem published at the time, 'Idan
(p. 57–88), written in 1965. 'Idanre' refers to the region with the highest elevation
western Nigeria (3,098 feet at the highest point), a region prominent in Yoru
mythology, 'a god-suffused grazing of primal giants and mastodons, petrified throu
some strange history, suckled by mists and clouds' (p. 57). The poem relates the poe
lone pilgrimage to the sacred hills and offers a validation of human individuality a
diversity.

872 **Kongi's harvest.**
Wole Soyinka. Oxford; London: Oxford University, 1967. 90p.

In this play, Soyinka's themes are the abuse of power by petty dictators and the cla
of tradition with the state. The drama takes place on the eve and day of the nation
celebrations of Isma of which Kongi is President. Kongi has imprisoned Oba Danlo
a traditional ruler and spiritual leader, but attempts to use him at the new yam festiv
to boost his own image. At the climax of the festival, Kongi is devastatingly surpasse
Kongi's harvest was performed first in August 1965 in Lagos by the 1960 Masks a
Orisun Theater, which was begun by Soyinka in that year. A film (colour, eighty-fi
minutes) directed by Ossie Davis using Soyinka's screenplay was made in 1974.

873 **Madmen and specialists.**
Wole Soyinka. Ibadan, Nigeria: University Press; London: Oxford
University, 1971. 77p.

Set in and around the home surgery of Dr. Bero, this play explores the destructi
horror of war and its dehumanizing impact on individuals. Dr. Bero, the 'speciali
returns home from the war in which he served as head of an intelligence section ('. . .
specialist is – well – a specialist. You analyse, you diagnose, you . . . prescribe', p. 32
His sister Si Bero is appalled by the changes in him. His father has been driven mad
the war and with a group of mendicants belongs to the perverted cult of As. Ultimate
destruction prevails as Bero kills his father in the play's climax. This play was fir
performed in August 1970 at the Eugene O'Neill Theater Center, Waterfor
Connecticut, but the present version had its debut in March 1971 at the University
Ibadan, Ibadan, Nigeria.

874 **The man died: prison notes of Wole Soyinka.**
Wole Soyinka. London: Rex Collings; New York: Harper & Row,
1972. Reprinted, New York: Noonday, 1988. 317p.

This autobiographical volume was written on the pages of smuggled books and pape
as 'the private record of one survival' (p. 25) while Soyinka was held in Lagos's Ki
Kiri Prison and in Kaduna from August 1967 to October 1969. The first 'letter
compatriots' was written 14 December 1971; the postscript is dated 15 January 197
The book's title was inspired by the death of journalist Segun Sowemimo, who died
a result of a beating he received while in detention. Soyinka writes: 'the man dies in
who keep silent in the face of tyranny' (p. 13); and 'In any people that submit willing
to the 'daily humiliation of fear', the man dies' (p. 16).

375 A shuttle in the crypt.

Wole Soyinka.   London: Rex Collings/Eyre Methuen, 1971;
New York: Hill & Wang, 1972. 89p.

A collection of thirty-four poems, most written while Soyinka was in solitary
confinement, a period of nearly two years. 'The shuttle is a unique species of the caged
animal, a restless bolt of energy, a trapped weaver-bird yet charged in repose with
unspoken forms and designs'. These poems are 'a map of the course trodden by the
mind, not a record of the actual struggle against a vegetable existence. . .' (Preface,
p. vii). Most recently the author has published *Mandela's earth and other poems* (New
York: Random House, 1988; London: André Deutsch, 1989. 70p.).

376 Collected plays.

Wole Soyinka.   London; Oxford: Oxford University, 1973, 1974.
2 vols. (Oxford Paperbacks, 296, 324).

Volume one contains *A dance of the forests* (1963), *The swamp dwellers* (1964), *The
strong breed* (1964), *The road* (1965) and *The bacchae of Euripides* (1973). Volume two
reprints *The lion and the jewel* (q.v.), *Kongi's harvest* (q.v.), *The trials of Brother Jero*
(Ibadan: Mbari, 1963. 33p.), *Jero's metamorphosis* (1973) and *Madmen and specialists*
(q.v.). Another collection is *Soyinka: six plays* (London: Methuen, 1984. 407p.
(Master Playwrights Series)) which contains: *The trials of Brother Jero*; *Jero's
metamorphosis*; *Camwood on the leaves* (1973); *Death and the king's horseman* (q.v.),
Madmen and specialists (q.v.); and *Opera Wonyosi* (q.v.). In *The trials of Brother Jero*
(Oxford: Oxford University, 1964), Soyinka satirizes religion in the person of
Jeroboam, a suave 'beach divine' who attempts to attract followers. In the sequel
Jero's metamorphosis (Eyre Methuen, 1973), Brother Jero has prospered and become
a spiritual empire builder and General of the First Church of the Apostolic Salvation
Army of the Lord. It was first performed in 1974. Among Soyinka's varied efforts is his
translation of the work of Yoruba playwright D. O. Fagunwa (1903–63) entitled *The
forest of a thousand daemons: a hunter's saga* (London: Nelson, 1968; New York:
Random House, 1982. 140p.), which was illustrated by Bruce Onobrakpeya.

377 Season of anomy.

Wole Soyinka.   London: Rex Collings, 1973; Walton-on-Thames,
England: Thomas Nelson, 1980. 313p. (PanAfrica Library).

In contrast to his first novel, this novel has a more straight-forward story line. The
story concerns the relationship of an isolated, self-sufficient commune Aiyéró, to the
larger society. Ofeyi, a cocoa productions man for the Corporation, is intrigued by the
community whose values stand in contrast to those of the larger society and is drawn to
Iriyise, his lover who is kidnapped. Through his characters and the events in the novel,
Soyinka continues his critique of modern society begun in *The interpreters* (q.v.).

378 The Bacchae of Euripides: a communion rite.

Wole Soyinka.   New York: Norton, 1974. 97p.

In this adaptation of *The Bacchae* of Euripides, Soyinka links Ogun, the Yoruba 'god
of metals, creativity, the road, wine and war' with Dionysos and incorporates lines
from traditional Yoruba praise-chants and from his long poem 'Idanre' (q.v.) which
celebrates Ogun's night of pilgrimage (Introduction, p. vi). In the introduction,
Soyinka explains that he sees *The Bacchae* as 'a prodigious, barbaric banquet, an
insightful manifestation of the universal need of man to match himself against Nature'

323

and as 'a communal feast, a tumultuous celebration of life', in which 'man re-affirm his indebtedness to earth, dedicates himself to the demands of continuity and invoke the energies of productivity' (p. xi). The play was first performed in August 1973.

879 Aké: the years of childhood.

Wole Soyinka. London: Rex Collings, 1981; New York: Random House, 1982; New York: Vintage/Aventura, 1983. 230p.

In this lyrical account of his first eleven years, Soyinka re-creates a child's fantas world of spirits and daemons, of Yoruba traditions, and of adults. He describes h relations with his mother 'Wild Christian' and his father 'Essay', his early educatio and his youthful perceptions of the broader events of the women's uprising i Egbaland. Yoruba words and short verses are translated into English throughout.

880 Opera Wonyosi.

Wole Soyinka. Bloomington, Indiana: Indiana University, 1981. 86p

Soyinka adapts Bertold Brecht's *The threepenny opera* to Africa to examine politic corruption in what was then the Central African Empire capital of Bangui. In h foreword, the author writes that this is an 'exposition of levels of power in practise – t a satirist's pen . . . The Nigerian society which is *portrayed*, without one redeemir feature, is that oil-boom society of the seventies which every child knows only tc well'. He also describes the writer's rôle and his own 'uncompromising concern for tł social values of literature'. *Opera Wonyosi* was first performed 16 December 1977 the University of Ife (now Obafemi Awolowo University), Ile-Ife, Nigeria.

881 A play of giants.

Wole Soyinka. London, New York: Methuen, 1984. 69p.

This play is a 'savage portrait' of four dictatorial African heads of state set at tł Bugaran Embassy of the United Nations, New York, a few years before the prese time. In the introduction, 'On the heroes of our time: some personal notes' (p. v–x Soyinka makes no secret of his models for the characters: ex-President for Life I Amin of Uganda; the late President for Life Macias Nguema of Equatorial Guinea; e Emperor for Life Jean-Baptiste Bokassa of the Central African Republic; and Lł President Mobutu Sese Koto of Zaire.

882 Death and the king's horseman.

Wole Soyinka. New York: Hill & Wang, 1987. 112p.

According to Oyo Yoruba tradition, when the Oba (king) dies, his horse, his dog ar his chief horseman must die also. This play is based on events which took place in Oy in 1946, set for dramatic effect two or three years earlier in wartime. Here confli occurs when Simon Pilkings, the District Officer, refuses to allow Elesin Oba, tł king's horseman, to commit suicide. Ultimately, Olunde, eldest son of Elesin, who h returned from studies in Britain, takes his place. According to Soyinka's note, 'Tł confrontation in the play is largely metaphysical, contained in the human vehicle whi is Elesin and the universe of the Yoruba mind – the world of the living, the dead ar the unborn, and the numinous passage which links all: transition' (p. viii). Sever photographs of the New York Lincoln Center Theater production in 1987 are includ as is a short glossary of Yoruba terms.

Amos Tutuola

883   **The palm-wine drinkard and his dead palm-wine tapster in the Dead's Town.**
Amos Tutuola.   London: Faber & Faber, 1952; New York: Grove, 1953. 130p.

Amos Tutuola (20 June 1922– .) of the Yoruba city of Abeokuta, began the modern era of Nigerian fiction published in English with this picaresque tale acclaimed in a review by Dylan Thomas as a 'brief, thronged, grisly and bewitching story, or series of stories, written in young English' (*Observer*, 6 July 1952, p. 7). In Tutuola's world nothing is too strange as he blends Yoruba folk tales with his fertile imagination in a phantasmagorical series of encounters. The story is that of a palm-wine drinkard who consumes 225 kegs of palm-wine a day who goes on a quest to find his deceased expert palm-wine tapster. To do so he travels to the Dead's Town, along Death's Road, meeting a gentlemanly Skull, 400 dead babies and assorted creatures. The woman he meets and marries bears him a son from her thumb whom he is forced to kill and he acquires a miraculous egg by which he feeds the world. The Grove Black Cat Edition (1984. 130p.) was introduced by Michael Thelwell. Tutuola provides a brief account of 'My life and activities' (p. 126–30) in which he describes his childhood, limited education and metalworking trade.

884   **My life in the Bush of Ghosts.**
Amos Tutuola, foreword by Geoffrey Parrinder.   London: Faber & Faber; New York: Grove, 1954. Reprinted, 1964, 1969. 174p.

Tutuola's second published story and perhaps his wildest reinterpretation of traditional mythology and themes. The narrator, a boy of seven becomes lost in the deep forest, the Bush of Ghosts, a spirit world full of towns of ghosts. For twenty-four years he wanders from town to town enduring adventures both morbid and terrifying, is changed into a cow and back again, builds a Methodist church, and is eventually shown the way home by a 'television-handed ghostess'. In the foreword, the Rev. Parrinder considers Tutuola's story 'more terrifying than Grimm' (p. 11) and the abnormal beings reminiscent of the creations of Bunyan and Dante. His stories 'are of the kind, lively, vulgar, frightening, which is common in the traditional Africa of the villages' (p. 10).

885   **Simbi and the Satyr of the dark jungle**
Amos Tutuola.   London: Faber & Faber, 1955. 136p. Reprinted, San Francisco: City Lights, 1988. 136p.

Simbi, a young woman, makes a quest in order to understand poverty and punishment. In this story Tutuola for the first time organizes his material into chapters and writes in the third person. Tutuola explores story-telling conventions further in *The brave African huntress* (London: Faber & Faber, 1958. New York: Grove, 1970. 150p), *Feather woman of the jungle* (London: Faber & Faber, 1962. 132p.), *Ajaiyi and his inherited poverty* (London: Faber & Faber, 1967. 235p.), and in his first-written novel of 1948 *The wild hunter in the bush of ghosts* (London: Faber & Faber, 1982, 2nd ed. 167p.; Washington, DC: Three Continents, 1987, 2nd ed. 150p.).

886 **The witch-herbalist of the Remote Town.**
Amos Tutuola. London: Faber & Faber, 1981. 205p.

In this novel, his first in fourteen years, Tutuola tells the story of the Brave Hunter of the Rocky Town. After four years of childless marriage, he decides to make the journey to the witch-herbalist of the Remote Town to obtain a remedy. During the six-year trip, he encounters strange creatures such as the Abnormal Squatting Wild Man of the Jungle, the Wild Jungle Wealthy People, the Crazy Removable-Headed Wild Man and others. He finally sees the Witch-Mother and is given the medicine. Nearly home again, he sips a little himself. Although his wife drinks the rest, they both become pregnant and are sacrificed to the river gods by the town. In they end, they survive and are happy with their new child. In 'The return of Amos Tutuola', *Africa Today*, vol. 29, no. 3 (1982), p. 65–69, Nancy J. Schmidt perceives a change in narrative style since his previous work. 'It appears that either Tutuola's creative imagination is flagging or his editor felt compelled to standardize and homogenize his English' (p. 69).

887 **Pauper, brawler and slanderer.**
Amos Tutuola. London; Boston, Massachusetts: Faber & Faber, 1987. 156p.

Two thousand years ago, in the town of Laketu of present-day Ogun State, the son of the king was exiled because the Babalawo, the priest of Ifa, prophesied his future of poverty and wretchedness. Similarly the daughter and son of the second- and third-ranking chiefs were expelled because of their natures, of brawler and slanderer. The story recounts their relations with each other and their adventures and ultimately explains the presence of poverty, brawling and slander in the world. Compared to Tutuola's earlier stories, this one lacks vigour and appeal. Nancy J. Schmidt clarifies the history of this volume and critically reviews it in 'Tutuola writes again', *Africa Today*, vol. 33, no. 4 (1986), p. 81–82.

Other major writers

888 **One man, one wife.**
T[imothy] M. Aluko. London: Heinemann, 1967. 156p. (African Writers Series, no. 30).

Aluko (1918– .) published a series of satirical commentaries on the rapidly changing Nigerian society. Others, all published in the Heinemann African Writers Series (AWS) include *One man, one matchet* (1964. 196p. (AWS, 11)), discussed in *Writers and politics in Africa* (q.v.), *Kinsman and foreman* (1966. 203p. (AWS, 32)), *Chief, the honorable minister* (1970. 214p. (AWS, 70)), *His worshipful majesty* (1973. 175p. (AWS, 130)) and *Wrong ones in the dock* (1982. 186p. (AWS, 242)).

889   **The concubine.**
Elechi Amadi.   London: Heinemann, 1966. Reprinted, 1978, 1985.
216p. (African Writers Series, no. 25).

This best-known work by Amadi (1934– .) tells the story of Ihuoma, a watermaid become human, and the disastrous consequences which befall her husband and her later loves as the Sea King, her spirit husband, takes revenge. It is set in an idealized traditional village of eastern Nigeria. *The concubine: notes* by Roger Ebbatson has been published as a study guide (Harlow: Longman, 1981. 64p.). *The concubine: a critical view* by Alastair Niven, edited by Yolande Cantù, (London: Collins in association with the British Council, 1981. 32p.) contains a brief bibliography and list of films. Amadi was born near Port Harcourt and studied maths and physics at University College, Ibadan. Heinemann has also published his other novels, *The great ponds* (1969. 217p. (AWS, 44)), *The slave* (1978. 160p (AWS, 210)), *Estrangement* (1986. 244p. (AWS, 272)) and his civil war diary *Sunset in Biafra* (1973. 184p. (AWS, 140)).

890   **The anonymity of sacrifice.**
I. N. C. Aniebo.   London: Heinemann, 1974. 115p. map. (African Writers Series, no. 148).

A novel of the Nigerian civil war telling the story of three days of tense confrontation between two Biafrans, Captain Benjamin Onwura, a career army officer, and Sergeant Cyril Agumo, a career enlisted man. Much of the war story is reconstructed through the thoughts of these men who because of class and temperament are brought inevitably to a fatal clash. The author was born in Port Harcourt, Nigeria, became a major in the Nigerian army and fought on the Biafran side. At the time of publication he was a writer at the University of California, Los Angeles. Aniebo's novel *The journey within* (1978. 242p. (AWS, 206)) tracing two Igbo marriages, one Christian, the other traditional, and his collection of sixteen short stories written in the 1960s and 1970s *Of wives, talismans and the dead: short stories* (1983. 153p. (AWS, 253)) were both published in Heinemann's African Writers Series.

891   **Shaihu Umar.**
Alhaji Sir Abubakar Tafawa Balewa, translated and introduced by Mervyn Hiskett.   London: Longmans, Green, 1967. 80p.

This popular story of Umar and his family set in the late-nineteenth century incorporates many details of Hausa culture, court life, the institution of slavery and Muslim education. In his enlightening introduction (p. 3–15), Mervyn Hiskett describes Umar as 'both an Islamic and a Hausa ideal' (p. 4), his mother as 'an ideal of womanhood' (p. 9) and the story as 'a tale of the *fin de siècle* – the last days of a century of turbulence, bloodshed, and slavery' (p. 15). The novel was originally published as *Shaihu Umar* in Hausa (Zaria: Gaskiya, 1946). The author was born in 1912 in Bauchi, Northern Nigeria, served as an educator and then entered politics. In 1960, he became Nigeria's first Federal Prime Minister and was assassinated during a coup on 15 January 1966. A play *Shaihu Umar* by Unaru Ladan and Dexter Lyndersay (London: Longman, 1975, 51p. (African Creative Writing Series)) has been adapted from the novel.

327

892 **Aissa saved.**

Joyce Cary. London: E. Benn, 1932. Reprinted, London: Michael Joseph, 1952. Carfax edition. New York: Harper & Row, 1962. 219p.

Cary's first novel is set in Northern Nigeria during the early-twentieth century and revolves around Aissa 'A half-bred Fulani girl with big soft eyes and a fine golden skin very attractive to any man' (p. 14), a convert to the Christian mission run by Mr. and Mrs. Carr. The novel relates the conflicts between 'pagans', Christian converts, missionaries and colonial administrator Bradgate and the ultimately tragic fate of Aissa and her child. The American edition contains Cary's prefatory essay written for the Carfax edition of 1952 in which the author describes his sources of inspiration for the novel which took him three years to complete. Cary wrote other novels set in Northern Nigeria: *An American visitor* (q.v.), *The African witch* (q.v.), *Castle corner* (q.v.) and *Cock Jarvis*, which he never finished, but which was edited by A. G. Bishop and published in its different versions recently (New York: St. Martin's 1975. 267p.).

893 **Mister Johnson.**

Joyce Cary. London: Michaël Joseph, 1939. Harmondsworth, England: Penguin, in association with Michael Joseph, 1962. 251p. (Penguin Modern Classics).

Joyce Cary's most famous African novel is set in Northern Nigeria and tells the story of Mister Johnson, the irrepressible chief clerk of Fada and assistant to J. H. Rudbeck, the Assistant District Officer. Johnson's schemes, ambitions and impecunious ways lead him from one dilemma to another as he takes a traditional wife, Bamu, negotiates with a host of associates, works for the merchant Sergeant Gollup, shows Rudbeck's wife Celia around and inspires hard labour among road workers. Cary portrays brilliantly the complexities and consequences of road building in rural Nigeria. In his 1952 preface to the novel, Cary describes Mister Johnson as 'a young clerk who turns his life into a romance, he is a poet who creates for himself a glorious destiny' (p. 7). Cary was the District Officer of Borgu Division, Northern Nigeria in 1917 and 1918, shortly after a major rebellion occurred.

894 **America, their America.**

J. P. Clark, foreword by E. U. Essien-Udom. London: André Deutsch, 1964; London: Heinemann, 1968. 224p. (African Writers Series).

The Nigerian poet and playwright offers an angry account of his experiences in the US in 1962–63 while a participant in Princeton University's Parvin Fellowship Programme. His story is full, not only of scathing commentary on the Americans of New York, Washington and Princeton, but also of perceptive observations on student life, race and politics by a young Nigerian intellectual. Throughout are poems capturing his feelings and experiences. Professor Essien-Udom, a political scientist who studied and worked in the US, provides additional insights in his foreword. Clark (1935– .) is one of Nigeria's most prominent writers. His other works include *The Ozidi saga* (q.v.) and *A decade of tongues* (q.v.). Clark is Professor of English at the University of Lagos, Lagos, Nigeria.

95 A decade of tongues. Selected poems: 1958–1968.

John Pepper Clark. Harlow, England: Longman, 1982. 104p.

A selection of seventy-four of the author's poems from *Poems* (Ibadan: Mbari Publications, 1962), *A reed in the tide* (London: Longman, 1965), *Casualties* (London: Longman, 1970) and 'Incidental songs for several persons'. Brief notes (p. 102–04) clarify some of the alusions. The distinguished poet is also known for his *Song of a goat* (Ibadan: Mbari, 1961. 43p.), *Three plays* (London: Oxford University, 1964. 134p.), comprising *Song of a goat, The masquerade* and *The raft*, and essays in *The example of Shakespeare* (London: Longman, 1970. 113p.).

896 Tefuga.

Peter Dickinson. New York: Pantheon, 1986. 256p.

An excellent novel which is about indirect rule and rural conditions in Northern Nigeria. The story revolves around the diary of artist Betty Jackland who joins her husband the District Officer at Kiti in 1923. Chapters of the diary alternate with an account of contemporary events occurring while her son Nigel Jackland makes a film of the diary and attempts to reconstruct the events which led up to the violent revolt at Tefuga. Dickinson (1927– .) born in Zambia, is a prolific author of adult and children's fiction.

897 The anthill.

Obi B. Egbuna. Ibadan, Nigeria; London: Oxford University, 1965. 60p.

This cleverly crafted play is set in London and the British Protectorate of Tongo in the 'immediate past'. Bobo, an African art student, obsessively paints anthills; his landlady's son returns from Tongo on leave from the army and mysteriously dies, revealing a series of 'catastrophic coincidences'. Among Egbuna's other works are his first novel *Wind versus polygamy* (London: Faber & Faber, 1964. 128p.) reissued as *Elina* (Glasgow: Collins/Fontana, 1978. 125p.), a collection of short stories *Emperor of the sea* (Glasgow: Collins/Fontana, 1974. 127p.) and *The minister's daughter* (Glasgow: Collins/Fontana, 1975. 96p.).

898 Double yoke.

Buchi Emecheta. London: Barrie & Jenkins, 1972. 158p.; New York: Braziller, 1985. 163p. London: Fontana, 1984. 159p.

Double yoke, Emecheta's sixth novel, is the story of two undergraduates, Ete Kamba and Nko, at the University of Calabar who struggle with the pulls of tradition and modernity, which are highlighted by the character of Professor Ikot. Emecheta (1944– .) was born in Lagos of Ibuza parents and has worked as Senior Research Fellow in the Department of English at the University of Calabar. She has written several other novels and children's books: *The slave girl* (1977. 179p.); *The bride price: young Ibo girl's love; conflict of family and tradition* (1976. 175p.); *Second-class citizen* (1975. 176p.; 1983. 175p.) and *Joys of motherhood* (1979. 224p.), all published by Allison and Busby, London, and Braziller, New York; *The wrestling match* (1981; 1983. 74p.) and *Moonlight bride* (1981; 1983. 77p.) both published by Oxford University, Oxford, and Braziller, New York; and *In the ditch* (1980. 128p.) published by Allison and Busby, London, and Schocken, New York.

899 Head above water: an autobiography.

Buchi Emecheta. London: Fontana, 1986. 243p.

This prominent Nigerian writer gives a personal and inspiring account of her life including her struggles as a single parent of five small children in London, her pursui of a degree in sociology and the results of serializing her first book, *In the ditch* (q.v.) in the *New Statesman* in 1972.

900 Forty-eight guns for the general.

Eddie Iroh. London: Heinemann, 1976. 224p. (African Writers Series, no. 189).

This popular writer has published a Biafran War trilogy, the first volume of which i about mercenaries flown in to help the Biafrans. *Toads of war* (1979. 144p. (AWS 213)) takes place in Owerri during the last days of the war, while *The siren in the nigh* (1982. 203p. (AWS, 255)) concerns events just after the war's end. He has als published *Without a silver spoon* (Ibadan: Spectrum, 1981. 112p.).

901 Behind the rising sun.

S[ebastian] O[kechukwu] Mezu. London: Heinemann, 1972. 241p. (African Writers Series, no. 113).

A substantial novel of the Nigerian civil war, much of it set in Europe and concerning efforts to provide supplies to embattled Biafra. In Paris Obiora Ifedi lives luxuriously and attempts to charter planes to carry ammunition to Biafra. Freddy Onuoha must return to his native Biafra; once there he encounters the tragedy of the losing battle. The international setting affords a panoramic view of the war. Mezu, born in Owerri in eastern Nigeria and educated in the United States and the Sorbonne, has written extensively on Leopold S. Senghor. In 1988, Festus Lyayi (1947– .) won the second Commonwealth Writers Prize for his civil war novel *Heroes* (Harlow, England: Longman, 1986. 247p.). His earlier novels were *Violence* (London: Longman; Washington, DC: Three Continents, 1979. 316p.) and *The contract* (Harlow, England: Longman, 1982. 217p.).

902 The only son.

John Munonye. London: Heinemann, 1966. 160p. (African Writers Series, no. 21).

In this story of conflict between tradition and a changing society, a Catholic missionary competes with a mother for the allegiance of her only son. Munonye (1929– .) is one of Nigeria's more popular, but unsung novelists. Among his many works are five others in the Heinemann African Writers Series: *Obi* (1969. 210p. (AWS, 45)); *Oil man of Obange* (1971. 186p. (AWS, 94)); *A wreath for the maidens* (1973. 248p. (AWS, 121)); *A dancer of fortune* (1975. 187p. (AWS, 153)); and *Bridge to a wedding* (1978. 228p. (AWS, 195)).

03 Danda.

Nkem Nwankwo.   London: Panther Books, 1966. 154p. London:
Collins, 1972. 157p. (Fontana Modern Books). London: Heinemann,
1970. 208p. (African Writers Series, no. 67).

Again, the theme for this novel is changing society. This time an Igbo son rejects the
authority of his father and the village elders. In the popular *My Mercedes is bigger than
ours* (London: Heinemann, 1975. 171p. (AWS, 173); London: André Deutsch, 1975;
New York: Harper & Row, 1975; London: Fontana/Collins, 1976. 127p.) which has
also been translated to French and Portuguese, Nwankwo confronts the corrupting
power of money in a rapidly changing society where luxury cars are important status
symbols. Nwankwo (1936– .) has also published *More tales out of school* (Lagos:
African Universities Press, 1965. 80p.) and *The scapegoat* (Enugu: Fourth Dimension,
1984. 125p.).

04 Efuru.

Flora [Nwazuruahu Nkeiru] Nwapa.   London: Heinemann, 1966.
281p. Reprinted, 1978. 221p. (African Writers Series, no. 26).

Efuru is a beautiful woman who marries Adizua and eventually has a baby, Ogonim.
After her husband deserts them, her child dies and other misfortunes befall her. She
then learns that a river goddess has chosen her as her honoured worshipper. Nwapa
(1931– .) born in Oguta, Imo State, creates a complex traditional world in this
popular first novel. Also by Nwafa in the African Writers Series is *Idu* (1970, 218p.
(AWS, 56)) a story about a woman's longing for children. In 1977 she founded her own
printing and publishing firms, Tana Press and Flora Nwapa & Co. She is 'the first
Nigerian woman to have published a novel and the first woman in Africa to have a
work of fiction published in London' according to Alison Perry in 'Meeting Flora
Nwapa', *West Africa*, no. 3487 (18 June 1984), p. 1262. Among her many other works
are *This is Lagos, and other stories* (Enugu: Nwamife, 1971), her account of the civil
war, *Never again* (Enugu: Nwamife, 1975; Enugu: Tana, 1986. 85p.), *One is enough*
(Enugu: Tana, 1981. 154p.), *Mammywater* (Enugu: Flora Nwapa, 1979. 32p.; 1984.
47p.) and *Wives at war, and other stories* (Enugu: Tana, 1984).

905 The voice.

Gabriel [Imomotime Obainbaing] Okara, introduced by Arthur
Ravenscroft.   London: André Deutsch, 1964. (African Writers Series,
no. 68); New York: Africana, 1970. 127p.

An important novel attempting to reconcile in European prose the author's Niger
Delta Ijaw idiom. This experimental novel tells the story of Okolo, which translates as
'The voice', who returns from his studies to his village. His questioning approach to
local traditions threatens Chief Ozongo and the village elders and eventually results in
Okolo's death. In the introduction (p. 1–21), Ravenscroft suggests reading the story as
an extended political parable (p. 10). Bernth Lindfors calls *The voice* 'a moral allegory
about man's quest for faith, truth, and the meaning of life in a corrupted world', in
African literatures in the 20th century: a guide (q.v.). Okara (24 April 1921– .) was
born in Bumodi, located in an Ijaw district of the Delta region, Nigeria, was educated
at Government College, Umuahia, and has worked as a printer and book-binder in
Lagos and Enugu.

906 **The fisherman's invocation.**
Gabriel Okara, introduced by Theo Vincent.   London: Heinemann,
1978. 63p. (African Writers Series, no. 183).
This is the first collection of Okara's poetry and offers thirty-three poems, includi:
'The call of the River Nun' from 1953 and others written in the later 1950s and 196C

907 **Labyrinths, with Path of thunder.**
Christopher [Ifekandu] Okigbo.   New York: Africana in association
with Mbari, Ibadan, 1971. London: Heinemann, 1971. 72p. (African
Writers Series, no. 62).
This slender volume contains famed poet Okigbo's only published collectic
Labyrinths, with a postscript, 'Path of thunder, poems prophesying war' (p. 61–72)
which he was working before he was killed on the Nsukka front in 1967 in the Nigeri;
civil war. The latter appeared first in *Black Orpheus* (q.v.), February 196;
Heavensgate (1962. 39p.), *Limits* (1964. 23p.) published in Ibadan by Mbari, 'Silences
Transition, vol. 8 (1963) p. 13–16 and 'Distances' *Transition*, vol. 16 (1964) p. 9–1
comprise the 'organically related' collection *Labyrinths* (1965) which is introduced b
the author (p. xi–xiv). Okigbo (16 August 1932– .) was born in Ojot
Anambra State. In 1986 Okigbo's *Collected poems* was published by Heineman
(99p.), introduced by Adewale Maja-Pearce, with a preface by Paul Theroux.

908 **The edifice.**
Kole Omotoso.   London: Heinemann, 1971. 121p. (African Writers
Series, no. 102).
One of Nigeria's powerful younger writers (1943– .), Omotoso tells the story of 'Del
who marries in Britain, returns home, and then deserts his wife for another whit
woman. In *The combat*, (1972, 88p. (AWS, no. 122)), he produces a clever, rapidl;
moving story of two men overcome by their circumstances. The prolific author has als
published *Fella's choice* (Benin City: Ethiope, 1974. 111p.), *The scales* (Ibadar
Onibonoje, 1976. 104p.), *The curse* (Ibadan: New Horn, 1976. 32p.), *Miracles an
other stories* (Ibadan: Onibonoje, 1978. 95p.), *Sacrifice* (Ibadan: Onibonoje, 1978
123p.), *Memories of our recent boom* (Harlow, England: Longman, 1982. 232p.), *Ju;
before dawn* (Ibadan: Spectrum, 1988. 345p.), and an account of his journey to th
Soviet Union, *All this must be seen* (Moscow: Progress Publishers, 1986. 92p.).

909 **Poems in Bini.**
Ikponmwosa Osemwegie, introduced in English by E. Ogieriakhi. New
York: St. Martin's; London: Macmillan, 1965. 58p.
These twenty-five poems, the first collection of poetry published in Bini (and withou
an English translation), include narrative, praise and prayer, historical, philosophica
and miscellaneous poems. The volume contains a brief introduction in English by E
Ogieriakhi. In 'Ikponmwosa Osemwegie: a young Bini poet', *Nigeria Magazine*, no. 9·
(Sept. 1967), p. 250–52, Dan Ben-Amos describes the poetry and the problems facin;
a writer using the vernacular, as well as the poet's art and traditionalism. He states tha
Osemwegie 'is the first Bini author whose book has been put into print by a majo:
publisher' (p. 250).

910 **Kolera Kolej.**

Femi Ọṣọfisan. Ibadan, Nigeria: New Horn, 1975. 113p.

Osofisan (1946– .) has written both this and other plays, including *The chattering and the song* (Ibadan: Ibadan University, 1977. 57p.); *A restless run of locusts* (Ibadan: Onibonoje, 1975. 51p.); *Once upon four robbers* (Ibadan: BIO Educational Services, 1982, 2nd ed. 82p.); *Morountodun and other plays* (Ikeja: Longman Nigeria, 1982. 138p.); *Two one-act plays: The oriki of a grasshopper and Altine's wrath* (Ibadan: New Horn, 1986. 90p.); and *Farewell to a cannibal rage* (Ibadan: Evans, 1986. 76p.). Of interest also are his essays in the Ife Monographs on Literature and Criticism Series produced by the Department of Literature and English, University of Ife, 'Beyond translation: (a comparatist look at tragic paradigms and the dramaturgy of Wole Soyinka and Ola Rotimi)' (40p. (3rd series, no. 1)), and, with Bayo Williams, 'The genre of prose fiction: two complementary views' (60p. (4th series, no. 3)).

911 **The gods are not to blame.**

Ola Rotimi. London; Ibadan, Nigeria: Oxford University, 1971. 72p. (A Three Crowns Book).

One of Nigeria's outstanding playwrights, Rotimi has also written and creatively produced *Kurunmi: an historical tragedy* (Ibadan: Oxford University, 1971. 95p.); *Ovonramwen Nogbaisi: an historical tragedy in English* (Benin City: Ethiope; Ibadan: Oxford University, 1974. 81p.); *Our husband has gone again: a comedy* (Ibadan: Oxford, 1977. 86p.); *Holding talks: an absurdist drama* (Ibadan: University Press, 1979. 42p.); and *If: a tragedy of the ruled* (Ibadan: Heinemann, 1983. 91p.). A useful publication is *Understanding The gods are not to blame: a detailed interview with Ola Rotimi on his award-winning tragedy* (Lagos: Kurunmi Adventures, 1984. 17p.) by Rotimi and C. Maduka.

912 **Monkey on the tree.**

Uwa Udensi. In: *African plays for playing.* Edited by Michael Etherton. London: Heinemann, 1976, vol. 2. p. 7–32. (African Writers Series, no. 179).

This play is set in the Niger Delta during the Nigerian civil war. The brutal war brings together Jane, a young white girl whose parents have just been killed, an elderly Roman Catholic priest and several mercenaries, two from East Africa, Scrum, a white captain, and Nkomo, a young black South African. Despair, rootlessness and the horrors of war are evoked powerfully in this short play.

The Arts

General

913 **Popular arts in Africa.**
Karin Barber (et al.). *African Studies Review*, vol. 30, no. 3, special
issue (Sept. 1987), p. 1–78. bibliog.
This lengthy, seminal essay, originally commissioned for the African Studies
Association meeting at Madison, Wisconsin, November 1986, defines popular arts as
distinct from traditional and élite arts, explores their production and consumption, and
creatively argues that 'through art – through the gaps, evasions and contradictions in
art – that popular consciousness stubbornly maintains and renews its independence'
(p. 68). Numerous examples from Nigeria are used including ones from popular
travelling theatre, television, and Onitsha market literature which is contrasted with
Kenyan popular fiction. Critical essays by Mary Jo Arnoldi, Donald Cosintino,
Bennetta Jules-Rosette and Frederick Cooper follow the main article and are in turn
responded to by Barber. An excellent bibliography (p. 113–32) completes this special
journal issue.

914 **African art in cultural perspective: an introduction.**
William Bascom.   New York: Norton, 1973. 196p. maps. bibliog.
(Norton Critical Studies in Art History.)
Professor Bascom discusses art of the entire continent in fifteen regional chapters. His
extensive experience in Nigeria makes the chapter 'Southern Nigeria' (p. 83–109),
which describes the art of the Nupe, Yoruba, Bini, Ijo, Igbo, Ibibio and Ekoi,
especially worthwhile. 'Northeastern Nigeria' (p. 111–12) receives little more than
brief mention. The volume is heavily illustrated and provides a short bibliography
(p. 189–91).

915 **The living culture of Nigeria.**
Edited by Saburi O. Biobaku, foreword by Akenzua II, Oba of
Benin. Lagos: Thomas Nelson (Nigeria), 1976. 55p.

An informative companion volume to *The living arts of Nigeria* (q.v.), this book
contains succinct essays on nine topics by, with two exceptions, Nigerians, each one an
expert in the field covered. Ekpo Eyo authored 'Sculpture'; S. Irein Wangboje, 'Arts
and crafts'; Akin Euba, 'Music'; Peggy Harper, 'Dance'; Titi Euba 'Dress'; Ola
Rotimi, 'Drama'; David Aradeon, 'Architecture'; Umaru Ladan, 'Hausa literature';
and Chinua Achebe, 'Contemporary literature'. Eighty-six brilliant colour photographs
by Peccinotti illustrate the topics. The distinguished editor was, at the time of
publication, Chairman of the National Antiquities Commission and had been Vice-
Chancellor of the University of Lagos.

916 **The traditional artist in African societies.**
Edited by Warren L. d'Azevedo. Bloomington, Indiana; London:
Indiana University for the International Affairs Center, 1973. 454p.
map. bibliog.

This volume contains an introduction, ten papers on traditional artists in nine African
societies presented at a 1964 Indiana University seminar, and four broader papers on:
African art, the anthropological study of art, aesthetics and 'Approaches to non-
western art'. Five of the ten papers provide excellent detailed analyses of traditional
art and artists in Nigeria: 'Yoruba artistic criticism' by Robert Farris Thompson
(p. 19–61); 'A Yoruba master carver: Duga of Meko' by William Bascom (p. 62–78);
'the role of the carver in Anang society' by John C. Messenger (p. 101–27); 'A
sociocultural view of Hausa musical activity' by David W. Ames (p. 128–61); and
'*aökyagu* as artists in Marghi society' by James H. Vaughan, Jr. (p.162–91). Each
article is illustrated with photographs by its author; a useful bibliography (p. 435–54)
concludes the volume.

917 **The National Theatre & makers of modern Nigerian art.**
Edited by Edith Uche Enem, Garba Ashiwaju, S. O. Oputa, B. J.
Abegunde. Lagos: Nigeria Magazine, 1977. [12]p. (Nigeria Magazine
FESTAC Publication).

This booklet describes Nigeria's National Theatre in Lagos, with its many facilities and
art works illustrated in colour photographs. In the second part, an essay describes the
florescence of Nigerian art from the 1950s, and includes photographs of numerous
artists from a wide range of specialties.

918 **The living arts of Nigeria.**
Edited by William Fagg. London: Studio Vista, Cassell & Collier
Macmillan, 1976. [100]p. bibliog.

First published in 1971 and reprinted as a companion volume to *The living culture of
Nigeria* (q.v.), this book introduces a sampling of Nigeria's arts and crafts set within
their social contexts. It is an account of 'a 14-day expedition by four people innocent of
anthropological or ethnological knowledge or training, but equipped with powers of
observation (and material equipment) worthy of the best journalism, and charged with
doing a reporting job on the state of traditional crafts in Nigeria'. Neither text book
nor encyclopaedia, 'it is exoteric and impressionistic, being intended primarily to

interest the general public. Yet ethnologists or ethnographers may learn from it too . . .' (Introduction). The volume is divided into seven sections, covering: beadwork; brass work; dyeing; leather; pottery; weaving; and carving. Each section has a description by Fagg, former Keeper of Ethnography at the British Museum, several pages of striking colour photographs by Peccinotti and annotated colour illustrations by artist Michael Foreman.

919   **20th century art of Africa.**
      Kojo Fosu.   Zaria, Nigeria: Gaskiya, 1986. 234p. bibliog.

Informative details on many contemporary Nigerian artists are found in this volume. Although the author's interests are broader, Nigerian artists dominate his perspective which emphasizes contemporary art of the 1960s and 1970s. The book contains 158 plates of art works, describes the Oshogbo Centre and its artists and the 'Zaria rebels'. See also the recent essays and eighty-one plates in Uche Okeke's *Art in development: a Nigerian perspective* (Nimo, Nigeria: Documentation Centre, Asele Institute; Minneapolis, Minnesota: African American Cultural Center, 1982. 90p.) available from the University of Minnesota Gallery, Minneapolis, MN 55455.

920   **A bibliography of African art.**
      Compiled by L. J. P. Gaskin under the direction of Guy Atkins.
      London: International African Institute, 1965. 120p.

A very complete and well-organized listing of more than 5,359 entries based on the holdings of the International African Institute and other major collections in London, Paris, Amsterdam, Cologne and Frankfurt. Nigeria-related entries are numerous (p. 29–39, entries 1,575–2,177) and are sub-divided under the headings 'Figures and masks', 'Buildings and furniture', 'Clothing and adornment', Rock art, 'Techniques', 'Utensils, tools and weapons'; 'Miscellaneous' and 'African art today'. Relevant publications appear throughout the other categories of the volume.

921   **Contemporary Nigerian artists: a bio-bibliography.**
      Compiled by Bernice M. Kelly.   Washington, DC: Smithsonian
      Institution Libraries, National Museum of African Art Branch, 1988.
      [n.p.] bibliog.

An invaluable resource and remarkably rich compendium of information on nearly 300 Nigerian artists, listed alphabetically. A brief introduction (18p.) with a useful general bibliography including audio-visual materials precedes the entries for the artists, each of which contains, to the extent available, information on the artist's birth date and location, training, experience, exhibitions, awards and a bibliography of works about the artist. The bio-bibliography is published in loose-leaf, unpaginated form facilitating its continuous revision as more information on the artists becomes available and as new Nigerian artists emerge. Babatunde Lawal's 'The present state of art historical research in Nigeria: problems and possibilities', *Journal of African History*, vol. 18, no. 2 (1977), p. 193–216, is a significant survey of the subject for the time. See Dele Jegede's important recent doctoral thesis, *Trends in contemporary Nigerian art: a historical analysis* (PhD thesis, Indiana University, Bloomington, Indiana, 1983. 456 leaves. bibliog. Available from University Microfilms, Ann Arbor, Michigan, 1983).

922 **The art of West African kingdoms.**
Edward Lifchitz, project director; edited by Dean Trackman, Anita
Mintz, Janet Stanley. Washington, DC: Smithsonian Institution,
National Museum of African Art, 1987. 48p. 6 maps. bibliog.
This well-illustrated, slender, educational volume is written for teachers at secondary,
and slightly lower, levels. It provides an overview of the kingdoms of the Western
Sudan (Ghana, Mali, Songhai and Hausa States) and individual chapters relating the
art and culture of the kingdoms of Asante, Dahomey, Benin and the Yoruba
kingdoms, with maps, a chronology and numerous illustrations for each. The
annotated bibliography (p. 47–48) by Stanley is very useful and includes suggestions
for curricular materials. Four posters, one for each of the kingdoms discussed,
accompany the book.

923 **African images: essays in African iconology.**
Edited by Daniel F. McCall, Edna G. Bay. New York, London:
Africana for the African Studies Center, Boston University, 1975.
326p. (Boston University Papers on Africa, vol. 6).
This volume contains ten major analytical essays of which four directly concern
Nigerian cultures: Philip J. C. Dark, 'Benin bronze heads: styles and chronology'
(p. 25–103); Herbert M. Cole, 'The history of Ibo *mbari* houses – facts and theories'
(p. 104–32); W. Perkins Foss, 'Images of aggression: *Ivwri* sculpture of the Urhobo'
(p. 133–43); and Paula Ben-Amos, 'Professionals and amateurs in Benin court carving'
(p. 170–89). Ninety-seven plates of photographs are included for the articles.

924 **Background to Nigerian classical art, select annotated bibliography and
glossary of terms.**
Compiled by Andre Nitecki, introduced by Julia D. Harrison.
Calgary, Alberta: Glenbow Museum, 1981. 23p. map.
This brief introduction, a highly selective bibliography of forty-nine items, and
glossary, serves as an informative companion guide to the major exhibit 'Treasures of
ancient Nigeria' for which it was compiled. The exhibit was at the Glenbow Museum in
Calgary 16 March–10 May 1981. Another excellent basic source for information on
Nigerian art is the *Catalogue of the Robert Goldwater Library, the Metropolitan
Museum of Art* (Boston: G. K. Hall, 1982, 4 vols.). Vol. three, p. 250–98, contains
items under 'Nigeria' and relevant entries appear elsewhere in the *Catalogue* as well,
such as under African art auction catalogues and exhibitions.

925 **Bibliography of Nigerian sculpture.**
Compiled by Oyeniyi Osundina. *A Current Bibliography on African
Affairs*, vol. 6, no. 1 (winter 1973), p. 4–32.
An excellent, unannotated listing of 530 references to Nigerian art, organized by types
of scuplture (general, stone carving, brass casting, mud, bronze casting, wood, ivory,
terra-cottas and cement) with a list of general references, and indexed by author. The
author was Librarian, Ibadan University Library, Ibadan, Nigeria, at the time of
publication.

926 **A bibliography of Yoruba art.**
Compiled by Carolyn Owerka. New York: Pace, 1981. 40p.

This unannotated alphabetical listing is divided into four parts: 'Yoruba art, religion, and history'; 'Ancient Nigeria and the Benin Kingdom'; 'General books'; and 'Appendix: writings by William Fagg'. The compiler has incorporated relevant works found in H. M. Cole and W. F. Thompson's 1964 279-item *Bibliography of Yoruba sculpture* (New York: Library of Primitive Art, 10p. (Primitive Art Bibliographies, no. 3.)). D. C. Western's *A bibliography of the arts of Africa* (q.v.) and L. J. P. Gaskin's *A bibliography of African art* (q.v.).

927 **Everyman's guide to Nigerian art.**
Pat Oyebola. Lagos, Nigeria: Department of Culture, Federal
Ministry of Social Development, Youth, Sports and Culture, 1980.
2nd ed. 133p. bibliog. (Nigeria Magazine Special Publication no. 1).

Offers a practical overview of Nigerian art and artists for the non-specialist. The book describes 'Traditional arts' (p. 2–47) and offers brief 'Historical notes on iron and bronze scuplture' (p. 48–51). The special value of this well-illustrated volume is its chapter 'The modern scene' (p. 52–129), which describes briefly the wood and metal sculpture, painting, etching and batik of numerous contemporary artists. There is no obvious difference between the second edition and the 1976 first edition.

928 **Introduction to African arts of Kenya, Zaire, and Nigeria.**
Fred J. Parrott. New York: Arco, 1972. 188p. map. bibliog.

This wide-ranging survey of African arts in three countries 'is intended to stimulate further study and investigation. Its general objective is to foster appreciation and understanding of the contemporary African renaissance and to stress the concept that African art, like all artistic expression, is essentially ambivalent – both unique and universal, revealing man's identity as an individual and also his status as a human being' (Foreword, p. vii). The author provides general information on the countries and describes their traditional arts; 'the fetish' and music; 'colonial arts', especially the bronzes of Nigeria; dancing; and contemporary arts, especially wood carving; and writing. Examples of traditional folklore, writing from the colonial and post-colonial periods and poetry are included. The volume contains a substantial bibliography (p. 177–82), 'A basic chart for the analysis of artistic expression' (p. 183–84) and an index; numerous black-and-white illustrations by Naomichi Kimura appear throughout the text.

929 **Observations and interpretations: 2000 years of Nigerian art.**
Edited by John Povey, Arnold Rubin. Los Angeles: University of
California, African Studies Center, 1981. 40p. (Occasional Paper,
no. 23).

A collection of brief critical essays by the editors, Herbert M. Cole, Daniel Crowley, Sarah Dickerson, William Fagg, Merrick Posnansky and Thomas Seligmann on the occasion of the exhibition '2000 years of Nigerian art' in Los Angeles. Writes Rubin: 'A concentric system of priorities is clearly operative in African art research, publication, and exhibition, with Nigeria at the center, and the Yoruba at the center of the center. . . I suspect that work done on the arts of southwestern Nigeria – of the Yoruba and Benin – is more than the rest of Africa put together' (p. 7).

930   **African art: a bibliographic guide.**
Compiled by Janet L. Stanley.   New York, London: Africana, 1985.
55p. (Smithsonian Institution Libraries Research Guide, no. 4).

An excellent critical guide to the 'best books' on the subject, intended for the initiate as well as the specialist, with informative annotations for each item. Criteria for inclusion are clearly spelled out and the 167 entries are arranged in nine categories: 'Periodicals'; 'Bibliographies and reference books'; 'General surveys'; 'Regional studies'; 'African crafts & utilitarian arts'; 'Architecture'; 'Rock art, stone sculptures & ancient terracottas'; 'Contemporary African art & tourist art'; and 'African art market & collecting African art'. While only twelve sources are listed for Nigeria in the regional studies section (p. 18–22), important references for the country are found throughout the guide. The compiler is Librarian, National Museum of African Art, Smithsonian Institution, Washington, DC.

931   **African art in motion: icon and act.**
Robert Farris Thompson.   Los Angeles; Berkeley, California:
University of California, 1974. 275p. map. bibliog.

This volume was written to accompany the exhibition of the Katherine Coryton White Collection at the Frederick S. Wight Art Galleries of the University of California, Los Angeles, and at the National Galleries of Art in Washington, DC, in the spring and summer of 1974. In it Professor Thompson uses photographic and videotape studies from his fieldwork, African criticism and historical accounts. He analyses the art, performances and motion of Dan masks in Liberia, the Ejagham (Ekoi) of southeastern Nigeria and western Cameroon (p. 173–88), the Yoruba of Nigeria (p. 191–207; 219–26) and the Banyang of western Cameroon. The result is a major study of dance and of the attitudes of standing, sitting, riding, kneeling, supporting and balancing as they appear in art works to produce 'a unified aesthetic . . . demonstrating how motion lends special stature to music, and to objects, while objects deepen the perception of music-drenched motion' (cover copy). This important study is profusely illustrated with ten colour and 274 black-and-white plates. The author studied Yoruba sculpture and dance in Nigeria and Dahomey during 1962–64, 1965, 1967–68, and art and dance in Ghana and Cameroon in 1969 and Liberia in 1967.

932   **Flash of the spirit: African and Afro-American art and philosophy.**
Robert Farris Thompson.   New York: Random House, 1983; New
York: Vintage, 1984. 317p. bibliog.

This fascinating, creative study 'begins the project of identifying *specifically Yoruba, Kongo, Dahomean, Mande, and Ejagham* influences on the art and philosophies of black people throughout the Americas' (Introduction, p. xiv–xv, italics in original). The author shows how the traditions, aesthetics and philosophies of these cultures as seen in their music, sculpture, textiles, architecture, religion and idiogrammatic writing, have been used by black people in the United States, Cuba, Trinidad, Haiti, Brazil and Mexico. Nigerian cultural influence appears in 'Black saints go marching in: Yoruba art and culture in the Americas' (p. 1–99) and 'Emblems of prowess: Ejagham art and writing in two worlds' (p. 225–68) and extensively in the chapter on vodun religion and art in Haiti (p. 161–91). Copious notes support the author's arguments; 164 plates and numerous drawings illustrate his associations.

933 **A bibliography of the arts of Africa.**
Compiled by Dominique Coulet Western. Waltham, Massachusetts: African Studies Association, Brandeis University, 1975. 123p.

This unannotated compilation is organized into sections on 'Art', 'Architecture', 'Oral literature', and 'Music and dance' in sub-Saharan Africa with each of these categories subdivided into a general listing and broad geographic areas. Under 'West Africa', there are separate divisions by ethnic groups (for Benin, Hausa, Ibo, Ife, Nok, Tiv, Yoruba) and by country. There is an author index but no table of contents; modern painting and sculpture are not included.

934 **African art: an introduction.**
Frank Willett. New York, Toronto: Oxford, 1971. Reprinted 1985. 288p. 4 maps. bibliog. (The World of Art Series).

Offers an outstanding introduction to the art of the continent, set in historical perspective. Chapters cover the history and development of the study of African art, as well as architecture, sculpture and 'African art today'. Extensive coverage is given to Nigerian art, especially that of the Yoruba, Igo and Ibibio, and of Ife and Benin; all are amply illustrated by many of the book's 261 plates, sixty-one of which are in colour. The author spent several years conducting archaeological excavations in Nigeria, wrote *Ife in the history of West African sculpture* (q.v.) and is currently Director of the Hunterian Museum and Art Gallery of the University of Glasgow. George Corbin's recent *Native arts of North America, Africa, and the South Pacific* (New York: Harper & Row, 1988) contains an excellent, illustrated chapter on 'Art in Nigeria' (p. 155–80).

Periodical

935 **African Arts.**
Los Angeles: University of California, African Studies Center, 1967– . quarterly.

Orginally *African Arts/Arts d'Afrique*, this is the premier publication in the field. Each issue contains exhibition and book reviews, as well as scholarly articles, each of which is profusely illustrated with colour and black-and-white photographs. A wide range of art topics and the sociocultural context of art throughout Africa are considered. Most issues contain at least one article on Nigerian art and many issues contain several relevant articles, a small selection of which have been included in this bibliography. For example, vol. 20, no. 1 (Nov. 1986), was a special memorial issue to Robert Plant Armstrong whose 'personal kindness and professional distinction made him revered in the field of African studies' (p. 30). It contained: 'Flaming crowns, cooling waters: masquerades of the Ijebu Yoruba' by Henry John Drewal (p. 32–41, 99–100), 'The Isoko ethos of Ivri' by Philip M. Peek (p. 42–47, 98), 'Nigerian thorn carvings: a living monument to Justus Akeredolu' by Frank Willett (p. 48–53, 98), and 'Art and trance among Yoruba Shango devotees' by Margaret Thompson Drewal (p. 60–67, 98). Vol. 21, no. 2 (Feb. 1988), is devoted to Igbo arts and contains the following important articles: Herbert M. Cole 'Igbo arts and ethnicity' and 'The survival and impact of Igbo Mbari' (p. 54–65, 96), Richard N. Henderson and Ifekandu Umunna 'Leadership symbolism in Onitsha Igbo crowns and Ijele', (p. 28–37, 94–96), Henry John Drewal 'Mermaids, mirrors and snake charmers: Igbo Mami Wata shrines', (p. 38–45, 96), John Picton 'Ekpeye masks and masking' (p. 46–53, 94), Eli Bentor 'Life as an artistic process: Igbo ikenga and Ofo' (p. 66–71, 94), and Simon Ottenberg 'Psychological aspects of Igbo art' (p. 72–82, 93–94).

Visual arts

36   African stone sculpture.
Philip Allison, foreword by William Fagg.   New York; Washington,
DC: Praeger, 1968. 71p. 3 maps. bibliog.

This volume discusses stone sculptures found in Nigeria, Sierra Leone, Guinea, the
Congo, Rhodesia, southern Ethiopia, and 'Worked stones of the Western Sudan and
the Sahara'. For Nigeria, the author surveys 'The Yoruba stone sculptures, including
the stone figures of Esie' (p. 11–24) and 'The Cross River *akwanshi*' (p. 25–35),
describing them as 'groups of stone-carvings which resemble no other works of art, in
any medium, in the whole of West Africa' (p. 25) and considering 295 stones in all.
Each chapter contains numerous black-and-white photographs. A bibliography
(p. 65–69) provides important references for each of the stone groups analysed.

37   William Bascom: in memoriam.
Edited by Robert Plant Armstrong.   *African Arts*, vol. 16, no. 2
(Feb. 1983), p. 26–27, 89–93. bibliog.

Most of this beautifully illustrated memorial issue is devoted to the appreciation of
William R. Bascom's contributions to the study of West African, especially Yoruba,
art and culture. The introductory essay contains reminiscences by his colleagues
(including R. P. Armstrong, David Ames, Barbara Ames, Philip E. Leis, Joseph
Greenberg, and Joe Moore). Other articles are: 'Oshe Shango and the dynamic of
doubling' by the editor (p. 28–33); 'The celebration of *oworu* among the Isoko' by
Philip M. Peek (p. 34–41, 98); 'Yoruba cloths with regal names' by Ruth M. Boyer
(p. 42–45, 98); 'Nike Olaniyi' (a prominent artist of Oshogbo) by Victoria Scott
(p. 46–47); 'Igbo and Yoruba art contrasted' by Simon Ottenberg (p. 48–55, 97); 'The
art and aesthetics of the Yoruba' by Justine M. Cordwell (p. 56–59, 93–94, 100); and
'An Ifa diviner's shrine in Ijebuland' by Margaret Thompson Drewal and Henry John
Drewal (p. 60–67, 99–100). Professor Armstrong is himself commemorated by scholars
in a special issue of *African Arts*, vol. 20, no. 1 (Nov. 1986) (q.v.).

38   Art in Nigeria, 1960.
Ulli Beier.   Cambridge: Cambridge University in collaboration with
the Information Division, Ministry of Home Affairs, Ibadan, Nigeria,
1960. [67]p.

The well-known author of this volume aims to convey 'some idea, at least, of the rich
and varied artistic activity that goes on in Nigeria in the year of Independence' (p. 4).
His survey touches on contemporary traditional art, the art of the new middle class,
Christian art, commercial art, European architecture, and the use of traditional carving
and forms in Nigerian architecture. He considers modern European artists in Nigeria,
particularly Susanne Wenger, the Austrian who 'has become completely absorbed into
Nigerian life; . . . and has so astonished the people with her spontaneous grasp of
Yoruba religious symbolism that she was made a priestess of Obatola, the Yoruba
creator god' (p. 23). Following the well-illustrated main text (p. 1–24) are seventy-
seven black-and-white plates of Nigerian art (p. 25–67).

939 **African mud sculpture.**
Ulli Beier. London; New York; Ibadan, Nigeria: Cambridge
University, 1963. 96p.

An interesting discussion of mud sculptures, a highly perishable traditional art form, l
an artist and art historian who had been resident in Yoruba areas for twelve years. Tl
author describes the ethnographic setting for religious and court-based mud figure a
among the Igbo, Yoruba and Bini of southern Nigeria, as well as in Abomey, tl
capital of the Dahomean kingdom. Seventy-seven black-and-white photographs, mc
taken in 1956, illustrate the mud art of Igbo Mbari houses, Bini Olokun mud shrine
sculptures for Eshu, Legba and Ogun and the royal palaces of Abomey and Ben
City. An excellent related article is Paula Ben-Amos's 'Symbolism in Olokun mud ar
African Arts, vol. 6, no. 4 (summer 1973), p. 28–31, 95.

940 **Contemporary art in Africa.**
Ulli Beier. New York: Praeger, 1968. 173p.

Although this volume discusses newer art and artists in Ghana, the Sudan, Ethiopi
Senegal, the Cameroons, South Africa, Zaire, Mozambique, Kenya and Rhodesia, tl
majority of the discussion focuses on Nigerians and their works. In part one 'Africa
renaissance' (p. 15–88) Yemi Bisiri, Ovia Idah, and Lamidi Fakeye are described a
transitional Nigerian artists. Demas Nwoko and Uche Okeke of the Zaria art schoc
and Ben Enwonwu are described as leading an artistic breakthrough in Nigeria. Pa
two, 'Changing images in an African town' (p. 89–164) presents the story of the artist
community in Oshogbo, featuring the Mbari Mbayo Club, Georgina Beier
workshops, Twins Seven-Seven, Susanne Wenger's works at the shrine of the riv
goddess Oshun and several individual artists. The works described are illustrated i
ninety-nine monochrome and eleven colour plates. The personal view presented b
Beier reflects his (at the time of publication) seventeen years as a tutor in th
Department of Extra-Mural Studies of the University of Ibadan, the last ten of whic
were spent in Oshogbo.

941 **The art of Benin.**
Paula Ben-Amos. London: Thames & Hudson, 1980. 96p. 2 maps.
bibliog.

An excellent and attractively produced introduction to the art, history, beliefs an
general culture of the traditional Kingdom of Benin in southern Nigeria. Combinin
archaeology, accounts by European travellers dating back to the sixteenth century an
her own anthropological fieldwork in Benin City since 1966, the author tells th
complex story of the rôle art plays in so many aspects of Bini life. A brief bibliograph
(p. 94) and notes are useful. In *Bibliography of Benin art* (New York: Museum c
Primitive Art, 1968, 17p. (Primitive Art Bibliographies, no. VI)), Dr. Ben-Amc
compiles 433 unannotated references. Among her several informative articles on th
Benin Kingdom are 'Men and animals in Benin art', *Man*, vol. 11, no. 2 (June 1976
p. 243–52; with Osarenren Omoregie, 'Ekpo ritual in Avbiama village', *African Art.*
vol. 2, no. 4 (summer 1969), p. 8–13, 79; 'Owina n'Ido: royal weavers of Benin
African Arts, vol. 11, no. 4 (July 1978), p. 48–53; and 'Artistic creativity in Beni
Kingdom', *African Arts*, vol. 19, no. 3 (May 1986), p. 60–63, 83–84.

942 **The art of power, the power of art: studies in Benin iconography.**
Edited by Paula Ben-Amos, Arnold Rubin. Los Angeles: Museum of
Cultural History, University of California, 1983. 111p. map. bibliog.
(Monograph Series, no. 19).

This volume, which accompanied the exhibition at the Museum of Cultural History
Gallery at the University of California, Los Angeles, 2 March–1 May 1983, is a
collaborative study of Benin iconography by a seminar of advanced graduate students'
(p. 8) and several specialists in Benin art. It includes a series of brief interpretative
essays on specific types or technologies of the art by the graduate students: three by
Barbara Winston Blackmun; 'A Benin bronze plaque of a single figure with leopard' by
Philip J. C. Dark; an introduction, 'The power of kings: symbolism of a Benin
ceremonial stool' and 'In honor of queen mothers' by the editor, and a preface
(p. 10–12) by Rubin. The selected bibliography (p. 109–11) provides a useful list of
references on Benin art. The study is generously illustrated with eighty-five figures and
photographs.

943 **The essential gourd: art and history in northeastern Nigeria.**
Marla C. Berns, Barbara Rubin Hudson. Los Angeles: Museum of
Cultural History, University of California, 1986. 190p. 4 maps. bibliog.

A profusely illustrated volume on the ethnography and art history of gourd use and
decoration in northeastern Nigeria. The study is based on 214 gourds collected in the
region by Hudson in 1969–71 and donated to the Museum of Cultural History, the
1980–82 fieldwork among the Ga'anda in the lower Gongola Valley, and the analysis of
Berns, the book's principal author and curator of the exhibit for which the book was
produced. The volume consist of six chapters: 'Introduction'; 'An ethnography of
gourd use'; 'An ethnography of gourd decoration'; 'The Ga'anda'; 'Decorated gourds
and history'; and 'Gourds and modern change'. An appendix of 'Word lists by
language family', notes and a substantial bibliography (p. 186–90) complete the book.
In a related article, 'Hausa calabash decoration', *African Arts*, vol. 19, no. 3 (May
1986), p. 45–47, 82–83, Judith [M.] Perani discusses the creativity of men in calabash
carving, particularly in Kode, a village south-east of Kano.

944 **Art as statecraft: a king's justification in ivory, a carved tusk from
Benin.**
Barbara Winston Blackmun. Geneva: Musée Barbier-Müller, 1984.
29p. map. bibliog.

The author provides a fascinating analysis of the meanings conveyed by the carving on
a single elephant tusk in the Musée Barbier-Müller. Her 1984 University of California,
Los Angeles, doctoral thesis was *The iconography of carved altar tusks from Benin,
Nigeria* (Ann Arbor, Michigan: University Microfilms, 1985, 3 vols.). Of an entirely
different order, but none the less interesting is the *Ekon society puppets: sculptures for
social criticism, 13 October to 17 December 1977* (New York: Tribal Arts Gallery Two,
1977. 14p.), an exhibition catalogue with an essay by Alfred L. Scheinberg,
photographs by Johan Elbers, and a bibliography (p. [14]).

The Arts. Visual arts

945 **From the hands of Lawrence Ajanaku.**
Jean Borgatti. Los Angeles: Museum of Cultural History, University of California, 197m 39p. map. bilbiog. (UCLA Museum of Cultural History Pamphlet Series, vol. 1, no. 6).

An account of the life and work of Lawrence Ajanaku, a master carver and maker c complex, brilliantly-coloured cloth appliqué costumes for the northern Edo of Bende State. The costumes are part of *Okakagbe*, 'a multi-media art form in cloth appliqué dance and music' adopted in the late 1920s (p. 3). The masquerade, its music and th artist Okeleke who made its first costume are described in this booklet whicl accompanied an exhibition by the same title at the UCLA Museum of Cultural Histor in the autumn of 1979.

946 **Ikenga figures among the north-east Igbo and the Igala.**
John Boston. London: Ethnographica in association with the Federal Department of Antiquities, Lagos, Nigeria, 1977. 120p. 2 maps. bibliog.

The author presents a description and functional analysis of the cult of *ikenga* amon the north-east or Nri-Awka Igbo and the Igala of eastern Nigeria. The varied carve representations of *ikenga*, or *okega* as the Igala call it, with their characteristicall stylized horns, are examined in detail. The author emphasizes the need to place th horned figure in its social and religious context for its rôle in reference not only t masculinity but to 'achievement in the social field, to competition between lineages lineage segments and individuals for status and prestige' (p. 115). Seventy-seve plates, eight in colour, of *ikenga* in village settings, in the Nigeria Museum, Lagos, an in the British Museum's Museum of Mankind, London, illustrate the volume.

947 **Nigerian traditional sculpture, Central Hall, University College, Cardiff, 23 April to 17 May 1974.**
Cardiff University Art Group, introduced by Raymond Eyquem.
Cardiff: University College, 1974. [48]p. bibliog.

An exhibition catalogue of 156 Nigerian sculptures, many presented in photograph and with a very brief bibliography (p. 9).

948 **Yoruba religious carving: pagan & Christian sculpture in Nigeria and Dahomey.**
Kevin Carroll, foreword by William Fagg. New York: Praeger, 1967. 172p. map. bibliog.

Father Carroll, S.M.A., began, in 1947, to oversee a centre experimenting with the adaptation of African crafts to Christian uses in in the north-eastern Yoruba area tow of Oye Ekiti. Here he describes the 'work of several of these carvers [Areogun 1880–1954, his son Bandele, b. 1910, Lamidi, b. 1925, son of Bendele apprentic Fakeye and the Ketu carver Otoọrọ, b. 1905] and of others who have worked in th area during the last seventy years, relating their work to its environment as it change from the close community life of the last century to the wide-eyed and turbulent life o today' (p. 1). The result is an important account of both Yoruba wood carving an carvers, and the relationship between 'pagan' arts and Christianity. Carroll conclude 'that the art of the Yoruba carver . . . is a humanistic rather than a deeply religious ar even when directly concerned with the creation of religious objects' (p. 53). Tw colour plates, twenty-two line drawings and 128 half-tones illustrate the volume whicl has a brief bibliography (p. 169).

344

949 **Decorated gourds in north-eastern Nigeria.**
T. J. H. Chappel. Lagos, Nigeria: Federal Department of
Antiquities; London: Ethnographica, 1977. 222p. map. bibliog.

Offers a fully illustrated artistic and ethnographic account of decorated gourds in the
former province of Adamawa in north-east Nigeria. The focus is on four ethnic groups:
the Muslim settled Fulani; the pastoral Fulani; the Bata of the Yola area; and the
Yungur. The author spent ten months in 1965–66 surveying the area for the Nigerian
Federal Department of Antiquities and gathering items for the department's museum
at Jos. In eight chapters he describes 'The area and its peoples'; 'The gourd and its
uses'; 'Decorative techniques and designs'; 'Gourd designs and their meanings';
'Carving as an individual activity'; 'Carving as a social and cultural activity'; 'The
appreciation of decorated gourds'; and 'Gourd-carving and modern change'. Notes (p.
208–16), a bibliography (p. 216–18) and an index increase the value of this attractive
volume.

950 **Mbari: art and life among the Owerri Igbo.**
Herbert M. Cole. Bloomington, Indiana: Indiana University, 1982.
261p. map. bibliog. (Traditional Arts of Africa).

An excellent study of the art and culture of Owerri Igbo of eastern Nigeria, which
seeks 'to describe mbari houses, not as isolated works of art but as monuments growing
out of and expressive of, the values beliefs, rituals and processes of Owerri Igbo
culture' (Preface, p. xvii). To do so the author provides the ethnographic context and
examines the form, inspiration, individuality, aesthetics and meaning of mbari houses,
which are elaborately decorated shrines filled with diverse sets of clay representations
of humans, deities and animals. *Mbari* in Igbo means 'decorated', 'beautiful', 'fine', or
'celebrated', 'a complex and long-term festival' and 'many different things' (p. 183).
Professor Cole, an art historian, did fieldwork in the Owerri area in 1966–67, when he
saw about 150 mbari houses. Twelve colour plates, seventy-six black-and-white plates,
thirty-one figures, a glossary (p. 221–24), appendices (p. 225–36), a bibliography
(p. 237–42) and notes (p. 243–57) give great depth to this fine work.

951 **I am not myself: the art of African masquerade.**
Edited and introduced by Herbert M. Cole. Los Angeles: Museum of
Cultural History, University of California, 1985. 111p. map. bibliog.
(Monograph Series, no. 26).

This monograph was published in conjunction with an exhibition of the same title and
includes short accounts, by thirteen scholars, of masking in eighteen cultures, mainly
from West Africa and Zaire. Relating to Nigeria, are: Debbie Randolph's 'Yoruba'
(p. 60–65), Richard Blades's 'Northern Edo' (p. 66–67), Arnold G. Rubin's 'A
Mumuye mask' (p. 98–99), and the editor's 'Introduction: the mask, masking and
masquerade arts in Africa' (p. 15–27). This latter includes a perceptive discussion of
masks in general with those of the Igbo and Yoruba among other groups. The volume
is well-illustrated with eighty-eight figures and seven colour plates (four of Nigerian
masks) and has a brief bibliography (p. 109–11). Of related interest is Emmanuel
Okechukwu Odita's 1970 doctoral dissertation at Indiana University entitled, *Igbo
masking tradition: its types, functions, and interpretations* (Ann Arbor, Michigan:
University Microfilms, 1971. 183 leaves.) which contains sixty-four photographic
illustrations.

952 **Igbo arts: community and cosmos.**
Herbert M. Cole, Chike C. Aniakor, foreword by Chinua Achebe.
Los Angeles: Museum of Cultural History, University of California,
1984. 238p. 2 maps. bibliog.

This profusely illustrated volume was published for an exhibition at the Frederick S. Wight Art Gallery of the University of California at Los Angeles (UCLA), in conjunction with the twenty-seventh annual meeting of the African Studies Association, and in honour of the twenty-fifth anniversary of the UCLA African Studies Center. The book's six chapters include brief contributions by four specialists (Alexander Okwudor Attah, Della Jenkins, Sidney Littlefield Kasfir and Bonnie E. Watson). They cover the topics: 'Introduction' (religion and world view); 'Art and the individual'; 'Art and the family'; 'Art and the community';'Masquerades'; and 'Cosmos, world view, and aesthetics'. Notes and an excellent bibliography (p. 233–38) conclude the volume.

953 **An introduction to Benin art and technology.**
Philip J. C. Dark. Oxford: Clarendon, 1973. 114p. 2 maps. bibliog.

This major work on Benin art is based on the author's several years of study in Nigeria and participation in the Benin History Scheme in the 1950s. The main text (p. 1–77) offers an excellent introduction to the range of Benin art, artists, artisans and craftsmanship available, though the bibliography (p. 83–85) only relates to works mentioned in the text and, therefore, is brief. Eighty full-page plates illustrate the art work, craftsmanship and designs and are fully described in notes (p. 87–109). Dark is Professor Emeritus of Anthropology, Southern Illinois University, Carbondale, Illinois. His *The art of Benin: a catalogue of an exhibition of the A.W. F. Fuller and Chicago Natural History Museum collections of antiquities from Benin, Nigeria* (Chicago: Field Museum of Natural History, 1962. [122]p.) discusses the discovery and collection of Benin art as well as the objects displayed at the exhibition.

954 **An illustrated catalogue of Benin art.**
Philip J. C. Dark. Boston, Massachusetts: G. K. Hall, 1982. [172]p.
bibliog.

The author, an authority on Benin art, provides a summary catalogue of some 5–6,000 objects organized by type with information on where the object is found and where it has appeared in illustrations. In addition, non-Benin ('Afro-Portuguese-Sherbo') objects and collections of Benin art are listed, and there is a subject catalogue. The entire catalogue is introduced by the author's lucid preface and his essay 'Collections of Benin art: their formation and study' (p. v–xix). A table (p. xxi–xxiii) lists 'some sales of Benin and related art objects by W. D. Webster between 1899–1901', providing a fascinating record of the previous prices of items which now command high prices. Eighty black-and-white illustrations and an extensive bibliography (9p.) accompany the catalogue.

955 **Traditional art of the Nigerian peoples: the Milton D. Ratner family collection.**
Henry John Drewal, foreword by Milton D. Ratner. Washington, DC: Museum of African Art, 1977. 58p. map. bibliog.
This catalogue was published to accompany the exhibition of the same title at the Museum of African Art. The author presents an essay 'Hidden presence and visual command' (p. 4–9) which focuses on Yoruba concepts of 'life force and its expression in art', using the thesis that 'ritual objects in many African societies are prepared with powers often concealed and alluded to in a variety of ways by the artist' (p. 9). Extensive notes on cultural context and meaning accompany the black-and-white illustrations of fifty-seven objects.

956 **The arts of the Egungun among Yoruba peoples.**
Henry John Drewal (et al.). *African Arts*, vol. 11, no. 3 (April 1978), p. 18–19, 97–98. map. bibliog.
This special issue is devoted to masquerades throughout Yorubaland; it contains eight articles. Drewal asserts that 'Egungun masquerades are elaborate ensembles of cloth and other media that pay homage to forces affecting the living' (p. 18). Egungun among many peoples is considered: the Remo Yoruba (p. 20–27, 100) and Oyo Yoruba (p.56–61, 99) by Marilyn Hammersley Houlberg; the Egbado (p. 23–39, 98) by Margaret Thompson Drewal and Henry John Drewal; the Igbomina Yoruba (p. 40–47, 99–100) by John Pemberton III; Iganna (p. 48–55, 100) by Marc Schiltz; and Owo (p. 65–76, 100) by Robin Poynor. Joel Adedeji writes about 'The poetry of the Yoruba Masque Theatre', popularly known as the Alarinjo (p. 62–64, 100). The bibliography on Egungun (p. 100–01) is useful and the many colour and black-and-white illustrations throughout the issue document Egungun in dramatic fashion. Professor Drewal's 'Flaming crowns, cooling waters: masquerades of the Ijebu Yoruba' in the special issue of *African Arts*, vol. 20, no. 1 (Nov. 1986) (q.v.) contains vivid illustrations.

957 **African artistry: technique and aesthetics in Yoruba sculpture.**
Henry John Drewal. Atlanta, Georgia: High Museum of Art, 1980. 100p. map. bibliog.
A perceptive essay on both the creative process and the technical aspects of Yoruba wood carving (p. 9–20) accompanies this catalogue from 'An exhibition of Yoruba art from the Arnett Collection' at the High Museum of Art, Atlanta, Georgia, 17 April–25 May 1980. The author, who apprenticed himself to two Yoruba sculptors and conducted other fieldwork on the subject while doing research in western Yorubaland in 1965, 1970–71, 1973, 1975 and 1977–78, offers notes on 163 illustrated objects. These fall into the categories of: posts, doors, staffs, containers, pedestals, twin figures, miscellaneous sculptures and masquerades.

The Arts. Visual arts

958 **Gẹ̀lẹ̀dẹ́: art and female power among the Yoruba.**
Henry John Drewal, Margaret Thompson Drewal. Bloomington,
Indiana: Indiana University, 1983. 306p. map. bilbiog. (Traditional
Arts of Africa).

A remarkably rich description and analysis of Gẹ̀lẹ̀dẹ́ masquerades is offered,
considering 'lavish spectacles of carved wooden headpieces, cloth costumes, dances,
songs, and drumming found principally among western Yoruba peoples in Nigeria and
Benin' (p. xv). 'Consisting of nighttime (Èfè) and daytime (Gẹ̀lẹ̀dẹ́) performances,
these masquerades represent a highly visible, artistic expression of a pan-Yoruba
belief: that women, primarily elderly women, possess certain extraordinary power
equal to or greater than that of the gods and ancestors, a view that is reflected in
praises acknowledging them as 'our mothers', 'the gods of society', and 'the owners of
the world' . . . They can bring health, wealth, and fertility to the land and its people,
or they can bring disaster – epidemic, drought, pestilence' (p. xv). It is based on twelve
years of research. The authors combine historical perspectives from elderly informants
with ethnographic and artistic data based on their observation of numerous Gẹ̀lẹ̀dẹ́
performances and thus provide a comprehensive view of the event. The volume
contains thirteen colour and 170 black-and-white plates, each with notes, and an
excellent bibliography (p. 293–99).

959 **Nigerian sculpture: bridges to power.**
Ellen F. Elsas, Robin Poynor, foreword by Gail Andrews Trechsel.
Birmingham, Alabama: Birmingham Museum of Art, 1984. 64p. map.
bibliog.

This catalogue is a guide to the exhibition of the same title, 15 April–3 June 1984.
Elsas's brief essay 'Nigerian sculpture: images of power' (p. 7–9) is followed by
Poynor's 'Nigerian sculpture: bridges to power' (p. 11–21) and informative notes on
the 100 objects exhibited, most of which are shown in photographs. Yoruba pieces
account for half of those included, but there are also Edo, Niger Delta, Igbo, Cross
River and Nigerian Plateau carvings as well.

960 **The living arts and crafts of Ile-Ifẹ.**
Ọmọtọsọ Eluyẹmi. Ile-Ife, Nigeria: Adasanmi Printing Works, 1978.
47p. map. bibliog.

The author has performed a welcome service by making available, to residents and
visitors alike, his illustrated study of contemporary arts and crafts in this ancient ritual
centre.- He describes the work of the families still engaged in wood carving, metal
casting, blacksmithing, bead-making, dyeing, ritual and utilitarian pottery-making and
crown-making. The location of each of these activities is shown on the enclosed fold-
out map of the city.

961 **Two thousand years Nigerian art.**
Ekpo Eyo. Lagos, Nigeria: Federal Department of Antiquities, 1977.
238p. map. bibliog.

A beautifully produced, folio volume 'intended to illustrate with examples the different
types of Nigerian scupltures in terracotta, metal, stone and wood' (p. 8). Objects are
shown in 111 full-page colour and 161 smaller black-and-white photographs by André
Held and Ursula Held. They range from Nok culture, dated between 900 BC and AD

200, to that of the twentieth century. An informative discussion of each culture and style is framed by an introduction to African art and an epilogue describing the future of Nigerian art. The author, highly regarded in this field, wrote his 1974 University of Ibadan PhD thesis on *Recent excavations in Ife and Owo and their implications for Ife and Benin studies* and at the time of publication had been Director of the Nigerian Federal Department of Antiquities since 1968. A perspicacious essay by Dr. Eyo is 'Primitivism and other misconceptions of African art', *Munger Africana Library Notes*, no. 63 (April 1982), 27p., in which he argues against use of the terms 'primitive', 'tribal' and 'tribality' to describe art from Africa.

962   **Treasures of ancient Nigeria.**
Ekpo Eyo, Frank Willett. New York: Knopf, in association with the Detroit Institute of Arts, 1980. 162p. map. bibliog.

This book was produced to accompany Nigeria's magnificent international exhibit of 100 works in bronze, ivory and terracotta. The works, spanning more than 2,000 years, are from ten cultures (Nok, Yelwa, Igbo-Ukwu, Ife, Owo, Benin, Tsoede, Yoruba, Esie and Ikom) and are depicted here in 137 photographs and plates, fifty-three of which are in colour. The introduction is by Dr. Eyo, then Director of the Nigerian Department of Antiquities; Willett, former archaeologist for the Nigerian Department of Antiquities and Curator of the Museum of Ife Antiquities, wrote the interpretative text. A German edition has been produced, *Kunstschätze aus Alt-Nigeria* (Art treasures from ancient Nigeria) (Mainz am Rhein: Philipp von Zabern, 1983. 203p.). Published at the time of the same exhibition at the Royal Academy of Arts (Oct. 1982–Feb. 1983) is a colourful booklet, useful for teachers and secondary school students, entitled *A glimpse of Nigeria's past* (London: Ethnographica, 1982. 28p.) by Stuart Hamilton and Eyo. This publication distils extensive information on the artistic styles and provides a fold-out historical chronology.

963   **Nigerian images: the splendor of African sculpture.**
William Fagg. London, New York: Praeger, 1963. 124p. map. bibliog.

One of the first books devoted exclusively to Nigerian art, this volume commemorates a series of exhibitions organized by the author and held in Britain, Germany and Switzerland in 1960–62. Accompanying the descriptive text, which is divided into 'The ancient arts' (p. 19–40, plates 1–76) and 'The recent period' (p. 117–24, plates 77–144), are 144 dramatic black-and-white photographs by Herbert List. A brief list of plates (p. 8–9) introduces the cultures and art styles represented and a useful glossary (p. 11–14) explains less familiar terms.

964   **Yoruba sculpture of West Africa.**
William Fagg, John Pemberton III, edited by Bryce Holcombe.   New York: Alfred A. Knopf, 1982. 209p. map. bibliog.

Represents the first art book to concentrate on the modern sculpture – the early-nineteenth to the early-twentieth centuries – of the 'most prolific art-producing people in Black Africa' (Foreword, p. xi), the Yoruba of south-western Nigeria. Fagg, former Deputy Keeper of the African Collections of the British Museum, contributed three chapters: 'On the art of the Yoruba', 'The Yoruba and their past', and 'The Yoruba artist: regional styles' (p. 5–49). They are illustrated by more than fifty photographs. John Pemberton III, Professor of Religion at Amherst College, Massachusetts,

349

authored the 'Descriptive catalogue' (p. 52–192) containing both seventy full–pag€ plates, of which thirty-five are in colour, and descriptive notes on each plate. Th€ editor, Holcombe, Director of Primitive Art, The Pace Gallery, New York City, als€ wrote the brief foreword. Carolyn Owerka compiled the excellent bibliograph; (p. 201–08).

965 **Benin art.**
W[erner] Forman, B[edřich] Forman, Philip Dark. London: Paul
Hamlyn, 1960. 59p. map. bibliog.

Dark provides a succinct, lucid introduction to Benin art and notes to the ninety-two black-and-white plates of photographs by Forman and Forman. Aesthetically culturally, and technically, Benin art has fascinated Westerners since their encounter with it in 1897. As Dark asserts 'The command of the *cire-perdue* technique by the bronzeworker at one stage in the art's development was quite exceptional for any culture' (p. 25).

966 **Royal Benin art in the collection of the National Museum of African Art.**
Bryna Freyer, foreword by Sylvia H. Williams. Washington, DC;
London: Smithsonian Institution for the National Museum of African
Art, 1987. 63p. 2 maps. bibliog.

This attractive catalogue was produced to accompany the exhibition of twenty-one works of art from the kingdom of Benin, part of the collection of the National Museum of African Art, Washington, DC. The author, an assistant curator of the museum, provides a brief but excellent introduction to the kingdom and its art history. She later describes the art works, predominantly copper-alloy castings, and their cultural contexts in the sections 'The Oba'; 'The court', and 'Foreigners'. The foreword by the museum's director explains that most of these objects were formerly in the Joseph H. Hirshhorn Collection; the provenance of each is described in footnotes. A brief glossary of Bini terms (p. 61), a bibliography (p. 62–63), and photographs taken in 1958 by W. B. Fagg enhance this high-quality publication.

967 **The arts of the Hausa: an aspect of Islamic culture in Northern Nigeria.**
David Heathcote. Chicago; London: University of Chicago, 1977.
61p. map. bibliog. (University of Chicago Press text-fiche).

Based on the first comprehensive exhibition of Hausa art held outside Africa, at the Commonwealth Institute, London, as part of the World Of Islam Festival, 1976. The author, a senior lecturer in the Department of Art History at Ahmadu Bello University in Zaria, Nigeria, introduces the main forms of art of one of the largest cultural groups in sub-Saharan Africa, and provides a glossary of Hausa terms and a bibliography (p. 55–61). Brief accounts of calligraphy and Quranic decoration, weaving, indigo dyeing, embroidery, basketry, calabash decoration, leatherwork, metalwork, horse trappings, woodcarving, musical instruments, pottery, wall decoration, and miscellaneous items are followed by notes on the 168 colour photographs which are reproduced on two micro-fiches and included with the book. A slightly longer version with the same title was published in 1976 for the exhibition (London: World of Islam Festival, 100p. bibliog.) with photographs integrated in the text. See also Heathcote's 'Hausa embroidery stitches', *Nigerian Field*, vol. 39, no. 4 (1974), p. 163–68, and 'Hausa hand-embroidered caps', *Nigerian Field*, vol. 40, no. 2 (1975), p. 54–73.

968   **Kalabari sculpture.**
Robin Horton.   Lagos: Federal Department of Antiquities, 1965.
127p. bibliog.

'This essay is an attempt to relate the form and content of a body of sculpture to its use in the culture that gave it birth' (Preface). The author presents an outline of Kalabari culture, an Ijaw (Ijo) people of the Niger Delta, before examining 'Sculpture and its uses', 'Carving, criticism and the carver' and the motifs used in the sculptures. Seventy-two black-and-white plates, most taken by the author and Noah Onwuka, supplement the text (p. 1–49). Professor Horton, a long-time resident of the area, is at the University of Port Harcourt; he has authored many articles on the Kalabari, including 'The Kalabari world-view' in *Africa*, vol. 32 (Oct. 1962), p. 197–220. An exhibition of Kalabari ancestral screens and of scuplture by Sokari Douglas Camp was held at the National Museum of African Art, Washington, DC, November 1988–January 1989 and is described in three publications: *Echoes of the Kalabari: sculpture by Sokari Douglas Camp* (Washington, DC: National Museum of African Art, Nov. 1988, 24p.), by the sculptor, Nigel Barley's *Foreheads of the dead: an anthropological view of Kalabari ancestral screens* (Washington, DC: Smithsonian Institution for the National Museum of African Art, Nov. 1988. 88p.) and his 'Pop art in Africa? The Kalabari Ijo ancestral screens', *Art History* (London), vol. 10, no. 3 (Sept. 1987), p. 369–80.

969   **The art of eastern Nigeria.**
G. I. Jones.   Cambridge; London; New York: Cambridge University, 1984. 230p. map. bibliog.

Dr. Jones, a student of Nigerian art and culture since the 1930s, delineates four major artistic styles of eastern Nigeria, that is Lower Niger, Delta, Anang/Ibibio and Cross River. He examines their social settings, religious beliefs, and secret societies and the masquerades with which they are associated. His detailed analysis considers the full range of media (mud sculpture, stone, ivory, wood and bronze) as well as architecture. This book, which contains 114 half-tones and six line drawings, won the 1984 Amaury Talbot Prize for African Anthropology. Jones is a Fellow of Jesus College, Cambridge University and has also published *The trading states of the oil rivers* (q.v.) and numerous articles.

970   **Images of power: art of the royal court of Benin.**
Edited by Flora S. Kaplan.   New York: New York Univeristy, 1981. 80p. map. bibliog.

This catalogue illustrates the sixty-eight works comprising 'the first museum exhibition devoted to the art of Benin' in the City of New York (p. 5), at New York University 23 January–21 February 1981. It provides several short essays on the subject: 'Benin art as power' by Richard W. Hull (p 8–11); 'Benin: the sack that never was' by William Fagg (p. 20–21); 'The king's ivories' by Rosalind R. Jeffries (p. 41); 'Benin City and the royal patronage of the arts' by Boniface I. Obichere (p. 48–51); and 'Reading the art of Benin' by George Nelson Preston (p. 62–63). The editor contributed 'Of symbols and civilizations' (p. 77–79), and has supplied a list of obas and queen mothers (p. 4), an introduction (p. 5–6) and a brief bibliography (p. 80). A critical review of the volume by Paula Ben-Amos and a response by the editor appeared in *African Arts*, vol. 16, no. 2 (Feb. 1983), p. 17, 19–23, 100; and vol. 16, no. 3 (May 1983), p. 28–29, 78, respectively.

The Arts. Visual arts

971 **Die Altertümer von Benin. (The Benin antiquities.)**
Felix von Luschan. Berlin; Leipzig [GDR]: Staatliche Museen zu
Berlin, Museum für Völkerkunde, 1919. Reprinted, New York: Hacker
Art Books, 1968. 522p. bibliog.

A monumental study and visual presentation of the objects in Berlin which were sen
from the conquest of Benin in 1897. The single-volume reprint has 889 illustrations and
129 plates of photographs. The short introduction (p. 1–26) contains an overview o
the Benin pieces and in one chart (p. 12–13) classifies 2,400 antiquities by type and by
museum holding. Of the 2,400, 580 were in Berlin, 280 in the British Museum, 227 in
the Pitt-Rivers collection, 196 in Hamburg, 167 in Vienna, 182 in Dresden, ninety
eight in Leiden, eighty-seven in Leipzig, seventy-three in Cologne, eighty in Stuttgart
fifty-one in Frankfurt and 379 were held in miscellaneous collections. The compositior
of the bronzes is described (p. 19–20, 24, 507–10) and most of the volume (p. 27–514,
consists of detailed examinations of the objects by type. The author reports that he
cannot explain why many of the 1897 photographs of Benin he publishes from Frau
Alma Erdmann in Hamburg also appear in H. Ling Roth's *Great Benin* (q.v.) as
photographs by R. K. Granville (p. 6). He also expresses the belief that the bronze-
casting methods of the Benin people had slowly diffused from Egypt (Foreword, p. x).

972 **The nucleus: a catalogue of works in the national collection on the
inception of the National Gallery of Modern Art.**
National Gallery of Modern Art. Lagos, Nigeria: Federal Department
of Culture, National Theatre, 1981. 113p.

This 'maiden catalogue of works in Nigeria's National Gallery of Modern Art' contains
a listing (p. 10–23) of the 301 works in the collection with plates, mostly in colour
(p. 25–113) of many of the paintings and sculptures.

973 **The arts of the Benue: to the roots of tradition.**
François Neyt, assisted by André Désirant, preface by Ekpo Eyo.
[n.p.]: Editions Hawaiian Agronomics, 1985. 215p. maps. bibliog.

A beautifully produced book, full of maps and photographs in both colour and black-
and-white of the arts of Benue State, Nigeria. The text is divided into four chapters,
each rich in history and cultural context: 'The Benue State'; 'The Igala. Art at the
service of kingship?'; 'The Idoma. Art at the service of the sacred'; and 'The Tiv. Art
and the cultural mutations'. The lavish volume was made possible by the patronage of
Roger F. Azar, owner of Hawaiian Agronomics, an American company working in
Benue State. The author, Father Neyt, OSB, is a lecturer at the Université Catholique
de Louvain-la-Neuve.

974 **Bruce Onobrakpeya: symbols of ancestral groves. Monographs of prints
and paintings, 1978–1985.**
Bruce Onobrakpeya, introduced by Babatunde Lawal, foreword by
T. A. Fasuyi. Mushin, Nigeria: Ovuomararo Gallery, 1985. 252p.
bibliog.

A major publication of perhaps the best-known contemporary Nigerian artist, (30
August 1932– .), who is of an Urhobo family near Ughelli in Bendel State. The
volume contains an introduction to his work (p. 11–14), a 1980 interview with the
artist, a description of the Ovuomararo Art Studio and Gallery (Lagos Annex, 39

Oloje Street, Papa Ajao, Mushin), and an explanation or the traditional sacred symbols from which he derives inspiration. Most of the book (p. 65–225) consists of notes and comments on the many illustrated artworks, biographical notes and a bibliography (p. 236–42) of commentary on the artist's work. The volume is reviewed by Jean Kennedy in *African Arts*, vol. 20, no. 1 (Nov. 1986), p. 90–91. Robert Barde and Wendy Lawrence produced *Bruce Onobrakpeya: Nigeria's master printmaker* (Toronto: Best of Africa, [1977]. 32p. bibliog.) in conjunction with an exhibition of his prints in Toronto, 10 March–10 May, 1977.

975 **Masked rituals of Afikpo: the context of an African art.**
Simon Ottenberg. Seattle; London: University of Washington for the Henry Art Gallery, 1975. 229p. 8 maps. bibliog. (Index of Art in the Pacific Northwest Series, no. 9).
This offers a full-scale description and interpretation – sociocultural, psychological and aesthetic – of the masks and masquerades of the Afikpo village-group, an Igbo subgroup in eastern Nigeria. It was written to accompany an exhibition at the Henry Art gallery, University of Washington, 24 May–21 June 1975. The data and analysis and most of the photographs are based on the author's fieldwork in 1951–53 and 1959–60. Among numerous topics of interest are a 'Portrait of an Afikpo carver' (p. 67–83), an analysis of the most popular Afikpo play (*Okumpa*) and general 'Interpretation of the Afikpo masqueraders' (p. 201–16). In addition to sixty-six black-and-white figures and sixteen colour plates, including several portraits by Johsel Namkung of masks, are a glossary (p. 217–21) and a bibliography (p. 223–29). Dr. Ottenberg is Professor of Anthropology at the University of Washington, Seattle, Washington.

976 **Mbari: art as sacrifice.**
John Okparocha. Ibadan, Nigeria: Daystar, 1976. 63p.
In this well-illustrated booklet, the author explains the purpose of *mbari*, sacrifice in its simplest definition. It is a type of appeasement to Amadioha, the Igbo god of thunder, or to other gods, resulting in prestige for the god and protection for the people who built the *mbari* house. He describes the construction methods and beliefs and the numerous figures of animals, humans, gods and spirits who may be represented in *mbari* statuary, as well as the 'Cult of Amadioha' (p. 39–57) and *Iri ji ohuru*, or New Yam festival.

977 **Antique works of art from Benin.**
Augustus [Henry Lane-Fox] Pitt-Rivers, introduction by Bernard Fagg. New York: Dover, 1976. 101p.
This edition is an unabridged and corrected republication of the volume originally printed privately in London in 1900 by Lieutenant-General Augustus Pitt-Rivers 1827–1900). It illustrates, in 393 annotated figures, the Pitt-Rivers collection of 240 pieces of Benin art, then the second largest collection in the world, bought by the General in 1897 when the 'punitive expedition' returned from the sack of Benin City. The brief introduction (p. iii–iv) by Fagg, then the Curator of the Pitt-Rivers Museum at Oxford University, describes the General's collections and re-identifies seventeen plates as non-Benin works.

The Arts. Visual arts

978   **Praise poems: the Katherine White collection.**
Edited by Lorna Price, with contributions by Arnold Jolles, Robert
Farris Thompson, Roy Sieber, Pamela McClusky.   Seattle,
Washington: Seattle Art Museum, 1984. 122p. bibliog.
This volume is a tribute to Katherine Coryton White for her generous bequest to the
Seattle Art Museum of African Art, much of it from Nigeria. The Museum Director,
Jolles, wrote a very brief foreword (p. ix); scholars Thompson and Sieber contributed
personal tributes to White (p. xi–xiv). The bulk of the book consists of an illustrated
introductory essay (p. 3–8) and commentary on each piece, accompanied by the
sensitive words of the donor, by McClusky, Associate Curator of Ethnic Art at the
museum. Of the fifty-three 'heroic works' featured in striking black-and-white
photographs from the collection of over 2,000 objects, twenty-one objects are from
Nigeria.

979   **Nigerian truck art.**
Jack Pritchett.   *African Arts*, vol. 12, no. 2 (Feb. 1979), p. 27–31.
No-one who has visited Nigeria has failed to notice the creative paintings which often
appear on trucks. Here with numerous photographs, Pritchett explains and interprets
the origins and meanings of the truck art. Ulli Beier described 'Signwriter's art in
Nigeria' in *African Arts*, vol. 4, no. 3 (spring 1971), p. 22–27, this being another highly
conspicuous form of popular creativity.

980   **Antiquities from the city of Benin and from other parts of West Africa in
the British Museum.**
Charles Hercules Read, Ormonde Maddock Dalton.   London:
Trustees of the British Museum, 1899. Reprinted, New York: Hacker
Art Books, 1973. 61p. bibliog.
This folio volume contains an introduction to Benin and those of its antiquities
(p. 1–32), chiefly brass panels, given to the British Museum by the Principal Secretary
of State for Foreign Affairs, which comprised two-thirds of the collection sent to
England by Sir Ralph Moor following the plunder of Benin. These and ivory carvings
of Portuguese influence are fully depicted in thirty-two plates and described in detail
(p. 33–61), providing a valuable visual and textual account of a large collection of
Benin art. Read was keeper of the Department of British and Medieval Antiquities
and Ethnography at the British Museum and Dalton was a senior assistant.

981   **Figurative sculptures of the Niger River Delta.**
Arnold Rubin.   Los Angeles: Gallery K., Barry A. Kitnick, 1976. 24p
map. bibliog.
This small catalogue illustrates twenty-nine carvings from the Niger Delta purchased in
Europe, the US, and Africa by Barry A. Kitnick and exhibited 28 September–2
October 1976 in Los Angeles. Art historian Rubin provides an informative essay
explaining the art's geographical, historical and cultural contexts and its form and
meaning. Detailed notes describe the Ijaw, Urhobo or Isoko, Igbo, Ekoi and one
Grebo (Liberia) figurative sculptures, personal shrines, masks and headpieces. The
bibliography (p. 24) is excellent for the culture area.

982 **Sculpture of Northern Nigeria.**
Roy Sieber. New York: Museum of Primitive Art, 1961. 32p. map.
bibliog.
On his 1958 survey fieldtrip to Nigeria, Sieber photographed and studied the little-known art of five cultures presented here in forty-five illustrations. Professor Sieber provides a brief description of the Igala and Idoma, which lie east of the Niger-Benue confluence, and the Montol, Goemai and Jaba, which are found generally between Jos and the Benue River.

983 **Traditional Igbo art: 1966. An exhibition of wood sculpture carved in 1965–66 from the Frank Starkweather collection.**
Frank Starkweather, foreword by Richard K. Beardsley.   Ann Arbor, Michigan: Museum of Art, University of Michigan, 1968. [64]p. map. bibliog.
This exhibition catalogue provides a general introduction to the Igbo, and considers a men's secret society (*Mmo*), masquerades, carving and costumes. The exhibition notes provide information on the 129 varied objects, most of which are shown in photographs. A bibiography (p. 60–64) is included.

984 *Ibeji*: **Zwillingsfiguren der Yoruba/Twin figures of the Yoruba.**
Mareidi Stoll, Gert Stoll, Ulrich Klever, translated by Donald Arthur. Munich: The Authors, 1980. 338p. maps. bibliog.
This is a detailed introduction to the Yoruba twin figures, *ibeji*, one of the most familiar types of Yoruba traditional art. The authors describe (p. 13–108) in German and in parallel English text the Yoruba generally, twins and the '*ibeji*' cult', the '*ibeji*' as an art object and the geographical distribution of the forms of the '*ibeji*'. Two hundred and forty-six illustrations, some in colour, show the numerous varieties of '*ibeji*' figures.

985 **Black gods and kings: Yoruba art at UCLA.**
Robert Farris Thompson. Bloomington, Indiana; London: Indiana University, 1976. [n.p.]. 2 maps. bibliog.
This heavily illustrated book illuminates one of the world's largest collections of Yoruba carving, brass and iron work, beadwork, crowns, textiles, domestic objects and architectural sculpture, held at the Museum of Ethnic Arts, University of California. In the author's view, 'The purpose of sculpture is to praise people and the gods with beauty. Yoruba . . . assume that someone who embodies command, coolness, and character is someone extremely beautiful and like unto a god' (Preface, p. 4–5). The appendix contains an 'X-ray fluoresence analysis of brass and iron artifacts' (p. 1–4) and the bibliography (p. 1–3) is useful. Lack of an index and continuous pagination hamper use of this rich volume originally published in 1971 (Los Angeles: Museum and Laboratories of Ethnic Arts and Technology, University of California, (Occasional Paper, no. 11).

The Arts. Visual arts

986 **Contemporary African arts.**
Maude Wahlman, introduction by Frank Willett. Chicago, Illinois:
Field Museum of Natural History, 1974. 124p. map. bibliog.
This generously illustrated catalogue accompanied a major exhibition of the same title
at Chicago's Field Museum, 20 April–3 November 1974. It describes a wide range of
arts, crafts and creative efforts from nine countries (Sierra Leone, Mali, Niger,
Nigeria, South Africa, Rhodesia (Zimbabwe), Kenya, Ethiopia and Egypt). From
Nigeria are featured: Asiru Olatunde, counter-repoussé artist; Akin Euba, composer;
Bruce Onobrakpeya, graphic artist; Ladi Kwali, potter; and Lamidi Fakeye and
Thomas Ona, sculptors. Not only is the bibliography (p. 111–17) most usefully
subdivided by artistic speciality, but there are also lists of African artists in the United
States, selected African and Afro-American dance, drama and music groups, films
about and by Africans, film distributors, and importers of contemporary African arts.
The author was a consultant in African ethnology to the Field Museum.

987 **The sculpture of Western Nigeria.**
Western Nigeria, Ministry of Information, introduced by Frank
Willett. Ibadan, Nigeria: Western Nigeria, Ministry of Information,
1966. rev. ed. [56]p.
Illustrated with excellent photographs by Frank Speed and with a brief introduction,
this volume serves as a good survey of terracotta, bronze and wooden objects from the
Yoruba region. It was first issued in 1960 by the Information Division of the Ministry
of Home Affairs. Dr. Willett describes 'Nigerian thorn carvings: a living monument to
Justus Aderedolu' in *African Arts*, vol. 20, no. 1 (Nov. 1986), p. 48–53, 98. John
Pemberton writes about 'The Yoruba carvers of Ila-Orangun' in *Iowa Studies in
African Art*, Iowa City, Iowa, vol. 2 (1987), p. 117–47.

988 **Ife in the history of West African sculpture.**
Frank Willett. New York: McGraw-Hill, 1967. 232p. 2 maps. bibliog.
(New Aspects of Archaeology).
The author, a prolific writer on the art and archaeology of the Yoruba, concentrates
here on the royal and sacred city of Ife, where he lived for several years as an officer of
the Nigerian Department of Antiquities. In Ife in 1938 a group of naturalistic, life-size
bronze sculptures of heads, unlike any other African art, were found first. Willet
describes the archaeological history of Ife art, from Leo Frobenius's claims in 1910 that
he had found evidence of a Greek colony in Africa to his own excavations in the late
1950s. He places Ife art in the context of Ife and Yoruba culture history and the
broader context of other Nigerian and West African art forms. The impressive volume
has thirteen colour plates, 110 monochrome plates and forty-one line drawings.
Detailed notes, an extensive bibliography (p. 216–26), a list of illustrations and an
index conclude the volume. Professor Willett explores Ife-Nok links in 'A missing
millennium? From Nok to Ife and beyond' in *Arte in Africa*, edited by Ezio Bassani
(Modena, Italy: Panini, 1986, p. 87–100).

989 **Three rivers of Nigeria: art of the Lower Niger, Cross and Benue from the collection of William and Robert Arnett.**
Marcilene K. Wittmer, William Arnett, introduced by Roy Sieber. Atlanta, Georgia: High Museum of Art, 1978. 112p. 4 maps. bibliog.
The authors prepared this attractive and informative catalogue with 259 black-and-white illustrations for the exhibition 'Three rivers of Nigeria' at the High Museum and at the Museum of African Art in Washington, DC. Sieber sets the value of the exhibition in perspective in his brief introduction (p. vii). Wittmer introduces the general area and provides descriptive notes for much of the art work pictured. Arnett, one of the collectors, also offers notes and an essay on 'Terracotta art of the three rivers region' (p. 105). The bibliography (p. 112) is short, but practical.

Nok terracottas.
See item no. 141.

Great Benin: its customs, art and horrors.
See item no. 346.

Textiles, dress and ornamentation

990 **African Arts, special issue. Death, ritual, and art in Africa**
Edited by Fred T. Smith. vol. 21, no. 1 (Nov. 1987), 88p. bibliog.
Martha Anderson's article in this issue, entitled 'The funeral of an Ijo shrine priest', (p. 52–57, 88) describes the ritual display and ceremony accompanying the death in 1979 of Oweikoroghawei, a Central Ijo shrine priest. Other brilliantly illustrated articles in the same issue include the editor's introduction 'Death, ritual and art in Africa' (p. 28–29, 84); Joanne B. Eicher and Tonye V. Erekosima's 'Kalabari funerals: celebration and display', (p. 38–45, 87–88); M. Catherine Daly's 'Iria Bo appearance at Kalabari funerals', (p. 58–61, 86); and Robin Poynor's 'Ako figures of Owo and second burials in southern Nigeria', (p. 62–63, 81–83, 86–87). See also 'Male and female artistry in Kalabari dress', *African Arts*, vol. 19, no. 3 (May 1986), p. 48–51, 83, by M. Catherine Daly, Joanne B. Eicher and Tonye V. Erekosima.

991 **Akwete weaving: a study of change in response to the palm oil trade in the nineteenth century.**
Lisa Louise Aronson. PhD thesis, Indiana University, Bloomington, Indiana, 1982. 248 leaves. maps. bibliog. (Available from Ann Arbor, Michigan: University Microfilms, 1983. Order no. ADD 83-01052).
This study of the Igbo village of Akwete in south-eastern Nigeria during 1977 and 1978 is unique in that it documents changes in weaving that took place more than a century earlier. The author shows the historical patterns of weaving as well as its socio-cultural context. An appendix describes 'Warping the Akwete loom'.

992 **Adirẹ cloth in Nigeria: the preparation and dyeing of indigo patterned cloth among the Yoruba.**
Edited by Jane Barbour, Doig Simmonds. Ibadan, Nigeria: Institute of African Studies, University of Ibadan, 1971. 104p.

'This book describes for the first time the resist techniques and the methods of dyeing used in the preparation of the indigo patterned cloth of Yorubaland in Nigeria. The word *adirẹ* means literally 'that which is tied and dyed' but it has come to be used as an omnibus word for all indigo-dyed cloth' (Introduction, p. 6). The articles and their authors are: 'Dyeing methods in western Nigeria' by Nancy Stanfield; 'The chemistry and general history of dyeing' by O. L. Oke; 'The origin of some *adirẹ* designs' by Barbour; 'The devolution of the jubilee design' by George Jackson; and 'Comments on *adirẹ* in western Nigeria' by 'Bisi Akpata. All authors were at the Universities of Ibadan or Ife at the time of publication. The appendix contains a list of methods, proverbs, and exclamations used as names of cloth and motifs in both English and Yoruba. Numerous photographs and drawings illustrate all phases of the process and the major motifs described. A well-illustrated, step-by-step guide to *adirẹ* cloth was developed by Vivian Derryck, Sharon Dunn, Anne Glickman, Hans Guggenheim, D. Hassfeld, and T. Lashile in *Yoruba blue: symbols on cloth* (Cambridge, Massachusetts: Education Development Center, 1972. 53p.).

993 **Yoruba beaded crowns: sacred regalia of the Olokuku of Okuku.**
Ulli Beier. London: Ethnographica in association with the National Museum, Lagos, 1982. 114p. map.

A fascinating account of the ritual headgear of Yoruba kings (obas) in general and of the twelve major crowns of the oba – the Olokuku – of the Yoruba town of Okuku. The elaborate crowns were photographed by Frank Speed and the Olokun festivals of 1956 and 1972 were photographed by the author.

994 **Cloth as metaphor: Nigerian textiles from the Museum of Cultural History.**
Jean Borgatti. Los Angeles: Museum of Cultural History, University of California, 1983. 63p. 3 maps. bibliog. (Monograph Series, no. 20).

A beautifully illustrated essay, description and analysis of the social meanings of cloth, focusing particularly on the northern Edo of Bendel State, and including a 'Catalogue of museum collection' by Borgatti and Betsy D. Quick (p. 46–62) and a useful bibliography (p. 62–63). Dr. Borgatti conducted fieldwork in southern Nigeria in 1971–74 and here describes 'The fabric of life', 'Cloth as symbol', 'Cloth as metaphor', 'The fabric of sculpture' and 'The making of a masquerade'. The book was produced for a special exhibition of the same title at the Museum of Cultural History gallery, Haines Hall, UCLA, 18 May–19 June 1983.

995 **Nigerian handcrafted textiles.**
Joanne Bubolz Eicher. Ile-Ife, Nigeria: University of Ife, 1976. 106p. map. bibliog.

An excellent overview and introduction to Nigerian weaving styles and methods. The author describes cotton and silk fibres and fabrics, looms and historical evidence of weaving, pattern-dyed and whole-piece dyed textiles, embroidery, appliqué work and drawnwork. An extensive bibliography (p. 95–103) is especially useful. Seventy-one black-and-white photographs and twenty-four colour plates accompany the text. Dr. Eicher lived in Nigeria from 1963 to 1966 and visited briefly in 1971 and 1974. *Nigerian textiles* (London: Commonwealth Institute, 1984. 3 vols.) is a major illustrated catalogue designed for the Nigerian textile exhibition held at London's Commonwealth Institute August–October 1984. S. A. Adetoro authored volume one, *Traditional woven fabrics*, Adunola Towry-Coker and Similola Towry-Coker wrote volume two, *Indigo dyed fabrics*, and C. S. Okeke produced volume three, *The legend that is Akwete*.

996 **Pelete bite: Kalabari cut-thread cloth.**
Joanne Bubloz Eicher, Tonye Victor Erekosima, Otto Charles Thieme. St. Paul, Minnesota: Goldstein Gallery, University of Minnesota, 1982. 32p. map. (Catalogue, no. 17).

This is a brief description of forty cloths exhibited May 1982 at the Goldstein Gallery. Thieme supplies a technical analysis. An illustrated account of the history and culture of weaving among the Igbo is A. E. Afigbo and C. S. Okeke's *Weaving tradition in Igbo-land: history and mechanism of Igbo textile industry* (Lagos: Nigeria Magazine, 1985. 99p. (Nigeria Magazine Publication Series)).

997 **Yoruba beadwork: art of Nigeria.**
William Fagg, edited and foreword by Bryce Holcombe, descriptive catalogue by John Pemberton. New York: Rizzoli, with the Pace Gallery, 1980. 99p. map. bibliog.

This volume examines beadwork among the Yoruba of Western Nigeria and Benin (Dahomey) in the nineteenth and twentieth centuries 'a wondrous flowering of their traditional art which is based on the sudden availability from Europe of 'seed beads,' tiny trade beads in an almost limitless palette of colors, and regular in size (about two millimeters)' (p. 9). Fagg wrote the general account of beadwork (p. 9–28). The brief foreword is by Holcombe, Director of the Pace Gallery in New York, from which came most of the beaded objects shown in thirty colour plates and described by Pemberton (p. 31–91).

998 **Nigeria's traditional crafts.**
Alison Hodge. London: Ethnographica, 1982. 96p. map. bibliog. (Ethnographic Arts & Culture Series, 3).

A well-illustrated survey, full of practical details, of Nigeria's traditional crafts. Individual chapters cover woodcarving, decorated gourds, matwork, basketry and related crafts, woven textiles, dyed textiles, leatherwork, brass casting and brass working, pottery, beads and beadwork, Bida glass, wall decoration, cicatrization, body decoration and hairdressing. Scholarly notes (p. 90–95) and a bibliography (p. 95–96) conclude the volume. The author hopes the Nigerian public pride can be cultivated and public taste educated to maintain high standards in these crafts, for at present 'foreigners keep the craftsman alive by artificial respiration: he is not breathing naturally. To do so, he must be needed by his own people' (Introduction, p. 6). Important also is Pat Oyelola's *Nigerian crafts* (London: Macmillan, 1981. 83p.) with its chapters on pottery, wood-carving, weaving, dyeing, embroidery and appliqué, beadwork, calabash decoration, metalwork, mat-making and basketry.

The Arts. Textiles, dress and ornamentation

999 Yoruba hairstyles: a selection of hairstyles in southern Nigeria.
Nina W. Gwatkin. Lagos: Craft Centre, National Museum
Compound, 1971. 42p.

Gwatkin's booklet is well illustrated with photographs by Ann Goodall. Other books,
all heavily illustrated, on this popular topic include: Titus Ajibade Ogunwale's *African
traditional hairdos* (Ibadan, Nigeria: Ogunwale, 1976. 44p.); Esi Sagay's *African
hairstyles: styles of yesterday and today* (London; Exeter, New Hampshire: Heinemann,
1983. 128p.); and 'Susie's' [Susan F. Akinnuoye's] *Nigerian hair styles* (Ibadan: Sketch,
[n.d.] 73p.) which offers brief descriptions and photographs of 128 different women's
hairstyles.

**1000 Crafts and cooperation in Western Nigeria: a sociological contribution
to indigenous economics.**
Michael Koll. Bielefeld, GFR: Bertelsmann-Universitätsverlag,
1969. 167p. maps. bibliog. (Materialien des Arnold-Bergstraesser-
Insituts für kulturwissenschaftliche Forschung, Freiburg. vol. 27).

A major sociological study of crafts in Ibadan, and, to a lesser extent, in Lagos and
throughout south-western [*sic*] Nigeria. The author provides a review of the literature
on Nigerian crafts, suggestions for the development of cooperative craft societies, and
an excellent bibliography (p. 157–67).

1001 Nigerian weaving.
Venice Lamb, Judy Holmes. Lagos, Nigeria: Shell Petroleum
Development Company of Nigeria, 1980; London: Alpha Books,
1980. 276p. 2 maps. bibliog.

A beautifully produced systematic survey of the major Nigerian weaving traditions
based on three years' fieldwork throughout the country and on the study of Nigerian
cloths preserved in English museum collections. Venice Lamb, an authority on African
weaving, wrote 'The horizontal loom' (used by men) (p. 25–169); Judy Holmes, who
used weaving in occupational therapy and lived for several years in Nigeria, the Sudan
and Libya, authored 'The vertical loom' (used predominantly by women) (p. 170–263);
they collaborated on 'Vertical looms used by men' (p. 265–71). Numerous colour and
black-and-white photographs by Peter Holmes and Alastair Lamb illustrate the volume
which has a useful bibliography (p. 271–73). Venice Lamb's *West African weaving*
(London: Duckworth, 1975. 224p. bibliog) and her publication with Alastair Lamb,
West African narrowstrip weaving, edited by Patricia Fiske (Washington, DC: Textile
Museum, 1975, 48p.) are also valuable books on the subject. An excellent illustrated
article by Colleen Kriger considers 'Robes of the Sokoto Caliphate', *African Arts*, vol.
21, no. 3 (May 1988), p. 52–57, 78–79, 85–86.

1002 Nigerian body adornment.
Eve de Negri. Lagos, Nigeria: Nigeria Magazine, 1976. 128p.
bibliog. (Nigeria Magazine Special Publication, no. 2).

An informative, well-illustrated volume describing 'Tribal marks and decorative cuts',
'Hairdressing in Nigeria', 'Craftsmanship in jewellery', 'Cloth manufacture in Nigeria',
'Robes of state (chiefs, *obas*, emirs, *olu*)', 'Costume and ornament associated with
ritual ceremonies', and traditional costumes in northern, western, Bendel State, and
eastern areas, for both sexes. A glossary provides 'Names of some costume and
accessories of the northern and western areas' (p. 124–26) and useful lists of relevant
articles (p. 5, 127–28).

1003 **Nupe crafts: the dynamics of change in 19th and 20th century weaving and brassworking.**
Judith [Marie] Perani. PhD thesis, Indiana University, Bloomington, Indiana, 1977. 186 leaves. 3 maps. bibliog. (Available from University Microfilms, Ann Arbor, Michigan, 1977. Order no. 77–22,705).

Dr. Perani provides a history of the Nupe with detailed emphasis on their craft organization and production and especially on weaving and brass work. The study includes numerous photographs and figures and a bibliography (leaves 177–84).

1004 **African textiles: looms, weaving and design.**
John Picton, John Mack. London: British Museum, 1979. 208p. 5 maps. bibliog.

Covering the entire continent, this attractive, illustrated volume has sections on the Nigerian vertical loom, the cloth woven by Yoruba, Hausa, Fulani and others in Nigeria and Yoruba *adire* cloth. It contains 208 illustrations of weavers and cloth and a short bibliography (p. 204–05). Another significant volume is *Textiles of Africa*, edited by Dale Idiens and K. G. Ponting (Bath, England: Pasold Research Fund, 1980. 210p.). Five illustrated essays are on Nigerian textiles: John Picton's 'Women's weaving the manufacture and use of textiles among the Igbirra people of Nigeria' (p. 63–88); Lisa Aronson's 'History of cloth trade in the Niger Delta: a study of diffusion' (p. 89–107); C. S. Okeke's 'Use of traditional textiles among the Aniocha Igbo of Mid-Western Nigeria' (p. 108–18); Jill Salmon's 'Funerary shrine cloth of the Anang Ibibio, South-East Nigeria' (p. 119–41); and Keith Nicklin's 'Annang Ibibio raphia weaving' (p. 142–62).

1005 **African dress II: a select and annotated bibliography.**
Compiled by Ila M. Pokornowski, Joanne Bubolz Eicher, Moira F. Harris, Otto Charles Thieme. East Lansing, Michigan: African Studies Center, Michigan State University, 1985. 316p. map.

Following essays on 'The study of African dress' by Thieme and Bubolz Eicher (p. 1–16) and 'Resource materials for the study of African dress' by Thieme (p. 17–26) are 1,260 numbered and briefly annotated references grouped by geographic area and by country. For Nigeria (p. 118–66) some 375 entries are included. Access is by an author index. The first edition was compiled by Bubolz Eicher (East Lansing, Michigan: African Studies Center, Michigan State University, 1970. 134p.) and contained 1,025 items, 261 of them specifically on Nigeria (p. 29–58).

The development of an export oriented dyed cloth industry in Kano Emirate in the nineteenth century.
See item no. 214.

Film and music

Film

1006 **Le cinéma au Nigéria. (Nigerian cinema.)**
François Balogun. Brussels: OCIC; Paris: L'Harmattan, 1984. 137p.
map. bibliog. (Collection Cinémédia. Cinémas d'Afrique Noire, 6).
The author discusses the history of Nigerian film, the structure of the film industry, list
thirty-six feature films made from 1970 to 1984, reprints brief newspaper articles and
editorials on Nigerian film, and describes several filmmakers and their work. He
covers: Francis Oladele and *Kongi's harvest*; Sonya Dosunmu and *Dinner with the
devil*; Ola Balogun; Adamu Halilu, Job Adu, Bankole Bello, Eddie Ugbomah and
three Yoruba filmmakers who work in Yoruba (Ade Folayan, Chief Hubert Ogunde
and Moses Olaiya Adejumo). The bibliography (p. 127–37) contains French and
English citations.

1007 **A filmography of the Third World, 1976–1983: an annotated list of
16mm films.**
Compiled by Helen W. Cyr. Metuchen, New Jersey; London:
Scarecrow, 1985. 275p.
This volume continues the author's *A filmography of the Third World: an annotated list
of 16mm films* (Scarecrow, 1976. 319p.). For Nigeria, twelve films are listed: *Africa is
my home*; *Djibo*; *The doctors of Nigeria*; *Festac '77*; *Journey towards peace*; *Kongi's
harvest*; *Religion in Nigeria: Christianity*; *Soro: the beating game*; *That our children will
not die*; *A thing of wonder*; *The tribal eye: (2) Behind the mask*; and *The tribal eye: (6)
Kingdom of bronze*. *Africa from reel to reel: an African filmography* (Waltham,
Massachusetts: African Studies Association, 1976. 144p.), compiled by Steven Ohrn
and Rebecca Riley, lists, with descriptive annotations, 1,300 16mm films on Africa
distributed in the United States and Canada. It is, in the compilers' words, 'a curious
mixture of some of the best and some of the worst films ever made about Africa and
Africans' (Introduction, p. i). Ninety-three films on Nigeria are listed in the
geographical and area index with another twenty-one listed under 'Western Africa'.
The annotated bibliography (p. 139–44) is especially useful.

1008 **Towards a development scheme for the Nigerian film culture.**
Hyginus Ekwuasi. *Nigeria Magazine*, vol. 54, no. 2 (April–June
1986), p. 56–67. bibliog.
The author, a lecturer in Film and TV in the Department of Theatre Art at the
University of Ibadan, reviews the structure of the Nigerian film industry of both pre-
and post-independence periods. He provides a catalogue of thirty-nine indigenous
Nigerian feature films from 1962 to 1984, made in English, Igbo, Yoruba and Hausa.
See also his short article on Yoruba language films 'The animated universe', *West
Africa*, no. 3698 (27 June 1988), p. 1162, in which he lists twenty films made in
Yoruba between 1975 and 1988. An interesting early description of rural Nigeria's
encounter with films is Peter Morton-Williams' *Cinema in rural Nigeria: a field study of
the impact of fundamental-education films on rural audiences in Nigeria* (Lagos: Federal
Information Service, [1952]. 195p.).

909   **Film in Nigeria: development, problems and promise.**
Onyero Mgbejume.   PhD thesis, University of Texas, Austin, Texas,
1978. 162 leaves. bibliog. (Available from University Microfilms, Ann
Arbor, Michigan, 1979. Order no. 7900608).

This study examines the development of films and the film industry in Nigeria from
1903, the first public showing in the country, to early 1978; it also sets the Nigerian
situation in a broader African context. In 1947 the Nigerian government established
the Federal Film Unit, replacing the Colonial Film Unit which had begun film
production in Nigeria. The author describes Nigerian filmmakers and their problems
and offers five reasons why film is the least developed of Nigeria's mass media. These
are: colonial constraints, bureaucracy, lack of funding, shortage of skilled filmmakers
and lack of recognition of the importance of film by Nigerians and their leaders.
Leaves 148–53 contain his useful bibliography. Adeola Solanke profiles Nigerian film-
maker Faith Isiakpere in 'A doer of deeds', *West Africa*, no. 3712 (3–9 Oct. 1988),
p. 1838–39.

910   **Sub-Saharan African films and filmmakers: an annotated
bibliography/Films et cinéastes Africains de la région subsaharienne:
une bibliographie commentée.**
Nancy J. Schmidt.   New York; Munich; Oxford: K. G. Saur/ Hans
Zell, 1988. 401p.

This remarkable compilation includes nearly 4,000 entries of all types published
between the early 1960s and mid-1987. Among them are articles and reviews from
African newspapers and magazines. There are indexes of actors and actresses, film
festivals, film titles, filmmakers, countries, and general subjects, and an introduction in
English and French. Dr. Schmidt's *Sub-Saharan African films and filmmakers: a
preliminary bibliography* (Bloomington, Indiana: African Studies Program, Indiana
University, 1986. 112p.) is a similarly well-indexed compilation of 1,690 books and
articles of which at least sixty concern Nigeria and fifteen the filmmaker Ola Balogun.

Music

1011   **Ibibio music in Nigerian culture.**
Samuel Ekpe Akpabot.   East Lansing, Michigan: Michigan State
University, 1975. 102p. map. bibliog.

This well-illustrated study provides descriptions of varied types of music and
instruments and their social contexts among the Ibibio of south-eastern Nigeria. The
work considers 'Ibibio musical instruments and their functions', 'Masquerade music',
'Orchestras with special functions', 'Music of social control', 'Choral patterns' and
'Ibibio instrumental rhythms'. The author includes a useful glossary for terminology, a
pronunciation guide, thirteen plates showing instruments and masquerades, and a
bibliography (p. 100–02). The author, an Ibibio from Ikot Abasi village, was a Fellow
of Trinity College of Music, London, at the time of publication and has also published
'Standard drum patterns in Nigeria' in *African Music*, vol. 5 (1971), p. 37–39.

1012 **Foundation of Nigerian traditional music.**
Samuel Ekpe Akpabot. Ibadan, Nigeria: Spectrum, 1986. 113p.
bibliog.

Presents a succinct account of the major features and instruments of tradition
Nigerian music. The author discusses, among other topics, talking drums, drum a
gong rhythms, the African orchestra, traditional African music in twentieth-centu
Western music, a musicological approach to oral poetry and the effects of social chan
on music. The author is on the staff of the Institute of African Studies, University
Ibadan, Ibadan, Nigeria.

1013 **Juju music: a study of its social history and style.**
Afolabi Alaja-Browne. PhD thesis, University of Pittsburgh,
Pittsburg, Pennsylvania, 1985. 137 leaves. map. bibliog. (Available
from University Microfilms, Ann Arbor, Michigan, 1986. Order no.
ADD 85-19449).

A history and analysis of juju music from its beginnings at Till Nelson Akamo Davies
motor mechanic workshop in Lagos in the late 1920s to the stars of the 1970s wi
special emphasis on Abdulrafiu Babatunde King. Includes photographs of ju
bandleaders and a discography of King's recordings in the 1950s.

1014 **Musicmakers of West Africa.**
John Collins. Washington, DC: Three Continents, 1985. 177p.
bibliog.

Offers an excellent illustrated description of popular music in Ghana and Nigeria, wi
briefer material on music in Sierra Leone, Zaire, the Ivory Coast and the People'
Republic of Benin. Nigerian pop is described in 'Nigerian juju music, apala, and guita
bands', 'Sir Victor Uwaifo', 'Fela – the 'chief priest of afro-beat', ''F'' promotion
(Faisal Helwani), and 'Segun Bucknor and popular music in Lagos'. In addition h
describes Nigerian music unions, and the West African recording industry. Collin
studied at the University of Ghana, had his own guitar band and has a recording studi
near Accra, Ghana. See also his *African pop roots: the inside rhythms of Afric*
(London: Foulsham, 1985. 120p.). Although in German, Wolfgang Bender'
Sweetmother: moderne afrikanische musik (Munich: Trickster, 1985. 241p.) survey
Nigerian highlife and provides a brief bibliography and discography for the count
(p. 234–35).

1015 **A bibliography of African music and dance – the Nigerian experience,
1930–1980.**
Compiled by Herbert O. Emezi. *A Current Bibliography on African
Affairs*, vol. 18, no. 2 (1985–86), p. 117–47.

Offers an extensive listing, following a brief introductory essay, of works in English or
Nigerian music and dance. In this, the first bibliography on the subjects, the autho
includes masters and doctoral theses. Emezi is at the Alvan Ikoku College o
Education, Owerri, Imo State, Nigeria. Akin Euba, head of the Department of Music
at what is now Obafemi Awolowo University, edited the first issue of the *Nigeria*
Music Review (Ife: University of Ife, Department of Music, May 1977, 108p.) which
provides articles on Igbo song, Yoruba music in Lagos and an overview of music in
Nigeria, with a bibliography and discography and list of Nigerian composers and thei
compositions.

1016 **Jazz in Nigeria: an outline cultural history.**
Chief Bassey Ita. Lagos; Calabar, Nigeria: Atiaya Communications, 1984. 99p.

The author, a veteran journalist and arts critic, presents an account of jazz in Nigeria from 1940 to the late 1960s. The study emphasizes Bobby Benson, who returned from abroad in 1947; Zeal Onyia and Eddie Okonta; the impact of Louis Armstrongs' visit to Lagos; and the emergence of Fela Ransome-Kuti. 'Jazz around the world' and 'Jazz-derived music of the young' offer a broader context by describing the music of Louis Armstrong and James Brown. Several of the short chapters were published earlier as critical reviews.

1017 **Popular culture and popular music: the Nigerian experience.**
Dele Jegede. *Présence Africaine*, no. 144 (4th quarter 1987), p. 59–72. bibliog.

This article is concerned with the meaning of the rapidly changing Nigerian popular music in Nigerian culture. Jegede describes popular music, particularly *juju* and *fuji* ('a modification of neo-traditional Yoruba *sakara* and *apala* music, with a large dose of inspiration from *juju*', p. 63); Millicent Small; Fela Anikulapo-Kuti (1938– .); the patronage, dissemination and criticism of popular music (including the taxes that musicians are required to pay); and the rôles of radio and television. He is critical of the 'wholesale consumption of foreign culture' (p. 69) and grapples with the lack of bearings which seems to characterize contemporary music. Dr. Jegede is at the Centre for Cultural Studies, University of Lagos, Lagos, Nigeria.

1018 **Fela Anikulapo-Kuti: the art of an Afrobeat rebel.**
Randall F. Grass. *The Drama Review*, vol. 30, no. 1 (spring 1986), p. 131–48.

A lengthy illustrated article about 'Africa's most challenging and charismatic popular music performer' (p. 131). Fela, born in Abeokuta to distinguished parents, returned to Lagos from the United States in 1970 and developed Afrobeat, a style described as 'amalgamated jazz, the funk of American soul singer and bandleader James Brown, highlife, traditional rhythms, and chanted declamatory vocals' which is written and sung in Yoruba and pidgin English. His unconventional habits, anti-authoritarianism and criticism of both civil and military governemnts have resulted in ongoing conflict with the state. In September 1984 he was arrested for illegal currency exportation and in October was sentenced to five years in prison; he was released 25 April 1986. The article describes the evolution of his music and includes lyrics from several songs. The author is a musician, writer and radio show host in Philadelphia who lived in Nigeria for three years.

1019 **Fela, Fela: this bitch of a life.**
Carlos Moore, translated by Shawna Moore. London: Allison & Busby, 1982. 287p.

A biography of Nigeria's famous musician, the originator of 'Afrobeat', Fela Anikulapo-Kuti. The author tells Fela's story, through transcriptions of interviews with Fela himself, his wives, his closest associates and childhood friends; press clippings; and his association with the artist since 1974. He chronicles the evolution of Fela from his training at the Trinity College of Music in England (1958–62) through the influences of James Brown and Ghanaian music, his trip to the United States in the turbulent late

1960s and his return to Nigeria where he created Afro-beat. Fela's political and social evolution is described: his rejection of authority; the attack on his Lagos compound, the 'Kalakuta Republic'; his twenty-seven wives; and his imprisonment in Nigeria. The story is illustrated with more than fifty photographs. The English edition was translated from the French *Fela, Fela – cette putain de vie*. Of special interest is the discography for Fela from 1970–81 (p. 285–87). Moore is a Cuban-born journalist and ethnologist who worked in Lagos from 1974–80.

1020 **Nigerian musical instruments.**
Mosunmola Omibiyi. *Nigeria Magazine*, nos. 122–23 (1977), p. 14–34.

This description of Nigerian instruments, with forty-three illustrations, is arranged in the four main 'organological' categories used in ethnomusiciology: idiophones, membranophones, aerophones, and chordophones. The author is a musicologist who was teaching at the Polytechnic in Ibadan at the time of publication. A lengthy illustrated article by Edith Enem, 'Nigerian dances' appeared in *Nigeria Magazine*, nos. 115–16 (1975), p. 68–115.

1021 **Jùjú: the historical development, socioeconomic organisation, and communicative functions of a West African popular music.**
Christopher Alan Waterman. PhD thesis, University of Illinois, Urbana-Champaign, Illinois, 1986. 458 leaves. bibliog. (Available from University Microfilms, Ann Arbor, Michigan, 1986. Order no. DA 8610996).

This anthropological study, based particularly on fieldwork in Ibadan in 1981–82, also examines popular music in Lagos. It provides a history of *jùjú* music 'an areal variant of the pan-urban Anglophone West African 'palmwine guitar' tradition' (author's abstract) hypothesizing that it emerged in the early 1930s. Primarily, the study examines the socio-economic organization of *jùjú* groups and the stylistic communication among *jùjú* performers and patrons, demonstrating that African popular syncretic music offers systems of social and aesthetic communication which are important in the emergence of urban African identity during periods of rapid change.

Horses, musicians, & gods: the Hausa cult of possession-trance.
See item no. 353.

Tiv song.
See item no. 394.

Sweet words: storytelling events in Benin.
See item no. 1024.

Tales of Yoruba gods and heroes.
See item no. 1025.

Folklore

1022 **The origin of life and death: African creation myths.**
Edited by Ulli Beier. London: Heinemann, 1966. 65p. (African
Writers Series, no. 23).
Among these eighteen creation stories from around the continent are six myths from
the Ijaw (Ijo), the Yoruba, the Bini, the Igbo, the Nupe and the Efik of Nigeria.

1023 **Yoruba myths.**
Compiled and introduced by Ulli Beier. Cambridge: Cambridge
University, 1980. 82p.
Forty-one Yoruba myths are compiled here, each of which is explained in notes
(p. 59–82). An introduction (p. x–xiv) gives a brief description of the collection and of
Yoruba mythology. The myths were collected by Yemi Elebu-Ibon, a practising
babalawo (Yoruba priest), Bakare Gbadamosi, Pierre Verger, and Beier, who spent
twenty years in Nigeria and translated most of the tales. M. I. Ogumefu's *Yoruba
legends* (London: Sheldon, 1929; Reprinted, New York: AMS, 1984. 87p.)
contains forty brief tales, nine of which are about Tortoises. Of interest also is Mike
Omoleye's *Great tales of the Yorubas* (Ibadan: Omoleye, 1977. 59p.).

1024 **Sweet words: storytelling events in Benin.**
Dan Ben-Amos. Philadelphia, Pennsylvania: Institute for the Study
of Human Issues, 1975. 93p. bibliog.
This book examines thoroughly the place of storytelling in Bini culture in Benin City of
Bendel State. The author explores the forms and contexts of folk narration and the
vital rôles of bow-lute (*akpata*) and the thumb-piano (*asologun*) which are used in
storytelling. He relates the marginal social position of storytellers to their association
with witches and other spirits. Especially valuable are the transcriptions of the music,
the narrative texts in both Edo and English, the photographs and line drawings and the
glossary of Edo terms. The original tapes used in this study are deposited at the Center
for African Oral Data at the Archives of Traditional Music, Indiana University,
Bloomington, Indiana. The author, a folklorist at the University of Pennsylvania,
Philadelphia, conducted fieldwork in Benin City in 1966, 1973 and 1975–76.

1025 **Tales of Yoruba gods and heroes.**
Harold Courlander. New York: Crown, 1973. 243p. map. bibliog.
Represents a valuable collection of thirty-two stories of the *orishas*, or deities, and
warrior heroes of the Yoruba of south-western Nigeria. They were gathered by the
author and his principal informant and researcher Ezekiel Aderogba Adetunji of Ilesha
and Lagos. Useful introductory material describes the Yoruba and their gods; notes on
each story add context (p. 177–207). The appendices contain 'Some Yoruba orishas
[*sic*] worshipped in the Americas' (p. 211–12), 'Yoruba myths and legends in Cuba'
(p. 213–23), and musical scores for 'Yoruba music in the Americas' (p. 224–30). A
glossary, pronunciation guide and selective bibliography (p. 241–43) conclude the
volume. Writer Amos Tutuola recently published seven stories in *Yoruba folktales*
(Ibadan, Nigeria: Ibadan University, 1986. 58p.) illustrated by Kola Adesokan. With
Ezekiel A. Eshugbayi, Courlander also published *Olode the hunter, and other tales
from Nigeria* (New York: Harcourt, Brace & World, 1968. 153p.).

1026 **Hausa tales and traditions: an English translation of Tatsuniyoyi Na Hausa, originally compiled by Frank Edgar.**
Frank Edgar, tran:ₘated and edited by Neil Skinner, foreword by M. G. Smith. Lo..don: Frank Cass, 1969. vol. I; Madison, Wisconsin: University of Wisconsin, 1977. vols. II and III.

This three-volume work translates a large collection of Hausa folktales and stories, anecdotes, 'tongue twisters', riddles, proverbs and Muslim legends, collected and published by Edgar in 1911 and 1913. Edgar (d. 1937) was one of the early British political officers serving in Northern Nigeria from 1905 to 1927. Professor Skinner provides cross-references to the original Hausa and Professor Smith sets the work in broader context in his foreword (p. vii–xxi).

1027 **Tales of land of death: Igbo folk tales.**
Uche Okeke. Garden City, New York: Zenith/Doubleday, 1971. 114p.

A collection of forty tales, twenty-three riddles and forty proverbs, first written down in 1950. The folktales are grouped as '*Iro* – tales that are spoken' and '*Iro/ita* – tales that are sung and spoken'. Prominent in the stories are animals, especially *Mbe*, the tortoise; *Anna mmuo*, the land of the dead, and the traditional Igbo spirit world also feature frequently. Romanus N. Egudu collected and translated *The calabash of wisdom, and other Igbo stories* (New York: Nok, 1973. 141p.).

1028 **Hausa folk-lore, customs, proverbs, etc, collected and transliterated with English translation and notes.**
R. Sutherland Rattray, preface by R. R. Marett. Oxford: Clarendon,
1913. Reprinted, 1969. 2 vols.

Rattray collected forty-six stories, and grouped them into those concerning heroes and heroines, animals, customs and art; there are also 133 proverbs recorded during 1907–11 by Malam Shaihu. They are reproduced in Arabic script, transliterated into the Hausa of Kano or Sokoto and translated into English; brief notes accompany them.

1029 **Magána Hausa. Native literature, or proverbs, tales, fables and historical fragments in the Hausa language to which is added a translation in English.**
J. F. Schön. London: Society for Promoting Christian Knowledge,
1885. Reprinted, Nendeln, Liechtenstein: Kraus Reprint, K. T. Organization, 1970. 2 vols.

The first of these two volumes contains, in Hausa, proverbs, letters, the life and travels of Dorūgu (p. 18–111) and narratives, tales and descriptions. They are chiefly by Dorūgu, a Hausa, who accompanied Heinrich Barth on his travels (discussed briefly in *Nigerian writing . . .* (q.v.)). The second volume is 'African proverbs, tales and historical fragments', (195p.) which is the Rev. Schön's translation of the preceding volume.

1030   **Stories of the Benin Empire.**
Joseph E. Sidahome.   Ibadan, Nigeria: Oxford University, 1967.
132p.

The school edition contains nine traditional stories of commoners, royalty, deities and spirits told by story-tellers to the author, a Nigerian. These are the oral traditions of the Benin Empire as told among the Ishan, an ethnic group living in the north of the old empire, today north-eastern Bendel State. The text is illustrated by J. K. Oyewole and the author includes a very brief introduction written in 1963.

1031   **Hausa superstitions and customs: an introduction to the folk-lore and the folk.**
A[rthur] J[ohn] N[ewman] Tremearne.   London: John Bale, 1913.
Reprinted, London: Frank Cass, 1970. 548p. map.

This large volume presents an early-twentieth century ethnographic account of the Hausa; one hundred tales, parables and their variants, illustrated by forty-one photographs and more than 200 figures are featured. Another work by Major Tremearne (1877–1915) is *The tailed head-hunters of Nigeria: an account of an official's seven years' experiences in the Northern Nigerian pagan belt, and a description of the manners, habits, and customs of some of its native tribes* (London: Seeley, Service, 1912. 2nd ed. Reprinted, Nendeln, Lichtenstein: Kraus Reprint, 1973. 340p.). Here he describes the Kagoro, Moroa, Kajji, Katab, Jaba and Kagoma groups, emphasizing their 'customs and superstitions', but also includes a broad range of observations and a chapter on 'Hausa folklore' as well as thirty-eight photographs and a fold-out map. For excellent collections of Hausa proverbs, see A[nthony] H[amilton] M[illard] Kirk-Greene's *Ai, Hausa ba dabo ba ne* (Ibadan: Oxford University, 1966. 500 proverbs) and C. E. J. Whitting's *Hausa and Fulani proverbs* (Lagos: Government Printer, 1940. 2000 Hausa and 600 Fulani proverbs).

1032   **The way we lived: Ibo customs and stories.**
Rems Nna Umeasiegbu.   London; Ibadan, Nigeria: Heinemann,
1969. 139p. (African Writers Series, no. 61).

In this volume the Igbo author preserves twenty-five customs and fifty-five folk-tales he learned as a youth from his father. 'Practically all the customs detailed in this book are now obsolete and are nowhere to be found amongst the Ibo today' (Preface, p. ix).

1033   **Words are sweet: Igbo stories and storytelling.**
Rems Nna Umeasiegbu.   Leiden, Netherlands: E. J. Brill, 1982.
140p. bibliog.

Dr. Umeasiegbu presents 100 folk-tales, grouped thematically, which he collected and translated from the Igbo during the 1960s and 1970s. In his introduction to Igbo life and storytelling (p. 3–20), he describes the storytelling event, Igbo aesthetics and his methods of collecting the tales. The author wrote his 1975 University of Pennsylvania doctoral thesis on *Folklore in Anglophone West African literature* and also published *Ask the humorist: Nigerian jokes* (Enugu, Nigeria: Koruna, 1986. 104p.) Another valuable collection by C. N. Ugochukwu, T. Meniru and P. Oguine is *Omalinze: a book of Igbo folk-tales* (Ibadan, Nigeria: New York: Oxford, 1977. 200p.). Here Igbo texts have been re-transcribed and edited and provided with an introduction and notes in English by E. Nolue Emenanjọ.

1034 **Nigerian folktales as told by Olawale Idewu and Omotayo Adu.**
Edited by Barbara K. Walker, Warren S. Walker. Hamden,
Connecticut: Archon, 1980. 2nd ed. 157p. bibliog.
The editors provide introductions (p. xiii–xvii; 1–9), extensive notes (p. 77–147) and a
bibliography (p. 149–57) to go with thirty-seven folktales told by Yoruba students, one
from Abeokuta, the other from Lagos. They are grouped as tales of demon lovers
pourquoi stories, moral fables, trickster tales and fertility tales. The first edition was
published in 1961 by Rutgers University. In Ashley Bryan's *Beat the story-drum, pum
pum* (New York: Atheneum, 1980. Reprinted, New York: Aladdin Books; London
Collier Macmillan, 1987. 68p.), he retells and illustrates five traditional Nigerian
folktales, two of which are Hausa in origin. The 1910 edition of Elphinstone Dayrell's
Folk stories from Southern Nigeria, West Africa, introduced by Andrew Lang, has been
reprinted (New York: Negro Universities, 1969. 158p.).

**The Yoruba-speaking peoples of the Slave Coast of West Africa, their religion,
manners, customs, laws, languages, etc., with an appendix containing a
comparison of the Tshi, Gā, Eẃe, and Yoruba languages.**
See item no. 405.

Festivals

1035 **The history and performance of durbar in northern Nigeria.**
Abdullahi Rofi Augi. Lagos: Nigeria Magazine, Cultural Division,
Federal Ministry of Information, 1978. 47p. bibliog. (Nigeria
Magazine Special Publication, no. 6).
This booklet, with both English and French text, describes the durbar or great
ceremonial festival of northern Nigeria, introduced in 1911 by Sir Frederick Lugard,
who linked it to pre-colonial forms of martial and equestrian display. Durbars were
also held in 1924, 1925, 1948, 1960 and 1972. Described and illustrated abundantly in
colour and black-and-white photographs, the 1977 durbar in Kaduna marked the
second World Black and African Festival of Arts and Culture (FESTAC) and brought
together 20,000 participants from nine states performing traditional music, dances, and
acrobatic feats, and horsemanship displayed on 3,500 horses and 500 camels.

1036 **Festivals in Nigeria: a bibliography.**
Compiled by G. D. Ekpenyong. *Nigeria Magazine*, no. 136 (1981),
p. 31–54.
Offers a most useful listing of 605 entries arranged in three sections: 'Nigeria-General',
the twelve states of 1967 and 'Northern Nigeria-General'. The illustrated introduction
describes the major festivals, the Pategi Regatta, the Argungu Fishing Festival and the
Oshun Festival. The author and title index accommodates the 1976 nineteen state reorganization. John Pemberton describes and includes colour photographs of three
annual festivals (for the ancestors, Ogun, and the Oba) in 'Festivals and sacred
kingship among the Igbomina Yoruba', *National Geographic Research*, vol. 2, no. 2
(1986), p. 216–33.

Architecture

1037 **Igbo architecture: a study of forms, functions and typology.**
Chike Cyril Aniakor. PhD thesis, Indiana University, Bloomington,
Indiana, 1978. 2 vols. 6 maps. bibliog. (Available from University
Microfilms, Ann Arbor, Michigan, 1979. Order no. 7916909.).
This highly informative Department of Fine Arts dissertation describes Igbo
architecture in detail. It surveys Igbo house and compound types and their distribution;
an ecology of house types and building technology; 'Igbo gates and compounds';
special forms; and the impact of modern forms on Igbo architecture. Volume one (339
leaves) has a bibliography (l. 328–39); volume two contains ninety-nine plates of maps,
diagrams and photographs. Fred T. Smith's 'Compound entryway decoration: male
space and female creativity', *African Arts*, vol. 19, no. 3 (May 1986), p. 52–59, 83,
compares compound portals and 'the nature of gender role differentiation and
complementarity among the Gurensi of northeastern Ghana and the Igbo of
southeastern Nigeria' (p. 52). Nancy Neaher discusses 'Igbo carved doors' in *African
Arts*, vol. 15 (1981), p. 49–55.

1038 **A history of Nigerian architecture: the last 100 years.**
Susan B. Aradeon. *Nigeria Magazine*, no. 150 (1984), p. 1–17.
bibliog.
An informative, well-illustrated survey of Nigerian architectural patterns, including a
discussion of the impact of British colonial rule on styles. The author is Senior Arts
Fellow in the Centre of Cultural Studies of the University of Lagos; her 1984 doctoral
thesis at Ahmadu Bello University was *Traditional mud-roofed architecture: a
provisional classification of structural systems and their resultant ceiling patterns.*

1039 **Da senzala ao sobrado: Arquitetura Brasileira na Nigéria e na
República Popular do Benin. From slave quarters to town houses:
Brazilian architecture in Nigeria and the People's Republic of Benin.**
Mariano Carneiro da Cunha, introduced by Manuela Carneiro da
Cunha. São Paulo, Brazil: Nobel Edusp, 1985. 185p. maps bibliog.
(Ed. da Universidade de São Paulo).
A fascinating, generously illustrated history in Portuguese and English of the freed
slaves who returned to Nigeria and Benin and their impact on local society, especially
as seen through their architecture. A bibliography (p. 114–16) is included, as is an
essay by Pierre Fatumbi Verger (p. 117–69) containing numerous photographs of the
urban Yoruba houses with Brazilian influences. Of interest also is *Brazilian houses
Nigeriane. Nigerian Brazilian houses* by Massimo Marafatto (Lagos: Istituto Italiano de
Cultura, 1983. 45p.), published in dual columns of Italian and English. It includes a
discussion of the Brazilian influence in architecture and forty-four figures, most of
which are photographs of houses in Lagos.

1040 **Hausa architecture.**
J. C. Moughtin. London: Ethnographica, in association with the Institute of Planning Studies, University of Nottingham, 1985. 175p. maps. bibliog.

An impressive, nicely produced and profusely illustrated volume which examines in detail the 'creation of the built environment in Hausaland', including its history and evolution, relationship to climate, manner of construction and decorations. The bibliography (p. 168–72) is excellent. The author taught at Ahmadu Bello University, Zaria, in the early 1960s.

1041 **Yoruba palaces: a study of Afins [sic] of Yorubaland.**
G. J. Afolabi Ojo, foreword by Adesoji Aderemi I. London: University of London, 1966. 110p. maps. bibliog.

This study of the *Àfin*, the royal residence of a Yoruba oba or king, describes their types, size, location, layout, and their architectural style as well as their builders, occupants, religious significance and changes in modern times. His Highness Adesoji Aderemi I, the Oni of Ife, wrote the foreword to this well-illustrated volume. S. O. Babayemi describes 'Oyo palace organisation, past and present' in *African Notes* (Ibadan), vol. 9, no. 1 (1986), p. 4–24.

1042 **Traditional housing in African cities: a comparative study of houses in Zaria, Ibadan, and Marrakech.**
Friedrich W. Schwerdtfeger, foreword by M. G. Smith. Chichester, New York: John Wiley, 1982. 480p. maps. bibliog.

This 'pioneer study' (Foreword, p. xi) blends sociology and architecture in an examination and comparison of housing in two Nigerian cities and one Moroccan. Zaria (p. 3–97) and Ibadan (p. 101–82) housing is well illustrated with photographs and diagrams. Each city is analysed according to 'context', 'land tenure and land use', 'demography', 'domestic groups and the house', 'occupation and income' and 'production, cost, and financing'. The author, of Ahmadu Bello University, Zaria, Nigeria, includes a wealth of data that is unavailable elsewhere.

Pottery

1043 **Itinate and Kwandalowa: ritual pottery of the Cham, Mwana and Longuda peoples of Nigeria.**
John N. Hare. London: Ethnographica, 1983. 45p. map. (Ethnographic Arts & Culture Series, 5).

A booklet on the figurative terracotta pots made by the Cham, Mwana and Longuda, who live in northern Nigeria near the Benue River. The pots, thirty-eight of which are described shown here in full-page photographs by Bernard Brandham, are used 'for divination, curing disease in both humans and animals, the protection of the foetus during gestation and well-being of the child until the age of puberty' (p. 7–8). The author describes the associated rituals in the brief introduction (p. 7–10).

1044 Folk pottery of Nigeria.
Josef Kandert. Prague: National Museum, 1974. 197p. bibliog.
(Annals of the Náprstek Museum, 7).
This major study in English of Nigerian pottery describes manufacture and trade,
technology and production, and types and culture areas. The book contains a
'Catalogue of the [179 specimens in the] collection of Nigerian pottery' (p. 129–66), a
list of published specimens of pottery by ethnic group (p. 167–85), 164 figures of pots,
and a bibliography (p. 187–94).

1045 Nigerian pottery: a catalogue.
Compiled by Sylvia Leith-Ross, foreword by Thurstan Shaw.
Ibadan, Nigeria: Ibadan University for the Department of Antiquities,
Lagos, 1970. 200p. maps. bibliog.
This catalogue, according to the remarkable compiler whose experience in Nigeria
dates back to 1907, 'should be looked on as no more than a first attempt at bringing to
light the unexpected wealth and interest of Nigerian pottery' (p. 15). This modest
assessment obscures her efforts of many years which resulted in the collection of
traditional pottery which became the Pottery Museum at Jos in the late 1950s and later
the Pottery Gallery of the Jos Museum. By 1970 the collection numbered 1,100 pieces,
a substantial number of which are pictured and described here, from seventy-one
cultures, divided into ten groups (p. 18–191). Michael Cardew describes 'Pottery
techniques in Nigeria' (p. 9–13), and Leith-Ross explains the 'Method of collection'
(p. 15), as well as the context of the pots presented in the catalogue. In the appendix
(p. 194–97) there are accounts of pottery-making among the Kofyar by Robert M.
Netting, and three notes on pottery of the Bassa Nge and Bassa Nkwomo. A glossary
(p. 198–99), a 'List of tribes' (p. 200) and a fold-out map of Nigeria showing ethnic
groups conclude the unique volume.

1046 Pottery making in Ilorin: a study of the decorated water cooler.
Ann O'Hear. *Africa*, vo. 56, no. 2 (1986), p. 174–92. map. bibliog.
This illustrated article relates the historical, social and technical aspects, and the
decline, of water cooler pottery in Ilorin, a largely Yoruba city of west-central Nigeria
known for its crafts. The author describes five types of water cooler and traces their
changes as potters adapted to new market conditions by streamlining and mass-
production. She discusses the disappearing craft as a women's industry handed down
within a largely patrilineal society. Also of interest is the 1969 article by Frank Willett
and Graham Connah, 'Pottery making in the village of Use, near Benin City, Nigeria',
Baessler-Archiv, vol. 17, p. 133–49.

1047 Pottery in Nigeria.
D. Simmonds. In: *Earthenware in Asia and Africa: a colloquium
held 21–23 June 1982.* Edited by John Picton. London: University of
London, School of Oriental and African Studies, Percival David
Foundation of Chinese Art, 1984, p. 54–92. (Colloquies on Art &
Archaeology Asia, no. 12).
A discussion of pottery manufacture, firing and distribution, and of potters in Nigeria,
based on observations made during 1960–70. It contains nineteen plates of photographs
of pots and pot-making.

Cookery

1048 **Nigerian cookbook.**
H. Olaitan Anthonio, Miriam Isoun. London; Basingstoke, England: Macmillan, 1982. 216p. bibliog.

A comprehensive cookbook with a wide variety of recipes drawn from all parts of the country, as well as a few 'introduced' recipes, which is designed to be both interesting and practical for both Nigerians and non-Nigerians. The book includes a glossary of food terms, weight and conversion tables, six colour plates and numerous drawings. Anthonio runs Ibadan University's Catering Department. The Federal Ministry of Information published *Cook with Nigeria* (Apapa, Nigeria, 1969. 30p.), a thirty-page booklet with twenty-three recipes and a glossary of terms.

1049 **Onjẹ fun oriṣa (food for the gods).**
Gary Edwards, John Mason. New York: Yoruba Theological Archministry, 1981. 143p. bibliog.

In this unusual book the authors describe the rôle of food in Yoruba religion providing ethnographic commentary and explanation to accompany the numerous recipes and sixteen photographs of the prepared dishes. Major categories are the warrior, the male and the female deities. Haitian gods and their foods are included, as are a glossary (p. 121–23) and a bibliography (p. 142–43). Edwards has published *Black gods: oriṣa studies in the New World* (Brooklyn, New York: Yoruba Theological Archministry, 1985. 80p.).

1050 **African cooking.**
Ola Olaore. London, New York: W. Foulsham, 1980. 96p.

A selection of recipes from all over Africa, in which Nigerian dishes appear prominently. A chapter on regional specialities from nineteen countries includes Nigeria (p. 47–55). A glossary of terms is included and eight colour plates illustrate several dishes. Adebisi Vincent, an inspector of education in Western Nigeria published *A cookery book for the tropics* (London: Allen & Unwin, 1962. 124p.) which serves as both a cooking handbook and as a source of diverse recipes. She followed this with *Food and nutrition* (Lagos: Macmillan, 1967. [n.p.]) which examines the nutritional value of West African foods.

1051 **Miss Williams' cookery book.**
[Rhoda Omosunlola Williams], foreword by G. Plummer. Ikeja, Nigeria: Longmans of Nigeria, 1957. Reprinted, 1962, 1967. 260p.

This gem is the 'first comprehensive work on Nigerian cookery' (Foreword, p. v). It contains information on everything from kitchens and markets to methods of cooking and 'the housewife hostess', and offers a very large number of recipes for all sorts of foods. The volume includes a glossary of terms, mostly Yoruba, (p. 249–55), an index and ten illustrations. Williams also published *About your cookery* (Ikeja, Nigeria: Longmans of Nigeria. 1960, 1966. 114p.). *The kudeti book of Yoruba cookery*, compiled by J. A. Mars and E. M. Tooleyò (Lagos: CSS Bookshops, 1979. 60p.). originally published in 1934 and now in its third edition, contains an assortment of basic recipes and a list of Yoruba terms.

1052 **A West African cook book: an introduction to good food from Ghana, Liberia, Nigeria and Sierra Leone, with reicpes collected and adapted by Ellen Gibson Wilson.**
Ellen Gibson Wilson. New York: M. Evans, distributed by J. B. Lippincott, Philadelphia, 1971. 267p. bibliog.
Presents an excellent compendium of West African recipes, most with their country of origin identified. The author discusses peppers, 'Cooking the West African way', 'Eating the West African way' and groups most recipes into 'Classic main dishes', 'Other main dishes', 'Other side dishes', 'Starters', 'After chop', and 'Small chop', 'Some feasts and rituals' and includes an annotated reading list (p. 249–54). The author expresses her debt to R. O. Omosunlola Williams's *Miss Williams' cookery book* (q.v.).

Museums

1053 **The museum and nation building.**
A[diele] E[berechukwu] Afigbo, S. I. O. Okita.   Owerri, Nigeria:
New Africa, 1985. 139p. bibliog.

This small but informative book offers nine essays (four by Afigbo, five by Okita)
containing a wealth of information about the history, philosophy, purposes and
potentials of the Nigerian museum system. The first essay 'The emergence of public
museums in Nigeria' by Okita has biographical data on the museum pioneers K. C.
Murray, E. H. Duckworth and B. Fagg. Others describe the rôle of the museum in
education, the museum as historical record and the position of the curator. Afigbo is
Professor of History, University of Nigeria, Nsukka; Okita is Senior Research Fellow,
Centre for Nigerian Cultural Studies, Ahmadu Bello University, Zaria. The publisher,
New Africa is at 24 Alaenyi Street, P.O. Box 1178, Owerri, Imo State, Nigeria.

1054 **The Nigerian museum movement.**
Kenneth Onwuka Dike.   Lagos: National Commission for Museums
& Monuments, [1983]. 7p.

This 'First Annual Museum Lecture, 1982, commemorating the silver jubille [*sic*] of
the National Museum, Onikan, Lagos', recounts the efforts of the individuals who
began conservation of Nigerian antiquities and culture in the 1930s. Leaders in this
movement were Kenneth C. Murray, who went to Nigeria in the 1930s as a fine arts
teacher, served as Surveyor of Antiquities and became the first head of the newly
created Department of Antiquities in 1953; and Bernard Fagg, who became
Government Archaeologist and Director of Antiquities in the 1950s. This brief lecture
was published soon after the death of Professor Dike on 26 October 1983, a
distinguished historian who had been the first indigenous Vice-Chancellor of the
University of Ibadan (1962–67) and the First Chairman of the Nigerian Antiquities
Commission (1954–67).

1055   **Guide to the Nigerian Museum, Lagos.**
Ekpo Eyo, Thurstan Shaw.   [Lagos]: Associated Press of Nigeria.
[Federal Ministry of Education, 1971]. 60p. map.
This guidebook provides a succinct overview of Nigerian traditional art. Eyo, then
Director, Department of Antiquities, offers 'A few words about your museum' (p. 1)
and Shaw, then Research Professor of Archaeology, University of Ibadan, describes
the invaluable work of archaeology in 'The Archaeology Gallery' (p. 2–4). The major
types of Nigerian art represented in the museum are reviewed and illustrated with
photographs. 'The Nigerian Museum was born from the idea of the conservation of
traditional works of art in Nigeria, first conceived in 1933 by E. H. Duckworth, a
former editor of *Nigeria Magazine*' (p. 1). In 1943 the Nigerian Antiquities Service was
begun and K. C. Murray was appointed Surveyor of Antiquities. The Lagos Museum,
established in March 1957, and has a 'first-class library of Africana with some 5,000
books and periodicals on archaeology, anthropology, ethnography, travel and history'
(p. 1), as well as more than 20,000 objects and between forty and fifty employees. See
also Philip Allison's article 'Collecting Yoruba art' in *African Arts*, vol. 6, no. 4
(summer 1973), p. 64–68.

1056   **Guide to the National Museum, Kaduna.**
[Federal Department of Antiquities], foreword by Ekpo Eyo.   Lagos:
CSS, [1977]. 47p.
The National Museum in Kaduna began its collections in 1972 and was opened in 1975.
This illustrated guide describes the gallery of Nigerian prehistory; the ethnographic
gallery of wooden masks, indigenous currency, musical instruments and textiles; and
the gallery of modern crafts which include pottery, leatherwork and calabash carvings.
In the compound of the museum is a Craft Village with potters, smiths, weavers,
wood-carvers and hairdressers working in tradtional styles, all of whom are described
briefly in this guide.

1057   **25 years of Jos Museum.**
Federal Department of Antiquities.   Jos, Nigeria: National Museum,
1978. 64p. 3 maps. bibliog.
This booklet is an expanded version of the catalogue for the exhibition entitled '25
years of Jos Museum' held in the Katsina Palace replica in 1977 to commemorate the
founding of Nigeria's first museum. The generously illustrated volume provides a
history of, and guide to, the museum and its ethnographic, archaeological and
architectural collections. In addition, it includes brief biographical sketches of fifteen
individuals who have been associated with the museum throughout its existence
(p. 53–61). The *Guide to the National Museum complex, Jos* ([Jos: National Museum,
1977, 13 leaves.] map) provides an overview of the collections.

Museums

1058 **Nigeria.**
Flora S. Kaplan, Nnennaya Samuel Ukwu, Emmanuel N. Arinze.
In: *Art museums of the world*. Editor-in-chief, Virginia Jackson;
Associate editors, Marlene A. Palmer, Eric M. Zafran; Assistant
editor, Ann Stephens Jackson. New York; Westport, Connecticut:
Greenwood, 1987, vol. I, p. 802–22. bibliog.
This article provides the best overview available of the national system of museums in
Nigeria, 'one of the best organized and coordinated museum systems in Africa'
(p. 802). The authors describe the various museums, and their histories, themes and
contents, as well as the history, organization and responsibilities of the National
Commission for Museums and Monuments which replaced the former Antiquities
commission and the Federal Department of Antiquities in 1979.

1059 **Preserving the past: a short description of the Museum of Nigerian
Antiquities, Traditional Art and Ethnography together with a note on
the principal art treasures and their sources of origin.**
K[enneth] C. Murray. Lagos: Information Division, Federal
Ministry of Research and Information, 1959. 31p.
This illustrated booklet, an expanded version of Murray's *Our art treasures* (Lagos:
Public Relations Department of Nigeria, [1953]) contains his original article (p. 13–31)
and an anonymous introduction (p. 5–12) describing the creation and growth of the
National Museum which opened in Lagos on 9 March 1957. Murray (1902–72) joined
the Education Department of Nigeria in 1927 as an art instructor, was appointed
Surveyor of Antiquities in 1943 and served as Director of Antiquities of Nigeria for
many years. He was known as the 'Father of Nigerian Antiquities' and died in a car
accident 22 April 1972 (*25 years of Jos Museum*, p. 58).

1060 **A guide to the Gidan Makama Museum, Kano.**
National Commission for Museums and Monuments, foreword by
Ekpo Eyo. [Ikeja, Nigeria: National Commission for Museums and
Monuments], 1985. 48p. maps.
A brief, room-by-room guide, with sixty-six plates, which gives a history of the city of
Kano and its environs and describes some arts and crafts in the city.

1061 **The story of the Old Calabar: a guide to the National Museum at the
Old Residency, Calabar.**
National Commission for Museums and Monuments, foreword by
Ekpo Eyo. [Lagos: National Commission for Museums and
Monuments], 1986. 228p. 5 maps.
This very full and informative history and guidebook to the Calabar Museum is
organized around a description of the themes in the five exhibition halls. The volume
contains a wealth of old photographs portraying the people and scenes of the times.
There is, however, neither an index nor a bibliography.

1062   **Guide to the National Museum, Oron.**
        Keith Nicklin, foreward [*sic*] by Ekpo Eyo.   [Lagos: Federal
        Department of Antiquities, 1977]. 79p. bibliog.

The Oron Museum near Calabar in south-eastern Nigeria, one of the country's finest
small museums, is described in this well-illustrated guidebook. Opened in 1959, with
about 800 ancestral figures of the Oron people, the museum was destroyed during the
civil war and 'the carvings were scattered, destroyed or stolen for sale abroad'
(Foreward [*sic*], p. ii). After the war the Federal Department of Antiquities recovered
about 100 pieces, which remain on display in a rebuilt museum which opened in April
1977. The guidebook provides a useful survey of the objects and their cultural contexts
and contains forty-one illustrations. The author was an ethnographer with the Federal
Department of Antiquities at the time of publication and is now Director of the
Horniman Museum in London.

1063   **The Benin Museum collection.**
        Frank Willett.   *African Arts*, vol. 6, no. 4 (summer 1973), p. 8–17,
        94. bibliog.

An informative account which considers both the establishment of the Benin Museum
and the distinctive works of Benin art it contains. 'The collection . . . has a quality and
importance all its own, for it includes a very high proportion of unique pieces, but
relatively few representations of the types which are commonly found in other
collections of Benin antiquities' (p. 8–9). Photographs of twenty-four objects are
included. The Bini historian Chief Jacob U. Egharevba, appointed museum curator in
1946, wrote a fifty-six-page *Descriptive catalogue of Benin Museum* in 1954 and first
published it in 1969; it is reprinted in his collected works (q.v.). In it he describes over
100 items held by the museum and mentions that 'the long delay on the part of Mr.
K. C. Murray the director of Antiquities Lagos Nigeria to print our joint Descreptive
[*sic*] Catalogue . . . has compelled me to the publication of this' (Preface). 'Mr. Death
can come at any time' (Preface).

Sports and Recreation

1064 **Football in Nigeria.**

S[amuel] E[kpe] Akpabot. London: Macmillan, 1985. 104p.

This small illustrated book gives a capsule history of Nigerian football. Exceptional players, such as 'bulldozer' Amusa, are noted, photographs are numerous and occasionally the names of the late famous players, such as Nnamdi Azikiwe, left wing for ZAC (Zik's Athletic Club) in 1938, appear.

1065 **The liege lord of Noxema.**

Curry Kirkpatrick. *Sports Illustrated*, vol 59, no. 23 (28 Nov. 1983), p. 106–10, [112], 114, [116, 118, 120, 124, 126, 128, 130, 132, 134–36].

A lengthy story about Hakeem Abdul Ajibola Olajuwon, 'Akeem the Dream', the seven-foot tall basketball superstar of the University of Houston, Texas, and the Houston Rockets. Most of the article and the colour pictures concern Olajuwon's family and life in Lagos, where he grew up; he later emigrating to the United States.

1066 **Ayo: a popular Yoruba game.**

A. O. Odeleye. Ibadan, Nigeria: Oxford University, 1977. 54p.

Ayo is the Yoruba version of the mancala board games played throughout Africa and found also in the New World. It is the most widespread board game among Yoruba peoples in south-western Nigeria and the Republic of Benin and is one of the greatest pastimes in a traditional social setting. Among the Igbo it is called *okwe*, among the Hausa it is *darra* and among the Bini it is *iyagbe*. The game is played by two players who move forty-eight seeds of the *Caesalpinia crista* plant around a board consisting of twelve cups or 'houses'. Each player moves his seeds according to a relatively simple set of rules and attempts to capture or 'eat' his opponent's seeds. Chief Odeleye, a former Secretary to the National Library Board of Nigeria and a master *Ayo* player, explains the strategies and subtleties of several variations of the game. A general article on games is Paul G. Brewster's 'Some Nigerian games with their parallels and analogues', *Journal de la Société des Africanistes* (Paris), vol. 24, no. 1 (1954), p. 25–48.

1067 **The development of Nigeria's participation in international sport competition and its effects on the nation.**
Daniel Ogungbenjo Ogunbiyi. PhD thesis, Ohio State University, Columbus, Ohio, 1978. 407 leaves. bibliog. (Available from University Microfilms, Ann Arbor, Michigan, 1978. Order no. 7812375).
Using library sources, questionnaires and interviews in Nigeria with some 300 athletes, coaches and sport administrators, the author presents a history of Nigerian international sport competition from 1950 to 1977. Nigeria's first international medals were won in 1950 at the Auckland, New Zealand, Commonwealth Games and the 1952 Helsinki Olympic Games. The author traces Nigerian participation in the All-African Games, West African Games and the University Games. He shows the rôles that sports play in promoting national unity and international relations, discusses Nigeria's strong sports (athletics, boxing, football, lawn tennis, table tennis and swimming), and weak sports (basketball and volleyball), and organizational problems and makes recommendations. Ebo Quansah reports on the 1988 Olympic Games (and Nigeria's disappointing results) in 'Africa in the long run', *West Africa*, no. 3713 (10–16 Oct. 1988), p. 1891.

Gods and goods in Africa: persistence and change in ethnic and religious identity in Yauri Emirate, North-Western State, Nigeria.
See item no. 438.

Libraries and Archives

1068 **Directory of law libraries in Nigeria (incorporating a practical classification scheme for Nigerian law libraries).**
Compiled by A. Adefidiya. Lagos, Nigeria: Federal Ministry of Information, Printing Division, 1970. 2nd ed. 110p. bibliog.

Gives practical information and statistics on thirty-three law libraries in Nigeria. In 1970 the largest was President Kennedy Library, Zaria, with 41,000 volumes, followed by the Ministry of Justice, Enugu, (30,000 volumes), the Federal Ministry of Justice, Lagos (26,000 volumes) and the High Court and Supreme Court Libraries in Lagos, each with 15,000 volumes. The compiler was the Librarian, Federal Ministry of Justice in Lagos at the time of publication. The first edition appeared in 1966.

1069 **The foundations of modern libraries in Nigeria.**
C. C. Aguolu. *International Library Review*, vol. 9 (1977), p. 461–83. bibliog.

This excellent article reviews pre-1948 library developments in Nigeria. The author emphasizes the long history of Islamic scholarship, the origins of printing and publishing by Scottish missionaries in the 1840s, early special libraries and the personal collections of Dr. Henry Rawlinson Carr whose 18,000-book collection was 'the largest personal library ever assembled by any West African' (p. 476) and of Herbert Macaulay, which had some 500 volumes. Finally, he describes the influence of the Carnegie Corporation of New York which financed the 1932 Lagos Library, the first Nigerian library open to the general public, as well as other libraries, and encouraged the development of a library training institute in West Africa. References cited in the notes are valuable for further research on the history of Nigerian libraries.

1070 **Public library services in Borno State.**
Christian C. Aguolu. *Annals of Borno*, vol. 3 (1986), p. 67–80.
bibliog.

This article surveys the nature and development of the library facilities in Nigeria's largest state, which serve c. four million widely dispersed persons. The author describes information resources, staffing and management control, continuing education and public library education. In *Annals of Borno* vol. 1 (1983), p. 17–28, he published 'Libraries as agencies of research and scholarship, with special reference to Borno State'. Aguolu is Professor and Head of Library Science at the University of Maiduguri and has been Dean of Education.

1071 **Libraries in West Africa: a bibliography.**
Compiled by Helen Davies. Oxford: Hans Zell; Munich: K. G. Saur,
1982. 170p.

Following an introductory essay, the author presents a list of 1,369 entries, some of which are briefly annotated, organized into 'West Africa in general' and then by country. Nigeria has the largest section with 729 entries (p. 67–136). Entries are subdivided into some twenty-five categories concerning librarianship and libraries. An appendix has a select list of library periodicals published in West Africa (p. 154–56), a conference index and a name index. One-third (p. 16–37) of A. O. Banjo's useful *Social science libraries in West Africa: a directory* (Lagos: Nigerian Institute of International Affairs, 1987. 63p. (NIIA Monograph Series, no. 13)) concerns Nigeria.

1072 **Library and archive collections in sub-Saharan Africa: a bibliography. Part 1.**
Peter Duignan. *A Current Bibliography on African Affairs*, vol. 2, no. 7 (July 1969), p. 5–19.

Annotated regional and country surveys of books, papers and articles on libraries and archives comprise this convenient bibliographical and archival tool. Nigerian sources (p. 14–19) are the most plentiful of those countries surveyed. Duignan and Lewis H. Gann's *A bibliographical guide to colonialism in sub-Saharan Africa* (London; Cambridge: Cambridge University, 1973. 552p.), volume five of their *Colonialism in Africa 1870–1960* (London: Cambridge University, 1969–74. 5 vols.) contains an excellent, very extensive listing and discussion of library and archival resources.

1073 **The non-book material resources of the Library of the Institute of African Studies, University of Ibadan, Ibadan, Nigeria.**
Adejoke O. Scott-Emuakpor. *A Current Bibliography on African Affairs*, vol. 9, no. 3 (1976–77), p. 202–12. bibliog.

The author describes the valuable collection of recordings, Yoruba music, the Ife literary corpus, Nigerian music, films, slides, illustrations, maps and manuscripts held by the Institute of African Studies. The appendices list eleven Nigerian cultural records and fourteen films, of a similar nature, noting especially those made by Frank Speed and others in the 1960s, which are available for showing at the Institute.

Libraries and Archives

1074 **Africana catalogue of the Ibadan University Library.**
University of Ibadan Library, preface by T. Olabis Odeinde.
Boston, Massachusetts: G. K. Hall, 1973. 2 vols.
The Ibadan University Library, with more than 260,000 volumes at the time of publication, was the largest library of its kind in tropical Africa. This catalogue is essentially an author catalogue to the 'heart' of the main collection. These two volumes are a photographic reproduction of over 35,000 cards representing Africana acquisitions from 1948 to April 1972.

The African book world & press: a directory. Répertoire du livre et de la presse en Afrique.
See item no. 1079.

Books and Publishing

1075 **Publishing in Africa: a bibliography.**
Compiled by Maduka W. Anyakoha. *A Current Bibliography on African Affairs*, vol. 8, no. 4 (1975), p. 296–319.
A most useful listing of 255 publications, grouped by region and indexed, with a list of sources consulted and an introduction. Books, newspaper and journal articles, government publications, unpublished conference papers and publishers' annual reports are included. A substantial number of the West African items concern Nigerian publishing. The author was at the Univeristy of Nigeria, Nsukka, at the time of publication.

1076 **Nigerian books in print 1970.**
Edited by J. A. Dosunmu, compiled by the staff of the National Library of Nigeria in co-operation with the Nigerian Publishers Association. Lagos: National Library of Nigeria, Dec. 1971. 3rd ed. 115p. (National Library Publication, 25).
This third edition lists over 1,000 titles of publications in two parts, the first an alphabetical author list and the second an alphabetical subject list. Bibliographic information, including date, price and publisher is listed. The second edition, *Nigerian books in print 1968* (May 1970. (National Library Publication, 19)), by the same editor, listed a similar number. The first edition appeared in 1966. *Serials in print in Nigeria*, issued annually by the National Library, lists all serial titles published in a particular year.

1077 **Publishing in Nigeria.**
Ethiope, foreword by Tayo Akpata. Benin City, Nigeria: Ethiope, 1972. 71p.
Ten short essays describe aspects of publishing in Africa generally and in Nigeria in particular. Among the articles are 'African books in print' and 'Book publishing in Africa: a check list' by Hans Zell, editor of the University of Ife Press at the time of publication. The booklet includes text up to page fifty-four, and then advertisements for publishers.

Books and Publishing. Periodical

1078 **Nigerian publications, 1950–1970.**
Compiled by O. G. Tamuno, G. A. Alabi. Ibadan, Nigeria: Ibadan
University, 1977. 433p. bibliog.

This professional bibliographical listing cites the 9,767 titles received by the Ibadan
University Library, as the major national depository for all publications, from April
1950–June 1970. By law, publishers were required to deposit at the library two copies
of every book produced in Nigeria. Of these titles, 3,511 or 35.8 per cent were official
publications in English; 4,577 or 47.1 per cent were non-official publications in English;
1,679 or 17.1 per cent were works representing forty-seven Nigerian languages, of
which thirty-nine per cent were Hausa, Igbo or Yoruba. The compilers point out the
notable publications of each five-year period in their introduction to this valuable
work.

1079 **The African book world & press: a directory. Répertoire du livre et de
la presse en Afrique.**
Edited by Hans M. Zell, Carol Bundy; associate editors Margaret
Curran, Robin Mortlock. Munich: K. G. Saur; Oxford: Hans
Zell, 1983. 3rd ed. 285p.

This volume brings together information on 4,621 institutions and organizations from
all sectors of the book and press world in fifty-one African countries. Hundreds of
printers in Nigeria are included, using the *Nigerian yellow pages* (Lagos: ICIC
directory, 2nd ed. 1980). Nigerian entries (p. 106–36, nos. 1,751–2,330) include
university, college and public libraries, special libraries, booksellers, publishers,
newspapers, printers and the government printer, for each of which there is an address
and other information. The fourth edition (1989. 306p.) includes nearly 5,000 entries.

Periodical

1080 **The African Book Publishing Record.**
Oxford: Hans Zell, Jan. 1975– . quarterly.

An invaluable publication with notes and news, reference sources, book, periodical
and magazine reviews, and full bibliographic and ordering information in both English
and French. Coverage is of recent imprints, accessed by subject, author and country
indexes.

The Sokoto Caliphate.
See item no. 201.

Guide to research and reference works on sub-Saharan Africa.
See item no. 1129.

**Colonialism in Africa, 1870–1960. Volume 5. A bibliographical guide to
colonialism in sub-Saharan Africa.**
See item no. 1130.

Niger Delta studies, 1627–1967: a bibliography.
See item no. 1138.

Bibliographies for African studies 1970–1986.
See item no. 1140.

A bibliographical guide to Borno studies, 1821–1983.
See item no. 1142.

The United States and Africa: guide to U.S. official documents and government-sponsored publications on Africa, 1785–1975.
See item no. 1147.

Nigerian publications: current national bibliography.
See item no. 1150.

Mass Media

1081 **The Nigerian press under civilian rule.**
Sylvanus A. Ekwelie. *Journalism Quarterly*, vol. 63, no. 1 (spring
1986), p. 98–105, 149. bibliog.
This article reviews the status of the Nigerian press during the years 1979–83. Several
challenges to the press's autonomy are examined with the overall conclusion that 'the
1979 Constitution seems to have provided a protective shield. It is now unlikely that
elected officials will in the future get successful prosecution only on the grounds that
press criticism was intemperate, violent or is likely to excite hatred or disaffection'
(p. 149).

1082 **African mass communications: selected information sources.**
Compiled by   Sydney W. Head.   *A Current Bibliography on African
Affairs*, vol. 10, no. 1 (1977–78), p. 32–66.
A brief discussion of mass communications in Africa precedes the listing of 460
periodical, bibliographical and yearbook sources, indexed by country and region. Fifty-
four items pertain to Nigeria, significantly more than for any other country.

1083 **History of the Nigerian Broadcasting Corporation.**
Olu Ladele, V. Olufemi, Olu Lasekan, foreword by Christopher
Kolade.   Ibadan, Nigeria: Ibadan University, 1979. 251p. bibliog.
Offers a history of the predecessors of the NBC, of its incorporation in 1957 and of its
development over the next twenty years. Fourteen photographs are included, and
appendices contain the relevant legislation and show the distribution and power of
transmitters. Another useful source is Luke Uka Uche's 'The politics of Nigeria's radio
broadcast industry: 1932–83', *Gazette*, vol. 35, no. 1 (1985), p. 19–29, which describes
the ways in which Nigerian radio was affected by political changes over fifty years.

1084 **The Nigerian press and the civil war in Angola.**
Onuora E. Nwuneli, Olatunji Dare. *A Current Bibliography on African Affairs*, vol. 9, no. 4 (1976–77), p. 302–16.

The authors, who were in the Department of Mass communications at the University of Lagos at the time of publication, assess the rôle of the Nigerian press coverage of the Angola civil war from several viewpoints. Five newspapers (the *Daily Times*, *New Nigerian*, *Nigerian Tribune*, *Nigerian Herald* and *Nigerian Observer*) were analysed during an eight-week study period, four weeks before Angolan independence and four after. They found that Nigerian newspapers relied on foreign news agencies for their news and made little attempt to interpret Angolan news to the public. They conclude, 'the fact that the Nigerian press has not improved significantly both in quality and sophistication in the past five years dating back to 1971, is what should be viewed with the uttermost concern' (p. 315) [*sic*].

1085 **Press and politics in Nigeria, 1880–1937.**
Fred I. A. Omu. Atlantic Highlands, New Jersey: Humanities; Harlow, England: Longman, 1978. 290p. bibliog. (Ibadan History Series).

This book, based on the author's PhD thesis at the University of Ibadan, is both a history of the newspaper press and a study of its impact on political development in Nigeria. The indigenous newspaper movement began with the establishment of the *Lagos Times and Gold Coast Colony Advertiser* on 10 November 1880. Between then and 1937, fifty-one newspapers were begun, eleven dailies, thirty-three weeklies, three fortnightlies and four monthlies, most in Lagos, 'the centre of the most developed newspaper industry in Africa' (p. 26). An epilogue describes several trends up to about 1974. An appendix lists the newspapers and provides circulation figures for most. The bibliography (p. 267–77) is a substantial listing of relevant sources for the study of Nigerian and West African newspapers.

1086 **Communication policies in Nigeria.**
Frank Okwu Ugboajah. Paris: UNESCO, 1980. 67p. map. bibliog. (Communication Policies Series).

This short informative book discusses aspects of the media in Nigeria. It includes: a history of newspapers with tables of the fifteen surviving national dailies and the twenty-eight surviving monthly magazines (1965–77); the founding and policies of the News Agency of Nigeria (NAN) in 1976; freedom of the press and legislation relating to the press; the Nigerian Television Authority (NTA), created in 1977; and the Nigerian Broadcasting Corporation, now the Federal Radio Corporation of Nigeria (FRCN). One chapter reports on characteristics of the top media managers and their attitudes. The appendix contains the Nigerian press code of conduct, circulation figures for newspapers and magazines and a list of the same from 1859 to 1965, drawn from I. H. E. Coker's *Landmarks of the Nigerian press: an outline of the origins and development of the newspaper press in Nigeria, 1859 to 1965* (Lagos: Apapa Nigerian, 1968. 126 leaves).

Mass Media

1087 **Mass communication, culture and society in West Africa.**
Edited by Frank Okwu Ugboajah. Munich; New York; London;
Oxford: Hans Zell, K. G. Saur for the World Association for
Christian Communication, 1985. 329p. bibliog.
Of the twenty-six informative articles in this volume, twelve are directly relevant for
Nigeria: Idowu A. Sobowale's 'The historical development of the Nigerian press';
David Omazo Edeani's 'Press ownership and control in Nigeria'; P. O. Elegalem's
'Economic factors in the development of mass communication in Nigeria'; Michael R.
Real's 'Broadscast music in Nigeria and Liberia'; Theo Vincent's 'Television drama in
Nigeria: a critical assessment'; O. O. Oreh's '*Masquerade* and other plays on Nigerian
television'; C. M. B. Brann's 'A sociolinguistic typology of language contact in
Nigeria: the role of translation'; E. Simpson's 'Translating in the Nigerian mass media:
a sociolinguistic study'; F. O. Ugboajah's 'Editorial professionalisation in the Nigerian
mass media' and 'Nigerian mass media in social crises'; and L. Uka Uche's 'Diffusion
of major crisis information among urban and rural opinion leaders in Nigeria'. Barbara
S. Monfils provides a bibliographic essay on mass media in West Africa (p. 285–308).

General Periodicals and Newspapers

1088 **African Concord.**
London: Concord Press of Nigeria, 1985– . weekly.

African Concord succeeded the *Concord Weekly*, which began in 1984. 'The premier pan-African weekly' is a reliable general news magazine with continent-wide coverage. Feature articles report on the most important news in Africa but also on issues elsewhere which are relevant for African nations. Nigerian news is reported in longer articles as well as in 'News briefs'. Both a pan-African and a Nigerian edition are published. The addresses for these, respectively, are: Concord Press of Nigeria, Ltd., 5–15 Cromer Street, London WC1H 8LS, and 42 Concord Way, Off Murtala Mohammed Airport, Ewu Tuntun, Ikeja, P.O. Box 4483, Ikeja, Nigeria. Aare M. K. O. Abiola is the publisher and Dr. Doyin Abiola is the managing director and editor-in-chief. Concord Press also publishes a daily newspaper, the *National Concord* (whose logo is 'Truth is constant'), the *Sunday Concord,* and the *Business Concord*, 'Your favorite business/financial newspaper'.

1089 **Africa Now.**
London: Pan-African; Banjul, The Gambia: Inter Africa, 1981– . monthly.

One of the major monthly news magazines, *Africa Now* is available both in Nigeria and abroad. Peter Enahoro is president and chairman. Another important news monthly is *New African* (London: IC Publications, 1966– .), the 'oldest pan-African monthly'.

1090 **Daily Times.**
Ikeja, Lagos: Daily Times Group, 1949– . daily.

'The independent newspaper', although it is sixty per cent government owned, provides reasonably good coverage of events in the country. With approximately 400,000, this paper has the largest circulation in Nigeria and claims to have the largest daily circulation in Africa. The editor is Oneyma Ugochukwu. The Daily Times Group publishes a large range of papers including weeklies: *Sunday Times*; *Lagos Weekend*; *Sporting Record*; *Business Times*; *Times International*; and a Yoruba-language paper, *Irohin Yoruba;* and monthlies: *Woman's World*; *Spear*; and *Home-Studies*.

1091 The Guardian.
Oshodi, Lagos: Guardian Magazines, 1983– . daily.

This is Nigeria's most sophisticated newspaper, with the most reliable reporting and highest quality writing, and a circulation of about 80,000. Its logo is 'Conscience, nurtured by truth'. In addition to current news and varied feature articles, it includes such items as a weather report, a crossword puzzle and television reviews. *The African Guardian* (Oshodi, Lagos: Alex Ibru, 1986– . weekly) 'newsfeature magazine', provides international and domestic coverage of important events. Andy Akporugo is editor-in-chief and managing director. The editor is Lade Bonuola; columnists listed on the magazine's masthead include Wole Soyinka and Femi Osofisan. Its address is Rutam House, Isolo Expressway, P.M.B. 1217, Oshodi, Lagos, Nigeria.

1092 New Nigerian.
Kaduna: Northern Nigerian Newspapers, 1966– . daily.

This government owned daily with a circulation of about 80,000 provides respectable news coverage, is distinctly northern and Islamic in contrast to the Lagos originated *Daily Times*, and has a variety of features in addition to the regular news stories. Its chairman is Professor Tekena Tamuno and the editor is Bilkisu Yusuf. Its address is Ahmadu Bello Way P.O. Box 254, Kaduna South, Nigeria.

1093 Newswatch.
Ikeja, Nigeria: Newswatch Communications, 1985– . weekly.

This highly regarded publication, 'Nigeria's weekly newsmagazine', reports on contemporary events in Nigeria and the world. Its outspoken coverage of sensitive issues has brought it into conflict with the government. Founding editor Dele Giwa (1947–86) was assassinated by a parcel bomb in October 1986 and his assassin never located. In May 1987, the magazine was banned for six months as a result of its publication of a confidential government document. Ray Ekpu is editor-in-chief and Dan Agbese is deputy editor-in-chief. Published in 62 Oregun Road, P.M.B. 21499, Ikeja, Nigeria, it has international offices at *Newswatch*, Lyntonia House, 7–9 Praed Street, London W2 3NJ.

1094 West Africa.
London: West Africa, Feb. 1917– . weekly.

The most respected and the longest running weekly news magazine for sub-Saharan Africa, *West Africa* features timely editorials and articles on the region. In addition to political and economic news, there are regular articles on literature, book reviews, interviews, a 'writers' diary', excerpts from issues fifty and twenty-five years ago, and 'Dateline Africa' in which brief news items from each country in West Africa and from most Nigerian states are reported. This magazine is essential reading for an understanding of contemporary events in the region. Recently, a series of special reports by Maxwell Nwagboso, Olugbenga Ayeni, Nuru Adio-Saka, Olu Akaraogun, Olaniyi Ola and Bola Olawo examined '25 years of republicanism' in Nigeria, *West Africa*, no. 3711 (26 Sept.–2 Oct. 1988), p. 1772–93.

Africa South of the Sahara 1989.
See item no. 1111.

Professional Periodicals

General

1095 **Publishing of learned journals in Nigeria.**
S. Olajire Olanlokun. *Libri*, vol. 35, no. 4 (1985), p. 333–40.
The author, Principal Librarian at the University of Lagos, Akoka-Yaba, Nigeria, describes the proliferation of learned journals, from the *Nigerian Field* (q.v.) which began in 1931 to the current 103 journals listed in the appendix. Of these more than fifty per cent were begun in the 1970s and 1980s and eighty per cent originate in higher educational institutions in the country; of the total number, 25.24 per cent are in the humanities, 25.24 per cent are in scientific and technological fields, 19.42 per cent are social science journals, 15.54 per cent are in education and 14.56 per cent are in law.

Periodicals

1096 **Africa. Journal of the International African Institute.**
Manchester: Manchester University for the International African Institute, 1928– . quarterly.
An important journal, each issue of which contains scholarly articles, sometimes in French, especially on historical and socio-cultural topics, as well as critical book reviews and 'shorter notices'. 'The International African Institute promotes international research, conferences and publications on African societies, cultures and languages and encourages the application of research and science to practical affairs in Africa'. The address of the IAI is Lionel Robbins Building, 10 Portugal Street, London WC2A 2HD.

Professional Periodicals. Periodicals

1097 **Africa Index to Continental Periodical Literature.**
Oxford: Hans Zell; Munich: K. G. Saur, 1976– . annual.
This periodical began as an annual serial but was issued in book form commencing with no. 3 (covering 1978) edited by Colin Darch and O. C. Mascarenhas in 1981. No. 4/5 (covering 1979–80, 392p.) was edited by Colin Darch in 1983; no. 6 (covering 1981, 215p.) was edited by Colin Darch and Alice Nkhoma-Wamunza in 1985. The index covers selected scholarly and semi-scholarly journals published but not necessarily printed within the African continent, excluding South Africa. Many relevant Nigerian journals are represented in each issue.

1098 **African Affairs.**
London: Royal African Society, 1901– . quarterly.
This distinguished journal is published by the Royal African Society, an organization founded in 1901 in memory of Mary Kingsley. Each issue contains articles by both African and non-African scholars on historical, political and economic topics; notes and news of the Society and its members; book reviews; a very useful bibliography of Africa-related articles; and a list of Africa articles in non-Africanist publications. It is an important source of articles and information on Nigeria. The editorial address is *African Affairs*, Institute of Commonwealth Studies, 27 Russell Square, London WC1B 5DS.

1099 **African Notes. Journal of the Institute of African Studies.**
Ibadan, Nigeria: Heinemann Educational (Nigeria) for the Institute of African Studies, University of Ibadan, 1963– . irregular.
This University of Ibadan journal contains articles on archaeology and antiquities, dance, history, medicine, oral traditions, religion, and social structure, among other topics. Vol. VIII, no. 1 (1979), p. 45–49, contains a subject and author index to volumes I–VII (1963–73). In 1986, its editor was Mabel Segun.

1100 **Africa Report.**
New York: African-American Institute, 1956– . bimonthly.
Africa Report, 'America's leading magazine on Africa', continues *Africa Special Report: Bulletin of the Institute of African-American Relations* which began with vol. 1, no. 1 (5 July 1956). Each issue has a theme, but also provides broad, balanced coverage for the continent. In addition to articles on current issues, and an 'update' section reporting briefly on several countries, a strength of the magazine is its interviews with heads of state and prominent officials throughout Africa. The editorial address is *Africa Report*, 833 United Nations Plaza, New York, NY 10017.

1101 **Africa Research Bulletin.**
Exeter, England: Africa Research, 1964– . monthly.
Each issue is extremely informative, providing continent-wide coverage of all significant events. The *Economic Series* includes a statistical supplement in each issue and surveys of policy and practice, development plans, commodities, and industries. The *Political Series* covers continental alignments, internal developments, national security, overseas relations, and social and cultural topics.

1102 **Africa South of the Sahara: index to periodical literature.**
Boston, Massachusetts: G. K. Hall, 1971, 1982; Washington, DC:
Library of Congress, African Section, African and Middle Eastern
Division, 1985. irregular.

This on-going publication began as the *Index to periodical literature, 1900–1970* (Boston, Massachusetts: G. K. Hall, 1971, 3 vols.). The *Second Supplement* (Boston, Massachusetts: G. K. Hall, 1982. 3 vols.) covered periodical literature from June 1972–December 1976. The *Third Supplement*, (Washington, DC: Library of Congress African Section, 1985) includes citations to African periodicals published in 1977 arranged in six broad subject categories and subdivided by country. The result is an indispensable resource. Also very helpful is *U.S. imprints on sub-Saharan Africa: a guide to publications catalogued at the Library of Congress* (Washington, DC: Library of Congress, African Section, 1985– . annual), compiled under the direction of Joanne M. Zellers.

1103 **Annals of Borno.**
Maiduguri, Nigeria: University of Maiduguri, 1983– . irregular.

This important journal for north-eastern Nigeria is a 'multidisciplinary periodical of research and documentation in the Human and Natural Sciences'. Each issue, vol. 1 (1983), vol. 2 (1985), and vol. 3 (1986), contains articles on geography and geology, history, social patterns, Kanuri language studies, the government and numerous other topics; book reviews; research notes; and bibliographic articles. In vol. 3, is 'Bibliography of writings on Borno by Ronald Cohen, 1961–1985'. The editorial address is The Editor, *Annals of Borno*, University of Maiduguri, Maiduguri, Nigeria.

1104 **The Conch: a Sociological Journal of African Cultures and Literatures.**
Buffalo, New York: Conch Magazine, 1969–81. semi-annual.

Founded, edited and published by Sunday O. Anozie, originally as *A Biafran Journal of Literary and Cultural Analysis*, the journal contains numerous thematic issues of value to Nigerian studies. Vol. 1, no. 1 (March 1969) is a special issue 'In memoriam Chris Okigbo'; vol. 3, no. 2 (Sept. 1971) is 'Igbo traditional life, culture & literature' edited by M. J. C. Echeruo and E. N. Obiechina; vol. 5, nos. 1 & 2 (1973) is devoted to Nigerian politics, culture and literature, and contains C. C. Aguolu's 'Bibliographic problems in Nigeria', p. 129–51; vol. 8, nos. 1 & 2 (1976) is on 'Traditional healing: new science or new colonialism? (Essays in critique of medical anthropolgy)' edited by Philip Singer; vol. 9, nos. 1 & 2 (1977), is 'Education and politics in tropical Africa', edited by Victor C. Uchendu.

1105 **Current Contents Africa.**
Munich; New York; London: K. G. Saur, 1976– . quarterly.

This publication consists of photocopies of the tables of contents of nearly 200 Africanist and non-Africanist periodicals supplied by the Frankfurt Stadt- und Universitätsbibliothek. It is edited by Irmtraud Wolcke, Head, Africa Collection, Stadt- und Universitätsbibliothek, Frankfurt-am-Main, GFR.

Professional Periodicals. Periodicals

1106   **Ikenga. Journal of African Studies.**
Nsukka, Nigeria: Institute of African Studies, University of Nigeria,
January 1972– . semi-annual.

Ikenga 'is a cult object of the Igbo-speaking peoples to which traditionally is attributed
success or good fortune in the professions or in life generally. It is also closely
associated with the right arm with which a man hacks his way through life. *Ikenga*
could therefore be briefly described as the Igbo god of achievement. The journal is
dedicated to the critical study of the fortunes of the black man down the centuries, and
of his contemporary problems and dilemmas. Its interest covers the entire spectrum of
African Studies' (Journal editorial policy). Most articles concern Nigerian topics. The
University of Nigeria's Institute of African Studies also publishes (irregularly) *Ikoro*,
July 1971– .

1107   **Nigeria Magazine.**
Lagos: Department of Culture, Federal Ministry of Social
Development, Youth and Culture, 1933– . quarterly.

A long-running, generously illustrated magazine which includes articles on 'any topic
related to Nigerian culture, languages, literature, religion, sociology, biology,
philosophy, any aspect of folklore and folklife, etc.' (Editor-in-chief's editorial
statement). From 1933–36 it was *The Nigerian Teacher*; from 1937–59, *Nigeria*; from
1960, *Nigeria Magazine*. The editorial address is 'Nigeria', National Theatre, Iganmu,
Lagos, Nigeria.

1108   **Nigerian Behavioral Sciences Journal.**
Ibadan: Nigerian Institute of Social and Economic Research, 1978– .
irregular

This journal publishes articles from the disciplines of sociology, cultural studies,
religion, economics, politics and health. NISER also publishes an annual report which
lists its current research projects and publications. The editorial address is Nigerian
Institute of Social and Economic Research (NISER), P.M.B. 5, University of Ibadan,
Ibadan, Nigeria.

1109   **Odu. A Journal of West African Studies.**
Ile-Ife, Nigeria: Obafemi Awolowo University Press, July 1964–68.
New series, April 1969– . semi-annual.

'The journal is meant to cover the entire spectrum of West African studies with an
emphasis on intensive local research' (Editorial statement). This valuable journal was
issued originally as *Odu. Journal of Yoruba and Related Studies*, nos. 1–9 (Jan.
1955–Sept. 1963) by the West Region Literature Committee, Ibadan, Nigeria. The
original series has been reprinted (Nendeln, Liechtenstein: Kraus Reprint, 1976).

1110   **Savanna. A Journal of the Environmental and Social Sciences.**
Zaria, Nigeria: Ahmadu Bello University, June 1972– . irregular.
An important journal, publishing articles on all aspects of the savanna area, from
studies of pollution, water, flora and fauna, and soils to human culture, and containing
book reviews. Each issue has a substantial 'current bibliography of the savanna states
of Nigeria' compiled by Anthony Olden.

Encyclopaedias and Directories

1111 **Africa South of the Sahara 1989.**
London: Europa, 1988. 18th ed. 1,163p. 10 maps. bibliog.
This invaluable annual publication covers political, social and economic developments of the previous year in essays by internationally recognized experts. Fifty-one 'country surveys' form the bulk of the volume (p. 219–1,163), each chapter covering standard topics: 'Physical and social geography'; 'Recent history'; 'Economy'; 'Statistical survey'; 'Directory', subdivided into numerous useful categories and 'Bibliography'. In 'Nigeria' (p. 777–819) appear essays by Akin L. Mabogunje, T. C. McCaskie, Paul Hackett and Simon Reynolds, data on population, agriculture, forestry, industry, finance, trade, transport and education, lists of political office holders and organizations, diplomatic representation, newspapers and periodicals, publishers, banks, organizations in trade and industry, unions and a bibliography (p. 818–19). In short, if a reader could only consult one source on contemporary Nigeria, this should arguably be that one.

1112 **Nigeria yearbook.**
Daily Times. Ikeja, Lagos: The Daily Times of Nigeria, 1952– . annual (A Daily Times Publication).
This annual publication contains a wealth of varied information on the country, covering business and finance, politics and government, history, resources and a daily record of significant events, plus numerous other topics. The most recent 1986 edition, edited by Gbenga Odusanya, had 349p., but no index. It is available from The Daily Times of Nigeria Publications Division, New Isheri Road, P.M.B. 21340, Ikeja, Lagos, Nigeria.

Encyclopaedias and Directories

1113 Information Lagos: a comprehensive reference/directory for business people in Nigeria.
Edited by Mark M. Ford, assistant editor Hedy Kalikoff, editor emeritus Leo G. B. Welt. Washington, DC: Welt, [1979] 165p.

A useful handbook with information on 'Doing business with Nigeria' (p. 12–76), 'Traveling to Nigeria' [*sic*], 'In Nigeria', 'Resources in the United States'. It has a directory of banks, health facilities, oil and gas companies and an index.

1114 Africa contemporary record.
Edited by Colin Legum. New York, London: Africana, 1968–69– . annual.

Represents a very useful annual survey and compilation of important documents. Each volume contains a series of essays on current issues, country-by-country reviews of events, documents and name and subject indexes.

1115 The Cambridge encyclopedia of Africa.
Roland [Anthony] Oliver, Michael Crowder, general editors.
Cambridge; New York: Cambridge University, 1981. 492p. 46 maps. bibliog.

This excellent, one-volume, profusely illustrated reference work by ninety-nine contributors surveys virtually all significant aspects of Africa. The book is organized into 'The African continent' (physical environment and peoples), 'The African past', 'Contemporary Africa' and 'Africa and the world'. Nigeria (p. 246–47) is described in overview, as are all other nations, and appears frequently throughout the volume. Nigerian historians J. F. Ade Ajayi and K. Onwuka Dike served as consultant editors. The *African encyclopedia* (London: Oxford, 1974. 554p.) contains an informative alphabetical guide from 'Aardvark' to 'Zulu language' in 1,850 brief articles, 500 photographs and 200 diagrams, maps and drawings, with much information on Nigeria. It was produced by advisory editors W. Senteza Kajubi, L. J. Lewis, C. O. Taiwo and dozens of contributors.

1116 Biographia Nigeriana: a biographical dictionary of eminent Nigerians.
S[tephen] A[demola] Orimoloye, foreword by J. F. Ade. Ajayi.
Boston, Massachusetts: G. K. Hall, 1977. 368p. (Bibliographies and Guides in African Studies).

An unindexed alphabetical listing of nearly one thousand prominent Nigerians, each afforded concise biographical data and a list, if appropriate, of major publications. This is an excellent source of information, especially on prominent academics, scientists, physicians, architects and educators. The author (1935– .) was Deputy University Librarian, University of Lagos Library, Yaba, Lagos, Nigeria, at the time of publication. Also particularly useful are *Who's who in Nigeria: a biographical dictionary* (Lagos: Daily Times, 1956, 1st ed. 277p.; 1983, 4th ed. 558p.) and *Who's who in Nigeria* (Lagos: Biographical Centre of Nigeria, 1981, 1st ed. 95p.; 1985, 3rd ed. 144p) with Hector Udunna Ukegbu as Chairman of the Editorial Board.

1117 **Who's who of Nigerian women.**
Edited by Clara Osinulu, Oluremi Jegede. Lagos, Nigeria: Nigerian
Association of University Women, 1985. 284p.

This first edition contains brief biographical sketches and often a small photograph of
prominent Nigerian women. Entered are 280 women, indexed by profession.

1118 **Historical dictionary of Nigeria.**
A[nthony] Oyewole. Metuchen, New Jersey; London: Scarecrow,
1987. 391p. 2 maps. bibliog. (African Historical Dictionaries, no. 40).

An important reference work, valuable for anyone interested in Nigerian politics and
history. The volume contains a 'Selected chronology' from 1788 to 1983 (p. viii–xii),
and an introduction (p. 1–9) providing a brief history. The dictionary (p. 11–345)
offers an alphabetical list and descriptions of people, events, ethnic groups, and places.
A selected bibliography of 668 works (p. 347–84) and brief addenda (p. 385–91),
bringing events up to the coup of 27 August 1985, conclude the dictionary. The author
is a senior lecturer in political science at Obafemi Awolowo University, Ile-Ife,
Nigeria. The book is reviewed by R. A. Myers in 'An uneven work of reference on
Nigeria', *Africa Today*, vol. 35, no. 2 (2nd quarter 1988), p. 67–68.

1119 **New African yearbook 1987–88.**
Edited by Alan Rake. London: IC Magazines, 1987–88. 7th ed.
412p. maps. (An IC Publication).

A highly informative annual publication, now reverting to a single volume covering all
sub-Saharan countries after four years of regionalized editions in which West and
Central Africa were combined. The 1987–88 edition covers forty-eight countries and
has a useful section on thirty African organizations (p. 9–18). 'Nigeria' (p. 243–68),
written by Keem Belo-Osagie, William D. Graf, Gavin Williams and Alan Rake,
covers general information, political history, economy, current events up to March
1987 and statistics from the mid-1970s to 1983–85.

1120 **African international organization directory and African participation
in other international organizations 1984/85.**
Edited by Union of International Associations. Munich; New York;
London: K. G. Saur, Nov. 1984. 604p.

Introductory material in English and French is followed by a description of numerous
African organizations, lists with addresses of international organizations of African
secretariat countries (Nigeria, p. 182–84) and international organizations with African
membership by country (Nigeria, p. 426–43). Multilateral treaty memberships and
statistical data on memberships are included.

399

Bibliographies

1121 **Nigerian contribution to humanistic studies, 1948–1975: a bibliographic survey.**
Compiled by B. Olabimpe Aboyade. Ibadan, Nigeria: Department of Library Studies, University of Ibadan, 1978. 157p. (Occasional Publication, 7).
An 'unannotated listing of 2,615 writings by scholars in Nigerian universities on humanistic subjects, not confined to works on Nigeria or Africa alone' (Preface, p. viii). Works by non-Nigerians written while they were employed in Nigerian universities are also included, but not those by Nigerian scholars abroad. The entries are grouped in nine broad headings: 'General Studies'; 'Oral tradition and oral literature'; 'The visual arts'; 'The performing arts'; 'Religion'; 'Philosophy'; 'Language'; 'Literature'; and 'History'. The 'Directory of some journals cited in this bibliography' (p. xiii–xxiv) contains useful addresses.

1122 **Nigeria: a comprehensive bibliography in the humanities and social sciences, 1900–1971.**
Compiled by Christian Chukwunedu Aguolu. Boston, Massachusetts: G. K. Hall, 1973. 620p.
A remarkable compilation of works on the country, which is organized topically with a large section devoted to works on Africa (p. 1–63). Juvenile literature, official publications, select Nigerian newspapers and periodicals, unpublished material such as theses and conference papers and Onitsha market publications are included, as are more standard works. Brief annotations and locations of book reviews are included for numerous items. In addition to the basic references there is a lengthy introduction considering 'A brief political history of Nigeria', 'Bibliographical problems', and 'Scope , purpose and arrangement' (p. ix–xxxviii). A 'Directory of major publishers, booksellers and booktrade organizations in Nigeria' (p. 569–75), 'Major sources consulted' (p. 577–83) and an author index conclude the invaluable volume. At the time of writing, the author was a graduate student at the School of Librarianship, University of California, Berkeley, California.

123 **A comprehensive periodical bibliography of Nigeria, 1960–1970.**
Compiled by Edward Baum. Athens, Ohio: Ohio University Center
for International Studies, Africa Program, 1975. 249p. (Papers in
International Studies, Africa Series, no. 24).
Presents an impressive compilation of journal articles in English on Nigeria published
between 1 January 1960 and 31 December 1970; entries are unannotated. The
references are grouped according to the Library of Congress subject classification
scheme and cover most topics in the social sciences and humanities, as well as science,
medicine, agriculture, forestry, technology, the armed forces and library science.
Baum was Associate Professor in the Department of Government at Ohio University,
Athens, Ohio, at the time of publication.

1124 **A world bibliography of African bibliographies.**
Compiled by Theodore Besterman, revised and updated by J. D.
Pearson. Oxford: Blackwell; Totowa, New Jersey: Rowman &
Littlefield, 1975. 4th ed. 241 columns.
This fourth edition contains 1,634 unannotated entries on African subjects up to 1973.
The listing for Nigeria (col. 136–48) is organized by topic and includes a note on the
number of references found in each entry.

1125 **Africa bibliography 1987.**
Compiled by Hector Blackhurst in association with the International
African Institute, London. Manchester, England; Dover, New
Hampshire: Manchester University, 1988. 4th ed. 303p. annual.
The fourth edition of this major annual bibliography records periodical articles, books
and essays in volumes published during 1987, and covering the continent and
associated islands. The works are chiefly from the social sciences, humanities and arts,
but works of creative literature are not included; they are located in the collections of
the John Rylands University Library of Manchester University and the International
African Institute, London. The Nigeria section (p. 124–48) includes 480 items arranged
by numerous topics. Author and subject indexes provide easy access to the material.

1126 **Nigerian women in development: a research bibliography.**
Compiled by Catherine M. Coles, Barbara Entwisle, with the
assistance of Margaret Hardner. Los Angeles: Crossroads, African
Studies Association, University of California, 1986. 170p.
This important bibliographic listing has an informative introduction (p. 1–7), but not
an index. Topics covered include: 'Economic roles of women' (266); 'Women in the
family and household' (308); 'Marriage and divorce' (284); 'Religion and ritual' (96);
'Associations and networks' (58); Education (139); 'Health and nutrition' (175);
'Fertility' (238); 'Family planning' (163); 'Migration and development' (243); and
'General works' (104). The numbers in parentheses indicate how many references
pertain to each topic.

Bibliographies

1127 Nigerian official publications, 1869–1959: a guide.
Compiled by Helen F. Conover. Washington, DC: General
Reference and Bibliography Division, Reference Department, Librar
of Congress, 1959. 153p.

After offering an 'Historical preface' (p. v–viii) and the introduction (p. ix–xi), th
compiler describes 1,204 items on Nigeria which are held by the Library of Congres
The items are divided into three time periods: 1947–59 (p. 1–101); 1923–4
(p. 102–29); and 1861–1922 (p. 129–42). Each part is subdivided by political regio
and/or types of documents. Publications pertaining to the Southern Cameroons
administered, at the time of writing, as a part of Nigeria since 1922, are include
(p. 97–101), as is a list of 'Bibliographic tools' (p. 142–44) and an index. Description
for some references and sectional introductions provide useful details. This work ha
been substantially revised by Sharon B. Lockwood's *Nigeria: a guide to officia
publications* (q.v.).

1128 Africa south of the Sahara: a selected, annotated list of writings.
Compiled by Helen F. Conover. Washington, DC: General
Reference and Bibliography Division, Reference Department, Library
of Congress, 1963. 354p.

The compiler provides excellent annotations and indexes 2,173 items covering al
aspects of sub-Saharan Africa, and arranged in topical sections and by country o
colonial area. The Nigeria section (p. 119–35) contains 125 well selected references.

1129 Guide to research and reference works on sub-Saharan Africa.
Edited by Peter Duignan, compiled by Helen F. Conover, Peter
Duignan, with the assistance of Evelyn Boyce, Lisolotte Hofmann,
Karen Fung. Stanford, California: Hoover Institution Press,
Stanford University, [1971]. 1,102p. (Hoover Institution
Bibliographical Series, XLVI).

This volume describes 'African library and archival materials important in reference,
research, and teaching' (Preface, p. xi) and is useful for both the student and the
librarian. Its 3,127 items serve as an excellent reference bibliography for the entire
field of African studies up to about 1970; most entries are annotated. Part I is a 'Guide
to research organizations, libraries and archives and the booktrade' (p. 1–87); Part II
has 'Bibliographies for Africa in general' (p. 91–152); Part III is a 'Subject guide in
general' (p. 155–400); and Part IV, the largest, is an 'Area guide (by former colonial
power, region, and country)' (p. 403–941). All references are indexed by author, title,
subject and geographical location (p. 945–1,102). Material specifically on Nigeria
appears in items 149–68 (p. 52–58) and 1,417–503 (p. 466–89), although numerous
other relevant sources are found throughout the large volume.

**1130 Colonialism in Africa, 1870–1960. Volume 5. A bibliographical guide to
colonialism in sub-Saharan Africa.**
Compiled by Peter Duignan, L. H. Gann. Cambridge: Cambridge
University, 1973. 552p.

One of the most valuable and extensive sourcebooks for Africa, this publication is
limited only by its timeframe and subject, although materials far exceed both. Among

the 2,516 fully annotated entries, many are relevant for Nigerian studies. The compilers describe libraries and archives in Great Britain (p. 50–54) and throughout Europe as well as general reference works for West Africa (p. 180–87) and provide an excellent listing of bibliographies, serials and reference works on Nigeria (p. 195–204).

1131 **Nigeria: Auswahlbibliographie/a selected bibliography.**
Compiled by Kurt Eitner. Hamburg, GFR: Dokumentations-Leitstelle Afrika, Institute für Afrika, Kunde, 1983. 2 vols. 3 maps.
(Dokumentationsdienst Afrika, Reihe A, 20/I-II. Africa Documentation Service, Series A, 20/I-II).

This excellent bibliography, published by the Africa Documentation Service of the Institute of African Studies, contains 1,883 references, briefly annotated, to items published between 1975 and 1982. Volume I, *Landeskunde. Politik. Recht/Country studies. Politics. Law* (131p.) has 908 references arranged in thirteen categories: 'Country studies'; 'History'; 'Contemporary history and politics'; 'Domestic policy'; 'Foreign policy'; 'Public health'; 'Education'; 'Research'; 'Information (libraries and media)'; 'Culture'; 'Religion'; 'Language'; and 'Law'. Volume II *Wirtschaft. Gesellschaft/Economy. Society* (135p.) has 975 references grouped into eighty subdivisions. Most of the items are in English and English-speaking users will appreciate the translations of the table of contents, explanatory notes and indexes in each volume. This valuable resource is available from: Institut für Afrika-Kunde, Deutsches Übersee-Institut, Dokumentations-Leitstelle Afrika, Neuer Jungfernstieg 21, D-2000 Hamburg 36, GFR.

1132 **Books about Nigeria.**
Compiled by [William] John Harris. Ibadan, Nigeria: Ibadan University, 1969. 5th ed. 83p. bibliog.

A most useful resource for books on Nigeria, organized into sixteen categories, including reference works, periodicals and official publications, and indexed by author and name. The compiler (1903– .), orginally from New Zealand, was Librarian, University of Ibadan (1946–68), Director of Caxton Press (1962–70) and Acting Vice-Chancellor, Univeristy of Benin (1972–74). The first edition appeared in 1959, with other editions in 1960, 1962 and 1963.

1133 **Women and development in Nigeria: a bibliography.**
Compiled by Mere Nakateregga Kisekka. Addis Ababa, Ethiopia: United Nations Economic Commission for Africa, 1981. 122p.
(African Training and Research Centre for Women/Ford Foundation, Bibliography Series, no. 4).

A bibliography of unnumbered and unindexed references, primarily journal articles, which is organized by topic: 'General studies'; 'Sex and puberty rites'; 'Marriage and the family'; 'Fertility and family planning'; 'Health'; 'Education'; 'Work and employment'; 'Law'; 'Politics'; and 'Religion'. Most items are annotated.

Bibliographies

1134 **Nigeria: a guide to official publications.**
Compiled by Sharon Burdge Lockwood. Washington, DC: General
Reference and Bibliography Division, Reference Department, Library
of Congress, 1966. 166p.

This guide is a complete revision, reorganization and updating of Helen F.
Conover's *Nigerian official publications, 1869–1959* (q.v.). Following a brief historical note, the
guide's 2,451 formally cited but unannotated items are arranged in four parts. 'Nigeria,
1861–1914' (p. 1–5) includes documents issued by the Colony of Lagos, 1861–86, the
Colony and Protectorate of Lagos, 1886–1906, the Protectorate of Southern Nigeria,
1900–06, and the Protectorate of Northern Nigeria, 1900–14. 'Nigeria, 1914–1965'
covers publications of the Federal Government and regional governments including the
Southern Cameroons, 1954–61. 'British publications relating to Nigeria and the British
Cameroons' (p. 135–40) lists seventy-eight documents, mostly published by H. M.
Stationery Office, London. The final part contains League of Nations and United
Nations publications on Nigeria and the Trustee Territory of the Cameroons
(p. 141–50). An index provides access to all the citations.

1135 **Annotated bibliography on Nigeria in the social sciences.**
National Library of Nigeria. Lagos: National Library of Nigeria, Jan.
1981. 51p. (Nigeria Since Independence History Project).

This compilation is particularly useful for accessing those works published in Nigeria.
Topic groups covered are: sociology, political science, economics, population,
urbanization, public administration, rural economics and development, local government, the police, law, education, history, culture and religion. There is neither
introduction nor index and the works are not numbered.

1136 **Retrospective index to Nigerian doctoral dissertations and master's
theses, 1895–1980. Vol. 1, Science & technology.**
Compiled by Patrick E. Ofori, Stephen A. Amune. Zaria, Nigeria:
Gaskiya Corp., 1984. 228p. map.

This bibliography lists 2,122 numbered works, many with brief annotations. Coverage
ranges from W. N. S. Stalikaart's *Malarial fevers, with reference to some types on the
West Coast of Africa*, MD dissertation, Edinburgh University, 1895, to those from
several Nigerian universities in September 1980, American dissertations listed in the
1980 volume of *Dissertation abstracts international* (Ann Arbor, Michigan) and those
British and Irish theses in ASLIB's *Index to theses*, vol. 28, part 1 (1980). Vol. 1 is
arranged by topic (including agricultural sciences, biological sciences, chemistry,
geology, mathematics, medical sciences, physical sciences, science education and
technical and applied sciences) and accessed by author and subject indexes. A second
volume on the humanities and social sciences is planned. B. O. Toye and S. O.
Oderinde compiled the volume of *Abstracts of Ibadan University theses and
dissertations, 1964–1975* (Ibadan, Nigeria: Ibadan University, 1979. 633p.) for 388 postgraduate degrees.

1137 **Lagos past & present: an historical bibliography.**
Compiled by A. Olu. Olafioye. Lagos: National Library of Nigeria,
1970. 2nd ed. 102p. (National Library Publication, 21).

With 403 entries this bibliography is more than twice the size of the 1968 first edition
which had 187 entries. It contains published books, official documents and pamphlets

404

and is not limited by period, language or place of publication. Each entry is given a location, there is an author index and several photographs of Lagos and Lagosian traditional figures are included.

1138 **Niger Delta studies, 1627–1967: a bibliography.**
Compiled by Jigekuma A[yebatari] Ombu, appendix by E. J.
Alagoa. Ibadan, Nigeria: Ibadan University, 1970. 138p. map.
(Ibadan University Library. Bibliographical Series, 2).

A fine bibliographical effort listing 1,724 items arranged topically, including works in Nigerian languages (Urhobo, Ijo, Nembe, Ogbia, Delta Edo, North-eastern Ijo and Ogoni), records of chieftaincy matters, intelligence reports, archival lists and annual reports; it is indexed by names of authors and chiefs. The appendix is entitled, 'A note on archival material in Nigeria relating to the Niger Delta' (p. 127–28). Ombu was on the staff of the Ibadan University Library at the time of publication.

1139 **Nigeria.**
Compiled by N. W. Posnett, P. M. Reilly, P. Whitfield. Surbiton,
England: Foreign and Commonwealth Office, Overseas Development
Administration, Land Resources Division, 1971. 3 vols. maps. (Land
Resource Bibliography no. 2).

An excellent unannotated, unnumbered listing of books, articles and reports mostly from the 1950s and 1960s covering a wide range of topics, many of which are not readily found in other sources. Vol. 1 (102p.) contains references on agriculture, animal science, crop science and forestry. Vol. 2 (111p.) covers botany, climatology, geoscience, natural resources, soil science, water resources and zoology. Vol. 3 (94p.) includes cultural studies, economics, land tenure, maps (p. 41–61), miscellaneous items and population (p. 87–94).

1140 **Bibliographies for African studies 1970–1986.**
Yvette Scheven. Munich; New York; London; Oxford: K. G. Saur,
Hans Zell, 1988. 615p.

This essential resource of nearly 3,300 entries indexed by subject and author covers fifty-seven geographical areas and nations and forty disciplines. It combines three of the compiler's earlier extremely useful publications: *Bibliographies for African studies 1980–1983* (Munich; New York; London; Oxford: K. G. Saur, Hans Zell, 1984. 300p) with 1,192 entries; *Bibliographies for African studies 1970–75* (1977. 159p.) and *Bibliographies for African studies 1976–79* (1980. 142p.), the latter two both published by Crossroads Press, Los Angeles (Archival and Bibliographies Series). In addition, bibliographies for 1984, 1985 and 1986 are included. Each entry notes the number of items in that bibliography as well as other basic information. Nigeria is well represented among the sources.

Bibliographies

1141 **Africa since 1914: a historical bibliography.**
Gail A. Schachter, editor; Pamela R. Byrne, executive editor;
J. Klass, Susan K. Kinnell, assistant editors. Santa Barbara, Denver;
Oxford: ABC-Clio Information Services, 1985. 402p. (Clio
Bibliography Series, no. 17).

This volume contains 4,329 well annotated journal articles published during 1973–82 which consider Africa since 1914. The references are organized by country within broad regions and in several general topics. For 'Nigeria' (p. 133–53), 307 entries appear, although many more of relevance appear throughout the topical sections and under West Africa. Extremely detailed indexing amplifies the ease of locating a subject or author.

1142 **A bibliographic guide to Borno studies, 1821–1983.**
Compiled by Wilhelm Seidensticker, Gizachew Adamu. Maiduguri,
Nigeria: University of Maiduguri, 1986. 205p. 4 maps.

An excellent listing of 1,647 numbered entries, divided into nine parts: 'Bibliographies'; 'Guides and published Arabic sources'; 'Nineteenth century external sources'; 'History and archaeology'; 'Anthropology, economics, education, ethnography, political sciences, sociology et al.'; 'Language, literature and linguisitcs'; 'Biological sciences, ecology, geo-sciences et al.'; 'Government publications'; and 'Archival materials'. Within most groupings entries are subdivided into published and unpublished materials, and include theses, final-year long essays, conference reports and symposia.

1143 **A selective bibliography of Nigerian government publications, 1973–1977.**
Compiled by Funmi Songonuga. *A Current Bibliography on African Affairs*, vol. 11, no. 4 (1978–79), p. 361–77.

The author, then a librarian at the University of Ife, Ile-Ife, discusses the difficulty of compiling lists of government publications and provides a selected bibliography of 256 items grouped by the state of publication. This listing supplements those of Sharon B. Lockwood, *Nigeria: a guide to official publications* (q.v.) and Janet Stanley, *Nigerian government publications, 1966–73* (q.v.).

1144 **Periodicals from Africa: a bibliography and union list of periodicals published in Africa.**
Standing Conference on Library Materials on Africa (SCOLMA),
compiled by Carole Travis, Miriam Alman, edited by Carole Travis,
foreword by Donald Simpson. Boston, Massachusetts: G. K. Hall,
1977. 619p. (Bibliographies and Guides in African Studies).

This massive compilation aims to provide a comprehensive list of periodicals published in Africa up to the end of 1973, with locations for those titles held in libraries in the United Kingdom. The periodicals are grouped by country (fifty countries and fourteen islands are covered) and there is a periodical title index. For Nigeria (p. 214–61) there are far more entries than for any other country except South Africa. Publications in Nigerian languages are included in the excellent listing. The *First supplement* to this work was compiled by D. Blake and Travis (Boston, Massachusetts: G. K. Hall, 1984. 217p.) and includes an additional 7,000 titles published in the period 1974–August 1979.

1145 **Nigerian government publications, 1966–1973: a bibliography.**
Compiled by Janet Stanley. Ile-Ife, Nigeria: University of Ife, 1975.
193p.
This bibliography is an attempt at a comprehensive listing of all publications of the
Federal Government of Nigeria, the four regional governments (Jan. 1966 to May
1967) and the twelve state governments (June 1967 to Dec. 1973), using a broad
definition of what constitutes an 'official publication'. It does not include local
government or university publications or those of the Biafran government. Author and
subject indexes allow ample access to the 2,660 items listed and grouped by state or
under 'Nigeria'.

1146 **Nigerian women: a bibliographic essay.**
Gloria D. Westfall. *Africana Journal*, vol. 5, no. 2 (summer 1974),
p. 99–138.
The author divides her discussion in this essay into: 'Ethnographic reference works',
'Tribal studies', 'Marriage', 'Fertility', 'Pregnancy, childbirth and childrearing',
'Participation in kinship groups', 'Social changes due to urbanization', 'Traditional
economic roles', 'Changes in occupational roles', 'Education', 'Political activities',
'Legal status', 'Role in traditional religion', and 'Image of women'.

1147 **The United States and Africa: guide to U.S. official documents and
government-sponsored publications on Africa, 1785–1975.**
Compiled by Julian W. Witherell. Washington, DC: Library of
Congress, USGPO, 1978. 949p.
Represents a valuable listing of 8,827 Library of Congress documentary and
government holdings on Africa, grouped by time periods and subdivided by country or
region. Among the items for Nigeria, of which there are over 653, (p. 13, 55, 111,
704–60) are a treaty between the US and the King and Chiefs of Lagos, 31 July 1854,
and a letter from Rev. Thomas J. Bowen concerning the early exploration of the River
Niger, dated 18 February 1857 (p. 13).

Periodicals

1148 **A Current Bibliography on African Affairs.**
Edited by Doris Hull. Farmingdale, New York: Baywood, 1968– .
monthly.
This publication, begun as a bimonthly in 1963, contains editorial features, articles,
bibliographic essays, book reviews and bibliographies on African topics. Each issue has
briefly annotated references arranged under forty-seven general subjects and by
country within regions of Africa. Until 1984 it was produced for the African
Bibliographic Center, P.O. Box 13096, Washington, DC 20009. It is an excellent
current source for Nigerian materials.

Bibliographies. Periodicals

1149 **International African Bibliography.**
Edited by David Hall. London: Mansell, 1971– . quarterly.
This publication includes current materials, books, articles and papers in African
studies compiled at the Library, School of Oriental and African Studies, University of
London. Each issue is geographically arranged and indexed by subject and has
numerous references to Nigeria.

1150 **Nigerian Publications: Current National Bibliography.**
Ibadan, Nigeria: Ibadan University Library; Lagos: National Library
of Nigeria, 1950/52– . annual.
Material in these issues is organized under works in English, works in Nigerian
languages, government publications and Nigeriana published outside the country and
acquired by the library. The 1972 edition (published in 1974) was the third volume
compiled by the National Library of Nigeria since it took over from the University of
Ibadan as the national depository in accordance with the legal deposit provisions of the
National Library Decree of 1970. Among the 624 items it lists are forty-four in
Nigerian languages (with twenty-four in Yoruba and seven in Hausa).

Le Nigeria contemporain.
See item no. 4.

Nigeria: a country study.
See item no. 21.

The Nigeria Handbook.
See item no. 34.

Geographical literature on Nigeria, 1901–1970: an annotated bibliography.
See item no. 35.

Nigerian archaeological literature: a classified bibliography, 1960–1983.
See item no. 140.

Nigerian perspectives: an historical anthology.
See item no. 159.

The Sokoto Caliphate.
See item no. 201.

The principles of native administration in Nigeria: selected documents, 1900–1947.
See item no. 260.

Nigerian civil war, 1967–70: an annotated bibliography.
See item no. 303.

Crisis and conflict in Nigeria: a documentary sourcebook, 1966–1970.
See item no. 308.

Nigerian population and urbanization, 1911–1974: a bibliography.
See item no. 320.

Bibliography of Nigeria: a survey of anthropological and linguistic writings from the earliest times to 1966.
See item no. 331.

Handbook of ethnic units in Nigeria.
See item no. 335.

Edo studies: a preliminary bibliogaphy.
See item no. 345.

Pastoralists of the West African savanna: selected studies presented and discussed at the fifteenth International African Seminar, held at Ahmadu Bello University, Nigeria, July 1979.
See item no. 348.

Hausa studies: a selected bibliography of B.A., M.A., and Ph.D. papers available in northern Nigerian universities.
See item no. 359.

The Hausa people: a bibliography.
See item no. 360.

The Ibo-speaking peoples of southern Nigeria: a selected annotated list of writings, 1627–1970.
See item no. 366.

The Igbo: a bibliographic essay.
See item no. 369.

The Tiv of central Nigeria.
See item no. 389.

The Yoruba of south-western Nigeria: an indexed bibliography.
See item no. 398.

The Yoruba-speaking peoples of south-western Nigeria.
See item no. 407.

Ife, the holy city of the Yoruba: an annotated bibliography.
See item no. 418.

A bibliography of Efik-Ibibio-speaking peoples of the Old Calabar Province of Nigeria, 1668–1964.
See item no. 421.

Foundations of the Bida Kingdom.
See item no. 432.

Language in education and society in Nigeria: a comprehensive bibliography and research guide.
See item no. 447.

The languages of Africa.
See item no. 448.

Bibliographies

The early study of Nigerian languages: essays and bibliographies.
See item no. 449.

Languages of West Africa.
See item no. 450.

Hausa.
See item no. 461.

Studies in Hausa language and linguistics, in honour of F. W. Parsons.
See item no. 463.

A reference grammar on Adamawa Fulani.
See item no. 483.

A select periodical bibliography on African traditional religion, with special emphasis on Nigeria, 1900–1970.
See item no. 488.

The development of Islam in West Africa.
See item no. 490.

Housing in Nigeria (a book of readings).
See item no. 515.

The WIN document: conditions of women in Nigeria and policy recommendations to 2,000 AD. [*sic*]
See item no. 518.

Silent violence: food, famine & peasantry in northern Nigeria.
See item no. 537.

Three decades of medical research at the College of Medicine, Ibadan, Nigeria, 1948–1980: a list of the papers published by members of the College of Medicine of the University of Ibadan from its foundation through 1980.
See item no. 544.

Mental health in Africa.
See item no. 550.

Nigeria: background to nationalism.
See item no. 577.

Nigerian political parties: power in an emergent African nation.
See item no. 581.

Nigeria elects '83: a brief guide to 1983 general elections in Nigeria for the foreign observer.
See item no. 585.

Nigeria: a bibliography of politics, government, administration, and international relations.
See item no. 590.

Class, ethnicity and democracy in Nigeria: the failure of the First Republic.
See item no. 597.

A bibliography for the study of African politics.
See item no. 631.

The Federal Republic of Nigeria.
See item no. 634.

Bibliography on the constitutions of Nigeria.
See item no. 644.

Nigerian legal bibliography: a classified list of materials related to Nigeria.
See item no. 645.

Nigerian legal studies: a bibliographical discussion of the sources and resources.
See item no. 649.

Selected bibliogaphy on the foreign policy of Nigeria, 1870–1977.
See item no. 665.

Nigeria and Cameroun: an annotated bibliography.
See item no. 666.

Nigeria's external relations: the first twenty-five years.
See item no. 671.

Nigerian foreign policy: alternative perceptions and projections.
See item no. 676.

IMF and Nigeria: a selected bibliography, 1960–1985.
See item no. 693.

The Nigerian petroleum industry: a guide.
See item no. 735.

The oil industry in Nigeria: an annotated bibliogaphy.
See item no. 736.

Transportation in Nigeria: a bibliography
See item no. 756

Bibliography on labour force participation in Nigeria, 1970–1976.
See item no. 761.

Urban planning and urban problems in Nigeria.
See item no. 772.

Abuja: the new Federal Capital of Nigeria: a selected list of references.
See item no. 773.

Education in Nigeria: a selected and annotated introductory bibliographical survey of current resources.
See item no. 775.

Bibliographies

Nigerian education: a classified bibliography of doctoral dissertations, 1946–1976.
See item no. 780.

Theses and dissertations on Nigerian education up to 1980.
See item no. 781.

Nigerian literature: a bibliogaphy of criticism, 1952–1976.
See item no. 794.

Chinua Achebe: bio-bibliography and recent criticism, 1970–75.
See item no. 801.

Critical perspectives on Wole Soyinka.
See item no. 802.

Wole Soyinka: a bibliography of primary and secondary sources.
See item no. 803.

A bibliography of literary contributions to Nigerian periodicals, 1946–1972.
See item no. 813.

Critical perspectives on Christopher Okigbo.
See item no. 821.

Research in African Literatures.
See item no. 837.

Popular arts of Africa.
See item no. 913.

A bibliography of African art.
See item no. 920.

Contemporary Nigerian artists: a bio-bibliography.
See item no. 921

Background to Nigerian classical art, select annotated bibliography and glossary of terms.
See item no. 924.

Bibliography of Nigerian sculpture.
See item no. 925.

A bibliography of Yoruba art.
See item no. 926.

African art: a bibliographic guide.
See item no. 930.

A bibliography of the arts of Africa.
See item no. 933.

The art of Benin.
See item no. 941.

412

African dress II: a select and annotated bibliography.
See item no. 1005.

A filmography of the Third World, 1976–1983: an annotated list of 16mm films.
See item no. 1007.

Sub-Saharan African films and filmmakers: an annotated bibliography/Films et cinéastes Africains de la région subsaharienne: une bibliographie commentée.
See item no. 1010.

A bibliography of African music and dance – the Nigerian experience, 1930–1980.
See item no. 1015.

Festivals in Nigeria: a bibliography.
See item no. 1036.

Libraries in West Africa: a bibliography.
See item no. 1071.

Library and archive collections in sub-Saharan Africa: A bibliography. Part 1.
See item no. 1072.

The non-book material resources of the Library of the Insittute of African Studies, University of Ibadan, Ibadan, Nigeria.
See item no. 1073.

Africana catalogue of the Ibadan University Library.
See item no. 1074.

Publishing in Africa: a bibliography.
See item no. 1075.

Nigerian publications, 1950–1970.
See item no. 1078.

The African Book Publishing Record.
See item no. 1080.

African mass communications: selected information sources.
See item no. 1082.

Publishing of learned journals in Nigeria.
See item no. 1095.

Africa index to continental periodical literature.
See item no. 1097.

African Affairs.
See item no. 1098.

Africa South of the Sahara: index to periodical literature.
See item no. 1102.

Bibliographies

Annals of Borno.
See item no. 1103.

The Conch. A Sociological Journal of African Cultures and Literatures.
See item no. 1104.

Current Contents Africa.
See item no. 1105.

Index

The index is a single alphabetical sequence of authors (personal and corporate), titles of publications and subjects. Index entries refer both to the main items and to other works mentioned in the notes to each item. Title entries are in italics. Numeration refers to the items as numbered.

A

Abba, I. A. 182
Abbeokuta; or sunrise within the tropics. . . 85
Abdalla, I. H. 570
Abdullahi, G. 154
Abdulraheem, T. 638
Abegunde, B. J. 917
Abegurin, 'L. 672
Abẹokuta 77, 85, 177, 226, 250, 555
   town plan 410
   traditional healers 541
   women 272
   see also Egba
Abeokuta and the Cameroons mountains: an exploration 77
Abercrombie, D. 476
Abernathy, D. B. 614
Abimbola, W. 401, 492, 808, 838
Abiola, A. M. K. O. 1088
Abiola, D. 1088
Abiri, J. O. O. 783
Aborisade, O. 652
Abortion 538
About your cookery 1051
Aboyade, B. O. 447, 783, 1121
Aboyade, Ojetunji 656, 685, 732
Abraham, R. C. 386, 456, 470, 475
Abstracts of Ibadan University theses and dissertations, 1964–1975 1136
Abu, J. A. 498
Abubakar, S. 162, 176
Abudu, F. 562
Abuja 27, 96, 699
   bibliography 773
   emirate 192, 194, 216
   political history 616
Abuja: the new Federal Capital of Nigeria, a selected list of references 773
Accelerated development in sub-Saharan Africa: an agenda for action 678
Achebe, Chinua 19, 528, 792, 796–801, 804, 807–09, 811, 815–16, 818–21, 823–28, 831, 833, 836
   bibliography 801, 804, 833
   works 528, 792, 848, 854, 857–64, 915, 952
Achebe, Christie Chinwe 795
Achebe's world: the historical and cultural context of the novels . . . 833
Adadevoh, B. K. 548
Adamawa 88, 194, 350, 428, 435, 485 Fulani 483
Adamawa past and present: an historical approach to the development of

a northern Cameroons province 350
Adamolekun, L. 653, 658
Adamu, G. 1142
Adamu, M. 174, 348
Adamu, S. O. 767
Adams, J. 31
Adapting to drought: farmers, famines, and desertification in West Africa 529
Addo, N. O. 318
Adebekun, O. 57
Adebayo, A. 169, 247
Adebayo, A. G. 695
Adebo, S. O. 713
Adedeji, A. 297, 656, 658
Adedeji, J. A. 815, 821, 839, 844–45, 956
Adede–Misinwaye, F. M. 791
Adediran, B. 169
Adefidiya, A. 1068
Adefuye, A. 198
Adejugbe, A. 701
Adekumo, M. O. 1006
Adekson, J. 'B. 622
Adekunle, L. V. 538
Adelabu, A. 579, 775
Adelẹyẹ, R. A. 175
Adelowo, E. D. 169
Adeloye, A. 539–40, 546
Adelugba, D. 802, 844–45
Ademoyega, 'W. 156, 302
Ademuwagun, Z. A. 541
Adeniji, Olu 668
Adeniyi, E. O. 42
Adenle, D. 418
Adenyemi, S. O. 788

415

425

435

436

444

461

462

Map of Nigeria

This map shows the more important towns and other features.

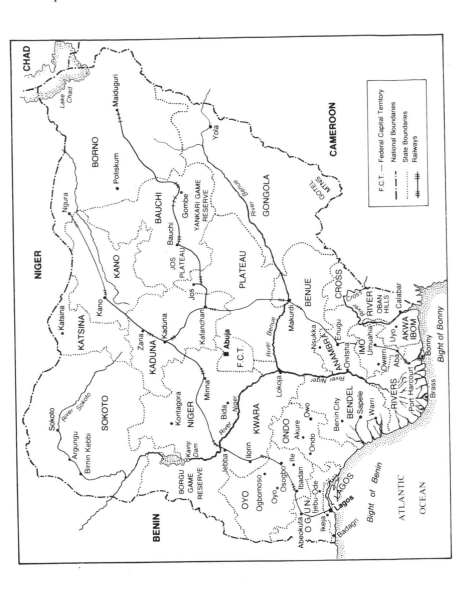
